Patrick B. Mahoney
Editor

The Eleventh Off-Campus Library Services Conference Proceedings

The Eleventh Off-Campus Library Services Conference Proceedings has been co-published simultaneously as *Journal of Library Administration*, Volume 41, Numbers 1/2 and 3/4 2004.

Pre-publication
REVIEWS,
COMMENTARIES,
EVALUATIONS . . .

"MANY OF THE CONTRIBUTORS ARE WELL-KNOWN NAMES IN THE DISTANCE LIBRARY SERVICES FIELD. The topics covered reflect many current and cutting-edge practices in the areas of librarianship and distance learning. Distance education and communication issues from a diversity point of view are covered in several chapters; also, several focus on the development of collaborations with online faculty. Many of the essays describe program development or the process of developing projects that would be useful to practitioners."

Mark Horan, MLS
Associate Professor
and Coordinator of College Librarians
University of Toledo

More pre-publication
REVIEWS, COMMENTARIES, EVALUATIONS . . .

"AN EXCELLENT RESOURCE . . . AND A GREAT SOURCE FOR IDEAS THAT CAN BE IMPLEMENTED ANYWHERE, from a small community college to a large research university library. The conference proved to be an unbelievably useful experience . . . and I have no doubt that distance education librarians will find these published proceedings equally useful. The papers included offer both practical advice and some theoretical discussions but the emphasis is definitely on the practical and includes such topics as the do's and don'ts of videoconferencing, creating a library CD to send out to students, setting up a virtual reference service, and everything you need to know about proxy servers, focus groups, and strategic planning for distance learning services—and more."

Stefanie Buck, MA, MLS
Librarian for Extended Education
Western Washington University

"IMPRESSIVE. . . . VALUABLE to anyone who offers library services to students at a distance or who doesn't work in a traditional library setting on a computer. . . . Provides thoughtful insights and concrete strategies for improving and expanding access to resources and services for students and faculty. The contributors touch on a wide range of overarching topics, including collaboration, marketing, and strategic planning, as well as specific technological issues such as electronic document delivery, usability testing, teaching with chat software, and videoconferencing. Many chapters also address working with diverse populations. LIBRARY PERSONNEL WILL BENEFIT GREATLY FROM THIS COLLECTION OF THOUGHT-PROVOKING, INFORMATIVE PAPERS."

Elizabeth Blakesley Lindsay, MA, MLS
Head, Library Instruction
Washington State University Libraries

More pre-publication
REVIEWS, COMMENTARIES, EVALUATIONS . . .

"A WONDERFUL INTRODUC-
TION TO EMERGING PRAC-
TICES and issues relating to library
services for distance education students. The contents are based on
solid empirical research projects
and are intellectually honest, providing thoughtful examinations of
real issues–not just upbeat 'how we
did it' stories. These proceedings
are especially strong and innovative in the chapters on using dedicated virtual references services
to provide library instruction, on
working with distance education
students from diverse populations,
on research readiness self-assess-
ments for distance education students, and on various proxy server
and remote authentication options.
Solid tips can also be found for conducting student surveys and focus
groups, for management of distance
education library services, and for
constructing tutorials for distance
learners. Readers will learn much
about new trends in distance education library services from these
proceedings. Very little here was
predictable or stale in its content or
approach, making it a rarity among
conference proceedings."

Kate M. Manuel, MS, MLIS
Instruction Coordinator
New Mexico State University

"PRACTICAL . . . SOLID. . .
EXCITING. . . . A NECESSITY
FOR LIBRARIANS INVOLVED WITH
DISTANCE EDUCATION. Librarians
serving any kind of distributed distance education program can find
great information covering the most
pressing issues in distance education library services in this book.
Topics include electronic reserves,
chat, collaborating across campus,
teaching students and faculty from a
distance, strategic planning, and
course management software. The
papers are well-documented and
researched, leading the eager researcher back to a multitude of other
good sources. Many are chock-full
of statistical data and examples of
program development, always important when trying to replicate a
program in your own library."

Michelle S. Millet, MA, MLS
Information Literacy Coordinator
Trinity University

More pre-publication
REVIEWS, COMMENTARIES, EVALUATIONS . . .

"**R**EQUIRED READING FOR ALL ACADEMIC LIBRARIANS, not just off-campus or distance learning librarians. . . . Relevant to any library or librarian providing electronic resources and services. The Off-Campus Library Services Conference deserves its reputation as one of the most relevant and useful professional conferences and these proceedings reflect that reputation. The contributing authors provide researched, practical, and innovative descriptions of, and solutions to, the emerging issues and pervasive challenges facing all public, technical, and instructional service academic librarians."

Darby Paige Syrkin, MLIS
*Academic Resource
Center Librarian
Florida State University
Panama City*

"**A**N ESSENTIAL RESOURCE for the practitioner looking for a snapshot of current trends and practical solutions to the challenges of providing library services to the distance learner. Chock full of practical case studies interspersed with research and theory, the thirty-six chapters offer everything from survey samples and technical tips to instructional ideas and advice for serving special populations."

Dan H. Lawrence, MLS
*Instruction Librarian
and Assistant Professor
of University Libraries
University of Northern Colorado*

The Haworth Information Press®
An Imprint of The Haworth Press, Inc.

M-GEN
Ne902

The Eleventh
Off-Campus Library Services
Conference Proceedings

The Eleventh Off-Campus Library Services Conference Proceedings has been co-published simultaneously as *Journal of Library Administration*, Volume 41, Numbers 1/2 and 3/4 2004.

626251930

The *Journal of Library Administration* Monographic "Separates"

Below is a list of "separates," which in serials librarianship means a special issue simultaneously published as a special journal issue or double-issue *and* as a "separate" hardbound monograph. (This is a format which we also call a "DocuSerial.")

"Separates" are published because specialized libraries or professionals may wish to purchase a specific thematic issue by itself in a format which can be separately cataloged and shelved, as opposed to purchasing the journal on an on-going basis. Faculty members may also more easily consider a "separate" for classroom adoption.

"Separates" are carefully classified separately with the major book jobbers so that the journal tie-in can be noted on new book order slips to avoid duplicate purchasing.

You may wish to visit Haworth's Website at . . .

http://www.HaworthPress.com

. . . to search our online catalog for complete tables of contents of these separates and related publications.

You may also call 1-800-HAWORTH (outside US/Canada: 607-722-5857), or Fax 1-800-895-0582 (outside US/Canada: 607-771-0012), or e-mail at:

docdelivery@haworthpress.com

The Eleventh Off-Campus Library Services Conference Proceedings, edited by Patrick B. Mahoney, MBA, MLS (Vol. 41, No. 1/2/3/4, 2004). *Examines–and offers solutions to–the problems faced by librarians servicing faculty and students who do not have access to a traditional library.*

Libraries Act on Their LibQUAL+™ Findings: From Data to Action, edited by Fred M. Heath, EdD, Martha Kyrillidou, MEd, MLS, and Consuella A. Askew, MLS (Vol. 40, No. 3/4, 2004). *Focuses on the value of LibQUAL+™ data to help librarians provide better services for users.*

The Changing Landscape for Electronic Resources: Content, Access, Delivery, and Legal Issues, edited by Yem S. Fong, MLS, and Suzanne M. Ward, MA (Vol. 40, No. 1/2, 2004). *Focuses on various aspects of electronic resources for libraries, including statewide resource-sharing initiatives, licensing issues, open source software, standards, and scholarly publishing.*

Improved Access to Information: Portals, Content Selection, and Digital Information, edited by Sul H. Lee (Vol. 39, No. 4, 2003). *Examines how improved electronic resources can allow libraries to provide an increasing amount of digital information to an ever-expanding patron base.*

Digital Images and Art Libraries in the Twenty-First Century, edited by Susan Wyngaard, MLS (Vol. 39, No. 2/3, 2003). *Provides an in-depth look at the technology that art librarians must understand in order to work effectively in today's digital environment.*

The Twenty-First Century Art Librarian, edited by Terrie L. Wilson, MLS (Vol. 39, No. 1, 2003). *"A MUST-READ addition to every art, architecture, museum, and visual resources library bookshelf." (Betty Jo Irvine, PhD, Fine Arts Librarian, Indiana University)*

The Strategic Stewardship of Cultural Resources: To Preserve and Protect, edited by Andrea T. Merrill, BA (Vol. 38, No. 1/2/3/4, 2003). *Leading library, museum, and archival professionals share their expertise on a wide variety of preservation and security issues.*

Distance Learning Library Services: The Tenth Off-Campus Library Services Conference, edited by Patrick B. Mahoney (Vol. 37, No. 1/2/3/4, 2002). *Explores the pitfalls of providing information services to distance students and suggests ways to avoid them.*

Electronic Resources and Collection Development, edited by Sul H. Lee (Vol. 36, No. 3, 2002). *Shows how electronic resources have impacted traditional collection development policies and practices.*

Information Literacy Programs: Successes and Challenges, edited by Patricia Durisin, MLIS (Vol. 36, No. 1/2, 2002). *Examines Web-based collaboration, teamwork with academic and administrative colleagues, evidence-based librarianship, and active learning strategies in library instruction programs.*

Evaluating the Twenty-First Century Library: The Association of Research Libraries New Measures Initiative, 1997-2001, edited by Donald L. DeWitt, PhD (Vol. 35, No. 4, 2001). *This collection of articles (thirteen of which previously appeared in ARL's bimonthly newsletter/ report on research issues and actions) examines the Association of Research Libraries' "new measures" initiative.*

Impact of Digital Technology on Library Collections and Resource Sharing, edited by Sul H. Lee (Vol. 35, No. 3, 2001). *Shows how digital resources have changed the traditional academic library.*

Libraries and Electronic Resources: New Partnerships, New Practices, New Perspectives, edited by Pamela L. Higgins (Vol. 35, No. 1/2, 2001). *An essential guide to the Internet's impact on electronic resources management past, present, and future.*

Diversity Now: People, Collections, and Services in Academic Libraries, edited by Teresa Y. Neely, PhD, and Kuang-Hwei (Janet) Lee-Smeltzer, MS, MSLIS (Vol. 33, No. 1/2/3/4, 2001). *Examines multicultural trends in academic libraries' staff and users, types of collections, and services offered.*

Leadership in the Library and Information Science Professions: Theory and Practice, edited by Mark D. Winston, MLS, PhD (Vol. 32, No. 3/4, 2001). *Offers fresh ideas for developing and using leadership skills, including recruiting potential leaders, staff training and development, issues of gender and ethnic diversity, and budget strategies for success.*

Off-Campus Library Services, edited by Ann Marie Casey (Vol. 31, No. 3/4, 2001 and Vol. 32, No. 1/2, 2001). *This informative volume examines various aspects of off-campus, or distance learning. It explores training issues for library staff, Web site development, changing roles for librarians, the uses of conferencing software, library support for Web-based courses, library agreements and how to successfully negotiate them, and much more!*

Research Collections and Digital Information, edited by Sul H. Lee (Vol. 31, No. 2, 2000). *Offers new strategies for collecting, organizing, and accessing library materials in the digital age.*

Academic Research on the Internet: Options for Scholars & Libraries, edited by Helen Laurence, MLS, EdD, and William Miller, MLS, PhD (Vol. 30, No. 1/2/3/4, 2000). *"Emphasizes quality over quantity. . . . Presents the reader with the best research-oriented Web sites in the field. A state-of-the-art review of academic use of the Internet as well as a guide to the best Internet sites and services. . . . A useful addition for any academic library." (David A. Tyckoson, MLS, Head of Reference, California State University, Fresno)*

Management for Research Libraries Cooperation, edited by Sul H. Lee (Vol. 29. No. 3/4, 2000). *Delivers sound advice, models, and strategies for increasing sharing between institutions to maximize the amount of printed and electronic research material you can make available in your library while keeping costs under control.*

Integration in the Library Organization, edited by Christine E. Thompson, PhD (Vol. 29, No. 2, 1999). *Provides librarians with the necessary tools to help libraries balance and integrate public and technical services and to improve the capability of libraries to offer patrons quality services and large amounts of information.*

Library Training for Staff and Customers, edited by Sara Ramser Beck, MLS, MBA (Vol. 29, No. 1, 1999). *This comprehensive book is designed to assist library professionals involved in presenting or planning training for library staff members and customers. You will explore ideas for effective general reference training, training on automated systems, training in specialized subjects such as African American history and biography, and training for areas such as patents and trademarks, and business subjects.* Library Training for Staff and Customers *answers numerous training questions and is an excellent guide for planning staff development.*

Collection Development in the Electronic Environment: Shifting Priorities, edited by Sul H. Lee (Vol. 28, No. 4, 1999). *Through case studies and firsthand experiences, this volume discusses meeting the needs of scholars at universities, budgeting issues, user education, staffing in the electronic age, collaborating libraries and resources, and how vendors meet the needs of different customers.*

The Age Demographics of Academic Librarians: A Profession Apart, by Stanley J. Wilder (Vol. 28, No. 3, 1999). *The average age of librarians has been increasing dramatically since 1990. This unique book will provide insights on how this demographic issue can impact a library and what can be done to make the effects positive.*

Collection Development in a Digital Environment, edited by Sul H. Lee (Vol. 28, No. 1, 1999). *Explores ethical and technological dilemmas of collection development and gives several suggestions on how a library can successfully deal with these challenges and provide patrons with the information they need.*

Scholarship, Research Libraries, and Global Publishing, by Jutta Reed-Scott (Vol. 27, No. 3/4, 1999). *This book documents a research project in conjunction with the Association of Research Libraries (ARL) that explores the issue of foreign acquisition and how it affects collection in international studies, area studies, collection development, and practices of international research libraries.*

Managing Multicultural Diversity in the Library: Principles and Issues for Administrators, edited by Mark Winston (Vol. 27, No. 1/2, 1999). *Defines diversity, clarifies why it is important to address issues of diversity, and identifies goals related to diversity and how to go about achieving those goals.*

Information Technology Planning, edited by Lori A. Goetsch (Vol. 26, No. 3/4, 1999). *Offers innovative approaches and strategies useful in your library and provides some food for thought about information technology as we approach the millennium.*

The Economics of Information in the Networked Environment, edited by Meredith A. Butler, MLS, and Bruce R. Kingma, PhD (Vol. 26, No. 1/2, 1998). *"A book that should be read both by information professionals and by administrators, faculty and others who share a collective concern to provide the most information to the greatest number at the lowest cost in the networked environment." (Thomas J. Galvin, PhD, Professor of Information Science and Policy, University at Albany, State University of New York)*

OCLC 1967-1997: Thirty Years of Furthering Access to the World's Information, edited by K. Wayne Smith (Vol. 25, No. 2/3/4, 1998). *"A rich–and poignantly personal, at times–historical account of what is surely one of this century's most important developments in librarianship." (Deanna B. Marcum, PhD, President, Council on Library and Information Resources, Washington, DC)*

Management of Library and Archival Security: From the Outside Looking In, edited by Robert K. O'Neill, PhD (Vol. 25, No. 1, 1998). *"Provides useful advice and on-target insights for professionals caring for valuable documents and artifacts." (Menzi L. Behrnd-Klodt, JD, Attorney/Archivist, Klodt and Associates, Madison, WI)*

Economics of Digital Information: Collection, Storage, and Delivery, edited by Sul H. Lee (Vol. 24, No. 4, 1997). *Highlights key concepts and issues vital to a library's successful venture into the digital environment and helps you understand why the transition from the printed page to the digital packet has been problematic for both creators of proprietary materials and users of those materials.*

The Academic Library Director: Reflections on a Position in Transition, edited by Frank D'Andraia, MLS (Vol. 24, No. 3, 1997). *"A useful collection to have whether you are seeking a position as director or conducting a search for one." (College & Research Libraries News)*

Emerging Patterns of Collection Development in Expanding Resource Sharing, Electronic Information, and Network Environment, edited by Sul H. Lee (Vol. 24, No. 1/2, 1997). *"The issues it deals with are common to us all. We all need to make our funds go further and our resources work harder, and there are ideas here which we can all develop." (The Library Association Record)*

Interlibrary Loan/Document Delivery and Customer Satisfaction: Strategies for Redesigning Services, edited by Pat L. Weaver-Meyers, Wilbur A. Stolt, and Yem S. Fong (Vol. 23, No. 1/2, 1997). *"No interlibrary loan department supervisor at any mid-sized to large college or university library can afford not to read this book." (Gregg Sapp, MLS, MEd, Head of Access Services, University of Miami, Richter Library, Coral Gables, Florida)*

Access, Resource Sharing and Collection Development, edited by Sul H. Lee (Vol. 22, No. 4, 1996). *Features continuing investigation and discussion of important library issues, specifically the role of libraries in acquiring, storing, and disseminating information in different formats.*

Managing Change in Academic Libraries, edited by Joseph J. Branin (Vol. 22, No. 2/3, 1996). *"Touches on several aspects of academic library management, emphasizing the changes that are occurring at the present time. . . . Recommended this title for individuals or libraries interested in management aspects of academic libraries." (RQ American Library Association)*

Libraries and Student Assistants: Critical Links, edited by William K. Black, MLS (Vol. 21, No. 3/4, 1995). *"A handy reference work on many important aspects of managing student assistants. . . . Solid, useful information on basic management issues in this work and several chapters are useful for experienced managers." (The Journal of Academic Librarianship)*

The Future of Resource Sharing, edited by Shirley K. Baker and Mary E. Jackson, MLS (Vol. 21, No. 1/2, 1995). *"Recommended for library and information science schools because of its balanced presentation of the ILL/document delivery issues." (Library Acquisitions: Practice and Theory)*

Monographic "Separates" list continued at the back

The Eleventh
Off-Campus Library Services
Conference Proceedings

Patrick B. Mahoney
Editor

The Eleventh Off-Campus Library Services Conference Proceedings
has been co-published simultaneously as *Journal of Library
Administration*, Volume 41, Numbers 1/2 and 3/4 2004.

The Haworth Information Press®
An Imprint of The Haworth Press, Inc.

New York • London • Victoria (AU)
www.HaworthPress.com

Published by

The Haworth Information Press®, 10 Alice Street, Binghamton, NY 13904-1580 USA

The Haworth Information Press® is an imprint of The Haworth Press, Inc., 10 Alice Street, Binghamton, NY 13904-1580 USA.

The Eleventh Off-Campus Library Services Conference Proceedings has been co-published simultaneously as *Journal of Library Administration*™, Volume 41, Numbers 1/2 and 3/4 2004.

Articles in this collection are © Central Michigan University Libraries and the CMU College of Extended Learning, and are reprinted here by permission, except where noted.

The development, preparation, and publication of this work has been undertaken with great care. However, the publisher, employees, editors, and agents of The Haworth Press and all imprints of The Haworth Press, Inc., including The Haworth Medical Press® and Pharmaceutical Products Press®, are not responsible for any errors contained herein or for consequences that may ensue from use of materials or information contained in this work. Opinions expressed by the author(s) are not necessarily those of The Haworth Press, Inc. With regard to case studies, identities and circumstances of individuals discussed herein have been changed to protect confidentiality. Any resemblance to actual persons, living or dead, is entirely coincidental.

Cover design by Jennifer M. Gaska.

Library of Congress Cataloging-in-Publication Data

Off-Campus Library Services Conference (11th : 2004 : Scottsdale, Ariz.)
The Eleventh Off-Campus Library Services Conference proceedings / Patrick B. Mahoney, editor.
    p. cm.
    Proceedings of the conference held May 5-7, 2004, Scottsdale, Arizona.
    "Co-published simultaneously as Journal of library administration, volume 41, numbers 1/2 2004 and volume 41, numbers 3/4 2004."
    Includes bibliographical references and index.
    ISBN-10: 0-7890-2784-4 (hard cover : alk. paper)
    ISBN-10: 0-7890-2785-2 (soft cover : alk. paper)
    ISBN-13: 978-0-7890-2784-9 (hard cover : alk. paper)
    ISBN-13: 978-0-7890-2785-6 (soft cover : alk. paper)
    1. Academic libraries–Off-campus services–Congresses. 2. Libraries and distance education–Congresses. 3. Academic libraries–Information technology–Congresses. 4. Distance education–Congresses. 5. Education, Higher–Effect of technological innovations on–Congresses. I. Mahoney, Patrick, 1964- II. Journal of library administration. III. Title.
Z675.U5 O36 2005
025.5–dc22
                                                     2004024741

Indexing, Abstracting & Website/Internet Coverage

This section provides you with a list of major indexing & abstracting services and other tools for bibliographic access. That is to say, each service began covering this periodical during the year noted in the right column. Most Websites which are listed below have indicated that they will either post, disseminate, compile, archive, cite or alert their own Website users with research-based content from this work. (This list is as current as the copyright date of this publication.)

Abstracting, Website/Indexing Coverage . . . . Year When Coverage Began

- *AATA Online: Abstracts of International Conservation Literature (formerly Art & Archeology Technical Abstracts) <http://aata.getty.edu>* 2004

- *Academic Abstracts/CD-ROM* 1993

- *Academic Search: database of 2,000 selected academic serials, updated monthly: EBSCO Publishing* 1995

- *Academic Search Elite (EBSCO)* 1993

- *AGRICOLA Database (AGRICultural OnLine Access) <http://www.natl.usda.gov/ag98>* 1991

- *AGRIS <http://www.fao.org/agris/>* 1991

- *Business & Company ProFiles ASAP on CD-ROM <http://www.galegroup.com>* 1996

- *Business ASAP* 1994

- *Business ASAP–International <http://www.galegroup.com>* 1984

- *Business International and Company ProFile ASAP <http://www.galegroup.com>* 1996

- *Business Source Corporate: coverage of nearly 3,350 quality magazines and journals; designed to meet the diverse information needs of corporations; EBSCO Publishing <http://www.epnet.com/corporate/bsourcecorp.asp>* 1993

- *Computer and Information Systems Abstracts <http://www.csa.com>* 2004

(continued)

- *Current Articles on Library Literature and Services (CALLS)* 1992
- *Current Cites [Digital Libraries] [Electronic Publishing]*
  [Multimedia & Hypermedia] [Networks & Networking]
  [General] <http://sunsite.berkeley.edu/CurrentCites/>. 2000
- *Current Index to Journals in Education* 1986
- *EBSCOhost Electronic Journals Service (EJS)*
  <http://ejournals.ebsco.com> 2001
- *Educational Administration Abstracts (EAA)*. 1991
- *ERIC Database (Education Resource Information Center)*
  <http://www.eric.ed.gov>. 2004
- *FRANCIS. INIST/CNRS <http://www.inist.fr>* 1986
- *General BusinessFile ASAP <http://www.galegroup.com>* 1993
- *General BusinessFile ASAP–International*
  <http://www.galegroup.com> 1984
- *General Reference Center GOLD on InfoTrac Web* 1984
- *General Reference Center INTERNATIONAL*
  <http://www.galegroup.com> 1984
- *Getty Conservation Institute (GCI) Project Bibliographies*
  <http://www.getty.edu>. 2004
- *Google <http://www.google.com>*. 2004
- *Google Scholar <http://scholar.google.com>* 2004
- *Higher Education Abstracts, providing the latest in research*
  & theory in more than 140 major topics 1991
- *IBZ International Bibliography of Periodical Literature*
  <http://www.saur.de> 1995
- *Index Guide to College Journals (core list compiled*
  by integrating 48 indexes frequently used to support
  undergraduate programs in small to medium sized libraries) 1999
- *Index to Periodical Articles Related to Law <http://www.law.utexas.edu>* 1989
- *Information Reports & Bibliographies* 1992
- *Information Science & Technology Abstracts: indexes journal*
  articles from more than 450 publications as well as books,
  research reports, and conference proceedings;
  EBSCO Publishing <http://www.epnet.com> 1980
- *Informed Librarian, The <http://www.informedlibrarian.com>* 1993
- *InfoTrac Custom <http://www.galegroup.com>*. 1996
- *InfoTrac OneFile <http://www.galegroup.com>* 1984
- *INSPEC is the leading English-language bibliographic*
  information service providing access to the world's scientific
  & technical literature in physics, electrical engineering,
  electronics, communications, control engineering, computers
  & computing, and information technology
  <http://www.iee.org.uk/publish/> 1986

(continued)

- *Internationale Bibliographie der geistes- und sozialwissenschaftlichen Zeitschriftenliteratur . . . See IBZ*. 1995

- *Journal of Academic Librarianship: Guide to Professional Literature, The* 1996

- *Konyvtari Figyelo (Library Review)* 1995

- *Library & Information Science Abstracts (LISA)* <http://www.csa.com> 1989

- *Library and Information Science Annual (LISCA)* <http://www.lu.com> 1997

- *Library Literature & Information Science* <http://www.hwwilson.com> 1991

- *MasterFILE Elite: coverage of nearly 1,200 periodicals covering general reference, business, health, education, general science, multi-cultural issues and much more; EBSCO Publishing <http://www.epnet.com/government/mfelite.asp>* 1993

- *MasterFILE Premier: coverage of more than 1,950 periodicals covering general reference, business, health, education, general science, multi-cultural issues and much more; EBSCO Publishing <http://www.epnet.com/government/mfpremier.asp>* 1993

- *MasterFILE Select: coverage of nearly 770 periodicals covering general reference, business, health, education, general science, multi-cultural issues and much more; EBSCO Publishing <http://www.epnet.com/government.mfselect.asp>* 1993

- *MasterFILE: updated database from EBSCO Publishing* 1995

- *Mathematical Didactics (MATHDI)* <http://www.emis.de/MATH/DI.html)* 2004

- *OCLC ArticleFirst <http://www.oclc.org/services/databases/>* 2003

- *OCLC ContentsFirst <http://www.oclc.org/services/databases/>* 2003

- *OCLC Public Affairs Information Service <http://www.pais.org>* 1990

- *PASCAL, c/o Institut de l'Information Scientifique et Technique. Cross-disciplinary electronic database covering the fields of science, technology & medicine. Also available on CD-ROM, and can generate customized retrospective searches* <http://www.inist.fr>* 1986

- *Referativnyi Zhurnal (Abstracts Journal of the All-Russian Institute of Scientific and Technical Information–in Russian)* 1982

- *SwetsWise <http://www.swets.com>* 2001

- *Trade & Industry Index* 1991

- *zetoc <http://zetoc.mimas.ac.uk/>* 2004

(continued)

Special Bibliographic Notes related to special journal issues (separates) and indexing/abstracting:

- indexing/abstracting services in this list will also cover material in any "separate" that is co-published simultaneously with Haworth's special thematic journal issue or DocuSerial. Indexing/abstracting usually covers material at the article/chapter level.
- monographic co-editions are intended for either non-subscribers or libraries which intend to purchase a second copy for their circulating collections.
- monographic co-editions are reported to all jobbers/wholesalers/approval plans. The source journal is listed as the "series" to assist the prevention of duplicate purchasing in the same manner utilized for books-in-series.
- to facilitate user/access services all indexing/abstracting services are encouraged to utilize the co-indexing entry note indicated at the bottom of the first page of each article/chapter/contribution.
- this is intended to assist a library user of any reference tool (whether print, electronic, online, or CD-ROM) to locate the monographic version if the library has purchased this version but not a subscription to the source journal.
- individual articles/chapters in any Haworth publication are also available through the Haworth Document Delivery Service (HDDS).

The Eleventh Off-Campus Library Services Conference Proceedings

CONTENTS

Preface   xix

Acknowledgments   xxi

Program Advisory Board and Executive Planning Committee   xxiii

Introduction   1
    Patrick B. Mahoney

CONTRIBUTED PAPERS

Educating the Educators: Outreach to the College of Education
    Distance Faculty and Native American Students   3
    Tina M. Adams
    R. Sean Evans

On Ramp to Research: Creation of a Multimedia Library
    Instruction Presentation for Off-Campus Students   19
    Michele D. Behr

Using Direct Linking Capabilities in Aggregated Databases
    for E-Reserves   31
    David Bickford

Blessing or Curse? Distance Delivery to Students with Invisible
    Disabilities   47
    Nancy E. Black

Institutional Challenges in Web-Based Programs: Student
    Challenges and Institutional Responses   65
    Elizabeth A. Buchanan

Where Is the Library in Course Management Software?   75
    Marianne A. Buehler

A Survey of Distance Librarian-Administrators in ARL
    Libraries: An Overview of Library Resources and Services   85
    Mary Cassner
    Kate E. Adams

Do's and Don'ts of Simultaneous Instruction to On-Campus
    and Distance Students via Videoconferencing   97
    Mou Chakraborty
    Shelley Victor

eBooks for a Distributed Learning University: The Royal
    Roads University Case   113
    Rosie Croft
    Shailoo Bedi

A Tale of Two Campuses: Providing Virtual Reference
    to Distance Nursing Students   139
    Ladonna Guillot
    Beth Stahr

User Instruction for Distance Students: Texas Tech University
    System's Main Campus Library Reaches Out to Students
    at Satellite Campuses   153
    Jon R. Hufford

Research Readiness Self-Assessment: Assessing Students'
    Research Skills and Attitudes   167
    Lana Ivanitskaya
    Ryan Laus
    Anne Marie Casey

Creating a Library CD for Off-Campus Students   185
    Marie F. Jones

Working Together: Effective Collaboration in a Consortium
    Environment   203
    Grant Kayler
    Paul R. Pival

Chat It Up! Extending Reference Services
    to Assist Off-Campus Students   217
    M. Kathleen Kern

Progressive Partnering: Expanding Student and Faculty Access
    to Information Services   227
    Linda L. Lillard
    Pat Wilson
    Constance M. Baird

Collaboration and Information Literacy: Challenges of Meeting
    Standards When Working with Remote Faculty   243
    Robin Lockerby
    Divina Lynch
    James Sherman
    Elizabeth Nelson

Collaborating on Electronic Course Reserves to Support Student
    Success   255
    Elaine Magusin
    Kay Johnson

Assessing the Library Needs and Preferences of Off-Campus
    Students: Surveying Distance Education Students,
    from the Midwest to the West Indies   265
    Evadne McLean
    Stephen H. Dew

Assessing Minds Want to Know: Developing Questions
    for Assessment of Library Services Supporting Off-Campus
    Learning Programs   303
    Lynn M. McMain
    Judy Ann Jerabek

Anything, Anytime, Anywhere: Proxy Servers, Shibboleth,
   and the Dream of the Digital Library   315
   Brian L. Mikesell

Taking Assessment on the Road: Utah Academic Librarians
   Focus on Distance Learners   327
   Rob Morrison
   Allyson Washburn

Tri-Institutional Library Support: A Lesson in Forced
   Collaboration   345
   Paul R. Pival
   Kay Johnson

Starting Small: Setting Up Off-Campus Library Services
   with Limited Resources   355
   Linda A. Reeves

The Impact of Distance Learning Library Services Experience
   on Practitioners' Career Paths   365
   Beth A. Reiten
   Jack Fritts

Ahead of the Game: Using Communications Software
   and Push Technology to Raise Student Awareness
   of Library Resources   375
   Tom Riedel

All in the Family: Library Services for LIS Online Education   391
   Susan E. Searing

Strategic Planning for Distance Learning Services   407
   Anne Marie Secord
   Robin Lockerby
   Laura Roach
   Joe Simpson

A Systematic Approach to Assessing the Needs of Distance
   Faculty   413
    Janette Shaffer
    Kate Finkelstein
    Nancy Woelfl
    Elizabeth Lyden

Learning to Teach in a New Medium: Adapting Library
   Instruction to a Videoconferencing Environment   429
    Sheri Sochrin

Providing Off-Campus Library Services by "Team":
   An Assessment   443
    Marcia Stockham
    Elizabeth Turtle

If You Build It, Will They Come? Creating a Marketing Plan
   for Distance Learning Library Services   459
    Terri Pedersen Summey

Yeah, I Found It! Performing Web Site Usability Testing
   to Ensure That Off-Campus Students Can Find
   the Information They Need   471
    Beth Thomsett-Scott

Pests, Welcomed Guests, or Tolerated Outsiders? Attitudes
   of Academic Librarians Toward Distance Students
   from Unaffiliated Institutions   485
    Johanna Tuñón
    Rita Barsun
    Laura Lucio Ramirez

80 Miles from the Nearest Library, with a Research Paper
   Due Monday: Extending Library Services to Distance
   Learners   507
    Allyson Washburn
    Jessica Draper

Selecting Electronic Document Delivery Options to Provide
    Quality Service   531
        Cherié L. Weible

Contributor Index   541

Index   547

ABOUT THE EDITOR

Patrick B. Mahoney, MBA, MLS, is an off-campus librarian with Central Michigan University. He works with the school's distance students in accessing information both online and in traditional print formats, and regularly teaches students to conduct research and use the school's databases. His professional interests include information use by nontraditional students and the implementation of assessment guidelines. Mr. Mahoney is active with the Distance Learning section of the Association of College and Research Libraries (ACRL). He also has conducted numerous presentations that pertain to information access for the Kansas City Metropolitan Library & Information Network, and the Kansas Library Association. In addition, he has written numerous book reviews for *Library Journal* and various library and business newsletters.

ALL HAWORTH INFORMATION PRESS
BOOKS AND JOURNALS ARE PRINTED
ON CERTIFIED ACID-FREE PAPER

Preface

Welcome to the Eleventh Off-Campus Library Services Conference Proceedings. Once again, the Central Michigan University Libraries and the Central Michigan University College of Extended Learning have provided generous support of both this conference and these Proceedings.

The papers included here were selected by a twenty-six member Program Advisory Board using a juried abstracts process. All of the contributed papers have been formatted consistent with the conference *Guidelines for Preparing Manuscripts* distributed to contributors. Typographical errors have been corrected and cited references have been formatted consistent with guidelines published in the *Publication Manual of the American Psychological Association* (5th ed.), *APA Publication Manual* Web site at http://www.apastyle.org/, and other reputable sources.

Patrick B. Mahoney
Editor

[Haworth co-indexing entry note]: "Preface." Mahoney, Patrick, B. Co-published simultaneously in *Journal of Library Administration* (The Haworth Information Press, an imprint of The Haworth Press, Inc.) Vol. 41, No. 1/2, 2004, p. xxv; and: *The Eleventh Off-Campus Library Services Conference Proceedings* (ed: Patrick B. Mahoney) The Haworth Information Press, an imprint of The Haworth Press, Inc., 2004, p. xix. Single or multiple copies of this article are available for a fee from The Haworth Document Delivery Service [1-800-HAWORTH, 9:00 a.m. - 5:00 p.m. (EST). E-mail address: docdelivery@haworthpress.com].

© 2004 by The Haworth Press, Inc. All rights reserved.

Acknowledgments

We are thrilled to have the many presenters participate in the OCLS Conference. Their knowledge of providing unique information services to distance students, faculty, and others who are not able to utilize a traditional library has helped make the Conference a success.

Thanks also go to the Program Advisory Board for reviewing dozens of submitted Conference paper proposals. As usual, a very special thanks goes to Connie Hildebrand, who again has served as Conference Coordinator. Her guidance is greatly appreciated.

Program Advisory Board
and Executive Planning Committee*

Kate Adams
Distance Education Coordinator
University of Nebraska-Lincoln

Constance Baird
Director
Distance Learning Programs
University of Kentucky

David Darryl Bibb
Distance Education Librarian
Southeast Missouri State University

Marianne Buehler
Library Coordinator for Distance
    Learning
Rochester Institute of Technology

Margaret Casado
Distance Education Library
University of Tennessee

Marissa Cachero
Reference and Instruction
    Liaison Librarian
George Mason University

Anne Marie Casey
Associate Dean of Libraries
Central Michigan University

Monica Hines Craig*
Off-Campus Librarian
Central Michigan University

Hazel Davis
Library Director
Rio Salado College

William Denny*
Off-Campus Librarian
Central Michigan University

Wes Edens
Electronic Resources Librarian
American Graduate School of
    International Management
(Thunderbird)

Daniel Gall*
Off-Campus Librarian
Central Michigan University

Julie Garrison*
Director
Off-Campus Library Services
Central Michigan University

Anne Haynes
Distributed Education Library
    Services Coordinator
Indiana University Libraries

Connie Hildebrand*
Conference Coordinator
Central Michigan University

Marie Jones
Extended Campus Services
    Librarian
East Tennessee State University

Patrick Mahoney*
Off-Campus Librarian
Central Michigan University

Jill Markgraf
Distance Education & Reference
    Librarian
University of Wisconsin-Eau Claire

Brian Mikesell
Manager of eServices
St. Johns University

James Nalen*
Off-Campus Librarian
Central Michigan University

Paul Pival
Distance Education Librarian
University of Calgary

Tom Riedel
Distance Learning Librarian
Head of Access Services
Regis University

Christy Rilette
Distance Library Services
Loyola University

Steve Schafer
Director Library Services
Athabasca University

Jason Vance
Extended Campus Librarian
Morehead State University

Pat Wilson
Distance Learning
University of Kentucky

Introduction

Patrick B. Mahoney

These contributed papers describe many problems and solutions to issues facing librarians providing service to faculty and students who do not have access to a traditional library. A major issue facing librarians who provide such services to nontraditional faculty and students is collaboration. Several contributors tackle this issue as they discuss how they worked with different people and departments both within and outside their organizations to enhance distance information services.

Another issue discussed by several contributors deals with how services are monitored, or assessed, to serve as a gauge for future improvement. Assessment of services is a rapidly growing concern of all information programs, and the papers that discuss this issue not only present the obstacles facing the profession but solutions that serve to motivate librarians to initiate similar assessment programs.

A hallmark of conference proceedings is to witness the progression of topics with each conference. This year's proceedings not only build from papers presented at previous conferences but enhance the profession by posing new solutions to current problems. The presentation of ideas and solutions to further promote service to distance information users in these contributed papers reflect the vitality of the profession, and will provide yet another platform for additional growth.

[Haworth co-indexing entry note]: "Introduction." Mahoney, Patrick, B. Co-published simultaneously in *Journal of Library Administration* (The Haworth Information Press, an imprint of The Haworth Press, Inc.) Vol. 41, No. 1/2, 2004, p. 1; and: *The Eleventh Off-Campus Library Services Conference Proceedings* (ed: Patrick B. Mahoney) The Haworth Information Press, an imprint of The Haworth Press, Inc., 2004, p. 1.

CONTRIBUTED PAPERS

Educating the Educators:
Outreach to the College of Education
Distance Faculty
and Native American Students

Tina M. Adams
R. Sean Evans

Northern Arizona University

SUMMARY. The focus of "Educating the Educators: Outreach to the College of Education Distance Faculty and Native American Students" is to examine and explore the relationship between the Library and the College of Education regarding provision and promotion of Library services to students and faculty taking and teaching classes virtually and at satellite campus and computer lab locations throughout the state. It will include an overview of the special challenges facing the Library in providing these services to a college that offers a large number of distance education classes, enrolls a large number of Native American students, and includes a majority of the institution's distance students and part-time distance faculty.

KEYWORDS. Distance education, faculty, library instruction

[Haworth co-indexing entry note]: "Educating the Educators: Outreach to the College of Education Distance Faculty and Native American Students." Adams, Tina M., and R. Sean Evans. Co-published simultaneously in *Journal of Library Administration* (The Haworth Information Press, an imprint of The Haworth Press, Inc.) Vol. 41, No. 1/2, 2004, pp. 3-18; and: *The Eleventh Off-Campus Library Services Conference Proceedings* (ed: Patrick B. Mahoney) The Haworth Information Press, an imprint of The Haworth Press, Inc., 2004, pp. 3-18.

http://www.haworthpress.com/web/JLA
Digital Object Identifier: 10.1300/J111v41n01_02

Specifically, the presentation will explore four areas:

- The nature of the programs, students and faculty of the College of Education;
- The unique conditions under which these courses are offered in rural and reservation locations;
- The special conditions of the reservation, including population, economic and educational considerations; and finally,
- How the library's services and promotion efforts have been adapted to be most effective in this unique environment.

ABOUT NORTHERN ARIZONA UNIVERSITY AND OUR NATIVE AMERICAN POPULATION

Over the last ten years Northern Arizona University (NAU) has embraced an ever more aggressive distance education program, serving students primarily in Arizona, but increasingly from an ever growing and diverse array of locations. Initially, NAU undertook this effort by establishing branch campuses around Arizona. Today, looking at the map of NAU IITV and computer lab locations gives an idea of the nature of the program as it was started, and to the extent it still exists today.[1] Early distance education models at NAU made use of local instructors or faculty, or had faculty travel from Flagstaff to the distance sites to teach classes. Today that model still exists, but an ever increasing number of classes are being offered by IITV and via the Internet. The challenge for the Cline Library historically has been to provide library service to users at a distance regardless of the format of their class. An additional challenge has been to do this for our students who are Native American and participating in classes via sites located throughout their respective Reservations.

NAU currently enrolls about 1,343 Native American students as of Fall semester of 2002, which is about 7% of the total student population. NAU ranks 4th of all colleges and universities in the nation in total enrollment of Native American students. In addition, NAU is ranked second in the nation for total degrees awarded to Native Americans. A majority of these students are from the Navajo tribe with the Hopi tribe being the next most common. An amazing 65% of the graduate students in the College of Education are Native American, so it is no wonder that one of NAU's primary goals is to be the nation's leading university serving Native Americans. With this goal in mind, the Cline Library's services to this population are vital to the mission of the University.[2]

VITAL STATISTICS[3]

Educational Enrollment

In Arizona, there are 1.4 million students over the age of three enrolled in some form of public or private education. This stands against a total population of 5.1 million in the state, or about 27% of the entire population. The single largest block of students fall into the grades 1-8, comprising 44.6% of the total student number. College or graduate school enrollees are next, at 23.6% of the total student population.

For the Navajo Reservation and Trust Lands area (which includes Arizona, New Mexico and Utah), the total population is 181,269. Of that number, 39% of reservation residents over the age of three are enrolled in public or private education The single largest block of students fall into the grade 1-8 category at 53.1% of the total student number, the next highest numbers are from the grade 9-12 category with 25.1% of total. College or graduate school enrollment accounts for only 7,573 students or 10.6% of the total.

All students over age 3	Arizona 1,401,840	Navajo Reservation and Trust Areas 71,172 (% change from Arizona)	
Nursery School/Preschool	81,923 / 5.8%	4,062 / 5.2%	(−.6%)
Kindergarten	77,930 / 5.6%	3,889 / 5.5%	(−.1%)
Elementary School (grades 1-8)	624,766 / 44.6%	37,757 / 53.1%	(+8.5%)
High School (grades 9-12)	286,122 / 20.4%	17,891 / 25.1%	(+4.7%)
College, Graduate School	331,099 / 23.6%	7,573 / 10.6%	(−13.0%)

Educational Attainment

In Arizona, for the population over 25 years of age, 26.4% has had some college education, with the next greatest number, 24.3%, having achieved a High School degree or equivalent. On the Navajo Reservation for the population over 25 years of age, the largest block of that population has achieved a High School degree or equivalent at 26.3%, with the next largest block being those with less than a 9th grade education at 24.4%.

Population over 25 years of age	Arizona 3,256,184	Navajo Reservation and Trust Areas 88,662 (% change from Arizona)	
Less than 9th grade	254,696 / 7.8%	21,612 / 24.4%	(+16.6%)
9th to 12th grade, no diploma	364,851 / 11.2%	17,457 / 19.7%	(+8.5%)
High school graduate	791,904 / 24.3%	23,333 / 26.3%	(+2.0%)
Some college, no degree	859,165 / 26.4%	15,048 / 17.0%	(−9.4%)

Associate degree	219,356 / 6.7%	4,748 / 5.4%	(−1.3%)
Bachelor's degree	493,419 / 15.2%	4,135 / 4.7%	(−10.5%)
Graduate or professional degree	272,793 / 8.4%	2,329 / 2.6%	(−5.8%)
Percentage high school graduate or higher	81%	55.9%	(−25.1%)
Percentage bachelor's degree or higher	23.5%	7.3%	(−16.2%)

As we can see, there are many similarities but also some significant differences between these segments of Arizona's populations. Generally, we can see that in comparison with the population of the State of Arizona, residents of the Navajo reservation have significantly lower educational attainment. Despite similar and often greater percentages of enrolled students, it can be inferred from this data that enrollment does not necessarily lead to degree completion.

Economic Conditions

Rather than examine the entirety of economic data available from Summary File 3 of the 2000 U.S. Census, we will focus on these key areas: employment and unemployment, and income and industry.

For the State of Arizona, there is a potential labor population of 3,907,229 (comprised of people over 16 years of age); of those 61.1%, are employed. Limiting employment status to just those in the civilian labor force lowers unemployment to 3.4%.

For Arizona, 18% of those employed are working in the education, health and social services industries.

Income for Arizona looks like this: median household income is $40,558, median family income is $46,723 and per capita income is $20,275, with median male and female year-round worker incomes being $35,184 and $26,777 respectively. Poverty status statewide for families is 13.9%.

For the Navajo Reservation and Trust Areas, the figures shift dramatically. The potential laboring population of this region is 114,966. Of that number, 44.7% are in the labor force. The percentage of that group that is unemployed is 11.2%.

The percentage of those working, work in the education, health and social services industries is 35.6% of all employed.

Income for the reservation and trust lands looks like this: median household income is $20,005, median family income is $22,392, per capita income is $7,269, with full-time male and female year-round workers earnings being $25,667 and $20,868 respectively. Poverty status for families on the Navajo Reservation is 40.1%.

Population over 16 years of age	Arizona 3,907,229	Navajo Reservation and Trust Lands 114,966	
Civilian labor force	2,387,139 / 61.1%	51,363 / 44.7%	(−16.4%)
Employed	2,366,372 / 60.6%	51,330 / 44.6%	(−16.0%)
Unemployed	133,368 / 3.4%	12,865 / 11.2%	(+7.8%)
Education, health and social service employment	402,183 / 18.0%	13,705 / 35.6%	(+17.6%)
Median household income	$40,558	$20,005	(−$20,553)
Median family income	$46,723	$22,392	(−$24,331)
Per capita earnings	$20,275	$ 7,269	(−$13,006)
Median male full-time earnings	$35,184	$25,667	(−$9,517)
Median female full-time earnings	$26,777	$20,868	(−$5,909)

Clearly we can illustrate two interesting economic realities in examining differences between the state of Arizona and the Navajo reservation. First, there is a huge disparity between the population groups in income which can have far reaching effects regarding what can be done educationally on the reservation. Second, that while the industries surrounding education, health and social services comprise the single largest block of employers in both the state and the reservation, but that the percentage increase for the reservation population is notable. On the Navajo Reservation education, health and social service jobs account for more than 35% of all available jobs (nearly double the percentage of the state as a whole).

INTRODUCTION TO THE LITERATURE

There is very little in the library literature regarding library services to Native American populations. What little research that has been done on this topic is no longer current. There are a few useful articles written in the mid-1990s that discuss public library services to this special population, but we have not found anything in the literature regarding academic library services to Native American student populations.[4] Much of what we have included in this paper is experiential and our own assessment although we have drawn on non-library related literature when appropriate.

NATURE OF THE COLLEGE OF EDUCATION PROGRAM

The NAU College of Education offered in Spring 2004 a total of 181 classes, 40 of which are undergraduate. Many of these classes were offered in multiple sections. There are a total of 119 full time on-campus faculty and 484 part-time distance faculty, for a total of 603 Education Faculty. For the purposes of this paper, we will be focusing on those classes offered on the Navajo Reservation, though it is important to note that only 29% of our Native American student population attends classes via Reservation sites. The majority attend the Flagstaff Mountain Campus. This Spring semester marks a turning point away from reliance on on-site instructors to provide classes locally (3) to instead offering classes via IITV and the Internet (9). All education classes offered on the Reservation for the Spring 2004 semester were graduate level classes.

HISTORY OF LIBRARY SERVICES TO DISTANCE LEARNERS AT NAU

In 1987 the Cline Library established the Field Services Office, which served as a reference unit and an interlibrary loan unit for NAU's distance students. As originally configured, Field Services through a variety of means took library services into the field, meaning to places where distance classes occurred. In those days before the Internet, this meant hauling paper copies of indexes and abstracts to the various field sites, and instructing users on how to perform literature searches in these titles. Once students located articles they needed, they contacted the Field Services office which would then obtain copies of materials students needed from the library's periodical collection, or through Interlibrary Loan. The arrival of PC and laptop technology helped in that CD-ROM-based databases could be taken and set up at field sites or classrooms for instruction sessions and student use. Field Services duplicated existing library services, but provided them to the distance student population.

Field Services began expanding its role in providing library services, and in the mid-1990s, changing its name to Distributed Library Services to both reflect a change in expansion of services, and also the beginning of its integration into the Cline Library's other units. DLS began by making use of the library's Interlibrary Loan unit to acquire, duplicate and ship materials to distance students rather than performing those tasks within their own unit. DLS was then better able to serve distance sites by focusing on on-site instruction, or distance phone (and later e-mail) reference service. DLS's unique service was gradually being integrated into the library's regular service. Processes were being put in place to ensure that all library users were receiving more equitable treatment and service regardless of their location relative to the University's main campus.

This process accelerated when the library's Reference department began to assist DLS in performing literature searches for students and performing on-site instruction sessions. Meanwhile, the library was also rapidly moving to make more and more of its resources available via the Internet which made mediated searching for students redundant. With the acquisition of more and more online, full-text databases, library users were not as reliant upon the library to perform searches, or to fax and mail them articles.

CURRENT LIBRARY SERVICES
TO DISTANCE LEARNERS AT NAU

As has been noted in the previous discussion, historically, the Cline Library has served the needs of distance students via a separate department, Distributed Library Services. However, in 2000 the decision was made by our administration to integrate the Distributed Library Services (DLS) Department into the main Reference Department, the philosophy being that on-campus and off-campus students should be provided with equitable services and served by all staff rather than by a separate department. This philosophy required staff to assume that all students needed the same services, though at times these services may be delivered in different ways.

In the past, DLS had provided what was perceived as separate but equal services by searching for and delivering materials directly to distance students. Pedagogically, this was not sound, as it was discovered that distance students were not gaining the benefit of becoming information literate. A shift in the provision of services occurred which realigned library services and the promotion of information literacy while still providing fast and effective delivery of materials.

To this end, the library's Interlibrary Loan service (now called Document Delivery Services or DDS) moved to a Web-based request form allowing users to request that the Cline Library obtain materials from other libraries from any location. DDS expanded services to include shipping library-owned materials to NAU students living more that forty miles from campus, thus making our collections available to our distance users in a way similar to our users based on or near campus. DDS had already instituted mailing or faxing of articles directly to users. Electronic delivery of articles had also been added by an initiative out of the Arizona State Library to make use of PCs and scanners to electronically deliver material via the Arial system.

To some extent, through these efforts the library is trying to re-create the traditional role of the library as information provider to students and faculty. We know now, and have known for a while, that setting distance users adrift to find their research via local libraries or the Internet has not served them well. The academic library's services have become nearly invisible for distance users. It is only through such programs that libraries can bring back and expand their patron base, and provide a quality service to all of their users. [5]

The final enhancement to our distance users was the creation of the library's Ask-A-Librarian (AAL) service (www4.nau.edu/library/reference/aal/askalibrarian.asp). While largely just an outgrowth of the e-mail service for distance students, AAL now allows library users on campus, in Flagstaff, or at a distance to use a Web-based e-mail form to formulate their reference question, and send it to us at the Reference Desk. As the Reference desk is open and staffed every day (more than ninety hours per week), we guarantee twenty-four hour response to questions. Those questions which we cannot answer immediately at the desk are referred to other library departments, librarians or subject teams as appropriate. For those more routine questions, we employ a set array of stationeries covering interlibrary loans, renewals, basic research, etc.

The aspect the service users do not see is the Web-based management system created in-house by our Library Technology Services unit that records the question, the user's contact information and status (NAU affiliated or not), and our response to the question. Additional information like time and date of the question and answer, and any referral data are recorded as well. The system allows the user to respond to the quality of the answer they receive by asking them if their question was in fact answered and by permitting them to ask for additional help. As this is an e-mail-based system, it is easy to track questions and answers as well as any questions we forward to teams. The system automatically scrubs user information from the database after two weeks, allowing us to keep track of questions and answers–a very useful training and analysis tool. One aspect of the service that needs some mention is the lack of a chat function. At this point AAL has purposely avoided chat. This is based upon a number of factors: service hours, experience with current commercial chat products, and technology issues with distance students.

Many of our students make use of our Ask-A-Librarian e-mail service. We average 200 questions a month via Ask-A-Librarian; this number has been steadily climbing. This is a fairly significant number, considering that NAU is a relatively moderate size university of about 19,000 students. During the last three months that we have kept statistics about our service, as much as 12% of our reference questions were asked via Ask-A-Librarian. One of the reasons may, of course, be that our turnaround time is, on average, under two hours, but the fact that we serve such a far-flung rural population may also account for these numbers. [6]

While we do not have any way of knowing whether these numbers include students from the reservation, the high number would indicate that we are probably serving many Native American students with this service. In addition to our Ask-A-Librarian service, we also provide a toll free phone number which anyone may use to call us long distance at no charge and ask a question.

Because our Ask-A-Librarian service is so successful, it may seem that the obvious next step would be to adopt some of the other electronic reference services such as chat or video conferencing. At this time, we do not have any plans to proceed with new technologies due to cost and the inadequate infrastructure within many of the communities that we serve.

LIBRARY INSTRUCTION
AND NATIVE AMERICAN DISTANCE LEARNERS

Instruction at distance sites via in-person, IITV, and, when necessary, in Internet class-based chat rooms, is vital, especially with regard to some of the special populations we serve off-campus, such as the Navajo and Hopi tribes. It is obvious that instruction is necessary to bridge the skills gap with this population who are less technologically and computer savvy due to more limited access to computers. The Reservation areas are heavily dependent upon the NAU computer labs, which are often shared with, and housed in, public schools. Due to the infrastructure challenge on the Reservations, these labs are sometimes the only place that people living on the Reservations are exposed to, and have the opportunity to use computers.

Instruction sessions held on the Reservation are very well attended. Students there are interested in developing their research skills. But even with such a motivated group of students, there are many challenges to providing services on the Reservation. Travel and travel costs are often an issue. Reservation instruction requires the use of a university fleet vehicle and often an overnight stay where lodging and food must be paid for. This can mean up to $200 per trip just to send one librarian to do one instruction session. Many of the population centers on the Reservation are more than a hundred miles from the main campus in Flagstaff, so even when an overnight stay is not necessary, librarians must travel part of each day to get to the sites and back. This means leave-time for one or more librarians for an entire day. In addition, there is a cost to NAU for use of the computer labs or IITV labs. Obviously, these costs can add up quickly.

As mentioned, the computer labs are often housed in local public schools. Most contain only about ten computers, are quite small, and may have limited hours of access. Usually there are not enough computers to accommodate an entire class. Three or four students must share a computer. In addition, sometimes librarians must bring their own equipment such as a laptop and projector because the labs are set up for student use but not for instruction, so there is often not an instructor station. Sometimes the equipment and Internet connections are not compatible so the equipment is of no use. Often the only way to conduct an instruction session is for the librarian(s) to walk around, looking over students' shoulders at their computer monitors indicating in steps, "Click here, now click there." It is also important to supplement the instruction session with a written handout that includes information on access, strategies, and contact information for both students and faculty.

Once the presentation part of the session is over, librarians incorporate hands-on time into the class, so that students can begin their research and consult us with any questions. Often these library instruction classes are three to four hours long, and these students may never see a librarian again while in their program, so it is important to use the time well to help students with their immediate need, but to also instill rapport so students will be more likely to contact the library when they need assistance later as well.

Third, as we mentioned before, these students are often less computer savvy due to the lack of computer access and because the average Native American student is older than the traditional non Native American student. Statistically speaking, the majority of Native American college students are twenty-five years of age or older. Both the age of the students and their lack of advanced computer skills means that the instruction session is more effective if there are two librarians present. In that instance, one librarian can present, while the other assists students individually with keeping up with the instruction session. When the hands-on part of the session begins, the second librarian is indispensable for helping to field questions and assist with individual consultations.

Another consideration when providing instruction to this particular population is cultural awareness and sensitivity. Many of the students that we teach on the Reservation are Navajo, although some are Hopi. We have found that in-person instruction is by far the most effective and culturally respectful form of instruction for this population. Native American students, in general, have expressed a preference for face-to-face instruction. We have found that Native American students often have a fear of asking questions. In addition, as the research on learning styles in Native American populations has shown, these students usually prefer to work in groups, prefer to approach the research in a holistic and global style of organization rather than a linear or sequential approach and learn best when material is presented with a visual component, like illustrations, multimedia or other visual aids. In general, Native American students also prefer observational and collaborative activities to lecture and textual learning.

When instructing students from these cultures, we try to take into account both cultural considerations and learning style preferences. We present the resources so students may observe how to use a particular interface. Then, we allow students to work in groups and have plenty of hands-on free time. At this time in the class, the librarians will visit the groups of students individually. In these smaller groups students generally feel more comfortable asking questions and we are able to answer the more complex questions. Of course, the research and our own experiential observations are all generalizations and there are exceptions. We do not want to imply that all Native American students–or even all Navajo students–are alike, but through our own experience we have found that these preferences for learning generally hold true for the students we have interacted with.

In addition to the manner of instruction, it is also important that we choose, or make available, culturally sensitive materials. For example, in one class involving research relevant to starting a small business, we chose to use a short video in addition to the standard review of finding and using relevant resources. We chose a video that we thought would be engaging and get the students interested. The video contained interviews with successful Native American entrepreneurs who answered insightful questions and gave advice. This was a great hit with the students who remarked that they liked it because it was produced by, for and about Native Americans. When choosing materials it is vital that you not choose condescending materials. This video was relevant and respectful, but not preachy, about what is needed to succeed as a Native American businessperson and had the added benefit of employing the students' preference for visual learning.

Choosing good materials is important, but students must also be made aware of collections that may be of special interest to them. For instance, often the students we instruct on the reservation who are enrolled in the College of Education are majors of our Bilingual and Multicultural Education program. These students find our special collections and archives materials very useful. The Special Collections and Archives at NAU Cline Library collect materials related to the history of the Colorado Plateau region of Northern Arizona. Students studying Bilingual and Multicultural Education through the College of Education can find a rich collection of materials related to Navajo and Hopi culture and history, including materials that are relevant for studying early white-motivated "education" programs and the related movement to assimilate Native Americans into white culture.

In another case, the library provided culturally relevant materials, via Document Delivery Services (DDS), to a Reservation-based IITV class. We worked with the instructor to identify and provide an array of biographies of famous Native Americans. If the library did not have a requested biography, we purchased it on rush order. It cannot be overstated how important it is for libraries to collect and provide culturally responsible materials to support and inform not only our Native American students, but to provide a realistic cultural representation of any ethnic group to all of our students.

Culturally speaking, though in-person instruction is the most effective, it is not the only way in which we instruct students on the reservation. IITV classes–broadcast from the home campus to satellite campuses across the reservation–are very popular, so librarians often attend these classes to teach research skills.

It is no surprise that librarians serving distance students must always be able to adapt. For instance, teaching library skills via IITV can be uncomfortable at first. One must interact with the students via television cameras, be prepared to write down all important information such as Web addresses, telephone numbers and other contact information and broadcast it via the pad cam, since students in this environment often prefer visual learning over auditory.

In addition to being comfortable with using a pad cam for writing notes, one must consciously remember to speak clearly and monitor all IITV screens, all showing different sites, to be aware of students' questions or to notice problems or confusion. One must also be comfortable with being a disembodied voice! Much of the session will be spent showing students how to navigate through the library Web page, while the narration goes over the image of the Web page that is being shown on the monitors.

INTERNET-BASED CLASSES AND WEB INSTRUCTION TOOLS LIKE *WebQuest*

Increasingly, NAU is moving away from IITV classes and even in-person Reservation classes in favor of Internet-based courses. This may have implications for Native American students who generally prefer IITV and in-person classes. In addition, there are a limited number of computers available to Reservation students and some computer skills issues.[7] How all of these factors will affect the way NAU and the Cline Library serves the students on the Reservation remains to be seen, as this is a new direction. However, it is clear that this change will again require librarians who serve off-campus students to find viable ways to instruct students at a distance.

One tool that we are in the process of developing and hope will have more instruction application than our current course resource page is the use of WebQuest modules. WebQuest is still in its infancy at the Cline Library, but may prove to be a tool which can be used to relate the research process to students through sequential modules. We will include illustrations, audio, and video files in these WebQuest modules to address students' many learning styles and compensate for the fewer opportunities for in-class library instruction as the University moves increasingly towards Web-based teaching in the distance learning environment. At the moment, the library has used subject or class-specific course pages to assist students with locating important resources for a particular class or assignment. Unfortunately, while these course resource pages are very popular and do address many of the needs of our distance learners for easy access to librarian vetted lists of resources, they are not designed to provide instruction about the research process. [8]

OUTREACH TO FACULTY AND STUDENTS

The library has developed many services for students and faculty in the home campus environment. Because of distances involved, the challenge has been to not only provide these same services equitably to students and faculty at a distance as we have discussed, but to generally increase faculty and student awareness of the services that the library can provide them.

In an attempt to educate faculty about our services, the librarians from the Education Team worked with the Assistant Dean of the College of Education and the College's Instructional Designer to arrange the library's involvement in the College of Education Faculty Development Workshop. After our presentation we met individually with interested faculty who wanted to discuss their needs with us one-on-one and arrange appointments.

The challenge is always, of course, enticing the faculty to attend such workshops. Although attendance was less than we had hoped for (only a dozen or so faculty were present), we deemed the workshop a success. Most of the faculty at the workshop subsequently asked for a course resource page, an instruction session or electronic reserve, as a result of the session. Many informed their colleagues who did not attend, who in turn contacted us for assistance. We administered an evaluation tool to the attendees. All of the respondents from the workshop rated the session as "Extremely Useful" with many giving us enthusiastic feedback such as:

"Extremely useful, yes! All of the faculty on campus would benefit by this presentation! People where gracious & go beyond the call of duty to be helpful! Thanks."

"Excellent Services! Very Impressive!" "I look forward to working with you."

In addition to the on-campus workshop we partnered with the College of Education to provide a workshop for distance faculty. The workshop was a grant-funded full-day orientation for part-time distance faculty packed with presenters on various topics of interest to Education faculty. The grant allowed the part-time faculty to travel from all over the state and be provided with lodging to attend the event. As part of the workshop, the College of Education developed a Web page to accompany the orientation. The Education librarians arranged to participate by providing a Web page to be included on the orientation site and the Assistant Dean of Education offered to present this site at the day seminar. See the Web page at: http://jan.ucc.nau.edu/~rse/LibraryServicesFaculty.html. While the event was only funded to allow about sixty part-time distance faculty to attend, it was definitely a step in the right direction for addressing the need to inform part-time distance faculty of the services and resources available to them at the home campus.

Another inexpensive and often used approach to communicating information concerning vital services is via e-mail. While not always a successful way to connect with faculty, it is just one of the many ways that the library attempts to inform faculty of new products or services, as well as frequently reminding faculty of our ability to assist them. We send reminder notices before the beginning of each semester encouraging faculty to contact us for course-related assistance. Faculty can request online course readings, the creation of a course resource Web page, or general or assignment driven library instruction online. The form is available from the library's Web site at: http://www.nau.edu/library/services/request/coursesupport.html.

Participation in orientation efforts, campus events and special events held by the College are also approaches used. In the process of getting the word out about the library to the students who attend these events, we also have the opportunity to network and meet some of the faculty in person. Visibility is highly important when trying to promote the library to the campus. When possible, getting on the agenda to present briefly at a college's departmental meetings is also a great way to remain visible and involved.

In addition to these various efforts, we still often rely on print publication materials to publicize the library in the many computer and IITV labs located throughout the reservation and the state. We send current brochures to the labs regularly in an effort to promote our services directly to students at their point of need in the labs. Brochures are also included in a direct mailing from the Graduate College to all new graduate students. We also attend IITV and lab technician orientations to give a brief synopsis of what the library can do for students and all the services available. This is especially important since often students at remote labs will ask the lab technician research questions. We want to give the lab techs a basic understanding of using the library Web site, but emphasize to them the many ways they can direct students to the library for assistance, such as our toll free reference phone number and our Ask-A-Librarian service.

Much of our outreach efforts are in transition as we shift from an organizational structure based on individual subject specialists supporting a college to a team-based approach supporting programs and implementing outreach efforts. We have met formally and informally with small groups of faculty demonstrating our services. We find outreach can occur just as effectively by "word-of-mouth." One faculty member impressed by library support can, through their communication with colleagues, lead to more interaction between librarians and faculty.

CONCLUSIONS

This paper has explored the unique relationship between the library and the College of Education regarding provision and promotion of library services to students and faculty taking and teaching classes at a distance. We have sought to explain the special cultural, technical and logistical challenges facing the library in providing these services to a college that offers a large number of distance education classes, enrolls a large number of Native American students and includes a majority of the institution's part-time distance faculty. We have shared our efforts, formal and informal, to address these challenges. We hope these attempts will contribute to anyone serving Native Americans, and will further the academic success of Native American students.

NOTES

1. For a map and location guide of NAU Distance sites, see: www.nau.edu/its/swlabs/labinfo.html.

2. For a more complete picture of Native American students and employees at Northern Arizona University, please see the NAU Office of Native American Student Services Report, "Fall 2001 Native American Student and Employee Report." http://www2.nau.edu/nass/.

3. All of the population and occupation information is pulled from the 2000 Census of the United States, specifically from the Summary File 3. This material was acquired from the American Factfinder (http://factfinder.census.gov/home/saff/main.html) Web site. The methodology employed involved collecting from Quick Tables the DP-2 Profile of Selected Social Characteristics 2000, DP-3 Profile of Selected Economic Characteristics 2000, and DP-4 Profile of Selected Housing Statistics for the entire State of Arizona, and the Navajo Nation Reservation and Off-Reservation Trust Land, AZ–NM–UT.

4. For a discussion of Public Library services see "Information needs and services of Native Americans." in *Rural Libraries* Vol. 15, 1995, pp. 37-44. and "Native Americans and library service: Washington examples." in *Alki* Vol. 11, March, 1995, pp. 6-7.

5. Ann Wolpert succinctly describes the situation in her article "Service to Remote Users: Marketing the Library's Role" in *Library Trends*, Vol. 47 (1), pp. 21-42. Specifically see the section entitled Academic Libraries.

6. The first assessment of the Ask-A-Librarian service came in April 2003. It confirmed much of what was known about the service, but there were some interesting elements. The report is entitled: *An Analysis of the Ask A Librarian Service June 2002 to April 2003.* and is available at: http://www4.nau.edu/library/reference/AALReportJune2002toApril2003.htm.

7. Among the unique aspects of the Navajo Reservation is the relative lack of Internet connectivity. This means for many of NAU's reservation based students that their only means of Internet access is at an NAU Computer Lab, or on a PC at one of the public schools. Private PC ownership is not very prevalent as slightly more than 60% of Reservation residences lack even telephone service according to Census 2000 Summary File 3, DP-4 Profile of Selected Housing Characteristics: 2000. See: http://factfinder.census.gov/home/saff/main.html for additional data.

8. See: *The WebQuest Page* at: http://webquest.sdsu.edu/ for more information and samples of WebQuest pages for student use. The essential implication for librarians attempting library research instruction at a distance is the need to find ways to add instructional text to the basic elements of the course pages already offered to replace the lack of in-person instructional opportunities. While the library is currently experimenting with the WebQuest model, it is possible that we may wind up with another product or some sort of hybrid entity.

REFERENCES

American Factfinder, summary file 3 quickfiles. Retrieved 17 November 2003 from United States Bureau of the Census, American Factfinder Web site: http://factfinder.census.gov/home/saff/main.html.

An analysis of the Ask A Librarian service June 2002 to April 2003. Retrieved 5 December 2003, from Northern Arizona University, Reference Services Web site: http://www4.nau.edu/library/reference/AALReportJune2002toApril2003.htm.

Fall 2001 Native American student and employee report. (2001). Retrieved 3, December 2003, from Northern Arizona University, Planning and Institutional Research Web site: http://www2.nau.edu/nass/.

Hilberg, R. Soleste, and Tharp, Roland. (2002). *Theoretical perspectives, research findings and classroom implications of the learning styles of American Indian and Alaska Native students.* (Report No. EDO-RC-02-3). Charleston, WV: ERIC Clearinghouse on Rural Education and Small Schools. (ERIC Document Reproduction Service No. ED468000).

Talakte, Catherine. (n.d.). *NAU factbook 2002-2003: Northern Arizona University student characteristics, Native American students fall 2002.* Retrieved December 2003, from Northern Arizona University, Native American Student Services Web site: http://www4.nau.edu/pair/Factbook/2002FactBook/FactBook2002-2003.htm.

Wolpert, A. (1998). Service to remote users: Marketing the library's role. *Library Trends, 47,* 21-42.

On Ramp to Research:
Creation of a Multimedia Library
Instruction Presentation
for Off-Campus Students

Michele D. Behr

Western Michigan University

SUMMARY. This paper discusses the planning and development process of a project to create a Web-based multimedia instruction tool for off-campus graduate students in Education. The project involves Macromedia Flash for animation, MP3 sound files for voice narration, text, still images, and Web screen shots. The tutorial uses several different forms of technology and media to appeal to any learning style a student prefers, and it offers non-linear navigation to allow students to select the section they need, and to repeat any section.

KEYWORDS. Library instruction, distance education, distance learners, library services

INTRODUCTION

For the off-campus student the library Web site *is* for all intents and purposes their library; they access nearly all necessary resources and services through those pages. It is therefore appropriate to have a Web-based solution for educating and assisting them with access and navigation. While in

[Haworth co-indexing entry note]: "On Ramp to Research: Creation of a Multimedia Library Instruction Presentation for Off-Campus Students." Behr, Michele D. Co-published simultaneously in *Journal of Library Administration* (The Haworth Information Press, an imprint of The Haworth Press, Inc.) Vol. 41, No. 1/2, 2004, pp. 19-30; and: *The Eleventh Off-Campus Library Services Conference Proceedings* (ed: Patrick B. Mahoney) The Haworth Information Press, an imprint of The Haworth Press, Inc., 2004, pp. 19-30.

http://www.haworthpress.com/web/JLA
Digital Object Identifier: 10.1300/J111v41n01_03

person instruction is always the most effective and valuable method of delivery, the realities of current economics for colleges and universities require that we look to use technology as a way to reach a wider audience in a more cost effective manner. This paper describes the process of one of these endeavors.

BACKGROUND

Western Michigan University (WMU) currently has approximately 3,000 students enrolled each semester in its off-campus programs offered through the Office of Extended University Programs (EUP). Classes are taught in person at seven branch campus locations throughout Michigan. In addition distance education programs are offered through compressed video, as well as online and self-instructional delivery methods.

While off-campus programs include both undergraduate and graduate offerings, the vast majority of off-campus students (87%) are enrolled in graduate programs. Masters programs represent 77% of off-campus students, with the remaining 10% being at the doctoral level. Academic programs offered at off-campus locations include Public Administration, Social Work, Business, Counseling, Engineering, multiple courses of study in Education, as well as several other disciplines.

WMU off-campus students are primarily non-traditional. According to a recent survey of students off-campus the majority of students are female (66%). The vast majority (88%) are employed full time. The average age of students is in the mid-30s, with more than one-third of students over the age of 35. Slightly less than half of the off-campus students pay all of their tuition by themselves (44%) with the remaining students receiving partial or full tuition assistance through employers (32%) or loans and grants (24%).

LIMITATIONS OF THE CURRENT LIBRARY
INSTRUCTION PROGRAM

The WMU Libraries provide an array of services to support students and faculty in off-campus programs. Services include electronic resources such as e-books, full-text databases, electronic journals, and online reference sources. Document delivery and interlibrary loan services are requested and handled using ILLiad software. Books are delivered to the students' home, and articles are scanned and mounted on the Web for the student to pick up. Reference services are provided over the phone, through e-mail and "chat" using the Docutek VRLplus software. In addition, librarians meet with students and faculty in person at locations throughout the state. The library's Web pages make available many guides, handouts, and instructional tools to help students find the information they seek.

Off-campus services librarians also conduct regular bibliographic instruction sessions in the computer labs at all of the WMU branch campuses. Typically, about eighty formal in class face-to-face instruction sessions per year are held in off-campus locations. In addition, librarians hold "drop-in" labs throughout the semester in all the WMU branch campuses. Through these efforts several hundred off-campus students receive in person library instruction each year.

While the current instruction program emphasizes face-to-face instruction, it has the following limitations:

1. The model is dependent on instructors to request a library presentation. While some faculty members routinely request instruction for their classes, others have never contacted the library to request instruction. In addition, depending on the academic program, the majority of the instructors are adjunct faculty who teach one class a semester and have no other connection with the University. These instructors are often not aware of the services the library can provide to their students. Because of this situation, students may have taken several classes requiring library research before they have attended a formal instruction session.

2. There are over 3000 students taking classes off-campus each semester and only 1.5 FTE librarians to provide instruction to these students. Given this ratio, there is simply no way to effectively provide instruction to all these students in person.

3. Normally, in class presentations are sixty to ninety minutes. While this may be longer than many "one shot" library instruction sessions on campus, sessions for off-campus students must also include basic information on how to connect to the library databases remotely, use of the document delivery system, and other services available to them. Sometimes explanation of these services alone takes close to half the time of the formal session.

4. Non-traditional students need additional help with the basic technology needed to access information remotely. As mentioned previously, WMU off-campus students are older than their on-campus counterparts. Therefore they often do not have the experience or comfort level with computers, software, and general Web navigation that younger

students possess. Library instruction for these students requires working with them on technology related skills as well as the use of databases and resources.

5. The most effective instruction would be at "point of need." As mentioned previously, the vast majority of WMU off-campus students are at work during the day and need to access library research services late at night and on weekends.

In addition to the limitations of the instruction program, students also had difficulty and required a great deal of assistance in accessing electronic resources through the library's proxy server. Remote access to the licensed databases and resources required that students configure their Web browser and then log in with their name and social security number. Off-campus services librarians, reference desks, and the WMU Help Desk logged hundreds of calls each semester from students having difficulty configuring their Web browser to access library resources. Problems ranged from students who did not know what version of the Web browser they had and therefore not able to get to the right set of directions, to those who had conflicts with their Internet Service Provider and the library proxy server. In addition, formal library instruction sessions required off-campus librarians to spend several minutes explaining how to configure the Web browser, and often much more time answering specific questions from students who had tried and failed to configure their Web browser successfully.

PROPOSED SOLUTION

Considering the limitations of our current instruction program, and the number of students we needed to reach, a Web-based solution seemed to have the most potential for improving services to students, being available when they needed it, and still remaining fairly cost effective. As many other authors have pointed out, "a clear and distinct advantage of using a Web-based tutorial is that it can be offered to anyone in the world at any time of the day or night, to the benefit of independent learners and those at a distance. Additionally, such a teaching tool requires no librarian intervention at the point of patron contact" (Dennis & Broughton, 2000, p. 32).

Western Michigan University has a relatively long history of developing and using computer assisted instruction among its library educational offerings. WMU librarians developed a HyperCard tutorial for incoming freshman in the early 1990s, and have also created other general and subject specific tutorials in recent years (Jayne, Arnold, & Vander Meer, 1998). Currently

SearchPath (http://www.wmich.edu/library/searchpath/index.html), an adaptation of the TILT tutorial from the University of Texas, is widely used in introductory courses on campus. These earlier experiences showed that while extremely useful and worthwhile, development of these Web-based modules could be time consuming, expensive, and require expertise not available in the library.

A good possibility for funding the development of a Web-based tool for off-campus students existed in the WMU Teaching and Learning with Technology (TLT) Grant program. This program provided up to $10,000 for individual projects. The primary goal of the TLT grant program was to "encourage and support faculty to make creative and effective use of technology to enhance teaching and learning." Grant monies could be used to purchase software and equipment and could pay for any additional staff needed to work on the project.

While the grant provided an opportunity to pay for the software and developmental expertise that did not exist at the time in the libraries, it did put some constraints on the project. Specifically, it required that the project be tied to a particular course, so an off-campus course which required library research needed to be identified. The ED601 class, Introduction to Research in Education Settings, was selected as a good candidate for this project. ED601 is required for most of the graduate programs in the College of Education, and is intended to provide students with an overview of major forms of research models used in educational settings and to provide them with skills in interpreting and evaluating educational research studies. One of the major course requirements is for each student to complete a research proposal including literature review. This course also seemed to be a good candidate for development of the project since it was taught off-campus nearly every semester and instructors often request library instruction in person to aid students in identifying and obtaining relevant research studies.

The Off-Campus Services Librarian who would serve as the Principal Investigator on the project approached one of the adjunct instructors who often taught the ED601 class off-campus about the possibility of being a Co-Principal Investigator. He agreed to participate, as well as to use his students to aid in the development of the content and usability. A series of meetings and exchanges of e-mails and phone calls took place as the grant application was written and the project goals defined.

Broadly defined at this point, the stated goals of the project were:

1. To answer basic questions from off-campus students about getting connected, getting books and articles, and finding research studies.

2. Prepare students to find the information they needed for the literature review portion of their required research proposal.
3. Introduce students to services available from the library for the ED601 class as well as the remainder of their course of study.
4. Enable them to know where to go for additional help and assistance with research and library use.
5. Make in person instruction as well as individual reference assistance more effective and productive.

The application was completed and the grant was accepted during the winter semester of 2002. The grant money would be available to be spent over the course of a year beginning April, 2002. The project proposal outlined thirteen topics to be covered and specified that the final product would involve multimedia including text, sound files, and animation.

LOOKING AT THE ROAD PREVIOUSLY TRAVELED

The next step was to assess and review the many tutorials and Web-based modules that had been developed and were being used by other libraries for various instructional purposes. As with many other tutorials, such as Bowling Green State University's FALCON, the presentation would model a standard library instruction session (Dennis & Broughton, 2000, p. 31). Like many others, our finished product was intended to provide users with remote, integrated, just-in-time help using the specialized, scholarly access tools and information purchased by the library for specialized research (Ardis & Haas, 2001). And as other authors have pointed out, the tutorial would not substitute for more traditional library instruction. "Rather it should be seen as an addition and an enhancement to the overall instructional plan" (Dennis & Broughton, 2000, p. 32).

Many Web-based instructional presentations were identified through the library literature as well as online clearinghouses such as the Internet Education Project (http://cooley.colgate.edu/etech/iep/default.html) sponsored by the ACRL Emerging Technologies in Instruction Committee. Review of these projects did not identify any existing product that matched our goals or was intended for use by a similar audience to ours.

The majority of other tutorials identified were designed for undergraduates, usually freshman or other lower division students. Also these products were designed primarily for a more general audience such as students in beginning composition courses. These tutorials also have broad goals with regard to furthering the efforts of information literacy on campus. Specifically, many tutorials reviewed aimed to help students gain skills in identifying and analyzing their information needs, locating and accessing information, and evaluating resources. Finally, the existing tutorials reviewed had a look and feel which was intended to appeal to students in the 18-22 age range, not our target population.

Very few tutorials identified were designed for a graduate student audience. Two notable exceptions are "Information Excavation," a tutorial for Graduate Students in Engineering at the University of Texas (http://www.lib.utexas.edu/engin/information-excavation/index.htm), and "The Education Tutorial" (http://www.nova.edu/library/dils/tutorials/education) designed for graduate students in Education at Nova Southeastern University.

The goals of the project were more mechanical and less "concept oriented" than most of the other projects reviewed. While the intention is for the concepts to be easily translated to multiple formats, the focus was for students to be able to use the libraries' Web site and the library databases to conduct the necessary research for their class and their continued assignments. FirstSearch was selected as the aggregator that would be used for the majority of the database examples since the WMU Libraries made ERIC available through FirstSearch. In addition the ILLiad system used for document delivery and interlibrary loan was integrated with the FirstSearch databases.

EARLY DECISIONS: HIGH ROAD OR LOW ROAD?

After reviewing other projects for content, functionality, and goals the next step was to determine the best technology and software options for this project. Required elements were that the application be able to include sound files and animation as well as text. Also flexible, nonlinear navigation was crucial. Students should be able to zero in on any particular section or sections they needed, to repeat sections and to skip through the tutorial to just those sections of interest.

Before any particular software package could be chosen an overall direction with regard to "low-end" or "high-end" technology needed to be settled on. Higher-end applications would require students to download necessary plug-ins and would require higher bandwidth for satisfactory performance. This higher-end option would, however, allow the finished product to be more engaging, dynamic, and allow greater flexibility in navigation. Lower-end options would run more easily on computers with dial up connections and without additional plug in software. However, this option would limit the way the information could be presented. The Off-Campus Services Librarian was mindful of the home computers and dial-in connections the off-campus students were using to access library resources. However, of primary importance was the ability to include multiple forms of media to appeal to any learning style a student prefers. A student who may be a more visual learner may choose to work primarily with the graphic and animated parts of the presentation. A student with a more auditory style may listen to the audio files with or without the other parts of the presentation.

Ultimately the higher-end technology direction was chosen and specifically Macromedia Flash MX was selected as the software. This application was chosen for its ability to include all types of media including text, sound, and video, as well as to provide animation. In addition, staff in the WMU Media Production Department had the necessary expertise with the software. While the finished product would require both high bandwidth as well as downloading of plug-ins, these problems could be solved if the finished product was also available on a CD-ROM in addition to delivery over the Web. While the grant would not pay for the files to be distributed on CD-ROM the Office of Extended University programs agreed to fund this part of the project. Having the files on CD-ROM solved the problems of the higher-end applications since students would not need to be connected to the Internet to use the product, and any necessary plug-ins could be included on the disc and would not have to be downloaded.

GETTING THE MOTORS READY

Next, to help determine the content of the presentation, a pretest was developed and distributed to students in two sections of the ED601 class in off-campus locations. The pretest included ten multiple-choice questions. The pretest showed that many students were unaware of the services the libraries offered them and had many misconceptions about how to do library research. This helped to focus on the issues that needed to be communicated with the project.

The faculty member acting as the Co-PI and the Off-Campus Services Librarian met to go over topics to be included and settle on content modules which would be of use to students in the ED601 class. The agreed upon six content modules were:

1. Overview of library services for off-campus students
2. Remote access to licensed resources (i.e., proxy server set-up)
3. Finding articles

4. Using ERIC
5. Finding books
6. Getting further information and assistance

A detailed outline was also developed to fill in the subsections for each of the modules. It was important that each subsection communicate a specific task that a student would need more direction on since it was designed so students could use the tutorial to get help at the point of need and not necessarily go through the whole presentation, or even a whole module.

The project was given the title "On Ramp to Research" to indicate the notion that this would help them to get started with their research. Also it was planned that the future marketing could tie into the concept of the "Information Highway." In addition, off-campus students commute to class often traveling many miles to access the program they want to pursue; a theme of commuting and traveling by car could be tied into future marketing.

The Off-Campus Services Librarian then met with staff in the Media Production Department of the University's Office of Information Technology who would be paid out of the grant money to do the design and development work. Prototypes of three basic screen and navigation designs were developed and reviewed. Student services staff in the branch campuses were asked to review the prototypes for ease of use and overall aesthetics. One of the three designs was ultimately chosen and a template was developed for the content to be added. The design incorporated a screen with sections for text, screen shots, photos, or animation, and buttons to turn the sound on or off, and to jump to other modules or sections as desired.

The Librarian began by writing out narrative scripts for each module. This proved problematic since each screen was limited to 600 characters and the information could not easily be logically broken up in sections. In working on the production of the modules it became important to "chunk" the information so a specific idea or concept was imparted on each screen.

A content entry template was designed in MS Word for the Off-Campus Services Librarian to write out the text for each screen. This text would be recorded in PP3 format and added at a later point. Screen shots of the library Web site, database, or other concept being described were taken in Fireworks and burned on CD-ROM for each module. The Web Librarian provided still shots of instruction sessions, library stacks, people using computers, etc. These images could be used for screens for which there was not a specific Web screen shot needed to illustrate a concept. Text files were sent as e-mail attachments to the developer in the Media Production Department. Screen shots and graphics were burned on CD and delivered in person since the files were too big to be sent as e-mail attachments.

BUMPS IN THE ROAD

As other authors have noted, the Web tutorial proved to be a very labor-intensive experience (Bracke & Dickstein, 2002, p. 36). Unfortunately original deadlines could not be met, and an extension of the grant was needed past the original twelve-month period. Because of the shortage of librarians to serve the WMU off-campus community, the Off-Campus Services Librarian had to find the time to work on the tutorial in addition to the other duties of the position. This proved to be more problematic than anticipated.

In addition, during the project development period there have been four changes in library services which have necessitated changes in the presentation and have delayed the completion of the project. First, document delivery and interlibrary loan services have transitioned from use of a Web form for request of materials, to use of the ILLiad software to set up accounts, request materials, and deliver articles. Second, three of the content modules used screen shots from the FirstSearch interface to illustrate finding articles and books. Changes were made to the FirstSearch interface in the spring of 2003 thus making it necessary to replace many of those images. Third, the WMU libraries have purchased EZProxy software to manage the remote authentication of licensed databases. Web configuration is no longer necessary. Therefore nearly one whole module which had been developed is now no longer necessary. Finally, the WMU Libraries will be launching a new Web site in winter of 2004. This is requiring further replacement of existing screen shots and text in the presentation.

Once these updates and changes are made the sound files can be recorded. At that point the presentation will be released on the web, and the CD-ROM product will be mastered, copied, and distributed. Further changes and maintenance will then need to be undertaken by staff in the library.

After the finished product is distributed and accessible assessment will begin. Evaluation of this project is planned to take a two-pronged approach. First, librarians will be tracking the quantity and quality of questions from off-campus students after the product is available and in use, and comparing them to the quantity and quality of questions before the presentation was available. Second, a survey is being designed to accompany the content modules on the web, and on the CD. This will assess the transfer of the information to the student, and gather data on how future versions of the tutorial can be improved.

CONCLUSIONS

A great deal of work has gone into this project and a great deal of work remains to be done. Whether or not the ends justify the means and the project meets its intended goals remains to be seen.

At least three valuable lessons have been learned so far. First, a project such as this should not be attempted unless the participants involved have dedicated time allocated to working on the development. Creation of a Web-based tool such as this is simply too time consuming and involved to be fit into an already full schedule of work commitments. Second, careful balance needs to be struck with regard to teaching concepts versus teaching mechanics. While the ideal product would contain some of each, it should emphasize concepts so that the lessons learned can be used in multiple settings. The reality is however, that students need examples of how to use *their* library Web site and *their* library databases. Inclusion of this kind of instruction and images of screen interfaces results in time-consuming maintenance and upkeep as changes inevitably occur. Finally, much is to be gained in this endeavor purely in the partnerships created. Librarian and teaching faculty working together toward development of an instructional tool has resulted in a new understanding of the role that each partner can play in the overall educational process.

REFERENCES

Ardis, S. & Haas, J. (2001, Fall). Specialized remote user education: Web based tutorials for engineering graduate students. *Issues in Science and Technology Librarianship, 32*. Retrieved November 12, 2003, from http://www.library.ucsb.edu/istl/01-fall/article3.html.

Bender, L. J. & Rosen, J. M. (2000). Working toward scalable instruction: Creating the RIO tutorial at the University of Arizona Library. *Research Strategies, 16*(4), 315-325.

Bracke, P. J. & Dickstein, R. (2002). Web tutorials and scalable instruction: Testing the waters. *Reference Services Review, 30*(4), 330-337.

Dennis, S. & Broughton, K. (2000). FALCON: An interactive library instruction tutorial. *Reference Services Review, 28*(1), 31-38.

Jayne, E. A., Arnold, J., & Vander Meer, P. F. (1998). Casting a broad net: The use of web based tutorials for library instruction (at Western Michigan University). In P. Steven Thomas & M. Jones (Comps.), *Off-Campus Library Services Conference Proceedings, Providence, Rhode Island, April 22-24, 1998* (pp. 197-205). Mount Pleasant, MI: Central Michigan University.

Koenig, M. H. & Brennan, M. J. (2003). All aboard the eTrain: Developing and designing online library instruction modules. *Journal of Library Administration 37*(3/4), 425-435.

Pival, P. R. & Tunon, J. (2001). Innovative methods for providing instruction to distance students using technology. *Journal of Library Administration, 32*(1-2), pp. 347-360.

Rutter, L. & Matthews, M. (2002). InfoSkills: A holistic approach to online user education. *Electronic Library, 20*(1), 29-34.

Swaine, C. W. (2001). Developing, marketing and evaluating Web-based library and information skills tutorials at Old Dominion University. *Virginia Libraries, 47*(3), 5-8.

Using Direct Linking Capabilities in Aggregated Databases for E-Reserves

David Bickford

University of Phoenix

SUMMARY. Libraries looking to realize the full value of their electronic resource purchases have the opportunity to link directly to content within aggregated databases. An examination of direct linking tools provided by four major aggregators show a varied landscape of features and capabilities. Despite differences from one platform to another, direct linking has become an important feature for database subscribers and is becoming a more straightforward process. In light of advances in direct linking technology, libraries should compare the costs and benefits of direct linking in comparison to traditional e-reserve methods based on securing permissions and scanning hard copy.

KEYWORDS. Reserves, technology, distance learners

INTRODUCTION AND PROJECT RATIONALE

The challenge of information retrieval involves not only the difficulty of finding relevant and authoritative information, but also the logistics of finding one's way back to such information after the conclusion of the initial research

[Haworth co-indexing entry note]: "Using Direct Linking Capabilities in Aggregated Databases for E-Reserves." Bickford, David. Co-published simultaneously in *Journal of Library Administration* (The Haworth Information Press, an imprint of The Haworth Press, Inc.) Vol. 41, No. 1/2, 2004, pp. 31-45; and: *The Eleventh Off-Campus Library Services Conference Proceedings* (ed: Patrick B. Mahoney) The Haworth Information Press, an imprint of The Haworth Press, Inc., 2004, pp. 31-45.

http://www.haworthpress.com/web/JLA
Digital Object Identifier: 10.1300/J111v41n01_04

session and of sharing valuable documents with others who do not participate in the initial research session. On the open Web, this process is difficult because of the unstable nature of some Web sites, a phenomenon obvious to anyone who has had the frustrating experience of seeing bookmarked documents lead only to "page cannot be displayed" errors. In a subscription aggregated database environment, however, this problem becomes more significant because most major aggregators use dynamically generated pages with session-based URLs.

Attempts to bookmark documents found in these database environments often fail. First, the user of the bookmark must authenticate as an authorized user. This process may fail if the user is attempting access from a different computing environment than the one in which he or she originally found the document. Second, even if there is no issue with authentication, the URL may lead only to an error message or a generic search screen.

At the same time that database users have contended with these limitations, many libraries have worked to create extensive electronic reserve (e-reserve) systems in order to facilitate access to required readings for academic coursework. These systems, whether outsourced or internally developed, have largely replaced the traditional reserve reading room at many academic libraries. Reserve readings are a significant component of most libraries' operations, representing 30% of all loan transactions, for example, at San Diego State University (Goodram, 1996). Since libraries often pay a premium price for scholarly journals based on the assumption of multiple users, libraries have attempted to realize the full value of their electronic subscriptions by enabling their use not only for keyword searching, but also for targeted linking in association with course required reading lists (Laskowski & Ward, 2001).

Most library e-reserve systems have focused on extensive scanning of documents and hosting of files in Portable Document Format (PDF). Since these files have generally originated with printed resources, libraries have had to invest considerable time, and sometimes funds, in securing appropriate permissions from publishers (Groenewegen, 1998). In many cases, permissions have become available only with a guarantee that libraries will delete files associated with specific courses at the conclusion of the academic term.

Given the considerable logistical, legal, and economic challenges associated with e-reserve systems based on the library's own scanning of print documents, it would seem logical for libraries to favor direct linking to content they already purchase in digital form, often through aggregated databases. Since aggregated database content resides on the vendor's servers and has already received copyright clearance, the library has only to build and maintain the link. The more challenging activities of hosting documents and securing permissions become the responsibility of the database producer.

An additional impetus for direct linking lies in the widespread use of popular "courseware" applications such as Blackboard, WebCT, and numerous homegrown alternatives by academic institutions. Some library administrators have expressed concern about the implementation of these systems with insufficient integration of library resources. While most courseware has readily accepted links to sites on the open Web, the complexities of direct linking to database content have sometimes rendered the academic library minimally visible in the online instructional environment (Machovec, 2001).

LITERATURE REVIEW

Until recently, the limitations of the dominant aggregators have made such direct linking either unavailable or unacceptably difficult. While the major aggregators are unlikely to change their dynamic, session-based site design in the short term, they have offered subscribing libraries various software tools to enable bookmarking and linking to database content by authorized users. ProQuest, for example, introduced in 1998 SiteBuilder, a tool that has allowed librarians and faculty members to build long-term links to database content. End-users (students and public library patrons) enjoyed the same ability with the links restricted to a 30-day expiration timeline. ProQuest enjoys a reputation of being the first major aggregator to develop and market a direct linking capability.

Initial evaluations of SiteBuilder were positive, largely because SiteBuilder solved so many logistical, economic, and legal problems associated with scanning-based e-reserves (Jasco, 1998). Usage grew in the years following the SiteBuilder product introduction, especially after ProQuest ceased charging most customers separately for SiteBuilder and instead built SiteBuilder capability into its product line for all subscribing institutions. While most usage occurred in higher education, reports of SiteBuilder usage in high schools (INFOhio and ProQuest, 2000) and corporations have emerged in the trade literature.

Although SiteBuilder was useful from a library administrator's point of view, this software tool proved too cumbersome for most end-users. In addition, the principal method of securing links constructed via SiteBuilder, expiration dates, proved insufficient for the needs of ProQuest and the publishers whose publications appeared in full text within ProQuest databases. As a result, with its July 2003 platform upgrade, ProQuest has discontinued SiteBuilder as a tool for building new links, although ProQuest will continue to support existing links until their expiration dates.

As a replacement to SiteBuilder, ProQuest has initiated a new system of direct linking based on OpenURL standards. This new method of linking, which has been available for only a few months to most ProQuest subscribers, appears to offer both improvements over SiteBuilder technology and some new challenges. While the construction, maintenance, and distribution of links has become easier for the average end-user in a typical campus environment in which all authorized users share an Internet Protocol (IP) address range, the prospects for remote, or off-campus, use appear less clear. While it is certainly possible to use proxy servers, referring URL authentication, and similar mechanisms to enable off-site access, some end-users may struggle with the administrative steps necessary to enable this access.

EBSCO, Gale, and other aggregators have responded with similar tools for their subscribers. EBSCO allows administrators to enable a feature allowing "persistent links" to articles. These links appear when the end-user selects the option to save marked items from the search results list. While EBSCO offers an optional page-building utility called "Page Composer," this utility is not mandatory for link building. Gale, on the other hand, offers the simplest linking of all the major aggregators. Users can simply copy the address that appears in the browser's address bar and paste that address into any environment in which the user wishes to provide a link to a specific article, journal, or search query.

These tools, like SiteBuilder, generally work most readily and seamlessly when the recipient of a link occupies the same computing environment as the link's creator. If both individuals share a common IP range associated with the subscribing institution's account, links are likely to work without error messages or the appearance of login prompts. The challenge for the direct linking tools of all aggregators, then, is enabling sharing links with other authorized users who may be using those links from outside the campus network. In this respect, the aggregators have a mixed record. All do support remote access to direct links, but the additional steps required to enable remote access may exceed the expertise and authority of most end-users, including faculty members. As a result, staff intervention in the e-reserve process is still necessary, albeit at a reduced level relative to "traditional," scanning-based e-reserve programs.

Despite the implementation of directly linking tools by some of the major aggregators, numerous specialized online information resources still fail to offer any direct linking mechanism at all. Some vendors feel that direct linking will dilute their brand identity by allowing users to bypass their clearly identified search interfaces and welcome pages, proceeding instead directly to a minimally adorned full-text article (Seaman, 2003). RDS Business Reference Suite, for example, offers no persistent address capability for its considerable trade journal content. The introduction of any sort of linking capability will likely wait until the RDS product line migrates to the dominant platform of its parent company, Gale Group (Catherine Friedman, personal communication, October 1, 2003).

While those tools that exist are growing in popularity and volume of use, there has been little in-depth examination of their efficacy and usability. In fact, a preliminary literature review has revealed no peer-reviewed literature specifically concerned with the evaluation and implementation of direct linking tools associated with aggregated databases.

PROJECT DESIGN AND IMPLEMENTATION

In pursuing this project, the author examined the linking tools provided by four major aggregators: EBSCO, Gale, Ovid, and ProQuest. Aggregators selected for the study were those readily available to the author for testing over a period of several weeks. The author's multiple affiliations with two academic libraries (University of Phoenix and Nova Southeastern University) and one public library (Phoenix Public Library) allowed access to a number of aggregator platforms. In some cases, it was possible to observe multiple configurations of the same platform at two or more subscribing libraries.

Examination occurred at both the administrative (librarian/faculty) level and the end-user (student/public library patron) level in those cases in which the vendor distinguished between the two user groups in the design of its direct linking capability. The author tested linking to individual articles, journals, and search queries with vendor-provided tools. Evaluation focused on results as measured from the points of view of both information retrieval and human-computer interaction. This initial evaluation also incorporated observations gleaned from prior use of these linking tools by the author and by library staff at the author's institution.

Additional areas of focus included the viability of such linking technologies for off-campus and distance education use, authentication strategies, and the prospects for standardization across platforms and vendors. The author performed testing as needed to determine link viability beyond the computing environment in which initial link creation had taken place.

Vendor documentation and discussions with appropriate vendor personnel offered supplementary source information to complement the author's own evaluation of these tools. Based on the findings of the initial evaluation, the author decided that ProQuest was an appropriate subject for an in-depth case study due to the substantial change in linking strategy that company made early during the course of project research. To enable a more in-depth analysis of ProQuest strategy, the author conducted telephone interviews with two ProQuest employees directly involved in the design and implementation of ProQuest's linking strategy.

RESULTS AND OUTCOMES

Initial results of testing and evaluation appear below for each vendor examined. A tabular representation of direct linking features appears in the Appendix.

EBSCOhost

The EBSCOhost platform uses session-based, dynamically generated URLs for the address of each page displayed to the end-user. These URLs are not effective in their original form as a direct linking tool and will often generate "session expired" messages if the cookie from the original session has expired or if someone attempts to follow the URL from another computer. As a result, any EBSCOhost links harvested directly from the browser's address bar are of limited utility. Such links generally endure for only a matter of hours and generally function only on the machine originally used for research.

As an alternate mechanism for linking, EBSCOhost offers users a folder function. This feature allows users to place selected articles in a folder by clicking a folder icon. This icon appears to the right of each document listed in the search results and also appears on the Web page displaying the full text or detailed bibliographic record for each document retrieved. Once the user has placed documents in the folder, the user can then open the folder and print, save, or e-mail the items stored within. As part of the save function, a user can display direct URLs, "persistent links" in EBSCOhost terminology, for all documents in the folder. The folder can store not only individual documents retrieved, but also search queries, including searches by journal name. The process for adding search queries to the folder is less obvious, requiring use of a folder icon that appears next to the query on the search results page. Nevertheless, once queries have been placed in the folder, they are available for direct link construction in the same manner as individual documents from search results.

While this process does involve several steps, there is an alternative available for linking to individual articles. If allowed by the account administrator, the EBSCOhost platform will display the persistent link URL in the full bibliographic record for each document. From this environment, the user can simply copy and paste the URL to the environment in which he or she wishes to store or distribute the link. This option is not available for linking to search queries and journals, both of which require use of the folder function.

Since the EBSCOhost folder capability is necessary for certain types of links and helpful for generating URLs for multiple articles in a single transaction, it is important to observe a significant usability challenge associated with folders in this platform. Specifically, some users seeing the folder icon assume that they are saving documents in a permanent repository, one to which they can return during subsequent research sessions. In actuality, this type of function is session-based. It offers a useful place to store documents for single-transaction printing, e-mailing, or saving, but is not useful for long-term storage unless the user invokes an optional personalization feature known as "My EBSCOhost." Since there is no clear warning language informing users that usage of My EBSCOhost is mandatory for long-term storage, library users at the author's institution have reported, often in a panic, that they had placed promising documents in a folder several days ago, returned expecting them all to be available in the folder, and found them missing. For users conducting research over several days with the intent of eventually harvesting direct links to all items saved in a folder, this issue could result in frustration and unexpected rework.

The principal cause of this usability challenge seems to be EBSCO's recent transition from the "marking" metaphor used by many aggregators to the current folder metaphor. The previous metaphor of marking suggested a whiteboard or other temporary means of storing information. One would logically assume that any information stored on a whiteboard would not persist. The new metaphor of a folder, on the other hand, suggests permanence since documents stored in both paper folders and computer folders tend to remain in the folders until deliberately removed. Given the implications of permanence associated with a folder, it would be helpful to display a warning message to the user when he or she is about to exit the database and thereby end the research session. A message along the lines of "You are about to end your current research session. Please print, e-mail, or save all documents in your folder" would minimize the number of misunderstandings associated with this feature. EBSCO has shown openness to feedback regarding this feature and may make appropriate modifications in future releases (Tim Collins, personal communication, October 21, 2003).

Despite this challenge, direct links to content in EBSCOhost work effectively with no observed errors. Direct links to specific articles, specific journals, and search queries all proceed without delay or intermediate steps to the targeted content as long as the user has followed one of the strategies outlined above in creating them. The EBSCO links endure as long as EBSCO retains rights to include the content in its databases and as long as the subscribing institution continues to purchase the appropriate databases from EBSCO.

For remote users, EBSCO provides account administrators with the ability to add login information at the end of persistent links created via the accounts they manage. The added login information at the end of the URL allows for IP authentication if the user is connected to an institutional network or for login via individual user name and password. A string to enable authentication by referring URL is also possible; however, this option is generally useful only at the administrative level since individual users are unlikely to place URLs on a page on file with EBSCO as a valid referrer for an institution's account. Given the flexibility afforded by this feature, it is a relatively straightforward task to enable remote access to direct links for an institution's authorized users.

Gale

Gale Group, a division of Thomson, supports direct linking in its InfoTrac product line of aggregated periodicals databases. In addition, Gale offers this capability in its various resource centers, all of which combine periodical content with selected reference book entries and primary source materials. Gale labels its direct linking capabilities "Infomarks."

Infomarks have the uncommon feature of requiring no additional steps or administrative intervention in order to target specific database content. If the user is viewing search results or a specific document, he or she may simply copy and paste the URL from the browser's address bar into an environment appropriate for storage and distribution of links. Similarly, the user can employ the browser's "bookmark" or "favorites" function to retain a direct link for return visits. From this point of view, Gale has come farther than most aggregators in allowing users an experience similar to bookmarking sites on the open Web. For most users, who may have more experience with free Web content than with proprietary subscription databases, the process of performing additional actions in order to link to database content may be counterintuitive.

Gale's Infomarks endure for a short period of time based on the presence of a cookie established as part of the user's initial research session. After the expiration of the cookie, the link will still function indefinitely as long as the person using the link has authenticated in a supported manner. Under these circumstances, the links should endure as long as Gale retains rights to the particular content targeted and as long as the subscribing institution continues to purchase access to the relevant Gale database. Gale's authentication programming looks automatically for the user's IP address, and if it does not detect an

IP range for a subscribing institution, the screen displays a prompt for user name and password. For users within the subscribing institution's IP range, access is seamless. For remote users, it is necessary to either use authentication by user name and password or to pass traffic to Gale's site through a proxy that allows Gale to see the page request as originating from a subscribing institution's IP range.

While Gale's direct linking process is remarkably simple, it does have some limitations. End-users can easily link directly to specific articles, specific journals, and search queries. The direct journal linking feature, however, is less robust than similar features offered by competing aggregators. Most aggregators allow a user targeting a specific journal to link directly to a list of available issues, which in turn offers links to tables of contents for each issue, and then finally to each article. This process allows users to navigate in a step-by-step manner to a known article from a previous issue. Gale, on the other hand, offers a link only to a list of all articles found in all available issues of a journal listed in reverse chronological order. As a result, a user linking to a Gale database from a library's electronic journal list would have to scroll and click through numerous screens to find a known article from a prior year. Gale's approach works satisfactorily for those users wishing to browse the most current issues, but is substantially less effective for finding older documents within a specific periodical.

Ovid

Ovid is a database producer that specializes in biomedical information. Because Ovid takes a broad approach to its specialization, including the literature of nursing, psychology, and sociology among its full-text offerings, Ovid products see widespread usage in academic and corporate environments. The Journals@Ovid platform hosts full-text periodical content that Ovid licenses to its subscribers.

From an account administrator's point of view, Journals@Ovid offers a rich array of possible direct link configurations as part of a feature known as "Jumpstarts." Jumpstarts allow account administrators to construct links that lead directly to specific articles, specific journals, and search queries. In addition to these standard linking capabilities, Ovid offers an extensive array of codes that are useful for customizing links. Some of the possibilities include inserting accounting comments to allow tracking of usage by location or department and automatically closing the user's session after a short duration. The latter option is particularly useful because Ovid bases its pricing model on number of simultaneous users. Institutions will want to close sessions attributed to direct article linking quickly in order to avoid turning away users attempting to establish sessions for open-ended research.

Ovid's Jumpstarts employ the same authentication methods as general access to the Journals@Ovid platform. Ovid will look for a subscribing institution's IP range and grant appropriate access based on the institution's subscriptions. In the absence of a page request from an approved IP range, Ovid will prompt the user to login with user name and password. For users within the subscribing institution's IP range, access is seamless. For remote users, it is necessary to either use authentication by user name and password or to pass traffic to Ovid's site through a proxy that allows Ovid to see the page request as originating from a subscribing institution's IP range.

Ovid links endure for as long as the Ovid maintains rights to the targeted content and as long as the institution maintains its Ovid subscriptions. Links are not otherwise subject to expiration.

Despite its impressive array of linking capabilities, Ovid's Jumpstart feature does have one significant limitation: It is currently available only to account administrators. End-users of the database do not see an announcement of the Jumpstart capability, and the browser's address bar always displays a URL of http://gateway1.ovid.com/ovidweb.cgi regardless of how deep into the database one maneuvers, suggesting that all Web content is dynamic with no prospect of direct access. For this reason, libraries that subscribe to publications via the Journals@Ovid platform must be willing and able to employ staff to build links to Ovid content in association with an e-reserve function. The cost savings and convenience associated with allowing end-users to build their own links are not available at the present time in association with the Journals@Ovid platform.

ProQuest

ProQuest has been offering direct linking longer than most aggregators. The initial version of SiteBuilder debuted in 1998 and evolved from a separately priced feature to a built-in component of ProQuest subscriptions. ProQuest also notes that it was first to market a "flexible linking solution" for building links from one vendor's platform to another in 2000 (John Law, personal communication, December 4, 2003). Nevertheless, as SiteBuilder has matured, the requirements of vendors and the clients they serve have evolved, necessitating reconsideration of linking strategy.

ProQuest's current direct linking strategy reflects new methods introduced as part of a July 2003 software release. At that time, ProQuest discontinued the original SiteBuilder platform as a method for building direct links. While ProQuest continues to support existing SiteBuilder links until their expiration dates, all new links must rely one of two capabilities offered in the latest ProQuest release. Specifically, ProQuest now presents direct article links at two strategic points in the research process. First, the page that displays the full text or the complete bibliographic record contains a URL for the article based on the emerging OpenURL standard. Using broadly accepted representations of title, author, and other significant fields, ProQuest offers an address that targets the article using OpenURL. This link is useful not only for building links to specific documents from course Web pages, but also for constructing cross-vendor links that allow documents identified in search results from one database to link seamlessly to full text contained in another vendor's database.

The second method is part of a new feature entitled "My Research Summary." This feature is similar to the EBSCOhost folder feature since it allows users to select specific documents, mark them, and place them in a designated workplace for printing, saving, e-mailing, or linking. When viewing marked items, a ProQuest user can see direct URLs to specific articles, specific journals, and to each search query used during the research session. The URLs offered within "My Research Summary" reflect a proprietary ProQuest syntax. By offering both links based on the OpenURL standard and links based on ProQuest syntax, the company seeks to compare the two methods and assess user preferences (Mike Hoover, personal communication, December 4, 2003).

Regardless of the method used to construct the links, the links differ from those built via the previous SiteBuilder software in two significant respects. First, newly built links have no expiration dates. SiteBuilder links, in contrast, lasted for up to five years for administrators and faculty members who obtained access via a "builder" account. Students, public library patrons, and other users without administrative rights could build links valid for just 30 days. These expiration dates were part of ProQuest's initial authentication strategy, which based article access on digital certificates. Although administrators could make links available only within specific IP ranges, there was no requirement to do so. As a result, an expiration date became the one mandatory method of minimizing the chances of unauthorized redistribution of database content to non-subscribers.

Second, since newly built links no longer use certificates and expiration dates, direct links to ProQuest content now require authentication at a level equivalent to that which governs access to the ProQuest search screen. Available authentication methods include IP address, user name and password, and referring URL. As with other aggregators examined, IP authentication works well for users on a campus network or linked to one via proxy. Referring URL offers another option for remote access that some institutions may wish to explore. At the same time that ProQuest introduced its new linking strategy,

ProQuest also introduced cascading authentication, allowing ProQuest's servers to look sequentially for IP address, referring URL, and a local authentication system before finally prompting the user to login if no other authentication credentials are available (Mike Hoover, personal communication, December 4, 2003).

John Law, Director of Systems and Product Development at ProQuest, summarized his company's motivations for the shift in strategy as originating in a desire to move toward the OpenURL standard and to include metadata within the link itself. In addition, ProQuest wished full extend link creation abilities to all database users instead of constraining most end-users to 30 days as it had done under the SiteBuilder program. Finally, the new strategy supports a wider variety of authentication methods and secures content more effectively than SiteBuilder (John Law, personal communication, December 4, 2003).

Of all the major aggregators, ProQuest has the most robust mechanism for direct linking to a specific journal. A journal link in ProQuest leads not only to a list of issues sorted by date, but also displays a helpful "search within publication" link. This feature is particularly desirable for enhancing library e-journal title lists. Despite recommendations by librarians that most users should search a broad array of content, many researchers prefer instead to search only certain recognized publications known within their disciplines. ProQuest's approach is likely to become a standard requirement for journal-level linking since it responds to end-user desires for both search and browse capabilities.

At this time, the full range of ProQuest's linking capabilities exists only for those resources offered via ProQuest's flagship platform. ProQuest hopes to extend this capability to content hosted on its Chadwyck-Healy platform, which currently allows linking at the journal level but not at the article level. In addition, ProQuest hopes to extend direct linking capabilities to its substantial offerings of electronic theses and dissertations (Mike Hoover, personal communication, December 4, 2003).

CONCLUSION AND RECOMMENDATIONS

In fairness to those vendors that require extras steps to generate a viable long-term link, it is important to note that the logistics of link creation and maintenance increase in proportion of the size and complexity of the database involved. Some publishers' own e-journal platforms offer linking without additional steps. For a publishers' own content, this process is relatively simple since it involves management of a locally developed and stored array of content. In many cases, the publisher may use digital object identifiers (DOIs), which offer a direct link to content hosted on publishers' sites. The use of DOIs is more problematic for aggregators since their products pool content from numerous publishers, host it at the aggregator's site rather than at the publisher's site, and may involve embargoes that restrict access to the latest issues of a publication. As a result, a simple process based on DOIs is not a viable strategy for most aggregators.

Given the need for aggregated database producers and their customers to use additional strategies and tools for direct linking, there are several trends that emerge from the preceding review of specific vendors. First, it appears likely that due to the complexity and size of their databases that most vendors will continue to rely on dynamically generated URLs for their products. The architecture of most aggregated databases currently requires special tools for direct linking. Nevertheless, the rapid emergence of the OpenURL standard may reduce the necessity of such tools. If vendors' default URLs begin to incorporate metadata, then the address displayed in the user's browser may become viable as a link under more circumstances than currently possible.

Where Open URL offers the greatest potential and the greatest challenges, however, is in cross-platform linking among multiple vendors. Link resolvers, an emerging trend in libraries' management of their electronic resources, are a sufficiently complex topic to warrant a separate research project. Nevertheless, it is evident that some of the same technologies developed for direct linking to content hosted on a specific vendor's platform may also be applicable to linking from one platform to another. Mike Hoover, product manager at ProQuest, has provided a worthwhile caveat by observing that linking between vendors may never be as reliable as linking within a single vendor's offerings. In particular, cross-vendor linking based on OpenURL will remain challenging as long as vendors use incompatible, inaccurate, or incomplete metadata. Since an OpenURL link carries metadata within it, any faulty metadata can cause the link to fail. A newspaper article with dummy values inserted for volume and issue number in order to allow its placement in a database designed for journal articles is an example of the type of metadata likely to cause failed links across platforms. (Mike Hoover, personal communication, December 4, 2003).

Despite the challenges associated with more ambitious cross-vendor linking strategies, several issues that previously complicated direct linking no longer present significant barriers. Expiration dates associated with links, most often seen as a result of ProQuest's previous SiteBuilder strategy, are no longer an issue in most databases. Subscribing libraries should remember, however, that even if URLs do not contain embedded expiration dates, link stability is still subject to the changing circumstances of publisher-aggregator relations. The recent decision by Sage to withdraw its journals from aggregated databases, for example, has resulted in links that point to abstracts rather than full text in both the EBSCOhost and ProQuest platforms. Libraries seeking links to articles with the highest degree of stability and permanence may still fare better with direct electronic subscriptions when available. Aggregation offers libraries convenience and cost savings, but the practice is inherently less stable than direct purchase from publishers.

Just as expiration dates have faded as a barrier to direct linking, remote access issues have also become less significant. All vendors examined support authentication of direct links via the same array of methods used for access to database search screens. In some situations, it may be necessary to affix a proxy string at the beginning of a URL. Some libraries will be able to present this prefix automatically to users; others may need to provide end-user training so that researchers can add the prefix themselves. Of those vendors examined, only one (Ovid) has a tool that is not currently available to end-users. Libraries seeking direct links to Ovid content must dedicate staff time to building links on behalf of faculty members and other customers of the e-reserves process.

PROSPECTS FOR FUTURE RESEARCH

Despite this exception, most libraries can reduce scanning, copyright clearance, and Web hosting costs by using direct links to realize increased value from their subscriptions to aggregated databases. One key prospect for future research is an in-depth cost-benefit comparison of traditional approaches to e-reserves with approaches based on direct linking to aggregator content. While it appears clear that direct linking to aggregated database content can bring substantial benefits to interested libraries, there is still no established method of these benefits to the costs in terms of decreased stability of content.

Likewise, there are many other aggregators whose direct linking capabilities fell outside the scope of this project. In-depth analysis of direct linking capabilities in platforms such as JSTOR, Lexis-Nexis Academic, and WilsonWeb offers an opportunity for expanded research in this area. Similarly, little research and evaluation has occurred in the linking capabilities of publisher-hosted platforms such as Emerald and Science Direct. Presumably, the use of DOIs would make direct linking more straightforward in these environments, but detailed analysis is necessary to confirm these impressions.

REFERENCES

Goodman, R. J. (1996). The E-RBR: Confirming the technology and exploring the law of "electronic reserves": Two generations of the digital library system at the SDSU Library. *Journal of Academic of Librarianship, 22*(2), 118-123. Retrieved January 24, 2002, from EBSCOhost Academic Search Premier database.

Groenewegen, H. W. (1998). Electronic reserves: Key issues and innovations. *Australian Academic & Research Libraries, 29*(1), 1-11. Retrieved January 24, 2002, from EBSCOhost Academic Search Premier database.

INFOhio and ProQuest database highlighted in Media & Methods. (2000). *Ohio Media Spectrum, 52*(1), 19. Retrieved August 3, 2003, from ProQuest database.

Jasco, P. (1998). UMI's digital vault initiative project. (1998). *Information Today, 15*(8), 15-16. Retrieved August 3, 2003, from ProQuest database.

Laskowski, M. S. & Ward, D. (2001). Creation and management of a home-grown electronic reserves system at an academic library. *Journal of Academic Librarianship, 27*(5), 361-372. Retrieved January 24, 2002, from EBSCOhost Academic Search Premier database.

Machovec, G. (2001). Course management software: Where is the library? *Online Libraries and Microcomputers, 19*(10), 1-2. Retrieved October 6, 2003, from ProQuest database.

Norman, D. A. (2002). *The design of everyday things.* New York: Basic Books.

Seaman, D. (2003, October). *From isolation to integration: Major trends in digital libraries.* Paper presented at the meeting of the Library and Information Technology Association, Norfolk, Virginia.

SiteBuilder users. (2003). Retrieved August 1, 2003, from ProQuest Training Resource Center Web site: http://training.proquest.com/trc/linking/SiteBuilder.htm.

UMI unveils SiteBuilder, adds to ProQuest Direct. (1998). *Information Today, 15*(6), 16-17. Retrieved August 3, 2003, from ProQuest database.

APPENDIX. Direct Linking Features Comparison as of December 11, 2003

Vendor/ Platform	Name of Direct Linking Feature	Direct Linking Available to End-Users	Direct Linking Available to Administrators	Direct Linking Available from Browser Address Bar	Journal Links Support Browsing and Searching
EBSCOhost	Persistent Links	Yes	Yes	No	No
Gale	Infomarks	Yes	Yes	Yes	No
Ovid	Jumpstarts	No	Yes	No	No
ProQuest	Durable Links	Yes	Yes	No	Yes

Blessing or Curse?
Distance Delivery to Students
with Invisible Disabilities

Nancy E. Black

University of Northern British Columbia

SUMMARY. The student with learning disabilities faces various challenges in an academic environment. As more students with learning disabilities enter post-secondary institutions, this poses a variety of considerations both for the student and for the librarian. The technology offers tremendous opportunities for disabled persons, and it stands to reason that more learning disabled persons may pursue distance education as a viable alternative to higher education. To date, there is very little literature examining the learning disabled student in a distance learning environment. This paper explores the implications for the distance librarian serving the needs of the distant student with learning disabilities by discussing the literature related to the learning disabled student in an academic environment, the profile of learning disabled students, challenges, models for success, and adaptive technology. The paper also makes reference to the standards, professional principles, and legislation that inform and guide the practices integrated into distance library service.

KEYWORDS. Library services, distance learners, technology, disabled students

[Haworth co-indexing entry note]: "Blessing or Curse? Distance Delivery to Students with Invisible Disabilities." Black, Nancy E. Co-published simultaneously in *Journal of Library Administration* (The Haworth Information Press, an imprint of The Haworth Press, Inc.) Vol. 41, No. 1/2, 2004, pp. 47-64; and: *The Eleventh Off-Campus Library Services Conference Proceedings* (ed: Patrick B. Mahoney) The Haworth Information Press, an imprint of The Haworth Press, Inc., 2004, pp. 47-64.

INTRODUCTION

As advocates for the distant student, distance librarians are concerned with removing barriers, providing library instruction, and ensuring accessibility to library resources in support of academic learning and research. To do so, we set high service standards, promote our accessibility, exploit the Web for its flexibility to create options and solutions. The distant student often represents a smaller user group and by virtue of the distance is sometimes "invisible," overlooked, or forgotten. To combat this, distance librarians make concerted efforts to identify and reach the distance students affiliated with our institutions. In the provision of distance library delivery we are guided by principles specific to our libraries, collaborations built with key individuals within the institution (faculty, student services, registrar), and the broader institutional mandates. For many of us the ACRL Guidelines for Distance Learning Library Services (Association for . . . 1998), or the CLA Guidelines for Library Support of Distance and Distributed Learning in Canada (CLA Services . . . 2000) represent key touchstone documents in the implementation and delivery of distance library services.

But who are these distance students? The typical profile of the distant student, age 35-49, female, employed full-time, married, with a family (Dewald, Scholz-Crane, Booth, & Levine, 2000; Black, 2001) with which most of us involved in distance education are familiar, represents only part of the picture. Who else is taking distance courses and what sorts of obstacles confront them? The technology now provides tremendous flexibility and opportunities for people who in the past have been marginalized, limited, or prevented from seeking educational, vocational, or employment opportunities (Rouse, 1999; Wall & Sarver, 2003). While effective library service for many such individuals–physically challenged, minority groups, economically disadvantaged–are of interest to librarians in general, for the purpose and context of this article, distance library service for individuals with learning disabilities in an academic setting will be the focus of this discussion.

There is a great deal of information available and ongoing research in the field of learning disabilities, however, there is very little literature exploring the issues of the learning disabled student in the distant learning environment of an academic setting. As more students with learning difficulties enter post-secondary institutions (Jax & Muraski, 1992), and with the advantages offered by the technology, it stands to reason that we will see the numbers of learning disabled distance students increase. For students with these various challenges, the practice of "equitable access" takes on new meaning for the distance librarian delivering effective library service to meet their needs. What is the role of the librarian in understanding the learning styles and needs of this particular group of students and where does our responsibility lie in helping them with their educational success? How do we build this awareness of their needs into our service, and what approach is effective, inclusive, and will avoid isolation and alienation? As distance librarians, it behooves us to educate ourselves about learning disabilities by reading and drawing on the literature across the disciplines (education, psychology, health, for example) in order to evaluate, make changes, and apply strong practices and enhancements to our services with the needs of these students in mind.

LEARNING DISABILITIES–DEFINED AND PROFILED

A learning disability is not a disorder or a disability that is immediately apparent or obvious to others, it is often referred to as a "hidden" disability (Olney & Kim, 2001). As Olney and Kim suggest, this presents a variety of dilemmas. As a hidden disability, people are less likely to make assumptions about the abilities of an individual, but may on the other hand, make different assumptions, such as presuming a person is "lazy" and unmotivated, when various difficulties become evident. In addition, with an invisible disability, the need for assistance and particular accommodations is not as apparent and may not be considered essential. There can also be issues around the label; some individuals may want the label since the identification legitimizes the need for accommodations, while others may be reluctant to disclose this personal and confidential information. Olney and Kim suggest that people with hidden disabilities "may exist in a netherworld, belonging solidly to neither the 'disabled' nor the 'non-disabled' class of people" (p. 564). For the learning disabled student who is also a distance student this situation has the potential of rendering the student invisible in two ways: the disability is not obvious, and sometimes distance students, as noted, are easily forgotten or overlooked. Some students are further disadvantaged by struggling with an undiagnosed learning disability. In a learning environment already filled with challenges–distance, isolation, possibly inconsistent support from the institution, technology issues–the student with a learning disability is confronted with even more barriers than the typical distant student.

According to the Learning Disability Association of Canada (LDAC), statistics estimate that one in ten Canadians has learning disabilities or over 3 million Canadians; 30% to 70% of young offenders have learning disabilities; 80% of children with Attention Deficit Hyperactivity Disorder (ADHD) have a specific learning disability while 30% of children with learning disabilities have ADHD; 30% of adults with severe literacy problems were found to have undetected or untreated learning disabilities (LDAC, 2001). According to the

National Institute for Literacy (NIFL), approximately 50-80% of students in Adult Basic Education and literacy programs are affected by learning disabilities (NIFL, 1995).

The LDAC Web site (LDAC, 2002) officially defines learning disabilities as:

> A number of disorders which may affect the acquisition, organization, retention, understanding or use of verbal or nonverbal information. These disorders affect learning in individuals who otherwise demonstrate at least average abilities essential for thinking and/or reasoning. As such, learning disabilities are distinct from global intellectual deficiency. (Official Definition page, para. 1)

> Learning disabilities result from impairments in one or more processes related to perceiving, thinking, remembering or learning. These include, but are not limited to: language processing; phonological processing; visual spatial processing; processing speed; memory and attention; and executive functions (e.g., planning and decision-making). (Official Definition page, para. 2)

Further, learning disabilities range in severity, are due to genetic and/or neurobiological factors or injury that alters brain functioning, and are life long. Early identification and interventions in the forms of specific skill instruction, accommodations, strategies, and self-advocacy skills, are critical in supporting individuals with learning disabilities. (Note: for the complete official definition adopted by the LDAC January 2002, see the Web site <www.ldac-taac.ca>.)

The National Institute for Literacy (NIFL, 1995) follows a similar definition. "Learning disabilities is a generic term that refers to a heterogeneous group of disorders manifested by significant difficulties in acquisition and use of listening, speaking, reading, writing, reasoning, or mathematical abilities, or of social skills" (The Interagency Committee section, para. 1).

There are many variations of learning disabilities and it is recognized as a life long condition. Adults with learning disabilities may experience low self-esteem, difficulties related to education, vocation, social interactions, and independent living. (Note: for a more complete definition, see the NIFL Web site <www.nifl.gov/nifl/ld/archive/definiti.htm>.)

But what do these definitions mean specifically? Because the disability ranges in severity and includes a cluster or a group of disorders, individuals may be affected in quite different ways and have a variety of difficulties, such as poor short term memory, or problems tracking the words along a page. Visual difficulties might include letter, word, or number reversals: "d" and "b," or "p" and "q"; or "saw" for "was"; or "she" for "the"; or "41" instead of "14." From personal experience and in talking with professionals in the field, I am aware that these reversals are often inconsistent, which contributes to further frustration. In other words, the letter "b" may not always be consistently reversed for the letter "d." An individual with a learning disability, for example might read this sentence: The boy dropped the popcorn on the table, as: She doy proqqed the dodcorn no the tadle. Again, from personal experience and from conversations with professionals, I am aware that chunking parts of words together with other words is another common pattern. As a result, an individual with a learning disability might read this sentence: The international environmental advocacy agencies with respect to growing concerns of global warming . . . in this way: Sheinter nation al envrion men talad vocacy a gencieswi thres pect to growing con cernsof globa lwarming. . . . As with the reversals, chunking the words in different orders does not occur consistently but certainly adversely affects the comprehension of the printed material.

Additional difficulties can include: auditory problems, auditory memory, auditory sequencing (confusion with number sequence), motor problems and poor hand eye coordination, time management problems, or an inability to organize tasks, or space, or conceptual problems such as rigid thinking, difficulty understanding figures of speech, or in anticipating the future (LDAC, March 2001). All of these various difficulties, depending of course on the range of severity, result in poor, or inconsistent academic performance.

LEGISLATION

As previously noted there are many standards in place guiding the professional principles and practices of the distance librarian. In addition to these standards, the librarian must also consider the legislation that regulates accommodations for people with disabilities. In Canada, Section 15 (1) of the Canadian Charter of Rights and Freedoms, (1982) states:

> Every individual is equal before and under the law and has the right to the equal protection and equal benefit of the law without discrimination and, in particular, without discrimination based on race, national or ethnic origin, colour, religion, sex, age or mental and physical disability.

This legislation has been criticized for its rather broad wording in terms of stipulating and regulating accommodations for the disabled and that it is open to interpretation (Griebel, 2003). The duty to accommodate is written into the federal legislation of the Canadian Human Rights Act (1985) as well as provincial and territorial human rights legislation. This legislation specifies the legal obligation to provide reasonable accommodation for disabled persons in educational institutions and places of employment. (Note, see LDAC, undated, Learning disabilities and the law <www.ldac-taac.ca/ld-law/start.htm>, which provides an excellent discussion, tailored to learning disabilities, explaining the legislation, defining various legal terms and the implications for disabled persons, parents, employers, and educators.)

In the United States, the Americans with Disabilities Act of 1990 (ADA, 1990), Title II, section 202 reads that, "no qualified individual with a disability shall by reason of such disability, be excluded from participation in or be denied the benefits of the services, programs, or activities of a public entity."

The act also details the type and nature of accommodations that are to be put into practice: modifications to architecture, communication practices, provision of auxiliary aids, and adaptive technology (ADA, 1990; Jax & Muraski, 1995; Wall & Sarver, 2003). Additional legislation, as noted by Wall and Sarver (2003), such as Section 508, the Assistive Technology for Individuals with Disabilities Act, and the Telecommunication Act outline standards and requirements to compatibility, usability, software standards, accessibility, performance issues specific to various technologies. (Note, the ADA home page <http://www.usdoj.gov/crt/ada/adahom1.htm> provides a wealth of information pertaining to the legislation, regulations, information, resources, and links to additional sites.)

The definitions, factors, statistics, and legislation related to disabilities in general and to learning disabilities in particular have implications, as we shall see, for the learning disabled distant student as well as for the librarian designing the service for these students.

THE DISTANCE EDUCATION ENVIRONMENT

The wealth of literature of distance education in general discusses: the culture of the learning environment, the learning behaviours of the distant student, and influential factors contributing to a positive academic experience (Niemi, Ehrhard, & Neeley, 1998; Potter, 1998; Wiesenberg, 2001; Rovai, 2003). With respect to course delivery, library services, and additional student support services, along with effective technological integration in course and service delivery, again the literature is rich with models (Luther, 1998; Potter, 1998; Barley, 1999; Dewald et al., 2000).

In more specific terms, while the technology has significantly reduced a number of barriers to education and as result provided individuals with tremendous flexibility with educational opportunities not previously realized, there remain nonetheless, the barriers of distance and isolation. Additional barriers identified in the literature include: situational, institutional, and dispositional barriers (Potter, 1998; Wiesenberg, 2001). These barriers can be defined as; personal barriers (finances, family); preventing or inconvenient access to materials; poorly designed courses or ineffective communication practices; and lack of provision of personal counseling, academic advising, learning skills; all of which contribute to feelings of isolation and alienation. The degree to which these various obstacles are minimized or eliminated depends largely on how well institutions manage the technology, course design, quality of the course, and the strength of the pedagogy. These factors along with seamless access to library resources, as well as seamless access to student support services, such as academic advising, course registration, or personal counseling are equally instrumental in removing barriers. The sense of isolation is also significantly reduced when effective communication and customer service practices are followed (Potter, 1998; Dewald, 1999; Black, 2001; Wiesenberg, 2001).

With respect to the profile of the distant student, the literature outlines various qualities and factors that contribute to academic success. Typically, because these students are older, they bring a higher degree of maturity and life experience into the learning environment. They are highly motivated, focused on goals, more independent, and are able to effectively employ a variety of coping strategies, such as time management techniques. As learners, they tend to show initiative, take control and responsibility for their learning and are able to be more self-directed and self-aware. In addition, they are generally computer literate and have access to the technology they require in order to access the courses and resources (Potter, 1998; Niemi et al., 1998; Black, 2001; Wiesenberg, 2001). The distant student who possesses these qualities is more likely to achieve academic success, and is less likely to be adversely affected by the various barriers.

THE LEARNING DISABLED STUDENT AND THE ACADEMIC ENVIRONMENT

The distance learning environment as described above refers to a typical or conventional pattern with which many of us involved in the practice are familiar. However, when we compare and contrast this learning environment with the profile and learning needs of a student with learning disabilities, a number of implications both for the student and the distance librarian emerge.

Services for adults with learning disabilities both in Canada and the United States have been developing over the past 10 years. This is partly due to the research in the field of learning disabilities, the efforts of advocacy groups, increased awareness in educators, and the legislation (Wiener & Siegel, 1992; Jax & Muraski, 1992; Fichten, Asuncion, Barile, Fossey, & de Simone, 2000; Wall & Sarver, 2003). Wiener and Siegel note, for example, that many Canadian "universities and colleges have special needs offices" (1992, p. 347). Two Fact Sheets on the LDAC Web site discuss options, factors, and suggestions for the learning disabled individual interested in pursuing higher education. The LDAC Fact Sheet (February, 2000), for instance, outlines specific details, considerations and strategies for selecting a post-secondary institution, along with the types of accommodations that should be available to the student. The LDAC Fact Sheet (March, 2003) describes the advantages of online distance learning for the learning disabled, by emphasizing the flexibility, accessibility, and convenience of online distance learning. This particular Fact Sheet provides a link to the Special Needs Opportunity Windows (SNOW) Project <http://snow.utoronto.ca>: a Web site devoted to online resources and professional development opportunities for educators and parents of students with special needs. The home page of this site provides links to information about: online workshops, best practices, research, adaptive technology, resources, and education (SNOW Project, undated). Following the education link <http://snow.utoronto.ca/resources/technology/techdised>, leads people to information about distance learning and Canadian institutions that provide distance education at the post-secondary level. Both of these LDAC Fact Sheets mentioned above emphasize that learning disabled individuals who are planning to pursue higher education require self-advocacy skills, an understanding of their own learning disabilities, should know their strengths and recognize the expectations of the academic environment.

In addition, individuals are cautioned to select an institution that is a good match for their abilities. These themes and characteristics are not only expressed throughout the literature discussing the learning disabled student, but are also present in the literature pertaining to the learning behaviour of distance students. It is interesting, in this respect, that there appear to be some commonalities between the two types of students and this suggests that this could be something upon which the distance librarian could capitalize in evaluating and designing distance service to accommodate the needs of the learning disabled distant student.

In their article exploring the attributes of highly successful adults with learning disabilities, Gerber, Ginsberg, and Reiff (1992) identified the following key characteristics and factors as being instrumental to success: control, a desire to excel, goal setting, reframing, persistence, goodness of fit, learned creativity, and social ecologies. Larkin (2001) considers some of these points and argues that in order for individuals to internalize and assimilate these characteristics to become successful both academically and in careers, appropriate support must be in place in school. She suggests that scaffolded instruction provides a supportive environment that allows students to build on their strengths, gain independence, learn coping skills, and break the failure cycle. Scaffolded instruction is described as a gradual decrease of support while increasing the independence for the student. The author outlines and describes eight elements and guidelines, some of which include: a shared goal, understanding and assessing the child's prior knowledge, positive feedback, minimizing frustration, help achieve success quickly, and recognize when it is time to stop. Larkin notes that although she presented examples from an elementary school setting, she believes this approach would be valuable for students of any grade. She does not suggest that this model may be useful for an academic setting; however, some of the tips may prove to be practical for the distance learning environment.

A different model for success discussed by Gerber, Reiff, and Ginsberg (1996) is a process of "reframing," discussed in an earlier article by the same authors and defined as "a set of decisions relating to reinterpreting the learning disability experience in a more productive and positive manner" (Gerber et al., 1992, p. 481). In other words, this is a process, or a technique whereby an individual can identify and build on strengths to achieve success in an academic setting, life, or employment. The authors argue that the reframing process is instrumental to independence, that it encompasses the lifespan, and "must be addressed in school-age and postsecondary programming, job training, parenting, counseling, and advocacy training" (Gerber et al., 1996, p. 98). The authors describe the reframing model as part of a larger pattern or model for success for the learning disabled adult. Reframing is an internal variable (a situation or circumstance that could be susceptible to change) yet linked to an external variable of adaptation. The process of reframing is comprised of four stages: (1) Recognition–the ability to recognize the disability; (2) Understanding–understanding the disability and the implications; (3) Acceptance–accepting the positive and negative of the learning disability; (4) Action–making a conscious decision to set a plan of action toward short term and long term goals. An individual who is able to move through and adopt this dynamic process is likely to have strong self-advocacy skills. With expectations of positive outcomes along with self-advocacy, the learning disabled adult will be able to clearly articulate the reasons for various needs, adjustments, and accommodations in the academic or employment setting (Gerber et al., 1996).

From the perspective of a distance learning environment, the implications are clear. The distant student with learning disabilities who is able to adopt this model, or a similar problem solving, action oriented model, along with self-advocacy skills, will be more likely to experience and achieve academic success. Further, if the distance librarian were able to integrate this awareness and understanding into the distance library service, this would provide a supportive learning environment for the distant student with learning disabilities.

THE ROLE OF ADAPTIVE TECHNOLOGY
AND LEARNING DISABILITIES

In the delivery of distance library service, distance librarians capitalize on the Web to deliver library service, accessible resources, and library instruction, thereby minimizing the isolation. Using the technology as an effective communication tool, we incorporate user-friendly directions, easy to use online forms, design intuitive Web pages, and employ many other innovative techniques to reach our audience and ensure our users can reach us. The inherent flexibility in the technology has completely changed the culture of distance education and the provision of distance library services. Students can be and are expected to be far more independent, resourceful, and self-directed in their course work, and in conducting library research.

For students with disabilities, the technology has opened up far more educational opportunities, due in part to the convenience and the accessibility. In this respect, the technology is truly a blessing. However, it must be remembered that technology cannot solve everything and depending upon the disability (visual, physical, auditory, or cognitive), it may, in fact, present a different set of challenges for an individual. This is when technology represents a curse. As Fichten et al. (2000) notes, disabled individuals can participate fully in society only if they have "equal access to education and the new computer and information technologies," but caution at the same time that the technologies have "the potential to enable or to create difficulties, making concerns about the accessibility of these technologies an evolving issue for the next decade" (p. 180). In other words, in implementing technological solutions to eliminate certain barriers, such as accessibility, we must make certain that more barriers are not created, such as compatibility difficulties. The challenge, therefore, for librarians in general, and distance librarians in particular in the context of this discussion, is to ensure that Web page designs and any other enhancements are as effective and inclusive as possible in order to avoid alienating any group of users who may have very specific or special needs. Additional challenges include keeping up with technological change, balanced against financial considerations, legislation, and issues such as compatibility, maintenance, and performance standards. These issues, too, represent a blessing and curse for the librarian trying to juggle all of the factors while striving for ease of use and minimizing barriers.

To determine the benefits of instructional computer technologies for disabled students in Canadian academic settings, Fichten et al. (2000) conducted three studies. The first study was a focus group and the second study was a phone interview of 37 students from 49 different institutions. The third study was broader again in scope and participants: 725 students responded (of which, 271 or 37% had learning disabilities, 11 respondents were enrolled in distance education), from over 200 Canadian colleges and universities. The authors note that "consistent with the North American trend, the largest group of students (37%) had a learning disability" (pp. 188, 189). This statement serves to reinforce previous comments about the growing numbers of learning disabled students entering post-secondary institutions.

With respect to how the technology was used by the respondents in the studies, the findings show that the enhancements and adaptations (scanners, portable note taking devices, spelling and grammar checking, diction software, for example) provided many advantages for the students: time management, editing work was easier, accessibility of information, communication was easier, helpful with physical mobility issues, and visual impairments. Disadvantages were noted as well: cost, compatibility, technical difficulties, upgrading, and availability, to name a few. The findings also showed two other trends: first, the cross-use of adaptations by students with different disabilities (learning disabled students, for example, benefited from adaptations designed for the visually impaired), and second, standard features of software such as spell-checkers, cut and paste, scanners, were being used as disability accommodations. The three studies took place between the fall of 1997 and spring of 1999, just on the cusp of the web explosion and there have been numerous notable advances to the technology since that time. Nonetheless, Fichten et al. (2000) concluded that there are many positive links between the use of the technology and the ability of disabled students to build on their learning, access education and information, and allowed them to prepare for the knowledge based society.

When it comes to the challenge of designing inclusive, effective Web pages, and integrating adaptive technologies, fortunately, there is a great deal of literature and numerous Web sites providing resource information upon which the librarian can draw. Fichten et al. (2000), and Wall and Sarver (2003), for instance, make a number of very good recommendations regarding Web page accessibility and usability. Both Bobby <http://bobby.watchfire.com/bobby/html/en/index.jsp> and the Web Accessibility Initiative (WAI) <http://www.w3.org/WAI> are excellent resources. Bobby is a free online program that will check Web page accessibility, and WAI has developed guidelines, recommendations, and standards for Web accessibility specifically with disabled users in mind. There are many, many Web sites on resources for learning disabilities, far too many to list here. However, a few helpful Canadian sites are included here. LDAC, the Learning Disabilities Association of Canada <www.ldac-taac.ca> has several Fact Sheets specific to assistive technologies and learning disabilities: Assistive Technology Examples (LDAC, March, 2003); Resources–Assistive Technology (LDAC, March, 2003); Myths and Realities of Assistive Technologies (LDAC, March 2003). The SNOW Project <http://snow.utoronto.ca> provides links to adaptive technology products and provides free trials of the products. There are many, many helpful Web sites in the United States, again, too many to acknowledge and list here. However, a few include: the ADA home page: http://www.usdoj.gov/crt/ada/adahom1.htm, General Disability Internet Resources: http://wally.rit.edu/internet/subject/disability.html, the NIFL Web site <www.nifl.gov> and Resources for the learning disabilities community home page: http://www.ldresources.com. Finally, the legislation of Canada and United States stipulates practices and the duty to accommodate the needs of disabled people with adaptive technologies.

In spite of the challenges to technology (change, cost, maintenance, compatibility) to ignore it is simply not possible. Technology represents an essential, critical, and substantial part of education. As noted previously, it provides flexible educational opportunities, tremendous accessibility to information, and in the delivery of distance education, offers individuals a viable alternative. Integrating adaptive technologies for the benefit of disabled persons can only improve and strengthen library service, further eliminate barriers, and help prepare all students (disabled or not) for a knowledge-based society.

AFTER GRADUATION–THE TRANSITION INTO CAREERS

The literature in the field of learning disabilities in the last 10 years has begun to present research on the subject of employment success and shows links between a successful post-secondary experience and successful employment outcomes (Gerber et al., 1992; Gerber et al., 1996; Madaus, Ruban, Foley, & McGuire, 2003). When one considers that a successful post-secondary experience is generally built upon a successful elementary school experience, along with factors such as: early intervention, a supportive environment at home and at school, appropriate accommodations, use of adaptive technology, this finding seems to follow logically.

In their article discussing employment satisfaction of university graduates, Madaus et al. (2003) noted two factors: self-efficacy and self-regulation that were influential in determining job satisfaction. Self-efficacy refers to how people perceive themselves and their abilities; a positive perception of self-efficacy, for example, encourages people to develop new competencies. In describing the quality of self-regulation, the authors refer to the research conducted by Gerber et al. (1992), and defines this as goal setting, reframing skills, goodness of fit, and social ecologies (support systems from family and friends). Additional compensation strategies include: cognitive learning strategies, self-advocacy, accommodations, study strategies, all of which were identified as instrumental to academic success, and overall life satisfaction.

In a study conducted to determine factors contributing to the success of highly successful learning disabled adults, Gerber et al. (1992) found that several influential patterns emerged. The subsequent model of success developed by the authors is based on the themes of "alterable variables" defined as "special circumstances in self, situation, influence, and interaction that may have had either an individual or a cumulative effect on success and that are susceptible to change" (p. 476). Although they caution that success is not automatic, the model seems to support the finding that "the greater the degree of control obtained, the greater the likelihood of success" (p. 485). The themes of the model include: Control, Internal decisions, External manifestations. Control is defined as making a conscious decision to take charge of one's own life. Internal decisions is sub-divided into: (a) Desire, as in a desire to excel; (b) Goal orientation, setting goals to excel and achieve what is desired, and (c) Reframing, as discussed earlier, is a set of decisions to regard the disability in a positive or more productive approach. The final theme, External manifestations pertains to adaptability and is also sub-divided: (a) Persistence, a consistent characteristic in highly successful learning disabled adults, and was the external expression of the internal decision of desire to excel; (b) Goodness of fit, also mentioned previously, is the ability and recognition of matching the work environment with the strengths and abilities of the individual; (c) Learned creativity, defined as the strategies and techniques to accomplish tasks in alternative methods; (d) Social ecologies, the various support systems (family, friends, mentors, improvement programs) established by highly successful learning disabled adults. The authors argue that the theme of Control is the critical piece of the model, from which everything else flows. They also suggest that the model elements are in themselves alterable and can be taught and learned. As such, in helping the learning disabled person learn to be successful, the model has implications for education, curriculum, counseling, and workplace training.

In view of these findings, it would appear to be critical that such supports and models should be built into academic settings. It would also follow that in a distance learning environment, building this awareness into the service would not only contribute to academic success but also future employment success and job satisfaction for the learning disabled person.

DISCUSSION AND IMPLICATIONS FOR PRACTICE

The literature across the fields of distance learning, learning disabled students in an academic setting, and the role of technology in education in general and for disabled persons in particular, presents a variety of common themes. Distance students are often faced with situational, institutional, and dispositional barriers. In addition, their educational environments can be less than favourable: isolation from resources and services of the main campus, juggling pressures of family, money, work and school, and possibly struggling with the technology (Potter, 1998; Wiesenberg, 2001). When the institution is committed to implementing student support systems, providing quality courses with strong pedagogy, seamless access to resources and student services, along with customer service standards and effective use of the technology, then the academic experience for distance students will likely be positive (Luther, 1998; Dewald, 1999; Black, 2001). This experience will be further enhanced when the distant student hones and assimilates such qualities as: goal setting, self-direction, self-motivation, advocacy skills, persistence, and independence. Additional factors instrumental to academic success include support systems for the student (family, friends), and a good match between the student's abilities, and the institution.

These patterns, noted above and discussed throughout this paper, are also echoed in the literature pertaining to the learning disabled individual. In struggling with a cognitive disability, they too are confronted by situational, institutional, and dispositional barriers with less than favourable educational environments. The services, supports, and accommodations they need may be inconsistent or non-existent. The literature also informs, educates, and raises awareness for educators, librarians, parents, and other professionals as to the many challenges these individuals face: visual, auditory, memory difficulties, poor physical coordination, cognitive processing, and time management and planning issues. Models that contribute to success (Gerber et al., 1992; Gerber et al., 1996; Larkin, 2001; Madaus et al., 2003) suggest that when such models are integrated into the curriculum (or the workplace), and when disabled persons are able to assimilate the skills, there is a greater likelihood that they will achieve academic success. However, the key difference, between the conventional distant student and the distant student with learning disabilities that must not be overlooked, is that the disability does represent a variety of challenges adding another layer of difficulty for the student.

As distance librarians, the high standards (guided by the various principles, guidelines, and mandates) that we have implemented and integrated into our services may well be beneficial to the learning disabled distant student. For instance, we already minimize barriers, attempt to reach our students, exploit the

Web for its communication strengths, apply innovative solutions and options to the technology, strive for user-friendly directions, and create intuitive easy to use Web pages. We already understand the culture of the distance learning environment and the learning behaviours of the distant student, and this knowledge can be applied to the context of providing service to the learning disabled student. However, there are still many factors to consider and many questions to ask before the delivery of distance library service truly meets the needs of disabled users.

So how do we do this? Finding and reaching learning disabled persons can be a challenge: some students may be comfortable with self-advocacy, some may not wish to disclose such personal information, while others may be struggling with an undiagnosed disability. To some degree, this can be addressed by simply assuming that disabled students will be among the distant student user group, and act on this assumption by implementing technological enhancements. Such enhancements do not just benefit the student with learning disabilities, they can be helpful to a broad range of students who may have disabilities, or who may be struggling with a steeper learning curve. The technology, after all, is the first line defense for both the student as well as for us, and we certainly cannot carry out our responsibilities without using it effectively and to its full potential.

In other respects, collaboration with knowledgeable people in the field, or with the disability services personnel of the institution, can heighten our awareness as to the special needs and accommodations. Familiarity with the legislation, exploring the many, many Web resources, along with reading the literature across the disciplines (psychology, education, health) to understand the issues and implications for improving our services is highly recommended. Finally, focus groups with disabled students, or pilot projects, are other methods to collect data, obtain feedback, introduce adaptive technologies, address concerns, and would be instrumental in strengthening and setting new directions for the service we provide.

Some of the commonalities between the conventional distant student and the distant student with learning disabilities have been previously noted. However, we must remember that there are still disparities. The various supports from librarians, educators, parents, the technology, along with the coping strategies developed by the student, do not cure the disability, it is still a life long condition and the supports can only provide conveniences and some advantages. Because of the lack of literature pertaining to the learning disabled student in a distant learning environment, many of the comments and observations throughout this paper have been speculative. Future study to identify more clearly the issues, problems, barriers, or positive advantages of this area would be beneficial to the practical practice of the field.

CONCLUSION

Moving forward on the implications discussed with respect to distance library service to learning disabled students will require some shift or transition to how we conduct our professional practices. As Gerber et al. (1996) notes "such a transition requires not only new attitudes from society as a whole, but, just as importantly, fundamental changes in the way many people with disabilities view themselves" (p. 98). Hopefully, with improved understanding of learning disabilities, further research, and intervention programs at the elementary school level and into higher grades as well as at the post-secondary level, the students who enter post-secondary institutions will be prepared with the desirable qualities to succeed and accomplish their goals. As distance librarians, we should make it our responsibility to recognize the needs, and provide support that will contribute to a positive academic experience. Let us ensure that our distance delivery service is a blessing, not a curse, just as we would for any other student.

REFERENCES

ADA, Americans with Disabilities Act. (1990). Home page. Retrieved December 1, 2003 from http://www.usdoj.gov/crt/ada/adahom1.htm.

ADA, Americans with Disabilities Act. (1990). *Title II*, section 202. Retrieved December 1, 2003 from http://www.usdoj.gov/crt/ada/pubs/ada.txt.

Association for Colleges and Research Libraries. (2000). *ACRL guidelines for distance learning library services*. Retrieved December 9, 2003 from http://caspian.switchinc.org/~distlearn/guidelines/guidelines_intor.pdf.

Barley, S. R. (1999). Computer-based distance education: Why or why not? *The Education Digest, 65* (2), 55-59.

Black, N. E. (2001). Emerging technologies: Tools for distance education and library services. *Journal of Library Administration, 31*(3/4), 45-59.

Canadian Charter of Rights and Freedoms, Department of Justice of Canada (1982). Retrieved December 1, 2003 from http://canada.justice.gc.ca/loireg/charte/const_en.html#egalite.

Canadian Human Rights Act. (1985). Retrieved December 1, 2003 from http://laws.justice.gc.ca/en/H-6/.

CLA Services for Distance Learning Interest Group. (2000). *Guidelines for library support of distance and distributed learning in Canada*. Canadian Library Association, http://www.cla.ca/about/distance.htm.

Dewald, N. H. (1999). Web-based library instruction: What is good pedagogy? *Information Technology and Libraries, 1*(1), 26-31.

Dewald, N., Scholz-Crane, A., Booth, A., & Levine, C. (2000). Information literacy at a distance: Instructional design issues. *Journal of Academic Librarianship, 26*(1), 33-45.

Fichten, C. S., Asuncion, J. V., Barile, M., Fossey, M., & de Simone, C. (2000). Access to educational and instructional computer technologies for post-secondary students with disabilities: Lessons from three empirical studies. *Journal of Educational Media, 25*(3), 179-201.

Gerber, P. J., Ginsberg, R., & Reiff, H. B. (1992). Identifying alterable patterns in employment success for highly successful adults with learning disabilities. *Journal of Learning Disabilities, 25* (8), 475- 487.

Gerber, P. J., Reiff, H. B., & Ginsberg, R. (1996). Reframing the learning disabilities experience. *Journal of Learning Disabilities, 29*(1), 98-101, 97.

Griebal, R. (2003). If Helen Keller lived north of the 49th: Canadian library services of people with disabilities. *Feliciter, 49*(3), 55-157.

Jax, J. J. & Muraski, T. (1992). Library services for students with disabilities at the University of Wisconsin-Stout. *Journal of Academic Librarianship, 19*(3), 166-168.

Larkin, M. J. (2001). Providing support for student independence through scaffolded instruction. *Teaching Exceptional Children, 34*(1), 30-34.

LDAC, Learning Disability Association of Canada. (February 2000). *Fact Sheet. They can get there from here: students with learning disabilities in Canadian colleges and universities.* Retrieved December 1, 2003 from http://www.ldac-taac.ca.

LDAC, Learning Disability Association of Canada. (undated). Home page. Retrieved December 1, 2003 from http://www.ldac-taac.ca.

LDAC, Learning Disability Association of Canada. (undated). *Learning disabilities and the law: A Canadian resource.* Retrieved December 1, 2003 from http://www.ldac-taac.ca/ld-law/start.htm.

LDAC, Learning Disability Association of Canada. (March 2001). *Fact Sheet. What is a learning disability?* Retrieved December 1, 2003 from http://www.ldac-taac.ca.

LDAC, Learning Disability Association of Canada. (October 2001). *Fact Sheet. Statistics on learning disabilities.* Retrieved December 1, 2003 from http://www.ldac-taac.ca.

LDAC, Learning Disability Association of Canada. (January 30, 2002). *Official definition of learning disabilities.* Retrieved December 1, 2003 from http://www.ldac-taac.ca.

LDAC, Learning Disability Association of Canada. (March 2003). *Fact Sheet. Assistive technology examples.* Retrieved December 1, 2003 from http://www.ldac-taac.ca.

LDAC, Learning Disability Association of Canada. (March 2003). *Fact Sheet. E-Learning as an assistive technology tool.* Retrieved December 1, 2003 from http://www.ldac-taac.ca.

LDAC, Learning Disability Association of Canada. (March 2003). *Fact Sheet. Myths and realities of assistive technologies.* Retrieved December 1, 2003 from http://www.ldac-taac.ca.

LDAC, Learning Disability Association of Canada. (March 2003). *Fact Sheet. Resources–Assistive Technology.* Retrieved December 1, 2003 from http://www.ldac-taac.ca.

Luther, J. (1998).Distance learning and the digital library. *Educom Review, 33*(4), 22-27.

Madaus, J. W., Ruban, L. M., Foley, T. E., & McGuire, J. M. (2003). Attributes contributing to the employment satisfaction of university graduates with learning disabilities. *Learning Disability Quarterly, 26*(Summer) 159-169.

NIFL, National Institute for Literacy. (Summer, 1995). *Adults with learning disabilities*. Retrieved November 25, 2003 from http://www.nifl.gov/nifl/ld/archive/definiti.htm.

Niemi, J. A., Ehrhard, B. J., & Neeley, L. (1998). Off-campus library support for distance adult learners. *Library Trends, 47*(1), 65-74.

Olney, M. F., & Kim, A. (2001). Beyond adjustment: Integration of cognitive disability into identity. *Disability & Society, 16*(4), 563-583.

Potter, J. (1998). Beyond access: Student perspectives on support service needs in distance learning. *Canadian Journal of University Continuing Education, 24*(1), 59-82.

Rouse, V. (1999). Making the Web accessible. *Computers in Libraries, 19*(6), 48-53.

Rovai, A. P. (2003). In search of higher persistence rates in distance education online programs. *Internet and Higher Education, 6*, 1-16.

SNOW Project, Special Needs Opportunities Windows (undated). *SNOW (Special Needs Opportunities Windows)*. Home page. Retrieved December 1, 2003 from http://snow.utoronto.ca.

Stanton, S. (2003). Going the distance: developing shared web-based learning programmes. *Occupational Therapy International, 8*(2), 96-106.

Wall, P. S. & Sarver, L. (2003). Disabled student access in an era of technology. *Internet and Higher Education, 6*, 277-284.

Wiener, J. & Siegel, L. (1992). A Canadian perspective on learning disabilities. *Journal of Learning Disabilities, 25*(6) June/July, 340-350, 371.

Wiesenberg, F. (2001). The roller coaster life of the online learner: How distance educators can help students cope. *Canadian Journal of University Continuing Education, 27*(2), 33-59.

Institutional Challenges in Web-Based Programs: Student Challenges and Institutional Responses

Elizabeth A. Buchanan

University of Wisconsin-Milwaukee

SUMMARY. Institutions, as we know, are quickly embracing distance education, in the forms of online or Web-based courses and programs at phenomenal rates. Oftentimes, however, significant institutional structures, including such areas as registration, advising, library, and technical support are overlooked until too late. Institutions must have clear, well-planned strategies in place in order to maximize their students' learning experiences and overall satisfaction with distance education programs to avoid attrition and maximize retention. This paper provides many useful and easy to implement strategies for institutions considering distance education, as well as for those already engaged in serving students online. In particular, this paper explores experiences of students pursuing the Master of Library and Information Science degree through a Web-based program. Their challenges will be described, and the institutional responses and solutions will be offered.

KEYWORDS. Internet, distance education, program development, distance learners

---

[Haworth co-indexing entry note]: "Institutional Challenges in Web-Based Programs: Student Challenges and Institutional Responses." Buchanan, Elizabeth A. Co-published simultaneously in *Journal of Library Administration* (The Haworth Information Press, an imprint of The Haworth Press, Inc.) Vol. 41, No. 1/2, 2004, pp. 65-74; and: *The Eleventh Off-Campus Library Services Conference Proceedings* (ed: Patrick B. Mahoney) The Haworth Information Press, an imprint of The Haworth Press, Inc., 2004, pp. 65-74.

INTRODUCTION

Who is remote when taking online coursework? It is easy to assume it is the student; he or she only "visits" the university via the Internet and course management packages. He or she communicates via e-mail, via chat room, via fax. He or she doesn't need to "know" fellow students. He or she doesn't use the library. Or students services. Or the career center. Or other services "real" students use on a daily basis. Or do they?

Distance education students, who now assume an increasingly larger percentage of our college and university enrollments, are not remote. Indeed, their presence is different, and thus, requires different considerations and services. How can institutions serve their distance students so that they experience a rewarding learning experience, so they do not feel they are attending "lone wolf university"?

This paper looks at the challenges experienced by graduate students pursuing their Master of Library and Information Science (MLIS) degree through a Web-based program. How the sponsoring school and institution as a whole have responded to these experiences will be described, with further recommendations for making the experiences of online graduate students more successful and rewarding.

INSTITUTIONS: PUTTING THE CART BEFORE THE HORSE?

What sorts of planning mechanisms are required to initiate a Web-based program? Unfortunately, Schrum and Benson (2002) note the paucity of program planning models in the growing body of distance education literature. Seemingly, institutions in this first wave of Web-based programs learn as they proceed, a trial by error approach. Programs are launched before critical planning occurs. This lack of planning contributes to serious consequences for students in particular, ultimately diminishing their educational experiences.

Schrum and Benson identify three major areas of planning that must be considered prior to establishing successful online learning courses and programs: factors related to educators, to learners, and thirdly, to program planners. In the realm of program planning, Schrum and Benson identify the need for faculty development, technical support, student services, curricular design, program technologies, course design, and finally, marketing and pricing. A sound consideration of these factors is critical before the implementation of an online program; of course, it is never possible to conceive of every scenario, situation, and yes–possible disaster–that may arise, but by adopting a remote student-centered perspective from the outset a smoother transition to a Web-based programmatic model will be achieved. How can this perspective be adopted?

Buchanan (2002) recommends that the faculty, staff, and administrators or program planners responsible for or participating in the Web-based program in any capacity should receive formal training in distance education pedagogy and its specificity. This can take place in the form of a one-day workshop or an online module. The training should include information from the distance education literature that explains how Web-based teaching and learning is different and what they can expect from it. After a general introduction to Web-based education, specific groups depending on one's role (faculty, administrator, etc.), should focus on unique issues related to these roles. For instance, faculty should focus on teaching and assessment strategies, administrators and planners on management, electronic communication, and programmatic strategies. For example, faculty must be cognizant of the time allotment in Web-based coursework. One area of particular concern among students is with asynchronous discussion fora: *"Keeping up with the discussions is like going to class daily"; "You have to work hard if not harder. You need to participate in discussion all the time"; "Very intense and time consuming"; "Must have good time management and not mind reading A LOT."* (For useful discussion of effective online discussions, see Palloff and Pratt, 1999.)

The research on Web-based education is replete with information on the importance of communication, and yet, a large majority of the problems facing online students revolves around barriers to effective communication. In this sense, communication entails effective planning and consultation between institution and student as well as within the institution itself. As part of the planning process, other institutional offices and services, such as the library, bursar's office, career center, and others, must be consulted. The School of Information Studies, for instance, created the position of distance education coordinator, who is responsible for overseeing such communication among the offices involved in serving the distance students.

Yet, consider a common example: Institutions launch online programs without informing the library, which later finds out that specific journals and materials are indeed necessary to support the program's mission. Faculty assigns reading from specific journals; the host library does not hold them or have access to them. Students may not have access to another research library, and are thus unable to attain the materials for learning. This creates frustration for all involved: students, librarians, and faculty.

Where students are able to access other research libraries, this one issue can be assuaged, if the institution has thought through others. Consider this example:

I live in Wisconsin and have learned that I can check materials out at my local UW library if I have a Milwaukee ID. Without it, I'm out of luck. I called to inquire about getting one, and was told that I must show up in person at Milwaukee to get one! One reason for being a DE student is to not have to actually go to Milwaukee! Even if one does not live in WI/have desire to get an ID to use at another university, there are any number of reasons to want one. . . . I realize the problem is creating a picture ID when you are not there to get a picture taken by the people that make the ID. But could we not either be allowed to send in a photo (they could specify any size requirement) or else get an ID that does not have a picture but names us as a student, provide our student ID number and says something about checking driver's licenses to verify you really are the student named?

Effective planning and communication across the institution could have alleviated this ID card program before it became an issue for the students. Perhaps the institution just never considered this issue? As a way to avoid missing such pertinent information, Buchanan (2002) recommends holding online focus groups and creating an online student advisory board to contribute to a true student-centered perspective. Much like a business model, these two approaches can provide unique insight into the needs and desires of the students; too, such forms of regular contact with the students can prevent potential problems from exploding into major institutional disasters. Such focus groups and consultations with the advisory board are not a one-time event, but should be held regularly, with students from various stages in the program participating. It is not possible to foresee every situation, but it is possible to respond to them effectively.

LET THE FRUSTRATIONS BEGIN: NAVIGATING THE INSTITUTIONAL MAZE

As noted, effective communication across an institution can contribute to a more successful student experience. Students frequently note the inability to find information easily and quickly; the inability to find the "right" person to answer questions; the difficulty in relying on e-mail or phone calls to negotiate a problem. A few examples typify these problems:

There does not seem to be a centralized location for information. I was very concerned my first semester about how to register, find out which textbooks to buy, etc. These things, which are very easy for on-campus students, can be quite mystifying for DE students. I tried searching the Web site but found little information for students who are actually enrolled. Finally I ended up e-mailing the DE coordinator and even my professors directly. I got no response from two teachers. One teacher sent me the textbook list, and I did also get a link to the official textbook list from the DE coordinator. How would I have known to look at that Web page if I had not requested the link? I have NO CLUE. It seems like there should be ONE Web page that has all those links on it: schedule & registration, textbooks, etc. This issue also came up again at registration time for UWinteriM and Spring semesters. Someone finds out (HOW???) when registration is supposed to start and posts it to the student chat board, and others confirm or contest the rumor. It all seems very random.

I also had trouble with my financial arrangements. While it looked to me on PAWS like everything was fine with my finances, my financial aid did not disburse as it was supposed to. I began getting statements with carrying charges. I tried calling the financial aid office and the bursar's office. First, it was VERY difficult to find their phone numbers on the school Web site. Second, when I did call, I got one of those baffling touch-tone mazes which left me desperately punching numbers in an attempt to get a real person on the phone. None of the automated options EVER match my problem! When I finally did manage to speak to a live person, each office referred me to the other. I had to repeat the whole maddening process several times. Finally, someone actually looked at my file and said, "Oh, that's odd!" There was a hold on my financial aid account because of something relating to my fellowship. I still don't understand exactly what happened, but the two departments did finally talk to each other and my aid disbursed the next day.

Financial issues have been by far the most frustrating. Without being able to sit down face to face with a real person, I feel I have very little understanding of what's actually going on. I know that these services are often bad for on-site students too, but at least the on-site student can "camp out" at an office until something is worked out or explained. DE students don't have that luxury. I don't really understand how much financial aid I'm getting (the amount I receive does not match any letter I got) or why I'm receiving it, or when it's supposed to happen. I just keep holding my breath and hoping that I don't get kicked out of classes.

Depending on the size of one's institution and the number of programs offered online, an office for distance education students should be created. The number of staff should be relative to the number of students and programs being served; as with other "specialized" student offices (Adult and Continuing

Students, Minority Students, etc.), who have a unique place to go for assistance, distance education students should as well. This office would serve as the mediary between students and the institution, with a special focus on communications and consultations: This office is the one-stop shop for information for distance students, or the "centralized location of information" desired by the student above.

One of the first orders of business from this office would be to provide each new student with an orientation video, cd-rom, web module, or paper manual, giving the student the choice of material. Students mentioned the lack of *"beginner's knowledge"* and expressed a sense of helplessness when first beginning: *"There is not a lot of support to help get you started"; "Difficult to get started and learn the ropes. It might be nice if there were an online training class before the new student begins. Or a generalized tutorial for the whole process."* Common sentiments including technical frustrations have been reported by Hara and Kling (1999), among others.

This "how to be an online student" manual would contain institutional tours (what office does what, as well as give the student a visual image of the institution), an overview of the technical issues involved in the online program, an overview of the services available to the distance student, recommendations on participating in online coursework, a list of important contact information (though the institution should have a toll free telephone line that permits transfers throughout the institution to avoid multiple calls and "run-around;" this phone line should also be accessible to international students), and information on institutional policies for registration, graduation, and similar issues. A review of the postings on the SOIS Virtual Student Lounge reveals a majority of them are questions revolving around "How do I register for classes?" "Where do I get the application for graduation?" "How do I sign up for fieldwork and internships?" "How do I sign up for the comprehensive exam?" Also, students expressed frustration in their lack of knowledge in where to obtain such information and thus, rely on each other.

Online students, especially if not part of a cohort, can feel very isolated and confused by the institutional maze, as this research has found. To minimize these feelings and experiences, a virtual student lounge and an online mentoring program were created.

HOLDING YOUR HAND FROM A DISTANCE: ONLINE MENTORS AND AN ONLINE LOUNGE

Institutions can respond to the needs and desires of their online students, but there is a large place for peer-to-peer information sharing and support. Online students miss out on the "hallway discussions" that take place during a break in an onsite class; they can not get together and talk about an instructor as their onsite counterparts can, and thus, are often shortchanged of pertinent information that could help them decide to take this class over that one, work with this professor over that one, and so on. It is this type of socialization that contributes to a sense of isolation and disconnect among distance students; yes, they meet in their classes and work together where required, but oftentimes, their socialization stops there:

> *DE Students are so scattered. We meet in a few classes but don't–didn't–have a place to get together and just exchange ideas and talk outside of class. Now, we can all get together over a cup of coffee and talk with each other. I haven't found a lot that makes me feel like I'm part of the University . . . so this virtual student lounge really makes me feel like UWM is starting to recognize the existence of DE Students.*

The virtual lounge to which this student refers was created by the School in response to recommendations by online students. The lounge is restricted to students and the School's distance education coordinator, but access by faculty is tightly controlled. The idea is simple: Provide the online students with a space that is entirely theirs, where professors can be "bashed," where friendships outside of a class can be formed, where information can be shared on an informal and formal basis. In addition to school-related postings, consider this posting to the lounge, which demonstrates one use of the lounge as a purely social networking tool, where personal information can be shared safely: *"Since the babyboomers have commented, are there any single mothers out there taking classes? I'm 27 and have a 6 year old. I also work at a public library branch. My travel time to work is a half an hour. I have a disgruntled ex-husband and ex-inlaws to deal with weekly. Anyone else in this situation?"*

This space is an outlet for students as well as a mechanism for dissemination of official information. If the School wants to share information regarding scholarships, research projects, new courses added, et cetera, it will be posted in the lounge and all students will have access to it. A student immediately attains access to the lounge upon his or her first enrollment in an online class; it will be listed along with his or her classes upon login.

The lounge has received an enthusiastic response, as one student expresses the sentiments of many: *"And this student lounge is a wonderful release valve; I have been reading along every day and smiling, knowing there are others out there who understand the same frustrations and joys I am feeling."* Students can also post anonymously in the lounge, and many take advantage of this ability to raise questions and discuss issues about professors and the school.

Students appreciate this factor, as they can argue, voice anger, and discuss political issues in a safe manner.

In addition to the lounge, an online mentoring program is underway to facilitate a more supportive experience for online students. While research still shows that generally, distance students are mature adults capable of working independently, this does not negate the need or desire for a mentor. A survey of 53 students in the Web-based MLIS program revealed that 62% wanted an online mentor. A mentor, it was felt, would *"Support from a mentor would probably help the newbies in learning the system," "An online mentor would help 'emerse' a student into the DE experience. There's a lot of simple things that aren't covered in some courses, like the availability of resources through UWM's library site," "An online mentor could help ease the isolation," "A mentor could advise the student of where to focus attention to learn the steps to get started. The mentor could answer questions and walk the student through the necessary steps to get started," and "An online mentor could discuss common pitfalls to help you avoid them . . . could answer miscellaneous questions as they arise . . . could provide a sense of connectedness that is otherwise absent."* Thus, a mentor's role is advisory, social, and supportive.

The administration of the mentoring program is carried out by the School's distance education coordinator. A simple approach has been used where new enrollees are given the name and contact information of a "veteran" student, and the new student contacts his or her mentor. The School is now, given the increased interest in a mentoring program, and based on the research study underway by Buchanan (2003), working on a more elaborate mentoring process, that matches students based on interests, geographical location, age, and other variables. Buchanan (2002) notes that such mentoring programs are quick, easy, and cost-effective ways of building support mechanisms for students while they also contribute to a more successful learning experience for students. And yet, Buchanan's ongoing research shows that few schools of library and information science with distance education programs have formal mentoring programs in place. It is likely that many online programs from other disciplines share in this and do not offer mentoring programs to online students.

CONCLUSIONS

This paper has reviewed the experiences of students in a graduate level MLIS Web-based program, and in particular, it has looked at institutional mechanisms and problems that contribute to the student experience, while offering suggestions for more successful distance education experiences. While the experiences of this student body will not be directly applicable to all online graduate students, many institutions can learn from the ideas expressed herein. Yes, institutions are learning to accommodate their distance students as they grow in their online programs and offerings. If we allow our students to share their experiences, listen to them and respond, and allow them a place of their own to participate in peer-to-peer networking, we are moving towards a greater understanding of online education. The days of discussing online learning in terms of "convenience" alone should be over; instead, we should raise the level of discourse and discuss how online education is a pedagogically unique and sound experience for students. Once the institutional mechanisms are in place to fully support distance students, the learning experience becomes focal and primary. This should be our goal.

AUTHOR NOTE

This paper is based on research from the School of Information Studies, University of Wisconsin-Milwaukee. The quotes and experiences included herein are from actual graduate students, whose names and identities are protected. This research is approved by the Institutional Review Board for the Protection of Human Subjects at UWM.

Students from the 2001 SOIS course, "Information and Library Sources and services for Distance Education" discussed the efficacy of this idea. Thanks go to them for encouraging its implementation.

Some of the comments used in this paper come from the lounge, but were obtained with permission and were gathered by one of the author's graduate student research assistants. This author never accessed the lounge directly, in respect for the DE students' space and privacy.

The author, in collaboration with two distance education graduate students, is conducting research on the role of online mentors and the learning experience of students. The research was funded by the UW-Milwaukee Center for Instructional Professional development's Student-Faculty Partnerships Grant Initiative.

REFERENCES

Buchanan, E. (2002). Institutional and library services for distance education courses and programs. In Discenza, R., Howard, C., & Schenk, K. (Eds.), *The Design and Implementation of Effective Distance Learning Programs*, 141-154. Hershey: Idea Group.

Buchanan, E. (2003). *Online students and the impact of online mentoring*. Research Funded by the UW-Milwaukee Center for Instructional Professional Development.

Hara, N., & Kling, R. (1999). Students' frustrations with a Web-based distance education course. *First Monday*, 4(12). Retrieved from the World Wide Web at http://firstmonday.org/issues/issue4_12/hara/index.html.

Palloff, R., & Pratt, K. (1999). *Building learning communities in cyberspace: Effective strategies for the online classroom.* San Francisco: Jossey Bass.

Schrum, L. & Benson, A. (2002). Establishing successful online distance learning environments: Distinguishing factors that contribute to online courses and programs. In Discenza, R., Howard, C., and Schenk, K. (Eds.), *The Design and Implementation of Effective Distance Learning Programs,* 190-204. Hershey: Idea Group.

Where Is the Library
in Course Management Software?

Marianne A. Buehler

Rochester Institute of Technology

SUMMARY. Course management software (CMS) or courseware products, such as Prometheus, FirstClass, Blackboard, and WebCT, do not include the Library as an essential, curricular component in their design. Consequently, the task falls to librarians to creatively partner with faculty to input library resources into courseware to support students effectively in their research endeavors. Distance learning students, who are off campus, will benefit as they are physically removed from the Library. Distance learners (DLs) can be intimidated by library Web sites and find it difficult and time consuming to navigate. Since the entire course content is in the course management product, the primary source for class information, it makes good sense to include library resources and services in the appropriate areas, such as the syllabus, assignments, projects, etc. Including research resources within courseware enables students to get started on their own in navigating the Library and can provide direct contact information to appropriate library staff for further and deeper resource assistance.

KEYWORDS. Distance learners, technology, library resources, Internet

Rochester Institute of Technology's (RIT) distance learning (DL) students are located in many places around the world, as far away as Hong Kong or as

[Haworth co-indexing entry note]: "Where Is the Library in Course Management Software?" Buehler, Marianne A. Co-published simultaneously in *Journal of Library Administration* (The Haworth Information Press, an imprint of The Haworth Press, Inc.) Vol. 41, No. 1/2, 2004, pp. 75-84; and: *The Eleventh Off-Campus Library Services Conference Proceedings* (ed: Patrick B. Mahoney) The Haworth Information Press, an imprint of The Haworth Press, Inc., 2004, pp. 75-84.

http://www.haworthpress.com/web/JLA
Digital Object Identifier: 10.1300/J111v41n01_07

close as living on the RIT campus. Students within 30 or so miles of the Campus prefer not to travel to take classes. These students share many commonalities, one of them is either they cannot easily or efficiently travel to RIT. Some on-campus students tend to prefer DL classes for the online environment and convenience. In the early development of CMS, the emphasis of providing an online venue was to reach DL students. Universities are discovering that a new audience is local students who prefer the online learning context (Machavec, 2001). "The lines between on and off-campus students and courses are blurring as technology is incorporated into all aspects of education" (Beagle, 2000, p. 367). Students who are isolated and scattered around the globe do not have the option of asking questions and sharing information amongst themselves in person regarding related coursework questions. The framework that all RIT DL students share is the use of two CMS products, FirstClass or Prometheus. FirstClass is used solely for DL classes. Prometheus is used for some DL classes, but also for on-campus, online, and blended learning classes (face-to-face with some online components). The courseware encompasses an entire professor's course content, including the syllabus, lectures, projects, and discussions. When it is time to do research, write papers, or create projects, DL students have to either locate information on their own or seek research assistance. Navigating library Web sites can be a time consuming affair, especially when resources are in an unrecognizable format, such as research databases, for which some students do not have a frame of reference. Since a majority of DL students are working and have families, they tend to do their coursework on weekends and nights when research help may not be available. Given this nontraditional profile, what can libraries, faculty, other university staff and CMS developers do to support DL student academic success within the parameters of using courseware?

Given the fact that courseware products are deficient overall in developing a built-in academic library component for student and faculty use, creative partnering with faculty is a good choice in assisting students with locating and learning how to use the Library. Librarians traditionally tend to work with faculty by purchasing suggested materials, teaching subject-specific classes, creating pathfinders, and doing research. In the online class environment that is structured within courseware, there are new opportunities and ways to present the required research information for students.

Students need general and specific library resources to be successful in finding course-related materials. On a continuum, some students prefer not to ask for research assistance and painstakingly search on their own, while other students like direct, detailed help. By presenting information directly in a courseware product, research assistance becomes a level playing field where all students are provided the same information to initially get started. Giving students more detailed research help in the form of a pathfinder is even better. DL students are grateful to have pointers and will sometimes e-mail librarians to thank them and say how they wish specific research information had been supplied earlier in their academic careers. How can librarians interact with instructors to achieve input of library-related information into CMS classes?

As librarians know, faculty own their own style and preferences in teaching. That said, there is no exception to the various ways that courseware is employed by instructors and the manner in which information is presented. Since there are multiple avenues for presenting library resources and services, it is best decided by faculty who teach a class as to how it fits their personal style. Librarians are knowledgeable regarding student information-seeking behaviors and what information is needed. They are experts in knowing when students are at the "point of need" in the information-seeking process to be aware of all resources to enable learners to be successful in their coursework. Libraries have also developed their Web sites so users can access their resources and services independent of time or location. Given the complementary expertise of both faculty and librarians to benefit DLs, it makes good sense for them to partner in furnishing the best and most useful resources and information available.

At RIT, two (instruction librarian and distance/online learning librarian) of the ten reference librarians teach Prometheus courseware classes in conjunction with the Online Learning Department, who sponsor the classes. The other librarians have a basic+ understanding of how the CMS works and how to use it. It is important for librarians to be knowledgeable about navigating and using courseware to solve occasional student questions and to work with faculty within the online class environment. Subject specialists are encouraged to offer library expertise in their respective topical areas to either input the information for faculty into Prometheus or demonstrate the resources for faculty to post the annotated links or other materials themselves. Some of the ways that RIT librarians have assisted faculty in posting information include: persistent links to e-books, writing and literature resources, librarian contact information, participating in monitoring and contributing to a discussion board topic on plagiarism, and other related topics. In the case of some courseware products, such as Prometheus, librarians can be added as Teaching Assistants with privileges to add or edit information.

An avenue that has provided guidance to RIT faculty on how and where to integrate library resources into an online course, was the development (and teaching of) a class within Prometheus by the Distance/Online Learning (D/OL) and Head of Information Delivery Services/Electronic Reserves Librarians, called *Integrating Library Resources Into myCourses*. The term, myCourses, was coined by RIT's Information Technology Services department, so when RIT migrates from one courseware product to another, faculty and students will not be confused by a new courseware name. In this case, Prometheus is the product "under the hood," so to speak, of myCourses. The class is offered on a quarterly basis and was also proffered at the 2003 spring faculty workshop, the *Faculty Institute on Teaching and Learning (FITL)*, an annual event precipitated in May 1998 by faculty who voiced a strong need for support in learning the latest teaching and learning technologies. The FITL class had a good turnout, with enthusiastic attendees.

Faculty and staff have come to every class offered, but there has not been an overwhelming attendance. RIT librarians have found that faculty usually attend offered classes or contact them when they have a specific "point of need." As an example, the RIT Library has used e-reserves since 1996. Many faculty are still not aware of the e-reserves service and are appreciative when they learn that such a service exists. Prometheus has an e-reserves template that instructors can use to request materials by filling out a citation for the item. If the Library has the article or book, the item is scanned and then posted wherever the instructor designates its location. If the Library does not own it, it is interlibrary loaned and then transmitted into the course. The demo class illustrates a model of how a course can best merge library information with the syllabus, the outline of weekly assignments, class projects, and lectures.

- Syllabus–provides contact information of the subject specialist by phone, e-mail, or by live reference; Turnitin, a plagiarism-fighting tool will be utilized for students to upload their papers
- Outline of assignments–library research databases supporting research for assignments; a link to Information Delivery Services (interlibrary loan); live reference contact information; library catalogs; e-reserve readings; Syndetics (more! button, that explains how to find full-text articles from an abstract or citation)
- Projects (writing a paper)–research database links; link to MS Word class; SmartForce learning modules that include MS Word
- Lectures–links to: online instruction guides on how to use research databases; the Research Tree that delineates how to do research at the RIT Library; citation formats; librarian-recommended resources by topic; *Plagiarism–You Can Avoid It* . . . tutorial; evaluating information from the Internet; career resources compiled by librarians

Because DL students are seeing library resources mingled with assignments and at other "points of need," they are able to more easily locate the requisite information or contact their librarian if assistance is necessary. Students can spend more time directly researching and writing instead of perusing the

Library's labyrinth Web site, or worse yet, surfing the Internet for information that may not be authoritative or available. The Library will gain an increased relevance for students if they see its presence in the courseware.

Recently, a librarian who manages the faculty/staff Educational Technology Resource Room at RIT's National Technical Institute for the Deaf (NTID), participated in a class, so he can support NTID faculty and staff who use Prometheus by using the demo class as an example. Garnering support of other university staff that foster relationships with faculty help spread the word of useful ways to incorporate library resources and services into a CMS. Even though every courseware has its own features, the ideas and examples here can be extrapolated for use in other courseware products.

Another valuable feature of Prometheus is its ability to create a Course Content Module. Modules allow faculty, librarians, or Online Learning (OL) staff to create a block of information, such as broad library research information, academic honesty/disability policies or another piece of information that can be shared among an instructor's multiple sections or with other faculty. In an attempt to forearm DLs with basic to intermediate library guidance available in every Prometheus course, the D/OL Librarian created a Course Content Module, *Navigating RIT Library*.

The Module encompasses Web links to doing library research, research guides and tutorials, librarian contact information and recommended resources by topic, more!–how to find full-text materials from abstracts and citations, E-Content Finder (a library-created tool to locate library full-text journals and books), library catalogs, and Information Delivery Services (see Figure 1). Faculty have expressed positive comments regarding the Module that enables students to independently commence their research. Since Prometheus is also used for on-campus and blended learning classes, all students benefit from the module that was intended for DL students.

OL and the D/OL Librarian worked together designing how the Module would be placed in the syllabus. OL was careful to convert the Module into a format that allows faculty to maneuver it within the syllabus or even delete it, if so desired. The OL Prometheus administrator also set the Module to appear in every RIT course by default (all RIT courses have a presence automatically created in the prior quarter), another creative and useful way of disseminating information in a CMS product.

RIT DL students who use FirstClass courseware also benefit from library resources and services that are disseminated globally in a manner similar to the Course Content Module in Prometheus. Every quarter, OL creates an alias and serves out the Wallace Library Conference on all FirstClass course desktops. FirstClass has a different paradigm of presenting information than Prometheus. It is comprised of conferences and folders, two types of locations

FIGURE 1

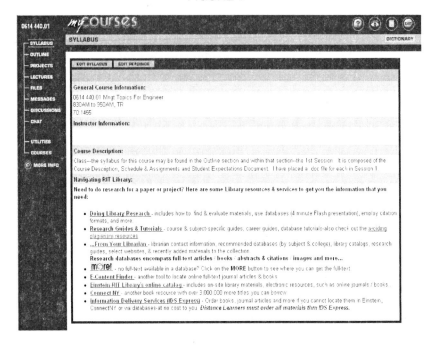

where faculty organize their course content. It also requires a client download (using the Web-based version is discouraged unless behind a firewall or if traveling) and has a built-in e-mail client. It is more robust than Prometheus, which makes it an excellent choice for DL faculty and students to communicate around the world. OL assisted the D/OL Librarian in setting up a course conference to delineate library resources in an easy to use format utilizing e-mail messages where the subject line clearly states what information is within. DL students can quickly scan the subjects to find the information they are looking for. The messages are succinct and contain links to the requisite materials on the Library's Web site (see Figure 2). There is a *history function* in FirstClass that provides the name, date, and time that a faculty member or student read a message. Some messages have been read by up to 200 users (during three quarters), a small percentage of which are faculty. DL students also reply to the FirstClass messages, therefore are able to directly contact the D/OL Librarian. Faculty and students have expressed appreciation of having a library resource on their course desktops.

Other DL and online students who may be using Prometheus are able to have Web access to the Wallace Library Conference. Every time the D/OL Li-

FIGURE 2

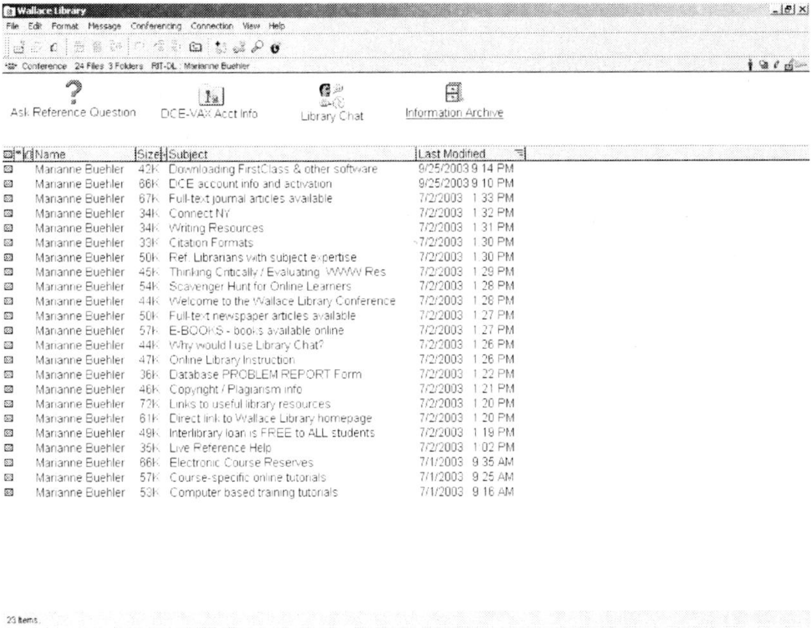

brarian updates a message in the Conference, it automatically updates the customized OL Web interface in the Student Resource Center <http://online. rit.edu/>.

To accommodate a need for logging in using one password at a single authentication point, another customized feature developed for DL students has been the e-reserves component in FirstClass. The FirstClass Administrator created a Conference with permissions for students to access reserve readings within the Courseware. Students have the ability to read the material without having to login to the Library's e-reserve site and having to know another username and password. This has eliminated frustration for students and staff time spent providing e-reserve usernames and passwords. Partnering with the OL department has been an asset for the Library to be able to assist DL students in various venues, enabling them to be aware of available research information and the ability to find and use it.

"By integrating and linking the Library's catalog and online databases [and more] into the courseware environment, students and faculty are only a click away from accessing many of the information resources relevant to their course assignments from within courseware" (Shank & Dewald, 2003, p. 3). A DL student-centered research tool was created to be used in FirstClass as a library pathfinder. Every fall quarter, the D/OL Librarian e-mails all DL faculty as a reminder of library resources and services for their course. Also, new DL faculty are e-mailed every quarter with the same information. One of the services offered by the D/OL Librarian, is the creation of a pathfinder for specific classes. It is comprised of general information regarding using the Library from a distance. It also entails working with a subject specialist for a particular class, having the librarian compile specific resources that target the class syllabus. Once faculty express an interest in the pathfinder and when assembled, the D/OL Librarian, as a sub-administrator in FirstClass, e-mails the Library Assistance guide into the class. Many DL faculty have taken advantage of this service. If more than two DL students contact the D/OL Librarian from a particular class who are struggling with navigating the Library, the professor is contacted asking if the he or she would like a pathfinder to assist students in navigating the Library. OL Instructional Designers also recommend and refer DL faculty to consult with the D/OL Librarian. Many pathfinders have been created from those contacts. There has been positive feedback from students and faculty in using the library guides. If all faculty partnered with librarians to create a course library guide to resources, students would be less stressed and more successful in their research endeavors and assignments.

Partnering within our own institutions with faculty and other support departments, such as an Online/Distance Learning or the campus IT department is essential to create optimal learning environments that benefit students. In most university and college settings, one or more departments work with the courseware folks who developed the CMS product that is used on campus. At RIT, there is a Courseware Management System team comprised of OL, Information Technology Services, and RIT Library members. One of our tasks is to choose an appropriate courseware for RIT when circumstances necessitate a change. OL is the main contact to the Prometheus and FirstClass courseware support staff. RIT Faculty, staff, and students have opportunities to provide functionality and usability courseware feedback by e-mailing suggestions or by participating in the annual spring distance learning survey. The OL administrators can make coding changes (Prometheus is open source) or request modifications for future version updates.

Libraries should play a discernible role in the evaluation and selection process of a campus CMS product (Beagle, 2000). Academic librarians also need to influence standards that include the library component, by determining ways in which CMS systems best use the expertise of librarians and library collections, both physical and online (Cohen, 2002). Overall, libraries have been absent in the design, development, and implementation of CMS. Consequently, faculty do not consider integrating library resources directly into their online courses. Authors Shank and Dewald (2003) believe that at a minimum, as faculty and librarians partner within a CMS, an instructor should at least link to a librarian's Web page. At a maximum, librarians can collaborate and assist in delivering the online class, with equal access to the courseware. The librarian adds customized links, leads chat discussions related to research, along with monitoring a message board with research-related questions throughout the term.

Many CMS companies have not incorporated an e-reserve system, a clickable library icon, or the library as a menu item that can be populated with research information or used as a pointer to more in depth library resources. The library is a missing element in most courseware products. Considering that a complete class is in a courseware environment, it makes sense to have curriculum research support placed in the same location for effective student use.

As an example of poor or lack of reliable resources, RIT used Blackboard (Bb), versions 2.0-5.0, until spring 2001. One of the obvious disadvantages of those versions was their rendition of a library component. It was a link that pointed to Bb-compiled informational websites that were not library-related. When CMS vendors point students to informational Web sites, some of which charge fees for their services, it is a concern of librarians because of the potential uneven quality of resources on the Web. Without integrating the library into a CMS, will students be aware of or find expensively purchased or leased online course material? Librarians spend much time and their expertise collecting authoritative sources and organizing information that is best for student use. To amplify the Library's online offerings, the integrating of these resources is essential to get maximum value from institutional monetary and expert investments (Cohen, 2002). There may be hope in future CMS updates and versions of courseware products, as mentioned in Bb's "Product Overview White Paper." The Bb company acknowledges the " . . . critical role that Library collections play in providing valuable e-Learning content." The Paper goes on to add new upcoming library features such as, Dublin Core metadata tagging for unstructured content, an e-reserves component, courses will have the ability to include subject-specific materials, and manage library content within an online course (Oerter, 2003, Library Digital Asset section, pg. 9).

Universities and colleges need to encourage and put pressure on courseware companies to incorporate the Library as a prominent feature for faculty and students to have direct access to library resources and services. Including a library component will enable DLs and other online students to realize the importance of reliable sources and equate their academic research success with the Library that resides in close proximity to where their courses are located.

From a constructivist's point of view, integrating library resources and instruction requires faculty to work with librarians in designing and creating learning tools that take into consideration a learner's understanding and thinking processes in using information to complete assignments and projects (Macklin, 2003). In utilizing a campus CMS system, faculty, and librarians can partner in providing the essentials for successful learning. By focusing on the interests of faculty and students who utilize the Library, librarians can succeed in producing and maintaining a relevant courseware presence.

REFERENCES

Beagle, D. (2000, July). Web-based learning environments: Do libraries matter? *College & Research Libraries, 61* (4), 367-79.

Cohen, D. (2002, May/June). Course-management software: Where's the library? *Educause, 37* (3), 12-13.

Machavec, G. (2001, Oct.). Course management software: Where is the library? *Information Intelligence Online Libraries and Microcomputers, 19* (10), 1-2.

Macklin, A. S. (2003, November). Theory into practice: Applying David Jonassen's work in instructional design to instruction programs in academic libraries. *College & Research Libraries, 64* (6), 494-500.

Oerter, L. (2003). *Blackboard content system-product overview white paper.* Retrieved December 9, 2003, from http://www.blackboard.com/docs/contentsystem/Content_System_wp.pdf.

Shank, J. D. & Dewald, N. H. (2003, March). Establishing our presence in courseware: Adding library services to the virtual classroom. *Information Technology and Libraries, 22* (1), 38-44.

A Survey
of Distance Librarian-Administrators
in ARL Libraries:
An Overview of Library Resources
and Services

Mary Cassner
Kate E. Adams

University of Nebraska-Lincoln

SUMMARY. The authors conducted a survey of distance librarian-administrators at Association of Research Libraries member libraries who plan for and manage distance learning library services. Survey questions included: What resources and services do ARL libraries currently offer to distance learners? What changes are being planned for in the immediate future? With libraries experiencing flattened budgets, what will be the impact on distance learners? Findings from the survey will inform librarian-administrators and library deans/directors of the current state of, and emerging trends in, distance learning library services.

KEYWORDS. Survey, library resources, library services, distance education

The literature is replete with articles and chapters describing the delivery of library services and resources to distance learners. A significant number of these are case studies that document how the library developed a distance learning library services program in accordance with the ACRL *Guidelines for*

[Haworth co-indexing entry note]: "A Survey of Distance Librarian-Administrators in ARL Libraries: An Overview of Library Resources and Services." Cassner, Mary, and Kate E. Adams. Co-published simultaneously in *Journal of Library Administration* (The Haworth Information Press, an imprint of The Haworth Press, Inc.) Vol. 41, No. 1/2, 2004, pp. 85-96; and: *The Eleventh Off-Campus Library Services Conference Proceedings* (ed: Patrick B. Mahoney) The Haworth Information Press, an imprint of The Haworth Press, Inc., 2004, pp. 85-96.

Distance Learning Library Services (rev. 2000). There is a need for empirical research on the provision of library resources and services to distance learners. Library deans/directors and distance librarian-administrators are often interested in seeing the range of distance learning library service offered by other institutions. The authors' study provides an overview of current practice and emerging trends in distance learning programs among a select group of academic libraries.

During the 1990s, academic libraries rapidly expanded the provision of remote access to electronic resources and services. Distance learners greatly benefited from this growth. Now, the fiscal situation has changed. The current economic picture presents challenges for academic libraries that are facing flattened or reduced budgets. Albanese (2001) reported how budget reversals at the state level affected university libraries. The fiscal outlook worsened during 2002 as states addressed revenue shortfalls, and university endowments declined (Albanese, 2002). An article in the August 8, 2003 issue of *The Chronicle of Higher Education* lamented the trend toward small increases in state appropriation for higher education, with no relief in sight for 2003/04 (Potter, 2003). While the state-aided budget improved slightly for some regions, other states experienced budget gaps for fiscal year 2004 (Hebel, 2003). The ACRL Focus on the Future Task Force gathered input from academic librarians on the major issues that shape library service. Higher education funding and support of new users (including distance users) are two of the top issues faced by academic libraries today (Hisle, 2002).

The authors conducted a survey of distance librarian-administrators who plan for and manage distance learning library services. The population studied is the Association of Research Libraries, an organization comprising over 120 large research libraries in North America. Several questions were posed. What resources and services do ARL libraries currently offer to distance learners? What changes are being planned for in the immediate future? What are the anticipated impacts of possible budget cuts on distance learners? Survey questions included those related to specific library services and resources, staffing, and budget. The authors believe that findings from the survey will inform librarian-administrators of current practice and emerging trends.

REVIEW OF THE LITERATURE

Numerous articles in the literature describe library services and resources delivered to distance learners. The discussion of budgetary or financial support for distance learning library services has often been quoted from the ACRL *Guidelines for Distance Learning Library Services* (rev. 2000) at http://www.ala.org/acrl/guides/distlrng.html. Budgetary support has frequently been covered as part of the planning process and start-up costs, or as part of a broader discussion of administrative function and oversight. Case studies typically discuss costs associated with delivery (phone, mail, the Internet). Looking ahead to the Millennium, Lebowitz (1997) forecast the impact of increasingly restrictive budgets on institutions. She asserted that how a library handles distance learning library services would be both a financial and philosophical decision.

An Association of Research Libraries SPEC Kit documented distance learning activity among ARL libraries (Snyder, Logue, & Preece, 1996). The 1996 survey primarily covered program administration, network management, and technical support. Of the 74 respondents, 46 reported that their institution was participating in distance education programs.

The Lebowitz article and 1996 ARL survey provided background for the authors' research. For the purpose of the 2003 survey, the authors defined distance education as the delivery of curriculum where the student and instructor are geographically separated, with the student receiving the course away from campus. The survey was intended to exclude the on-campus or residential user who is remotely accessing the library.

METHODOLOGY

The authors developed the survey drawing upon their previous research on ARL libraries' distance education Web sites, and adapting questions asked in the ARL survey in 1996. The survey was submitted to the university's Institutional Review Board for required approval. Data for the study were collected by a self-administered survey distributed in fall 2003. Surveys were sent to 112 academic members of the Association of Research Libraries. This number constitutes all ARL academic institutions whose primary language is English. The initial mailing included a cover letter addressed to the library dean/director, the survey, and a self-addressed stamped envelope. Approximately three weeks after the initial package was sent, a second packet was sent to non-respondents. This packet included a cover letter, survey, and self-addressed envelope. Seventy-six surveys were returned for a 68% return rate.

Initial questions on the survey asked whether the university offered for-credit distance curriculum and, if so, whether the library offered distance learning library services. The researchers asked questions related to access and delivery options, models of staffing, and collaboration of librarians with distance teaching faculty. Other questions asked the respondent to predict whether budgets that support library services and resources will increase, decrease, or have no change in the next two years.

The survey consisted of thirteen questions. The majority of survey questions were partially close-ended. Suggested answer choices were provided for these questions, although respondents had the option of adding their own comments. Three questions had multiple parts, and three questions were completely open-ended. Several questions were completely close-ended and called for concrete answers, such as "Does the library have a Web page dedicated to distance learners?"

A spreadsheet was developed using an Excel program. Data was manually compiled using raw numbers and percentages. Statistics were tabulated using simple percentages.

RESULTS

Of the 112 surveys sent, 76 responses were received, for a 68% return rate. Three of the 76 libraries declined to participate for various reasons, leaving 73 responses as the basis of analysis. Although the packet was addressed to library deans/directors, it was expected that the surveys would be given to distance learning librarians and/or to appropriate library personnel to complete.

Q1. Does the university offer for-credit distance curriculum?

Classes and degree programs for undergraduates?	Yes = 46/73 (63%)
Classes and degree programs for graduates?	Yes = 50/73 (68%)
For-credit distance certificate programs?	Yes = 34/73 (47%)
	No = 17/73 (23%)

29 universities offer all 3: distance classes at the undergraduate and graduate levels and distance certificate programs

14 universities offer distance undergraduate and graduate classes but no distance certificate programs

3 universities offer only for-credit distance classes at the undergraduate level (no graduate level distance classes or distance certificate programs)

5 universities offer only for-credit distance classes at the graduate level (no undergraduate level distance classes or distance certificate programs)

2 universities offer graduate level distance classes and distance certificates (no undergraduate level distance classes)

3 universities offer only for-credit distance certificate classes (no undergraduate level or graduate level distance classes)

Q2. Does the library offer distance learning library services?

Library services to distance undergraduate students

Yes   45/73 (62%) of total respondents
45/56 (80%) that offered distance classes/programs

Library services to distance graduate students

Yes   49/73 (67%) of total respondents
49/56 (88%) that offered distance classes/programs

No distance library services

5/73 (7%) of total respondents
5/56 (9%) that offered distance classes/programs

5 libraries do not offer distance learning library services (7% of total respondents)

51 of the 73 libraries (69% of respondents) do offer distance learning library services. This number–51–forms the basis of analysis for the remainder of the study.

Q3. Does the library have a Web page dedicated to distance learners?

Yes   36/51 (71%)

In a 2002 study, the authors found that 48 of the academic ARL libraries had links or Web pages for distance learning library users (Adams & Cassner, 2002). This was determined by checking Web sites of the ARL academic member libraries in fall 2001.

Q4. Of the following <u>library resources</u> for distance learners, indicate whether you expect the budget that supports these resources will increase, decrease, or have no change in the next two years.

Mark NA if not applicable.

Online catalog
Increase 13   Decrease 1   No Change 31   NA 4   No Response 2

Online indexes and databases
        Increase 29   Decrease 2   No Change 16   NA 2   No Response 2

Cross-database searching
        Increase 28   Decrease 0   No Change 15   NA 6   No Response 2

Internet reference materials
        Increase 26   Decrease 2   No Change 18   NA 3   No Response 2

E-books
        Increase 22   Decrease 2   No Change 21   NA 3   No Response 2

Electronic full text journals
        Increase 37   Decrease 1   No Change 8   NA 2   No Response 3

Electronic journal locator
        Increase 19   Decrease 1   No Change 24   NA 5   No Response 2

Electronic reserves
        Increase 25   Decrease 2   No Change 19   NA 4   No Response 1

One respondent reported that overall funding will not increase, and likely would decrease, although the proportional allocations will shift. Other libraries indicated that their distance learning budget is not separated out from other expenditures.

Q5. Of the following <u>library services</u> for distance learners, indicate whether you expect the budget that supports these services will increase, decrease, or have no change in the next two years.

Mark NA if not applicable.

Access to Materials

Delivery of books from the library's collections
Increase 15   Decrease 2   No Change 26   NA 7   No Response 1

Delivery of Photocopies from the library's collections
Increase 16   Decrease 6   No Change 22   NA 6   No Response 1

Consortial (system-wide or state-wide) borrowing of books
Increase 19   Decrease 1   No Change 23   NA 7   No Response 1

Consortial (system-wide or state-wide) borrowing of articles
Increase 19   Decrease 1   No Change 24   NA 6   No Response 1

Interlibrary loan (borrowing) of articles
Increase 17   Decrease 2   No Change 26   NA 5   No Response 1

Interlibrary loan (borrowing) of books
Increase 16   Decrease 2   No Change 27   NA 5   No Response 1

Reference Assistance

Chat-virtual
Increase 34   Decrease 0   No Change 11   NA 5   No Response 1

Consultation with librarian
Increase 16   Decrease 2   No Change 27   NA 4   No Response 2

E-mail
Increase 19   Decrease 1   No Change 26   NA 4   No Response 1

Phone
Increase 10   Decrease 4   No Change 28   NA 3   No Response 1

Toll free phone number to reference desk
Increase 10   Decrease 1   No Change 17   NA 22   No Response 1

Videoconferencing
Increase 9   Decrease 0   No Change 17   NA 23   No Response 2

Library Instruction

Class Web pages
Increase 24   Decrease 0   No Change 18   NA 8   No Response 1

Face-to-face
Increase 11   Decrease 7   No Change 27   NA 5   No Response 1

Live broadcast
Increase 5   Decrease 1   No Change 22   NA 22   No Response 1

Online tutorials
Increase 24   Decrease 0   No Change 22   NA 4   No Response 1

Print handouts
Increase 3   Decrease 18   No Change 26   NA 3   No Response 1

Videotape
Increase 2   Decrease 5   No Change 20   NA 23   No Response 1

Web-based course management software: (e.g., Blackboard, WebCT)
Increase 27   Decrease 0   No Change 11   NA 12   No Response 1

One respondent expected instruction via chat to increase. Another forecast more instructional activity without corresponding increases in funding. One respondent noted the shift from print to PDF format. One librarian said that if any increases occur, they would likely be due to reallocation of existing funds.

Q6. Which of the following access and delivery options are available for distance learners?

Automated request form via database, e.g., FirstSearch–27
Automated request from opac–30
Automated request from union/shared opac–16
Online request forms for delivery of materials from home institution–43
Online request forms for delivery of materials from system-wide or consortial institutions–26
Courier–17
Desktop delivery–42
Expedited delivery, e.g., FedEx, UPS–29

While 42 respondents reported the option of desktop delivery, one individual anticipated the arrival of desktop delivery in spring.

Q7. What model of staffing does the library use?

Distance librarian-administrator and staff dedicated to serve distance learners–12
Librarian and staff serve both on-campus (residential) and distance students–34

Respondents were given the option of "other." One respondent said the digital library services department serves all remote users. Two characterized their staffing pattern as hybrid, with a distance librarian position, and public services/reference librarians providing service to distance learners.

Q8. Does the library plan to increase or decrease the number of staff allocated to serving distance learners, in the next 12 months?

Increase–3
Decrease–0
No change planned–47

The results suggest a modest increase in the number of staff allocated to serving distance learners. No respondents mentioned the impact of prospective budget constraints.

Q9. Does the library have a separate permanent budget for distance learners?

Yes–8
No–43

This finding is quite similar to the 1996 survey, which reported that 6 respondents said the library had a permanent budget for distance education, and 38 said there was not a separate budget (Snyder, Logue, & Preece, 1996). None of the open-ended responses revealed this to be a significant issue.

Q10. Please describe efforts the library makes to serve new distance students.

Forty-two respondents provided a range of comments. Twelve specifically mentioned orientation sessions. Several mentioned distance learning (library) Web pages. Print continues to be a mode of communication to reach new distance students, whether as a brochure or handout summarizing services. Another respondent reported working with the registrar to find ways to inform new distance students of library services.

One respondent stated that the "key is working with faculty in targeted areas." At another library, individual subject specialists develop strong ties with distance education programs in their areas, and in several cases, the librarian has created customized information literacy components for entry-level classes.

Another respondent characterized the population as "fluid–going between on and off campus–that it is difficult to identify who are 'new' distance students." One librarian noted, "we have not targeted new students specifically," while another indicated serving distance students through existing library services, such as interlibrary loan.

Q11. Does the distance librarian-administrator and/or liaison librarians work collaboratively with distance teaching faculty to incorporate library resources into course management software used for distance courses? (ex., Blackboard and WebCT)

> Yes, distance librarian-administrator collaborates with teaching faculty–20
> Yes, liaison librarian collaborates–21
> No collaboration–8

This is an area where activity is starting–"collaboration is in the planning stages" and "this is a new initiative, and early results are encouraging." One respondent has created Web-based bibliographies and resource guides that are linked from course Web sites, and also that many instructors link to the library's electronic reserves from the course website. Another respondent indicated that library pages are a routine part of the request process for their course management software course space. Another library has created a generic library tutorial for use with the university's distance education software.

For some institutions, this is an area that requires future development. Some work on an "as requested" basis when invited by faculty.

Q12. What do you see as the major trends in library services to distance learners in the next several years?

Half a dozen respondents forecast further integration of library resources and services into online course delivery software. One asserted the importance of maintaining librarian involvement with course management systems.

Several respondents predicted the creation of additional online tutorials to assist distance learners in understanding and navigating electronic resources. One commented there would be more interactive, multimedia tutorials. Another individual predicted the development of tools that provide electronic access to a wide range of library resources and services, including information literacy. An individual forecast additional marketing of library services to distance learners.

Moderate growth in the use of chat services that offer application sharing was expected. Another predicted increased reliance on Internet chat for reference and troubleshooting. Several expected an increase in desktop delivery of articles to distance learners.

Respondents forecast more collaboration between librarians and teaching faculty, instructional designers, and other units on campus. One said there would be greater collaboration with local libraries and librarians, with a possible fee structure to support that.

One suggested there would be less demand for document delivery since more full text would be available. Others expected an increase in document delivery. Only one respondent predicted there would be more service delivery via library consortia. An individual noted a trend toward improved federated searching, which will benefit distance learners. One observed that in the future, "we will still be delivering documents–can't get away from it." Another expected to see fast document delivery and information retrieval with minimum effort on the part of the user.

A respondent forecast more computer savvy students among the distance population. This would be a shift from the earlier model of non-traditional distance students.

A significant number of respondents indicated distance learning library service would be blended into library services for all users. "Everyone can be a distance learner–and many are. Distance learning will become e-learning as distance is irrelevant" and "Distance education becomes indistinguishable from everyday service " summed up the sentiment.

CONCLUSION

Respondents' answers to questions 4 and 5, about library resources and services, reflect the ARL libraries' utilization of new technological developments. Library budgets now support cross-database searching, chat reference, class Web pages, online tutorials, and course management software, for example. Library budgets will support new technologies that have been adopted, while older technologies such as delivery of photocopies and print handouts are being phased out. Since many respondents indicated they did not expect to see any change in budgetary support for library services and resources, it can be concluded that libraries are addressing the challenge of flattened or minimally-increased budgets.

REFERENCES

Adams, K., & Cassner, M. (2002). Content and design of academic web sites for distance learners: An analysis of ARL libraries. *Journal of Library Administration*, *37*(1/2), 3-13.

Albanese, A. (2002). Academic library budgets squeezed by lowered revenue. *Library Journal*, *127*(19), 16.

Albanese, A. (2001). Looking back, looking ahead. *Library Journal*, *126*(20), 72-74.

Association of College & Research Libraries. (rev. 2000). *Guidelines for distance learning library services*. Retrieved November 5, 2003, from http://www.ala.org/acrl/guides/distlrng.html.

Hebel, S. (2003, December 19). State appropriations: Still scarce, but better budgets may be near. *The Chronicle of Higher Education*, p. A22.

Hisle, W. L. (2002). Top issues facing academic libraries. *College & Research Libraries News, 63*, 714-715+.

Lebowitz, G. (1997). After the millennium: Library services to distance education. *Journal of Library Services for Distance Education*. Retrieved December 16, 2003 from http://www.westga.edu/~library/jlsde/vol1/1/Glebowitz.html.

Potter, W. (2003, August 8). State lawmakers again cut higher-education spending. *The Chronicle of Higher Education*, p. A22.

Snyder, C., Logue, S. & Preece, B. G. (1996). *Role of libraries in distance education.* Washington, DC: Association of Research Libraries.

Do's and Don'ts
of Simultaneous Instruction
to On-Campus and Distance Students
via Videoconferencing

Mou Chakraborty
Shelley Victor

Nova Southeastern University

SUMMARY. Achieving the transition from Bibliographic Instruction (BI) to Information Literacy (IL) is particularly hard for institutions because it requires librarians to actively collaborate with a variety of administrative programs and this is all the more challenging when serving distance students. At Nova Southeastern University, the Speech-Language Pathology (SLP) department employs several delivery methods to impart graduate education. This case study describes transition from one-shot library BI to a three-day format for the SLP program, with instruction that builds sequentially and developmentally, incorporating a variety of assessment techniques (e.g., in-class exercises, puzzles, quizzes, take-home assignments). The paper discusses the innovative delivery of the course format: the issues and challenges of teaching local and distance students simultaneously via compressed video. Solutions are offered based on the presenters' experience of what worked and what did not, the quality of teaching and learning comparing videoconferencing to face-to-face instruction. The co-presenter, a faculty member teaching the course, provides a unique perspective to the presentation, thus exemplifying a librarian-faculty collaboration.

[Haworth co-indexing entry note]: "Do's and Don'ts of Simultaneous Instruction to On-Campus and Distance Students via Videoconferencing." Chakraborty, Mou, and Shelley Victor. Co-published simultaneously in *Journal of Library Administration* (The Haworth Information Press, an imprint of The Haworth Press, Inc.) Vol. 41, No. 1/2, 2004, pp. 97-112; and: *The Eleventh Off-Campus Library Services Conference Proceedings* (ed: Patrick B. Mahoney) The Haworth Information Press, an imprint of The Haworth Press, Inc., 2004, pp. 97-112.

http://www.haworthpress.com/web/JLA
Digital Object Identifier: 10.1300/J111v41n01_09

KEYWORDS. Library instruction, technology, distance learning

INTRODUCTION

Distance education has evolved through the ages in many different forms. What makes it a viable alternative to the traditional face-to-face setting is the dramatic advent of the Internet and computer technologies which are reinforcing interactivity and interpersonal communication in a distance learning environment. There is no doubt that recent technological advances have opened up exciting opportunities for information dissemination to distance learners. Convenience and flexibility are cited as the most common reasons for students seeking distance education. On the flip side, lack of interaction among students, and between the instructor and the students has been regarded as a major disadvantage.

LITERATURE REVIEW

Earlier studies show concern amongst students who feel isolated because of the physical distance from the instructor and other fellow students. "There has been little consideration of the lack of peer group interaction between distance students" (Rangecroft, 1998, p. 75). She further states that educators should introduce innovative ways to support social interaction into their online courses. A similar sentiment is also expressed by Bates when he says that interaction among the learners which is probably the most significant form of interaction for many learners, has been neglected in distance education (Bates, 1990). Recent studies also acknowledge the interactivity problem or a lack thereof. The studies emphasize that interaction amongst students themselves and between students and their instructor has a major impact on the quality of computer-assisted education programs (Muirhead, 2001). Alesandrini cites Miller and Bork when she laments that " . . . too many of today's distance learning courses suffer from low levels or weak forms of interaction with students and from overly verbal approaches to instruction as the limitations and inadequacies of traditional courses are repeated with new delivery methods" (Alesandrini, 2002, para. 1). The student in a distance learning environment is no longer a mere recipient of the instruction but an active participant as well. In recent times, Computer-Mediated Learning (CML) is enhanced with interactive activities like synchronous chats, e-mails, interactive assignments, etc. The use of a compressed video system to deliver instruction is one of the ways that the student may be more interactive.

One of the most annoying dilemmas following the introduction of computers in education has been assessing the effectiveness of technology in enhancing the quality of teaching and learning. At the same time, there has been some concern to develop flexible learning methods that combine technology with effective teaching methods in order to achieve the students' needs, objectives, and expectations. Research reveals that videoconferencing is being widely used in higher education and can bridge the gap by providing innovative services (Watkins, 2002). However, there are some issues revolving around the quality of instruction being delivered to remote sites.

Academic libraries actively strive for students to become information literate, but making the transition from providing one-shot bibliographic instruction (BI) to training students to be information literate (IL) is neither easy nor a process that's success can be assured. One of the most important but difficult components of successfully achieving this transition is obtaining "buy-in" from the various stakeholders. Achieving the transition from BI to IL is particularly hard for graduate institutions because it requires librarians to actively collaborate with a variety of administrative programs and this is all the more challenging when serving distance students. Being a pioneer in distance education, Nova Southeastern University has always provided excellent support for its distance students. The library has been recognized as providing high quality service to the remote students in terms of instruction, reference assistance, document delivery, online help sheets and tutorials.

This case study describes transition from one-shot Bibliographic Instruction (BI) to a three-day format with instruction that builds sequentially and developmentally, incorporating a variety of assessment techniques (e.g., in-class exercises, puzzles, quizzes, take-home assignments). The librarian has taught the library component of this class using different modalities, but the most challenging one has been teaching the local students face-to-face and the distance students via compressed video simultaneously. This has been compounded by the fact that the library has different services for local and distance students. The focus of the presentation will be on the innovative delivery of the course format: the issues and challenges of teaching the local and the distance students simultaneously. Solutions will be offered based on the presenters' experience of what worked and what did not. The presentation will also touch upon the quality of teaching and learning comparing videoconferencing to face-to-face instruction. A newly developed online tutorial complementing and supplementing the lecture class will also be showcased.

WHAT IS VIDEOCONFERENCING?

Compressed video provides two-way live audio and video even when the participants are geographically separated. According to Burge and Roberts

(1998, para. 2), "Compressed Video Learning occurs when instructor and learners use microphones, cameras and other television equipment to exchange verbal and moving color images to engage in discussions, exchange messages and access experts as part of a formal or informal learning process. All such interactions occur in real-time, which means learners and instructors are present at the same time and must coordinate their schedules."

Videoconferencing is an exciting medium but could be challenging as a modality of teaching and learning. Virginia Ostendorf posits that:

> Student acceptance of the live video class depends on three factors: (1) the instructor's informed and thoughtful preparation for each class, (2) the instructor's skill in conducting the class, and (3) the personal involvement of each student in the lesson at hand. (1994, p. 1)

She elaborates that it is not easy to achieve the third factor because in most cases distance students are not 'included' in the class; even if the instructor has interactive teaching style, he/she needs to integrate proven instructional strategies as part of his/her teaching style when delivering the class in a two-way compressed video environment.

There are several terms that identify this activity: interactive television, interactive videoconferencing, compressed video. For the purpose of this paper, videoconferencing or via compressed video will be used for consistency.

BENEFITS OF VIDEOCONFERENCING
FOR LIBRARY INSTRUCTION

- Establishes a synchronous voice and video interaction–librarian and students can see and hear each other in real time; communication can be enhanced by body language and dialog rather than just the instructor lecturing. When the librarian encourages participation, remote students can feel a sense of belonging, and feel that they are included in the class
- Multiple remote sites can easily be supported–eliminates the cost of the librarian traveling to different sites
- Enables connection with external resources–remote experts, in this case–the librarians can help validate understanding, provide feedback, and introduce practical examples. This real-world connection validates the course content placing it in practical perspective. Since the course-professor is also present, he/she can comment/expand on the subject content
- Improves use of computer demonstrations–the 'live' search on the computer can convey a difficult concept and simplify instructions. Docu-

ment cameras allow transmission of high-quality still pictures. Drawing diagrams on the smartboards, where possible, or white boards, certainly clarify additional concepts

Pival and Tuñon (2002) identify the following as to 'What compressed video does not do well for the library':

- High cost equipment and trained personnel make this an expensive option for synchronous interaction
- The compressed video system is only as good as its weakest link
- Interaction between sites constrained to group interactions

The authors would like to add the following:

- Lack of facilitator and a technician at remote sites may impede the learning experience
- Additional expenses incur if the projection did not go smoothly, as the librarians would have to make follow-up trips to the sites, thereby defeating the initial purpose of providing BI via compressed video

FACE-TO-FACE vs. COMPRESSED VIDEO

Both traditional face-to-face and compressed video has its advantages and disadvantages. Combining a face-to-face class seems to be a challenge for students at both the near and far end. Students at the near end feel that compressed video creates a time delay in the transmission of information. When there are technology glitches, the class may stop temporarily until the technology is running efficiently. Students at the far end may feel that the near end students have an unfair advantage if questions are directed to the near-end students. It is a challenge for the instructor to engage both sets of students equally. Teaching via compressed video requires the instructor to switch from a lecture style to abbreviated lecturettes interspersed with group discussion. Traditional lecturing in a compressed video format is a difficult mode for learning because students at the far end cannot maintain focus for an extended period of time in front of a monitor. A change to an interactive mode of teaching is an unexpected benefit of teaching via compressed video. When near-end and far-end students are combined into one class, they learn from one another. When different geographic regions are represented, students are exposed to differing viewpoints. In this particular course, the students in the near-end tend to have less clinical experience than the students at the far-end so the near-end students are able to learn from those that are more experienced.

The hypothesis of Knipe and Lee's (2002) research study shows the quality of teaching and learning using videoconferencing as a delivery method is not as good as the traditional face-to-face classroom delivery. The study revealed that there were significant differences between the local and remote site students in their learning behavior and classroom activities. The local students received more information and explanations from the instructor; they read and reviewed materials more than their remote counterparts; and they were more involved in group projects and presentations. The availability of the instructor at hand was considered the main cause for this. The remote students lacked the supervision that the local students enjoyed. Physical distance was a challenge in forming groups to work together and, due to this factor being beyond the instructor's control, group work was not a prominent class activity. The remote students were more involved with technology, and received more instructions and used worknotes from the lectures. Unlike the local students, they worked directly with the I.T. and the videoconferencing equipment, and relied on PowerPoint slide handouts when technology was down. Not surprisingly, cognitive outcomes for the distance students were reported to be poorer than the local students. Being part of larger groups, local students were able to engage in cooperative learning thereby maximizing their learning outcomes. Remote students were constrained to the same small group which restricted relationships. The distance students also felt isolated and lacked the sense of "belongingness" to the class, more so if there was no eye contact or if questions were not directed towards them. This lack of concentration and interest had an adverse effect on their learning process. At the same time the distance students could have experienced reduction in learning time. This was due to the fact they were more involved in setting up the videoconferencing equipment and troubleshooting; this took time away from actual learning.

NOVA SOUTHEASTERN UNIVERSITY–
HISTORICAL BACKGROUND

Nova Southeastern University (NSU) started experimenting with compressed video in 1994, serving the Graduate Teacher Education Program (GTEP) and the Pharmacy programs. The equipment selected was PictureTel and a couple of rooms on the main campus in Ft. Lauderdale and at some of the NSU student service centers around the country were set up for this purpose. After careful evaluation, PictureTel was selected because it was at the time the best manufacturer and the best equipment. The first units that were bought are still in operation, as they were made to last. The first batch of units bought was the Systems 4000, later upgraded to 4000EX and 4000EZ. As videoconferencing became popular, more and more rooms across NSU were equipped with these machines. New generations of PictureTel, Vennues 2000, and Concorde 4500 were added to the system. At this time multipoint video-conferencing was dawning, and NSU bought a videoconferencing server, Montage MCU, capable of handling up to 32 sites at the speed of 128 kbps and nicknamed it "the bridge." This bridge could also handle conferences at a higher speed rate. To take advantage of higher speed rates, NSU had to revamp its ISDN network and videoconferencing rooms to handle speed up to 384 kbps. With the expansion of the university and popularity of distance educa-tion using newer technologies, other programs, like undergraduate Education, Speech-Language Pathology (SLP) started delivering their courses using compressed video. The students in the doctoral program in SLP utilize com-pressed video technology but instead of receiving the instruction in a group format, each student has a camera and software which allows the instruction to be delivered into their home. Another big challenge has been the Pharmacy program when it started delivering its doctoral degree on this modality in 2000 to large operations in West Palm Beach, Florida, and Puerto Rico.

Today NSU has over ten videoconferencing rooms on main campus and at least two rooms in each one of the student service centers around the country. The videoconference operations handles approximately sixty rooms on the NSU network, which includes other sites like Puerto Rico and thirteen hospi-tals in Florida and Georgia as part of a project that the College of Osteopathic Medicine has. The equipment continues to be upgraded to meet the growing needs of the university. Until the year 2000, PictureTel was the preferred equipment; however Polycom, a relatively new company, then came out with a better product. PictureTel soon caught up with their technologically ad-vanced product called iPower systems and NSU switched back to PictureTel iPowers. In 2001, PictureTel was bought by Polycom. Today, NSU has the Polycom Ipower system and plans to add more of this hi-tech equipment. In 2001, the bridge was upgraded for an Accord bridge, which has enhanced features and the capacity to conduct videoconferencing over IP technology–something that NSU is taking a closer look as it is the trend that video-conferencing is moving towards.

As far as the library training was concerned, with distance sites this new de-livery format was a failure; the images of the computer screens were lousy and not very legible to the distance students. There were problems with frame re-fresh rates making it difficult for the distance students to keep up with the pace needed for demonstrating online searching. The compression/decompression compounded to the problem making the transmission of the small fonts on the computer screen almost unreadable (Pival & Tuñon, 2002).

At Nova Southeastern University, the Speech-Language and Pathology (SLP) department employs several delivery methods to impart graduate education: traditional face-to-face, online, and via interactive compressed video. The research course is typically offered to the students in their first or second semester of this 52-credit graduate program. The emphasis of the course is to teach the student to become a competent consumer of the research literature and to provide the student with life-long learning skills. A comprehensive research paper which focuses on a clinical topic is the culminating assignment in this course. One of the skills that the student needs to successfully complete this assignment is the ability to search the databases. Although the instructor could teach this information, the librarian is best suited for this task. The librarian has taught this information to each section for the past three years and thus has a grasp of the topical areas in the area of communication disorders. Use of the examples representative of the field enhances students' learning. Most of the students in the graduate program have been out of school for 5-10 years; therefore their computer proficiency and acquisition of research knowledge is limited. The library instruction for the SLP courses had originally started out as one-shot, face-to-face BIs. However, this has been proven less than adequate in producing information-literate students. The profession also has two components: education and medical. Because the students need to access medical and educational databases and they have limited familiarity with research, the BI has been extended to three sessions.

HOW IT STARTED

The library has always been very active providing bibliographic instructional sessions in different programs. The library had developed relationship with the Programs in Speech-Language Pathology and Communication Disorders Department. Initially it started out as 1-1/2 hr BI session presenting the students with a quick overview of the SLP databases including Linguistics & Language Behavior, MEDLINE, etc. However, as the instructor-librarian had predicted, this was not effective. Students' evaluations revealed that they were overwhelmed. They did note that it was a highly useful session but complained about the amount of information provided in such a short time span. Especially the distance students via video conferencing did not get much out of it as it was too quick, and they were not in front of the computers, therefore lacking the hands-on experience. This case study describes the transition from one-shot BI to a three-day format with instruction that builds sequentially and developmentally, incorporating a variety of assessment techniques (e.g., in-class exercises, puzzles, quizzes, take-home assignments).

While teaching the library research component for the SLP courses for different faculty members over the last couple of years, the librarian has fostered a positive rapport with the SLP faculty members. The co-presenter, a faculty member teaching a core course, SLP 6070 'Research Methods in Speech-Language Pathology,' provides a unique perspective to the presentation, thus exemplifying a librarian-faculty collaboration.

IMPORTANCE OF FACULTY–LIBRARIAN COLLABORATION

Collaboration between the faculty and librarian is imperative in maximizing the student's learning. In this research methods course, the librarian was the content expert in the area of bibliographic instruction. Prior to the first class, the faculty member and the librarian met to discuss the content of the course and the specific needs for the sessions that the librarian would be teaching. The focus of those class sessions were teaching the students to learn which databases were appropriate to their discipline, and to learn search strategies for each database. After the librarian presented the information to the class, the librarian and faculty member would debrief to discuss improvements that could be incorporated the following semester. The librarian should have basic knowledge of the subject matter and the faculty member should be a participant in the process so that he/she can answer questions relative to bibliographic instruction as they arise throughout the course.

EXTENDED BI CLASSES

The librarian has taught the library component of this class using different modalities but the most challenging one has been teaching the local students face-to-face and the distance students via compressed video simultaneously. This has been compounded by the fact that the library has different services for local and distance students.

The librarian went back to the professor with the evidence and they decided a multi-part class would be more beneficial. The librarian reassessed her course materials and came up with a new agenda. Instead of a one-shot BI session, the course professor and the instructor librarian agreed on doing two classes for library research. The librarian mailed class handouts to the distance students before. The librarian usually starts her class with a PowerPoint presentation, providing the students with an overview of the Electronic Library and discussing the different services available to each group. As per the SACS guidelines library training to the distance students should be timely and ongoing. ACRL also recommends that services to distance students should be equal or equivalent. The Distance and Instructional Library Services (DILS) department at the Alvin Sherman Library, Research, and Information Technology Center in Ft. Lauderdale, FL, strives to meet these goals by delineating the services in library handbooks–one for the local students, and one for the distance students. During the lecture the librarian constantly told the local students to refer to the local handbook, and distance students were referred to the distance handbook. This slightly complicated the process because the page numbers are different in the handbooks and the services to the distance students differ from those offered to the local students. This pertains mostly to the document delivery services.

DOCUMENT DELIVERY/INTERLIBRARY LOAN

At NSU, the Alvin Sherman Library, Research, and Information Technology Center has decided that it will be responsible for ensuring that distance students are provided with the resources to meet students' research needs rather than trying to negotiate contracts with local libraries where site-based classes are offered. In order to meet the research needs of distance students, the library provides all distance students with free document delivery for up to 25 documents per week. These include free photocopying and mailing or faxing of journal articles as well as the mailing of books and free microfiche copies of ERIC ED documents, NSU Major Applied Research Projects (MARPs) and practicums. Doctoral students are also provided with two free copies of non-NSU dissertations. If NSU does not have the requested materials in the university's library collection, these materials are obtained through interlibrary loan, commercial document delivery services, and host agreements with Wayne State University and the University of Michigan at no cost (Chakraborty & Tuñon, 2002). Under the supervision of the Head of the department, Interlibrary Loan (ILL) Department deals with the local and the public users, while Document Delivery (Doc Del) Department caters to the distance students.

Over the last few years, the librarian has done several classes via video conferencing in different SLP locations. Her first experience was at the Speech-Language Pathology's clinic site with portable equipment. There were some local face-to-face students as well as students dispersed in 4 different sites in Mississippi. The experience, though novel, was not a satisfying one. The students could not see the screen; it was very fuzzy, and the audio was very poor as well. Because of the transmission problems, librarians had to do follow-up site visits and re-did the classes face-to-face. Next time this session was done in the TV studio in the Mailman-Hollywood building where the transmission to the distance sites was much better. The past few times, the classes have been held in a state-of-the art technology classroom in the new library facility and the quality of the transmission has been much better.

In December 2001, NSU built a new state-of-the-art library building known as the Alvin Sherman Library, Research and Information Technology Center (ASLRITC). The new 325,000 sq. ft. joint-use facility with Broward County, is Florida's largest library building with capacity to hold 1.4 million volumes. This academic/public library has: a children's area; a 500 seat auditorium; a café; 14 electronic classrooms; wireless technology, numerous group study rooms; conference rooms; space for an art gallery and technology exhibits; and a 1500 space parking garage. The classrooms were equipped with newer and better video conferencing equipments as described above.

From the authors' experiences and the information gleaned from students' evaluations, the following problems were identified:

- Lack of facilitator and technician at the remote sites. Facilitators are hired at some of the sites based on availability of a facilitator and the number of students at any given site. The management of the class including the receiving and distribution of handouts is better when a facilitator is available.
- The students were not in computer labs–the compressed video was set up in a different room; unfortunately the distance students could not follow along on their computers unlike their on-campus counterparts.
- Less interactive for distance students–not having the computers in front of them, they are often lost. Even though the librarian often directed questions to them and asked if they were following along okay, most of them were quiet.
- Situation if the class handouts had not reached the distance students before the scheduled class–in one instance the handouts didn't reach the students before the first class; when the librarian found out this, she e-mailed the course professor all the handouts to be sent to the students for the next class.
- At some sites, it was difficult for the distance students to see the actual search on the screen–this has been the major problem for the past few years. When the instructor was just a talking head, it didn't matter as the students could see and hear her. But as soon as the librarian went live online demonstrating the search, the screen was fuzzy and the students at the remote sites were not able to see the screen as clearly as their on-campus counterparts did.

- A little fast paced for some students—not having the computers in front of them—made it extremely difficult for some students to follow along. The librarian kept refering to relevant page numbers in the handbook and the handouts, but students who were not that computer savvy found it difficult to keep up the pace with the instructor.

LESSONS LEARNED

After teaching the class for the first few times, the librarian consulted with the course professor and recommended some changes. The faculty member gladly agreed and the following modifications were made.

Instead of a single shot BI, it was first changed to two-part class. Even when that did not suffice, the instructors went on a three-part class. On the first day, after the introductions a short pre-test was given to the students. This helped the librarian assess the students' library research skills. Following this the librarian explained the NSU Electronic Library Web page, touching upon primary, secondary and tertiary research, continuing with in-depth lecture on SLP and research databases, e.g., Linguistics & Language Behavior, ERIC, E* Subscribe, ProQuest and finding full text articles in general. The first segment concluded with handing out the assignment and explaining the student presentations that were to follow in the third class.

The second day of the class included MEDLINE, CINAHL, Health and Wellness Resource Center & Alternative Health Module, and an overview of other related health and drug databases. The librarian also discussed the difference between journals and magazines, highlighting peer-reviewed journals. At the professor's request and the students' interest, Ulrich's database was also demonstrated.

The students did their presentations on the third and the final day of the library portion of the class. They had selected their own topics which they were to use for rest of the course. Each student selected a topic that compared and contrasted intervention strategies, or described the effect of a variable on a speech and language disorder. The local students came up one by one to the instructor's podium and using the computer, demonstrated their search strategy. The student was ready to answer questions from the audience. At the end of each presentation, the librarian provided feedback, explaining how the search could have been refined. The distance students also did their searches from the remote site, and as needed, the librarian reconstructed the search and provided step-by-step feedback. With the pilot project, the librarian had expected that the students would grumble about doing individual presentations! But to her pleasant surprise, the students remarked on the evaluation sheets that the presentations and the individual feedback provided by the librarian were the most helpful part of the class! At the end of the presentation, they handed in their assignments. The librarian graded the presentation on the overall clarity, style and effective search strategy.

The assignment was graded on the search strategy and the use of relevant databases (students had to justify why they chose that specific database/s). The scoring rubric (which was given to students beforehand) included choice of keywords, subject heading, use of Boolean Operators, limits, database specific features, number of relevant citations retrieved, etc. After grading the assignment, the librarian submitted the scores to the faculty member, who integrated these in her final grades. Each week the students were graded on an in-class assignment so the library assignment was incorporated into these grades. The students were also given a crossword puzzle and a short quiz which recaptured everything covered in the class. So far, the librarian has felt that the crossword puzzle has been well received. Both the local and the distance students do these as in-class activity and in the end the librarian goes over the answers. Even after these extended three-class formats, a few students noted that lot of information was presented in a short amount of time. An in-depth tutorial was developed and shown in the class. The tutorial included everything covered in the class and more (e.g., SLP Web sites, evaluating Web sites, etc.). The students were highly encouraged to go through this tutorial at their leisure.

In the librarian's experience, it seems that the on-campus students fare better on their graded assignments than their distance counterparts. Out of a total of 20 points, most were getting 16 and above. One major reason is that they have hands-on experience in the computer lab and they can follow along with the librarian, while unfortunately the distance students just keep taking notes. Another reason may be that by having the librarian instructor in front of them, the local students ask more questions. They also stop by at the reference desk later and come to see the librarian to clarify their questions or concerns. Even though they were repeatedly encouraged, some distance students did not take the advantage to contact the librarian by e-mail or phone. As a result they did not do the assignments correctly. Some distance students started their search from the NSU library's Full-text Journal Title Search from Serial Solutions in spite of the librarian emphasizing in class to start in subject-specific databases. Nor did they follow the assignment instructions correctly, and did not submit everything they were supposed to. For the future classes, these shortcomings will be considered and more emphasis will be given on how to do the assignment properly.

As for the faculty member, the information on BI that has been provided has been exceptional. The in-depth coverage of the databases is crucial to the students' success in completing their research assignment. The expanded number of classes has been essential to cover the breadth of this topic.

SOLUTIONS

From the lessons learned in the past classes, it is obvious that a multi-part class, especially three classes, is better than two. Some students wanted the librarian instructor to slow down a little so that they could keep up; this will allow the librarian to slow down thereby having more time dedicated to the explanation of the databases. After talking to the appropriate authorities, there seems to be a ray of light as far as the computer experience for the distance students: the future classes in the remote sites will most likely be held in computer labs and the compressed video portable unit will be brought into the lab. The authors are optimistic that there will be dramatic changes in the distance students' performances as their chief complaint was that they did not have computers to follow along with the librarian instructor. The authors will also make sure that the respective facilitators are present and they have received all the class materials in advance. If the distance students still feel that they were lacking in understanding, depending on budget, the librarian will make an attempt for follow-up on-site visits.

RECOMMENDATIONS

- Plan, plan, and plan well in advance.
- Send the class materials to the distance students in advance, and make sure they have everything before the class.
- Go slowly over the content, and repeat often. Also go over the class materials, making sure the local and the distance groups have all of the necessary handouts.
- Be patient and ask questions.
- Include the distance students by keeping eye-contact. This is probably the most important way of being effective with the distance students. To achieve this, look directly into the camera and direct questions at them.
- If possible, try to remember their names and address them personally.
- Make sure the students have your contact information, and encourage them to contact you with questions/concerns.

- Prepare yourself. Learn the equipment well in advance. Training from a technical expert helps in being comfortable using the equipment in class.
- Pay attention to clothing, accessories and make-up. Business attire or clothing for regular teaching is most appropriate. Professional appearance is desirable.

CONCLUSIONS

Technology is undeniably a dominant influence in today's educational world. Certainly virtual or distance learning environments have dramatically changed the way we teach and learn. However, many students participating in distance or virtual learning environments need to acquire a set of skills in order to be successful and to live and work in a technologically advanced world.

Similarly, educators have to evaluate their strategies and not only focus on reducing costs and increasing the amount of students participating in virtual learning environments, but also need to meet the learners' objectives and expectations. The most effective way to help these students to be successful is to increase the communication and interaction between the learners and teachers. Another approach is to avoid making assumptions that students possess these adequate skills that are required for the virtual world. Sometimes they need time to adapt in order to avoid frustrations, anxiety, and negative attitudes towards the technology and the virtual learning environment.

The challenge is for libraries that provide services for distance students to ensure that the distance students receive equivalent services to those offered to students attending classes at the main campus. Videoconferencing, as a medium itself, is not solely responsible for a poorer quality of teaching and learning. If it is to be used effectively and efficiently, a more involved relationship needs to exist between the organizers of the local and remote sites. The remote site needs to be set up accordingly so that it is conducive to a positive learning process. It needs to be realized that coping with technology is itself an adjustment; when compounded with lack of preparation and planning, inept teaching methods, and an inexperienced facilitator, the quality of teaching and learning via compressed video is bound to be of inferior quality than the traditional face-to-face class. The authors concur with Ostendorf's (1994, p. 5) following observation: "Only when we design lessons to include all learners instead of presenting one-way 'shows' or lectures, will students become truly involved. Distance education will achieve its potential as uniquely interactive instruction only when no learner is left on the outside looking in."

REFERENCES

Alesandrini, K. (2002). Visual constructivism in distance learning. *USDLA Journal, 16*(1). Retrieved October 15, 2003, from http://www.usdla.org/html/journal/JAN02_Issue/ED_JAN02.PDF.

Bates, A. (1990). *Interactivity as a criterion for media selection in distance education.* Paper presented at the Annual Conference of the Asian Association of Open Universities, Jakarta, Indonesia.

Burge, E., & Roberts, J. (1998). Compressed video learning: How do we create active learning? In *Classrooms with a Difference* (pp. 106-11, 113-16). Montreal: Cheneliere/McGraw-Hill. Retrieved October 26, 2003 from World Bank Global Distance Educationet http://www1.worldbank.org/DistEd/Technology/interaction/videoconf01.html.

Chakraborty, M., & Tuñon, J. (2002). Going the distance: Solutions and issues of providing international students with library services. AAOU Pre-Conference Seminar 2002 entitled *"Outreach Library Services for Distance Learner."* Indira Gandhi National Open University, New Delhi, India. Available at http://www.ignou.ac.in/aaou-pre/indexpap.htm.

Knipe, D., & Lee, M. (2002). The quality of teaching and learning via videoconferencing. *British Journal of Educational Technology, 33*(3), 301-311. Retrieved March 13, 2003 from Wilson Education Full-text database.

Muirhead, B. (2001). Interactivity research studies. *Educational Technology & Society, 4*(3). Retrieved October 15, 2003, from http://ifets.ieee.org/periodical/vol_3_2001/muirhead.html.

Ostendorf, V. (1994). *The two-way classroom.* Littleton, CO: PictureTel Corporation.

Pival, P., & Tuñon, J. (2002). *How well do you spell "support"? Multiple methods of library support to distributed education programs.* Paper presented North American Regional Distance Education Conference, ICDE/Canadian Association of Distance Education, Calgary, Canada.

Rangecroft, M. (1998). Interpersonal communication in distance education. *Journal of Education for Teaching, 24,* 75. Retrieved January 25, 2002, from Academic Elite database.

Watkins, C. (2002). Videoconferences can bridge the gap. *American Libraries, 33*(11), 14. Retrieved September 15, 2003 from Library Literature and Information Science Full-text database.

eBooks
for a Distributed Learning University:
The Royal Roads University Case

Rosie Croft
Shailoo Bedi

Royal Roads University

SUMMARY. Royal Roads University library, in implementing the institution's distributed learning model, purchased its first eBook collection in April 2000. Now, three years into subscription commitments and active development of an eBooks collection, the library conducts a study to determine: *Who is accessing the collection? For what purposes is it being used? Is the collection adequate to meet the academic program needs? Is there a preference for the open access model over single user access? How does the learning community find reading on screen versus print? In short, is an eBook collection a vital resource for distributed learning?* This paper focuses on the discoveries made through a quantitative and qualitative research study.

KEYWORDS. Library resources, Internet, study

INTRODUCTION TO ROYAL ROADS UNIVERSITY

Royal Roads University (RRU) was founded in 1995 following the closure of Royal Roads Military College (RRMC). The provincial government of

[Haworth co-indexing entry note]: "eBooks for a Distributed Learning University: The Royal Roads University Case." Croft, Rosie, and Shailoo Bedi. Co-published simultaneously in *Journal of Library Administration* (The Haworth Information Press, an imprint of The Haworth Press, Inc.) Vol. 41, No. 1/2, 2004, pp. 113-137; and: *The Eleventh Off-Campus Library Services Conference Proceedings* (ed: Patrick B. Mahoney) The Haworth Information Press, an imprint of The Haworth Press, Inc., 2004, pp. 113-137.

http://www.haworthpress.com/web/JLA
Digital Object Identifier: 10.1300/J111v41n01_10

British Columbia, through the proclamation of the Royal Roads University Act, conferred on RRU a mandate to grant applied professional undergraduate and graduate degrees to mid-career professionals. RRU offers specialized programs in four "pillar" areas: Leadership and Training; Conflict Analysis and Management; Business; and Science, Technology, and the Environment. Most RRU programs of study (including all of the graduate level programs) are delivered using a hybrid-learning model that combines short on-site campus residencies with online course delivery. This allows learners to participate on- or off-campus at any time and from anywhere for the bulk of their program. Most programs have at least one on-campus residency that lasts between 2 to 4 weeks, but some have up to three residencies and others, rarely may not have a face-to-face component at all.

On any given date, about 80 percent of RRU learners are working at a distance on Web-based online courses. RRU does not operate according to the traditional academic calendar: programs begin in every month of the year, with particularly high levels of program intake during the summer months. RRU does have a resident undergraduate population of learners in the Bachelor of Commerce in Entrepreneurial Management and the Bachelor of Environmental Studies degrees. The undergraduate programs are accelerated degrees combining the third and fourth years of undergraduate education into one full calendar year. These are the only programs that are held entirely on-campus (though there are also two-year online versions of both these degrees) and comprise the learner base at RRU that has daily access to the physical library collections as well as the online resources.

Similar to its ever-changing learner body, RRU has a large group of contract faculty who also work primarily at a distance. These faculty members are only on campus for brief periods and have competing demands on their attention, much like RRU's adult learners. In addition, the university employs a small group of core faculty members who work on campus full time, many of whom visit the library and use its online resources regularly. Familiarizing the faculty with the library's online resources is at least as, if not more, difficult than acquainting the learners with them.

One of the primary missions of RRU is to offer market-driven graduate degrees for adult learners, so an applied approach is heavily emphasized in the programs. Research conducted by the learners for their major projects or organizational consulting papers must provide a theory-based analysis that links directly to a real and practical organizational or industry situation. Most graduate learners are working full-time and use their own organizations as focal points for their research.

It is possible that the graduate learner may not hold an undergraduate degree. Prior learning assessments are employed as part of the admissions process for graduate program candidates at RRU. Related work, particularly management experience, is recognized as adding critical value to a graduate degree program application. From a library perspective this poses a challenge. Lack of undergraduate experience or stale post-secondary experience means that many mid-career learners begin their degree programs with limited or no computer literacy and lack basic knowledge of how to conduct research. Learners who are missing these foundational skills pose a serious challenge for the instructional librarians who are tasked with remedying the information literacy gap. It is a further challenge to balance the instructional needs of learners with varying levels of experience. Instruction in library research is essential in any university program, and its importance is magnified to an even greater extent in an online milieu where the physical separation between the learner and the physical library and its staff exacerbates the steepness of the information literacy learning curve.

At RRU, the educational environment focuses on lifelong learning, experiential learning, and learning-centered delivery and support. Reflecting these priorities, the library is strongly committed to a learning-centered delivery model that exposes learners to the resources immediately and helps to teach learners about information, not just about the tools that are available via the RRU Library. During almost all of the short on-site campus residencies, the library conducts computer lab-based instructional sessions to teach or expand information literacy skills. These sessions are mandatory and are part of the formal residency schedule. The goal of these sessions is to introduce the learners to the RRU library services and resources or to update returning learners on what's new. Conceptual and applied approaches to conducting research are also discussed and reviewed. Each of the library's instructional sessions is customized, based upon the needs and focus of the program and the learners.

In all our instructional sessions for first residencies, learners are introduced to finding, accessing, and retrieving material from both the library's print and electronic resources. Those resources are from a mixture of sources. Interestingly, RRU library's original print collection was inherited from the military college that preceded it. The military college offered a full complement of undergraduate programs and acted in all respects as a conventional undergraduate academic library for an on-campus learner population. RRU librarians evaluated the legacy collection in the early years of the university and an inventory and weeding project was conducted. At the end of the project, a core collection of print materials were retained to support the anticipated new disciplines. Since 1995, the library has collected materials to directly support the programs offered, and the composition of the current collection of print books is a mixture of approximately 50% RRMC and 50% RRU books.

After its inception, because the focus of RRU is distributed learning, the library quickly turned its attention to collecting electronic resources to support the information needs of its distributed clientele. This emphasis coincided with the proliferation in the late 1990s of online versions of what were formerly print journals, newer journals that were "born online," and online reference works. We explored these new formats with success and good feedback. We found that materials were used which would have remained unconsulted had they been in our print collection. When eBooks emerged they appeared to offer a natural extension of this collections emphasis.

RRU eBOOK COLLECTIONS

Royal Roads University Library purchased its first eBook collection in April 2000. This was a consortial purchase of 1078 netLibrary eBooks. The purchase could not have been afforded without the help of consortial purchasing power, and was an experiment in a new format for RRU Library. The 1078 title list was developed by netLibrary in consulting with representative librarians from the Council of Prairie and Pacific University Libraries (COPPUL), based on our budget and the subjects/publishers of interest that were submitted by the participating libraries.

Subsequently, in June 2001, RRU benefited from another consortial purchase of a set of 580 netLibrary eBooks. This set was developed by BC's Electronic Library Network (ELN), in conjunction with academic librarians in the business section of netLibrary. Titles were selected for their relevance to business school programs in the Canadian context.

netLibrary also made it possible for RRU Library to begin its own collection of eBooks books by reducing the required volume of the initial buy required to order directly. The library began an institutional collection with approximately 30 titles of our own selection in the summer of 2002, and has continued to add netLibrary titles as they are available, usually in preference to print, in the natural course of collection development.

The statistics in Figure 1 demonstrate both the rate of user uptake as well as significant turning points in the service.

After what appears to be an initial burst of activity that was probably reflective of testing and implementation, usage seems to have grown steadily, with a big jump in the summer of 2002, and has leveled out over the past year. netLibrary MARC records were added to the library catalogue shortly after purchase of the database. No correlation has been found between the spike in usage in Summer 2002 and any particular actions on the part of the Library to improve access, though it is possible that incorporation of eBooks into li-

FIGURE 1. RRU netLibrary Statistics

Period	Total Accesses
April-June 2000	188
July-September 2000	21
October-December 2000	36
January-March 2001	74
April-June 2001	61
July-September 2001	60
October-December 2001	78
January-March 2002	79
April-June 2002	93
July-September 2002	241
October-December 2002	221
January-March 2003	203
April-June 2003	243
July-September 2003	204

brary instruction sessions may explain it, at least partially. The most frequently accessed titles during Summer 2002 are mostly leadership oriented, which would correspond to the subject interest of the learners in on-campus residency at that time. As mentioned, RRU Library also began purchasing netLibrary titles on its own beginning in August 2002, so the corresponding increase in material of particular relevance to RRU learners was very likely a factor. RRU now has 114 netLibrary eBooks that have been selected and purchased by RRU and this collection will continue to grow if the vendor sustains a viable title-by-title selection model.

RRU Library also purchased the ITKnowledge collection from Earthweb in Fall 2000. This collection was 2200 titles strong, and while the subjects covered were primarily related to the IT field, this was much more than a collection of computer help manuals, and included many excellent business and education titles. Unfortunately, ITK, as with many other eBook services, did not survive the technology stock decline of 2000/01, and though statistical reports were intended for release in Jan 2001, the service was defunct in February 2001. The Library did receive positive anecdotal feedback from learners regarding this service, but no numerical data regarding the use of this resource was retrievable.

The most recent of RRU's forays into eBook collections is with the ebrary collection. RRU purchased a pre-set collection of approximately 13,000 titles covering all subject areas. The title list varies as titles are periodically added and deleted by ebrary. The ebrary model of simultaneous access for an unlimited number of users per title makes this an ideal resource and interface to demonstrate during instructional sessions, and it has become a standard part of our instructional curriculum during RRU's very busy summer residency season. It also lends itself well to supporting online courses with required or recommended readings, as netLibrary does not. As the statistics reveal, use of the ebrary collection has grown profoundly, and reflects our demonstration of it in instruction. There was, however, a lag of several months between acquiring ebrary and importing the MARC records into the RRU Library catalogue. This import was completed in September 2003, and the highest number yet of accesses/month was recorded during October 2003 (over 600) (Figure 2).

Unfortunately, RRU has no control over the content of the ebrary collection and cannot develop it in the same way that netLibrary eBooks can be selected on a title-by-title basis. Moreover, there is some redundancy between RRU's netLibrary and ebrary collections, and although multiple copies of titles may be of use, not being able to exercise control over the content of our collections in the most fiscally efficient manner is frustrating.

Cost is a significant factor in the current size and possible future growth of RRU Library's eBook collection. While we have more resources in this area than many other academic libraries within our consortia, especially those of similar size, our collection is small in comparison to those of large U.S. institutions, like the University of Texas that has collected extensively in netLibrary eBooks as noted in the eBook studies by Dillon (2001). Our collection is still very much a complement to our book collection rather than an attempt on our part to revolutionize it. In part, this reflects the relative availability of current eBook titles versus print titles in subject areas emphasized by our programs. You can't buy it if it isn't there. However, as Chu (2003, p. 345) points out "there is no indication that the printed book is dead or dying. Electronic books are unlikely to replace printed books."

FIGURE 2. RRU ebrary Statistics

Period	Documents Viewed
January-March 2003	284
April-June 2003	360
July-September 2003	1134

THE SURVEY/DATA COLLECTION

We were interested in investigating a number of issues concerning our eBook collection and our user groups. Online surveys using a homegrown survey tool from RRU were created that combined quantitative and qualitative questions to solicit responses from learners and faculty regarding:

- Who is using the RRU Library's eBook collection?
- Why are they using eBooks?
- Does the existing collection of eBooks satisfy their needs?
- How did they find out about eBooks?
- Do they prefer any particular eBook model (e.g., netLibrary vs. ebrary)
- Is there a preference for a print copy over the electronic version?

Participation in the survey was strictly anonymous. The link to the online learner survey was sent out by e-mail to the learner population at the end of August 2003. This was a last minute decision on our part, in the suspicion that we might capture more, and more thoughtful, responses from the undergraduate learners who were about to complete their programs than if we did the same survey in the fall with learners who were only a couple of months into their program. Moreover, at RRU, August is the month when we have the most number of learners on campus and many online courses are in full swing. In addition, we anticipated receiving a high level of response from the graduate learners who had just completed on campus residencies and those who had just completed a number of online courses. This precipitated a more hurried approach to the survey than we had initially decided, and in retrospect, may not have been the best choice. We did get what we feel is a high response rate to the survey. We had over 460 out of a possible approximately 2,500 learners fill out the survey, about 1,500 of who were in degree programs and have familiarity with and requirements involving library resources. As it turned out, we also ended up with many new undergraduate learners responding to the survey. These learners were actually enrolled for the September start date for their programs, so had neither library training nor the need to use library resources as yet.

The learners were asked 11 questions and had an opportunity to provide comments. The survey was deliberately kept brief and easy to answer to encourage learner response and full survey completion. (For learner survey, see Appendix A.)

A similar online survey was sent out to the core and associate faculty at RRU later in the fall. The faculty survey was almost identical to the learner survey, except that a question was added regarding whether faculty were accessing the eBooks via the Library catalogue or from the link to the eBook resource from the Library's database list. Respondents were also asked to identify themselves by department rather than by program to help maintain their anonymity. (For faculty survey questions, see Appendix B.)

As well as our timing, we have also viewed our choice and wording of survey questions in a new and more critical light than when we first developed the survey. In our rush to do the survey earlier than initially planned, our questions were not as well thought out as we would have liked. What has occurred as a result is redundancy in some areas and a general lack of specificity and distinction in others.

SURVEY RESULTS

We had 462 learners respond (Figure 3). The highest number of respondents came from the Masters of Leadership and Training learners, closely followed by the Masters of Business and Administration learners. These two programs also represent the majority of our graduate learner population, so their response rate is comparable to those learners in other more established programs such as the Masters in Conflict Analysis and Management and the Masters of Environmental Science Programs. The Applied Communications, Justice, Environmental Education, Peace and Human Security are all new programs in their inception year. Consequently awareness of library resources of both learners and their faculty lacks the continuity and learning between years that other well-established programs (and the Library) benefit from. RRU's Executive courses run from 2 weeks to 6 months. Executive program learners have little or no exposure to library resources, and while representing a significant portion of the numerical count of learners, have more modest expectations of service from the university library than those learners in degree programs.

Of the core and associate faculty solicited, 28 responded (Figure 4). We had an equal number of responses from the Organizational Leadership and Learning and the School of Business faculties at 33.33%. This corresponds with the learner responses as whose highest number of responses also came from the programs that are taught by the Organizational Leadership and Learning and the School of Business divisions.

Figure 5 illustrates faculty and learners who reported using the eBooks databases (ebrary and/or netLibrary) available via the RRU Library. This question is indeed one for which we wish we had chosen our wording more carefully. On viewing the results, we realized that our own assumptions as investigators about what the word "use" encompasses were quite different from

FIGURE 3. Learner Respondents by Program

Learners by Program	%
Bachelor of Commerce	14.75 (48/461)
Bachelor of Commerce (online)	5.86 (27/461)
Bachelor of Science	3.25 (15/461)
Bachelor of Justice	1.30 (6/461)
Bachelor of Applied Communications	1.08 (5/461)
Masters of Knowledge Management	1.30 (6/461)
Masters of Applied Communications	0
Masters of Environmental Ed. & Communication	0.22 (1/461)
Masters of Conflict Analysis & Management	4.34 (20/461)
Masters of Distance Learning	5.64 (26/461)
Masters of Leadership and Training	28.20 (130/461)
Masters of Business & Administration	25.16 (116/461)
Masters of Environmental Management	6.51 (30/461)
Masters of Peace & Human Security	0.22 (1/461)
Executive course (non-degree certificate or diploma)	0.22 (1/461)

FIGURE 4. Faculty Respondents by Department

Faculty by Program	%
Science, Technology, and Environment	14.81 (4/27)
School of Business	33.33 (9/27)
Organizational Leadership and Learning	33.33 (9/27)
Peace and Conflict Studies	7.41 (2/27)
Global and Executive Programs	11.11 (3/27)

FIGURE 5. Have You Ever Used eBooks?

	Yes	No
Learners	32.82% (150/457)	67.18% (307/457)
Faculty	33.33% (9/27)	66.67% (18/27)

each other, let alone what the word meant to learners and faculty, as revealed in their survey comments. One of us, like some of the respondents, assumed that use meant trying the product at all, while the other, interpreted "use" as using an item found within one of the eBooks databases rather than just trying to search it.

It is interesting to note that one-third of our learners have used (in some capacity) eBooks, and that figure is, interestingly, matched by our faculty users.

For those who answered no, we asked them to indicate why they had not used eBooks (Figure 6).

Many learner and faculty respondents indicated in the comments that they were not aware of the eBooks collection. Many of the undergraduate learners commented that they neither knew of nor used the eBooks resources because they were new to the university and would not be starting their programs until September. We were not intending to solicit responses from the new undergraduate intake and it is unfortunate that they seem to comprise the bulk of undergraduates who responded. Many graduate learners made mention that they had just completed an on campus residency and were shown the resource in a research instructional session. In fact, 73.49% of the learner respondents had seen a demonstration of the eBook resources in a library research instructional session (Figure 12).

For the respondents who answered yes to having used the eBooks resources, specific questions were asked about how they liked using different eBook (ebrary vs. netLibrary) resources (Figures 7 and 8). Very few comments were made that illuminated any particular preference between the ebrary and netLibrary databases. Also, only one mention was made about the netLibrary one book per user model vs. the ebrary simultaneous user-open access model. The learner indicated: " . . . I can appreciate the convenience for multiple users [sic]. I found the checkout system (24 hours only, which isn't useful when you spend several months writing a thesis) . . . " Figures 9 and 10 both involve preferences as to format.

Some respondents mentioned that they preferred online versions not only for the ease of access but to conserve paper and to support the university's own goal to reduce waste. But in the comments there were many anecdotal references to preferences for print. Such as: "My older eyes DO prefer print material. In my case, it has nothing to do with technophobia or level of computer literacy . . . " Another said: "I'm still a paper guy–I think the concept of ebooks

FIGURE 6. For Those Who Answered No to Using eBooks, Why Not?

Reason	Learners	Faculty
Didn't know about them	37.30% (138/370)	45.83% (11/24)
Preferred print books	11.62% (43/370)	12.50% (3/24)
Too much trouble	5.14% (19/370)	8.33% (2/24)
Didn't find anything on topic	5.68% (21/370)	4.17% (1/24)
Don't like reading on screen	11.89% (44/370)	16.67% (4/24)
Couldn't print out easily	1.62% (6/370)	0.00%
Other	26.76% (99/370)	12.50% (3/24)

FIGURE 7. Did You Like Using ebrary?

	Learners	Faculty
0 = Not at all	3.51% (6/171)	10.00% (1/10)
1	7.60% (13/171)	0.00%
2	7.60% (13/171)	0.00%
3	29.82% (51/171)	20.00% (2/10)
4	26.90% (46/171)	40.00% (4/10)
5 = Very much	24.56% (42/171)	30.00% (3/10)

FIGURE 8. Did You Like Using netLibrary?

	Learners	Faculty
0 = Not at all	3.11% (5/161)	22.22% (2/9)
1	4.97% (8/161)	0.00%
2	10.56% (17/161)	0.00%
3	28.57% (46/161)	11.11% (1/9)
4	29.29% (47/161)	33.33% (3/9)
5 = Very much	23.60% (38/161)	33.33% (3/9)

FIGURE 9. Did You Have to Use an eBook Because That Was the Only Available Format?

	Yes	No
Learners	45.98% (80/174)	54.02% (94/174)
Faculty	33.33% (3/9)	66.67% (6/9)

FIGURE 10. Would You Have Preferred the Print Version?

	Yes	No
Learners	43.80% (60/137)	56.20% (77/137)
Faculty	37.50% (3/8)	62.50% (5/8)

is great, but I don't like to read them on my screen (too hard on my eyes)." The majority of the comments regarding a preference for not reading on the screen came from the MBA learners. There was also a correlation between those who had not used the eBooks resources and those who then indicated they had not because they preferred the print.

There were a number of comments regarding the adequacy of the eBook collection from the learners (Figure 11). The percentage of those who thought the collection was adequate is marginal over those who felt it was not. Faculty were

FIGURE 11. Were the eBook Collections Adequate for Your Program?

	Yes	No
Learners	51.95% (80/154)	48.05% (74/154)
Faculty	12.50% (1/8)	87.50% (7/8)

much stronger in their opinions on the strength of the collection in their areas, with only one reporting that they found the collection adequate. Figures 15 and 16 illustrate by program the thoughts about the adequacy of the eBooks collection.

The majority of the written comments about the collection pertain to why it is not adequate. Some examples include: "The format of ebooks is limited, is not robust in subjects that are of interest to me . . ."; "I found some [of] the materials to be less than 'research based and academic.'" "The database did not feature many of the major titles that I wanted." "I found many ebooks needed were not available . . ."; "Some of the books that I am looking for are often compilation books with chapters on particular subjects (example: a book on international business with a chapter on managing multicultural workplaces). I find it more difficult to find those kinds of book[s]." "I was actually surprised initially by the offering, but while doing other research in the field of human rights, there was not information at all, which disappointed me." "There are not enough appropriate books on the ebooks system regarding political science, human security, and peace building. If this subject area were to be increased, we would use the service even more." "I found many books needed for my program were not available through the service." An MBA learner indicated, "My personal experience with ebook is the disappointment of its limited offerings. I have tried to find some books about service marketing. However, the returned titles could not feed my needs. I have just used it once and abandoned since then." Another MBA learner who is in the 2nd year of their program made a reference to the possible development of the collection: "I'm an MBA 2001 learner–maybe it has improved."

Figure 12 shows that nearly three-quarters of the learners noted seeing a demonstration of eBooks resources in a library instructional session, whereas only a small percentage of faculty were told about the resources through a library session. Some faculty commented that they would like to find out more about eBooks and hoped for the opportunity to follow up with a visit with a librarian.

"I really like the features on ebrary (the highlighting and bookmarking and the instant citation when I copy!). I am not as comfortable with the netlibrary as I haven't found as many useful books there!" As for the set up of accounts in either or both of the eBook databases and making using of the added features (Figure 13): 35.33% of learners had and 64.67% had not. A few comments

FIGURE 12. Were You Shown eBooks During a Library Research Instruction Session?

	Yes	No
Learners	73.49% (122/166)	26.51% (44/166)
Faculty	10.00% (1/10)	90.00% (9/10)

FIGURE 13. Did You Set Up an Account with Either/Both eBook Databases and Use the Added Features?

	Yes	No
Learners	35.33% (59/167)	64.67% (108/167)
Faculty	55.56% (5/9)	44.44% (4/9)

made mention of some difficulties in setting up accounts to use the extra features. For example: "I have used mostly eBooks–but have been unable to use the added features (i.e., Bookshelf, saving, highlighting, or bookmarks)." Another said, "Setting up an account was frustrating and I have stopped the use of eBooks and the eBook db."

As for faculty preference for ebrary or netLibrary, the results do not specifically point to any one particular resource. Almost half had created accounts with either or both eBook databases and used the added features.

About half of both students and faculty used eBooks for Research (Figure 14). One learner was particularly eloquent on why she or he was drawn to using the eBooks databases: "As an online student e-books provide a source of information not typically available. I entered the program not to just receive my degree but for the opportunity to learn. E-books are an opportunity to learn beyond what we are given. I want and have the desire to learn to be curious, e-books help fill this need. E-books shorten the division between conventional education and distant learning. As a distant learning facility the question of the need for e-books is a no brainier as they say. Now the trick is many of my fellow students are not aware of the source and how to use it and as such I have showed many of them how to access the information."

It was encouraging to note that a quarter of faculty who had used eBooks were looking for recommended/required readings in these databases, which will hopefully help the library to promote these resources to learners in the future.

One question that we unfortunately did not ask of learners but did ask of faculty was how they had accessed the eBooks databases. Of seven faculty respondents to that question, two chose via the RRU library catalogue, two via the databases directly, and three said they accessed eBooks both ways. We re-

FIGURE 14. For What Purpose Did You Use eBooks?

	Learners	Faculty
Research	49.13% (142/289)	50.00% (8/16)
Quick information	21.45% (62/289)	12.50% (2/16)
Recommended/required reading	14.19% (41/289)	25.00% (4/16)
Pleasure/personal interest	13.84% (40/289)	12.50% (2/16)
Other	1.38% (4/289)	0.00%

gret not having evidence from our learner population as to how they are accessing the eBook databases, though given the similarities in the response rates between faculty and learners on other questions, one wonders if the numbers would not be similar in the learner population.

Figures 15 and 16 provide more detail as to exactly who is using eBooks and what they think of the collection.

We manually broke down some of the data by respondent type (Figure 15 and 16). Very few responses were recognized as spoiled during this compilation of the data and were thrown out at that point. A few learners also identified themselves more clearly in the comments than in the self-identification question so their responses were assigned to the appropriate program accordingly.

These charts give a better idea of who is using the eBook collections and how adequate they think that the collections are to support their areas. The Masters of Leadership and Training and Bachelor of Commerce learner respondents were more pleased with the collections than were the respondents for any other program. MBA learners were evenly split on how adequate they felt the collection was for their program, as were some others, though it is difficult to make assumptions given the low number of responses for some of the programs.

ANALYSIS OF DATA

Prior to conducting this study, we anticipated a number of issues regarding the eBooks collection. We were interested in knowing more about:

- who was accessing the collection;
- what purpose were they using it;
- the general adequacy of the collection;
- was there a preference for the open access model rather than single user access;
- and was there a strong leaning towards print over reading materials online.

FIGURE 15. Use and Opinion of eBook Collections by Learners

	Yes used %	Not used %	Coll. good %	Coll. not good %
BCommerce	1.97 (9/458)	12.88 (59/458)	4.76 (7/147)	1.36 (2/147)
Bcom (online)	0.47 (2/458)	5.46 (25/458)	0.68 (1/147)	0.68 (1/147)
BScience	0.87 (4/458)	2.40 (11/458)	0.68 (1/147)	2.04 (3/147)
BJustice	0.47 (2/458)	0.87 (4/458)	0.00 (0/147)	0.68 (1/147)
BAppl Comm.	0.47 (2/458)	0.66 (3/458)	0.68 (1/147)	0.68 (1/147)
MKnowledge Mgt	0.66 (3/458)	0.66 (3/458)	1.36 (2/147)	0.68 (1/147)
MAppl Comm	0.00 (0/458)	0.00 (0/458)	0.00 (0/147)	0.00 (0/147)
MEnv Ed & Comm	0.00 (0/458)	0.29 (1/458)	0.00 (0/147)	0.00 (0/147)
MConflict Analysis	2.62 (12/458)	1.53 (7/458)	3.40 (5/147)	4.76 (7/147)
MDist Learning	1.09 (5/458)	3.93 (18/458)	0.68 (1/147)	2.72 (4/147)
MLeadership & Train	13.10 (60/458)	15.07 (69/458)	23.81 (35/147)	13.61 (20/147)
MBusiness Admin	9.61 (44/458)	16.16 (74/458)	13.61 (20/147)	13.61 (20/147)
MPeace & Hum Security	0.44 (2/458)	0.29 (1/458)	0.00 (0/147)	1.36 (2/147)
MEnvironmental Mgt	2.84 (13/458)	2.62 (12/458)	4.08 (6/147)	3.40 (5/147)
Exec programs	0.66 (3/458)	2.18 (10/458)	0.68 (1/147)	0.00 (0/147)

FIGURE 16. Use and Opinion of eBook Collections by Faculty

	Yes used %	Not used %	Coll. good %	Coll. not good %
Sci Tech & Env	3.70 (1/27)	11.11% (3/27)	0.00 (0/8)	12.50 (1/8)
Sch of Business	0.00 (0/27)	33.33% (9/27)	0.00 (0/8)	0.00 (0/8)
Org Lead & Learn	14.81 (4/27)	18.52% (5/27)	12.50 (1/8)	37.50 (3/8)
Peace & Conflict	3.70 (1/27)	3.70% (1/27)	0.00 (0/8)	12.50 (1/8)
Global & Exec	7.41 (2/27)	3.70% (1/27)	0.00 (0/8)	25.00 (2/8)

One of our initial suspicions were that the eBook collections were being used primarily by learners and faculty in the Business department because our collections included more relevant material in that subject area than for any other field of study. Indeed, one study of librarians by netLibrary as written up by Connoway (2001) indicated that 98.5% of 135 librarians thought that management as a subject area specifically was the discipline best suited to the eBook format. We also expected that the majority of the learning community was using the eBooks for reference and quick information. Furthermore, we anticipated that the users would prefer the multiple simultaneous access model of ebrary rather than the single user model of netLibrary, and that learners who were not near a major urban center would be particularly appreciative of books online. However, some surprising results came to light through the survey.

Who is using the eBook collections? From the learners who responded, only the Masters of Conflict Analysis learners exceeded the number of users over the number of non-users. However, a disproportionately high number of Masters of Arts in Distributed Learning learners had not used eBooks, and it is significant to note that this is the one group of learners who never have an on-campus residency and therefore receive no structured library instruction. Many more MBA learners had not used eBooks than had, with much commentary stating that they preferred not to read on screen. It is also important to note that MBA learners are given much more of their course material in print than are other programs, leading one to consider whether this group has an innate preference for print or whether a preference for print has been fostered by the program itself.

Furthermore, immediately apparent from the response rates was that learners in all new programs areas at RRU responded to our survey in extremely low numbers, and therefore we have very little data on their use of eBooks. This is perhaps a reflection of a lack of awareness of library resources among the faculty, as a relationship is still developing with new program faculty and the library; and little endorsement of those resources, as well as no transfer of learning amongst learners of different stages in the program.

The learners in the leadership focused program had a majority of learners who found the collection for their area of study adequate, as well as those in the Bachelor of Commerce, but the other programs were fairly evenly split on the adequacy of the collection for their areas. Faculty were unanimous and almost unequivocal in their feelings about the collection's inadequacy, but that is not entirely surprising given that faculty perceive the possibilities of collections for their areas beyond trying to meet the demands of individual assignments. An eBooks study conducted by Snowhill (2001), however, suggests that subjects like business and leadership are well represented in eBooks resources like ebrary and netLibrary. This presents the possibility that in these areas at least our collection could be quickly expanded (given resources) to meet the needs of learners and faculty.

Here were comments in the survey from both the Conflict Analysis and Management and the Human Security and Peace Building programs about the lack of content in the eBooks resources to support their research interests. There was concern expressed about the lack of diverse content in ebrary and netLibrary in the literature as well. Armstrong et al. (2002) and Edwards (2002) mention that the critical mass and diversity in eBook content is not yet available to appeal to a wide variety of disciplines. Furthermore, the feeling is that availability and diversity of academic content is needed in order to ensure overall success for eBook resources.

Some of the advantages of using eBooks is the perceived availability and accessibility of a resource; we assumed that the survey results would indicate a strong preference for ebrary over netLibrary because of the access model. It was certainly a perception of the RRU librarians that the ebrary model offers better overall access and therefore we anticipated that a preference would exist for ebrary over the netLibrary single user at a time, 'neo-print' model that has potential to create frustration for users. Much has been written on the netLibrary model in the literature. The limited availability can create a negative impression for users. Jeanette McVeigh (2000) and Edwards (2002) mention that in situations where libraries may only buy one access per eBook copy at a time then only one reader at a time can check the book out and if it happens to be a consortium purchase further limits are placed on access and availability. In the case of our survey results, this did not appear to be a concern for our users. It seemed as though most users were quite pleased to just find a copy of what they needed online. Only one learner made reference to the restrictive loan periods. The faculty users on the other hand did not seem to notice the access models.

Surprisingly, the survey results did not indicate a preference for print over the electronic version although comments from the MBA indicated that this was a rationale for not wanting to use eBooks. Even the faculty was comfortable with the electronic version. Overall, the results seem to reflect that the learners and faculty are pleased to find the content that they need and the format it comes in is not much of an issue. Falk (2003) refers to a study conducted at the University of Rochester's Rush Rhees Library. A comparison was done between eBooks and print books for 10 courses. The 17 titles needed for the courses were acquired in print and electronically in netLibrary. MARC records were added to the library catalogue for the netLibrary books. Students were referred to both the print and electronic versions. The study results indicated that the students opted for the electronic version over the print 3 to 1 citing that convenience and accessibility outweighed having to read on screen. Also, the results indicated that the RRU learners and faculty used eBooks for more than quick reference and research, marginally for pleasure and general interest. This is similar to what was revealed in other studies. In studies by Rosy (2002) and Summerfield et al. (2001), the eBooks were used more specifically for research and reference and less for leisure reading.

We also missed the opportunity to ask the learners whether they were accessing the eBooks resources either through the library catalogue or by going to the resource directly from the list of library subscription databases. We did ask the faculty and the results indicated that they were using both access routes equally. As the ebrary records had just been added to the library catalogue, it would have been useful for us to discern more from the learners about how they came across the eBook resources.

The survey results revealed for us the significance of library instruction and the corresponding use of the eBooks resources. Learners in the online Bcom and Masters of Distributed Learning programs had not made much use of the eBooks resources and did not see a demonstration of netLibrary or ebrary. For the learners who attended instructional sessions where eBook collections were featured, there was a definite correlation to using the resources at a later point. It is clear to us that we need to enhance the awareness and use of such resources by providing instruction. It appears likely that greater use of the collection would result.

Considering that RRU is a distance-based university, we should have included a specific question about how vital learners and faculty think that eBooks collections are to support distance education. Although we did not add this question, fortunately we did receive some comments about this in the comments portion of the survey. For example, "The ebooks are a great idea–I love them! I prefer these to having to come into the library and borrowing books physically plus [they are] accessible at all times of day, particularly late in the evening and early in the morning when I require them the most." Others said: "I am starting my program in 2 weeks, so I haven't had an opportunity to explore the library's resources at all. However, I am sure that I will find any and all resources available on-line very useful as I am remotely located away from ANY source of current information." "I think they are an essential element of a library that supports online learning programs. I prefer using ebooks since I can access information from home and not have to travel to the nearest university library to look in person." "Given the distance learning component of Royal Roads the ebooks is a great tool to assist those of us with limited access to high quality resources." "I think the ebook initiative is a very good way for some of us who are in remote places to have access to good information." "Please keep up the great work in updating the database as it is truly a vital part of the online learning environment."

One of the most interesting results of the survey was that, from the comments, students did not distinguish between different kinds of online resources: "We were shown during our residency how to access journals and info. Is this the same as ebooks?" "An explanation of what an ebook is would be helpful. I've answered these questions as if they refer to the journals and articles that I accessed through the LRC site." "I think that I used eBooks. For sure, I searched for articles. For some limited material, I had access to a whole book. I must confess that I am unsure by exactly what you mean by elibrary and netlibrary!"

CONCLUSION

To Summarize Our Findings

- RRU business learners are more reluctant to use eBooks than we had anticipated.
- Only slightly over 30% of our faculty and learners had used eBooks, but those who had were generally enthusiastic in their comments about the concept of eBooks while not necessarily finding the collection adequate for their needs.
- Instruction on how to use eBooks seems to be key in promoting their use to learners and faculty.
- There was a surprising lack of preference among RRU eBook users between the two eBook services and their access models. Overall satisfaction occurred in simply finding a needed resource, regardless of the format it came in.
- There were generally mixed feelings regarding the adequacy of the eBooks collections by learners. Faculty, however, were unequivocal as to the collection's inadequacy.

Goals for the Future

- Conduct a follow-up study on eBooks in our learning environment, perhaps with the help of focus groups.
- Turning our attention toward developing the eBook collections in support of other program areas like the Conflict Management, Human Security, and Environmental Sciences by examining alternatives to netLibrary.
- Explore new models for hosting and delivering eBook resources.
- Investigate ways to reinforce the value and use of eBooks to learners beyond formal instruction, including a possible library listserv. In addition, we need to explore ways to promote the resource to learners who do not have campus residencies and do not have the opportunity for library training on the resource in a face-to-face library instructional session.

Overall, we were pleased by both the willingness of learners to participate in a survey of their needs and their interest in eBooks specifically. Learner comments such as: "I did not learn about eBooks until my second year res[idency]. I am so totally thrilled with this access because of the immediacy, ease of use, and variety of books. I cannot believe how useful it has become in doing research. It truly is an awesome tool to be able use." The many other comments like it, were a powerful affirmation of the value of eBooks in our distance learning environment, and encourage us to continue to build our eBook collections.

REFERENCES

Armstrong, C., Edwards, L., & Lonsdale, R. (2002).Virtually there? E-books in UK academic libraries. *Program: Electronic Library and Information Systems, 36*(4), 216-227.

Chu, H. (2003). Electronic books: Viewpoints from users and potential users. [Electronic Version]. *Library Hi Tech, 21*(3), 340-346.

Connaway, L. S. (2001). A Web-based electronic book (e-book) library: The netLibrary model. [Electronic Version]. *Library Hi Tech, 19*(4), 340-349.

Dillon, D. (2001). E-books: The University of Texas experience, part 2. [Electronic Version]. *Library Hi Tech, 19*(4), 350-362.

Edwards, L. (2002). Shaping a Strategy for E-books: The JISC E-books Working Group. *Liber Quarterly, 12,* 240-244.

Falk, H. (2003). Technology corner-electronic campuses. *The Electronic Library, 21*(1), 63-66.

McVeigh, J. (2000, November). What's happening to the book and why you should care. *Library Issues: Briefing for Faculty and Administrators, 21*(2), 1-4.

Snowhill, L. (2001, July/August). Ebooks and their future in academic libraries: An overview. *D-Lib Magazine,* from http://www.dlib.org/dlib/july01/snowhill/07snowhill.html.

Rosy, R. L. (2002). Ebooks for libraries and patrons: Two years of experience. *Liber Quarterly, 12,* 228-233.

Summerfield, M., Mandel, C., & Kantor, P. (2001). Perspectives on scholarly online books: The Columbia University online books evaluation project. *Libraries & Electronic Resources: New Partnership, New Practices, New Perspectives, 35*(1/2), 61-82.

APPENDIX A

eBooks Survey for Learners

Survey Form

Survey Information: eBooks Use by RRU Learners

This survey is essential to the library's evaluation of our electronic book databases ebrary and netlibrary and their usefulness to students.
Responses from this survey will help the library evaluate the usefulness of eBooks to distance learners.
This Survey is anonymous.

eBooks–Survey Form

1) Who are you? Please tell us a little about yourself.
   What program are you in? (Required)
      BCom
      BCom online
      BSc
      BJus
      BAAC
      KM
      MAAC
      MAEEC
      MACAM
      MADL
      MALT
      MBA
      MEM
      PHS
      Executive course (non-degree certificate or diploma)

2) Have you used eBooks?
   Please tell us whether or not you have used eBooks during your program at RRU.
   Have you used the eBooks databases (ebrary and/or netlibrary) available via the RRU Library?
   Yes   ☐
   No   ☐

APPENDIX A (continued)

3) Only for those who answered "No," why not?
   Didn't know about them ☐
   Preferred print books ☐
   Too much trouble ☐
   Didn't find anything on topic ☐
   Don't like reading on screen ☐
   Couldn't print out easily ☐
   Other ☐

For those who answered "Yes" to using eBooks, please continue with this section. Our thanks to those who answered "No."

Please tell us about your experiences using eBooks.

4) Did you like using ebrary? (0 = Not at all, 5 = Very much)
   0   1   2   3   4   5

5) Did you like using netlibrary? (0 = Not at all, 5 = Very much)
   0   1   2   3   4   5

6) Did you have to use an eBook because that was the only available format?
   Yes   ☐
   No   ☐

7) If so, would you have preferred the print version?
   Yes   ☐
   No   ☐

8) Were the eBook collections adequate for your program?
   Yes   ☐
   No   ☐

9) Were you shown eBooks during a library research instruction session?
   Yes   ☐
   No   ☐

10) Did you set up an account with either/both eBook databases and use the added features?
    Yes   ☐
    No   ☐

11) For what purpose did you use eBooks?
     Research   ☐
     Quick information   ☐
     Recommended or required course reading   ☐
     Pleasure/personal interest   ☐
     Other   ☐

Please give us any comments you wish to make about the eBooks databases available via RRU Library. Thank you very much for your participation!!

(Maximum 4000 characters)

```



```

APPENDIX B

eBooks Survey for Faculty

Survey Form

Survey Information–eBook Use by Faculty

This survey is essential to the library's evaluation of our electronic book databases ebrary and netlibrary and their usefulness to students and faculty. Responses from this survey will help the library evaluate the usefulness of eBooks to distance learners.
This Survey is anonymous.

eBook Use by Faculty–Survey Form

1) Who are you? Please tell us a little about yourself.
    Which department do you work in? Please choose just the one you work in most. (Required)
        Science, Technology, and Environment   ☐
        School of Business   ☐
        Organizational Leadership and Learning   ☐
        Peace and Conflict Studies   ☐
        Global and Executive Programs   ☐

APPENDIX B (continued)

2) Have you ever used eBooks?
Please tell us whether or not you have used eBooks while employed at RRU.
Have you used the eBooks databases (ebrary and/or netlibrary) available via the RRU Library?

Yes ☐
No ☐

3) Only for those who answered "No," why not?

Didn't know about them ☐
Preferred print books ☐
Too much trouble ☐
Didn't find anything on topic ☐
Don't like reading on screen ☐
Couldn't print out easily ☐
Other ☐

For those who answered "Yes" to using eBooks, please continue with this section. Our thanks to those who answered "No."

Please tell us about your experiences using eBooks.

4) Did you like using ebrary? (0 = Not at all, 5 = Very much)
0 (Not at all)   1   2   3   4   5 (Very much)

5) Did you like using netlibrary? (0 = Not at all, 5 = Very much)
0 (Not at all)   1   2   3   4   5 (Very much)

6) Did you have to use an eBook because that was the only available format?
Yes ☐
No ☐

7) If so, would you have preferred the print version?
Yes ☐
No ☐

8) Were the eBook collections adequate for your subject interest?
Yes ☐
No ☐

9) Were you shown eBooks by a librarian?
   Yes   ☐
   No   ☐

10) Did you set up an account with either/both eBook databases and use the added features?
   Yes   ☐
   No   ☐

11) For what purpose did you use eBooks?
   Research   ☐
   Quick Information   ☐
   Looking for a required reading for learners   ☐
   Pleasure/personal interest   ☐
   Other   ☐

12) Did you find eBooks via the RRU Library catalogue or through the ebrary and/or netlibrary database(s) directly?
   RRU Library Catalogue   ☐
   Databases Directly   ☐
   Both   ☐

Please give us any comments you wish to make about the eBooks databases available via RRU Library. Thank you very much for your participation!!

(Maximum 4000 characters)

A Tale of Two Campuses: Providing Virtual Reference to Distance Nursing Students

Ladonna Guillot
Beth Stahr

Southeastern Louisiana University

SUMMARY. This paper describes the collaborative efforts of Southeastern Louisiana University librarians and faculty working on two campuses to provide one-on-one research coaching via digital reference service. In the fall of 2002, the University's Sims Memorial Library instituted a Virtual Reference Desk (VRD) for library patrons. In the summer of 2003, the Library began offering dedicated online VRD service to undergraduate and graduate Nursing students. Librarians worked with Nursing faculty to promote this service to students in two courses, the undergraduate Research in Nursing and the graduate Theoretical Foundations of Advanced Nursing. The purpose of dedicated VRD is to augment traditional bibliographic instruction with dedicated virtual reference sessions once students refine their research objectives and to enhance library access for graduate students who participate in a three university consortium.

KEYWORDS. Library services, distance learners, distance education, Internet

[Haworth co-indexing entry note]: "A Tale of Two Campuses: Providing Virtual Reference to Distance Nursing Students." Guillot, Ladonna, and Beth Stahr. Co-published simultaneously in *Journal of Library Administration* (The Haworth Information Press, an imprint of The Haworth Press, Inc.) Vol. 41. No. 1/2, 2004, pp. 139-152; and: *The Eleventh Off-Campus Library Services Conference Proceedings* (ed: Patrick B. Mahoney) The Haworth Information Press, an imprint of The Haworth Press, Inc., 2004, pp. 139-152.

http://www.haworthpress.com/web/JLA
Digital Object Identifier: 10.1300/J111v41n01_11

In the 20 years between 1975 and 1995, Southeastern Louisiana University doubled its enrollment and earned "the reputation as the 'fastest growing university in the nation'" (Public Information Office, 2001, para. 7). During this same time period, distance learning was emerging as a way of meeting the needs of non traditional and part time students. Like many regional state universities, distance learning initiatives at Southeastern pushed the library to investigate new methods of providing resources to users. The ability to successfully adapt to changes in instructional design and delivery have likewise prompted librarians to seek new methods of delivering quality reference and instructional services at a distance. This paper describes our efforts at meeting those needs.

Distance learning at Southeastern consists of several instructional delivery formats: courses held at two branch campuses, remote site courses held at K-12 facilities, compressed video courses, and Internet-based courses. Currently, the majority of the distance courses are those held at the remote campuses and those taught over the Internet or using a combination of Internet and Compressed Video.

The main campus of Southeastern Louisiana University is located in Hammond, Louisiana, at the intersection of two Interstate highways. The Hammond Chamber of Commerce touts the city's location as "the crossroads of the South." Actually, the tremendous increase in university enrollment can most likely be attributed to New Orleans urban sprawl. Hammond is located within easy commuting distance of New Orleans, the suburban North Shore, and the state capital, Baton Rouge.

Southeastern's two remote-site campuses are located in St. Tammany Parish and Baton Rouge. The St. Tammany Center includes classrooms, science laboratories, and a computer productivity lab, but no library. Courses scheduled at the St. Tammany Center are typically entry-level classes. Conversely, the Baton Rouge Center, located about 40 miles from the Main Campus, primarily serves the upper classmen in the School of Nursing, and includes classrooms, laboratories, computer lab, and a branch health sciences library.

In 1998, Southeastern selected Blackboard as its Internet-based instructional courseware. In the spring semester 2003, less than five years later, the university course catalog offered 173 100% Blackboard courses and an additional 20 courses that use Blackboard to deliver over 50% of their class content. The average enrollment in a Southeastern Blackboard course is 22 students. Southeastern Louisiana University is the second largest distance education provider in Louisiana. Although distance learning library services are provided for students at both remote site campuses, as well as those who are enrolled in electronic and compressed video courses, and those who take classes at many other remote sites, the rest of this paper will consider some special services provided to Nursing students.

Sims Memorial Library is located on the Main campus. One of the 18 professional library positions has been designated as the Distance Learning Librarian. The Baton Rouge Nursing Library is a branch library, specifically intended to provide services and resources for nursing students and faculty, and employs a full-time Health Sciences Librarian. Since some of the Nursing students attend classes in Hammond, the Health Sciences Librarian works with students and faculty on both campuses. Likewise, since all the graduate level Nursing courses are taught using a combination of Blackboard courseware and compressed video, the Distance Learning Librarian interacts with Nursing students. Together, the two librarians work to ensure that the needs of all the Nursing students and faculty are met. Over the past several years, these enhanced services have included the implementation of an Article Delivery Service between the two campuses in addition to collaborative efforts with the Ask A Librarian Services and user instruction, which builds upon the instructional model described below.

THE SOUTHEASTERN LOUISIANA UNIVERSITY LIBRARY INSTRUCTIONAL MODEL

Traditional library user instruction at Southeastern Louisiana University centers on a one-hour credit information literacy course, LS 102, and faculty requested single-session bibliographic instruction sessions. In addition, the Ask A Librarian Web page, as seen in Figure 1, is the point of entry for patrons using the library's e-mail, telephone, and chat reference services as well as research consultation appointments. Students and faculty may receive some user instruction when they direct reference queries through one of these services.

Reference/Instruction librarians teach approximately 70 sections of LS 102 per year, a required course for half of the academic majors on campus. Students receive 15 hours of library user instruction in a fairly typical classroom setting, enhanced with hands-on instruction technology. A series of in-class and homework assignments reinforce both lower level "buttonology" and higher level critical thinking skills. Increasingly popular is the online section of this class, where 75% of the instruction is conducted via Blackboard.

One-hour bibliographic instruction sessions, commonly referred to as one-shot BIs, are scheduled at the request of faculty and are usually discipline specific. Frequently, a library research assignment is tied to the BI session. For some students this session will be their first experience with an academic library. Often, however, BIs serve as refresher sessions for upperclassmen or for

FIGURE 1. Ask A Librarian Home Page

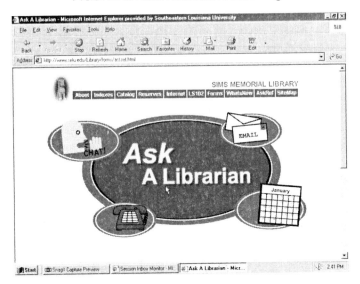

students who have taken LS 102. Librarians demonstrate specific database searching, familiarize students with library services and encourage students in need of further help to follow up with additional reference services. For the academic year 2002-03 (the most recent statistics that are available), 247 bibliographic instruction sessions were conducted for Southeastern students. Both the Distance Learning Librarian and the Health Sciences Librarian teach traditional BIs.

Live online reference service became a reality at Sims Memorial Library in the fall of 2002 when "chat" became the fourth component of the Ask A Librarian service. Southeastern partnered with the University of New Orleans in 2002-03 academic year and with Loyola University of New Orleans in the 2003-04 academic year, forming the Southeastern Louisiana Collaborative Digital Reference Service. In its initial year, the Service operated for 36 hours per week using the then LSSI software, recently acquired by Tutor.com. In the current year, this Service is the first 24/7 virtual reference service in the state of Louisiana, with 19 librarians from Southeastern and Loyola providing 47 hours of coverage per week and outsource librarians providing nighttime and weekend coverage.

In the spring of 2003, the Distance Learning and Health Sciences Librarians envisioned taking virtual reference service one step further for distance and non traditional learners. The librarians saw the instructional potential inherent in the cobrowsing feature of the Tutor.com program. Cobrowsing, as shown in Figure 2, allows the reference librarian to manipulate the patron's browser for the purpose of guiding the user through a reference query. The query may include anything from browsing the library's catalog to an in-depth search and viewing of full-text journal literature on the student's narrowed topic. The objective then became to design a pilot program that would extend the digital service beyond chatting in answering simple reference queries to the use of cobrowsing for online bibliographic instruction through dedicated virtual reference meetings. Since the software was already in place to schedule group meetings, the challenge lay in identifying and coordinating with a university population that would benefit from this service.

As the Distance Learning and Health Sciences Librarians sought a test group for the pilot program, they conceptualized the benefits of this new service. Five points were identified as enhancements of the year-old chat online reference service. First, it would be discipline specific with a reference subject specialist providing services. Second, it would be instruction oriented, augmenting traditional library user instruction and tied to a specific research assignment. Third, it would be appointment based with private group meetings, as seen in Figure 3, scheduled in advance. Fourth, it would entail a collaborative effort between faculty, students, and librarians. Most important, it would provide a value-added service for distance learners.

FIGURE 2. Cobrowsing in Sims Library Virtual Reference Service

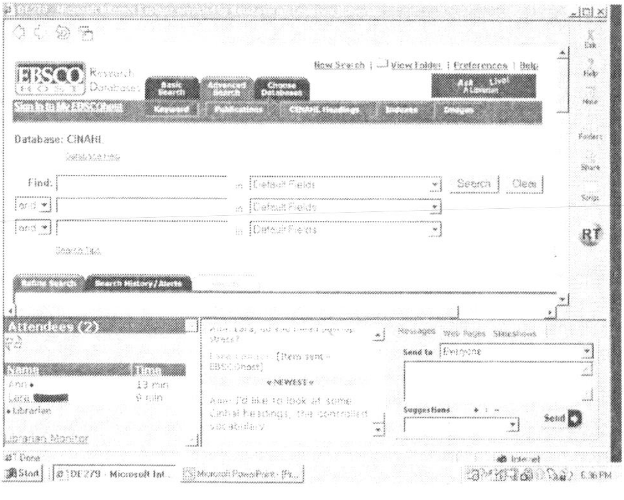

FIGURE 3. Group Instruction Session, Librarian View

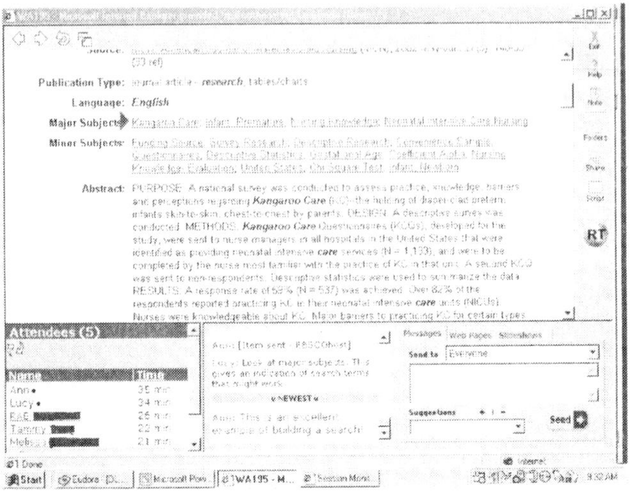

THE PILOT PROGRAM

The Sims Memorial Library dedicated virtual reference service pilot program was developed in the spring of 2003 and implemented in the summer of that year. It was expanded for the fall semester 2003 and continues to be an ongoing effort of the Distance Learning and Health Sciences Librarians.

Undergraduate and graduate classes from the Southeastern University School of Nursing were chosen for the pilot program for several reasons. Southeastern offers one of the fastest growing nursing programs in the United States with nearly 1500 students enrolled in the fall of 2002. Undergraduate nursing majors are required to complete their pre-clinical training at the main campus and their last three semesters at the Baton Rouge Center. They are required to take the one-credit hour information literacy (LS 102) class prior to admission to nursing school, ensuring at least a rudimentary knowledge of information retrieval skills and the library's resources. The selective admissions process in nursing generally yields a more intrinsically motivated and independent learner. Graduate students who participate in a three university Intercollegiate Consortium for a Master of Science in Nursing (ICMSN) were also suitable candidates. In addition, an excellent working rapport already existed between the nursing faculty and the Distance Learning and Health Sciences Librarians as a result of prior collaborative efforts in bibliographic instruction sessions and a graduate orientation program.

Many nursing students also fall into the non traditional category. Nearly all of the graduate students work full time. Currently, slightly over 20% of the graduate nursing students have been out of school for ten years or longer, and 8% have not attended university classes in 15 years or longer. In addition, nearly 90% of Southeastern students live off campus, 75% are employed, and 30% have children under age 18. Finally, library hours at the Baton Rouge Center Health Sciences Library often do not meet the needs of nontraditional and graduate students. Librarian access is crucial to these students who often require additional instruction in "buttonology," search strategy formation and evaluation of sources.

Distance learning components are involved in both the undergraduate and graduate nursing programs at Southeastern. Students use Blackboard in varying degrees ranging from 100% online courses to those using it primarily for course administration and enhancement. Compressed video usage within the ICMSN is an increasingly popular instructional option. Graduate students are true distance learners involved in a consortium that employs multiple distance learning technologies.

Planning the Pilot Program

The pilot program involved four phases. These included planning, implementation, session follow-up, and evaluation. Each of these is described below. Planning for the pilot program began in the late spring and early summer of 2003 and entailed more time than first envisioned. Early in June, the Distance Learning and Health Sciences Librarians met with the Coordinator of Graduate Education for the School of Nursing to determine how dedicated virtual reference services could best meet the needs of students in the ICMSN. Soon other faculty expressed interest in the pilot. Faculty buy-in was considered crucial to the success of the trial. The nursing faculty indicated that three courses emphasizing research methodology would be the ideal trials for dedicated virtual reference. Nursing 378, Research in Nursing, is an undergraduate course focusing on the history, terminology, and process of nursing research. Nursing 600, Theoretical Foundations of Advanced Nursing, and Nursing 602, Design and Methodology of Nursing Research, emphasize scientific research and analysis. The development of forms and handouts for administration of the program was tackled next. They seemed important to the success of any endeavor involving three-way communication between faculty, students, and librarians. Librarians created individual and group sign-up sheets and form e-mails that were used to distribute meeting keys and URLs.

A one-hour bibliographic instruction session was incorporated into the planning phase of the pilot program and preceded every dedicated virtual reference session. The BI session was course specific and focused on reacquainting students with the health sciences electronic databases, library services, and introducing the concept of dedicated virtual reference. Dedicated virtual reference seemed a logical follow-up to classroom reference instruction and an opportunity for augmenting research skills once students had the opportunity to refine their research objectives. Approximately one third of each BI session was allocated to the procedural details of scheduling virtual group meetings. Consideration was given to the work and class schedules of student participants and librarians. For the Nursing 378 undergraduate course, the culminating assignment is a collaborative research effort to produce a literature review on a nursing topic. Dedicated group meetings were offered to these students, since they worked in groups of two to three to produce the final assignment. For the Nursing 600 graduate course, students were offered the opportunity for one-on-one virtual reference instruction, targeting the specific needs of each individual, in a sense creating "designer instruction."

One of the easier tasks of the planning phase was setting up virtual group meetings in the Tutor.com software. Group meetings may be conducted independently of the ongoing chat reference service provided by the Loyola and Southeastern libraries reference departments. Participants were sent e-mails with a URL for connecting to Tutor.com and given a meeting key allowing them to join the dedicated reference meeting at the appointed date and time.

Implementing the Pilot Program

Once the planning phase was completed, implementation promised to be easier; however, invariably complications arose that could not be anticipated. Students encountered problems in connecting to the Tutor.com software when they failed to cut and paste the entire lengthy URL in the address line of Internet Explorer. In many instances, this was resolved when students telephoned the Reference Department for assistance. On one occasion, the University server unexpectedly crashed, precluding students from meeting at the appointed time. Occasionally problems occurred with the software that necessitated technical support from Tutor.com.

Follow-Up in the Pilot Program

Each virtual reference session was followed with further communication with faculty and students. Faculty were advised as to which students participated and the level of success thought to have been achieved with each group or individual. Each student received an automatically generated transcript of the online session via e-mail, providing an exact account of the session. This enabled students to independently pursue search strategies and review instructional components of the session at their own pace. Students were also thanked for participating in the pilot and offered alternative reference venues to ensure success with their research efforts.

ASSESSMENT OF THE PILOT PROGRAM AND THE FUTURE OF DEDICATED REFERENCE SERVICE AND VIRTUAL INSTRUCTION

In evaluating the pitfalls and successes of the dedicated virtual reference pilot program, the following six factors were taken into consideration: technology, library personnel, students, scheduling, marketing, and costs.

Technological Considerations

Success of the individual dedicated virtual reference sessions was closely tied to a favorable technological environment. Students with DSL or cable Internet access were more successful in achieving and sustaining communication and cobrowsing during a session. Bandwidth, institutional server downtime, and software problems occurred unexpectedly and impacted the success of individual dedicated meetings. Another example of unanticipated technology problems occurred when the library's online database provider made a minor change that interrupted the Tutor.com cobrowsing feature. It took several weeks for the problem to be resolved. In the interim, librarians improvised and found a temporary solution that enabled cobrowsing.

Library Personnel Considerations

Individual temperament and technological competence play a role in determining librarian suitability for this fast-paced service. Librarians must be capable of multitasking and manipulating multiple browsers while in nearly constant communication with patrons. Simultaneously formulating a response to reference queries while manipulating the virtual reference software and engaging in dialog with patrons is a daunting task for many. In addition, providing dedicated virtual reference service is a labor intensive. It must be evaluated in terms of its potential cost/benefit to any library. In the Southeastern pilot program, two librarians were engaged in providing this service. In one instance, the Health Sciences and Distance Learning Librarians spent six hours assisting 18 undergraduate nursing students over two days. The use of a well-trained graduate assistant working in tandem with a librarian was considered a less costly option, though it was never used in the pilot program.

Student Considerations

Five factors were identified in assessing student considerations. First, access to adequate technological components greatly impacted student success. Second, individual technical competency played as important a role for students as it did for the librarians. The most successful students were those whose familiarity with technology was greater, as troubleshooting was as likely to be initiated by the student as by the librarian. Third, the level of commitment and individual student responsibility affected the outcome of the virtual reference experience. On several occasions, students failed to attend their appointed dedicated virtual group meetings. Also, students were asked in the bibliographic instruction sessions to refine their research goals and select several relevant search terms prior to the virtual sessions. When carried out, this advance preparation ensured optimum use of the allocated virtual meeting time. Fourth and unexpected, student-faculty communication affected the perception of a session's success, particularly on the faculty's part. Occasionally students communicated assessment of a virtual reference session that differed greatly from that of the librarians, leaving a bewildered faculty member to seek further clarification. Student satisfaction with the dedicated reference experience appears to be correlated with their individual or group experience. Student impressions are currently being evaluated with a follow-up survey.

Scheduling Considerations

Scheduling dedicated virtual reference sessions was time consuming. Students' work and class schedules as well as the librarians' work schedules were considered when planning sessions. For the Nursing 600 participants, the librarians rearranged their schedules to conduct meetings in the evenings to best meet the needs of graduate students who are employed full-time. In the case of the Nursing 378 students, scheduling dedicated group meetings was even more difficult due to the collaborative nature of their research assignments. Librarians muddled through sign-up sheets to determine when group meetings could be scheduled. Once an appointed time had been determined, the librarians e-mailed confirmation.

Marketing Considerations

Sims Library began to market the 24/7 online chat reference service almost from its inception. A media blitz aimed at the Southeastern Louisiana University community began in the fall of 2002. Library faculty liaisons touted the service to their respective academic departments, and it was introduced at the annual fall faculty library orientation. Chat reference was advertised in traditional media venues including the campus newspaper, radio station, and television station. Posters were placed in all the campus computer labs. The Ask A Librarian logo, as seen in Figure 4, was linked to the library's online catalog and electronic databases.

The successful marketing of the chat online reference service paved the way for the introduction of dedicated virtual reference service. Faculty and student recognition of the existence of virtual services favorably impacted their willingness to use dedicated virtual reference software as an instructional tool, particularly for distance and non traditional learners. Nursing faculty and students immediately demonstrated an enthusiasm to participate in the pilot program at Southeastern.

Cost Considerations

Monetary and personnel costs weigh heavily in the decision to implement any virtual reference service. The initial chat reference service was funded by a University technology grant written by two reference librarians and the Library Director. The annual renewal fee is now part of the library's budget. Tutor.com supplies outsourced librarians under a contractual agreement. In the nearly six months that the 24/7 service has been provided, the number of queries addressed by outsourced librarians has been greater and more costly than expected. In addition, personnel costs, though not precisely calculated, are certainly significant enough to impact any decision regarding implementation of the service. The dedicated digital reference services for distance learners remain librarian labor intensive while meeting the user needs of a relatively small number of patrons. Still, libraries already know that serving distance learners is expensive. Distance Librarian Carol Goodson wrote, "We know of course that as the number of distance education programs increase, the cost to the library is greater, just as it is when enrollment increases. In fact, the costs of supporting distance education students is often higher, since the level of services provided is usually greater than that available to on-campus learners, and thus correspondingly more expensive" (Goodson, 2001). Yet Stephen

FIGURE 4. Ask A Librarian Logo

Parnell wrote that "the full costs of providing quality library services to support programs offered by universities through distance education are either overlooked or underestimated by libraries and their parent institutions" and that "research currently underway into the costs of higher education needs to be extended to include the full costs borne by institutions, their students and other libraries, in meeting the information needs of distance learners" (Parnell, 2002).

CONCLUSION: A GROWING POSSIBILITY

Despite the technological barriers, the excessive cost, the unknown scalability, virtual instruction using the digital reference software may be a possible way to fulfill the institution's responsibility to provide library instruction for all students. Many librarians who serve distance learners and who endeavor to meet the guidelines and standards of academic accrediting agencies and the Association of College and Research Libraries (ACRL) are frustrated. Existing technologies including online tutorials, e-mail service and Web-based courseware do not adequately provide service at the point of need. Virtual reference software systems like the one used in this study present another avenue for serving distance learners:

> New software designed for collaboration between computer users, however, points to a larger conception of the digital library that includes not only electronic access to sources, but electronic access to services as well. In this vision, it is assumed that electronic access to sources by itself does not obviate the need for librarian-patron interaction. In fact, access to an array of sources that differ in terms of accessibility, interface, organization, and content increases the need for interaction, especially when patrons are not physically in the library. (Meola & Stormont, 1999, p. 30)

A recently released international study considered ways to incorporate traditional library functions into electronic learning. Among other recommendations written for the entire academic community (instructors, librarians, IT departments, and instructional designers), the OCLC Task Force unanimously expressed a need to implement "easy access to virtual reference services at the point of need" and noted a lack of effective policy and fiscal models to sustain the e-learning environment (OCLC, 2003 p. 15). We are encouraged with our initial experiences in virtual instruction with undergraduate and graduate nursing students and look forward to additional opportunities to evaluate the practicality of this service.

REFERENCES

Association of College and Research Libraries. (2000). *Guidelines for the Distance Learning Library Services.* Retrieved November 21, 2003, from http://www.ala. org/Content/ NavigationMenu/ACRL/Standards_and_Guidelines/Guidelines_for_ Distance_Learning_Library_Services.htm.

Association of College and Research Libraries. (2000). *Information Literacy Competency Standards for higher education.* Retrieved November 21, 2003, from http://www.ala.org/Content/NavigationMenu/ACRL/Standards_and_Guidelines/ standards.pdf.

Ault, M. (2000). Thinking outside the library: How to develop, implement and promote library services for distance learners. In P. B. Mahoney (Ed.) *Distance Learning Library Services: The Tenth Off-Campus Services Conference.* Binghamton: The Haworth Press, Inc., 2002.

Caspers J. S. (2000). Outreach to distance learners: When the distance education instructor sends the students to the library, where do they go? *The Reference Librarian, 67/68,* 299-311.

Coffman, S. (2001). Distance education and virtual reference: Where are we headed? *Computers in Libraries, 21*(4), 21-25.

Goodson, C. (2001). *Providing library services for distance education students.* New York: Neal-Schuman.

Higher Learning Commission of the North Central Association. (2000). *Best practices for electronically offered degree and certificate programs.* Retrieved December 3, 2003, from http://www.sacscoc.org/pdf/commadap.pdf.

Hope, C., Peterson, C. & Silveria, B. B. (2003). *Reach out and touch someone: Instructional uses of virtual reference.* Presentation at Association of College and Research Libraries 11th National Conference, April 12, 2003. Retrieved December 3, 2003, from http://home.csumb.edu/s/silveriajanie/world/ACRL.ppt.

Hill, J. B. and Stahr, B. (2003). *Instructional opportunities in virtual reference.* Presentation at THE (Teaching in Higher Education) Forum, Louisiana State University, April 2002. Retrieved December 3, 2003, from http://www.celt.lsu.edu/CFD/E-Proceedings/index.htm.

The Institute of Higher Education Policy. (2000). *Quality on the line: Benchmarks for success in Internet based distance education.* Retrieved December 3, 2003, from http://www.ihep.com/Pubs/PDF/Quality.pdf.

Jaworowski, C. (2001). *There's more to chat than chit-chat:Using chat software for library instruction.* Presentation at Information Strategies 2001 conference. Retrieved December 3, 2003, from http://library.fgcu.edu/Conferences/infostrategies01/ presentations/2001/jaworowski.htm.

Johnston, P. E. (2003). Digital reference as an instructional tool: Just in time and just enough. *Searcher, 11*(3), 31-34.

Kraemer, E. W. (2003). Developing the online learning environment: The pros and cons of using webCT for library instruction. *Information Technology and Libraries, 22*(2), 87-92.

Meola, M. & Stormont, S. (1999). Real-time reference service for the remote user: From the telephone and electronic mail to Internet chat, instant messaging, and collaborative software. *The Reference Librarian, 67/68,* 29-40.

OCLC E-Learning Task Force. (2003). *Libraries and the enhancement of e-learning.* Retrieved December 3, 2003, from http://www5.oclc.org/downloads/community/ elearning.pdf.

O'English, L. (2003). 24/7 *Instruction: Why should reference get all the fun or how a pilot project never made it out of flight school.* Presentation at Virtual Reference Desk Conference 2003. Retrieved December 3, 2003, from http://www.wsu.edu/ ~oenglish/loe-vrdfinal/loe-vrdfinal.PPT.

Office of Institutional Research and Assessment. (2004, January). *Electronic factbook: Enrollment by class, Fall 1925-Fall 2003.* Retrieved February 5, 2004, from Southeastern Louisiana University Web site: http://www.selu.edu/Administration/Inst-Research/Student/totenroll.htm.

Parnell, S. (2002). Redefining the cost and complexity of library services for open and distance learning. *International Review of Research in Open and Distance Learning, 3*(2). Retrieved December 3, 2003, from http://www.irrodl.org/content/v3.2/ parnell.html.

Public Information Office. (2001, December 7). *Moffett appointed President of Southeastern by ULS Board.* Retrieved February 5, 2004, from Southeastern Louisiana University Web site: http://selu.edu/NewsEvetns/PublicInfoOffice/Moffett-President.htm.

Race, S. F. & Viggiano, R. G. (2001). It's not BI, it's VI-Virtual instruction for distance learners [from the Florida Distance Learning Reference & Referral Center]. In *National Online 2001:proceedings* (pp. 377-383). Information Today. Presentation retrieved December 3, 2003, from http://www.rrc.usf.edu/pres/nom/index_files/v3_ document.htm.

Roccos, L. J. (2001). Distance learning and distance libraries: Where are they now? *Online Journal of Distance Learning Administration, IV.* Retrieved December 3, 2003, from http://www.westga.edu/~distance/oidla/fall43/roccos43.html.

Williams, C. R. & Walters, T. O. (2003). Reference and instruction services go virtual as a form of outreach: Case studies from academic libraries. *Information Outlook, 7*(8), 20-4, 26-7.

User Instruction for Distance Students: Texas Tech University System's Main Campus Library Reaches Out to Students at Satellite Campuses

Jon R. Hufford

Texas Tech University

SUMMARY. Texas Tech University recently established satellite campuses in the Texas Hill Country area northwest of San Antonio. Basic library support for students was in place when the Hill Country campuses began enrolling students in distance courses in June, 2002. In July, Texas Tech Library's Distance Learning Team assisted Hill Country staff in preparing for a Southern Association of Colleges and Schools accreditation review. After visiting the campuses, the Team wrote a report that addressed the SACS criteria related to library support. The recommendations made in that report served as the basis for developing a comprehensive library support program for the Texas Tech Hill Country campuses. Among other things, the report emphasized encouraging Hill Country students to take the University's Web-based course, "Introduction to Library Research." This paper discusses the SACS review experience and, in particular, the efforts made to develop, advertise, and implement the Web-based course for students at the Texas Tech satellite campuses.

[Haworth co-indexing entry note]: "User Instruction for Distance Students: Texas Tech University System's Main Campus Library Reaches Out to Students at Satellite Campuses." Hufford, Jon R. Co-published simultaneously in *Journal of Library Administration* (The Haworth Information Press, an imprint of The Haworth Press, Inc.) Vol. 41, No. 1/2, 2004, pp. 153-165; and: *The Eleventh Off-Campus Library Services Conference Proceedings* (ed: Patrick B. Mahoney) The Haworth Information Press, an imprint of The Haworth Press, Inc., 2004, pp. 153-165.

http://www.haworthpress.com/web/JLA
Digital Object Identifier: 10.1300/J111v41n01_12

KEYWORDS. Library instruction, distance learners, outreach, library services

A transformation is occurring in how universities teach students. New technology, changes in the makeup of student bodies, and distance learning are major components in this transformation. The potential for the adult population in the United States to participate in distance learning is great. Distance learning has become an appealing alternative for working adults with career and family responsibilities who want to enhance their education. There also exists a fast and consistent growth of jobs in occupations requiring more education and an increased number of American households that have access to technology-based instruction (*Lifelong Learning Trends*, 1998, pgs. 23, 79, 85). As part of a general effort to participate as a leader in the transformation and become significantly involved in distance learning, Texas Tech University gave high priority to the goal in its strategic plan for 2001-2005 of developing additional educational sites to meet the needs of rural Texans, utilizing advanced instructional technologies and forming regional partnerships to accomplish this goal (Texas Tech University, 2000).

About the same time that Texas Tech was developing its strategic plan, city and county governments located in the Texas Hill Country northwest of San Antonio established a Higher Education Steering Committee whose purpose was to seek cooperation from Texas' public universities in establishing educational sites in its "educationally underserved" region (Paton, 2002). The need for a higher education presence in the Hill Country had already been determined through a variety of surveys undertaken over a period of several years. In July, 2000, the Hill Country Higher Education Steering Committee approached its local state legislative delegation and presented the results of the most recently conducted market survey. This led to one of the delegates inviting representatives from all Texas state university systems to a meeting where they were encouraged to become involved in a program of higher education in the Hill Country. The Chancellor of the Texas Tech University System attended the meeting and was impressed with the level of Hill Country community support for higher education that was demonstrated at the meeting. Owing to the Chancellor's subsequent efforts, it was not long before the Texas Tech University System Board of Regents approved the establishment of off-campus programs to serve the Texas Hill Country.

However, realizing the need for more comprehensive data on potential student enrollments, Texas Tech University conducted its own survey in the fall of 2001 to determine the level of interest in higher education in the Hill Country region. Approximately 10,000 surveys were distributed, and 3,414 people responded. The largest proportion of respondents were school district employees (50 percent of all respondents), followed by high-school seniors (36 percent), community college students (6 percent), the general public (5 percent), and hospital and clinic employees (3 percent). A majority of the respondents (69 percent) indicated that they planned to take college courses in the future. The main educational goals of these respondents were to obtain a master's degree (31 percent), a bachelor's degree (28 percent), or professional certification (17 percent). The curriculum areas showing the highest level of interest in the survey were education administration and leadership, curriculum and instruction, general business, and guidance and counseling. In addition, high school seniors responding to the survey expressed considerable interest in the visual and performing arts. The results of the survey were presented to the Dean's Council and the Senior Administrative Council of Texas Tech University, and planning soon began within the Colleges of Education and Arts and Sciences to offer master's degrees in Educational Leadership and Curriculum and Instruction and a bachelor's degree in General Studies. The College of Visual and Performing Arts is presently evaluating its options for offering courses and degrees in the Hill Country (Paton, p. 4).

Not long after the survey was completed, Texas Tech University education centers were established in Fredericksburg and Marble Falls. A Hill Country site at Junction, already used for several years as a place where Texas Tech main campus students take intensive spring and summer courses, was used as a base of operations for all the activities associated with the creation of the new education sites and also was developed as a third distance learning site (Texas Tech University, 2003). Within a relatively short time, the three centers became a distributed network of classrooms, connected to each other and to the main campus in Lubbock by interactive video technology. A year-round academic program began in the summer of 2002. Today, Texas Tech University offers education and general studies programs at the Hill Country sites that build on core courses offered by its Hill Country community college partners—Austin Community College, Central Texas College, and Howard College.

LIBRARY SERVICES FOR HILL COUNTRY STUDENTS

A significant factor that will contribute to the success of these new Hill Country courses and programs is the ease with which students can accomplish the library research needed to complete the assignments their professors give them (Edge, 1995, p. 10). Texas Tech Library personnel are expected to assist Hill Country students in several ways to bring about this success. Generally, the University's library support program for distance learning includes reference services, information literacy instruction, and document delivery services. To a great extent, the successful implementation of these services depends on the library staff projecting its traditional ethos of service to the patrons to include distance learning students.

Texas Tech University Library's Distance Education Team was assigned responsibility for making sure that the library services provided Hill Country students were exemplary. The Team was established in December, 1998 to function as an advisory body to the Associate Dean of the Libraries in all matters relating to library services provided to students and faculty in the distance education programs of Texas Tech University. In addition to functioning as an advisory board, the Team has taken the lead in creating and providing library services to all distance students, including those at the recently established Hill Country sites.

An important means of providing these services to the Hill Country sites is through a Web page created by the Team and accessible from Texas Tech University Libraries' Web site (Texas Tech University Libraries, 2003). The Web page introduces Hill Country students to all the services available to them. A summary of information found on this electronic resource is also available as a printed handout. The Web page provides access to reference assistance. Distance students can submit questions on the Internet and expect to receive answers either on the same day the questions are submitted or the morning of the next workday. Additional links on the Web page provide current news about the Libraries, a staff directory, and links to Internet resources compiled by the Libraries' subject librarians. The staff directory includes e-mail links to subject librarians for those students interested in subject-specific assistance. There is also a tutorial available on how to conduct library research and online forms for document delivery requests. Both the library-owned and interlibrary loan materials that are requested using these forms can be mailed or faxed to a distance student's home or office. Distance students also have access to scanned materials placed on reserve by their instructors at the Reserve link on the Libraries' Web site, and there are countless full-text resources available on the site and throughout the Internet. Finally, renewal of books, requests for "recalls" of books and other material checked out to someone else, the provision of TexShare cards that permit the holder to borrow materials from other Texas academic libraries, and accessing personal borrowing information, such as information on books currently checked out or overdue items, are other electronic services that Texas Tech University Library provides Hill Country students.

A critical review of all library services for the Hill Country sites began shortly after the Southern Association of Colleges and Schools informed the Director of Texas Tech University-Hill Country that it would conduct an accreditation review of all its facilities and services in October, 2002. Not long after this notification, the Director of TTU Hill Country asked the Chair of the University Library's Distance Learning Team if he would be willing to visit all three TTU Hill Country centers and assist her and her staff in preparing for the library requirements listed in the SACS preparatory documentation. The Director asked that the result of this visit be a report from the Team Chair that included recommendations. The Chair agreed, received permission from the Library Dean to go, and asked some colleagues to accompany and assist him during this visit.

Two librarians visited the TTU Hill Country sites in July, 2002 to assess library resources and services available to Hill Country students, faculty, and staff. The team used the then current "SACS Criteria" as a guide in conducting its assessment. The assessment process included examining facilities, reviewing documents, and meeting with Hill Country faculty, staff, students, and regional librarians. In addition to the Texas Tech Hill Country sites, the library team visited county libraries in Kimball, Gillespie, and Burnet counties, as well as the library at Schreiner University in Kerr county.

The recommendations that the visiting Team made in their report to the Director of Texas Tech University-Hill Country were that the TTU Hill Country hire a full-time librarian to provide instruction, reference, and collection development services to Hill Country students, faculty, and staff; that small traditional print reference and reserve collections be established at all three centers; and that all TTU Hill Country undergraduate students be encouraged to take LIBR 1100, the one credit hour library research course: "Introduction to Library Research" (Hufford, 2002). In addition, the librarians on the Team volunteered to create a distance learning handout for Hill Country students that would be available on the TTU Libraries' Web site and as a printable handout. Also, until a librarian is hired to support the TTU Hill Country centers, the Team agreed to organize and give interactive television (ITV) library orientation sessions from the Lubbock campus to students and faculty in the Hill Country. These sessions began in late August of 2002.

WEB-BASED LIBRARY RESEARCH COURSE

The Library Research course (LIBR 1100) had been created six years earlier as a traditional classroom course for undergraduates, particularly freshmen. The course's goal is to introduce students to basic library research. Normally, three sections, with up to twenty-five students in each section, meet each fall and spring semester. In addition to class lectures, demonstrations, and mid-term and final exams, five of the class meetings take place in the University Library's reference room where the students are assigned practicum exercises that provide them with hands-on experience finding reference and research resources.

The LIBR 1100 course was taught successfully for several semesters because of proactive advertising to students and their advisors. The need to limit the course to three sections each semester was due more to not having enough librarians available to teach the sections than to a lack of interest on the part of students. This success and the desire to encourage more students to take the course without having to assign more librarians to teach it led to the decision to develop a Web-based version that main campus students could take for one-hour of academic credit. The Web-based version was developed using WebCT. Students taking the Web-based version can complete all the requirements of the course on their own without having to attend classes, though they are encouraged to consult with the librarians teaching the course via e-mail, office appointments, or by telephone whenever they need help. Though students determine their own schedule for completing their course work, they have to complete all assignments by the end of the semester. Most of the course work consists of reading assignments and taking online tests. However, the practicum exercises belonging to the traditional classroom course have been kept in the Web-based version. The reason for this is that the librarians who developed the Web-based version felt that students need to become familiar with print resources as well as online resources, and they need to be familiar with how a physical library is organized.

Texas Tech University Hill Country students began enrolling in the Web-based Library Research course about one semester after the course began being offered to main campus students in Lubbock, and it became immediately apparent that some changes would have to be made to accommodate Hill Country students. Because Hill Country students do not have access to a large university library like the one on Texas Tech's main campus, a large majority of the Web-based course's reading assignments and online tests were edited so that all resources discussed in the assignments were available online and all questions in the tests required the use of online resources. Three of the five practicum exercises were changed so that they also required the use of online resources to find answers; however, two of the practicum exercises that required a visit to a library remained in the course. These two practicum exercises were changed somewhat, though, so that Hill Country students could use their nearest public library, not a college library, to complete them. The librarians teaching the Web-based version felt that it was important for all students taking "Introduction to Library Research" (LIBR 1100) to go to a library and use some of the print resources. They still saw the traditional resources as an important part of library research.

PROMOTING WEB-BASED COURSE

From the very beginning when LIBR 1100 was first offered at the three Hill Country sites in June, 2002, the librarians responsible for teaching it promoted the course to Hill Country students. The two librarians who visited the Texas Tech University Hill Country in July, 2002 to help prepare for the SACS accreditation visit promoted the Web-based course to the staff, faculty, and students they met at all three sites. During the visit, the Director of the TTU-Hill Country program indicated that she thought the course should be required for all Hill Country undergraduate students and began looking into the possibility of doing that. The promotion continued from one academic term to the next as librarians talked about the Web-based course during all on-sight and Interactive Television (ITV) orientations and encouraged students to enroll. Also, the Director of TTU-Hill Country and her staff promoted the course, and Texas Tech University Library's Distance Learning Web site and handout helped to advertise it.

Any talk of making LIBR 1100 a required course ended abruptly when the Director of TTU-Hill Country was promoted to a vice provost position in the fall 2002 and moved to Lubbock where she now works on the main campus. Her increased responsibilities have precluded any plans she may have had for making the course required for all Hill Country undergraduates. Further, despite all the promotion to Hill Country students that has taken place, LIBR 1100 has attracted only two or three Hill Country students each semester since July, 2002. This low level of interest contrasts significantly with the much larger number of Texas Tech students enrolled on the main campus in Lubbock who opt to take the Web-based version of the course.

One reason why both the traditional classroom sections and the Web-based section of LIBR 1100 have been as successful as they have among students enrolled on the main campus is that librarians made a point of promoting the course via e-mail messages to undergraduate advisors on the main campus shortly before students registered for class each semester and to parents of incoming freshman students during the summer orientations for new students. This kind of direct promotion by librarians to advisors and parents has not taken place at the Hill Country sites thus far. For one thing, it would be very difficult or impossible for main campus librarians to visit the three Hill Country sites during each class registration period. Perhaps, once a full-time librarian is hired for the Hill Country sites, this approach to promoting LIBR 1100 in the Hill Country will turn out to be just as successful as it has been on the main campus.

CONCLUSION

A new Dean of the Texas Tech University Libraries was hired in 2002. One of the Dean's early decisions was to restructure some of the Libraries' departments. The Information Services Department was one of the departments that was restructured, and, since librarians from Information Services had been responsible for the Library Research course and for library services to distance learning students, the restructuring had an impact on the Web-based course, distance learning services, and staffing responsibilities in these areas. New librarians were assigned responsibility for the course, and a new group of librarians were appointed to the Distance Education Team. Some of these librarians are junior colleagues not long out of graduate school and with little or no experience in distance education. The expectation is that younger, fresher librarians will bring new ideas to the course and to services for distance learning students. The Web-based version of the course is presently being upgraded, and library services for distance learning students are also being changed.

The new librarians involved in providing support to Hill Country students have continued pursuing the goal of developing enrollment of Hill Country students in the Web-based version of the library research course. A greater effort to advertise the course to students, faculty, and staff will play a major roll in making the goal a reality. However, thus far enrollment of Hill Country students in the Web-based course is still quite low. One important reason for the low numbers is that the Hill Country sites are new. They are only a little more than a year old, and overall enrollment in classes and programs at the sites is still low. In time, as enrollment increases in Hill Country courses and programs, LIBR 1100 may also experience increased enrollment. However, this expectation (or hope) does not preclude the need for the Texas Tech University Library to conduct a high powered advertising campaign to encourage enrollment in LIBR 1100 among Hill Country students. This is what the librarians presently responsible for the Web-based version of "Introduction to Library Research" have undertaken to do.

REFERENCES

Edge, S. (1995). Library support for distance learning: The University of Louisville's experience. *Kentucky Libraries, 59,* 8-14.

Hufford, J. (2002). *Texas Tech University–Hill Country library assessment, conducted July-October 2002.* Unpublished manuscript.

Lifelong learning trends: A profile of continuing higher education (5th ed.). (1998). Washington, DC: University Continuing Education Association.

Paton, V. (2002). *Texas Tech University substantive change prospectus; Texas Tech University–Hill Country, Fredericksburg and Highland Lakes Centers.* Unpublished manuscript.

Texas Tech University. (2000). *A clear vision for the future: The strategic plan for Texas Tech University; 2001-2005.* Unpublished manuscript.

Texas Tech University. (2003). *Texas Tech University–Hill Country, history.* Retrieved September 4, 2003, from the Texas Tech University Web site: http://www.depts.ttu.edu/hillcountry/history.htm.

Texas Tech University Libraries. (2003). *Distance learning services.* Retrieved September 4, 2003, from the Texas Tech University Libraries Web site: http://library.ttu.edu/distance/.

APPENDIX

Introduction to Library Research (LIBR 1100)

Syllabus

Instructors: Professional librarians selected from the Texas Tech University Library's Information Services Dept.

Telephone: 806-742-2238 X277/(toll free) 888-270-3369

E-Mail: jon.hufford@ttu.edu

Office Hours: By appointment

Credit Hours: one

Any student who, because of a disabling condition, may require special arrangements in order to meet course requirements should contact Jon Hufford (888-270-3369; jon.hufford@ttu.edu) as soon as possible so that the necessary accommodations can be made.

COURSE EXPLANATION

The necessary skills of an information-literate person are those required to access, analyze, and use information to solve a problem or make a decision. Confusion surrounds the definition of information literacy, with some placing heavy emphasis on computer skills. Although computer literacy is vital, it is not enough. Information literacy involves making students aware of information so that they become educated information consumers. Too many students who graduate from universities today are not information-literate. This is one reason why businesses are turning to universities and demanding graduates

APPENDIX (continued)

who can identify problems and solve them creatively using the same skills that librarians have identified as information literacy skills. The course is designed to teach students these skills.

Introduction to Library Research is designed to teach students how to do research using both traditional and online library resources. Information comes in a variety of forms. The plethora of printed publications (e.g., books, newspapers, magazines) and resources available online and on microform can be overwhelming. That is why it is so important to learn which resources are most appropriate and how to find and use them. It is also important to know how to evaluate information. Introduction to Library Research has three main objectives. They are to provide an overview of the range of resources that a university library provides, to examine how several reference resources are used, and to outline a systematic plan for using these resources for a research paper or project. Only a small number of the resources available in a university library are specifically cited in the assignments. However, the librarians teaching this course can direct you to resources that are most appropriate for your specific needs.

During the course you will be reading and studying your assignments, taking quizzes related to each assignment, reviewing for the practicum tests at your local public or college library, and taking five practicum tests and two exams. Fifty percent of your grade will be based on the quizzes and practicum tests, and 50% will be based on scores received on the two exams: a short answer mid-term and a short answer final.

Please feel free to consult with the librarian assigned as the class instructor regarding any questions you have that pertain to Introduction to Library Research.

COURSE REQUIREMENTS

1) Read and study assignments, beginning with number one and moving on sequentially to number twelve.
2) Quizzes after each assignment (12 quizzes) worth 25% of grade.
3) Practicum tests at designated times during the course (5 tests) worth 25% of grade.
4) Mid-term exam (40 short answer questions covering chapters 1 through 6) worth 25% of grade.
5) Final exam (40 short answer questions covering chapters 7 through 12) worth 25% of grade.

WAYS TO STUDY FOR THE COURSE

1) Read your assignments.
2) Take the chapter quizzes.
3) Go to your local library to review the practicum tests at the end of each chapter.
4) Regularly consult with your class librarian on any questions or problems you have regarding the course.

FINAL GRADE SCHEDULE

POINT
AVERAGE GRADE

94-100 = A

90-93.9 = A–

87-89.9 = B+

84-86.9 = B

80-83.9 = B–

77-79.9 = C+

74-76.9 = C

70-73.9 = C–

67-69.9 = D+

60-66.9 = D

Below 60 = F

The following is an outline of the reading assignments:

Assignment 1 Introduction to Library Research. This assignment introduces you to the ideas, practices, and terminology involved in library research, in particular, the kind of research related to developing a term paper.

Assignment 2 Critical Evaluation of Sources. This assignment explains how to go about evaluating, from a scholarly and research point of view, the sources that you find using catalogs, indexes, abstracts, subject bibliographies, the Internet, and other reference tools.

APPENDIX (continued)

Assignment 3 The Texas Tech University Libraries' Web Page and Online Catalog. This assignment introduces you to the Libraries' online catalog. Procedures for searching the catalog by author, title, subject, and keyword; using the information found in bibliographic records; using the *Library of Congress Subject Headings* to find subject headings to search for in the catalog; developing search strategies; and using a library's Interlibrary Loan service are covered.

Assignment 4 Online Periodical Indexes and Abstracts. This assignment explains how to find magazine, newspaper, and journal articles using electronic indexes and abstracts available on the Libraries' Web page. Electronic full-text databases and some non-bibliographic electronic databases are also covered. One part of this chapter explains how to develop search strategies, and another part explains how to use the TTU Libraries' online "Periodicals database" at the "Call numbers and location of Magazines, Periodicals, and Journals at the University Library" link.

Assignment 5 Print Periodical Indexes and Abstracts. This assignment explains how to find periodical articles using indexes and abstracts in print format that are available in a typical library reference room.

Assignment 6 Using Netscape and a Search Engine to Find Information on the World Wide Web. This assignment introduces you to strategies for finding all kinds of information located on the Internet. Much of this is the same kind of information you can find in the print sources, however, you can find it faster on the Internet.

Assignment 7 Using Encyclopedias. This assignment covers general and specialized encyclopedias. It discusses the value of articles in these sources and the importance of the bibliographies which appear at the end of many of the articles.

Assignment 8 Subject Bibliographies. This assignment defines and illustrates this important kind of research source.

Assignment 9 Newspapers. This assignment describes the scope of a library's newspaper collection and illustrates the use of *Newspaper Abstracts*, an online FirstSearch database, and the *New York Times Index*, a print index. Other newspaper indexes in the library are also referred to.

Assignment 10 <u>Other Approaches to Researching Current Events</u>. This assignment identifies sources that are useful for finding out what is happening in the world. Some of the types of sources covered are news digests and summaries, biographical sources, almanacs, and yearbooks.

Assignment 11 <u>United States Government Documents</u>. The term "government documents" is defined, and use of *GPO*, an online index for identifying documents, is illustrated. Also mentioned is an important print index titled: *Monthly Catalog of U.S. Government Publications*.

Assignment 12 <u>Social and Economic Statistics</u>. Covered in this assignment are methods for finding statistics on topics in health, welfare, criminal justice, education, economics, etc. Four important statistical indexes are examined.

Research Readiness Self-Assessment:
Assessing Students' Research Skills
and Attitudes

Lana Ivanitskaya
Ryan Laus
Anne Marie Casey

Central Michigan University

SUMMARY. Librarians and learning researchers at Central Michigan University collaboratively developed an online tool that assesses how student research attitudes and perceptions correlate to their actual research skills in order to educate them about state-of-the-art library resources and prepare them to write high-quality research papers. This article describes the reasons for developing the assessment as well as the design process and technical characteristics.

KEYWORDS. Assessment, library instruction, distance learners, information literacy

INTRODUCTION

Access to information quickly and easily has become a fact of life for most people in developed countries today, through the Internet. The ease and speed with which we can find information on the latest prescription drug; buy birthday presents; conduct research for a school project; or make travel plans has

[Haworth co-indexing entry note]: "Research Readiness Self-Assessment: Assessing Students' Research Skills and Attitudes." Ivanitskaya, Lana, Ryan Laus, and Anne Marie Casey. Co-published simultaneously in *Journal of Library Administration* (The Haworth Information Press, an imprint of The Haworth Press, Inc.) Vol. 41, No. 1/2, 2004, pp. 167-183; and: *The Eleventh Off-Campus Library Services Conference Proceedings* (ed: Patrick B. Mahoney) The Haworth Information Press, an imprint of The Haworth Press, Inc., 2004, pp. 167-183.

led to the belief, held by many, that all information is available at the end of a keyboard or mouse.

This attitude among the general population to the information superhighway has developed a generation of students who bypass libraries, both real and virtual, in the belief that Google or Yahoo will reveal all they ever need to know. In spite of the fact that students are often required to participate in library instruction sessions where information literacy skills and the location of electronic peer-reviewed or scholarly materials are taught, many students seem to perform very simple research on the World Wide Web (WWW). When reference librarians instruct students in research techniques that are more advanced and assist them to find scholarly materials in licensed electronic databases, students often show surprise at the amount and complexity of research available to them.

John Lenger, a professor of journalism at the Harvard University Extension School, described an interesting experience with a class assignment (Lenger, 2002). He assigned a project designed to teach students to report in teams. He warned the students that almost no information on the subject would be found on the Internet. Yet, at the next class, he learned that most of the students had spent their time researching the subject on the Internet. He also learned that, "the youngest students had difficulty imagining a pre-Internet world . . . Researching what Harvard was like in the 1730's, for example, members of a small group had typed variations of 'Harvard in the 1730's' into a search engine, found nothing, and concluded that no records existed" (Lenger, 2002, p. 2).

During the 2000-2001 academic year a survey was administered to 180 students at Wellesley College to measure how they react to information on the Internet. The authors of the survey wrote:

> The findings were remarkable. Regarding students' reliance on the Internet, it became apparent that students are very eager to use the Internet–and only the Internet–in conducting research. Though the survey was not in any way limited to Internet resources, less than 2% of students' responses to all questions included non-Internet sources. (Graham and Metaxis, 2003, p. 72)

Historically, term paper banks and services have been available to students who chose to plagiarize for class assignments (Moore, 1988), but the ability to cut and paste information from documents on the Internet into the body of a student's research project is so easy that many students plagiarize without truly understanding what they are doing or with the idea that they won't be caught. McMurtry (2001) sums the situation up well in the following:

No longer must a student retype an entire paper just to add in a paragraph or even a footnote. No longer must a student visit a library to use a card catalog for research. But also, no longer must a student retype a paper that someone else has written in order to put their name on it. The student can just copy the text from the Web, paste it into their word processing program, type their name at the top, print it out and hand it in; or in some classes, submit it digitally to the professor online or by e-mail. (p. 1)

Twenty-five years ago, a middle school student could carry basic research skills, such as finding books through a card catalog and locating articles through indices of periodical literature, into high school, college and lifelong research because the methods remained static for so long. This is clearly no longer the case.

In the last ten years the Internet has made a wealth of information available to anyone at the end of a mouse or keyboard. Many people believe that all of the information they need is available quickly on the Internet. Yet no search engine or combination of search engines provides access to all Web pages on the Internet. In addition, most search engines have somewhat different searching protocols, vary in what they consider relevant, and do not provide access to copyrighted material that is housed behind password-protected screens (Garnsey, 2002). Several students in the Harvard journalism class admitted during a discussion about their choice to use the Internet for research, despite the professor's warnings, that, "... they were not sure how to use archives, ... [and] that using actual libraries was burdensome" (Lenger, 2002, p. 1).

In a 2000 article on the changes that the Web is making on our work and educational lives, John Seely Brown, stated:

The new literacy, beyond text and image, is one of information navigation. The real literacy of tomorrow entails the ability to be your own personal reference librarian–to know how to navigate through the confusing, complex information spaces and feel comfortable doing so. (p. 14)

In the 21st century, the real challenge for academic librarians and everyone involved in information literacy is to educate our students to understand and be familiar with the research process. This involves teaching students and other lifelong learners how to navigate through the information spaces, as Mr. Brown terms it, so that they know when the best answer is at the end of a search engine and when it is in a database that is password protected by their libraries and when it is in the microforms collection or at the fingertips of the librarian in the reference area of the library.

In distance learning programs this lack of understanding of the research process and dependence on the Internet in the isolated situations in which many distance students find themselves can be magnified. Students researching from remote locations may have fewer opportunities for reference consultations, in which they may learn better research skills. In addition, a significant number of distance learners are older than the traditional college age and feel anxiety about asking for reference assistance since they believe they should already know how to conduct research efficiently.

At Central Michigan University (CMU), students enrolled in off-campus and distance learning courses through the College of Extended Learning (CEL) receive library services from a special unit dedicated to their needs, Off-Campus Library Services (OCLS). OCLS librarians incorporate a library instruction session into the required research classes of the Master of Arts in Education (MAE) and Masters of Science in Administration (MSA) programs, as well as into a variety of other undergraduate and graduate classes with research projects. With the exception of the Web-based courses where instruction is done via an online synchronous discussion, using chat software, all instruction is done face-to-face in the classrooms where the students take classes or in nearby computer labs. Librarians also provide reference assistance by phone, e-mail, and chat. The OCLS Document Delivery Office (DDO) loans books and provides copies of articles by mail, fax, and electronically to students enrolled in CEL courses.

The OCLS librarians had experienced a 25% drop in reference statistics over a three-year period ending in June 2000. Anecdotal evidence from professors was revealing that more students seemed to be using only Internet search engines for research purposes. Since all master's degree students and a majority of undergraduate students received at least one library instruction session in their programs, the OCLS librarians were searching for other ways to instruct students. Often librarians were learning from students in reference interviews that they had turned to OCLS as a last resort after all of the Internet searches had failed to yield the research materials that professors were requiring. A significant number of students, who had participated in a library instruction session that was geared to learning how to complete a specific class assignment, expressed a complete lack of understanding of the assignment during reference interviews conducted less than a week after the library instruction presentation. The impression that the librarians were receiving was that students thought they knew how to conduct research but often lacked basic information literacy skills. Because students' perceptions of their own information-seeking skills were often inflated, they apparently did not see the need to pay close attention to librarians in instruction sessions or to avail themselves of reference services.

In preliminary discussions about constructing a survey to determine students' library instruction needs, the OCLS librarians hoped to find an assessment tool that would measure areas where skills were lacking rather than measure only whether students knew how to use a library. In a cursory review of the literature, many of the sample library instruction pretests and posttests that we examined appeared to measure objective outcomes such as understanding how to use an online catalog or how to locate a periodical article. Although measuring these skill levels was important, the OCLS librarians also wanted to assess students' perceptions of their abilities to effectively use library resources and their understanding of the research process. Many of us believed that a significant number of students tuned us out during our instruction sessions because they perceived that they knew all there was to know about an effective research process using library resources. We thought that if we could devise an assessment tool that would help students to understand areas in which their skills were lacking, they would be motivated to pay attention in library instruction classes and to use reference services more effectively.

In the summer of 2000, OCLS approached the Center for Adult Learning (CRAL) in CEL to discuss creating an assessment tool that would measure students' information seeking skills and perceptions of their own abilities. CEL, which was established in 1971, delivers degree programs and courses to students off-campus in over 60 centers throughout North America as well as through Web-based courses. CRAL oversees all research activities in the College, including the creation of assessment tools.

In the initial discussions between staff in OCLS and CRAL, the groups decided to develop an online Research Readiness Self-Assessment tool (RRSA). This tool would be designed to help students assess their skills based on the *Information Literacy Competency Standards for Higher Education* (ACRL, 2000). Students would be asked to complete several problems and respond to questions that would reveal research skills in which they were strong and others in which they were weak. The results of the assessment would be delivered to the students within a short time of completion. In addition, when specific skill deficiencies were identified, students would be directed to explanations and places to go for further instruction. The ultimate outcome of this assessment tool would be to alert students to areas in which they needed to improve their research readiness skills in order to successfully complete a degree program and to be lifelong learners as well as to direct students to Web-based instruction and to OCLS for help in the areas in which they showed lack of skills.

INITIAL STAGES OF RRSA DESIGN
AND AN OVERVIEW OF RRSA CONTENT

The RRSA instrument was designed in multiple stages, beginning with a comprehensive literature review of information literacy competencies and conceptual models that provide a framework for the development of information skills. At the same time, we conducted a focus group to gather input from the OCLS librarians. The librarians shared information regarding specific skills that differentiated advanced information users from novices and provided critical incidents that illustrated particularly effective and ineffective strategies for finding and evaluating information resources.

The literature review, combined with the findings from a focus group, led to the formulation of key skills and attitudes that were targeted by the assessment. Over the next several months, we designed three classes of assessment items: (1) multiple choice questions, (2) skill-based problems, and (3) measures of students' attitudes (e.g., attitudes toward the use of the general Internet and attitudes related to requesting help from reference librarians). For a complete list of measures included in RRSA see Table 1.

The multiple-choice questions included in RRSA represented several knowledge domains, ranging from research-related terminology to identification of plagiarized sentences. For example, students are asked to select correct definitions of commonly used concepts, such as a bibliography or an abstract. In addition, the students are provided with a direct quote and asked to identify its plagiarized versions–passages that make use of the same idea without the proper acknowledgement of its source.

The skill-based problems require a test taker to demonstrate information skills by manipulating databases, evaluating the quality of multiple published documents, and conducting database searches that require them to employ multiple search strategies.

In addition to multiple-choice questions and skill-based problems, RRSA incorporates attitudinal measures. An attitude is defined as a state of mind or feeling with regard to the use of the general Internet or a disposition to seek librarians' assistance. The decision to measure attitudes was motivated by the following characteristics of attitudes:

1. *Attitudes are demonstrated through behaviors.* For instance, students who hold strong attitudes regarding the usefulness of information found on the Internet may refer to the general Internet for all of their research needs.
2. *Attitudes are learned through experience and, once formed, may not change easily.* For example, a learner who has recently discovered the

vast amount of documents available via the Internet may accept a position that "the Internet is the most sophisticated library that offers quality information at one's fingertips," leading him or her to be a reluctant user of traditional or virtual libraries.

3. *Negative attitudes can be changed through new experiences or when one encounters evidence that conflicts his or her mental position.* RRSA can be used as a diagnostic tool to detect attitudes that have negative implications and to provide students with corrective feedback.

Next, the initial draft of an online assessment was reviewed by Subject Matter Experts (SMEs), represented by experienced librarians and university professors who taught research intensive classes. Following a review of SMEs' comments and a small-scale pilot test, RRSA was revised to address specific concerns related to item wording and to resolve some technical issues.

TABLE 1. Research Readiness Components: Skills and Attitudes Measured by RRSA

Skill or attitude	Definition
Online research skills	Ability to use online library catalogue, online library databases (e.g., FirstSearch) and their Boolean operators.
Knowledge of information resources	Ability to identify and use best scholarly resources, knowledge of terminology (e.g., abstract and bibliography) and citation rules.
Understanding of plagiarism and copyright issues	Ability to identify plagiarism and copyright violations.
Attitudes toward Internet research	Measures the extent to which a student relies on the Internet and search engines (e.g., Yahoo and Google) to obtain scholarly resources for class research projects (e.g., papers, research assignments).
Evaluation of information	Ability to evaluate the quality of full-text articles from scholarly journals.
Motivation to supplement readings	Motivation to supplement instructor-assigned readings with additional materials.
Frequency of library use	Contacts with librarians, access to OCLS Web site, use of document delivery services, and general use of libraries.
Likelihood of contacting a librarian	Likelihood of contacting a reference librarian.
Research experience	Writing papers, citing sources, using bibliographies, encyclopedias, periodical indexes and subject headings, summarizing ideas and other research behaviors.

At the same time, an online feedback function was added that provided immediate, individualized information on assessment takers' skills in a variety of areas, such as knowledge of information resources, understanding of plagiarism, database search skills, evaluation of information, and self-reported reliance on the Internet search engines (see Table 2 for sample feedback given upon completion of RRSA).

MULTIDISCIPLINARY
AND HEALTH PROFESSIONS VERSIONS OF RRSA

Because there was a need to test students in a variety of disciplines, two versions of RRSA were created, one for the Health Professions students and one for a diverse group of students most of whom specialized in Administration or Education. In the summer of 2003, an *RRSA-Health Professions* version was administered to a group of 26 students entering a Doctoral program in Health Administration at CMU and an *RRSA-Multidisciplinary* version was administered to 95 individuals. The majority of these students were enrolled in the required research class of the MSA program at CMU off-campus centers in suburban Detroit and Flint, Michigan, Ohio, Hawaii, and California. The remainder consisted of a small group of undergraduate library student employees who participated in two stress tests and one entry level undergraduate class at a CMU off-campus center in suburban Detroit. Most of the students participated in a library instruction class after taking the RRSA so were able to discuss their results with OCLS librarians and provide feedback. Individual responses were recorded in a database and subjected to statistical analyses. Based on the findings, two items were eliminated and 14 other items were revised in order to ensure clarity, to provide an exhaustive list of responses, and to increase item difficulty. Analyses of descriptive statistics resulted in the fine-tuning of written feedback messages displayed upon the completion of RRSA. In particular, we were able to establish preliminary norms and create personalized feedback, corresponding to three levels of performance (top third, middle third, and bottom third).

VALIDATION OF RRSA

Validation is an evaluation of the accuracy or appropriateness of drawing inferences from RRSA scores. Although a thorough evaluation of RRSA will not be complete until a large number of students will have taken the assessment, we conducted several preliminary evaluations of RRSA.

TABLE 2. An Example of Immediate Feedback Provided upon RRSA Completion

Skill or attitude	Example of feedback (is determined by the level of performance)
Online research skills	Your score has indicated that your online research skills may not be as strong as you need in order to successfully conduct research in college. Understanding some of the techniques for efficient searching, such as how to choose the right databases for a particular topic and how to find out which terms are used in a particular database will help you to find more precise information more quickly.
Knowledge of information resources	Congratulations! You have demonstrated knowledge of information sources. You are able to identify and use the best scholarly resources, understand terminology, and cite information correctly. This knowledge will help you to find information more efficiently, identify the research that is being published on your topic, and cite your references professionally.
Understanding of plagiarism and copyright issues	Your score has indicated that you may not thoroughly understand what constitutes plagiarism or a violation of copyright law. These are serious issues. Plagiarism can be anything from incorrectly citing a reference to turning in a paper that someone else has written. It can be intentional or unintentional. Many people do not understand how much information is protected under copyright law. Making multiple copies of pages from books or articles or copies of music or videos to give to others is an infringement of the copyright law. Plagiarizing or breaking copyright law, whether or not it is done intentionally, may subject you to some serious consequences, such as losing credit for the course in which you are enrolled or paying legal fines.
Attitudes toward Internet research	Congratulations! You have shown that you understand that there are a wide range of resources available on the Internet to help with your research. You are able to distinguish between general search engines on the WWW and password protected databases that offer you access to scholarly and research articles. This will help you find appropriate articles from the many online databases that are licensed by CMU for your use.
Evaluation of information	Your score has indicated that you have some knowledge about the evaluation of information gathered in the research process. You may know that peer-reviewed journals are generally a good source of accurate research findings and the opinions of experts in the field. You may know it is important to verify the accuracy of the information you have found or establish the authority of the author, but you probably do not routinely evaluate the material by all of the criteria necessary to consistently find the most accurate resources for your research project. It is important to know if the author of the piece you are using is someone with experience in the field and to find out how the information was developed. Some of the questions you can ask when evaluating the literature you find on a topic are: Is there information on the author that sets out his/her expertise in the field? Are the sources for factual information listed clearly so they can be verified in other sources? If you are using an article, is it from a peer-reviewed journal? It may take a little more time to be sure that the information you are using has been written based on research or by someone with known expertise in the field. It is worthwhile to do this because the quality of your research projects will be better.

TABLE 2 (continued)

Skill or attitude	Example of feedback (is determined by the level of performance)
Motivation to supplement readings	Your score indicates that you may do some supplemental readings but do not do them for all of the classes in which they are recommended. Supplemental readings often can provide a more thorough background on the subjects taught in the class. By reading extra material, you may gain a more solid knowledge of the subject matter by the end the class.
Frequency of library use	Your score indicates that you do not use libraries or virtual libraries often. You may tend to rely on free Internet search engines for much of your research. Libraries purchase or license print and electronic books, journals, and other sources of information that support the curricula of their institutions. Much of what you need to research is generally available freely and more easily through your library.
Likelihood of contacting a librarian	Your score shows that you are not likely to contact a reference librarian whenever you have questions on your research projects. Many students assume that they know how to conduct research effectively and efficiently on their own. This is probably true in some cases and not in others. Students also hesitate to contact librarians for fear of being perceived as ignorant. Resources in libraries, especially online resources, change at a dramatically quick pace. Reference librarians are information professionals who, as part of their jobs, learn about these changes and are able to teach them to researchers. Reference librarians also have ready information on the correct terminology to use in setting up the most effective search strategies and are able to assist students to find the exact information they need quickly. Please consider consulting your reference librarian for help on future research assignments. They will help you to conduct your research efficiently and save you much time and aggravation.
Research experience	Your score indicates that you do not have extensive research experience. The more practice you have in using any research resource, the more accomplished you will be. Your research experience will help you to be more effective in your coursework.

First, we examined content validity of the instrument. Content validity is the degree to which RRSA covers all of the competencies essential to research readiness and information literacy. For the purposes of RRSA development and evaluation, we adopted the American Library Association's definition of information literacy. The Presidential Committee on Information Literacy of the American Library Association defined information literacy as the ability to "recognize when information is needed and have the ability to locate, evaluate, and use effectively the needed information" (American Library Association, 1989, p. 1). The concept of research readiness encompasses information literacy within a specific knowledge domain (e.g., an academic discipline) deemed essential for locating, evaluating, and using that discipline's body of research. Throughout RRSA development, care was taken to ensure that the assessment contained a representative sample of questions or problems covering all information literacy competency standards, as outlined by ACRL (2000). Judgments by two independent evaluators were used to determine if RRSA had a mix of items covering each standard within the context of a specific discipline. Additional items were written for underrepresented competency standards.

Concurrent criterion-related validity was investigated by correlating student scores on the assessment with proxy measures of library use and information skills. For example, we expected RRSA items that measured knowledge of information resources and database search skills would correlate *positively* with exposure to library instructional services. On the other hand, these items should correlate *negatively* with self-ratings of the extent to which the Internet Search engines (e.g., Yahoo and Google) provided everything one needs for writing scholarly research reviews. The obtained correlations were statistically significant and in the expected direction. Our preliminary validity studies led to generally positive conclusions regarding the instrument's ability to discriminate between advanced users of scholarly resources and novices who generally rely on the Web search engines. It would be important, however, to replicate these initial findings on a larger and more diverse group of assessment takers.

One of the outcomes of the validation was a redesign of the individualized feedback. In its present form, the written feedback on one's performance in several categories is referenced against the performance of the 95 people who completed this assessment in the past.

In sum, the complex and rigorous design of the RRSA tool led to the creation of an online application that provides students with an opportunity to check their skill level by completing an assessment that combines a survey and a skill test, to receive immediate feedback on areas of strength and weakness, and to obtain a list of resources for self-study.

RRSA TECHNICAL OVERVIEW

The original construction of the RRSA Web-based assessment began in 2001. During the planning phases, it was decided that RRSA needed to meet three criteria:

1. The program must have real world adaptability
2. Have an easy to use administrative interface for modifying users, questions, and score measuring scales
3. Be portable enough so that it could work on various server operating systems without large modifications.

In order to achieve these goals, it was decided that RRSA should be programmed in PERL/CGI. CGI is one of the most widely used scripting languages on the Internet. It is very platform-neutral, meaning platforms such as Windows, Linux, MacOS, Solaris, and many more, have no problem interpreting the language. Best of all, CGI is very easy to learn. PERL is used for creating the dynamic Web pages and works hand-in-hand with CGI. PERL also excels in tasks like database interaction, form field validation, and text parsing.

After choosing the programming language, the next logical step was selecting the operating system for the server. There are a variety of OS choices available, all with distinct advantages and disadvantages, including Windows 2000, Windows XP, Linux, and Solaris. In the end, Linux won out. Linux is a free, open-source, and very powerful OS that has a wide range of capabilities. The system requirements for Linux are also considerably less than other operating systems like Windows or Solaris so Linux can run fine on an older machine which saves money when compared to upgrading a server or purchasing a brand new one. Because Linux is open source, it has an abundance of documentation and support via the Web, making it easier to troubleshoot and fix any problems with little effort. The Linux commands are very similar to any of the other UNIX-like operating systems, so chances are if a person is familiar with the commands to a UNIX-like operating system, the same or similar commands can be applied on Linux.

Once we had our programming language and OS in mind, we needed a database program to store all of the information for RRSA and serve as the backbone for the program. Like OSs, there are a number of database servers available. Since we decided on Linux, Microsoft's SQL Server was immediately ruled out. Oracle also had prohibitively high costs associated with it. Oracle and MS-SQL server are both very powerful database servers that would have easily handled our needs, but also are very expensive. Instead, we choose to use MySQL as our database server. Also a free, open source program, MySQL is able to run on a variety of platforms such as Windows, IBM AIX, Linux, Solaris, HP-UX, and many others. MySQL also has the security conscious administrator in mind, giving the administrator tight control over users and various database table permissions. Documentation is also excellent and can be viewed via the Web, as well as user forum with solutions to common problems and questions.

With everything else in place, we needed just one final piece to put it all together, a Web server. Again, since we were dealing with a Linux box, Microsoft's IIS was not a viable option. The Apache HTTP server was the only logical choice. Like all of the other pieces of software used so far, Apache is open source and free to download. Currently, Apache is the most widely used Web server, accounting for over 63% of all Web servers. It also runs on various platforms such as Linux, IRIX, Windows, and IBM AIX. Documentation and support for Apache are also excellent, making it easy to solve most problems that arise.

The RRSA project has had several programmers over its long history. Sherzod Ruzmetov did the original programming for the RRSA project in 2000, which included the design of the administrative interface, implementation of the scales, and interfacing the Web pages with the MySQL database. The main challenge at this point was the creation of a simple, but user friendly administrative interface that would allow someone with limited programming knowledge to make changes and maintain the RRSA assessment. The result was a menu driven interface that gave the administrator control of almost every aspect of the RRSA assessment, including questions, e-mail responses, and even how the scores were calculated. It also allowed the user to view the overall results for each person that took the test and to download an Excel file of the results for later analysis.

Kedar Apsangikar picked up where Sherzod left off in the summer of 2002. He worked on ways to download the user results from the survey and also fixed the many bugs that still plagued the program after Sherzod left. Xinxin Wu and Ryan Laus took over the main programming duties in February 2003. They were able to successfully create a downloadable Excel file that could be plugged into SPSS to analyze the results of the survey. They also implemented a security system for the administrative module so that only specified people could perform administration functions to the assessment. They also fixed numerous bugs that cropped up during live testing with the students.

Our current environment for the RRSA assessment is as follows:

OS: AIX 4.3.3
PERL 5.6.0

MySQL 4.0.15
Apache 2.0.47
Server: IBM RISC 6000, 43P Model

The RRSA program itself is fairly small, only requiring about 10 MB of hard drive space. Like any database, as more users and data are added, the greater the space requirements of RRSA. Still, even with a large amount of data in the database, the RRSA program will probably never grow to more than 50-100 MB. With everything in place, RRSA should be able to handle at least 30 simultaneous users on a moderately powerful system.

In order to ensure the smooth operation of RRSA, the systems administrator should have several key skills to help him solve some of the various problems that may creep up from time to time. First, the administrator needs to be familiar with programming in PERL/CGI. Sometimes a change might need to be made to the way the program functions, so not knowing at least a small amount of PERL/CGI could lead to inefficiencies. Second, the administrator should be familiar with using SQL commands. This will come in handy if data somehow becomes corrupted in the database and the administrator needs to manually delete records or even whole tables from within the database. Lastly, the administrator needs to make sure that the database information is backed up on a regular basis. In our current setup at CMU, our database files are backed up on a daily basis. If this is done properly, the administrator should be able to tackle many of the problems that could occur from RRSA.

USES FOR RESEARCH READINESS SELF ASSESSMENT (RRSA)

The RRSA can be used in a variety of ways to enhance the education process. In its initial conception, the tool was developed as a means to help off-campus graduate students measure their information seeking skills and attitudes in an attempt to guide them to available library services when they were needed. To some degree this proved successful in the trials conducted in CEL classes in the summer of 2003. All of the OCLS librarians who offered library instruction sessions to students who were required to take the RRSA reported that at least one student in each class discussed being surprised at a lower than expected level of knowledge, which motivated them to pay attention to the library instruction session (M. C. Craig, personal communication, July 23, 2003, D. P. Gall, personal communication, June 16, 2003, and P. B. Mahoney, personal communication, June 30, 2003 and July 16, 2003).

The RRSA is a versatile tool that can easily be adapted to specific disciplines and to different levels of students. Since it measures skills and attitudes, it can be readily used as a pretest and posttest. Students receive feedback on their achievement in a number of areas that are made up of a combination of questions. They do not receive the answers to individual questions so there is very little chance that the memorization of correct answers from the pretest will skew the results of the posttest.

Although the focus of the first two versions of the RRSA has been to measure information seeking skills in order to encourage students to take better advantage of available library services in order to increase their research abilities, the assessment has wider applications. As higher education embraces the concepts of outcome assessment more thoroughly, a tool such as RRSA can offer a valuable way to measure the teaching outcome of any research oriented class. It is very simple to administer because the student takes it in his or her own time and receives immediate feedback.

CONCLUSION

The RRSA is a versatile tool that can be adapted easily in many educational assessment situations. The RRSA program can also be ported to a number of different operating systems such as Unix, Linux, or AIX, making it technologically feasible for most academic institutions to implement. Since RRSA does not have steep hardware requirements and uses open source software, the startup costs of RRSA will be minimal. Within the libraries at CMU, we have begun discussion with the acting Instruction Librarian to adapt a version of the RRSA to be used as a pretest and posttest for LIB 197, the one-credit library instruction class offered on campus. In addition, OCLS librarians plan to expand the use of RRSA into other research classes and have begun conversations with colleagues in CEL about using the RRSA more broadly to assess academic outcomes. As many new students complete RRSA, we continue to fine-tune the assessment and gather evidence regarding its validity.

REFERENCES

American Library Association. (1989). *Presidential committee on information literacy: Final report.* Chicago: Author.

Association of College and Research Libraries (ACRL). (2000, January 18). *Information literacy competency standards for higher education.* Retrieved September 10, 2003, from http://www.ala.org/Content/NavigationMenu/ACRL/Standards_and_Guidelines/Objectives_for_Information_Literacy_Instruction__A_Model_Statement_for_Academic_Librarians.htm.

Bar-Ilan, J. (2002). How much information do search engines disclose on the links to a web page? A longitudinal case study of the 'cybermetrics' home page. *Journal of Information Science, 28*(6), 455-466.

Benefiel, C. R., & Jaros, J. (1989). Planning and testing a self-guided taped tour in an academic library. *RQ, 29*(2), 199-208.

Bodi, S. (2002). How do we bridge the gap between what we teach and what they do? Some thoughts on the place of questions in the process of research [Electronic version]. *The Journal of Academic Librarianship, 28*(3), 109-14.

Brown, J. S. (2000). Growing up digital: How the Web changes work, education, and the ways people learn. *Change, 32*(2), 11-20.

Budd, J. M. (2001). Information seeking in theory and practice: Rethinking public services in libraries. *Research and User Services Quarterly, 40*(3), 256-63.

Bundy, A. (2000, February). *Drowning in information, starved for knowledge: Information literacy, not technology, is the issue.* Paper presented at the 10th VALA Conference, Melbourne, Australia. Retrieved July 5, 2001 from http://www.library.unisa.edu.au/PAPERS/drowning.htm.

Central Michigan University Library Off-Campus Library Services Guide. (2002). Retrieved July 30, 2002 from Central Michigan University, Off-Campus Library Services Web site: http://ocls.cmich.edu/htmlguide.htm.

Coombs, M., & Houghton, J. (1995). Information skills for new entry tertiary students: Perceptions and practices. *Australian Academic and Research Libraries, 26*, 260-70.

Copyright basics. (n.d.). Retrieved July 30, 2002 from the Library of Congress, Copyright Office Web site: http://www.copyright.gov/circs/circ1.html.

DuMond, J., O'Brien, J. P., & Paoletti, R. (2001, June). *Developing expectations for information literacy competencies.* Paper presented at the AAHE Assessment Conference, Denver, CO.

Fenske, R. F., & Clark, S. E. (1995). Incorporating library instruction in a general education program for college freshmen. *RSR: Reference Services Review, 23*(3), 69-74.

Fister, B. (1992). The research processes of undergraduate students. *Journal of Academic Librarianship, 18*, 163-9.

Fowler, R. (1990). *Assessment of library skills and traits of entering and lower level English students, Northern Michigan University, Olson Library.* Marquette, MI: Northern Michigan University. (ERIC Document Reproduction Service No. ED339370).

Garnsey, M. R. (2002). What distance learners should know about information retrieval on the World Wide Web. *The Reference Librarian, 77*, 19-30.

Goett, J. A., & Foote, K. E. (2000). Cultivating student research and study skills in Web-based learning environments. *Journal of Geography in Higher Education, 24*(1), 92-99.

Graham, L., & Metaxis, P. (2003). Of course it's true; I saw it on the Internet! Critical thinking in the Internet era. *Communications of the ACM, 46*(5), 71-75.

He, P. (1996). What are they doing with the Internet? *Internet Reference Services Quarterly, 1*, 31-51.

Hinchcliffe, L. (1998). *Cut and paste plagiarism: Preventing, detecting and tracking online plagiarism.* Retrieved July 30, 2002 from http://alexia.lis.uiuc.edu/~janicke/plagiary.htm.

Koehler, B., & Swanson, K. (1988). ESL students and bibliographic instruction: Learning yet another language. *Research Strategies, 6*(4), 148-160.

Lenger, J. (2002). Research: If a tree doesn't fall on the Internet, does it really exist? [Electronic version]. *Columbia Journalism Review, 41*(3), 74.

Lindauer, B. G. (1988, Winter). Rethinking instructional assumptions in an age of computerized information access. *Research Strategies, 6,* 4-7.

McCarthy, C. A. (1995). Students' perceived effectiveness using the university library. *College & Research Libraries, 56*(3), 221-34.

McMurtry, K. (2001). E-cheating: Combating a 21st century challenge [Electronic version]. *T.H.E. Journal, 29*(4), 36-41.

Moore, T. H. (1998, November 9). Colleges try new ways to thwart companies that sell term papers. *The Chronicle of Higher Education,* A1, A36.

Rasmussen, E. M. (2003). Indexing and retrieval for the Web. *Annual Review of Information Science and Technology, 37,* 91-124.

Taylor, D. C. (1989). Undergraduates use of periodicals–Implications for library reference work. *The Reference Librarian, 27-28,* 51-65.

Tiefel, V. M. (1991, October). The Gateway to Information: A system defines how libraries are used: Ohio State University's knowledge-based "Gateway" offers access with unprecedented ease. *American Libraries, 22,* 858-60.

Toifel, R. C., & Franklin, G. (1998-1999). Using technology to teach preservice students about locating information in the academic library. *Journal of Educational Technology Systems, 27*(2), 133-145.

Ury, C. J., Johnson, C. V., & Meldrem, J. A. (1997, Winter). Teaching a heuristic approach to information retrieval. *Research Strategies, 15,* 39-47.

User Access to Services Committee, RUSA Machine-Assisted Reference Section. (2001). Users' information-seeking behavior: What are they doing?: A bibliography. *Reference & User Services Quarterly, 40*(3), 240-50.

Web search evaluation checklist. (n.d.). Retrieved July 30, 2002 from University of Louisville Libraries, Information Literacy Program Web site: http://www.louisville.edu/infoliteracy/evaluate.htm.

Creating a Library CD
for Off-Campus Students

Marie F. Jones

East Tennessee State University

SUMMARY. During 2002, the Extended Campus Services Librarian and the Instruction Librarian at East Tennessee State University created tutorials that were compiled on a CD to be distributed to online students. This workshop presents a simple process using PowerPoint to create interactive HTML-based tutorials, as well as menu and auto-run programming specific to use on a CD. Discussion of the other technologies used for the CD (Dreamweaver for Web editing and customizing open source tutorials from TILT) is included. An overview of the pedagogical theory underlying tutorial design is provided, and the rationale and distribution method for the CD-ROM format is discussed.

KEYWORDS. Technology, distance learners, library instruction, distance education

BACKGROUND

The Setting

East Tennessee State University is a regional state university with approximately 11,000 students, and over 5,000 who take off-campus courses. The Extended Campus Services (ECS) department consists of one full-time pro-

[Haworth co-indexing entry note]: "Creating a Library CD for Off-Campus Students." Jones, Marie F. Co-published simultaneously in *Journal of Library Administration* (The Haworth Information Press, an imprint of The Haworth Press, Inc.) Vol. 41, No. 1/2, 2004, pp. 185-202; and: *The Eleventh Off-Campus Library Services Conference Proceedings* (ed: Patrick B. Mahoney) The Haworth Information Press, an imprint of The Haworth Press, Inc., 2004, pp. 185-202.

http://www.haworthpress.com/web/JLA
Digital Object Identifier: 10.1300/J111v41n01_14

fessional librarian, whose office is located on the main campus, two staff members who work at a branch library at an off-campus site, and a number of student workers. There is no dedicated ECS budget, and many services are provided by way of other departments in the main library.

Because of the budgetary and staff limitations, as the ECS librarian, I've worked hard to create relationships with administrative units across campus, in hopes of using those connections to enhance services to our students. In this case, my networking attempts paid off with cooperative arrangements where other departments paid for the distribution of the CD.

WHY A CD?

For a number of years, I have been working closely with our instruction librarian to create online tutorials for library resources. Our idea was that these tutorials would be available at any time for any student, on or off-campus, and that they would be particularly useful for training students in online courses. Most of these tutorials are already available on our library's website, in one form or another (see http://sherrod.etsu.edu/tutorials/tutorialshome.htm). However, we realize that our students and our campus have perpetual bandwidth problems, and that packaging the tutorials on the CD could act as a PR device as well as a training tool. We reasoned that students are not likely to come to the library Web site to see what's available without some outside impetus; however, if we send them a CD in the mail with other documents, they might pop it into their computer and give it a look. Alternatively, they can add the CD to their collection of AOL disks and create some really great art. Seriously, I believe in hitting them in as many venues as possible in order to try to catch their attention and let them know what the library has to offer.

The CD idea was part of a joint project with our faculty mentoring center (FMC). ETSU has no instructional technology designers on tap for faculty or others to use to help create instructional materials for online or on-ground courses. Instead, the Faculty Mentoring Center works with faculty one-on-one in the use of technology for improved instruction. The FMC, with the assistance of faculty members on campus, develops online training modules including modules on the appropriate use of multimedia in Internet-based instruction, training modules on Web-based resources, and creates tutorials and resources to help students successfully access and succeed in Internet-based and Web-enhanced courses. This project was part of the center's goal to create resources for students, and is part of the FMC's ongoing program to involve faculty in developing materials.

PLANNING THE CD

I'm a theory glutton. I like to read widely as I start any project that's new to me, to learn a bit of what others have said that relates to what I'm doing, and to give me a basis from which to start. For a number of reasons, around the time I started this project, I had been reading a lot of educational theory related to educational technology and teaching using technology. The ideas behind the design of this CD, therefore, were grounded in a number of theorist's work. The pedagogy involved is also based in adult learning theory, which I believe is important when working with the predominantly adult student body that participates in many of our off-campus programs.

Based primarily in Gagne's and Brigg's (1974) "Nine Events of Instruction," each tutorial includes the following components:

Event 1: Get Their Attention

In the Information Processing Model, the first step in processing information is selection. We want people to see what we want them to see, and to pay attention to the information that we think is important so that they can then organize the information they receive, integrate it into what they know, and move it from short-term to long-term memory. In order to do that, we organize our online lectures in ways that catch attention before cognition is consciously engaged, and that continue to keep attention once conscious attention is engaged (Fleming & Levie, 1993).

Pre-Attention Strategies

- *Use a horizontal-vertical orientation*. Readers tend to follow horizontal or vertical orientations more easily than diagonal orientations. English readers tend to look from left to right.
- *Carefully select changes*. Changes in color, texture, size, and placement grab attention. Use such changes judiciously to put attention where you want it, but without making too many changes that overload the senses.
- *Draw clear boundaries*. Make sure that it is easy to differentiate between objects in the foreground and objects in the background. High contrast makes it easier to pick out what is the important information; lower contrast allows text or images to recede into the background. High contrast is also helpful to the visually impaired.
- *Visually organize into meaningful parts*. A designer can direct the eye through appropriate groupings of items which go together, organizing

content into units. This organization affects the way cognitive processes operate and help learners to keep related items together in memory.

Voluntary Attention Strategies

- *Avoid irrelevant information.* One of the hardest things for many of us to do is to simplify processes by leaving out irrelevant information. You can always add detail once a basic framework is in place, but students will tune out very quickly if there is too much detail that seems overwhelming.
- *Draw attention by using contrast.* Related to the pre-attention point above, it's important to use layout, color, and fonts to draw attention where you need it.
- *Avoid extremes.* Although contrast draws attention, extremes can also cause people to tune out, or to be so jarred that they pay attention only to the extreme medium, not the content. Sounds should not be too high or too low, colors not too bright or too dull, textures not too smooth or rough.
- *Use composition, lines, and arrows to control order.*
- *Cluster related pieces of information.* Memory research indicates that people optimally process seven pieces of data at a time. If individual parts are clustered together, then more information can be learned, with seven clusters of items rather than seven individual items (Doerner, n.d.).
- *Don't overload the number of attention-getting strategies used in a single presentation.* Attention theory also talks about the fact that if there are too many stimuli, people can't pay attention to any of them. For example, if you vary your fonts in every slide, there is no single thing to which attention is drawn. However, if you are consistent in using larger fonts for headings and smaller fonts for sub-headings, with the same typeface throughout, but vary color and font style on one very important point, then you will draw more attention to that point than if you had varied many things throughout the presentation.

Event 2: Inform Them of the Learning Objectives for the Tutorial

Letting learners know what they should expect to learn during a particular session functions in a few ways. First, it lets them know what's most important in the coming lecture, and alerts them to pay attention to those items that fit those learning objectives. Second, it becomes a way to introduce concepts without being boringly repetitive. A speech teacher I had once used to say:

"Tell them what you're going to say, say it, and tell them what you said–but try not to let them know that you're repeating yourself."

Third, if your objectives are good, the students will be able to see a direct correlation between what they're about to learn and how they will apply that learning to everyday life. According to Knowles (1984), the practical application of learning is of particular importance to adult learners. Since many of our off-campus students are adults with a vast store of experience and responsibilities beyond the classroom, it is particularly important that we engage them in the learning process early on in the tutorial. Providing concrete objectives that are likely to appeal to adults is one way of engaging them.

Event 3: Recall Prior Knowledge

Memory theory indicates that we process information better when we can connect it and synthesize it with what we already know. For adult learners, who have much experience to draw on, it is particularly important to connect to that experience. Recalling prior knowledge is easier in a classroom setting, where you can ask individuals if they remember a particular event, or where you can connect with a specific class assignment. In a generic tutorial, it is more difficult to find ways to recall prior knowledge. However, some ways of making these connections include:

- Use popular culture references as search examples
- If you know you are working with a largely older population, draw parallels between library research in a print-based environment (paper indexes, card catalogs) to those of the online environment (databases, OPACs)
- Use regional or local examples that students will relate to

Events 4 and 5: Present Material and Provide Guided Learning

I see Gagne's events four and five as being inextricably intertwined (although I'm sure Gagne would disagree), so both are included here. While presenting the material may be more about organizing content, and guided learning may be more about interactivity, these two things become woven together in practice. While you're presenting the material you want them to learn, you need to keep the learners' attention and keep their brains as actively engaged in the learning process as possible. We used a variety of strategies to keep students attentive to the material and to help them learn it along the way, including using multimedia, organizing the presentations with care, cutting out irrelevant details, and using humor.

Use Multimedia

Different media types cause various parts of the brain to respond in different ways. Moving images gain attention and may stimulate particular areas of the brain for enhanced learning (cf. Gerlic and Jausovec, 1999). And individuals each have a learning style which responds differently to various kinds of learning stimuli (cf. Gardner, 1985). Some learn more from visual stimulus and others from auditory stimulus. Therefore, using a variety of types of media, including text, moving images, and sound, will probably help increase learning, as long as the media is not overused (in which case, it causes sensory overload).

For practical reasons, we chose not to use much audio in our tutorials. We included some sounds for attention-getting purposes, but we did not include informational audio elements. While it might be a pedagogically sound practice, at the time we created these tutorials, we found that most of our students did not have audio capabilities on their home computers. As students catch up with technological trends, however, audio can become an important part of the learning process. (For a good discussion of effective ways to use audio in multimedia presentations, see Joy, n.d.)

Be Organized

The organization of the presentation helps learners to "file" the information that they are being given in an orderly way and therefore to more easily remember it. We've all had the experience of listening to a poorly organized lecture that had individual points that were very interesting, but which was lost to you as a whole because the speaker didn't put it together in a coherent whole.

Keep It Short

Part of organization is also about culling out the irrelevant parts of the training. While it may be fascinating to you to know how George Boole died, your learners don't even care that AND, OR, and NOT are called Boolean operators, let alone the biographical tidbits of the man for whom the operators are named. Remember that online tutorials should be relatively short. How long would you want to sit and read a computer screen? Break your lessons up into digestible parts.

Use Humor (Maybe)

If you are the sort of person who enjoys being humorous, joking with your learners can be an excellent way to lighten the learning process, relieving some of the library anxiety prevalent among students, and establishing a friendly relationship (Steele, 1998; Tatum, 1999). Mind you, using humor can be counterproductive if it: (a) offends people; (b) distracts from the learning; or (c) isn't funny. The latter problem is probably the most difficult to address, since responses to humor are very individual, but you can try out your jokes on colleagues or friendly students in order to test responses before you deploy a tutorial. Humor that is related to the subject at hand can enhance rather than distract from the learning while humor that is completely off-topic may be distracting. To avoid offending anyone, always stay away from humor that makes fun of individuals or groups of people, no matter how innocuous it may seem to you.

The type of humor you use will depend on your style. My style is more along the lines of self-deprecation and strange examples. (Yes, I'm the dumpy librarian hiding in the corner doing searches on people who eat buttered cigarettes in their sleep.) Other people prefer bad puns and wordplay. Cartoons and visual humor work particularly well in online tutorials, as well.

Event 6: Elicit Performance

This is the point in the process in which learners are asked to do what they have been taught. Ideally, library instruction should be linked to in-class assignments, in which case students will have a chance to transfer their knowledge to real research. But before they get to that point (if they ever get to it at all), *interactive quizzes* are one way to ask students to practice what they've learned. We use quizzes with all of our tutorials both as a strategy for reviewing what was taught in the tutorial and as a method of eliciting performance.

Event 7: Provide Feedback

Our quizzes always tell whether answers are correct or incorrect. Many offer additional information as to *why* an answer is incorrect and some offer a chance to keep trying until the right answer is found. This feedback point is a place where gentle humor can be used to lighten tension about being wrong.

Event 8: Assess Performance

Ideally, a tutorial would not only tell whether individual answers were correct or incorrect, but would give a student an overall picture of how well they did with the quiz. Some of our quizzes have this capability; others are limited by our technological knowledge (or lack thereof). Students' performance is also assessed in the classroom, if related activities are assigned after library instruction.

Event 9: Enhance Retention and Transfer

This step should aid learners in remembering and applying the new learning. The ideal way to do this would be to have students complete library research assignments using the tools taught in the tutorial. But when the tutorial is not linked with coursework, additional research questions could be appended to the end of the tutorial, or a sample assignment might be included with the tutorial. We hope that students who take the time to go through a library tutorial will have assignments in the future related to library research, and that research will enhance retention in the future. (But that's a pretty lame hope, isn't it?) I'd say that as a whole, this is the point where we, as instruction librarians, have to work closely with the faculty that make assignments. Otherwise, tutorials like ours can be useful, but the long-term retention and transfer are likely to be minimal if students don't use what they learn.

WHAT'S ON THE CD?

The CD is set up to auto run so that when the CD-ROM is inserted into the CD drive, it loads automatically, and a HTML-based menu appears on the screen (using Internet Explorer). The following is a list of the materials contained on the CD and a description of why we included each item.

TILT

Our library has adopted the Texas Information Literacy Tutorial as our preferred method for offering online instruction in information literacy. TILT contains three modules that discuss information sources, how to find them, how to choose them, skills for effectively searching library databases and the Web, including choosing and combining terms, and criteria for assessing the credibility of sources as well as why and how to cite sources. TILT has an open publication license, and our instruction librarian has adapted TILT's tutorial to fit our individual library's needs. Shuttle (2003) provides more details about adapting TILT in his conference presentation, "Resources for Creating Online Information Literacy Materials."

Two Minute Tour

This animated Power Point presentation converted to HTML provides a quick overview of our library homepage. Words like "library catalogs" often mean little to students; this tour lets them know what each major item on the page can do for them when they are researching.

Library Services for Off-Campus Students

This page is actually one of the pages available on our Extended Campus Services Web site. It lists the services we provide for all off-campus students, faculty, and staff (online collections, proxy access to databases, reference services by phone, e-mail, live by appointment or online chat, document delivery, electronic reserves, interlibrary loan, use of other libraries, and collections at regional centers). Descriptions of each service are given in language that avoids library jargon as much as possible.

Voyager Library Catalog

This is an interactive tutorial created in HTML using Dreamweaver. The tutorial provides an overview of searching in the library catalog and includes a quiz to reinforce learning.

InfoTrac Tutorial

Because InfoTrac is our most commonly used database among undergraduates, and we have a number of databases using this same interface, it was chosen as the first database for which we would develop a tutorial. This tutorial is also interactive in nature and includes a quiz to test knowledge.

Music Video/Building Tour

I took an instructional technology course during the year before this CD was created, and one project in that class was to create a digital video. This video gives a sort of visual tour of the physical library building at ETSU, with information about services provided, in a music video format, with a garage rock band grinding out a tune called "Library Dance." The video was created in iMovie; therefore, it requires Quicktime.

THE TECHNOLOGY

The materials on the CD were all created over a span of a year or more, using primarily HTML written with Dreamweaver or saved as HTML from PowerPoint. Other materials were created using PowerPoint. The CD was designed for a Windows platform, consistent with ETSU's required configuration for online students. The CD was designed so that it would automatically boot when placed in the CD drive of most Windows computers.

Since this presentation is being offered in a workshop format, attendees will use the following directions to create their own CD during the workshop time. These instructions are detailed in order to prepare for a variety of ability levels.

Dreamweaver/CourseBuilder

Macromedia Dreamweaver is the HTML editor which we used for creating our initial library catalog tutorial and InfoTrac OneFile tutorial. Quizzes were created using the free CourseBuilder extension to Dreamweaver (see http://www.macromedia.com/support/coursebuilder/ for technical information, downloads, and support). Due to time constraints, this software will not be discussed in any detail during this workshop.

PowerPoint

The primary focus of the hands-on portion of this workshop relies on using PowerPoint to create interactive tutorials. It's amazingly easy to create dynamic, interactive PowerPoint presentations that can be used online or on a CD of this sort. Going beyond basic PowerPoint presentations, this process uses the interactivity capabilities available with action buttons, animations, and the ability to save as HTML for more universal access. The following directions apply to PowerPoint XP. Earlier versions of PowerPoint have these same capabilities, but step-by-step may work slightly differently.

The example that will be used in the workshop will be that of a "Two-Minute Tour" of a library Web site. Participants can use their own library Web sites or a "canned" Web site provided by the facilitator.

Begin to Create Your PowerPoint Presentation

1. Open PowerPoint.
2. To be sure that we are all looking at the screen the same way, pull down **the view menu → toolbars**, and make sure that *standard, formatting, drawing,* and *task pane* toolbars are all checked.
3. At the right side of the toolbar, click on the **design** button.
4. Choose a template that you like

   • Remember that the slide show will be viewed on a computer screen, not projected in a room

- Color choices are therefore more flexible (when projected, dark backgrounds work well; this is less important on-screen)
- High contrast is most easily viewed by the visually impaired

5. Type your tutorial **title and subtitle** in the appropriate boxes.

List Your Objectives

It's important to learners to know the objectives of any learning endeavor before they begin (see "contents" below for more information). It also helps you to keep a tutorial organized if you know what it is you plan to teach before you begin.

1. Click the **new slide** button to begin making your slide.
2. Make a list of your objectives for this tutorial. Because we are building a very short tutorial, your objectives should be simple.

Make a Screen Shot

A screen print (aka, "screen shot") takes up a lot of memory and is often a bit fuzzy. However, it is a very simple method to include visual representations of computer screens in a tutorial. For better screen captures, use a program like SnagIt. Using either capture method, you can use PhotoShop or another graphic editing program to work with your image once it is captured. For the purposes of this workshop, we will use simple screen prints.

1. Open the program you want to copy and maximize it to your full screen.
2. Press **Cntrl-PrntScrn** to copy what you see on the screen to the clipboard.

3. In PowerPoint, click the **New Slide** button and then choose the **blank** slide layout. (Roll your cursor over the different layouts to see the names of each layout style.)

4. Click on the slide. Press **CNTRL-V** (or use **edit → paste**) to paste the image into PowerPoint. Drag the item the way you want it to appear on the slide. Use crop in the drawing tools as needed. (For more information about manipulating graphics in PowerPoint, see http://www.fgcu.edu/support/office2000/ppt/graphics.html.)

Adding AutoShapes

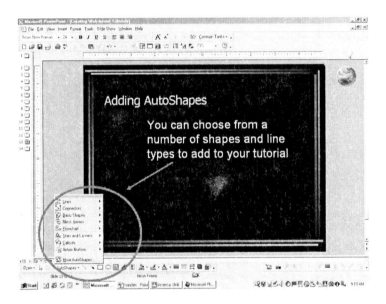

Add a Call-Out to Your Slide Show

1. Click on **AutoShapes** in the drawing toolbar at the bottom of your screen and select **Callouts** (or use the slideshow menu at the top of the screen).
2. Choose the **shape** of callout you would like to use.
3. **Click and drag** to make the callout the size and shape you would like. Use the **yellow square** at the tip of the callout's point to move the shape to point to the part of the slide you want to highlight.
4. **Type text** in the callout.
5. If you like, you can change the color of the callout background by clicking on the paint bucket icon on the drawing toolbar on the bottom of the screen. Use the text color button (the A with a colored line under it) to change the color of the text.

Adding Animation and Effects

Animation adds interest and some interactivity to your slide shows and can be used for emphasis. You want to be sure not to overdo it, as too much can be distracting. For more detailed information on effects, see: http://www.fgcu. edu/support/office2000/ppt/slideeffects.html.

1. Select **Slide Show** → **Custom Animation** from the menu bar.
2. Select the object on the slide that will be animated, then click **add effect** in the task pane at the right of the screen.
3. Choose an animation type that you prefer (example: entrance → fly in).
4. You can also change the direction, speed, and timing on the animations using the task pane. On click means that the learner will have to click to make the animation begin; otherwise, you can set up the animation to begin after a specific period of time, or at the same time as another animated item.
5. To preview your animation, click the **play** button at the bottom of the task pane.

Action Buttons

Because students will be completing this tutorial on their own, you will want to make the tutorial easily navigable. One way to do this is to add action buttons to the slides.

1. Click anywhere on a slide.
2. Use the **AutoShapes menu** at the bottom of the screen (or pull down the **Slide Show** from the menu).
3. Choose **Action buttons**.
4. **Choose a button** from the fly out menu.

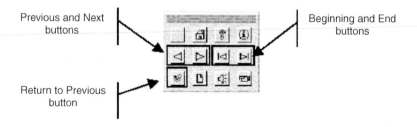

Previous and Next buttons

Beginning and End buttons

Return to Previous button

5. Notice that when you point at the slide now, the mouse pointer changes to a black cross. Move the mouse pointer where you want the button and **click and drag** the mouse to draw the button.

6. The action settings box should appear. Make sure that the action is what you intend to occur when someone clicks on the icon. (For example, the home button should hyperlink to first slide.) If it needs to be changed, choose the desired action setting and click OK.
7. Follow the directions above to put a **next** button on the lower right-hand corner of each page of your slideshow.
8. Use the directions above to create one **home** button on the lower left corner of one slide. Copy and paste it to all of the other slides, except the title slide.

Creating a Quiz

Create a Question Slide

1. Click on the **New Slide** button on the tool bar.
2. Click in the **Title** and type **Question 1**.
3. Click in the **Text**.
4. Click on the **Bulleted List** button on the formatting toolbar to turn off bullets.
5. Type your quiz question in the text box.
6. Click on the **Bulleted List** button to turn it back on.
7. Type multiple choice answers to your question as a bulleted list.
   Example:
   Which of the following library resources would you use to find out if your school has a copy of *War and Peace*?
   • Databases
   • Library Catalog
   • Chat with a Librarian

Create Answer Slides

1. Click on the **New Slide** button on the toolbar.
2. Choose the **Title** layout.
3. Click in the title area and type: **Sorry, that's not correct. Please try again.**
4. Add a **Return action button** to the "incorrect" slide (see Action Buttons, above, for directions on adding an action button). This button will take the learner back to the question page, forcing them to choose the correct answer before completing the tutorial. Leave the **hyperlink to** setting at **Last Slide Viewed** and click **OK**.
5. Repeat steps 1-3 to create a correct answer slide that says, **Correct!!!**
6. On the correct answer slide, add a **next** button. This button will take the learner to the next question slide.

Link Question Slide to Answer Slides

1. Pull up on your screen the **question slide** you created earlier.
2. **Highlight** the text of the correct answer to your quiz question.
3. **Right click** while pointing your cursor at the highlighted text and choose **hyperlink** from the menu.
4. Click on the **place in this document** button at the left of the dialog box.
5. Click on the slide title **"Correct Answer!!"** Click **OK**.
6. Highlight the text of an incorrect answer, and follow the same process to link to the "Sorry that's not correct" slide. Repeat this step until all answers are linked.

Creating "Branches" in a Quiz

Rather than giving a quiz with simple correct and incorrect answers, you can have "branches" of your tutorial that personalize the learning content to the answers given. For example, if a student correctly answers that a *War and Peace* is found in the library by using the library catalog, the next slide might ask how that student would search for *War and Peace* (by title, keyword, or subject). If they answer that question correctly, another, more advanced question can follow.

On the other hand, if a student gives an incorrect answer, you might backtrack to slides that provide the answer to the question, or you could create new slides that offer the information in a new way.

Turn Off Advance on Mouse Click

To keep learners from clicking through the tutorial without using the action buttons (this is particularly important when you have quizzes or branching paths), you need to turn off the option that allows the user to click with the mouse to advance to the next slide.

1. From the menu, choose, **Slide Show** → **Slide Transition**.
2. On the right side of your screen, a slide transition menu should appear. At the bottom, under advance slide, click the checkbox to **deselect on mouse click**.
3. Click on the **apply to all** button at the bottom of the task pane.

Save as Web Page

Easier to access later if you give it a one-word name. PowerPoint creates a file that starts the presentation and a folder of files the presentation uses. You need to put both of these on your CD in order for your slideshow to run.

Creating the Menu

To have more than one tutorial or other material available on your CD, you must create a menu file to be the initial screen that is available when the CD is loaded. Any HTML editor can be used to create such a file. For the purposes of this workshop, we will use PowerPoint to create the file.

1. Open a **new** PowerPoint presentation and choose a **template**.
2. Select the **title and text** layout (with bullets).
3. In the **title** portion of the screen, type a title for your CD (example: Introduction to ETSU Library Services).
4. In the bulleted list section, **type the titles** of the tutorials or information files you plan to include. If you don't want your menu to have bullets, highlight the entire list and click the bulleted list button to remove the bullets.
5. Highlight the first item on your list. **Right-click** and choose **hyperlink** from the menu.

6. Click on **existing file or webpage** button.
7. In the address box, type **filename.htm**, where filename represents the name you have given the file you wish to link to. Although you can use the browse feature to find the file, I've found that you'll have to do less troubleshooting later, if you just type the filename this way.
8. Continue this process until all your menu items are linked.
9. Select **file → save as web page**. Name your file **menu.htm**.

AutoRun

After all of your files are created and linked to your menu, the final file you need to create is the one that causes the CD to load automatically when it's put into the CD drive. I used a free program downloaded from downloads.com that contained a "helper" program that opens Internet Explorer in order to run the HTML applications. There are many programs of this type available for free download.

Because we used PowerPoint as our design tool, IE is the preferred browser; it is also the browser specified for our online classes. We also included information about installing an appropriate version of IE with the CD, in case people needed to install a recent version of Internet Explorer on their computers.

Testing the CD

Once you've put together a prototype CD or even as you create individual tutorials, you want to test your tutorials to be sure that they make sense to someone other than you, the author. Use the same kind of strategies you would for Web usability studies. Zhang (n.d) provides a good resource for designing your usability evaluation. A quick-and-dirty way to test is simply to ask a few students to work their way through the tutorial, talking out loud as they do so about what they see and what they think about parts of the tutorial. You'll get some excellent feedback by just watching what works for them and what doesn't, and listening to their responses to the tutorial.

WHAT I'D DO DIFFERENTLY

It turns out that my attempts to make the tutorials interactive by using layers and behaviors in Dreamweaver didn't work for people with different screen sizes or resolutions. I found that every computer that I have access to in the library and at home is configured similarly enough that I couldn't trust my tests to show me the bugs that our students would encounter when they ran the tutorial. And the minute that an interaction doesn't work, most students will just give up and not complete the tutorial.

I've haven't heard any complaints or problems with the tutorials that I've created subsequently using PowerPoint. Using animations and other high-end PowerPoint tricks can make a tutorial just as interactive as my HTML work, and is much easier to do for someone with average technology skills. In addition, if there are materials (like quizzes) that are easier to create in Dreamweaver using Extensions, then those materials can be linked from a PowerPoint tutorial.

I'd also make each of my tutorials shorter, more along the lines of the "Two Minute Tour." I've found that the attention span of students–even the graduate students that I teach–is relatively short, and that having them complete a number of short tutorials is better than a single long tutorial. It also makes updating the presentations much easier. In the time since we created our first batch of tutorials, almost all of the interfaces described have been changed, and none of us have had the time to update the lengthy HTML tutorials to bring them in line with the new interfaces. As we begin to create shorter tutorials using PowerPoint, perhaps we'll be able to share the work with colleagues who have fewer skills with HTML.

REFERENCES

Doerner, M. (n.d.). Attention: Getting it. In *Encyclopedia of Educational Technology.* San Diego, CA: San Diego State University. Retrieved December 1, 2003 from http://coe.sdsu.edu/eet/.

Fleming, M., & Levie, W. H. (1993). *Principles from the behavioral and cognitive sciences.* Englewood Cliffs, NJ: Educational Technology Publications.

Gagne R. M., & Briggs L. J. (1974). *Principles of instructional design.* New York: Holt, Rinehart & Winston.

Gardner, H. (1985). Frames of mind: The theory of multiple intelligences. New York: BasicBooks.

Gerlic, I. & Jausovec, N. (1999). Multimedia: Differences in cognitive processes observed with EEG. *Educational Technology Research and Development, 47*(3), 5-14.

Joy, D. (n.d.) Audio: How much is too much? In *Encyclopedia of Educational Technology.* San Diego, CA: San Diego State University. Retrieved December 1, 2003 from http://coe.sdsu.edu/eet/.

Knowles, M. (1984). Andragogy in action: Applying modern principles of adult education. San Francisco: Jossey Bass.

Shuttle, J. (2003). *Resources for creating online information literacy materials.* Retrieved December 1, 2003 from http://faculty.etsu.edu/shuttle/Resources%20for%20Creating%20Online%20Information%20Literacy%20Materials.htm.

Steele, K. E. (1998). *The positive and negative effects of the use of humor in the classroom setting.* Salem, WV: Salem-Teikyo University. (ERIC Document Reproduction Service No. ED426929).

Tatum, T. (1999). Cruel and unusual punishment (LOW humor is better than NO humor). *English Journal, 88*(4), 62-64.

Zhang, Z. (n.d.) *Usability evaluation.* Retrieved November 20, 2003 from http://www.pages.drexel.edu/%7Ezwz22/UsabilityHome.html.

Working Together:
Effective Collaboration
in a Consortium Environment

Grant Kayler
Paul R. Pival

University of Calgary

SUMMARY. This paper describes innovative library services to distance students negotiated through a geographically dispersed consortium, the Council of Prairie and Pacific University Libraries (COPPUL). The Distance Education Forum (DE Forum) is one of the most active member groups within COPPUL, and has had a number of successes in collaborative services over the years. This paper provides an overview of how the DE Forum works, its Web site, and its ways of working through small sub-teams coordinated via an annual meeting. We describe a number of projects, looking both at what was successful and what didn't work as well, and discuss what we learned.

KEYWORDS. Collaboration, Internet, library services, distance learners

INTRODUCTION

Several recent papers have discussed the accomplishments of consortia in assisting distance education students (Subramanian, Brunvand et al.), but for

[Haworth co-indexing entry note]: "Working Together: Effective Collaboration in a Consortium Environment." Kayler, Grant, and Paul R. Pival. Co-published simultaneously in *Journal of Library Administration* (The Haworth Information Press, an imprint of The Haworth Press, Inc.) Vol. 41, No. 1/2, 2004, pp. 203-215; and: *The Eleventh Off-Campus Library Services Conference Proceedings* (ed: Patrick B. Mahoney) The Haworth Information Press, an imprint of The Haworth Press, Inc., 2004, pp. 203-215.

http://www.haworthpress.com/web/JLA
Digital Object Identifier: 10.1300/J111v41n01_15

the most part these articles focus on the end result, and not the process that lead to that result. In this paper we will document how the Council of Prairie and Pacific University Libraries (COPPUL) Distance Education Forum was successful in reaching a number of its goals. While not necessarily revolutionary, we feel our approach is a solid one, and one that other consortia may wish to emulate.

Thomas Peters, Dean of University Libraries at Western Illinois University, writes, "I firmly believe that collaboration involving libraries is crucial to the continued success of libraries. This is not a bold prediction, because libraries have been collaborating successfully for decades. Perhaps the question is not whether or not to collaborate, but how to collaborate and with whom" (Peters, 2003). This paper will describe the successful collaboration of a large number of academic libraries in planning distance services in Western Canada, and will discuss both how we've collaborated, and why this collaboration has lead to success for our group.

The Council of Prairie and Pacific University Libraries is currently comprised of 22 university libraries located in the four western provinces of Canada–Manitoba, Saskatchewan, Alberta, and British Columbia, a geographic area roughly equivalent to one third of the continental United States. The institutions range in size from very small (FTE < 500) to very large (FTE > 30,000). Member libraries cooperate to enhance information services and reduce costs through resource sharing, collective purchasing of online resources, document delivery, and many other similar activities. Many of COPPUL's activities are of direct benefit to distance students.

COPPUL AND THE DISTANCE EDUCATION FORUM

COPPUL has established a number of Working Groups to help it accomplish its goals. Currently there are Working Groups for collections, data resources, public services, systems, interlibrary loan, digitization, the Virtual Western Canadian University Library, and our group, the Distance Education Forum. The DE Forum is one of the most active of these working groups. It was established in 1989 as a means for COPPUL members to share information about the provision of services to off-campus and distance education students and faculty. From 1989 to 1995, the Forum held a number of meetings. During that time, COPPUL Directors revised COPPUL's strategic plan and gave the Forum a more specific mandate: to bring greater consistency to the services offered by each member Library to its distance students, and to pursue the endorsement of the Canadian Library Association Guidelines for Library Support of Distance Learning in Canada. There was a sense that greater equity needed to be established, not only between on- and off-campus students but also in the level of service that COPPUL's members offered to their distance students. For several reasons however, one being the lack of a Chair, the Forum went on hiatus from 1995 to 1998. Since distance learning and online instruction seemed to be expanding rapidly at that time, a proposal was submitted to COPPUL Directors to reactivate the Forum. The proposal was supported by all attending the October 1998 Directors' meeting.

The Forum reconvened in 1999 under new leadership and met in Vancouver, British Columbia in May of that year. Each institution in COPPUL with a distance education program (19 out of 22) appointed a representative to the Forum. At this first meeting of the reactivated group, members agreed that in addition to exchanging information, the Forum needed to be more of a working group that would undertake specific projects on a cooperative basis. The overall aim was to carry out projects that would enhance the level of service provided to distance students by all COPPUL libraries–not just by member libraries to their own students, for which they have primary responsibility, but also to distance students from other COPPUL institutions who were located near enough to their library to use it in person. Thus, distance students would benefit from a wider range of services from their home institution, and from access to specified services from COPPUL libraries that were physically accessible to them. The overall result would be a higher lever of service for all students in the consortium, regardless of home institution, or to which library they happened to be closest. To this end, the members developed new goals and objectives, which were subsequently approved by COPPUL Directors.

As stated on the Forum's homepage, our goals are as follows: The Forum will promote, within the context of COPPUL's mission and strategic plan, the development of cost-effective library services that support the distance and distributed learning activities of COPPUL institutions. In doing so, the Forum will emphasize (1) cooperative service development and resource sharing among COPPUL libraries, as well as among other types of libraries, and (2) real-time information accessibility and materials availability, regardless of the origin of the information, or the location of the library user.

We have the following objectives:

Share Information

To enable COPPUL distance education librarians to collaborate by sharing information about issues and problems relating to distance delivery of library service, and to promote a cooperative resolution of procedural and practical issues, including that of staff development.

Promote Service Development

To promote the development by COPPUL libraries of services to distance learners that are consistent with (1) CLA's current Guidelines for Library Support of Distance and Distributed Learning in Canada, and (2) collaborative endeavours which lend themselves to the "sharing of staff expertise"; as identified by the COPPUL Board of Directors in their 1999-2001 Strategic Plan.

Promote Equity of Access

To promote equity of access for all COPPUL distance education students by working to ensure that they are able to take advantage of the total information resources of COPPUL in a timely fashion.

Facilitate Advocacy

To assist COPPUL distance education librarians in advocating for effective library support for distant and distributed learning among their library and institutional colleagues, and among external partners from the wider distance education community.

Assist and Advise COPPUL Directors

To proactively assist COPPUL Directors and Institutional Administrators by informing and advising them about issues and problems associated with library service for distance learners.

To accomplish these objectives, the Forum holds an annual meeting in the spring of each year. At this meeting we develop an action plan for the upcoming year based on discussion over the Forum's mailing list and at the annual meeting, and establish small teams to work on individual projects during the upcoming year. We should note here that Directors of COPPUL libraries have established some criteria to help ensure that the projects undertaken will be successful and contribute positively to COPPUL as a whole. These criteria deal with questions such as: How does the project contribute to COPPUL's overall vision? Will the project result in cost savings? What is the long-term viability of the new or enhanced service, and what would be the implications if the service were to be discontinued? What impact would the service have on existing agreements or technical operations within COPPUL?

FRUITFUL DE FORUM PROJECTS

On the following pages we will describe some of the bigger and more successful projects worked on by the DE Forum. For each project we will provide background information, and discuss the role of the DE Forum in that project, in particular how it helped promote a consortium-based approach to developing and implementing new distance services. It is this final aspect where we feel the DE Forum truly shines.

Examination of Commercial Library Alternatives (e.g., Questia, netLibrary, etc.)

When commercial services like netLibrary and Questia began appearing in the late 1990s, they made claims that they were much faster and easier to use than traditional bricks and mortar libraries, and that they contained all the material a student would need, so they could actually replace a student's traditional library. For a subscription cost. Since we want to offer our distance students as many academic full text articles as possible, Forum members felt that they needed to know more about these products–what they actually contained, how they worked, what they cost–and what role resources of this nature could play in distance service. Much of the focus on e-resources development had been on journal articles. These new services were focused on books and thus represented a new area that needed investigation for its potential impact on DE service. The more we knew about them, the better we could respond to questions from students or administrators.

This project illustrates one of the advantages of working together in a consortium–that in the larger group, there is a greater likelihood that one of the members will have interest and expertise in the project area, and be willing to take leadership of the project team. This was indeed the case with this project, and one member agreed to lead the Work Team. Several others volunteered for the Team, each one to investigate a separate product. The products examined were netLibrary, Questia, ebrary, XanEdu, and Jones e-global library.

The Team Lead developed a set of questions that each member asked the publisher when researching their respective product, including:

- What are the key subject content areas of the product?
- How does the student and/or Library obtain access to it?
- How do the key functions work (e.g., searching, printing, downloading)?
- What is the product's business plan, and how are costs determined?
- Is the product easy to use?
- What is the overall quality of the product?
- How does the product contribute to distance library support?

With representatives from several member libraries, we had the staff to divide the work so that each member of the Team could concentrate on a single product and do a more detailed assessment of it, resulting in a better understanding of the product. As members of a consortium, Team members were seen to represent potentially substantial purchases of a product, either institutionally, perhaps even consortium-wide, or from students directly, so publishers were helpful in providing the information we were seeking. This project gave us all a better understanding of the e-book side of distance service, to complement our understanding of e-journal resources.

The full report was presented at the Forum's 2002 annual meeting and served as a valuable source of information not only for Forum members, but also for others in our respective libraries, for example those with collection development responsibilities.

Reciprocal Borrowing

A reciprocal borrowing agreement had existed in COPPUL for many years, allowing faculty and graduate students to borrow materials directly from other COPPUL libraries when they were away from their home libraries, for example on sabbatical or doing thesis research. It had become an important element in service to individuals who were temporarily at a distance from their home institutions. With distance learning moving more strongly into undergraduate curricula, a majority of COPPUL Directors felt that the time had come to look at expanding the agreement to include undergraduate students. However, certain members had long-standing concerns that this expansion would "unleash the hordes" and create uneven and/or unsustainable demand. Thus, while there was a strong feeling that something needed to be done, expanding the project to include undergraduates was seen as a sort of Pandora's Box that some were afraid to open.

When the DE Forum was reconvened in 1999, the Directors asked the Forum to take the lead on this project, knowing that the reciprocal borrowing service was becoming an increasingly important element of distance service, and that the Forum would have the interest needed to move it forward. Thus, the DE Forum took the lead on a service development that, if implemented, would benefit all undergraduate students in COPPUL institutions. The Directors also saw the Forum as having sufficient members and representation from each institution, two elements that would enable us to conduct a pilot project, to gather data on actual usage and address any other issues that arose.

The Forum established a Reciprocal Borrowing Work Team at its annual meeting of May 1999 consisting of 4 members, one representing each province. This Work Team developed a proposal for a pilot project for undergraduate reciprocal borrowing, and obtained approval from the other members of the Forum. The Forum Chair presented the proposal to the Directors for consideration, and the Directors gave approval for a one-year pilot, to run from September 2000 to August 2001. They did ask that a specific implementation plan be developed, and this was done prior to the implementation of the pilot. The plan proved to be a very useful tool as there were many logistical details to work out. The plan was posted on the Forum's Web site so that it could be checked anytime clarification was needed.

The decision was made to include a local contact at each Library from front-line staff, e.g., Circulation Supervisor. This helped to get buy-in at local level and address issues quickly. Local contacts and DE Forum representatives also kept their individual Directors informed of progress, so the Director was prepared in case any problems arose. The Directors were provided with a six-month progress report, and were so assured of the results that they approved the service on an ongoing basis after the first six months. The success of this local expansion eventually led to the expansion of the reciprocal borrowing service for all levels of students among all the other consortia across Canada, making this a nation-wide service. With a few exceptions, undergraduates, graduate students, and faculty at Canadian universities can now borrow in person from other Canadian university libraries coast-to-coast.

This project helped show that concerns among different sized libraries within a consortium—in this case, concern about the uneven impact of a new service—could be addressed by means of a clear process that generated clear data. The data gathered showed that while there were some differences, they were not significant enough to merit pulling out. This project also showed that proactive communication could help ensure the success of a project by addressing concerns before they had a chance to escalate and undermine the project.

Information Literacy Web Site

When the Forum met in 1999, members indicated strong interest in providing users with a fuller range of online instruction tools, to promote more effective library research from a distance, but also to help distance students gain access to the collective resources of COPPUL libraries, either from their home library or from COPPUL libraries they could use in person. As there were a number of issues to consider, it was decided that some background exploration of possible options was needed before a decision could be made, in order to be sure that we developed something we could all use.

As a result, we established an Electronic Instruction Team to investigate options and report back to members. The Team developed some questions for each Forum member to answer, e.g., what kind of instruction tools they were currently using; whether any of these tools could be adapted for use beyond their institution; what they felt were the top three kinds of tools needed; and whether they felt it was possible to develop shared tools that would still be effective for local needs. Responses to these questions indicated that an online tutorial in basic research skills was something everyone could use effectively as a shared resource.

During this fact-finding phase, the Team discovered that the Coalition of Atlantic University Libraries (CAUL), another Canadian consortium, had already developed a tutorial of this nature, which, given that it had been developed for a consortium, had some of the structure and features we wanted, for example Web links to each member's distance service pages, online reference assistance, and other resources to complement the instructional content. At the Forum's meeting the following year, 2000, the Team's proposal to adopt the CAUL tutorial and adapt it for COPPUL use was accepted. One of the members offered to host it at her Library and do the development work needed. The tutorial went live in the fall of 2001. This project illustrates some of the benefits of the consortium approach: pooling feedback to identify the most useful product to develop; the likelihood that at least one of the members will be in a position to host the site; all members making sure their respective links are kept up-to-date.

Virtual Western Canadian University Library (VWCUL)

The VWCUL project grew from a joint meeting in January 2001 in Victoria, BC between the Directors and Systems groups. The outcome of that meeting led to the formation of the VWCUL Steering Committee in March 2001. The VWCUL project originally consisted of six steps resulting in a virtual "Research Assistant." These steps are:

1. develop tools that will allow users to select an appropriate starting point;
2. develop authentication mechanisms that will ensure that users gain access to resources;
3. develop tools that will allow effective subject or known item searches;
4. develop better mechanisms to check availability of items online or in print;
5. develop better mechanisms to get items remotely if not available locally; and
6. develop tools to incorporate citations and/or articles into personalized library services.

All of these steps are currently commercially available individually, but no package seemed to contain the entire research process as envisioned for this project. In addition, utilizing local programming expertise throughout the consortium would allow this product to be made available in an affordable package to COPPUL members, a very real concern when Canadian dollars are used to purchase commercial services from the U.S. The success of this project would be of obvious benefit to students studying at a distance.

Shortly after the VWCUL Steering Committee was formed, a member of the DE Forum was asked to participate to ensure that the interests of distance students were addressed in the planning and implementation of this project. This DE representative attended all Steering Committee meetings and participated in the listserv discussion of the project, informing and consulting with DE Forum members when necessary and appropriate. One of the biggest areas of concern for distance students is to ensure that step 5, mechanisms to get items remotely if not available locally, takes into account the unique situation of the distance student. As we know, distance students often request items held by the home library, and we needed to ensure that distance students wouldn't be barred from requesting items the system thought they could obtain for themselves. This project is still underway, and has evolved to some extent based on feedback from the various stakeholders.

The existence of the DE Forum gave us a group from which a member could be drawn to represent the needs of distance students on the VWCUL Steering Committee. Early on it seemed apparent to the Steering Committee that what would make a successful product for distance students (remote access, full text, ease of use w/o guided instruction) would also make a good product overall.

The consortium approach of this project has been particularly interesting because over the course of the project (now approaching three years), several commercial products have matured, and several members of COPPUL have essentially purchased components of the VWCUL to serve their own students, but not those of the rest of the consortium. It remains to be seen just what the final product, now known as reSearcher, will mean to COPPUL distance students.

MISSES

The Forum has not been successful in every attempted project. The following are three examples of areas where the Forum faced challenges and did not enjoy as much success as we would have hoped.

DE Survey

During the early 1990s, the Forum carried out a survey of its students that gathered data on a number of different issues, e.g., other kinds of libraries the respondents had used, difficulties they had encountered in obtaining materials or service, how often respondents had used the catalogues of other COPPUL libraries, etc. When the Forum was reactivated in 1999, it was proposed that another survey be conducted. A proposal was developed and taken to the Directors but was not approved, and the survey did not go ahead. Looking back on why this happened, there appear to be several reasons. The original survey had been a useful scan of a number of issues and had helped us understand the nature of library use by distance students at that time. With the reconstituted group, however, there was a sense that a new survey should facilitate our focus on specific projects, by gathering data that would help identify specific needs or issues as well as the kind of project that would be best suited to addressing them. A survey of this nature was more complex than the previous one, particularly with new issues to address such as electronic access, Web-based delivery, and inter-institutional course delivery. Unfortunately, in this case the Forum's structure of a one-day meeting plus discussion via our list for the rest of the year did not allow sufficient time for the in-depth discussion needed to resolve these and other questions, and develop an appropriate design. Thus, when questions arose about sample size, ethics reviews, as well as overall purpose, it became apparent that more work was needed. While the consortium environment certainly offers fertile ground for surveys, there needs to be a structure that can adequately support the design and implementation process, and give sufficient time to deal with the diversity of opinions that will inevitably arise in a project of this nature.

Direct-to-Student Document Delivery

One of the biggest problems faced by distance students is the time it takes to receive hard copy materials. The Forum wanted to explore methods of reducing this time, and a suggestion was made that if we could cut out the "middle man" library and have books shipped directly from the lending library to the distance student, regardless of home institution, this transaction would be greatly sped up.

This project was an example of a synergistic opportunity presented by a joint meeting of the DE Forum and the COPPUL ILL Forum in May 2002. Because members of the ILL Forum were present at the DE Forum's annual meeting, they were able to provide insight into what would be necessary to make this initiative work with the various ILL systems found throughout the

COPPUL consortium. A joint subcommittee was established with members from both the DE and ILL forums to further examine the feasibility of this initiative.

A pilot project was begun to test whether a "flag" could be set in the various ILL systems to notify ILL staff that they were receiving a distance education request. This flag would include the patron's mailing address, and would need to be obvious enough to catch the eye of staff processing a large number of requests. Participating libraries would also need to ensure that materials were delivered via comparable means, i.e., one library couldn't ship via express post while another shipped via parcel post, as this would mean disparate service to students based on the sending institution.

The pilot was run but quickly showed that the various automated ILL systems used by COPPUL member libraries were not up to the task of thinking outside the box. The members of the pilot team determined that there is no simple or effective way of flagging requests to be routed directly to distance students, and thus this pilot has been terminated. We do hope to revisit the project and discuss the results at the next annual meeting in the hopes that member libraries might try to work outside the automated ILL systems to make this project a reality.

Resources

The Forum has also faced some resourcing issues. The COPPUL consortium has an Executive Director, who himself has a part-time staff assisting him and an office at one of the member libraries, but there are no other staff dedicated to the work of the consortium. COPPUL is essentially a grass roots approach where staff of the member libraries do most of the work involved in carrying activities forward. While this is to be expected to some extent, local priorities often supersede consortium projects, which can result in a loss of momentum on a project. As well, because we are working cooperatively in a consortium environment, members must consult with and involve each other as much as possible, yet inevitably, some members contribute more than others, so it can sometimes be difficult maintaining a balance and moving forward.

WHAT MAKES THE DE FORUM WORK?

There are a number of factors that have contributed to the success of the DE Forum, as marked by the implementation of a number of initiatives that have increased service to our students.

First and foremost is the spirit of collegiality. We serve on this committee to improve service to our primary clientele, and to make our jobs easier and more efficient, if at all possible. Forum members share ideas freely, both through the online discussion list, and in person at the annual meeting. This annual meeting provides an important connection for us, as we suffer the same problem we do when dealing with our faceless students trying to put a face to the name.

We have been fortunate to have good leadership in the forum, and in recent years a DE Librarian has filled the position of Executive Director of COPPUL, which makes it easy to keep our cause visible.

We also feel it is vitally important that we have the trust and ears of the institutional Directors. Little of what we have accomplished could have been done without their support, both philosophically and in many cases financially. Directors' support also makes it easier for members of the Forum to have their project work recognized formally in their position objectives, which helps ensure they have the time needed to keep projects moving forward, and thus helps address the resourcing issues noted above.

CONCLUSIONS

COPPUL and the DE Forum together have proven to be an effective mechanism for cooperative projects. DE librarians from several institutions are working together on various projects in small sub teams that set specific objectives, work together during the year communicating via a listserv, then come together for work meetings and decision-making at an annual meeting each May. One of the more interesting results of working within a consortium environment is the synergy between the DE Forum and other COPPUL groups. We hope this paper has illustrated the benefits and power of working as a group, rather than in isolation, as is so often the case with the typical distance education librarian.

REFERENCES

Brunvand, A., Lee, D., McCloskey, K. (2001). Consortium solutions to distance education problems: Utah academic libraries answer the challenges. *Journal of Library Administration, 31*(3/4), 75-92.

Canadian Library Association (2000).*Guidelines for library support of distance and distributed learning in Canada*. Retrieved December 8, 2003 from http://www.cla.ca/about/distance.htm.

COPPUL (2003). reSearcher home page. Retrieved December 8, 2003 from http://theresearcher.ca.

COPPUL DE Forum (2003). *Action plan.* Retrieved December 8, 2003 from http://library.athabascau.ca/copdlforum/action02-03.htm.

COPPUL DE Forum (2000). *Doing research at a distance.* Retrieved November 26, 2003 from http://www.royalroads.ca/coppul/.

COPPUL DE Forum Web site. Retrieved November 26, 2003 from http://library.athabascau.ca/copdlforum/.

COPPUL DE Forum (2002). *Report on commercial library alternatives.* Retrieved November 26, 2003 from http://library.athabascau.ca/copdlforum/taskreport2.htm.

COPPUL home page. Retrieved November 26, 2003 from http://www.coppul.ca/.

D'Andraia, F. (2002). High, wide and cooperative: Academic library cooperation in the Rocky Mountain West and Northern Great Plains. *Resource Sharing and Information Networks, 16*(1), 21-32.

Peters, T. (2003). Consortia and their discontents. *Journal of Academic Librarianship, 29*(2), 111-115.

Subramanian, J. (2002). The growing and changing role of consortia in providing direct and indirect support for distance higher education. *The Reference Librarian 77,* 39-62.

VWCUL Web site. Retrieved November 26, 2003 from http://www.lib.sfu.ca/vwcul/.

Chat It Up!
Extending Reference Services
to Assist Off-Campus Students

M. Kathleen Kern

University of Illinois at Urbana-Champaign

SUMMARY. A virtual reference service is likely to attract both on-campus and off-campus students and providing one service for all users can extend the hours of availability to all students. The needs of these two student populations may differ and off-campus users may present some specific challenges to the reference staff. While some libraries do have a specified distance education librarian, it is unlikely at many institutions that there will be reference staff dedicated only to answering questions from off-campus students. Reference services for off-campus students do present special issues about which general reference staff may not be aware. With awareness of these challenges and proper training, an existing virtual reference service can be extended (or improved) to help off-campus students, or a new chat service can be developed with the objective to assist all user groups with equal success.

KEYWORDS. Distance learners, library services, distance education, information resources

INTRODUCTION

Distance education librarians have long used e-mail and telephone to support the research needs of distance education students. E-mail and telephone

[Haworth co-indexing entry note]: "Chat It Up! Extending Reference Services to Assist Off-Campus Students." Kern, M. Kathleen. Co-published simultaneously in *Journal of Library Administration* (The Haworth Information Press, an imprint of The Haworth Press, Inc.) Vol. 41, No. 1/2, 2004, pp. 217-226; and: *The Eleventh Off-Campus Library Services Conference Proceedings* (ed: Patrick B. Mahoney) The Haworth Information Press, an imprint of The Haworth Press, Inc., 2004, pp. 217-226.

http://www.haworthpress.com/web/JLA
Digital Object Identifier: 10.1300/J111v41n01_16

provided a direct link to the librarian dedicated to support of these programs. In libraries where contact with distance programs is distributed among librarians by subject expertise, distance students could be provided with e-mail and telephone access to specific librarians. E-mail inquiries arriving at a general reference mailbox could be easily forwarded to a specific librarian, without being apparent to the user or seeming to delay response to a question. Telephone calls from distance patrons that came to a general reference number more closely resemble chat inquiries arriving at a virtual reference service in that the patron expectation is for immediate assistance from the librarian answering the call. In the case of chat reference, as with the telephone, a general reference service can be used to support the research needs of distance students. Support of distance students may be an extension of an existing virtual reference service, or something that is planned for in the creation of a virtual reference service.

Chat reference allows for real-time, synchronous communication with a reference librarian. The advantage to the patron is manifold: immediate assistance at the time of need, a more rich communication medium allowing for better understanding between the patron and librarian, and in some cases enhanced features (i.e., co-browsing, voice-over-IP) that allow for even better communication and instruction. These same advantages exist for the reference librarian. Chat reference is not without its challenges in terms of communication and management and there have been many articles written recently that address the implementation of chat reference services.[1] This paper focuses on the intersection of chat reference and support of students enrolled in distance education programs.

Chat reference has a natural attraction for the distance student as it is a no-cost service that allows for synchronous communication. Additionally, chat reference may have hours that extend beyond those of the distance education librarian or subject specialist supporting the distance education program, and the chat technology can allow students without a dedicated Internet connection to talk with a librarian at the same time as they access online library resources.

In many interactions, the patron's location is irrelevant. The reference interview and the access to library resources can be seamless. Providing chat reference service for distance students has many similarities to chat reference for on-campus patrons who are accessing the library from home or other off-campus locations. Off-campus access to electronic resources is the same if the patron is one block off-campus or 2000 miles away. There are times when the patron's location becomes an issue, as with problems in access to electronic resources, or when the patron's status as a distance education student becomes important. It is these situations about which the librarians staffing the virtual reference desk must be aware and trained to handle. Virtual reference service policy is also affected by distance education students. Policies may be written with the assumption that the patrons using the service have other recourse for interaction with a reference librarian, specifically access to the physical library and in-person or telephone assistance. When virtual reference supports distance education programs, training and policy need to encompass situations specific to this population.

DEFINITIONS

Distance students–Students who are permanently or temporarily enrolled in off-campus/distance education programs and do not have easy in-person access to the home library. This differentiates from "off-campus students" or "remote users" access the library from off-campus locations but take courses on-campus as residential or commuter students.

Home library–The library of the institution at which the distance education student is enrolled.

Virtual reference–"Reference service initiated electronically, often in real-time, where users employ computers or other Internet technology to communicate with librarians, without being physically present. Communication channels used frequently in virtual reference include chat, videoconferencing, Voice over IP, e-mail, and instant messaging" (*"Draft Guidelines,"* 2003, section 1.1). This paper mainly addresses synchronous (i.e., chat, videoconferencing) methods of providing reference services, but many of the suggestions apply to asynchronous (i.e., e-mail) services as well.

SERVICE POLICY

Service to students in distance education programs may require adjustments or exceptions to a library's general virtual reference services policy. It is not uncommon for libraries to limit, either by policy or practice, the extent of service that will be provided to students via virtual reference services. This limit might be a limit on the amount of time that a chat interaction should take, or a limit on the types of questions that will be answered by a service. Some example policy statements that set limits on service are:

> Questions which require typing paragraphs or long lists of information, or assignments which require in-depth research (e.g., locating two books, two journal articles, and two primary sources for history class) are not appropri-

ate for Ask A Librarian. Please visit the Library in person for assistance with these questions. (Felix. G. Woodward Library, 2003, About Ask A Librarian section, para. 4)

This service is not intended for providing answers to "factual" questions (e.g., "What is the G.D.P. of China?"). We may instead suggest the resource(s) to help you answer your question. (Newman Library, About Chat Reference section, para. 5)

1. Patrons physically present in the library take precedence over I-Ref users. 2. This service is intended to offer brief reference assistance, extensive research assistance is not available via I-Ref. (Feinberg Library, Important Conditions section, paras. 1-2)

A suggested limit of 15 minutes will be placed on individual chat sessions. . . . Extensive research questions are beyond the scope of this service. (University of Illinois at Urbana-Champaign, Real Time Reference section, para. 6)

This is not to imply that these policies are inappropriate, but rather to provide examples of policies which may need reconsideration or exceptions when providing service to distance students.

Extensive research assistance is easier to provide in person and the library may wish, for reasons of efficiency and pedagogy to encourage on-campus students to work with a librarian in person. While it may be reasonable, and even desirable, to set such limits on service for on-campus students, the same rationale does not apply for distance students. A limit of time or extent of service can shut the distance education student out of virtual reference when they need it most. A distance MBA student in Poland does not have the option to come into the home library for assistance with locating articles on just-in-time manufacturing. Local resources in Poland may be not existent, inadequate, or not in the correct language for the patron. Availability of reference services in other locales may very, even when resources are accessible. Complexity of question, lags due to technology, and extent of assistance needed may all contribute to a transaction that would normally fall outside of a library's time and scope limits for virtual reference. But the student in Poland cannot come into the home library and cannot or will not want to call. Referral to the distance education librarian may not immediately help the patron, depending on time of day, and may require referring the patron to another, less preferable, mode of communication such as telephone (expensive) or e-mail (a "thinner" medium of communication than chat). Virtual service policy and practice must be able to accommodate the research assistance needs of distance students.

Change to service policy to accommodate distance education students can be explicit or internal. An internal policy change would leave the policy that all users see on the library's Web site unchanged, but alter the librarians' level of service for distance students. The advantage of this approach is that users are unaware that there are two levels of service, one for on-campus patrons and one for distance students. The disadvantage of this approach is that a posted policy that states a time limit or a service restriction may deter distance students with extensive research needs from even approaching the virtual reference service. An external policy change will clarify the extent of service that is available to distance students but may result in a perception of inequality for on-campus students (who may not understand the different needs of distance students). Additionally, on-campus students could attempt impersonation of distance students, which might then necessitate the process of verifying the status of patron professing to be distance students. A third possibility is a separate entry-point into the virtual reference service for distance education students, such as from a Web page about library services for distance education students. This would allow for posting of a virtual reference policy tailored for this user group, but would not be seen by distance education students if they entered the service through a link from elsewhere on the library's Web site.

There are some limitations to all of these ways of communicating changes in virtual reference service policy to accommodate distance students. Nonetheless, virtual reference services need to accommodate this user group and determine the best way to communicate policy. At a minimum, librarians staffing the service need to know how to differentiate between distance and on-campus students and be able to offer the most appropriate level of service. Discussion among the staff of service needs of distance education students and training lead by the distance education librarian (where one exists) would facilitate the adoption of policy that supports distance students.

DOCUMENT DELIVERY AND ACCESS TO PRINT COLLECTIONS

Reference librarians generally stay away from the arena of document delivery. On-campus patrons have access to materials by visiting the library and non-affiliated off-campus patrons are referred to the interlibrary loan process. All libraries with distance education programs should have in place a service to deliver photocopies and book loans to distance students. Since document delivery is an important service for distance students, it is important that reference staff be aware of the options to avoid inappropriate referrals to interlibrary loan or send the patron to a local library. Librarians who are not involved directly with these support services may be unaware of their existence, particularly if all distance education services have been traditionally handled by a single librarian. While existing librarians likely already know about document delivery service, it needs to be part of regular training for new staff. It is also important that librarians know how to determine distance education students from on-campus students who may merely be temporarily off-campus and do not fall under the auspices of distance education support services. Here again, training is essential for general reference librarians to understand and make these distinctions.

ASSISTANCE WITH LOCAL COLLECTIONS

There may be times when document delivery and shipment of books from the home library does not best meet the needs of the distance patron. Distance education students are as open to procrastination as other patrons and the time to ship a book may be too long for the student's needs. The item that a student needs might be checked out of the home library and unavailable for photocopy or loan. If the student has unreliable or slow Internet access, remote use of library databases and services might be cumbersome. It is impossible for a librarian to be familiar with all of the libraries that are local to each distance education student. However, reference librarians are adept at searching library catalogs and at navigating the home pages of other libraries. This can be a great benefit to the distance patron who may be unfamiliar with their local library or may assume it inadequate for their research needs. In fact, the local library may even have resources that the home library does not.

A simple referral to a local library might seem sufficient, but going the extra step to confirm that a local library has something for the student is an exemplar of good service. A distance student in Manchester, England researching art history might find it helpful to know that the University of Manchester has Art Bibliography Moderne and Art Abstracts and several special collections in art history. The local library might have the book that the patron needs sitting on the shelf when it is unavailable at the home library or when shipping would take too long to make that option useful. This is information that it takes the virtual reference librarian a matter of minutes to find, but which may not have occurred to the student. The student or librarian may have to determine if walk-in access to these resource exists at the local university. Another way in which it is good to make distance students aware of local resources is that if they are in different time zones, particularly when they are several time zones away, using a local library can give them additional hours of access to a reference librarian. There are, of course, distance students for whom a local library is not an option due to distance or accessibility issues. Librarians unused to serving distance education students may not already be aware of the positive and negative aspects of recommending local options and should develop the ability to discern when this will be practical and to make the referral as specific and useful as possible.

TROUBLESHOOTING ELECTRONIC ACCESS

Access to a library's subscription resources is generally the same for distance education students as it is for on-campus students who are using them from off-campus locations. Patrons gain access to these resources through a proxy server, a university ID and password, a VPN, or a password specific to a particular resource. A number of different things can go awry that cause a patron to not be able to access an electronic resource. The fault may lie with the vendor, the library, or even the student and the library staff member assisting the off-campus patron must ask questions to determine the source of the problem. In this respect, librarians may have experience with troubleshooting access for on-campus students which is directly applicable to trouble-shooting access for distance students.

When the problem with access is due to the vendor, it may be the responsibility of one librarian (i.e., electronic resources or acquisitions) to resolve the problem; when there is a problem with the technology that supports remote access, it is often the library's systems office that must provide the solution. Reference staff should know when to pass the problem to another unit and to whom the problem should be directed. In these cases, resolution of the problem might not be quick enough to meet the needs of the patron, especially when the access problem occurs in the evening or on the weekend. Where it might not be standard practice for the virtual reference service to provide document delivery, problems with access to electronic resources may necessitate this, particularly in the case of distance students. Since distance students do not have recourse to come into the library and access problems may not be solved within the timeframe that they need, the reference librarian should have the discretion to e-mail a specific article for the student. If this falls outside of the normal scope of the reference service, it should be made clear to the student that this is an exception based on extenuating circumstances.

Frequently, the problem with access is due to error on the patron side and with some questioning and patience the librarian can direct the distance student to the correct path into the resource. Troubleshooting access to electronic resources is always an important service, but is particularly vital for distance students as they do not have recourse to visit the library in person (where on-campus access may be uninterrupted). Additionally, the need may be for specific online articles for basic course readings where substitution of a different, accessible, resource is not acceptable.

Electronic access problems due to patron error are usually from taking the wrong path into an electronic resource. There are two common causes for patrons taking an incorrect path into a resource. First, patrons are not aware, for instance, that the homepage for LexisNexis will not gain them access to the library's LexisNexis subscription. They have heard, or read, references to LexisNexis and found the Web site through an Internet search engine rather than through the library. This incorrect access sometimes works for on-campus patrons because the campus IP address is recognized by the vendor as cleared for access, but it does not work for off-campus patrons. Second, patrons may be using a bookmark or a direct link into a specific article. Again, this will sometimes work from on-campus (depending on the resource) but will not work for off-campus patrons. This is a particular problem when on-campus faculty teach distance courses and do not realize that off-campus access for their students is different and requires entry through a proxy server or other means of authentication. The resolution for the individual student is guiding them to the correct path to the article. The long-term solution is to contact the faculty member and explain the situation for off-campus students and provide a more appropriate path to the article, or suggest the use of e-reserves. The librarian assisting the patron might not be the person to contact the faculty member (this being the area of the distance education librarian or a subject liaison), but the librarian should be aware of who in the library to contact.

With either of the scenarios, questioning the patron about their location and the path they took to access the electronic resource will reveal the source of the problem and allow for an easy solution. Librarians staffing the virtual reference service need to be aware of the modes of access for off-campus patrons, the faculty liaisons for the distance education programs, and the basics of troubleshooting remote access problems. Depending on the current organizational structure of the library this might all be old news for your reference librarians or new territory altogether. Those librarians directly involved with distance education programs as well as the systems staff or librarian responsible for electronic subscriptions have knowledge to share through training or by writing troubleshooting guides for the reference staff.

KNOWLEDGE OF PROGRAMS

Distance education programs may encompass academic areas which are not a strength of on-campus programs. Librarians staffing the virtual reference service should be aware of what these programs are and what resources are available. If the distance education librarian or a subject specialist has heretofore provided all of the research support for these students, the general reference staff may need training on the best research tools for these disciplines.

Faculty teaching distance education programs often use courseware to support the delivery of course content. It is not up to the librarian to troubleshoot this software, but it is essential that they know the terminology so that they understand what a student means if they refer to the courseware package or certain features of the courseware system. Distance education programs may also set up their own proxy servers for access to electronic resources and courseware. These may or may not be compatible with library technology and can further complicate the access troubleshooting process. It is unlikely that general reference staff will have access to enter an electronic course; the distance education librarian or subject specialist may be granted access. This can be a useful thing for all of the reference staff to be aware, particularly in some instances of troubleshooting access to electronic materials or if it would be useful to view the text of a specific assignment.

CONCLUSIONS

The basics of providing reference service to on-campus students and distance students are identical. Reference librarians can apply those things which they do best—a good reference interview and assistance with the research process—to virtual reference interaction with distance students. There are some specific differences in the needs of distance students that require awareness and flexibility in order for librarians to best support this group of students (Table 1). Reference generalists and subject specialist who staff the virtual reference service can be prepared to assist all patrons with excellence regardless of location, with attention to training and policy.

TABLE 1. Similarities and Differences of Providing Virtual Reference Service to On-Campus/Off-Campus Patrons and Distance Education Students

SAME	DIFFERENT
Reference interview skills	Virtual reference policies
Instruction in use of resources	Document delivery options
Troubleshooting electronic access	Troubleshooting electronic access
Our desire to provide excellent service to all users through all modes of communication	Academic program areas of emphasis
	Availability of local resources

When a library has a distance education librarian, this person can be invaluable in training reference colleagues to provide support to distance students. Additionally, this librarian and the virtual reference service can define when the virtual reference service should make a referral to the distance education librarian. In libraries without a dedicated distance education librarian, staff will need to work together to determine ways in which the virtual reference service can support distance students and make sure that all reference staff have the same level of training in this area.

NOTE

1. For general discussion of planning for virtual reference service, see for instance: Meola, M. and Stormont, S. (2002). *Starting and Operating Live Virtual Reference Services.* New York: Neal-Schuman; Kibbee, J., Ward D., and Ma, W. (2002). Virtual Service, Real Data: Results of a Pilot Study. *Reference Services Review. 30 no. 1.* 25-36; and MARS Ad Hoc Committee on Digital Reference Guidelines. (2003) *Draft Guidelines for Implementing and Maintaining Virtual Reference Services* at http://www.ala.org/rusa/mars/dig_ref_guidelines.htm.

REFERENCES

Feinberg Library. *Welcome to I-Ref.* Retrieved December 5, 2003 from Plattsburgh State University of New York, Feinberg Library Web site: http://www2.plattsburgh.edu/acadvp/libinfo/library/iref.html.

Felix G. Woodward Library. (2003) *About Ask A Librarian.* Retrieved December 5, 2003 from Austin Peay University, Felix G. Woodward Library Web site: http://library.apsu.edu/5_0.htm.

MARS Ad Hoc Committee on Digital Reference Guidelines. (2003) *Draft Guidelines for Implementing and Maintaining Virtual Reference Services.* Retrieved December 5, 2003, from American Library Association, Reference and User Services Division, Machine Assisted Reference Section Web site: http://www.ala.org/rusa/mars/dig_ref_guidelines.htm.

Newman Library. *Online Chat Guidelines.* Retrieved December 5, 2003 from Baruch College, Newman Library Web site: http://newman.baruch.cuny.edu/e_ref/chat_guidelines.htm.

University of Illinois at Urbana-Champaign Library. (2002) *Frequently Asked Questions: Real Time Reference.* Retrieved December 5, 2003 from University of Illinois at Urbana-Champaign Library, Ask-A-Librarian Web site: http://door.library.uiuc.edu/ugl/faq_files/faq.htm#rtr.

Progressive Partnering: Expanding Student and Faculty Access to Information Services

Linda L. Lillard
Pat Wilson
Constance M. Baird

University of Kentucky

SUMMARY. A distance learning team, including select faculty, a distance learning librarian, and a distance learning administrator, worked closely to develop a pilot study which actively involves the distance learning librarian as co-instructor in an online library science course. This paper details the results of the study and highlights the successful collaboration among academic, administrative, and support units.

KEYWORDS. Collaboration, distance learners, faculty, library resources

Because library resources and services in higher education must support the needs of faculty, students, and staff, regardless of location, the Association of College and Research Libraries' (ACRL) 2000 Guidelines for Distance Learning Library Services (Philosophy section, para. 1) were designed to "delineate the elements necessary to achieving these ends." Attempting to respond to

[Haworth co-indexing entry note]: "Progressive Partnering: Expanding Student and Faculty Access to Information Services." Lillard, Linda L., Pat Wilson, and Constance M. Baird. Co-published simultaneously in *Journal of Library Administration* (The Haworth Information Press, an imprint of The Haworth Press, Inc.) Vol. 41. No. 1/2, 2004, pp. 227-242; and: *The Eleventh Off-Campus Library Services Conference Proceedings* (ed: Patrick B. Mahoney) The Haworth Information Press, an imprint of The Haworth Press, Inc., 2004, pp. 227-242.

http://www.haworthpress.com/web/JLA
Digital Object Identifier: 10.1300/J111v41n01_17

these Guidelines, librarians have designed a variety of services to meet the needs of students and faculty in the distance learning environment. Examples of this response include such real-time reference services as instant messaging software; remote access to electronic resources through a proxy server; online tutorials and distance learning library services Web pages; and electronic reserves (Calvert, 2000; Wilson, 2002).

However, even with all of these services, recent research from a study conducted by the Online Computer Library Center (OCLC) (2002) indicates that many of the library services developed thus far are apparently not sufficiently meeting the needs of remote users in academe. The OCLC study (2002) found that 78% of the students surveyed preferred to access the Web remotely using their home computers. Even with a preference for remote access, students preferred face-to-face assistance rather than online or telephone assistance when they had problems using the Web to complete assignments. In 61% percent of the responses, students first asked friends or classmates for help, even though they preferred remote access. Furthermore, 62% of the students indicated that online assistance from librarians is something they would certainly use. Indeed, services must be developed that are *"close enough"* to meet students' needs for face-to-face assistance (Lillard, 2003).

With this in mind, a distance learning team, including select faculty, a distance learning librarian (DLL) and a distance learning administrator, worked closely to develop a pilot study which actively involves the DLL as co-instructor in online library science courses. The DLL had instructor privileges in the online course management system Blackboard. These access privileges allowed the librarian to be always available for assistance in students' research projects. She had full access to all course materials and could make announcements or contact students when she thought she might be of assistance. As library and information science literature is replete with studies showing that students are hesitant to ask librarians for assistance in the research process, the ability to contact students within the online course environment is a significant step in the provision of library services. In addition, this type of service is something very unique to the online classroom experience, as the librarian does not have the ability to walk into the on-campus classroom at any time and provide the same. At best, distance learning librarians are able to provide an orientation and/or workshop for a particular class as requested by a faculty member and then can be available via e-mail for follow-up questions. Being part of the online teaching team not only increases and enhances student/librarian interaction; it identifies the librarian as a faculty member active in the teaching process.

FIRST PHASE OF THE STUDY

Preparations for the study actually began prior to the beginning of the spring 2003 semester in which the course, Information in Society, was actually offered online. Information in Society is an introductory course that touches on the various topical areas related to library and information science. As the online course was developed, "Library Use" was included as the study module for the third week of the class. During the collaboration sessions, the DLL and the course instructor determined the type of assignments that would require students to do library research. It was decided that the Reading Summary assignments would require the most library research. These assignments were described in the course syllabus as follows:

> Over the course of the semester, read articles from *three different journals*. Each article is to be in a particular topical area (see calendar). Provide a complete citation to what you read. *Summarize* what the author says in 200-400 words, double-spaced. Where appropriate, note what other work the author uses (through references and discussion). Quote from the work only if you think the exact wording is important or particularly well-put. Most important points: *critique* what the author says; *connect* what you read to your own experience if possible. *Pose questions and make comments* about the topic or conclusions in a *section labeled "Discussion."* Aim for a variety of journals and for articles of substance; do not choose regular columns or reviews of books or other media. Do not select articles from American Libraries–those articles are too brief to be merely summarized. For the same reason lean towards the longer, more substantive articles from other journals. Be prepared to discuss what you learned in class.

The DLL provided information and designed tutorials for the Library Use module that directly related to the Reading Summaries course assignments. Figure 1 shows the first level of the Library Use Module. The first item on this screen describes the Library Use Module and the second item allows the student to click to yet another level of information resources to complete this assignment. The second level of this module is shown in Figures 2 and 3.

The instructor of the online course was also teaching a section of the same class in the face-to-face format during the same semester. Students were scheduled for hands-on library instruction with the DLL for two class periods during the third week of class. Our thoughts were that the on-campus workshops were of more benefit to the students because of the face-to-face interaction. This is especially important to note because the questions asked by many of the online students indicated that they had not looked at the instruction module provided for them.

FIGURE 1. First Level of Library Use Module

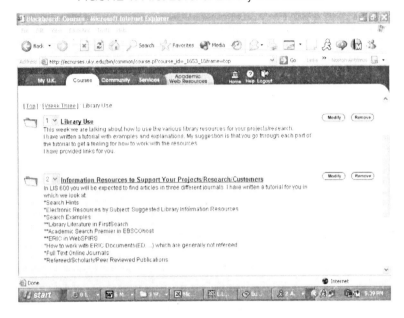

FIGURE 2. Second Level of Library Use Module

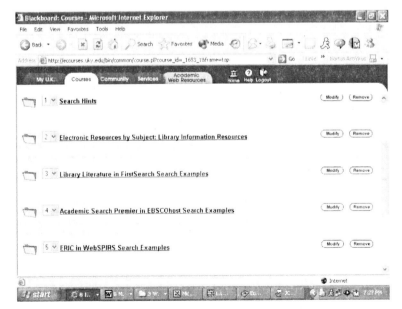

FIGURE 3. Second Level of Library Use Module

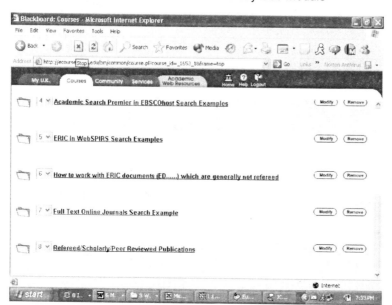

Students in both classes were given a library assignment that was worth 15 points of extra credit. The purpose of this assignment was to ascertain whether the students had benefited from the instructional sessions. Twelve of the 30 (40%) students in the online class and five of the 18 (28%) students in the on-campus class, however, did not submit these assignments. Our thoughts were that the point value attached to the assignments was not significant enough to make the extra effort for some students.

EXPLANATION OF CONSTRUCTION OF DLL's MODULE SHOWN IN FIGURES 1, 2, AND 3

The Information Resources to Support Your Projects/Research/Customers was written to emulate the topics covered in an on-site workshop. These workshops have three primary foci:

- Connectivity to remote resources
  - Off-campus access instructions were given in Topic/Module One
    - Students were told to request a library card from Distance Learning Library Services

- Proxy server information was given
- Library assignment for the week was to actually connect to data-bases remotely
- Contact information was given for help/problem solving
- Bibliographic databases
  - What is a bibliographic database
  - How does one know which one to choose
  - Why is the same database available from more than one place
- Construction of search statements

ASSIGNMENT GIVEN TO STUDENTS BY DLL

The following announcement was made in Blackboard to the online class:

Wed, Jan 29, 2003–*Library Use and a Tutorial*
Please look at the Week 3 Course Material.
I have made available a tutorial for your class focusing on information Resources available in the library.
I have also posted 3 assignments which are worth 5 extra points each for a total of 15 points.
My suggestion in working with the tutorial is that you print each part and then actually do the searches as you follow it.
I have links to the tutorials within the various parts of the Week 3 course material. I also have a link under External Links on the top screen for the class.

If you have questions, please let me know at pwilson@uky.edu
Pat Wilson
DLL

Keeping in mind that a myriad of bibliographic databases are available from multiple vendors it was decided that the students should be exposed to a variety of databases with different foci and from more than one company. The librarian chose databases for search examples based on assigned topics for the reading summaries.

SECOND PHASE OF THE STUDY

The next time the course, Information and Society, was offered online was during the summer of 2003. At this time the course, which is normally a 16 week course, was offered in the 8-week summer session. Some of the assignments were altered and while the three reading summary assignments remained, a poster session and book summary were replaced with a research paper. The inclusion of the research paper added yet another assignment that would require students to do major library research.

Because of the shortened schedule for the class, the fourth module, *Library/Information Resources-Use for Reading Summary Assignments*, was a requirement for the second week of class. The information presented in this module was altered considerably from the first iteration of the class. Figure 4 shows the Table of Contents for the Library/Information Resources module.

For this iteration of the course, the library use assignments were required. Three screen capture assignments, each tied to one of the three reading summary assignments, were worth 10 points each out of a total of 500 points for all course work. This time the assignments had a much better completion rate. Out of 34 students, three students did not complete one of the three assignments, and one student completed none of the library use assignments (this student subsequently took an incomplete in the course).

FIGURE 4

THIRD PHASE OF THE STUDY

Information and Society was offered again online during the fall semester of 2003. The course instructor was also teaching another online course, Instructional Services. The DLL was involved with both classes. The course instructor and the DLL again worked together to plan the assignments that promoted use of information resources and that promoted student collaboration with the librarian. The same resources that were used in the summer semester as shown in the Table of Contents in Figure 4 were used for both fall courses. During the course planning session, the instructor and the DLL decided that the students would be required to consult with the librarian when doing their research for course projects. In the Information and Society course, the librarian consultation assignment was worth 100 points or 10% of the final course grade. The description of the librarian consultation as detailed in the course syllabus was:

Librarian Consultation (100 points)

In the course of searching for items for your research paper and presentation, you will be required to consult with Pat Wilson, the Distance Learning Librarian who is participating as a co-instructor in this class. The details of completing this assignment will be discussed in the classroom discussion board and will be posted in the class materials at the appropriate time.

The librarian consultation assignment in the Instructional Services course was tied to the bibliography assignment. This assignment was worth 50 points out of 1000 total points for the course or 5% of the final grade. The bibliography and consultation assignments were described as follows in the syllabus:

Bibliography (75 points)

You will prepare a 25 item bibliography of articles, books, and Web sites pertinent to a particular topic pertaining to instructional services. Choice of topic for this assignment will be discussed in class.

Librarian Consultation (50 points)

In the course of searching for items for the bibliography assignment, you will be required to consult with Pat Wilson, the Distance Learning Librarian who is participating as a co-instructor in this class. The details of completing this assignment will be discussed in the classroom discussion board and will be posted in the class materials at the appropriate time.

The bibliography assignment and the librarian consultation were further described in the class discussion board as follows:

> Your 25 item bibliography can contain a variety of media: books, articles, Web sites, videos, etc. You can prepare this bibliography on instructional services in general, but it is best to limit it somehow . . . maybe by type of library or maybe by type of service, etc. You will be required to consult with Pat Wilson, the distance learning library about your plans for searching for the items for your bibliography. While Pat is here to help you with your information needs throughout the course, the purpose of the consultation is for you to receive one on one assistance with your searches. So, you will make an initial appointment with her for this assignment. This does not mean that you cannot contact her again with any questions you might have. The initial appointment is required. This also does not mean that you cannot begin searching until you consult with Pat since many of you are quite a way through the program and have searching skills. However, Pat may be able to help you refine your searches if you aren't finding exactly what you want . . . This assignment will be due on December 7.

REPRESENTATIVE QUESTIONS/PROBLEMS/COMMENTS FROM STUDENTS BROKEN DOWN INTO CATEGORIES

Connectivity Issues

- The student stated that she tried her password with the userID xxxx and the proxy authentication and that it had failed. She further commented that her computer was set-up according to the instructions on the DL library homepage. Help! (Spring '03 Student)

  - *Solution: DLLS Technician helped problem solve*

- Another student tried logging into FirstSearch using the ID and Library card number provided. When attempting to log in, a message was received that the authorization id must be nine characters long, and it refused to accept the ID. She asked for thoughts? (Spring '03 Student)
- A student inquired: I am having trouble getting into FirstSearch to do the tutorial for the LIS 600 class. I printed the screen that I get when I try to log in and attached it. Please let me know if I am heading in the right direction. Thank you so much. (Spring '03 Student)

- *Solution: Student not going through the proxy server. DLLS Technician responded.*

- Explanation: Some students cannot access proxy server because of firewalls, etc. In that case DLLS sends a handout with ID/Passwords for some of the databases available to UK affiliates.

Success

- It was really fun working with the following student. He was so excited once he had everything working. Notice the greeting. He was at work and couldn't get through our proxy server so was letting us know he was successful and needed some help getting articles.

  - The student inquired: Afternoon Pat,
    I did an ERIC search in WebSPIRS (using the search techniques I've learned) and found some journal articles I'd like to read. . . . can you help me get hold of these articles? Thanks! (Spring '03 student)

- Another student having success:

  - The student attached her third screen capture for the last reading summary and wanted make sure the DLL received it. Then she went on to say . . . Pat, thanks so much for all of your help this summer for this class. I feel that I have learned so much about databases, and I know if I take another blackboard course, it will be much easier! Thanks again. (Summer '03 student)

Students Wanting to Improve Searches

- This is a message from a student who found an article for the assignment due that week, but was interested in looking at different databases for the next two assignments. She found this one by going to the distance learning page and clicking on "Full-text online Journals." Then she typed in "Library Journal" and searched from there until she "got lucky." Ha ha.
  She then went on to say . . . this is a learning exercise in searching the databases, and since I may be doing this for others someday, I would like to know different ways to find these articles. What database should I look in next time? Thanks for your help. I am happy with the article I found for this assignment, so if you are helping others this

week, don't worry about my request until later. Thanks again. (Spring '03 student)

- *Response: From Librarian*

  - *There are a couple of ways of approaching this. One is the way you took and maybe that isn't so bad since you were looking at a specific journal. By the way Congratulations!! On finding what you needed.*
  - *You could do that for your next assignment or I can direct you to a database, make some suggestions for searches, have you work with the database and then we can go from there.*
  - *Your next assignment deals with changes in the library/information science world due to technology and I will tell you that there have been tons of changes. I think that there are several databases we could use, Library Literature (FirstSearch), Academic Search Premier (EBSCO), etc.*
  - *I did some things in EBSCO's Business Source Premier. Let me show you. . . .*

- *Student's Response:*

  - Thank you so much!!! You are a fountain of information.
  - Then she asked for information sources re: medical information transmission/communication, etc., that would be great since that is her field. (Spring '03 student)

- *Response: Librarian suggested databases, sent examples of searches*

Fall 2003 Semester Student/Librarian Dialog

- A student was . . . interested in doing his paper on the topic of privacy . . . and was not entirely certain which direction he wanted to go with the broad topic, but was thinking about focusing on public libraries. . . .

  - *Librarian Response:*

    - I have some searches and databases to suggest to you. You can access these databases off of my home page if you wish. http://www.uky.edu/Libraries/dislearn.html. . . .
    - Try searching the ERIC database (EBSCO or WebSPIRS) for patriot act and librar* (use the * to search for the root of the word). Also try searching for patriot act and privacy.

- Try the same searches in the Academic Search Premier (EBSCO) database and in the PAIS database (FirstSearch).
- I think that you will want to look at the ALA home page http://www.ala.org. Click on the Issues and Advocacy tab. This should get you going . . .

- *Student Response:*

  - The student got back to the DLL . . . wanted to thank you for all your help. With the databases and search strategies you suggested I was able to find more than enough relevant materials. Now, if I can just condense this info and my ideas. Thanks Again!

SURVEY FALL 2003

During this semester, students in both classes were given a survey to record their reactions to the librarian consultation assignment. From the Information and Society class, 13 out of 24 students responded to the survey. From the Instructional Services class, 20 out of 29 students responded to the survey. The questions and responses from this survey are as follows:

Question 1. Strictly from your role as a student, what is your opinion of the librarian consultation assignment?

Out of thirteen responses to this question from the Information and Society class, students thought this was a good assignment. Words such as "good," "extremely helpful," "comforting," "painless," and "good idea and good practice" were used to describe their reactions to the assignment. Only one student answered in the negative saying that he/she "honestly did not find the librarian consultation necessary."

Question 2. Was the librarian consultation helpful to you in completing your assignment?

Most of the thirteen respondents thought that the consultation was helpful. Positive comments such as: "I found it helpful bouncing ideas for my project off of the consultant and getting some guidance. This is a critical step before doing a search," "Yes, I was surprised at how much attention the librarian gave to me," "Yes, she gave me insight in how to fine tune my search," and "Pat Wilson even called me at home to assist me with my paper and with getting my computer configured to access the UK library system," were plentiful while the only negative comment was "It wasn't counterproductive but it wasn't really helpful either."

Question 3. Would you have consulted the distance learning librarian if it had not been a course requirement?

Ten of the thirteen respondents said they would "probably not" have consulted with the distance learning librarian if it had not been a course requirement. One student expanded on this to say "I might not have because I would not have known it was available." These responses coupled with the positive responses in the first two questions indicate that students just do not realize that they can contact a librarian online.

Question 4. As a result of the student/librarian interaction in this class, how likely would you be to contact the distance learning librarian on your own for help in future classes in which this consultation is not a requirement?

All thirteen respondents stated that they would be much more likely to contact the distance learning librarian as a result of this assignment. Some students qualified the statement saying that they would contact her if they were stuck. Again this answer might be a result of the fact that these students are Library Science students.

Question 5. In your role as a future librarian or information specialist, what is your opinion of the library consultation assignment?

Students were now asked to step out of the role of student and look at the assignment from their role as a future librarian or information specialist. All thirteen students saw some benefit to this assignment, though comments indicated that some students thought it was more beneficial than others. Positive comments included: "It's good, I think it should be required," "I think it is extremely helpful," "I think it is good, because it encourages using the librarian as a resource . . . ," "I think it would greatly benefit someone unfamiliar with those online databases. It would have saved my life if I hadn't already known how to access them," while slightly negative comments were: "Not bad. Could have done the paper without, but appreciated the help I was given," and "For me, it underscores the inadequacy of some types of learning–I'm not fond of the 'distance learning' concept. E-mail responses sometimes don't answer the question at all, or don't answer it in terms that the student can understand. You have to be persistent in asking for clarification, and time can be a constraint."

Question 6. Since students traditionally shy away from asking a librarian for help, do you think requiring this assignment is beneficial?

Every respondent answered "Yes" to this question.

Question 7. Do you think this assignment would work to help alleviate student fear of asking for librarian assistance?

Nine respondents answered an unequivocal "yes" to this question. Two respondents were not sure and one of these students said that he/she thought it more likely "to ask someone in person for help than to e-mail someone I can't see. But I'm not sure if others are like me. I would probably suggest that the assignment be done in person if this is possible." Finally, one respondent answered no because "You would force the issue one time and for the rest of the time the student would still shy away from the librarian"

Question 8. Do you think the librarian consultation assignment could promote the development of a research relationship throughout the life of a project?

Eight respondents thought this assignment could promote the research relationship, while two respondents thought it would be a "case-by-case scenario." Nobody had a negative response, though one person thought that a research relationship wouldn't be needed for a term paper but might be for a person working on a thesis.

The unique aspect of this survey overall was that special questions needed to be included because the students themselves are future librarians. This could possibly bias their responses to this type of assignment, so future research would be useful where students in other classes were asked the first four questions.

CONCLUSION

The online instruction environment is providing many opportunities for librarians to provide research instruction for students. While comments from some students revealed the fact that they did not know they could ask for librarian assistance during an online course, the required librarian consultations highlighted this possibility. Even students who believed they had adequate or exceptional research skills found that the personalized attention from the librarian gave them additional guidance and found it helpful to bounce their ideas off of a knowledgeable consultant. This direct involvement with students, even though remote, allowed students to know the librarian personally resulting in students' responding that they would consult the DLL for future projects in future online classes.

The biggest drawback to providing the high quality personalized service in this project is that one DLL could very well be overwhelmed with requests for individualized assistance and fails to provide this assistance in a timely manner. Also because the students who had the face-to-face instruction sessions appeared to be more knowledgeable about library resources while some of the students in the online class asked questions that revealed they had obviously not looked at tutorial information, a solution might be to combine services that mirror these two different approaches. One week might be allotted in the online class to a synchronous instruction session in Blackboard's Virtual Classroom followed by librarian posed questions in the discussion board and questions from the students. After this time period, students would know what the librarian can do for them and could ask for more assistance on a case-by-case basis when necessary. This would alleviate the need for the librarian to be present in the class all semester, except when deemed necessary, and provide students with the personal contact necessary to develop a comfort level with contacting the librarian. This scenario probably more closely mirrors the one time Bibliographic Instruction session commonly offered on most college campuses, that is intended to provide students with research skills related to a particular class and hopefully make them comfortable contacting the librarian. However, a week long module provides more interaction and therefore might increase the possibility that the students would avail themselves of the librarian's assistance throughout the rest of the course and in the future. Another approach would be to compare and contrast the distance learning librarian role and student perception of such in an online course for library and information science students with an online course populated by students in a different discipline–using similar assignments and opportunities for interaction with the librarian. The authors want to build and expand upon the initial success of this first effort–comparing and contrasting these teaching techniques with new strategies for diverse student populations.

REFERENCES

Association of College & Research Libraries. (2000). *Guidelines for distance learning library services*. Retrieved January 8, 2004, from http://www.ala.org/ala/acrl/acrlstandards/guidelinesdistance.htm.

Calvert, H. M. (2000). Document delivery options for distance education students: An electronic reserve service at Ball State University Libraries. In P. S. Thomas (Ed.), *The Ninth Off-Campus Library Services Proceedings* (pp. 73-82). Mount Pleasant, MI: Central Michigan University.

Lillard, L. L. (2003). *Personalized library services for distance learners: Cultivating a research relationship*. Manuscript submitted for publication.

OCLC, Inc., (2002, June). *How academic librarians can influence college students' Web-based information choices*. Retrieved April 30, 2003, from http://www2.oclc.org/oclc/pdf/printondemand/informationhabits.pdf.

Wilson, P. (2002). The ins and outs of providing electronic reserves for distance learning classes. In P. B. Mahoney (Ed.), *The Tenth Off-Campus Library Services Conference Proceedings* (pp. 413-422). Mount Pleasant, MI: Central Michigan University.

Collaboration and Information Literacy: Challenges of Meeting Standards When Working with Remote Faculty

Robin Lockerby
Divina Lynch
James Sherman
Elizabeth Nelson

National University

SUMMARY. The National University Library Information Literacy Plan has been in place since 1999. Following a slow start, information literacy has begun to be accepted throughout the University. Faculty collaboration, dogged determination of librarians, and impressive assessment results have helped pave the way for this program. In this paper, a program overview will be briefly discussed followed by the National University LIC Librarians (virtual librarians at the regional learning centers) discussing faculty collaboration efforts, a University core curriculum class on information literacy, and information literacy assessment.

KEYWORDS. Collaboration, faculty, distance education, information literacy

INTRODUCTION

Since its humble beginnings in 1972, the National University Library System (NULS) remains proactive in developing its library programs to meet the

[Haworth co-indexing entry note]: "Collaboration and Information Literacy: Challenges of Meeting Standards When Working with Remote Faculty." Lockerby, Robin et al. Co-published simultaneously in *Journal of Library Administration* (The Haworth Information Press, an imprint of The Haworth Press, Inc.) Vol. 41, No. 1/2, 2004, pp. 243-253; and: *The Eleventh Off-Campus Library Services Conference Proceedings* (ed: Patrick B. Mahoney) The Haworth Information Press, an imprint of The Haworth Press, Inc., 2004, pp. 243-253.

http://www.haworthpress.com/web/JLA
Digital Object Identifier: 10.1300/J111v41n01_18

rapid growth of the University, which now has 17,200 students at 29 academic learning centers and over 3,000 online students. In 2000, the NULS Central Library moved into a new state-of-the-art facility that showcases the library resources (print and electronic) and its emphasis on information literacy; the 21st Century Cybrary Model was born. The library collections became centralized at the main library in San Diego and virtual libraries, named Library Information Centers (LICs), were established in the regional academic learning centers. Today we have 9 regional LICs supporting remote faculty and students with 11 professional librarians. These librarians are our advocates for the faculty and students. They preach the good news of information access and information literacy.

The NULS Information Literacy Plan, established in 1999 and revised in 2000, has evolved from traditional one-hour-stands (bibliographic instruction) to a systematic delivery of three levels of instruction incorporating information literacy: basic orientation to library services and resources; introduction to discipline specific research and resources; and advanced project/thesis instruction in developing a review of the literature. None of the library instruction is required by administration, but most programs now use the ACRL *Information Literacy Competency Standards for Higher Education* outcome language in some of their course objectives and recommend that classes meet with a librarian. The success of this has been the result of the collaboration between the library's department liaisons and LIC librarians, and the faculty. The NULS Information Literacy Plan is a dynamic process which means the Library has not arrived, but has made giant strides forward. The following stories by three LIC librarians demonstrate the issues, concerns, and successes of the library's program through the eyes of the regional librarians. It is interesting to note, that none of the concerns identified by the LIC librarians reflect problems generated by the fact that the LICs do not have their own collections, and must rely on fast document delivery and on electronic resources. National University Library System has truly become a Cybrary.

CHALLENGES

The NULS Information Literacy Plan aims to meet ACRL Information Literacy Standards by integrating these standards with curriculum objectives, combined with online tutorials, classroom instruction, and individual consultation. Implementation of the plan has met with varying levels of success in the Library Information Centers. This is not surprising for, as Iannuzzi (1998) has said, campus culture, and information literacy programs take time to develop (p. 97). Successful implementation requires the acceptance and support of, and collaboration with administration and faculty.

A survey of LIC librarians has identified a range of successful collaborations as well as challenges in meeting Information Literacy (IL) standards. One of the challenges is the fast pace of the one-month class format, where a class starts and finishes in four weeks. This contributes to a difficulty in communicating and connecting with faculty, especially adjunct instructors. On the other hand, some adjunct instructors recognize that their teaching would be more effective with help from the librarian. Some instructors call one or two weeks before the scheduled class session to make arrangements for Information Literacy Instruction (ILI), as well as to ask for assistance in doing research and getting access to materials they need. Last minute requests for instruction also do occur, which may not give the librarian adequate time to prepare for a particular class. In such a case, the librarian usually does the instruction because there may not be another opportunity to work with that class. In any event, this may still be a connection that could lead to a stronger relationship in the future.

Another challenge is the limited time for instruction. Time allotted may be too short to do active learning activities and cover all the IL standards adequately. The problem may come from two places: (1) the instructor's limit on time; and (2) the librarian's desire to cover as much as possible in one session. This problem makes it imperative that librarian and instructor work together to have ILI integrated into the course rather than taught as a separate module. It also shows the need to cooperatively decide what is to be covered, in order to make the instruction more effective and relevant. As Grassian (2001) says, "The decisions about what to include and what to leave out can become very painful indeed" (p. 294). She continues on to state the importance of and difficulty in fitting the amount of material to the timeframe.

Certain perceptions, assumptions, and misconceptions also present a challenge. Some of these may be characterized by the following statements:

- "I (librarian) do not get the impression that I am considered on the same level as faculty."
- "These are graduate students; they should know what they are supposed to do."
- "The students already know what they need to know about the library."

In some of these instances, the best that the librarian can do is to remind the faculty of his or her availability and willingness to help. At other times it may be possible to ask instructors to take a brief (librarian-supplied) survey of the class to determine the need for information literacy instruction. In any event, the librarian should continue to keep contact and take every opportunity to connect, and not give up.

Another challenge on certain occasions is the lack of technological resources. There are times when there are no computer classrooms available for hands-on learning. The librarian may have to use a laptop and a portable projector. This means instruction would mainly involve a lecture or demonstration, with perhaps a PowerPoint presentation, if the classroom does not happen to have an Internet connection.

In general, solutions to the problems mentioned above involve the fostering of better communication and stronger continuing relationships with faculty and administration. Raspa and Ward (2000) encourage librarians to listen and reach out, for "building relationships allows us to build stronger bridges" (p. 17). To promote information literacy and information literacy instruction, all of the LIC Librarians are involved in building relationships through a variety of activities such as providing reference and research assistance; attending faculty orientations, meetings and training sessions, as well as doing presentations or conducting an occasional workshop; and just engaging in conversations. They also send informational memos and e-mails to keep the faculty abreast of library services, resources, and other items of interest. These activities are important basic steps. According to Buchanan, Luck, and Jones (2002), "Developing initial connections with faculty is the necessary foundation upon which to build collaborations" (p. 144).

As important as they are, the activities mentioned above, comprise only the initial steps. For collaboration to truly occur, it will be necessary for the librarian to put in extra outreach and a stronger marketing effort on an ongoing basis. It is incumbent upon the librarian to find a faculty member who would be willing to work with him or her on a joint project that would integrate subject matter assignments with the acquisition of information literacy skills. If successful, the collaboration would demonstrate to the rest of the faculty the librarian's dedication to achieving shared educational goals.

SUCCESS

This paper presented the challenges the LIC librarians face in their efforts to collaborate with faculty. It will now also present some of their successes. Here are some examples of cooperation or collaboration from the San Jose, Fresno, and Sacramento Academic Centers of National University in California.

San Jose (Divina Lynch): Working with Administration and Faculty

The Associate Regional Dean at the San Jose Academic Center has been very supportive of efforts to promote information literacy instruction. She made time to meet with me, gave comments, and suggested activities for an MBA Project class and a graduate level research class in education. I provided the instructors with updates and asked for comments. About two weeks before the MBA Project class started, I e-mailed the students and encouraged them to do the library online tutorial. Instruction for this class focused on relevant resources, as well as evaluation of articles and Web sites. The writing center director also talked about plagiarism. Additional help was provided with the use of handouts. At various times during the class month, I answered e-mailed questions and gave the rest of the class additional information as needed. A reminder for them to get in touch with me for assistance was appreciated by the students. One of the MBA students included me when sending out an e-mailed update of his work to the instructor. This gave me an opportunity to remind the student of some things which would help him. I asked the instructors for comments on students' work and effectiveness of instruction and reminded them that I would be happy to continue to work with them and their students. Although there is a lot more work to do before real collaboration is achieved, the Dean has shown her strong support and additional lines of communication with faculty have opened up.

Another thing I count as a success is seeing members of the faculty who have had a fear of technology, become more comfortable with it. It is heartening to work with those instructors who have avoided computers but who now are excited about the research they can do online. I have been invited to join some of them in training sessions involving technology. I know that I was asked to participate so I could help them if necessary, after the training was over. If that helps the faculty to see the library's services as indispensable, that's another step towards collaboration.

Fresno (James Sherman): Teaching an Information Literacy Course at an Off-Campus Facility

One of the major challenges at an off-campus facility is the teaching of information literacy at that location. I have the distinct pleasure of teaching a course called "Information Literacy and Report Writing" at the Fresno Campus of National University. I team teach the course with a staff member of our Writing Center, herself also an English instructor and a writer. All National University locations include a Writing Center, wherein students can obtain help from a staff of writers in improving drafts of their compositions and gaining strategies for improving their writing. I, as a librarian, teach research-related material, and my colleague teaches writing methods. Our collaboration came about when the Associate Regional Dean for the Fresno Academic Center learned that this course would be offered in Fresno in February, 2003, and every six months thereafter.

I was immediately asked if I would like to teach it, to which I expressed an interest. However, upon seeing the requirements of the course in the University's abstract, I informed the Dean that I wasn't equipped to teach major parts of the course. I could handle the library/research skills aspects, but not so much the writing skills.

The Dean came up with the idea of having both the Writing Center person and myself teach the course jointly. Now, this course is a requirement within the School of Arts and Sciences of the University.

In a nutshell, the research aspect of the course covers National University's online resources in the humanities, business and science, plus an observation of government Web sites. The course also covers instruction in Microsoft PowerPoint and Excel. I begin the course by reviewing different university Web sites' definitions of information literacy. We also do extensive studies of methods for selecting topics for research and discovering the best materials and methods for selecting sources and doing research on those topics. Included in the coverage are field research methods, using interviews, surveys, and observations. We cover the refinement of topics, the evaluation of resources and information that has been gathered, and careful and complete citation of sources and the avoidance of plagiarism. This includes the coverage of legal responsibilities and moral responsibilities to authors, including copyright, and the need for accurate quoting. We also cover ways to evaluate Web sites for authority, accuracy, reliability, objectivity, currency, and completeness of coverage. I give the students a skills evaluation questionnaire right at the beginning of the first class to see where they place themselves as far as their abilities in doing online research using the Web and National University's online library resources. I then give them the same evaluation on the last day to see how they feel they have progressed throughout the class. I also spend some time with the students in dispelling their fears of libraries and librarians. As Van Scoyoc (2003) states, students perceive librarians as unfriendly, unapproachable, or too busy, so I try to make the students feel that librarians want to help them and support them.

The writing aspect of the course includes the writing of a prospectus on a major research/writing project, the evaluation and completion of that project, including in-class group discussions and peer reviews of the work that the student has done while it is in progress. The ALA and MLA writing methods are covered during the course.

The course requirements include a mid-term and final exam, both of which include a section on research and sections on writing, proper English grammar, word usage and sentence structure, and the evaluation of resources. The students must also submit their major research/writing project, and each must do a PowerPoint presentation to the class, which includes the use of Excel.

Generally, the class has been very well received by the students. The difference in the quality of their work between the start of the term and the end is always very evident. I always feel very confident that the students have gained skills that will carry them throughout their careers.

Sacramento (Elizabeth Nelson): Outreach and Assessment: Keys to the Successful Information Literacy Model for Remote Campuses

From the perspective of an Information Center in Sacramento, the issues we are finding important are: bridging the barriers between the remote campus and the Central Library, and finding solutions which are both time-efficient and comprehensive within the accelerated pace of the National University System.

OUTREACH

Sharing the passion for education is the lubricant which oils a slow-moving wheel. Although we think our faculty may be slow to join the Information Literacy momentum, I always ask myself: "Am I thinking of myself as isolated, or have I adopted the model expressed by Steven Bell (2000) who speaks of 'The Seamless Learning Culture?' " How can this be achieved in a remote setting? Part of my solution is "Collaborate, Integrate, and Appreciate." All three represent the passion for education. All three are at the root of *outreach*.

In the article entitled "Integrating Information Literacy into the Virtual University: A Course Model," *Library Trends*, Fall 2002, the authors (Buchanan, Luck, and Jones) state:

> Librarians, in collaboration with faculty, need to develop workable, mature methods for integrating IL concepts into traditional coursework and assignments instead of teaching them in a related but isolated fashion. . . . Librarians must continue to better educate themselves and teaching faculty on IL concepts, standards, learning outcomes, and objectives. (pp. 160, 161)

As fresh ideas ignite into a shared vision, we will reach an integrated, collaborative appreciation and outreach which will meet the needs of faculty and students in a unique way for each classroom. It is difficult to formulate a perfect model which will mold all disciplines in its framework. Rather, I strive to carve a unique niche in each classroom or group of students or faculty member requiring our services. This can be done through collaborative outreach and assessment.

Some examples of outreach are meeting faculty at monthly faculty meetings where librarians give a brief update on the LIC. These talks can help to ignite the flame and spread the passion.

The elements which compose this type of outreach are:

1. Introducing memorable examples which help faculty grasp our sphere of activities and possibilities.
2. Discussing a clear learning objective which constitutes a "shared vision," combining the library, faculty, and the university missions.
3. Explaining how we have reached our goals.
4. Illustrating how one enlightened idea has made the path easier for student achievement.
5. Reminding the faculty: "Our ultimate goal is student success!"

Sharing the vision of a great educator or management theorist, such as Peter Drucker (1974), who states in his classic book, *Management: Tasks, Responsibilities, Practices*, "The test of the organization is the spirit of performance" (p. 455).

OUTREACH WITH RESULTS

Capturing the moment is not exclusive to the marketing and sales professional; it also applies to us–remote campus librarians.

Example

A new faculty member walks into my office. She wants to order a video for a beginning accounting class. I also tell her about our other services, including the opportunity to instruct students on the use of our electronic library resources. "Oh no, I frankly do not have any extra time. Perhaps another month in the future. Do you realize what I must accomplish in one month?"

After I process her video request, I comment that I recently had an opportunity to see the new interface of Mergent Online, which is very useful for accountants. I give her a brief demonstration. She is very impressed. "When can you share it with the class?" The next week I was demonstrating it to students in a 15 minute presentation in a computer-assisted classroom. Later she came in to say that the students loved learning Mergent, and she had plans to ask the Lead Faculty to incorporate this module into the syllabus for that class.

Another example of successful faculty outreach which resulted in integration of learning outcomes and student success, was my work with the instructor of the IL680, the Master's Thesis class for Education. I e-mailed and visited with the faculty member for quite some time prior to this presentation. She shared her goals and learning outcomes with me. It was a privilege to work with her and the students who had reached this level and were highly motivated to complete their program. I gave an hour presentation on research methods, both in PowerPoint and interactively in the computer-assisted classroom. We explored the scholarly publications, assessed their value; learned the formulation of a thesis statement, literature review preparation, and shared the value of their own contributions to the field of scholarship.

After the presentation, I joined the class and the instructor at their break at a nearby restaurant where the instructor and I answered student questions and further discussed their Master's thesis proposal. The formal presentation followed by an informal gathering proved to be fruitful. I met with students informally after this on a consultation basis.

Another presentation took me to a middle school campus, where an NU class was being conducted. I presented a library orientation and Master's thesis proposal introduction for Sacramento teachers who were working on the advanced degree. The strategy used for this class was a PowerPoint presentation using a laptop computer. There was no access to the Internet, but the presentation was understood and very well received. The keys to the success of this presentation were flexibility and clarity of explanation.

ASSESSMENT WITH A FOCUS

Types of Assessment

Self-assessment is an analysis of the student's perception of his/her own skills and Information Literacy abilities. The skill scale is 1-5 (not at all, poor, fair, good, excellent). The questions are multiple choice. The purpose of this type of assessment is to achieve student "buy-in." Students perceive their own needs, and this paves the way to a successful information literacy instruction session. This is followed by a second self-assessment, where the students generally rate themselves much higher. A graph from Excel illustrating the progress is given to each student. Their scores are then visible to themselves and their instructors.

Outcome Assessment is another type of test. It is given after instruction and must meet the following criteria to be effective.

1. Does it measure relevant factors?
2. Does it measure the skills taught?
3. Does it measure the effectiveness of instruction in Information Literacy?
4. Does it engage the student in the critical thinking and analysis skills which Information Literacy incorporates?

Authentic Assessment is defined by the *Glossary of Education Terms and Acronyms* (2003) as: "An assessment presenting tasks that reflect the kind of mastery demonstrated by experts. Authentic assessment of a student's ability to solve problems, for example, would assess how effectively a student solves a real problem."

The role of the librarian is changing in a virtual environment. The ability to adapt to changing roles lies in librarians' willingness to experiment with new ways to accomplish their libraries' missions. . . . Boldly experimenting with new modes of instructional delivery can invigorate librarians and the services they offer. (Buchanan et al., 2002, p. 163)

CONCLUSION

The effective integration of information literacy into the curriculum is an ongoing process. Responsibility for making this happen lies with everyone involved in education. Librarians must continue to build relationships with administration, faculty, and staff to foster collaboration. Common educational goals can be achieved by meeting challenges head-on and building upon successful interactions.

REFERENCES

Bell, S. J. (2000). Creating learning libraries in support of seamless learning cultures. *College & Undergraduate Libraries, 6*(2), 45-58.

Buchanan, L. E., Luck, D. L., & Jones, T. C. (2002). Integrating information literacy into the virtual university: A course model. *Library Trends, 51,* 144-166. Retrieved May 27, 2003, from ProQuest Education Complete database.

Drucker, P. F. (1974). *Management: Tasks, Responsibilities, Practices.* New York, NY: Harper.

Grassian, E. S., & Kaplowitz, J. R. (2001). *Information literacy instruction: Theory and practice*. New York: Neal-Schuman.

Iannuzzi, P. (1998). Faculty development and information literacy: Establishing campus partnerships. *Reference Services Review, 26*, 97-102, 116. Retrieved November 25, 2003, from EBSCOhost EJS.

North Central Regional Educational Laboratory. Pathways. (2003). *Glossary of Education Terms and Acronyms*. Retrieved November 14, 2003, from http://www.ncrel.org/sdrs/areas/misc/glossary.htm.

Raspa, D., & Ward, D. (2000). Listening for collaboration: Faculty and librarians working together. In D. Raspa & D. Ward (Eds.), *The collaborative imperative: Librarians and faculty working together in the information universe* (pp. 1-18). Chicago: American Library Association.

Van Scoyoc, A. M. (2003). Reducing library anxiety in first-year students: The impact of computer-assisted instruction and bibliographic instruction. *Reference and User Services Quarterly, 42*, 329-41. Retrieved October 17, 2003, from Library Literature and Information Science database.

Collaborating on Electronic Course Reserves to Support Student Success

Elaine Magusin
Kay Johnson

Athabasca University

SUMMARY. As we move into an era in which an increasing amount of information is available in digital form and more universities and colleges are providing distance education courses, electronic course reserves are becoming an essential part of library services. The Digital Reading Room (DRR), an Athabasca University collaboratively developed e-reserves system, facilitates immediate student access to faculty selected, course specific resources in a variety of media and promotes increased use of electronic information resources. To encourage student success in a digital environment, the Library has worked with Faculty to create information literacy tools designed to help students become better researchers and information consumers.

KEYWORDS. Collaboration, reserves, distance learners, technology

INTRODUCTION

As librarians discover, develop, and implement best practices for delivering services and resources to distance learners, one area that has seen considerable experimentation is electronic course reserves. Whether we use commercial

[Haworth co-indexing entry note]: "Collaborating on Electronic Course Reserves to Support Student Success." Magusin, Elaine, and Kay Johnson. Co-published simultaneously in *Journal of Library Administration* (The Haworth Information Press, an imprint of The Haworth Press, Inc.) Vol. 41, No. 1/2, 2004, pp. 255-264; and: *The Eleventh Off-Campus Library Services Conference Proceedings* (ed: Patrick B. Mahoney) The Haworth Information Press, an imprint of The Haworth Press, Inc., 2004, pp. 255-264.

http://www.haworthpress.com/web/JLA
Digital Object Identifier: 10.1300/J111v41n01_19

products such as Docutek's ERes or in-house systems, we face similar challenges in bringing the course reserves desk to the desktops of our students. Technology offers many possibilities, but providing convenient access to resources that teaching faculty have prescribed for a course is only the beginning. "Student success" is a lofty goal, and the one we reach for, as librarians, teaching faculty, and other institutional partners work together to ensure that students not only have access to resources, but are provided with opportunities to grow as independent life long learners. Athabasca University's Digital Reading Room project offers one model for delivering e-reserves and learner support.

FROM PRINT TO ELECTRONIC

Athabasca University (AU) delivers distance and online education across Canada and internationally to over 26,000 students, and offers over 500 individual courses and approximately 60 programs at masters, bachelors, diploma, and certificate levels. AU offers undergraduate courses primarily in individualized study mode, with online grouped study representing the primary mode of delivery at the graduate level.

When students register in a course at AU, their course package, containing resources such as textbooks, study guides, student manuals, assignment manuals, and reading files, is automatically sent to them. Students are also generally required to use material beyond the contents of the course package. Many course study guides list "Supplementary Materials," a resource list that encourages students to further investigate various topics. Students are directed to contact the Library to request Supplementary Materials, which may be photocopied articles, books, or audio-visual resources, and are intended to help them in completing course assignments, writing papers, or expanding their knowledge of the course content. Master copies of reproducible readings are filed in Supplementary Materials cabinets, and are photocopied upon request and sent out to students through the postal system at the Library's expense.

Delivery of instruction and learner support has evolved in response to advances in information and communication technologies. As AU undergraduate courses are revised and updated the goal, expressed in the Strategic University Plan, is to include "proven, online-learning and online-assessment activities and resources," using "appropriate e-learning pedagogy." The objective for the Library is to "increasingly provide support to students using digital resources by acquiring and developing online resources and deploying resources (human and other) to facilitate learner access" (Athabasca University, 2002, p. 11). With demand for access to digital resources growing at the undergraduate level, as well as at the graduate level with the introduction of new programs, the Library initiated a project in 2002 to develop an electronic course reserves system to enhance, and in some cases replace, the traditional Supplementary Materials system.

In 1999, the Library explored the course reserves and electronic reserves capabilities of the Innovative Interfaces Inc. library system. The initial plan was to enter course reserves data (bibliographic citations) for the Supplementary Materials Lists (SMLs) for courses with more than 150 enrollments and/or high library use. Given that the number of journal database providers offering full text had grown and that online content appeared more stable, the Library anticipated that creating persistent links to the databases would be the preferred method of offering supplementary material online. It was recognized that much of the print based supplementary material on file would not be available through the databases and that this material would need to be scanned and mounted online in order for delivery to be electronic. Some e-reserves work was completed, but the project bogged down due to a number of variables including demands on library staff time, the costs and time associated with obtaining copyright clearance for digitization of print based resources, and minimal faculty involvement or student interest. By 2002, the decision was made to abandon this project and to develop a more effective, flexible system, one that would capture the imaginations of the teaching faculty and better serve student needs: the Digital Reading Room (DRR).

WHAT IS THE DIGITAL READING ROOM?

The Digital Reading Room (http://library.athabascau.ca/drr/) is an electronic course reserves system developed in-house using open source software. It provides for electronic search and retrieval of course and supplementary resources selected by teaching faculty. The DRR consists of a "Student View" in which students can access resources and an "Admin View" in which "Digital Reading Files" are created for courses, and faculty are provided with a means for easily updating the files. A Digital Reading File may be divided into "Required Readings" and "Supplementary Materials" and further partitioned into units, lessons, or weeks that correspond with the study schedule for the course. Areas are provided for course descriptions, links to course or Library pages, and DRR help files. Resources in the DRR are identified by media type such as Web site, audio clip, video clip, PDF, table, diagram, or database article and may include annotations, descriptions, or instructions.

The DRR operates along the principal of open access and is in this respect quite different from many other e-reserve systems. There are, of course, different levels of access. The DRR and the Digital Reading Files, and some of their contents, are accessible to the public. Access to articles from licensed databases requires authentication through the Library's proxy server. Professors may elect to password protect certain materials such as lecture notes. The rationale behind this openness is that the DRR is meant to function as a multidisciplinary knowledge database. The Library's traditional Supplementary Materials system is very closed. A student registered in a women's studies course receives a study guide that contains a Supplementary Materials List for that particular course. But, what if there is another women's studies course, or a psychology course, or a business course that has a Supplementary Materials List of use to that student? It may also happen that a professor who is writing a course could benefit from accessing materials filed away under other courses in the Supplementary Materials cabinets, but the task of browsing through these cabinets is too daunting. The DRR has a search engine that makes it possible for students and faculty to search across Reading Files and access faculty-selected resources from other courses.

As courses are developed and revised Digital Reading Files are being built into course structures replacing and/or enhancing the traditional Supplementary Materials system. The DRR currently supports more than 50 courses at the undergraduate and graduate levels and contains more than 3,000 online learning resources and course materials. Both of these numbers are continually growing.

COLLABORATION AND THE DRR

The Library's initial e-reserves project was a "library project." The DRR is a collaborative project involving the Library, the Educational Media Development (EMD) unit, and teaching faculty. Librarians have performed key roles in developing the DRR. The Director of Library Services, acting as project director, has overseen all stages of the project, and his responsibilities include liaising with management and securing funding for resources and infrastructure. His task is to further the Library's progress in meeting the University's online learning goals, to bring faculty and staff on board the DRR project, and to continue the transition from "ownership to access," migrating from a print-based collection to one that is more digital. One of the key elements of his role is to translate the vision and use of the DRR from a useful electronic reserves tool to a University-wide system for incorporating digital resources, and searching and researching into the curriculum.

The Electronic Resources Librarian, as the project leader, has conceptualized and established the technical requirements of the project and coordinates the activities of the DRR developers. His responsibilities include providing strategic planning, marketing, and end-user training. The Reference Librarians, acting as consultants, provide feedback regarding integration of the DRR with public services library operations and test and critique the user friendliness of the DRR interface and functions.

The University's Educational Media Development unit has played a crucial role in the collaboration. The Director of EMD recognized the potential of the DRR to increasingly become an important component in relation to course packages–enhancing and, in some cases, replacing the Supplementary Materials List–and she supported the project through the contributions of a number of EMD staff. An Instructional Webspace Designer has brought his expertise to the database and interface design, programming using HTML, CSS, and JavaScript for the front-end and PHP scripting language and MYSQL database software for the back-end. The project has also benefited from the input and assistance of a visual designer, the AU Photographer, a course materials editor, an instructional media analyst, and the Copyright Officer.

From the beginning, and throughout the project, AU Faculty have played a consulting role in the development of the DRR, particularly its "Admin View" and functionality. The Director of the Master of Arts-Integrated Studies (MAIS) program provided a good deal of the inspiration behind the project as he conferred with Library staff to find better ways to deliver online readings and resources to students. As word spread about the DRR, faculty from other AU Centres came to the Library to ask if certain features could be built in. As a result, the DRR is responsive to end user needs and concerns. This has resulted in the inclusion of various functions: a search engine for searching and retrieving DRR resources across courses, a broken link checker to insure that links to Web-based resources are still valid, the ability to easily search and reuse learning resources, functions that permit the use of hanging indents and italicization for formatting bibliographic citations, and a statistical tracking mechanism that counts the number of times a resource has been accessed.

A number of faculty concerns have arisen and have been addressed. A key issue is the openness of the DRR to public view and to cross-course searching, and the legitimate concern of faculty to protect their intellectual property. Early in the collaboration the Library found it necessary to emphasize that the DRR is about sharing "reading or resource lists," and facilitating access to resources, and is not intended to replace the detailed instructions student receive in the course study guides and assignment manuals. Another area of concern pertains to faculty workload and the entry of resources into the DRR. In some cases faculty have taken this on themselves, but many have delegated to assistants or have asked the Library to enter the data. During the early phases of the project the goal was to stimulate faculty interest and get courses into the DRR, but as the project has expanded the Library has worked with EMD to resolve the data entry issue. The Director of EMD has offered the services of the Educational Media Typesetters.

After the initial design phase of the Digital Reading Room was completed it became the task of the Library to support the DRR and disseminate information. Support Staff are responsible for determining the availability of print-based materials and ordering needed material, filling student requests for print-based resources and responding to inquiries from learners. The Librarians have been charged with the task of resolving access issues, providing instruction and training to students, faculty and staff, and disseminating information about the DRR both internally and externally through workshops, presentations, conferences and papers.

The scope for collaboration has expanded and the Library is a primary participant in an Athabasca University-eduSource Canada project to develop a learning objects repository that provides access to "searchable and reusable digital resources for technology-supported learning" (http://edusource. athabascau.ca/). The Digital Reading Room has been adopted as the model for the repository which is being developed using meta tags that conform to the IEEE Learning Object Metadata (LOM) standards and use the CANCORE implementation guidelines to insure consistency and search capability across other online repositories. A MARC-to-LOM converter (http://marc-lom. athabascau.ca/marc/index.html) that takes a MARC record and converts it into LOM format is in development which will enable XML-based digital repositories to interact with MARC-based harvested metadata from library systems. The project draws on the expertise of programmers and designers as well as librarians, particularly the cataloguing and metadata knowledge of the Technical Services Librarian.

BENEFITS TO STUDENTS

The DRR improves and enhances access to course reserves, enabling students to access online resources from any location and at any time. The Library's subscribed journal databases are a key source of content for the DRR. The DRR uses persistent URLs to link students directly to full-text journal articles. In addition to having quick access to online materials, students need to be aware of the wide range of scholarly materials that are not available electronically. Canadian copyright law requires that permission be obtained in order to scan and mount copyrighted materials online. Faculty tend to avoid this route due to cost and time constraints and have preferred an alternative offered by the DRR. The DRR supports the inclusion of non-digital resources by linking to Web-based request forms. This simplifies the requesting of offline materials, such as books and print-based articles. The forms contain full bibliographic information for an item and students need only enter their name, student ID, and mailing address. When a student submits a Web form, a request for the item is e-mailed to the Library Information Desk where staff process the request and mail out the material. This is considerably more convenient for students than the print based Supplementary Materials system that requires them to provide a list of bibliographic citations to the Library by phone or e-mail.

It has long been recognized that people learn in different ways (Burdett, 2001; Smith & Woody, 2000; McCarthy, 1997). The Digital Reading Files have the potential to reach visual and auditory learners as they often include resources in different media, such as video and audio clips. Not only are students made aware of the range of resources available for their course, they are also able to search the Digital Reading Files from other courses for additional materials. One of the greatest difficulties that both librarians and educators face is teaching students where they can find relevant information for their papers. The inclusion of faculty selected resources, whether they are from a journal database or the Internet, helps to introduce students to a variety of different material that has been assessed for quality and authority.

To increase the convenience of access to resources in Digital Reading Files, the Library is experimenting with proxy-less access to licensed resources: students enter the course learning management system (e.g., WebCT or Lotus Notes or Bazaar) with login and password and this is their authentication. They are not prompted for a Library ID number when accessing journal database content as they have already been authenticated at the course level. The University's implementation of uPortal will further streamline student access to information and resources, providing students with a personalized interface.

In order to more concretely determine the benefits of the DRR, AU Librarians and the Manager of Special Projects are engaged in a research project to evaluate the impact of the DRR. Semi-structured interviews will be used to assess the effectiveness of the DRR in delivering course and supplementary resources to students and to assess the impact of implementing the DRR into course materials on faculty and library staff workloads. It can be expected that findings from this research will provide valuable insight into the impact of the DRR on student learning and satisfaction with course resources and the successfulness of the DRR in meeting its objectives to increase accessibility of, and stimulate interest in, these resources. This research will highlight any areas in which changes may be required in the current DRR system, from student, faculty, or library staff perspectives.

INFORMATION LITERACY

Student success is affected by many factors, including technological issues such as access to online resources and the library can help facilitate this through effective e-reserves systems. The Digital Reading Room increases student awareness of the variety of material available to them in digital format by providing them with faculty-selected resources. However, if information literacy is to be achieved, it is also important to provide students with opportunities to search for their own research materials and to develop the skills they need to be successful in this task.

Information literacy is a key goal of librarians and educators alike. We are all aware of the importance of teaching learners the basics of research and writing. In this age of information overload, when more and more materials are becoming available in electronic format, it is essential to teach learners how to construct effective search strategies for library catalogues, journal databases, and the World Wide Web, as well as how to navigate the plethora of database platforms and interfaces. As a library in an entirely distance education institution, we are continually faced with the issue of providing the necessary information in an effective manner for students we never meet.

Librarians can play an important role, especially in partnership with teaching faculty, in promoting skills that bring students into the world of scholarship, such as critical thinking, evaluation, and reflection. Encouraging students to engage in effective information-seeking behaviours is challenging. To aid students, AU Librarians and Faculty have created a variety of information literacy tools designed to help students become better researchers and information consumers.

HELP CENTRE

The majority of AU Library information literacy tools are housed in the "Help Centre" on the Library's Web site. The Library is working with faculty to encourage integration of some of these tools into the Digital Reading Files to promote a more independent learner approach to locating information. The Help Centre contains resources created in-house, as well as some carefully chosen resources from other institutions. It contains information about citation styles, e-books, Internet searching, accessing and searching journal databases and library catalogues, and researching and writing papers.

The Library is engaged in a number of projects to develop discipline-specific research guides in collaboration with faculty from the various academic centers at AU. Much of the library instruction in traditional institutions with campus-based classes is done either in face-to-face reference transactions or in library instruction classes offered on campus. Athabasca University's geographic location and the fact that students are located across Canada and internationally, makes in-person instructional opportunities rare. To compensate for this, detailed information and instruction normally imparted in-person is provided through the Library Web site. Because students often learn best not in isolation with a Web tutorial but through interaction with a librarian, the Library provides a toll-free number within North America and reference services via e-mail.

To ensure that research guides are tailored to the disciplines and relevant to students, librarians obtain topics and examples from the collaborating faculty members or from course guides and confer with faculty on questions of evaluation criteria, research methodologies and so on. Search examples and screen shots are developed using databases that are appropriate to the discipline. Undergraduate guides (e.g., http://library.athabascau.ca/help/wmst/intro_wmst.htm) contain information about the steps involved in the research process: from thinking critically about a research topic, to constructing search strategies using a range of online tools, to evaluating information resources, citing them appropriately, and writing an academic paper. The main goals are to help undergraduate students to establish a logical thinking process from the beginning and not get overwhelmed by the task of writing a research paper and to provide them with a basic information literacy skill set.

Graduate level guides (e.g., http://library.athabascau.ca/help/mais/main.htm) focus less on basic steps for research and more on the types of resources available in the discipline, including archives and research collections. Whereas the undergraduate guides may include a few examples, primarily from full text databases, undergraduate guides typically deal with a larger number of databases, including abstracting and indexing tools. Collaboration plays an even greater role at this level and the faculty member's subject expertise is essential in directing students to resources that provide students with access to opposing viewpoints and alternative sources, and that the pedagogy for the discipline is soundly entrenched in the guide.

CONCLUSION

The Digital Reading Room provides Athabasca University with a means to improve the way course reserves are delivered, facilitating access to learning material in a variety of formats and supporting and promoting use of quality digital resources. Building the DRR has brought many opportunities for collaboration, increasing the Library's visibility within the institution and encouraging an environment in which all partners involved think more proactively about ways to promote student success, including not only access to resources, but also information literacy.

REFERENCES

Athabasca University. (2003). eduSource at Athabasca University. Retrieved November 13, 2003, from http://edusource.athabascau.ca/.

Athabasca University. (2002). Strategic university plan. 2002-2006. Retrieved November 13, 2003, from http://www.athabascau.ca/sup/sup_19_06.pdf.

Athabasca University Library. (2003). AU library guide to researching topics in women's studies. Retrieved November 17, 2003, from http://library.athabascau.ca/help/wmst/intro_wmst.htm.

Athabasca University Library. (2003). Digital reading room. Retrieved November 13, 2003, from http://library.athabascau.ca/drr/.

Athabasca University Library. (2003). MAIS research guide. Retrieved November 17, 2003, from http://library.athabascau.ca/help/mais/main.htm.

Athabasca University Library. (2003). Marc-Lom converter. Retrieved November 13, 2003, from http://marc-lom.athabascau.ca/marc/index.html.

Burdett, S. (2001). What's your style? *Journal of Audiovisual Media in Medicine, 24*(2), 70-74. Retrieved November 3, 2003, from Academic Search Premier database.

McCarthy, B. (1997). A tale of four learners: 4MAT's learning styles. *Educational Leadership, 54*(6), 46-51. Retrieved November 3, 2003 from Expanded Academic ASAP database.

Smith, S. M., & Woody, P. C. (2000). Interactive effect of multimedia instruction and learning styles. *Teaching of Psychology, 27*(3), 220-223. Retrieved November 3, 2003, from Academic Search Premier database.

Assessing the Library Needs
and Preferences of Off-Campus Students:
Surveying Distance Education Students,
from the Midwest to the West Indies

Evadne McLean

Mona Campus
University of the West Indies

Stephen H. Dew

University of Iowa

SUMMARY. In order to have a successful library program for distance education students, librarians must understand who their students are, as well as what their students want and need. Of course, the best way to get this information is to ask the students. The ACRL *Guidelines for Distance Learning Library Services* emphasize this point, encouraging librarians to regularly survey students involved in distance education and off-campus programs. This paper is based on two student surveys, one conducted by the Coordinator of Library Services for Distance Education at the University of Iowa and the other conducted by the Distance Librarian at University of the West Indies, Mona Campus. The paper focuses on the issues that librarians confront when they conduct a survey of distance education students. In addition, it covers details on writing and developing a survey instrument, including the need to ask the right

[Haworth co-indexing entry note]: "Assessing the Library Needs and Preferences of Off-Campus Students: Surveying Distance Education Students, from the Midwest to the West Indies." McLean, Evadne, and Stephen H. Dew. Co-published simultaneously in *Journal of Library Administration* (The Haworth Information Press, an imprint of The Haworth Press, Inc.) Vol. 41, No. 1/2, 2004, pp. 265-302; and: *The Eleventh Off-Campus Library Services Conference Proceedings* (ed: Patrick B. Mahoney) The Haworth Information Press, an imprint of The Haworth Press, Inc., 2004, pp. 265-302.

http://www.haworthpress.com/web/JLA
Digital Object Identifier: 10.1300/J111v41n01_20

questions in a proper manner and the need to arrange the questions and information in a user-friendly format. The results of the two surveys are presented, including a comparison of some data between the two programs.

KEYWORDS. Assessment, distance learners, survey, library services

INTRODUCTION

The authors of this paper originally met at the Tenth Off-Campus Library Services Conference in Cincinnati, Ohio, in 2002. As happens quite frequently among the attendees of the Off-Campus Library Services Conference, the authors conversed at length about the similarities and differences in their experiences with distance education students, and in this case, after the conference, the authors continued their contact, exchanging e-mail messages about a wide variety of matters concerning library services and distance education. During the spring of 2003, as both authors were discussing past student surveys and efforts to conduct new surveys, they shared ideas about questionnaires and considered the possibility of comparing data. From these developments, the idea for this paper was born.

First, the paper will review the literature on user surveys; then it will summarize the University of Iowa Libraries' experience in developing a survey and tabulating results; and then it will address the survey experience at the University of the West Indies, Mona Campus Library. The paper concludes with a comparison of some of the data and experiences between the two programs.

REVIEW OF THE LITERATURE ON USER SURVEYS

An interdisciplinary review of the literature on user surveys shows that, as a tool to assess quality of service and customer satisfaction–key indicators of an organization's performance, user surveys are increasingly popular in many institutions, especially academic libraries. Hiller (2001) points to the substantial body of literature developing on library surveys. The qualitative and quantitative data secured periodically from such surveys allows librarians to keep current about client issues and concerns, otherwise, without the use of surveys, librarians would "ignore user perceptions of library service quality at their peril" (Cook & Thompson, 2001, p. 586). According to Talbot, Lowell, and

Martin (1998), by completing library surveys, users "help determine (the) future direction" of the library.

Surveys can take many forms, but one of the most popular instruments is the self-administered questionnaire (SAQ). If its findings are to be statistically valid, however, its proper design is critical. According to Labaw, "a questionnaire is not simply a series of questions, nor is a question merely a series of words" (as cited in Synodinos, 2003). Suggestions on the art of good questionnaire design abound in the literature of the various professions.

Having decided on the SAQ as the instrument by which quantifiable data will be obtained, the researcher should bear in mind that "one size does not fit all," so it might be necessary to gear the questionnaire and the method of administering it to each user group to be surveyed. In addition, a sample of the population to be surveyed should be asked to provide input, identifying issues to be examined in the survey (Talbot et al., 1998). To hold the users' attention, the reason for the survey must be made clear early. He/she should be provided, either at the beginning of the questionnaire or in a cover letter, with a motivating reason for wanting to complete the questionnaire (Dolle, 2001).

In addition, a careful crafting of each question is critical for good quality data. The choice and order of the words, the form of the question, as well as the design of the response categories will affect respondents' answers. Questions should have a simple structure, words should be familiar, and slang or jargon should be avoided (Lockyer, 1998). Open-ended questions, which allow respondents to give their own replies, should be used sparingly, because as Fowler points out, they tend to produce "inconsistent and often uninterpretable answers from respondent to respondent" (Lockyer, 1998, p. 60). Close-ended questions on the other hand, allow respondents to select answers from a wide range of alternatives. However, when appropriate, respondents should also be given the option of a blanket category "other" in order to accommodate unexpected responses. Close-ended questions are more difficult to construct, but they are usually the most suitable response format and are relatively simpler to analyze; therefore they should be used (Synodinos, 2003). So as not to skew results, respondents should never be asked to limit their choice to only two options (Dolle, 2001). The sequencing of the questions is also very important. Synodious (2003) emphasizes that the questions should be in a logical order–similar questions should be grouped together, items should be arranged topically, and within a topic, they should begin with the general and end with the specific.

Another important consideration is the appearance of the questionnaire. Font size and spacing should be attractive; instructions should be clear and should be distinguishable from the questions. In addition, the tone should be polite and conversational (Lockyear, 1998). Each question should be brief, simple, and unambiguous, so that all respondents interpret it as intended. Furthermore, a question should ask for no more than one piece of information and be easy to answer (Dolle, 2001).

After the questionnaire has been constructed, it should be pre-tested before use, so that any flaws can be spotted early and ironed out. An excellent method of doing this is to distribute the questionnaire to a small sample of the target population (Stone, 1993; Hafner, 1998). Take extra steps to improve response rate. After the survey has been distributed, responses have been received, and it appears that only a few more responses will be received, if at all possible, the researcher should aim at a higher response rate by sending non-respondents a reminder and a copy of the questionnaire (Stone, 1993). All work done to improve the questionnaire and the response rate is well worth the effort. Through such efforts, the survey will be a better experience for the students, and library staff will be better informed by the results.

THE UNIVERSITY OF IOWA SURVEY, 1998-99

In the fall of 1998 and the spring of 1999, the University of Iowa (UI) conducted a survey of students enrolled in its distance education programs, and the results of that survey were presented at the 9th Off-Campus Library Services Conference in Portland, Oregon (Dew, 2001). The 1998-99 survey instrument was based on a previous survey conducted in 1992 at the University of Northern Iowa (Rose and Safford, 1998). The UNI questionnaire was used as a template; it was slightly revised, and a few new questions were added. The 1998-99 survey was rather expensive: it was distributed through a general mailing using the United States Postal Service. The mailing (to 706 individuals) consisted of the survey instrument, a cover letter, and a stamped return envelope, which was addressed to the Coordinator of Library Services for Distance Education. Expenses included photocopy charges for the survey instrument and cover letter, the cost of the envelopes, postage for the initial mailing, and the postage for the return envelopes. Although relatively expensive, the survey did pay off with a rather good return rate of almost forty percent, and it proved very useful in helping library staff understand distance education students. It was especially helpful to the Coordinator of Library Services for Distance Education, who had been hired for the newly created position just two months prior to the distribution of the survey. Importantly, the results showed that distance education students valued highly a number of library services, especially access to electronic resources, access to e-mail and toll-free reference help, and access to a document delivery service. Informed by the opinions and values expressed through the student survey, library administrators strongly supported the Coordinator's efforts to develop new library services for distance education students. Such new developments included a separate Web site for distance education students, an e-mail reference service, a toll-free telephone number for reference assistance, a fee-based document delivery service, and an electronic reserve service.

The 1998-99 survey was quite significant for the distance learning library services at the University of Iowa. The survey was conducted immediately after the Coordinator of Library Services for Distance Education had been hired, and its results supported a range of new library services for distance learners. Any follow-up or new survey could never have quite the impact that the first survey had, but nevertheless, three years after the first survey had been conducted, the Coordinator felt it imperative that another survey be planned. Regular evaluation is necessary in order to understand the constantly changing community of distance learners; so in 2002, the Coordinator began an effort to undertake another survey.

THE UNIVERSITY OF IOWA SURVEY, 2003

In the spring of 2002, at the Tenth Off-Campus Library Services Conference in Cincinnati, the Coordinator attended two informative presentations concerning surveying practices for distance education library services (Jerabek & McMain, 2003; Harrell, 2003), reinforcing the idea that a new survey was a "must." During the fall of 2002, using the previous survey instrument as a template, the Coordinator worked with the staff in the Division of Continuing Education and the campus Audio-Visual Center to develop a new questionnaire. A few questions were dropped; several were revised; and a number of new ones were added (see Appendix A). The new questions included usage and evaluation of particular library services (Web pages, handouts, instruction, e-mail and telephone reference, document delivery, etc.), as well as the level and type of connectivity students have (access to the Internet, e-mail, FAX, etc.). Some questions were edited to remove unnecessary jargon; in several cases, primary subjects and key words were highlighted in **bold print** to assist the reader; and the option to answer "do not know" was added to appropriate questions.

In early 2003, the Coordinator originally planned to set up the survey in *WebCT*, which would allow for students to fill out and submit the survey entirely online. Unfortunately, a complication arose over how distance education students would access the survey. During the 2003 spring semester on the Iowa campus, *WebCT* required each student-user to submit a campus-assigned ID (called HawkID) and a password in order to gain access. For on-campus students, that was certainly a reasonable requirement–on-campus students generally used their HawkIDs for library services and many other matters. For off-campus students, however, this was a different situation–off-campus students rarely had a need to use their HawkIDs, and only a rare few even knew there was such thing as a HawkID. Since few distance education students knew their HawkIDs and since instructions in how to find that information would have been complicated, the Coordinator and the Division of Continuing Education reluctantly decided on another alternative. The survey was placed on the Web in PDF as an *Adobe Acrobat* document. Students with access to electronic mail were sent a message with a link to the survey instrument, and for a few students without access to e-mail, a print version was sent through the U.S. Postal Service (see Appendix B). Every student enrolled at that time in a distance learning class through the Division was contacted (over sixteen hundred students). When the data was received, it was loaded into *Microsoft Excel*.

Unfortunately, the process for completing the survey was a bit cumbersome, which no doubt affected the response rate. Students were asked to print the survey off of the Web site, then fill it out with a pen or pencil, and then mail it to campus–a process that some might find too demanding or time consuming. As a result, only about eleven percent responded to the survey. Compared to the 1998-99 survey, which had a return rate of about forty percent and was conducted entirely by regular mail, the 2003 survey was significantly less expensive. Unfortunately, the return rate was also significantly less. In spite of the low return rate, one can be encouraged by the opinion of J. A. Krosnick (1999, p. 540), who observed that "recent research has shown that surveys with very low response rates can be more accurate than surveys with much higher response rates." Even though the return rate was very low, the data nonetheless proved useful, providing an insight into the opinions and values of Iowa's distance education students (for a summary of the data, see Appendix A).

The 2003 survey provided some significant information that was not obtained in the 1998-99 survey. Several of the questions were new in the 2003 survey, but also, the sample included a very large group of distance education students with newly acquired library privileges. The 1998-99 survey did not include students enrolled in the Guided Independent Studies (GIS) Program (mainly traditional guided correspondence classes, however, including an ever growing number of fully Web-based classes). At the time of the first survey, GIS students did not have access to library services–this was due to the Registrar's determination that their tuition was not large enough to fully enroll them for library and other privileges. In the spring of 2002, however, accompanying a slight increase in tuition, GIS students finally became eligible for library resources and services–meaning that, over the next year, approximately three-to-four-thousand additional students became eligible for library services. In the 2003 survey, not surprisingly, GIS students comprised a large percentage of the survey respondents. Seventy-five percent of the respondents had taken a GIS class at one time or another; fifty percent of the respondents were currently taking their first class; and fifty-seven percent had never enrolled in a class that required use of library resources–a characteristic of many "self-contained" GIS classes. These numbers indicate a definite need to promote the library among GIS faculty and to better inform GIS students about their privileges.

For the respondents who have used library services, however, the survey reflects an overall satisfaction with the resources and services. Over seventy percent graded the Distance Education Library Services Web site as "good" or "excellent," and none rated it as "below average" or "poor." Over eighty percent graded the student handouts summarizing distance education library services as "good" or "excellent," and none rated the handouts as "below average" or "poor." Eighty-seven percent rated the toll-free telephone reference service as "good" or "excellent"; however, about eight percent rated it "below average." Seventy-seven percent rated the e-mail reference service as "good" or "excellent;" however, about ten percent rated it "below average" or "poor." Over ninety percent rated the document delivery service as "good" or "excellent," and none rated it "below average" or "poor." The statistics reflect a good overall satisfaction with resources and services, but there is certainly room to improve the telephone and e-mail reference services (speed of response may be a key factor).

In the 2003 survey, in observing the ranking of library services that students value most, access to electronic resources ranked highest, followed by access to document delivery, followed by access to reference help, followed finally by instruction. Although this was similar to the earlier survey, in the 1998-99 survey, reference assistance and document delivery services actually ranked slightly higher than a couple of the electronic services. This higher ranking for reference assistance and document delivery was probably due to the fact that graduate students made up a larger percentage of the first sample; their classes tend to require research papers; and they tend to value these services more than undergraduates. If one looks at only graduate and professional students in the 2003 survey, eliminating the GIS students from the sample, the rankings of all library services fall into a list that looks very similar to that from the 1998-99 survey.

Regarding Internet connections, according to the 2003 survey, the vast majority of students have Internet access from home (over ninety percent), about half have access from their offices, and over forty percent use the access provided at their local public library. About sixty percent have access through a telephone modem, twenty-five percent have access through cable, and less than twenty percent have T-1 access to the Internet. How one accesses the Internet affects the loading speed for certain electronic and Web-based resources, especially electronic reserves and other PDF files–many Web resources load much slower through a telephone modem or cable connection than through a T-1 line. Since such a large percentage of UI distance education students depend on home computers and modems to access the Web, library Web pages and electronic reserve modules should keep bandwidth and file sizes to a minimum in order to speed access for users.

From the experience with the 2003 survey, the Coordinator and the Division of Continuing Education determined that the best option for future surveys was to develop a fully Web-based survey using *WebCT*. Importantly, beginning in the fall semester of 2003, all UI distance education students were informed about their HawkIDs and passwords, and since August 2003, they have been required to use those IDs in order to access the Libraries' electronic resources. Therefore, since distance education students are now familiar with the use of HawkIDs and passwords, *WebCT* appears to be the most viable option for conducting a future survey. Through *WebCT*, the survey instrument is easily accessible from a link that will be provided in a general cover letter, which will be e-mailed to students. Students can fill out and submit the questionnaire totally online–there is no need for printing or mailing, so expenses are kept to an absolute minimum. Importantly, through *WebCT*, the Coordinator will be able to tell which students have completed the survey. The Coordinator, however, will not be able to tell which student completed which particular survey, so the survey process remains anonymous, and students will be informed about that. However, by being able to tell who has (and who has not) completed the survey, the Coordinator can send follow up e-mails to those students who have not completed the survey, in hopes of gaining more in-put and a higher return rate. The University of Iowa has set up a schedule to conduct another survey in the spring of 2004, and the survey will be based in *WebCT*. The survey instrument will largely be the same as the instrument used in 2003, with few additional questions–at least two regarding employment (an idea borrowed from the UWI survey) and two regarding the evaluation of *Library Explorer*, the UI Libraries' online tutorial.

THE UNIVERSITY OF THE WEST INDIES

The University of the West Indies (UWI) is the successor institution to The University College of the West Indies (UCWI), founded in 1948 at Mona, Jamaica to cater to the tertiary education needs of the English-speaking Caribbean countries. In 1960, St. Augustine in Trinidad and Tobago became the site of the second campus, and two years later, in 1962, the institution received full university status. UWI's third campus opened at Cave Hill in Barbados in 1963. As one of two regional universities in the world (the other being the University of the South Pacific), UWI serves the three countries where campuses are located, as well as the non-campus countries (NCCs) in the Organization of Eastern Caribbean States (OECS)–Anguilla, Antigua and Barbuda, the British Virgin Islands, Dominica, Grenada, Montserrat, St. Kitts/Nevis, St. Lucia and St. Vincent, and the Grenadines–and those in the Northern Caribbean–Belize, the Bahamas, the Cayman Islands, and the Turks and Caicos Islands.

DISTANCE EDUCATION AT UWI

UWI has been involved in distance programs for more than two decades. Its offerings, which are at both the undergraduate and postgraduate levels, are faculty-driven and, in most cases, mounted and delivered by its Distance Education Centre (UWIDEC), which was established in 1996. For most courses delivered by UWIDEC, the primary medium of instruction is print, supported in varying degrees by face-to-face tutorials and interactive audio-teleconferences at the twenty-seven UWIDEC sites spread across the region. Each of the sites is equipped with a number of computers, and importantly, most have Internet access. At the moment, the program delivery method is undergoing restructuring, and the facilities are being upgraded with loan and grant funding from the Caribbean Development Bank. According to the UWI Office of Panning and Institutional Research, in the 2002/2003 academic year, 2,486 students were registered in the various UWI distance programs, and of this total, 669 were attached to Mona.

DISTANCE LIBRARY SUPPORT AT UWI, MONA

For all programs delivered through UWIDEC, students are encouraged to and expected to access library services and resources, in order to broaden and deepen their knowledge gained from course material. Each of the three campus libraries is responsible for distance library services to the various sites assigned to its Campus. Mona Library, therefore, has responsibility for services to the Northern Caribbean, as well as ten intra-Jamaica sites. To better meet this responsibility, in 1997, the Mona Library created a new library position–Distance Librarian; however, since the position is not full-time, the amount of attention given to distance library support has been limited. Nevertheless, the Distance Librarian has been involved in the implementation of a number of library services and resources to support the research needs of the Mona distance learning community.

BACKGROUND TO USER SURVEY

The distance library services and resources introduced by the Mona Library between 1997 and 2000 were selected intuitively and not as a result of the analysis of data obtained empirically through a user survey. Consequently, in late 2000, Mona's Distance Librarian undertook a review of services and resources for distance students because, from a review of the literature, she concluded that the best way for libraries to provide quality service and satisfaction to users is to "understand who and what their clients are" (Shouse, 1995, p. 352), "question them about their needs" (Kelly, 1987, p. 65), and "search for methods to meet those needs in a reasonable and cost effective manner" (Pettingill, 1998, p. 221). In addition, the Distance Librarian found strong support in the ACRL *Guidelines for Distance Learning Library Services*, which strongly recommends that students be surveyed to determine library service needs and user satisfaction. In the absence of separately published guidelines for places such as the Caribbean, many libraries, such as Mona and the other UWI libraries, have embraced the ACRL *Guidelines*. At the same time, the Distance Librarian, who had by then enrolled in the Masters in Library and Information Studies program at the UWI School of Library and Information Studies, decided to use the research findings as the basis of her research paper.

OBJECTIVES AND METHODOLOGY

The objectives of the survey were to assess distance students' use of and satisfaction with current services, to determine the extent distance students were using other libraries, and to determine their new service requirement. Distribution of the survey was limited to the students enrolled in the print-based programs sponsored by the UWIDEC (the Library has not been involved with the other groups of distance students in any meaningful way). The methodology of data collection was a print self-administered questionnaire (SAQ). Some of its questions were borrowed from various other survey instruments, some were informed by the literature reviewed, and some were informed by the input provided by students themselves.

In keeping with advice from the literature, several steps were followed. The questionnaire was piloted at three sites in order to ensure that the items were unambiguous and relevant to the objectives of the survey. After some alterations, a final draft of the questionnaire was developed (see Appendix C). In order to encourage response, a cover letter explaining the purpose of the study and requesting participation was attached to each questionnaire (see Appendix D). The Distance Librarian then informed the Site Coordinators of her intention to administer the questionnaire and solicited their help. Several Site Coordinators informed her that students were not amenable to questionnaires, hence the likelihood of a low response rate. As proof, some showed folders of other questionnaires from course coordinators and various UWI departments which students had refused to complete. However, the Distance Librarian decided to proceed with the SAQ, since it stood the best chance of gathering the desired data. After some amount of skepticism, the Site Coordinators finally agreed to administer the questionnaire.

UWIDEC staff administered the questionnaire at the sites throughout November 2000; the Distance Librarian was personally involved in its administration at two sites. Convenience sampling was used to select the participants, as it was the surest way of securing willing participants. Students who were early for their tutorials or teleconference sessions were requested to complete the questionnaires while they waited for their classes. This method ensured the return of the questionnaires, since they were completed at the sites. Constant follow-up by telephone calls and e-mail had to be done to improve the response rate, however. The site coordinators returned the completed questionnaires to the Distance Librarian by courier.

THE NATURE OF THE QUESTIONNAIRE

The final instrument comprised twenty-one questions, most of which were partially close-ended (see Appendix C). This means that suggested answer choices were provided but respondents had the opportunity to add their own answers. A five-point Likert-type scale with response categories was used for three questions. However, a neutral category was not included in the scale as it was the researcher's intention to force respondents to choose one of the specific responses. One question was fully open-ended in order to allow the respondents to give suggestions for improving Mona's distance library services.

In keeping with suggestions from the literature, the questionnaire was divided into four sections: profile of the distance students; use of Mona's distance library services and level of satisfaction with the services; use of other libraries; and new services required and recommendations for the improvement of existing services.

THE SAMPLE, RESPONSE, AND DATA ANALYSIS

The sample population targeted for the survey comprised 148 individuals, 37% of the 400 students who had completed at least one year in the usual UWIDEC program—it was felt that this sample would sufficiently reflect the views of the entire population. Unfortunately no questionnaires were received from a few sites, despite telephone calls and e-mail messages sent by the researcher. Nevertheless, seventy-nine questionnaires were returned, so the percentage of returned surveys was a respectable 52%—well above forty percent, the minimum response rate that many researchers feel necessary in order to judge results as accurate (Clougherty et al., 1998).

The Distance Librarian was aware of the many statistical and analytical programs readily available to make data analysis less challenging (SPSS, SAS, etc.); however, the researcher did not have access to any of those programs at the time. After the data was collected, the seventy-nine questionnaires were coded and entered into *Microsoft Excel*. The program was then used to generate frequency tables, and cross tabulations. A few examples of the findings are looked at here (for a summary of the data, see Appendix C).

KEY FINDINGS AND RECOMMENDATIONS FOR UWI

The data shows that females make up 66% of the sample, while males account for 25%. Women therefore outnumber men by about 2.5:1. The age range 25-50 accounts for 71% of the sample, while those in the under 25 and the over 50 age groups make up 29%. Females dominate every age category, with the highest percentage (20%) in the 25-35 age-range. The highest concentration of males, 10%, is in the 36-45 age-range. The findings also indicate that the on-campus trend of female dominance at UWI, the 70-30 ratio is replicated in the distance education segment.

Sixty-three percent of the students are enrolled in social sciences, particularly management studies, no doubt for career advancement in either the private or the public sector, or to facilitate a career switch to the private sector. Thirty-five percent are in education, and these are no doubt teachers seeking to upgrade themselves for positions, possibly as school principals, as subject specialists, or as leaders in other areas of education. According to Wulf (1995), lifelong learning for career improvement is taking place because "the period during which particular skills are relevant is shortening." The resources most used by students are textbooks at sites (72%), photocopies of articles and chapters of books from the Mona Library (63%), as well as book loans from the Mona Library (53%). Many book loans are accessed from the Mona Campus Library because students do not have a set text or a supplementary reader at the local site. This data indicates the significance of book loans to students. Reference service (49%) had average access, while the Mona Library collections enjoyed less than average usage (37%), this is no doubt due to the correlation between library use and distance from the Mona Campus. Only thirteen percent of those who visited the Mona Library accessed user instruction, perhaps because they were unaware of the service. Interlibrary loan (8%) is grossly under-subscribed. The reason could be that the service is marketed to the postgraduate students, but hardly to the undergraduates.

According to the literature, students tend to use other libraries in addition to their host libraries, so the students were asked to indicate other libraries used in addition to the Mona distance library services. The majority of respondents (36.6%) indicated that they had used public libraries while (12.5%) used workplace libraries, which are usually special libraries provided by employers. Just over thirty percent used school libraries, community college libraries, and teachers' college libraries. The implication for the Library is that a significant number of students are using other services, especially public libraries. The Distance Librarian should therefore have discussion with the public libraries with an eye to collaboration of some sort.

Fifty-three percent of the sample said they have access to the Internet, while just under a half (47%) said that they had no access. Although most of the sites have Internet access, the large percentage without access implies that a significant number of respondents are unaware of the availability of this important service at the sites. There is therefore a need for greater publicity of the service by the site administrators. Home (36.6%), work (25.4%) and UWIDEC sites (20.6%) are the chief access points. The above findings are not surprising as many private sector companies and educational institutions have Internet access. Additionally, with the price of computers decreasing, more individuals now own computers. The implication for the library is that the majority of students have access to the Internet, therefore the Library's Web resources should be accessible to them.

Access to the three primary electronic resources (the Mona catalogue, databases, and electronic journals) received approximately the same rating (extremely useful 1.6 to useful 1.8), indicating the sample's high level of interest in them. "Supplemental reading at sites" and "research consultation with Distance Education Librarian" are the two additional services most highly ranked by the sample (1.5-1.8–"extremely useful" to "useful"). Here again is an indication of two other services that are highly desirable. Visits to UWIDEC sites by the Distance Librarian are considered "useful" (2.0), while information literacy was ranked only "moderately useful" (2.6). At a time when information literacy is seen as critical for lifelong learning, it is important that the library sensitizes students to the need for instruction and develops effective methods for providing this instruction.

Students were asked to rate the usefulness of three electronic resources to their studies. To get an indication of how useful at least one of these resources, electronic databases, which was being enjoyed by on-campus students, would be to different age categories, the ratings and age groupings were correlated. The findings show that all age categories considered access to electronic databases useful. However, to the under thirty-fives it was "extremely useful" while to the over thirty-fives it was "useful." The lower rating given by the latter group could be attributed to the fact that older persons tend to find electronic resources intimidating. Students in this category would therefore need technical and instructional support.

Age categories and ratings given to usefulness of supplemental reading at sites were correlated for the same reasons that age and usefulness of electronic databases were correlated. The findings show that this resource is also important to all age categories. However, students above age thirty-five gave it the higher rating of "extremely useful," while those below thirty-five rated it as "useful." One can conclude that all age categories recognize the importance of supplemental texts at the UWIDEC sites, but that the older students consider them more useful, as they are more comfortably familiar with print than electronic for finding information to satisfy their research needs.

Peters (1998) advises that the best way to know whether a customer is satisfied with a product or service is to ask the customer. With this in mind, students were asked about their level of satisfaction with the distance library services. Overall, the average satisfaction rating given by the distance students ranged between "satisfied" and "moderately satisfied" on the five-point Likert Scale. The highest level of satisfaction was with copies of journal articles and chapters of books (2.1–"satisfied"); following were reference services, book loans and the UWI Mona Library collection, which were rated similarly ("satisfied" to "moderately satisfied"–2.5, 2.5, and 2.6 respectively). Interlibrary loan proved to be a little used service, and those who used it were only "moderately satisfied" (3.0). Library instruction received a rating of only "moderately satisfied" (3.0), no doubt because students who visited the Mona Library and tried to access this service might have received less than adequate library instruction because of staff constraint. Timeliness of response to requests and availability of core texts at site received ratings of 3.3, indicating less than moderate satisfaction. The other service with which students were "moderately satisfied" to "dissatisfied" was the provision of core texts at sites (3.3). The rating given to this service is no doubt a response to the inadequate number and variety of titles available at the sites. This situation has arisen, no doubt, not only because of the need to acquire more core texts for the sites, but also because poor management of site collections by some site personnel has resulted in depletion.

Based on the results of the survey, the Distance Librarian made several recommendations for the improvement of the distance library service. The most significant of these are as follows:

- Create a distance-learners Web site, from which a variety of electronic resources and services can be accessed.
- Give distance learners access to the electronic databases to which the Library subscribes.
- Increase the number of titles and copies of supplementary texts.
- Provide students with information literacy.
- Improve the turnaround time for the delivery of material to the sites for use by students.

The Distance Learners Web site is in an advanced stage of construction, and distance learners have been given access to three of the databases to which the Library subscribes. When completed, the Web site will be available at http://mona.uwi.edu/library/distance_learners.html. The Information Literacy Unit (MILU) is working on Web tutorials for the Library so that distance learners will benefit. In addition, new titles in multiple copies are being added as recommendations come in from tutors and site coordinators. However, to send requested material to the UWIDEC sites, a consistent turnaround time of three days was recommended, but it is yet to be achieved.

IOWA AND THE WEST INDIES: A COMPARISON OF DATA AND EXPERIENCES

A comparison of the data between the University of Iowa and the University of the West Indies, Mona Campus, shows a number of similarities; however, some significant differences can be noted, as well. Regarding similarities, first of all, both institutions offer a range of undergraduate and graduate level programs. In addition, at both institutions, women make up a sizeable majority of distance education students (UI 76.8%, UWI 66%), and for both institutions, the vast majority of students are older than the traditional on-campus student (UI 89.4% over the age of 22, UWI 71% over the age of 25). Although the majority of students in both programs use the resources and services of their home institution, many of them also use public libraries and other academic libraries to support their studies. Importantly, students at both institutions appeared to value the resources and services available to them through their home institutions. Students tended to rank most resources and services favorably, but at both institutions, they found more value in technology than in instruction–students tended to rank electronic resources quite high, while they ranked instructional services significantly lower. Importantly, however, those students who had received library instruction tended to rank such services highly.

Probably the most significant difference for UWI students and Iowa students concerns their access to the Internet–a major factor in how successful a library can be in providing electronic resources and services. Almost ninety-five percent of Iowa students have convenient access to the Web (from their homes, work, public libraries, etc.), whereas only fifty-three percent of UWI students have convenient access to the Web (nevertheless, a majority of students and a number that will certainly continue to increase). Over ninety percent of Iowa students have Internet access from their homes, but only about thirty-seven percent of UWI students have Internet access from home. Regarding future surveys, with a vast majority of its students having easy access to the Web, Iowa can confidently plan on developing a Web-based student survey that will be cheap and accessible to practically all of its students. For the near future, however, student surveys at UWI will need to take into consideration the lack of Web access by a significant number of its students, and paper-based surveys will remain an important tool for some time. Undoubtedly, however, Web access will continue to increase at UWI, and library staff are focusing on the continued development of Mona Library's Web presence.

In some ways, the University of Iowa and the University of the West Indies, Mona Campus, are worlds apart; however, in other ways, the two institutions are inside the same ballpark working at the same game–providing the best library resources and services possible for their students. In order to be successful at that game, each institution must address the needs and wants of its students, and that requires a knowledge of the student population that can only be gained by asking and assessing the right questions. The University of Iowa and the University of the West Indies, Mona Campus, undertook separate projects to survey distance education students. Each survey helped lay a foundation for understanding student needs, and from that foundation, better library service can be built. Communication and cooperation among two librarians facilitated the development and evaluation of those surveys. Similar communication and cooperation among librarians will help facilitate the assessment and development of library services wherever distance learning programs are offered–from the Midwest to the West Indies and beyond.

REFERENCES

ACRL *guidelines for distance learning library services.* (2000). *College & Research Libraries News, 61,* 1023-1029. Retrieved November 19, 2001, from the Distance Learning Section of the Association of College and Research Libraries Web site: http://caspian.switchinc.org/~distlearn.

Clougherty, L, Forys, J., Lyles, T., Persson, D., Walters, C., & Washington-Hoagland, C. (1998). The University of Iowa Libraries' undergraduate user needs assessment. *College & Research Libraries, 59,* 572-584.

Cook, C. & Heath, F. M. (2001). Users perceptions of library service quality: A LibQUAL+ qualiative study. *Library Trends, 49,* 548-584.

Cook, C., & Thompson, B. (2001). Psychometric properties of scores from the Web-based LibQUAL+ study of perceptions of library service quality. *Library Trends, 49,* 585-604.

Dew, S. (2001) Knowing your users and what they want: Surveying off-campus students about library services. *Journal of Library Administration, 31,* 177-193. Simultaneously published in A. M. Casey (Ed.). (2001). *Off-Campus Library Services* (pp. 177-193). New York: The Haworth Press, Inc. First published in A. M. Casey (Ed.). (2000). *The Ninth Off-Campus Library Services Conference Proceedings* (pp. 119-132). Mount Pleasant, MI: Central Michigan University.

Dolle, R. (2001). Who wants to try a questionnaire? *Journal of Environmental Health, 63,* 38-40.

Guidelines for distance learning library services: A draft revision. (2003). *College & Research Libraries News, 64,* 265-271. Retrieved April 26, 2003, from the Distance Learning Section of the Association of College and Research Libraries Web site: http://caspian.switchinc.org/~distlearn.

Hafner, A. W. (1998). *Descriptive Statistical Techniques for Librarians* (2nd ed.). Chicago: American Library Association.

Harrell, K. J. (2003). Reducing high anxiety: Responsive library services to off-campus nontraditional students. *Journal of Library Administration, 37,* 355-365. Simultaneously published in P. B. Mahoney (Ed.). (2003). *Distance Learning Library Services* (pp. 355-365). New York: The Haworth Press, Inc. First published in P. B. Mahoney (Ed.). (2002). *The Tenth Off-Campus Library Services Conference Proceedings* (pp. 277-285). Mount Pleasant, MI: Central Michigan University.

Hiller, S. (2001). Assessing user needs, satisfaction and library performance at the University of Washington Libraries. *Library Trends, 49,* 605-625.

Jerabek, J. A. and McMain, L. M. (2003). The answer you get depends on who (and what) you ask: Involving stakeholders in needs assessment. *Journal of Library Administration, 37,* 387-395. Simultaneously published in P. B. Mahoney (Ed.). (2003). *Distance Learning Library Services* (pp. 387-395). New York: The Haworth Press, Inc. First published in P. B. Mahoney (Ed.). (2002). *The Tenth Off-Campus Library Services Conference Proceedings* (pp. 301-307). Mount Pleasant, MI: Central Michigan University.

Kelly, G. J. (1987). Collection development and acquisitions in a distance learning environment, I: The development of acquisitions and collection services for off-campus students in Northeastern Ontario: An important library collection development issue or merely an issue of a more efficient materials handling and delivery system? *Library Acquisitions: Practice and Theory, 2*, 47-66.

Krosnick, J. A. (1999). Survey research. *Annual Review of Psychology, 50*, 537-567.

Lockyer, J. (1998). Getting started with needs assessment: Part 1–The questionnaire. *The Journal of Continuing Education in the Health Professions, 18*, 58-61.

Peters, T. A. (1998). Remotely familiar: Using computerized monitoring to study remote use. *Library Trends, 47*, 7-20.

Pettingill, A. (1998). Off-Campus resources: Collection development for distance education and its impact on overall library collection goals. In P. S. Thomas & M. Jones (Comps.), *The Eighth Off-Campus Library Services Conference Proceedings, Providence, Rhode Island, April 22-24* (pp. 221-229). Mount Pleasant, MI: Central Michigan University.

Rose, R. F. & Safford, B. R. (1998). Iowa is our campus: Expanding library resources and services to distant education students in a rural state. In P. S. Thomas & M. Jones (Comps.), *The Eighth Off-Campus Library Services Conference Proceedings, Providence, Rhode Island, April 22-24* (pp. 231-237). Mount Pleasant, MI: Central Michigan University.

Shouse, D. L. (1995). Library needs of rural distance education students. In C. J. Jacob (Comp.), *The Seventh Off-Campus Library Services Conference Proceedings, San Diego, California, October 25-25* (pp. 355-362). Mount Pleasant, MI: Central Michigan University.

Stone, D. H. (1993). How to do it: Design a questionnaire. *British Medical Journal, 307*, 264-266.

Synodinos, N. E. (2003). The art of questionnaire construction: Some important considerations for manufacturing studies. *Integrating Manufacturing Systems 14*, 221-237. Retrieved December 2, 2003, from the Emerald Group Publishing Web site: http://Giorgio.emeraldinsight.com.

Talbot, D. E.; Lowell, G. R.; Martin, K. (1998). From the users' perspective–The UCSD Libraries user project. *The Journal of Academic Librarianship, 24*, 357-364.

University of the West Indies, Mona Campus. Office of Planning and Institutional Research. (2001). *Official Statistics*.

Unwin, L; Stephens, K; Bolton, N. (1998). *The role of the library in distance learning: A study of postgraduate students, course providers and librarians in the UK* (pp. 41-103). London: Bowker-Saur.

Westbrook, L. (2001). *Identifying and analyzing user needs: A complete handbook and ready-to-use assessment workbook with disk*. New York: Neal-Schuman Publishers.

Wulf, W. A. (1995). Warning: Information technology will transform the university. *Issues in Science and Technology, 11*, 46-52.

APPENDIX A. University of Iowa Libraries, Survey of Distance Education Students: Survey Instrument and Summary of Results

2003 185 responses from 1,662 students contacted, 11.1% return rate **1998-99** 272 responses from 706 surveys mailed out, 38.5% return rate

Personal Characteristics

1. Student Status

	2003		1998-99
	Percent		Percent
Undergraduate (Part-time)	48.4	Undergrad	43.7
Undergraduate (Full-time)	17.3		
Graduate (Part-time)	21.2	Graduate	56.3
Graduate (Full-time)	7.6		
Graduate, Doctoral Level	1.6		
Other	3.7		

2. What gender are you?

	2003	1998-99
	Percent	Percent
Male	23.2	34.2
Female	76.8	65.8

3. What is your ethnicity?

	2003	1998-99
	Percent	Percent
American Indian/Alaska Native	0.5	NA
Asian/Pacific Islander	0.5	NA
Black, non-Hispanic	1.0	NA
Hispanic	2.1	NA
White, non-Hispanic	91.9	NA
Race/ethnicity unknown	3.8	NA

4. What age category are you in?

	2003		1998-99
	Percent		Percent
18-22	20.6	18-21	0.7
23-29	22.8	22-30	28.5
30-39	14.7	30+	70.7
40-49	26.6		
50+	15.2		

APPENDIX A (continued)

5. What is your program or major?

	2003 Percent	1998-99 Percent
Computer Science	1.0	1.1
Education	11.4	7.0
Electrical & Computer Engineering	0.0	1.5
Guided Independent Study	17.3	NA
Liberal Studies (BLS)	20.5	36.4
Library & Information Science	2.7	4.4
Nursing	15.1	11.1
Public Health	2.7	NA
Social Work	8.7	13.2
Pharmacy	NA	4.0
Business	NA	28.0
Other	20.5	NA

Coursework

6. How many distance education courses have you taken from the UI in recent years?

	2003 Percent	1998-99 Percent
This is my first one.	50.5	18.7
2 to 5	29.4	39.5
6 to 10	9.8	17.6
10+	10.3	14.2

7. What types of delivery modes were used for your courses (Check **all** that apply)?

	2003 Percent	1998-99 Percent
Face-to-Face	18.2	NA
ICN (state-wide, fiber-optic television)	19.3	NA
GIS print	74.4	NA
GIS Web	13.1	NA
Web, semester-based	14.2	NA
Cable Television	4.6	NA
Microwave Television	0.0	NA
Videotape	8.5	NA

8. How many of your University of Iowa distance education courses have required the preparation of papers/reports/presentations?

	2003	1998-99
	Percent	Percent
None	25.8	9.7
1 to 3	49.5	45.8
4 to 8	13.2	22.8
8+	11.5	21.7

Library Use

9. How many of your distance education courses have required the use of library materials?

	2003	1998-99
	Percent	Percent
None	57.7	34.7
1 to 3	26.4	53.8
4 to 8	8.2	17.5
8+	7.7	11.9

10. For those courses that have required the use of library materials, which libraries or types of libraries have you used? (Check **all** that apply)

	2003	1998-99
	Percent	Percent
U of Iowa Libraries	51.9	34.7
ISU Libraries	5.1	4.0
UNI Libraries	3.8	2.8
Other Academic Library	45.6	62.5
Public Libraries	55.7	68.2
Special Libraries	13.9	22.2
Area Education Agency	1.3	5.7
Personal Library	39.2	47.7
Instructor Materials	43.0	33.5

11. Which type of library have you **used most frequently** to complete the requirements of your distance education course(s)? (Check one)

	2003		1998-99
	Percent		Percent
U of Iowa Libraries	36.3		NA
Another academic library	13.7	Academic	47.2
Public library	30.0		29.0
Special library	6.3		10.2
Personal library	5.0		13.6
Materials instructor provided	8.8		NA

APPENDIX A (continued)

12. How **satisfied** have you been with the adequacy of the **collections** (electronic resources, databases, books, journals, etc.) of the library you have used the most? (Circle one)

	2003	1998-99
	Percent	Percent
Very Satisfied	40.0	24.0
Somewhat Satisfied	43.8	56.6
No Opinion	7.5	7.4
Dissatisfied	6.3	8.6
Very Dissatisfied	2.5	3.4

13. How **satisfied** have you been with the adequacy of the **services** (reference help, instruction, document delivery, etc.) of the library you have used most?

	2003	1998-99
	Percent	Percent
Very Satisfied	49.4	33.7
Somewhat Satisfied	36.7	46.9
No Opinion	8.9	9.1
Somewhat Dissatisfied	2.5	8.0
Very Dissatisfied	2.5	2.3

Library Services for Distance Education Students

14. How **often** do you use the UI Distance Education Library Services Web site?
   http://www.lib.uiowa.edu/disted   (Circle one)

	2003	1998-99
	.Percent	Percent
Once a week	15.0	NA
Once a month	15.0	NA
Once a semester	10.0	NA
Never	60.0	NA

15. If you have used the Web site, how would you **judge** it? (Circle one)

	2003	1998-99
	Percent	Percent
Excellent	9.7	NA
Good	61.3	NA
Average	29.0	NA
Below Average	0.0	NA
Poor	0.0	NA

16. How **often** do use other UI Web pages? (Circle one)

	2003	1998-99
	Percent	Percent
Once a week	28.6	NA
Once a month	28.6	NA
Once a semester	14.3	NA
Never	28.6	NA

17. Among the following UI Library Web pages, please judge those that you have used.
    (Circle one judgement for each that you have used)

The U of I Libraries Catalog	2003 Percent	1998-99 Percent
Excellent	28.1	NA
Good	56.3	NA
Average	15.6	NA
Below Average	0.0	NA
Poor	0.0	NA
InfoHawk Gateway	Percent	Percent
Excellent	18.9	NA
Good	46.0	NA
Average	32.4	NA
Below Average	2.7	NA
Poor	0.0	NA
Hardin Library (Health)	Percent	Percent
Excellent	36.4	NA
Good	41.0	NA
Average	22.7	NA
Below Average	0.0	NA
Poor	0.0	NA
Psychology Library	Percent	Percent
Excellent	7.1	NA
Good	71.4	NA
Average	14.3	NA
Below Average	7.1	NA
Poor	0.0	NA

18. Have you used one of the **handouts that summarize library resources and services** for
    distance education students? (Circle one)

	2003	1998-99
	Percent	Percent
Yes	69.2	NA
No	30.8	NA

APPENDIX A (continued)

If yes, how would you **judge** the handout?

	Percent	Percent
Excellent	29.2	NA
Good	62.5	NA
Average	8.3	NA
Below Average	0.0	NA
Poor	0.0	NA

19. Have you ever attended a **lecture** or observed an **instructional session presented by a UI librarian**? (Circle one)

	2003	1998-99
	Percent	Percent
Yes	83.3	NA
No	16.7	NA

If yes, how would you **judge** the instruction?

	Percent	Percent
Excellent	46.7	NA
Good	53.5	NA
Average	0.0	NA
Below Average	0.0	NA
Poor	0.0	NA

20. Have you used the **toll-free telephone number** to receive reference assistance or ask for help? (Circle one)

	2003	1998-99
	Percent	Percent
Yes	87.2	NA
No	12.8	NA

If yes, how would you **judge** the service?

	Percent	Percent
Excellent	53.9	NA
Good	23.1	NA
Average	15.4	NA
Below Average	7.7	NA
Poor	0.0	NA

21. Have you used **electronic mail** to receive reference assistance or ask for help? (Circle one)

	2003	1998-99
	Percent	Percent
Yes	69.2	NA
No	30.8	NA

If yes, how would you **judge** the service?

	Percent	Percent
Excellent	30.8	NA
Good	46.2	NA
Average	11.5	NA
Below Average	7.7	NA
Poor	3.9	NA

22. Have you used the **Distance Education Document-Delivery Service**? (Circle one)

	2003	1998-99
	Percent	Percent
Yes	67.1	NA
No	32.9	NA

If yes, how would you **judge** the service?

	Percent	Percent
Excellent	77.8	NA
Good	18.5	NA
Average	3.7	NA
Below Average	0.0	NA
Poor	0.0	NA

---

23. **Most useful services**	**Rank 1, 2, 3**

Please consider the following eleven library services. **Check each** service that is important to you in your coursework, and **rank** the **three services (1, 2, & 3)** that are the **most important** to you.

23-1. Remote access to full-text articles and journals

	2003	1998-99
	Percent	Percent
An Important Service	83.5	65.1 (2nd)
Ranking	Percent	Percent
1st	34.3	22.4
2nd	25.4	11.8
3rd	4.4	11.8

APPENDIX A (continued)

23-2. Remote access to the UI library catalog

	2003	1998-99
	Percent	Percent
An Important Service	65.7	49.1 (6th)
Ranking	Percent	Percent
1st	3.0	5.9
2nd	4.4	7.0
3rd	20.9	8.1

23-3. Remote access to electronic indexes and databases

	2003	1998-99
	Percent	Percent
An Important Service	65.7	42.3 (8th)
Ranking	Percent	Percent
1st	4.4	4.0
2nd	12.0	6.3
3rd	13.4	6.6

23-4. Distance Education Document-Delivery Service (articles and books, involves a basic charge of $3 per item)

	2003	1998-99
	Percent	Percent
An Important Service	50.8	60.7 (3rd)
Ranking	Percent	Percent
1st	10.4	9.2
2nd	7.4	11.4
3rd	10.4	8.1

23-5. Toll-free telephone number for reference help

	2003	1998-99
	Percent	Percent
An Important Service	47.8	49.3 (5th)
Ranking	Percent	Percent
1st	12.0	7.0
2nd	3.0	5.1
3rd	3.0	7.0

23-6. Web-based e-mail services for reference help

	2003	1998-99
	Percent	Percent
An Important Service	47.8	71.3 (1st)
Ranking	Percent	Percent
1st	10.4	15.1
2nd	4.4	17.3
3rd	4.4	9.6

23-7. Remote access to reserve reading materials for class

	2003	1998-99
	Percent	Percent
An Important Service	46.3	NA
Ranking	Percent	Percent
1st	5.9	NA
2nd	7.4	NA
3rd	4.4	NA

23-8. Interlibrary loan of books and articles

	2003	1998-99
	Percent	Percent
An Important Service	44.8	43.8 (7th)
Ranking	Percent	Percent
1st	7.4	4.8
2nd	5.9	5.1
3rd	4.4	10.7

23-9. Guides for doing library research in a subject area

	2003	1998-99
	Percent	Percent
An Important Service	35.8	30.9 (10th)
Ranking	Percent	Percent
1st	3.0	2.6
2nd	1.5	2.6
3rd	5.9	6.6

APPENDIX A (continued)

23-10. Computer-assisted instruction in doing library research

	2003	1998-99
	Percent	Percent
An Important Service	25.4	27.9 (11th)
Ranking	Percent	Percent
1st	0.0	1.5
2nd	1.5	1.8
3rd	3.0	2.2

23-11. Librarian-provided instruction in doing library research (in person or over the ICN)

	2003	1998-99
	Percent	Percent
An Important Service	20.9	20.2
Ranking	Percent	Percent
1st	1.5	2.2
2nd	1.5	2.9
3rd	3.0	0.7

Connectivity

24. What kind of **computer** do you usually use? (Circle one)

	2003	1998-99
	Percent	Percent
PC	86.9	NA
MacIntosh	6.6	4.8
Other	1.1	NA
Do not use one	5.5	NA

25. Do you have convenient access to the **Internet**? (Circle **all** that apply)

	2003		1998-99
	Percent		Percent
	NA	Yes	83.8
at home	93.5		NA
at work	48.4		NA
at local library	43.5		NA
other	6.5		NA

26. What kind of **connection do you have to the Internet**?

	2003	1998-99
	Percent	Percent
T-1-line or other direct connection	17.9	NA
Television or other cable connection	25.0	NA
Telephone/modem connection	58.3	NA
Do not know	6.0	NA

27. Does your computer have the capacity to use **CDs**? (Circle one)

	2003	1998-99
	Percent	Percent
Yes	92.7	75.3
No	0.6	24.7
Do not know	6.7	NA

28. Do you have convenient access to **electronic mail**? (Circle all that apply)

	2003		1998-99
	Percent		Percent
	NA	Yes	85.2
at home	92.9		NA
at work	48.8		NA
at local library	29.8		NA
other	9.5		NA

29. Do you have convenient access to a **FAX machine** for sending and receiving documents? (Circle **all** that apply)

	2003		1998-99
	Percent		Percent
	NA	Yes	73.8
at home	26.2		NA
at work	55.4		NA
at local library	11.3		NA
other	10.7		NA

Comments

30. The input that we get from you and other distance education students like you is very helpful to us. From it, we hope that we can continue learning about how students use library resources and services, how they judge and value those resources and services, and how we might improve them. Do you have any further comments that you would like to express regarding library services for distance education students?

Thank you for your input!

APPENDIX B. University of Iowa Libraries Cover Lettter for Survey

Dear Distance Education Student:

We are requesting your participation in a Library Services survey that is posted on the Web at **www.uiowa.edu/~ccp/survey**. The objectives of this survey are to assess the effectiveness of the information services that are currently available to distance education students and to identify areas for potential improvement. **We are aware that you are very busy with your academics and other matters, but we hope that you take time to respond.**

Your participation in this survey is completely confidential. No names are associated with individual responses. You were chosen to participate in this survey through the use of a random selection process, and each distance education student had an equal chance of being selected. **Your participation in this survey is completely voluntary, but it is crucial to the success of our project. Your response will give us an idea of how well we are currently meeting your information needs, and it will help us improve future services.**

The University of Iowa Libraries is committed to creating a learning environment that encourages quality research and scholastic achievement. Your participation in this survey provides us with the type of feedback required to achieve this goal. In addition, should you later have a question about library services or need assistance with any library matter, please feel free to contact me. My university address, a toll-free telephone number, and my e-mail address are provided below.

Access the survey at: www.uiowa.edu/~ccp/survey

Please print the survey, complete the questions, and mail it to us in the provided envelope.

It will take you approximately five-to-ten minutes to complete this survey.

Thank You,

Stephen H. Dew, Ph.D., Coordinator
Library Services for Distance Education
100 Main Library
University of Iowa
Iowa City, IA 52242-1420
Tel: 877-807-9587
FAX: 319-335-5900
E-mail: stephen-dew@uiowa.edu

APPENDIX C. University of the West Indies, Mona Campus, Survey of Distance Education Students: Survey Instrument and Summary of Results, 2000

QUESTIONNAIRE
SECTION ONE
PROFILE OF DISTANCE STUDENTS

1. **What is your gender?**
   Male
   Female

2. **What is your age category?**
   Over 50
   46-50
   36-45
   25-35
   Under 25

*Age Range	GENDER			
	Male	Female	Not Stated	
>50	2	8	2	15%
46-50	2	9	2	16%
36-45	8	10	0	23%
25-35	6	16	3	32%
<25	2	9	0	14%
Totals	20	52	7	79
%	25	66	9	100%

*Seven participants did not indicate their ages.

3. **Are you employed?**   **Percent**
   Full time   92
   Part time   5
   Not working   3

4. **In which sector are you employed?**   **Percent**
   Education   58
   Finance   16
   Civil Service   11
   Police Force   5
   Utilities   4
   Tourism   1
   Transport   1
   Other   4

APPENDIX C (continued)

5a. At which institution did you study last?	Percent
Teacher Training College	33
University	22
High School	20
Professional institution	4
Community College	6
College of Agriculture, Science, and Education	5
Other	10

5b. What program did you study?	Percent
Education	33
Management	33
High School curriculum	7
Computer studies	3
Agriculture	3
Other	21

5c. Which qualification did you obtain?	Percent
Tertiary Diploma	42
Post High School Certificate	29
General Certificate of Education Advanced Level Certificate	6
General Certificate of Education Ordinary Level Certificate	6
Associate Degree	3
Other	14

5d. When did you graduate?	Percent
1970s	8
1980s	27
1990-1994	25
1995-1999	25
Other	15

6. Why did you choose to study by distance education? Please tick all relevant answers.	Percent
Distance from Mona Campus	56
Work commitment	38
Home commitment	32
Career advancement	38
Change of occupation	25
Flexibility (time, place, pace)	13
Other	10

7a. Which is your distance education site?	Percent
Mona	24
Denbigh	18
Morant Bay	13
Savana-la-mar	10
Ocho Rios	9
Montego Bay	8

Brown's Town	5
Vere	5
Mandeville	4
Turks and Caicos Island	4
Cayman Islands	1

7b. In which distance education programme are you enrolled?

UWIDEC Programme	% of Sample
B.Sc. Management Studies	42
B.Ed. Educational Administration	29
Certificate Public Administration	9
Certificate Adult Education	6
B.Sc. Public Administration I	8
B.Sc. Agri-Business	4
B.Sc. Accounting I	1
Not Stated	1
Grand Total	100

8. How far do you travel to get to the UWI Mona Library? Please tick the answer that applies to you.

	Percent
10 miles/16km or less	17
11-25 miles/18-40km	8
26-50 miles/41-80km	30
Over 50 miles/80km	43
Other	2

9. How often do you visit the Mona Library? Please tick the answer that applies to you.

	Percent
At least once per week	10
Every 2-3 weeks	6
Every 4-5 weeks	6
Every 6-7 weeks	4
Once per semester	23
Never visited	51

10. If you visit the Mona Library, when are you most likely to do so?

	Percent
Weekdays (8:30 a.m.-4:30 p.m.)	18
Saturdays	19
Evenings (4:31 p.m.-10:00 p.m.)	11
Other	52

APPENDIX C (continued)

SECTION TWO
USE OF DISTANCE LIBRARY SERVICES

11. Which of the following library services have you accessed? Please tick all that you have used.

Services	% of Sample
Core Textbooks at site	72
Photocopies of articles and chapters of books	63
Book Loans from Mona Library	53
Reference Services	49
Mona Library Collections	37
User Instruction	13
None (have not used any)	13
Inter-Library Loan	8

12. How do you submit your requests to the Mona Library? Please tick the methods that you have used.

	Percent
FAX	8
E-mail	6
Telephone	14
Tutors	5
Site Coordinator	3
Administrative Assistant	32
Personal visit to Mona Library	26
Other	5

13. How did you learn about the distance library services? Please tick all that apply.

	Percent
Brochure	13
Site Coordinator	15
Student Orientation	35
Tutors	5
Student Handbook	27
Administrative Assistant	4
Other	1

14. How satisfied are you with the library services provided? Please circle the relevant number as indicated in the scale below.

Scale: 1 = very satisfied; 2 = satisfied; 3 = moderately satisfied; 4 = dissatisfied; 5 = very dissatisfied

Item Rated	Weighted Average Rating
Timeliness of response to requests for materials	3.3
Number and variety of core textbooks at site	3.3
Inter-library loans	3.0

Item Rated	Weighted Average Rating
Library instruction	3.0
UWI Mona Library collections	2.6
Book loans	2.5
Reference service	2.5
Photocopies of journal articles and chapters of books	2.1

15. **Why haven't you used the distance library services? Please tick all answers that apply to you.**

	Percent
I get books and resources elsewhere	53
I was unaware of the library services	31
Reading outside course materials not required	16
Other	5

SECTION THREE
USE OF OTHER LIBRARY SERVICES

16. **In addition to the Mona Distance Library Services, which of the following other libraries have you been using in your research? Please tick all the answers that apply to you.**

Type of Library	% of Other Library Usage
Public library	36
None (no other library used)	14
Workplace library	13
School library	13
Community college library	10
Teachers' college library	8
Other university library	4
Other libraries	2

17. **What are the factors responsible for your choice of library? Please tick all the answers that are relevant to you.**

	Percent
Convenient opening hours	26
Close to home	37
Library owns books I need	16
Library owns journals I need	6
Helpfulness of staff	16
Other	6

18a. **Do you have access to the Internet?**

	Percent
Yes	53
No	47

APPENDIX C (continued)

18b. If yes, tick the places from which you have access.

Access Points	% of all Responses
Home	37
Work	25
UWIDEC Site	21
Other	9.5
Home of friend/relative	7.9

SECTION FOUR
NEW SERVICES

19. **Do you think the following services would be useful to you in your studies? Please circle the relevant number as indicated by the scale.**

Scale: 1 = extremely useful; 2 = useful; 3 = moderately useful; 4 = somewhat useful; 5 = not useful at all

Services	Weighted Average Rating
Access to Mona catalogue	1.6
Access to electronic databases	1.8
Access to electronic journals	1.8
Supplemental reading at sites	1.5
Research consultation with Distance Education Librarian	1.9
DEC site visits by Librarian	2.0
Information literacy (Research Skills instructions)	2.6

Age Range	Access to Electronic Databases Weighted Average Rating
>50	2.5
46-50	2.7
36-45	2.3
25-35	1
<25	1.4

20.   **How useful would the following additional services be to your course of studies? Please circle the relevant number as indicated by the scale.**

Scale: 1 = extremely useful; 2 = useful; 3 = moderately useful; 4 = somewhat useful; 5 = not useful at all

         Supplemental reading at sites
         Research consultation with Distance Education Librarian
         Site visits by librarian
         Information Literacy (research skills instruction)

Age	Supplemental Reading at Sites Weighted Average Rating
>50	1.7
46-50	1.3
36-45	1.1
25-35	1.8
<25	2.0

21.   **What recommendations would you like to make to the Mona Library to help us to serve you better?**

THANK YOU FOR YOUR PARTICIPATION

APPENDIX D. University of the West Indies, Mona Campus Cover Letter for Questionnaire

University of the West Indies, Mona
Department of Library and Information Studies

August 20, 2000

Dear Distance Learner:

I am pursuing a Master's degree in Library and Information Studies and my area of interest is library services for distance learners. As part of the requirement for the degree, I am conducting a survey to ascertain how the Mona Campus Library is serving you and the new services you would like to see introduced. I will not use the information you provide for study purposes only but also to develop the Library's distance library service in order to serve you better.

I am therefore seeking your participation in the survey by requesting that you complete the attached questionnaire. Your answers will be treated with strict confidentially.

Thank you for your cooperation.

Yours sincerely

Evadne McLean (Mrs)

Assessing Minds Want to Know:
Developing Questions for Assessment
of Library Services
Supporting Off-Campus Learning Programs

Lynn M. McMain
Judy Ann Jerabek

Sam Houston State University

SUMMARY. This paper discusses requirements for constructing balanced questions for surveys when assessing library services for off-campus learning programs, including criteria for creating good questions. After exploring research goal and objective setting, the discussion turns to defining research type, selecting research format, and constructing questions. The next section focuses on question structure and wording issues with attention given to characteristics of open-ended and closed-ended questions and their application, double negatives and stating questions in the negative, use of time, eliciting a summary judgment, and bias exhibited in questions. Finally, consideration is given to a list of issues to note and avoid in question formation.

KEYWORDS. Assessment, library services, distance learners, distance education

---

[Haworth co-indexing entry note]: "Assessing Minds Want to Know: Developing Questions for Assessment of Library Services Supporting Off-Campus Learning Programs." McMain, Lynn M., and Judy Ann Jerabek. Co-published simultaneously in *Journal of Library Administration* (The Haworth Information Press, an imprint of The Haworth Press, Inc.) Vol. 41, No. 1/2, 2004, pp. 303-314; and: *The Eleventh Off-Campus Library Services Conference Proceedings* (ed: Patrick B. Mahoney) The Haworth Information Press, an imprint of The Haworth Press, Inc., 2004, pp. 303-314.

http://www.haworthpress.com/web/JLA
Digital Object Identifier: 10.1300/J111v41n01_21

INTRODUCTION

Recently television networks have added a number of shows involving competitions to see which person or group can build, cook, or decorate "better" than the other or others. Such shows include *House Rules, Iron Chef*, and *Knock First*. The reason for noting this trend, is not to comment on popular mass media, but rather to call attention to a factor which unifies all of these shows; that is, it is not what the contestants have, but how they put it together that makes the difference, and calls forth different responses. For example, the chefs on *Iron Chef* start out with the same theme ingredient. It is the selection among various other ingredients, the amount of each, the order in which they are combined, and how they are presented that produce different results and receive different reactions from the judges.

The same general principle applies when constructing questions for a survey or assessment of library services that support distance learning programs. It is not simply the words that are used, but how those words are selected, combined, ordered, and presented that produce different responses and thereby different results. This paper discusses requirements for constructing balanced questions for surveys when assessing library services for off-campus learning programs, including criteria for creating good questions. After exploring research goal and objective setting, the discussion turns to defining research type, selecting research format, and constructing questions. The next section focuses on question structure and wording issues with attention given to characteristics of open-ended and closed-ended questions and their application, double negatives and stating questions in the negative, use of time, eliciting a summary judgment, and bias exhibited in questions. Finally, consideration is given to a list of issues to note and avoid in question formation.

ASSESSING MINDS WANT TO KNOW
WHAT OTHERS HAVE SAID–
OVERVIEW OF THE LITERATURE

Fowler defines a good question as one " . . . that produces answers that are reliable and valid measures of something we want to describe" (1995, p. 1). Since reliable, valid measures are the hallmark of high quality research, how do researchers develop that 'good' question? The process of developing good questions begins with the research issue itself. Paul Burton states that the "researcher must have a clear definition of the objectives of the research before being able to ask the appropriate questions" (1990, p. 63). Westbrook agrees and states the research questions must be created first and that they function as goals to guide the creation of questions for the survey (2001, p. 51). Arlene Fink notes that " . . . selection and wording of questions are strongly influenced by the survey's context: its purposes, who asks the questions, how they are asked, who answers them, and the characteristics of respondents and responses" (1995, p. 3). Dillman says the " . . . writing of questions can be conveniently divided into three parts, each of which requires separate decisions. They are (1) the kind of information sought, (2) the question structure, and (3) the actual choice of words" (1978, p. 79). Fink and Kosecoff refer to this as setting the survey's boundaries, or defining its content. The researcher must know and understand the purpose of the survey and its goals in order to create and write effective questions.

Understanding how question wording or word choice affects the response is another key issue when constructing questions. Fowler observes "one standard for a good question is that all the people answering it should understand it in a consistent way and in a way consistent with what the researcher expected it to mean" (1995, p. 2). Questions must be written in such a way that surveyors and responders both interpret the question in a similar manner. Consistent understanding of the questions on the part of the responders leads to consistency of the responses which, in turn significantly improves the reliability of the survey instrument. Wording should be simple and readily understandable by any potential responder (Converse & Presser, 1988, p. 9). Salant and Dillman (1994, p. 77) declare that emotionally charged and biased questions cause problems in survey credibility and render the question responses useless.

Not only the wording but also the structure of the question affects the response. Salant and Dillman note that " . . . question structure may confuse the respondent thereby making it impossible for him or her to answer 'correctly'" (1994, p. 18). This is particularly true when there are not mutually exclusive responses.

Cox suggests avoiding compound or doubled-barreled questions (1996, p. 11), questions which are really two questions in one sentence. Compound questions serve only to mislead and confuse the responder and thereby the response. In his principles Fowler states that "A question should end with the question itself" (1995, p. 87). In other words, if there are choices or definitions included in a question, make sure they come first and the actual question is last. Czaja & Blair advise that questions must be structured to be "unadorned and uncomplicated" (1996, p. 62); and that the survey question is a "special construct with a clearly focused purpose" (1996, p. 63). The purpose is to elicit a response that is a reliable indicator of the true and real opinions and perceptions of the respondents.

ASSESSING MINDS WANT TO KNOW
ABOUT RESEARCH METHODOLOGY–
QUANTITATIVE OR QUALITATIVE?

There are two basic types of research: quantitative and qualitative. Quantitative research addresses things measurable, providing numerical results which are precise and therefore are easier to summarize and to compare with the results of other's quantitative research (Tague-Sutcliffe, 1995, p. 17). Questions such as "how often," "how much," "of what duration," "how many" are examples of questions appropriate for quantitative research surveys. The results of these questions, lend themselves to various statistical analysis methods; numbers are grist for the statistical mill. A variety of statistical analyses can be performed on the data generated by quantitative research. These various analyses fall into the larger categories of descriptive statistics which summarize and describe and inferential statistics which are used to predict or infer the characteristics of a larger population (Powell, 1997, p. 190).

In contrast to quantitative research, qualitative research, "centers on understanding rather than on predicting" (Westbrook, 1997, p. 144). The results of qualitative research are not numerically precise and therefore are not as easily expressed as the results of quantitative research. Glasier and Powell describe the characteristics of qualitative research as:

- viewing experiences from the perspective of those involved,
- trying to understand why individuals react or behave as they do,
- attending to the subjective aspects of human experience and behavior,
- taking a natural approach to the solution of research problems (1992, p. xi).

Content analysis, defined by Moser and Kalton as a "systematic analysis and description of the content of communication media" (1972, p. 414), is the primary data technique of qualitative research (Westbrook, 1997, p. 153). As "[a] group of formal and, especially, statistical techniques used to analyze texts . . . " (Calhoun, 2002, p. 92), content analysis involves counting frequency of word and phrase repetition, and the sorting and coding of significant words. Questions appropriate to qualitative research ask about the perceptions and feelings of the person being surveyed, using open-ended questions or asking for a narrative response. An example of an appropriate question for qualitative research would be "How would you describe your experiences with the Reference Desk personnel?"

The chosen type of research (quantitative or qualitative) greatly influences the nature and character of the questions being asked in the survey. Once the type of research has been selected it is time to move on to develop the questions themselves.

ASSESSING MINDS WANT TO KNOW ABOUT DEFINING THE RESEARCH OBJECTIVE– WHAT DO YOU WANT TO KNOW?

The first and primary act by a researcher is to define the specific question(s) the research is intended to answer; based on the reason for conducting the research. Fowler states the most difficult action in the questionnaire design process is for " . . . researchers, people who want to collect data, to define their objectives" (1995, p. 9). Defining the objectives of the questionnaire or survey will determine the type of information needed and point to the appropriate questions to elicit that information. Burton agrees, saying "Once the objective of the survey has been established, it is possible to determine the questions which will elicit the required information" (1990, p. 63). Goals and objectives help researchers to focus on the data desired and helps to eliminate superfluous questions.

When surveying participants in off-campus learning programs one must define what specific library services supportive of those programs should be the focal point of the questions. For example, the Acquisitions Department, while always vital and valuable to all library users, exemplify a secondary level service to off-campus learners. A secondary level service does not directly interface with or provide services to off-campus learners, whereas a primary level service does directly interface with, or provide services to off-campus learners. Relevant library services on a primary level include Reference, Interlibrary Loan, and Copy Services as well as any library-based computer support services.

Ask only those questions some action can be taken on or about, or as Fink and Kosecoff advise " . . . do not ask for information unless you can act on it. . . . Why raise hopes you cannot fulfill?" (1998, p. 11). Asking questions about services that are not available such as, "Would you use a real time chat type format reference service?" would lead to responders anticipating this service being provided by the library in the future.

Be aware of the context of a question. Look at the question that proceeds and the question that follows each individual question. Are there statements before that would influence a response, or could a statement in this question influence the question that follows it? Czaja and Blair point out that researchers "underestimate the impact of context while writing individual questions . . . "

(1996, p. 7). The order of the questions can also influence a response. It is important to maintain consistency in question order. Do not change the order of the questions in mid-survey, or for the purposes of changing format. If there are to be two or more research formats employed, remain consistent, ask face-to-face interview or telephone survey questions in the same order as the written survey questions. Powell notes "Changes in question order can produce 'context errors' resulting in substantial differences in responses to the same question" (1997, p. 102).

ASSESSING MINDS WANT TO KNOW
ABOUT RESEARCH FORMATS–
HOW ARE YOU GOING TO ASK IT?

Along with research methodology, the type of research format that will be used (i.e., written questionnaire, telephone survey) also influences the character and nature of the questions asked, what wording will be used, the structure of the questions and the structure of the survey itself. Method effect describes the difference between questions read to a respondent (what the respondent hears) and questions the respondents will read for themselves. As Salant and Dillman point out, respondents reading a survey or questionnaire have control over the pace and sequence of the questions (1994, p. 18) and they can take as little or as much time as they want in responding. Respondents can read through the whole survey before answering any questions and obtain a sense of the overall context of the survey. Not so in a telephone or face-to-face survey. In those settings the surveyor/interviewer sets both the pace and the sequence of questions. Respondents have only the time allotted by the interviewer to consider and answer the question, and they cannot look ahead to perceive the overall content of the survey. Additionally, interviewers can interject emotion through intonation, facial expressions, and body language, thereby influencing respondents. Conversely, interviewers can also observe respondents and note their intonation, facial expressions, and body language.

ASSESSING MINDS WANT TO KNOW
ABOUT QUESTION TYPES–
OPEN-ENDED AND CLOSED-ENDED

Questions can be either open-ended or closed-ended. Open-ended questions require the respondents to fashion an answer in their own words. Some examples of open-ended questions would be:

- How would you describe the service you receive from the Interlibrary Loan department?
- What would improve Copy Services?

This is the preferred type of question for qualitative research; the response provides the words and phrases for content analysis. However open-ended questions place demands on the respondents with which they may be unwilling or unable to comply. Respondents, for whatever reason, may feel uncomfortable thinking about a subject, placing feelings, thoughts, and experiences on paper, or vocalizing them. Open-ended questions take extra time for respondents to answer and may add significantly to the survey time. From a researcher's perspective there is another consideration. While open-ended questions do provide a wide range of answers, that variety of answers can cause problems when assigning codes to words and phrases. Because of their narrative nature open-ended questions are usually inappropriate for quantitative research.

Closed-ended questions do not allow respondents to use their own words. Instead each closed-ended question is followed by a list of responses from which the respondent must choose. Examples of closed-ended questions would be:

- How often last semester did you access the library's electronic databases remotely?
  1. >10 times
  2. >5 times
  3. 2 to 5 times
  4. once
  5. never

- How many times did you use Interlibrary Loan last semester?
  1. > 5 times
  2. never
  3. once
  4. 2 to 5 times.

Lists of responses can be ordered, as in the first example above, or unordered, as in the second example above. An ordered list of responses is characterized by a progression in a concept. Unordered lists do not provide this progression and consist of disconnected and sometimes unrelated selections. Closed-ended questions are best for ranking and scaling, lending themselves easily to quantitative analysis. However, closed-ended questions force the respondent to choose a response pre-determined by the researchers. On the other hand, pre-determined answers allow the researchers to control the set of responses and assign a numerical value to each given response. Closed-ended questions are usually inappropriate for qualitative research.

ASSESSING MINDS WANT TO KNOW ABOUT SURVEY STRUCTURE– HOW DOES IT GO TOGETHER?

Both Burton (1990, p. 73) and Powell (1997, p. 103) state that the survey or questionnaire should begin with general questions and proceed to more specific questions, providing a context for the questions. Some sources recommend beginning the questionnaire with simple, mundane questions and advancing to more complicated and sophisticated questions, as a way to make respondents comfortable and thus are more likely to complete the survey. Cox (1996, p. 14) suggests grouping questions by type and placing all open-ended questions together in one section and all closed-ended questions in a separate section. Dillman (1978, p. 123), by contrast, advises ordering a questionnaire " . . . along a descending gradient of social usefulness (or importance)." In other words the most important or relevant questions would come first and the simpler questions last. Dillman (1978, p. 124) also suggests grouping questions "similar in content together, and within content area by type of question" and that question topics "should build on cognitive ties" between topics. Powell (1997, p. 103) agrees that " . . . questions of similar context should be placed together." Not addressed is the issue of segues between question topics and how they can be created. Most researchers divide survey/questionnaires into sections, whether by topic or by question structure, and have a set of instructions for each. Additionally segmentation allows for a sense of progression through the survey for the respondents.

ASSESSING MINDS WANT TO KNOW ABOUT OTHER ISSUES TO CONSIDER– WHAT TO NOTE AND AVOID

There is much to consider and avoid in question creation. Salant and Dillman (1994, p. 91) instruct "Don't talk down to respondents." Keep language simple, but not at a level that is insulting. Avoid jargon specific to your area of research as well as scientific terms and use everyday language. An excellent example of jargon is the abbreviation OPAC. Every librarian knows what an OPAC is, but very few library users have any idea that OPAC stands for "On-Line Public Access Catalog." So asking questions about the frequency of accessing the OPAC would be meaningless to the distance learner using remote access to use the library catalog. Payne (1951, p. 233) says to "word your question according to principles of good grammar, but don't make it sound stilted." Use uncomplicated language and words in creating questions.

Double negatives should be avoided at all costs as they create unnecessary misunderstanding on the part of the respondent (Converse & Presser, 1986, p. 13). Double negatives can unintentionally show up in convoluted and complex questions. Many researchers avoid stating questions in the negative. Fink (1995, p. 29) suggests avoiding negative questions altogether, as they " . . . require an exercise in logical thinking." A good rule is to be judicious when stating a question in the negative and if it is a must, make sure to emphasize the negative by the use of italics, bolding, upper case, or a combination.

The time period referred to in a question should be restricted to a reasonable length (Czaja & Blair, 1996, p. 66). Fink (1995, p. 21) advises "periods of a year or more can be used for major life events . . . " The respondent will have forgotten specifics if the time period being surveyed is too long past and the event, behavior, or action, has become less significant. Fowler (1995, p. 85) says "A time period referred to by a question should be unambiguous." Clearly defining a period within a reasonable length of time allows the respondent to recall as accurately as possible a specific behavior, action, or occurrence of an event.

The use of qualifiers such as "overall," "in general," and "for the most part" ask respondents for a summary judgment (Czaja & Blair, 1996, p. 66). A summary judgment helps respondents overcome remembering specifics through long periods of time, and allows a general answer. Summary judgment phrases should not be overused, as the specificity and perhaps the usefulness of the survey answers will be lost.

Questions need to be stated in a non-biased manner. Dillman observes "A biased question is one that influences people to respond in a manner that does not accurately reflect their position on the issue under investigation" (1978, p. 101). Biased questions created either intentionally or unintentionally on the part of the surveyor influence the respondents to answer in a certain way, skewing the results in one direction or another. Questions exhibit bias by:

- insinuating a particular behavior on the part of the respondent,
- providing unequal comparisons,
- using emotional, highly charged words,
- exhibiting a lack of balance in answer choices,
- adopting a subjective tone in the question (Salant & Dillman, 1994, pp. 94-95).

The best way to prevent bias proves to be creating balanced questions. Payne (1951, p. 26) suggests the effective way to create sensible and balanced questions is to ask Who? Why? When? Where? and How? as a template for question creation. Submitting the questions to several colleagues to read and edit also will assist in eliminating bias and help produce balanced questions. Pre-testing questions on a small group of respondents helps researchers identify and eliminate problems and biases in order to produce a set of balanced and reliable questions for any survey instrument.

CONCLUSION

Question creation for surveys and needs assessments involves hard work. Attention must be paid at every level of question creation to ensure a set of quality questions that address the purposes and goals of the researchers. To that end researchers need to identify and clearly state the purpose and goals of the survey. Clearly defining the purpose and goals will focus the researchers as they determine what they really want to know and work to create viable questions. Once the purpose and goals have been defined, researchers then determine the nature of the research. Will the research require a quantitative or qualitative approach? Which approach will serve best to provide responses that directly address the purpose and goal of the survey or assessment?

The next step is to decide on the most appropriate type of research format or formats using the previously defined purpose and goals of the survey or assessment to provide direction for that decision. Personnel, time, and money constraints will all impact format selection which in turn determines the type and nature of the questions that comprise the survey instrument. Researchers must also keep method effect in mind when considering whether to use multiple formats. Questions appropriate to the selected formats can then be created.

At this point the researchers consider the use of open-ended versus closed-ended questions, based on the decisions and selections made up to this point: purpose and goal of the survey/assessment, type of research approach, research format/formats to be used; the researchers begin to construct questions in the chosen style.

There are many issues to consider or avoid in question creation, as previously noted in this paper. A short list of the issues to consider and practices to avoid are:

- Keep language simple
- Do not use jargon

- Do not use double negatives
- When at all possible frame questions only in the positive
- Clearly state time periods
- Set reasonable time periods
- Cautiously use qualifiers that call for a summary judgment
- Construct questions that are non-biased
- Aim at creating balanced questions
- Ask colleagues to edit questions
- Pre-testing on small groups.

Along with all the previously mentioned issues to keep in mind, the above list will help set assessing minds at ease as researchers create survey questions that elicit the information needed for assessment and decision making regarding the library services needed to support off-campus learning programs.

REFERENCES

Burton, P. (1990). Asking questions: Questionnaire design and question phrasing. In M. Slater (Ed.), *Research methods in library and information studies.* (pp. 62-76). London: Library Association Publishing.

Calhoun, C. (Ed.). (2002). *Dictionary of the social sciences* (p. 92). New York: Oxford University Press.

Converse, J. M., & Presser, S. (1988). *Survey questions: Handcrafting the standardized questionnaire.* Beverly Hills, CA: Sage Publications.

Cox, J. (1996). *Your opinion please!: How to build the best questionnaires in the field of education.* Thousand Oaks, CA: Corwin Press, Inc.

Czaja, R. & Blair, J. (1996). *Designing surveys: A guide to decisions and procedures.* Thousand Oaks, CA: Pine Forge Press.

Dillman, D. A. (1978). *Mail and telephone surveys: The total design method.* New York: John Wiley & Sons.

Fink, A. (1995). *How to ask survey questions.* Thousand Oaks, CA: Sage Publications.

Fink, A. & Kosecoff, J. (1998). *How to conduct surveys: A step-by-step guide* (2nd ed.). Thousand Oaks, CA: Sage Publications.

Fowler, F. J. (1995). *Improving survey questions: Design and evaluation.* Applied Social Research Methods Series (Vol. 38). Thousand Oaks, CA: Sage Publications.

Glaser, J. D. & Powell, R.R. (1992). *Qualitative research in information management.* Englewood, CO: Libraries Unlimited.

Moser, C. A. & Kalton, G. (1972). *Survey methods in social investigation* (2nd ed.). New York: Basic Books.

Payne S. L. (1951). *The art of asking questions.* Princeton, NJ: Princeton University Press.

Powell, R. R. (1997). *Basic research methods for librarians* (3rd ed.). Greenwich, CT: Ablex Publishing.

Salant, P. & Dillman, D. A. (1994). *How to conduct your own survey: Leading profes-sionals give you proven techniques for getting reliable results*. New York: John Wiley & Sons.

Tague-Sutcliffe, J. (1995). *Measuring information: An information service perspec-tive*. New York: Academic Press.

Westbrook, L. (1997). Qualitative research. In R. R. Powell (Ed.). *Basic research methods for librarians* (3rd ed.) (pp. 143-162). Greenwich, CT: Ablex Publishing.

Westbrook, L. (2001). *Identifying and analyzing user needs: A complete handbook and ready-to-use assessment workbook with disc*. New York: Neal-Schuman.

Anything, Anytime, Anywhere: Proxy Servers, Shibboleth, and the Dream of the Digital Library

Brian L. Mikesell

St. John's University

SUMMARY. Students and faculty have come to expect off-campus access to the full portfolio of electronic resources made available by their library. They demand, and should be provided, simple access to electronic information sources 24 hours a day, 7 days a week, regardless of their location. Proxy servers have been the solution of choice for remote authentication for some time now, but library users tend to have difficulty with manually configured proxies, and there are beginning to be robust alternatives that can provide secure off-campus access to library resources. Remote authentication should not be a matter of getting a proxy server running and then forgetting about it. New developments should be investigated to ensure the easiest, most reliable and most secure access possible–in the interests of libraries and their users.

KEYWORDS. Technology, Internet, distance education, library services

The dream of the vast, authoritative, easy-to-use virtual library is not only the dream of librarians–our patrons very much share this dream. For some, the ability to access library resources anywhere, anytime is an issue of conve-

---

[Haworth co-indexing entry note]: "Anything, Anytime, Anywhere: Proxy Servers, Shibboleth, and the Dream of the Digital Library." Mikesell, Brian L. Co-published simultaneously in *Journal of Library Administration* (The Haworth Information Press, an imprint of The Haworth Press, Inc.) Vol. 41, No. 1/2, 2004, pp. 315-326; and: *The Eleventh Off-Campus Library Services Conference Proceedings* (ed: Patrick B. Mahoney) The Haworth Information Press, an imprint of The Haworth Press, Inc., 2004, pp. 315-326.

http://www.haworthpress.com/web/JLA
Digital Object Identifier: 10.1300/J111v41n01_22

nience and portability. In fact, though, distance learners and others have every right to insist upon its availability not as a convenience, but as a necessity. Increasingly, this dream–and need–is being fulfilled. As more and more publishers and content owners make their materials available via the Internet, library patrons benefit. Libraries have worked to develop the relationships with publishers and vendors that facilitate the provision of electronic information and must continue to ensure that the necessary trust inherent in those relationships is maintained. Part of this process is ensuring that access to these electronic resources is secure and available only to those for whom the licenses are purchased. In libraries and on campuses, this is a relatively simple matter–after all campus networks and workstations can be secured.

When library patrons are not on campus or in the library, though, some method must be employed to both grant them access to the information sources they need as well as to maintain the necessary security. Proxy servers are a widely used solution to the problem of secure remote access. In fact, 60 out of 74 respondents to a survey about proxy server use in 2000 indicated that they were using a proxy server for remote patron authentication (Rogers, 2001, p. 7). As there has not yet been any technology development to supplant proxy servers, there is no reason to assume that the trend has not continued, with even more libraries relying on proxy servers today. A proxy server can provide a legitimate method of remote access, but they are not a complete or perfect solution. A simple, frank discussion of proxy servers and other remote access methods must take place in order to continue to move libraries forward in pursuing the dream of the anything, anytime, anywhere, digital library.

WHAT HAPPENS WHEN LIBRARY USERS ARE ON CAMPUS?

In most academic libraries, patrons may never know that they are using licensed resources that require some form of authentication. This is because libraries have widely adopted IP (Internet Protocol) authentication. "IP validation . . . continues to be the most practical method for securing and validating access to the online products libraries offer. It has become the standardized method for large-scale user validation" (Webster, 2002, p. 20). Simply put, IP authentication (or validation) works this way: (1) each organization or institution is assigned a block or blocks of IP addresses–a series of digits that uniquely identifies a computer to the local network and to the Internet at large; (2) the library communicates to its vendors the range of IP addresses used by their institution; (3) the vendor creates on its server(s) a file that says "these IP addresses" are allowed access to these resources; (4) when a student sits down at a computer on campus and clicks on a licensed library resource, the vendor's server checks the incoming IP address against its file of subscribers' IP addresses; (5) if a match is made, the user is allowed to use the resource, if not, access is denied (see Figure 1).

There are several advantages to IP authentication: users are not required to log in to electronic resources, therefore it is transparent to the users; it is an efficient way to authenticate large numbers of students, faculty, administrators, and staff who want to use library resources online; and it is easy for libraries to administer–all that is required is that the library submit a range of IP addresses to each vendor.

Of course, for users who are not on campus, IP authentication will not work at all. Their IP address is coming from a different source, usually their ISP (Internet Service Provider, such as AOL, RoadRunner, or EarthLink), and when the vendor's server checks their IP address against its list of authorized users, it will not make a match and deny access to the resource (see Figure 2).

THE NEED FOR REMOTE AUTHENTICATION

"In a perfect world, network security wouldn't exist. It's a barrier and, generally speaking, has an inverse relationship with functionality. Librarians and other users of information systems usually find network security to be a nuisance. But just as we understand we should lock our cars when we leave them in parking lots, so we know that we must secure our networks" (Cain, 2003, p. 246). Libraries have worked long and hard to convince publishers that they can safely make their materials available online, and libraries must work to maintain the level of trust necessary to continue the trend. Unfortunately, that means various levels of network security. In addition, "The problem of integrating disparate resources so that they are readily available to the user is both growing and pressing" (Law, forthcoming, para. 16). More and more users are demanding remote access to library resources.

IP authentication is a transparent method of authenticating users to vendors' databases when users are in our libraries or on our campuses. But how do we validate those users who want or need to do research from some other location? There are a range of reasons to want to do this–a graduate student doing

FIGURE 1. Seamless IP Authentication

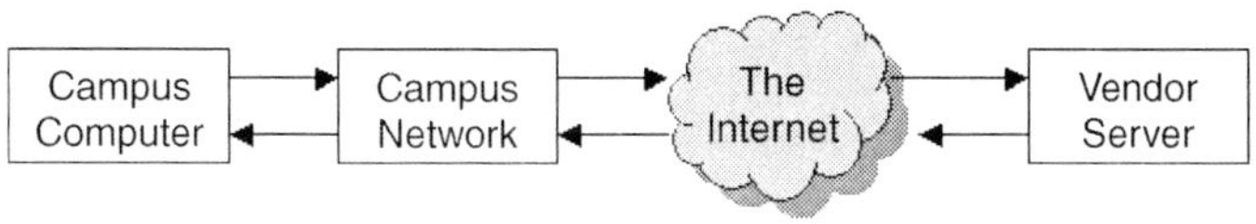

FIGURE 2. IP Address Not Registered–Access Denied

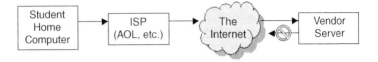

fieldwork; a faculty member at a conference; a student working from home at the end of a day of classes. There are also, of course, library users for whom it is a requirement to have off-campus access to electronic library resources–distance learners; people with disabilities for whom it is difficult to make a trip to campus to do research; students who work full time while taking classes and thus cannot spend much time on campus other than when they are attending class.

No matter what the reason for wanting or needing off-campus access to electronic resources, though, libraries have found various ways of making this possible. Some libraries give out usernames and passwords to particular databases only when requested; other libraries use vendor-developed authentication methods, which require the user to have different accounts for various vendors' databases; perhaps the most widespread method is to use some variety of proxy server.

WHAT IS A PROXY SERVER AND HOW DOES IT WORK?

"The proxy server is not unlike the modern librarian, serving as a helpful and discreet intermediary between users and online information" (Webster, 2002, p. 20). Some users (and librarians) would not agree with this statement. Some types of proxy servers are difficult to use and support, but all can provide an effective means of authenticating remote users into libraries' licensed electronic resources:

A proxy server is a computer on-site at a library that users can connect to over the Internet. This server acts as an intermediary between the remote users and the database servers that the library makes available. The remote users cannot access the vendors' databases directly from their home PCs. But they can connect to the proxy server, which then passes information back and forth from the remote users to the vendor database, making it appear as if they were working from valid IP numbers at the library rather than from their homes or offices. (Webster, 2002, p. 20)

Simply put, a proxy server relays commands from the patron's (off-campus) computer to and from the vendor server. The proxy server is recognized by the vendor's server because the proxy server is on campus and, therefore, has an IP address within the approved range. In "real world" usage: (1) when a library user who is off campus has her browser settings properly configured to use a proxy server (some require manual configuration, others do not) and is connected to the Internet (via her ISP) she can; (2) click on a link to her library's licensed resources; (3) she will be asked to log in to the proxy server; (4) if she has entered a valid username and password, she will be authenticated into the proxy server and can; (5) use any licensed resource that is configured to use IP authentication. In most proxy server installations, the user is logged into the proxy server for the duration of that session–that is, until she closes her browser or specifically logs off the proxy server. This allows the user to browse among the full range of licensed resources made available by the library, regardless of the vendor (see Figure 3).

PROBLEMS WITH PROXIES

An inherent problem with proxies is the issue of security. For example, " . . . any personal computer on a campus network can be set up as a Web server . . . It is also possible to find free proxy server software . . . If the computer is left on, and if a hacker can discover this machine, he has an open door to whatever Web-enabled databases that machine can access" (Cain, 2003, p. 247). It was this kind of "back door" that allowed " . . . an unauthorized user or users exploited unprotected proxy servers from participating JSTOR sites to download illegally more than 51,000 articles from 11 JSTOR journals" (Albanese, 2003, p. 20). This, of course, is not how libraries are using proxies, but relying on a combination of IP authentication and a proxy server makes this kind of abuse possible.

Another aspect of security is authenticating users into the proxy itself. Most vendor licenses authorize only persons currently affiliated with a college or university to access the materials in their databases. This means that it is the li-

FIGURE 3. Proxy Server IP Address Recognized–Access Granted

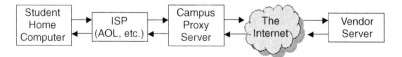

brary's responsibility to make sure that the list of authorized users against which the proxy server is authenticating remote users is current and valid. Many times, this means periodic extractions of data about current students and faculty from the student information system and subsequent uploads of that data to the proxy server for authentication. Of course, this list must either be updated regularly or risk improperly validating users who should no longer have access (i.e., students who have graduated, etc.) or denying access to users who should be granted access (i.e., newly hired employees, etc.). One way around this particular problem is to authenticate from a "live" source of this data–possibly integrating the proxy server with the student information system, e-mail servers, or some other source that is constantly being updated with the latest data about employees and enrollment. Many libraries, though, lack expertise to make these kinds of links or cannot access these data sources and must rely instead on potentially stale patron data.

One other issue that makes proxies a less than ideal solution is bandwidth consumption. "Remote resources access is the most popular use of proxies in libraries today, but it represents a cumbersome and inefficient way to solve the remote resource access problem. These proxies can be complicated to set up, both for the user and the library, and cause content for the remote resource user to cross an institution's Internet connection twice" (Murray, 2001, p. 176). The fact that off-campus users are logging into a server on campus creates the initial connection to the campus network–they then transmit all of their search commands to the vendor's server via the proxy and the vendor's server then sends data back to the patron via the proxy. This extra layer of data transmission could ultimately create excessive demands on the server and the network. A solution that does not require this extra connection would certainly be preferable.

One final problem with proxy-based solutions is that access is an all-or-nothing proposition. If a user can sign on to the proxy, they can have access to any resource that uses IP authentication. There is no way, really, of allowing access to a particular subset of resources only to a specific group of individuals. This may not be an issue for every library, but getting around it would require a certain amount of creativity and probably extra resources to make the adjustments. One solution might be to run multiple proxies, with separate authentication databases.

As mentioned above, there are a variety of different proxy solutions with different software and relatively widely varying setups. Some libraries choose to use a proxy server that must be configured manually by the user, others use URL-rewriters such as EZproxy, which do not require the user to do any configuration. There are also solutions other than proxies–each with their advantages and disadvantages. Some of these proxy and non-proxy authentication methods are described in the following sections.

REMOTE AUTHENTICATION METHODS

Proxies That Require Users to Configure Browser Settings

A manually configured proxy works basically as above, but users must first alter their browsers' Internet preferences/options so that the browser knows (1) that the user wants to connect to a proxy server and (2) the URL of the proxy server to be used. For example, to configure Internet Explorer 6.6 to use a proxy server, the user would need to: (1) open the browser; (2) click "Tools" in the menu bar; (3) go to "Internet options" in that menu; (4) click on the "Connections" tab; (5) choose the connection they want to configure (usually whatever ISP they use from home); (6) click "Settings"; (7) place a checkmark in the box next to "Use a proxy server for this connection"; and (8) enter the URL and port number of the proxy server they want to use.

To complicate matters, if the user has cable or DSL Internet access, the process is a bit different. Also, the steps are somewhat different for each version of Internet Explorer and Netscape. For an experienced computer/Internet user who has the appropriate instructions for their browser as well as the correct URL and port number, this is a relatively simple matter. For many users, though, this is an enormous hurdle to using library resources from off campus. These users then require additional support from their library. It is possible to write a script that will configure a user's browser for them. This approach has been adopted by some libraries, but requires the programming resources necessary to create and maintain the script properly.

EZproxy

More and more libraries are finding EZproxy to be an easier approach for their patrons. All a user must do is: (1) click on a link to a licensed resource; (2) embedded in such a link is the URL of the EZproxy server, so that; (3) the EZproxy server determines whether the incoming request is from a computer that is on campus or off campus; (4) if the user is on campus, EZproxy steps out of the process and forwards the user to the appropriate database URL; (5) if the user is off campus, EZproxy asks them to log in; (6) if the user inputs a valid username and password, EZproxy will then forward them to the appropriate database URL:

EZproxy works by dynamically altering the URLs within the web pages provided by your database vendor. The server names within the URLs of these web pages are changed to reflect your EZproxy server instead, causing your users to return to the EZproxy server as they access links on these web pages. The result is a seamless access environment for your users without the need for automatic proxy configuration files. EZproxy only alters references to your database vendors' Web pages, so if your database vendor provides additional links to other free web pages on the Internet, these are left as-is. In this manner, if your users elect to follow one of these links, the EZproxy server is automatically taken out of the communication loop. (EZproxy Overview, n.d., The solution section, para. 2)

There are several advantages to using a URL-rewriter like EZproxy: "(1) users aren't required to make any browser configurations and (2) the proxy server operates transparently, intervening only to authenticate and proxy data for remote patrons" (Bertrand, 2002, p. 135). On the other hand, EZproxy is not without its challenges. For example, the server must have a list of the URLs of resources to which the library subscribes. Creating and keeping this list up-to-date requires steady maintenance.

Onelog

An elegant step forward is a product just beginning to be available in the United States: Onelog, a system produced by ITS Ltd. Onelog might most properly be termed an access management system. At its core, Onelog works in much the same way as EZproxy–that is, it is not invoked until a user clicks on a link to a resource and then it checks to see whether the user is on or off campus, asks for a login as necessary, then forwards the user on to the database. "The Onelog service also features highly advanced IP parsing for offsite access that does not require the user to make any changes to their browser" (Law, forthcoming, para. 9). So, like EZproxy, access to electronic resources is seamless and transparent to the end user.

There are some things that Onelog does in addition, though. For example, "All web-resource scripting is undertaken by ITS as part of the service, thus giving the benison of removing some administrative overheads from the organization" (Law, forthcoming, para. 12). In practice, what this means is that all the library must do is notify ITS (the company that produces Onelog) to which resources they subscribe and ITS takes care of the configuration. Any resource not in their database is added upon request and any access idiosyncrasies worked out by ITS, freeing the library up to do other things. Another big benefit of Onelog is that it can be integrated with one's campus portal and with course management systems. Finally, Onelog can provide the library with extensive statistics about electronic resource usage.

Virtual Private Networks

A virtual private network is " . . . a network that is constructed by using public wires to connect nodes. For example, there are a number of systems that enable you to create networks using the Internet as the medium for transporting data. These systems use encryption and other security mechanisms to ensure that only authorized users can access the network and that the data cannot be intercepted" (VPN, n.d., para. 1). In practice, when a student connects to a virtual private network and, through that, to their library's electronic resources, they are using a more sophisticated version of the proxy server idea. "VPNs extend the institution's IP addresses to machines outside the local area network by tunneling traffic through the general Internet. As such, VPNs work at a network infrastructure layer below that of a Web proxy server, but can accomplish the same result as a Web proxy server for remote resource access" (Murray, 2001, p. 175). The user is still authenticated into the vendor's resource by IP address and still must both have their own ISP and log in to the campus network. The main advantage of a VPN is security. The main disadvantage is the required networking and other technical expertise as well as the hardware and other resources required to set up and maintain the VPN. A VPN may not be the best solution for a library looking to provide remote access to its electronic resources, unless the institution has an interest in providing remote access to their network for other reasons as well.

Athens

Athens, a product of EduServ in the United Kingdom, is a service that manages access to web-based licensed resources by students and other off campus users. "Athens is, fundamentally, a central repository of organisations, usernames and passwords with associated rights. It has extensive account management facilities for organisations to create and manage usernames and passwords, and to allocate rights to individual usernames" (Athens Access Management Services, n.d., Welcome to Athens section, para. 2). Athens is not a proxy-based solution, but rather relies on its centralized system to grant or deny access to a particular resource requested by a user. Athens allows the library to have granular control over who has access to which electronic resources. Also, because it is centralized, the library is not required to maintain the hardware and software, but only to keep its profile of users and resources up to date.

One item of significant note is that, in addition to the educational institution or library, publishers and vendors must also cooperate with the Athens protocols and be integrated into the system. This, then, requires a level of cooperation beyond merely licensing their materials to libraries. Athens has been in place in the UK since 1996 and, apparently, it is becoming increasingly difficult for a vendor to be successful in the academic library market if they are unwilling to participate in Athens (Athens Access Management Services, n.d., Education section, para. 1).

Shibboleth

A project of Internet 2, Shibboleth is still very much an emerging product. Some limited installations are in place, but it is not ready or available for wider distribution at this time. On its Web site, it is described thus:

> Shibboleth is an initiative to develop an open, standards-based solution to the needs for organizations to exchange information about their users in a secure, and privacy-preserving manner . . . The organizations that may want to exchange information include higher education, their partners, digital content providers, government agencies, etc. The purpose of the exchange is typically to determine if a person using a web browser (e.g., Internet Explorer, Netscape Navigator, Mozilla) has the permissions to access a resource at a target resource based on information such as being a member of an institution or a particular class. (Shibboleth Introduction, n.d., para. 1)

The Shibboleth project was begun after Athens began to show that cooperative methods could be successfully employed for remote access to electronic resources. It does differ from Athens in at least one fundamental respect–it is distributed rather than centralized. Rather than having a centralized depository, an institution must install the software on its own server while also being a member of the Shibboleth community. One similarity to Athens, though, is that publishers and vendors must also participate in the process as members of the Shibboleth community. Shibboleth is based on digital attributes that are exchanged–this is how the "trust relationship" is established between the user's browser and the vendor's server–they must recognize each other. As Shibboleth develops, it may eventually come to replace proxy servers, VPNs, and other remote authentication methods. This is, in part, because it is being developed with the full awareness of the limitations and difficulties inherent in these methods. Solutions to these problems are being integrated into the end product while it also addresses fundamental issues that cannot even be considered with proxy servers.

DIFFICULTIES WITH NEWER NON-PROXY METHODS

There are, though, certain difficulties with these non-proxy methods of remote authentication. One issue with a solution such as Shibboleth is that many libraries may lack the technical expertise to implement and maintain the technology. Of course, this too may change if Shibboleth becomes a standard, widely implemented solution–especially if provision is made to ensure its simplicity not only for users, but for the institution implementing it. It is likely, though, that there will be libraries–especially smaller ones–that continue to use proxy-based solutions like EZproxy because of the low cost and ease of implementation and use.

The biggest issue, though, is that because of their cooperative nature, there will for some time exist the situation that only a part–whether greater or smaller–of a library's resources will be able to utilize them. For example:

> If the resource is ATHENS protected the user is forced to logon using their ATHENS credentials. This seemed an optimal solution but has proved to be only a partial answer. While it is very satisfactory if all the available resources are ATHENS enabled, it becomes much less convenient if the user intends to move through a variety of resources. (Law, forthcoming, para. 2)

Athens has been available for about seven years, but there are still publishers who do not participate and, thus, libraries using Athens must still have some additional remote authentication procedure for those vendor resources that are not Athens-enabled. The situation is the same, of course, for Shibboleth, especially since it has not yet established itself as a standard solution. As these products continue to mature, it is likely that the vast majority of publishers will come to recognize the benefits of participating, but it is difficult to say when that will ultimately happen.

> Librarians strive to provide transparent systems, with a minimal amount of barriers between the user and the information she or he is seeking. Librarians also want to ensure user privacy and academic freedom. These

are all laudable values. But the publishing community has legitimate concerns as well . . . To protect our interests, we must protect theirs. (Cain, 2003, p. 247)

Obviously, none of these solutions are perfect, but librarians must continue to investigate new technologies and methods for providing secure, reliable access to the electronic information sources they make available to their patrons. Doing so will help ensure the continuation–and expansion–of the availability of these essential resources while also improving the transparency, integration, and ease-of-use about which library patrons and librarians alike, dream.

REFERENCES

Albanese, A. (January 1, 2003). Open proxy servers victimize JSTOR [Electronic version]. *Library Journal, 128*(1), 19-20.

Athens access management services. (n.d.). Retrieved December 7, 2003 from Athens Access Management Services Web site: http://www.athensams.net/.

Bertrand, G. (2002). Providing access to remote patrons can be ez [Electronic version]. *Feliciter, 48*(3), 134-136.

Cain, M. (July 2003). Cybertheft, network security, and the library without walls [Electronic version]. *Journal of Academic Librarianship, 29*(4), 245-248.

EZproxy overview. (n.d.). Retrieved December 7, 2003 from Useful Utilities Web site: http://www.usefulutilities.com/support/overview.html.

Law, D. (in press). Simplifying access to electronic resources: The changing model of information provision. *The Computer Journal.*

Murray, P. (Dec. 2001). Library web proxy use survey results [Electronic version]. *Information Technology and Libraries, 10*(4), 172-178.

Rogers, M. (Winter 2001). Proxy servers in wide use [Electronic version]. *Library Journal, 126*(1), 7. *Shibboleth introduction.* (n.d.). Retrieved December 7, 2003 from Shibboleth Project Web site http://shibboleth.internet2.edu/shib-intro.html.

VPN. (n.d.). Retrieved December 7, 2003 from Webopedia.com Web site: http://www.webopedia.com/TERM/V/VPN.html.

Webster, P. (Sept. 2002). Remote patron validation: Posting a proxy server at the DIGITAL doorway [Electronic version]. *Computers in Libraries, 22*(8), 18-23.

Taking Assessment on the Road: Utah Academic Librarians Focus on Distance Learners

Rob Morrison

Utah State University

Allyson Washburn

Brigham Young University

SUMMARY. This paper presents the results of focus groups conducted by Utah academic librarians at branch campuses in Utah. Librarians met with distance learners on-site to gain insights into their information-seeking behavior and to learn if they are using library services. Students rely heavily on the Web for information and also utilize known resources in friends and family. Marketing and publicizing library services through classes and at the delivery sites is vital. Students appreciate the services libraries offer and strongly prefer face-to-face instruction and direct assistance from a librarian.

KEYWORDS. Assessment, distance learners, focus groups, Internet

INTRODUCTION

The state of Utah has a population of 2,233,169 residents. Approximately three out of every four, or about 76%, live in four urban Wasatch front counties. The 1.7 million people living in these four counties occupy less than 5%

[Haworth co-indexing entry note]: "Taking Assessment on the Road: Utah Academic Librarians Focus on Distance Learners." Morrison, Rob, and Allyson Washburn. Co-published simultaneously in *Journal of Library Administration* (The Haworth Information Press, an imprint of The Haworth Press, Inc.) Vol. 41, No. 1/2, 2004, pp. 327-344; and: *The Eleventh Off-Campus Library Services Conference Proceedings* (ed: Patrick B. Mahoney) The Haworth Information Press, an imprint of The Haworth Press, Inc., 2004, pp. 327-344.

of the state's land area. The remaining residents live in 25 mostly rural counties that comprise the remaining 95% of the land area of the state (State of Utah, n.d.). Three public institutions have traditionally served distance learners in Utah: Utah State University (USU), the land grant institution, with the extension mission, delivers more than thirty degree programs and enrolls 10,000 distance learners annually; the University of Utah's Spencer S. Eccles Health Sciences Library also has an outreach mission to provide library services for health care professionals in the state; and the College of Eastern Utah operates through two separate campuses in the eastern and southeastern parts of Utah in Price and Blanding, respectively. Today, nearly every Utah public and private higher education institution serves distance learners on-site, via online courses, or by using the Utah Education Networks' microwave and satellite delivery system (www.uen.org).

The Utah Academic Library Consortium (UALC) was formed in 1973 and has a long history of cooperative efforts in the state of Utah. The purpose of the consortium is to "cooperate in continually improving the availability and delivery of library and information services to the higher education community and to the State of Utah." Methods employed for achieving that goal include the following:

a. Fostering research, developing and implementing cooperative library programs;
b. Providing a means for the exchange of information on cooperative library ventures;
c. Maximizing limited resources by improving library methods and avoiding expensive duplicate purchases;
d. Maximizing information delivery through shared use of technology and human resources;
e. Acting as an advocate for excellence in library resources and services.

The librarians in the Utah's higher education institutions are committed to providing library services to all higher education students in Utah regardless of location as evidenced by the fact that one of the eight standing committees of the consortium is the Distance Education committee. While not every institution employs a full-time distance education librarian, most institutions have a librarian who works with distance learners and is available to address their needs. The Distance Education committee actively strives to meet the needs of Utah's distance learners by maintaining a Web page (http://medlib.med. utah.edu/ualcdl/) with links to the distance librarians at each institution and current resources available to students and faculty. In addition to surveying libraries on services they provide to distance learners, the committee has made an annual trip to distance learning sites since the mid 1990s for the purpose of becoming better acquainted with the site, its faculty and students. These trips afford the committee an opportunity to better understand the needs of the students and develop programs and services to meet those needs. These visits are valuable for establishing personal contact with staff in community education centers hosting distance-delivered classes. Librarians learn how the centers operate, how courses are delivered, and the characteristics of the student population.

WHY FOCUS GROUPS

Focus groups were viewed as a means to enrich these visits as they are a means of gathering much more in-depth data, with the potential to provide information about user needs, habits, research (Shoaf, 2003). The advantage to focus groups is that unlike an impersonal survey, librarians can interact with participants and obtain much more detailed information and insights. It was obvious that discussion would be preferred, and indeed richer (Schafer, 1998) than any survey and bring out beliefs, ideas, and emotions that are difficult, if not impossible to determine from a questionnaire (Cavill, 2002). Moreover, using a focus group would be a more effective vehicle to investigate complex behaviors and to determine why people do or do not use a service (Verny & Van Fleet, 2001).

The primary objective of these focus groups was to learn more about the information-seeking behavior of Utah distance learners and through this, gain insights into how they utilize library services. Answers to the following questions about distance learners were sought:

- What do they know about information resources available in the library, on the Web, etc.?
- How do they find information that they need for school research/assignments?
- What qualities in information sources and services do they value?
- What do they find useful and why?
- When and how do they seek help?
- What barriers do students face?

THE FIRST FOCUS GROUPS

In late April of 2002, nine librarians from the Distance Education committee visited the College of Eastern Utah/Utah State University education center in Moab for the purpose of conducting focus groups. At that time, USU operated joint education centers with the College of Eastern Utah at sites in southeastern Utah in Price, Moab, Monticello, and Blanding. In Moab, the total student enrollments numbered around 300 with only 9 FTE USU students; this translates to a headcount of about 25 students.

The committee held two focus groups at the Moab Education Center to gather input that would form a foundation to strengthen statewide library services for all Utah higher education distance learners and to also lay the groundwork for future surveys and focus groups. This site was selected because it is located in a rural area with a public library but no on-site academic librarian. There were three main objectives of these focus groups: to gain a more thorough understanding of the information-seeking behaviors of distance learning students in a center that does not have an on-site academic librarian; to gauge their awareness and level of their library use; to determine their needs for information resources and library use instruction.

Methodology

The participants in the focus groups comprised one student attending classes from College of Eastern Utah and Utah State University in Moab and two of the staff at this education center. The format consisted of a one-hour focus group in which the committee first asked predetermined questions. This was followed by open-ended questions to clarify or obtain more detailed information. At the conclusion the committee visited informally with the participants to answer their questions. More students were not available due to illness and the timing of the sessions being held the last week of classes in the semester.

As none of the committee members had formal training in conducting focus groups, one member identified several articles on conducting effective focus groups and these were distributed to the committee for review. The following process was established for operating the focus groups:

a. Focus groups consisted of a primary interviewer, a note taker, a secondary interviewer (process observer), and participants.
b. A list of predetermined questions was given to each participant and the ground rules were explained. Each participant was asked to respond to each question with any follow-up queries.
c. Students introduced themselves by providing their name, school, degree sought and status (full or part-time).
d. Focus groups would be held in the evening.

e. Each group was recorded. A written report was created from both transcripts and notes.
f. The committee furnished refreshments, tape recorders, notepads, and name tags for participants.

The following questions were used for the focus groups:

1. Do you have: home computer and Internet access?
2. Do you use a computer other than at home to do research?
3. When do you usually conduct research outside of class?
4. How often do you use your local public library?
5. Are you aware of library services available to you as an academic student?
6. What sources do you use for research–rank in order of usefulness: Internet (Web sites); Textbook/syllabus; Public library; Academic library (online); Other?

Summary of Responses

The student did not have a home computer and Internet access at home and used computers at the center to complete assignments. She also used computers at the public library to conduct research and usually conducts research late at night, after class when she had time and everything else is done, typically around 1:00 a.m. and sometimes has stayed at the Center until it closes at 11:00 p.m. Occasionally, if a professor indicated that the students had until 11:59 p.m. to turn in the assignments, the Center staff would let students stay later. This student had used the public library about four times per year for print materials.

She was somewhat aware of the services available to her as a student because a professor "walked them through some searches." She had used reference services via e-mail and knew that she could borrow books through Interlibrary Loan, but did not know how to initiate a request. Her professors usually made course readings available on their course Web site, so she was unaware of electronic reserves. The student was also unaware that USU would deliver needed documents to her. One business professor provided the class some instruction, i.e., showing them how to search a database using Boolean operators. She knew about the USU library Web site, because the computers were programmed so that it popped up on the screen when the computer started, but if the computer was already logged on, it required some searching to find it.

When asked about sources used for research ranked in order of usefulness, she mentioned the Internet as being critical especially since distance students access everything via USU. She identified her class text as the next important source, followed by the public library. She used the public library when the center was closed and accessed videos, print reference materials, books, and magazines.

A follow-up question that provided valuable information was: do you have assignments in your courses that require research? She answered yes, that all had some degree of research. One class required students to compile a portfolio of articles, another to write a research paper; and a third to read a book and write a report on it. She also mentioned difficulties in logging into the USU proxy server and did not pursue help when it did not work. This student also volunteered several suggestions on how libraries could help students:

- Librarians should come to class on the first day and explain the services and how they are accessed.
- Create a Web site that tells how to do things or a brochure that explains how to access services.
- Not knowing who to ask for help is a big challenge for distance students.
- Place large posters in the center detailing what services students can get and how to do it.
- Initiate a chat reference service–her son connected her to a commercial service and she liked the fact that someone was right online even late at night.

The second focus group was composed of the Head Teaching Assistant and the CEU-USU Advisor. The same questions were asked, but focused on their perception of student behavior. Most students had full-time jobs and used the center in the evening, often staying until it closed between 10:30-11:00 in the evening. Their perception was that 90% of the students have computers at home and they surmised that students were doing some research at home. The staff indicated that the public library does not often have the materials students need and are not able to obtain them through Interlibrary Loan in a timely manner, so they mainly use the USU library online or perhaps travel to Price to use the CEU library or to Blanding to use the CEU branch library there.

The staff seemed to be aware of some of the library services available for the students, but indicated that things kept changing so often that it was hard to keep up with it. They were aware of electronic reserves and databases and indicated that about once a year they received training over the satellite system from a USU librarian. They also mentioned training sessions delivered over the satellite system and handbooks and other information on where to access library resources, but not specifically instruction aimed at students.

When asked about sources students used for research, the staff members listed the Internet, specifically the dot gov and dot edu sites, the toll-free number for the USU library, Interlibrary Loan of books, article databases available via USU, and local bookstores and government agencies. Word-of-mouth was also mentioned as a research source. Research assignments seemed to be limited to a few research papers in the Family Sciences, English, and History majors and job exploration papers.

Analysis of Responses

Obstacles to Library Service. Several impediments to using library services were identified. (1) Students do not know where to start finding information: they need orientation to being a distance learner and how to use various support services. Center staff cannot effectively assist students without receiving similar instruction. (2) On-site resources are insufficient: public libraries and education centers are not equipped to provide materials immediately. (3) Work and family are distractions. (4) Hours students are likely to conduct research may not match hours libraries offer reference services. (5) Web sites can be complicated and may not provide information very easily. Education center staff struggle to keep up with constant changes in technology and Web sites. (6) Students do not know how to begin information searching and do not differentiate between Web sites and online library databases. (7) Students give up quickly if materials are not readily available or login procedures are complicated.

Awareness of Library Services. Students were not aware of CEU library services and USU publicity was inadequate. Many instructors are not requiring research assignments that need library resources. Point-of-service contact is essential. Students seek help when they need it and when research is required for classes.

Communication and Publicity. These are vital services and apply to students and to faculty. Library services must be advertised in-class and prominently publicized at the centers. Students do not always know where to go for help when they are enrolled in a distance course. The USU student became aware of library services after an instructor incorporated databases and search strategies into the class. Small posters at the center advertising library services competed with many larger ones and were not visible.

Staff employed at this center had also taken courses, and were keenly aware of the challenges faced by distance learners. They make copies of course syllabi and follow along with the students in the course to help them keep on track and complete assignments on time. Staff are often able to direct students to resources that they may not be aware of. They seemed eager to help students and often do some searching of their own to help students find materials. They corroborated the late evening research patterns of students and their general lack of awareness of library resources and services available to them. Public library use was mentioned and research assignments seemed to be minimal in most courses.

The committee is cognizant of the fact that the information gained from this particular student and her information-seeking behavior may not necessarily apply to other learners in Utah. Separate conversations with the public library director and the high school librarian, however, revealed similar information-seeking behaviors among their respective groups. The committee felt that the information garnered from this focus groups trip will provide useful ways to improve library marketing and instruction. Several ideas were generated by these sessions:

- Create one Web page on how to get started on library research that would be prominently displayed on library and university Web sites.
- In-class presentation by librarian on the first day of class.
- Establish toll-free numbers to facilitate library contact.
- Place larger, highly visible posters and stickers on lab computers to alert students to library services and detailed brochures.
- Create an online tutorial for center staff and students addressing how to use library services at a distance.

Summary of the Experience

The experience was extremely productive and the small number of participants worked out very well as a first test group. The center staff work more closely with the students than any academic librarians and they were able to provide additional insights into student behavior. The solitary student fit the profile of a typical distance learner in Moab: a single adult (female) working full-time with a family.

The committee gained insights into how some students actually use library services and also learned how to conduct more effective focus groups in the future. New committee members had a valuable, first-hand look at a distance learning center. The committee felt this was a good start but realized additional focus groups would be necessary before making generalizations on student information-seeking behavior in Utah. The Moab sessions provided baseline data and experience for future endeavors. Improvements for future focus groups include: work with larger groups in quiet, enclosed rooms; employ a transcription machine; conduct usability studies on the committee's Web site.

THE SECOND FOCUS GROUPS

In March of 2003, four academic librarians from the Distance Education Committee held focus groups at Utah State University's Uintah Basin Branch Campus (UBBC) consisting of two separate campuses in Roosevelt and Vernal, Utah. The campus is located in eastern Utah, approximately 200 miles from the main campus in Logan and 100 miles from Salt Lake City. The UBBC enrolls close to 2,000 students and has 20 on-site faculty. Classes are delivered face-to-face and originate from this campus in addition to receiving classes from the main campus. The campuses are 30 miles apart and classes often alternate every week since many students travel from western Colorado and other parts of Utah.

This campus was selected for the focus groups, in part due to the presence of a small academic library. This facility was established in the early 1990s in Roosevelt and in 2001 moved into a state-of-the-art building. For a time, a room was utilized in the Vernal campus to house materials but was never developed into a full-scale, staffed library. A librarian for the UBBC is based in Roosevelt and serves on the Distance Education Committee and participated in the focus groups. The main campus provides document delivery and access to electronic databases and journals and both towns have public libraries. This mix of libraries and services plus the presence of an on-site librarian was felt to be conducive to recruiting participants.

Methodology

Since focus groups constitute using human test subjects, permission was needed from the subjects and from the university. USU librarians had already received permission to conduct on-campus focus groups and usability studies from the USU Institutional Review Board as part of a needs assessment for an online tutorial project. Permission was extended to include the committee's focus groups at this branch campus, greatly facilitating the process.

The on-site librarian helped publicize the focus groups and recruited participants. Advertisements used to promote the on-campus focus groups were adapted and posted at the Roosevelt campus. Several sessions were scheduled at each campus in the day and evening to accommodate students' schedules and to attract traditional and non-traditional students. The Vernal campus did not receive the ads but faculty helped recruit students. Despite the publicity and advance preparation, some participants had to be "rounded up" at both sites. Rooms were reserved at both campuses to facilitate the sessions and to ensure privacy.

Participants signed an "informed consent" form and were paid $10 for their time. The sessions were recorded and transferred to written transcripts. A note taker wrote down major points of interest during the sessions. Each focus group consisted of four students; one person left early in each. One student was under the age of eighteen and parental consent is required for their participation; since this was not initially sought, all data provided by this individual was scrubbed. Librarians served as facilitators and note takers since skill or training does not appear to be a qualification, only an interest or desire to work with users (Cavill, 2002).

There were three questions that framed the inquiry into information-seeking behavior, using the critical incident technique: (1) students were asked to briefly describe a research assignment, (2) discuss when they usually conduct research outside of class, and (3) detail specific library services that are the most helpful. The librarian-facilitators asked follow-up questions to probe for more details. As a reminder and prompt for the librarian-facilitators, a checklist of follow-up questions was provided. The librarian-facilitators asked follow-up questions to probe for more details (see Appendix A). The questions were much more detailed and were revised after the experience with the first focus groups. Debriefing sessions were then held at the conclusion of each session to answer student's questions in-depth and to engage in an informal discussion.

Results from Preliminary Survey

Participants completed a survey prior to the focus group to: obtain demographic information; determine how far they live from campus and an academic/public library; rank the usefulness of specific resources; list services used from an academic library at a distance; and identify the method they feel most comfortable to contact a librarian (see Appendix B). The results were then compared to data gleaned from the focus groups.

Demographics Summary

Age	Participants ranged from early 20s to the 30s.
Gender	Females: three Males: four
Majors	Humanities, Special Education, Business, and Nursing
Distance from campus	Roosevelt: 1 to 25 miles Vernal: 1 to 15 miles
Distance from academic library	Roosevelt: 1 to 25 miles Vernal: 3 to 25 miles

Survey Questions

Usefulness of Resources for Library Research. Participants ranked 10 different categories of sources, using 1 to designate most useful and 10 as the least useful. Data combining both focus groups resulted in Web sites ranked as most useful, and library catalogs as the least useful. The Roosevelt focus group ranked Web sites as the most useful and Course Notes/Syllabus as the least useful. The Vernal focus group ranked Course Notes/Syllabus as the most useful and as the least useful three sources were tied: Articles, Lectures, and Library catalogs. The overall ranking of Web sites as most useful was not surprising as this was a common resource identified in the focus groups. What is surprising is that the Vernal students, most of whom were in a nursing program and realized the limitations of the Web for information, did not rank articles higher. Many responses were tied, indicated by the letter "T."

Source	Roosevelt Ranking	Vernal Ranking	Overall Rank
Web sites	1	4	1
Newspapers	3T	2T	2
Books	4T	2T	3
Textbooks	4T	3	4
Other Students	5T	2T	5
Articles	2	5T	6
Lectures	3T	5T	7 T
Course Notes/Syllabus	6	1	7 T
Library Catalogs	5T	5T	8

Services Used from an Academic Library. Participants identified specific library services they had used as a distance learner. A majority had used research assistance from a librarian and none used the Live Chat software that UALC had introduced the prior fall.

Library Service	Roosevelt	Vernal	Total # students who used
Document Delivery	0	1	1
Research Assistance (from a librarian)	4	2	6
Electronic Course Reserves	1	2	3
Live Chat	0	0	0

Most Comfortable Method for Contacting a Librarian. Participants identified the method they felt most comfortable with for contacting a librarian. All but one felt most comfortable with face-to-face contact, and that preference was strongly echoed in the focus groups.

Method	Roosevelt	Vernal	Total
Face-to-Face	4	3	7
Phone	0	1	1
E-mail	0	1	1
Computer: Chat or Conferencing	0	0	0

FOCUS GROUP SUMMARY

Insights into distance learners information-seeking behavior:

- Use sources and people familiar to them and utilize the most convenient and quickest routes to obtain information and materials (Internet, fellow students, friends, and family).
- Prefer face-to-face contact with a librarian. Working with a live person was ranked as the most comfortable method on the pre focus group survey. Live chat/phone were ranked next, depending on the immediacy of a response.
- Acknowledge they do not know enough about the research process and using library databases; recognize that they are "learning how to learn." One student remarked, "Cause sometimes we just have to rely on each other and sometimes that don't work. Sometimes it falls through and so . . . "
- Find library Web pages confusing (design, library terminology).

What do distance learners know about information resources available in libraries:

- Learn about journals as valid sources in class.
- Several participants had used academic libraries in Salt Lake.
- Realize they will require greater access to library materials and resources as they progress in their studies.
- Most were unaware library resources and databases available–interested in learning more about using library resources.

What qualities in information sources and services do they find useful and value:

- Personal assistance from a librarian or an instructor and timely access to materials: Students do use public libraries but recognize the limitations of their collections.

- Consider librarians to be very helpful; students recognize they are "learning how to learn."
- Many expressed a dislike for distance learning technologies–prefer live instruction.
- Want and appreciate on-site collections.

When and how do they seek help:

- Prefer face-to-face communication with a librarian.
- Conduct research whenever there is time after class, work, or on weekends.
- Contact depends on information need and urgency: in-person and live chat for immediate response; e-mail if it can wait.

What barriers do students face:

- Lack of an on-site academic library collection and librarian; local public libraries collections are inadequate to meet their needs.
- Materials that are not available through a local library or are not available in a timely manner through document delivery.
- Home Internet access not great–faster network at the campus.
- Confusing library Web pages–need first-time user instructions.
- Local public libraries do not have adequate materials (especially journals) to support their curriculum.

DEBRIEFING SESSIONS

These sessions were also very productive. Students reiterated that they wanted and needed an on-site library and preferred receiving research help from a live librarian. In the words of one student, "I'm just more of a hands-on learner so I need to . . . have a contact person there." Questions concerning specific library services were answered and librarians engaged in a positive dialogue with participants. The Roosevelt students have a library, librarian, and staff available and appreciated their service; they also referred to library staff as "librarians." The Vernal students expressed a strong desire to have their own academic library and librarian and even asked for advice on how to ensure one is included in plans for a new campus. These students were the most homogenous group and also expressed a strong preference for live classes and listed many problems with distance learning classes. Both groups emphasized the need for training in using libraries and a desire to work directly with a live librarian for when they want immediate help.

FUTURE FOCUS GROUPS

The committee decided that the data and experience gained from these sessions was valuable and that additional focus groups in urban areas are necessary. Future focus groups are planned for the Salt Lake area in 2004 to broaden the data pool and to provide a comparison with the rural students. Participants from other Utah schools will also be included in these sessions. Participants were primarily older students and Utah has a large number of high school students taking university courses in concurrent enrollment programs to shorten their time in the higher education system. Parental permission is required for tests involving students under the age of eighteen and the committee has not decided how to address this population. Approval for testing human subjects will be sought under a multi-site research project. This will be accomplished through Utah State University's Institutional Review Board and all librarians participating in future focus groups will undergo formal training.

CONCLUSION

The focus groups were extremely productive and informative. The significant insights from these focus groups are that students tend to rely on the Web for information and will use alternative sources if services are not timely. The second group revealed a strong preference for an on-site academic library and librarian. In Moab, the need for a more visible academic library presence was also identified. Utah academic libraries opened a 24/7 Live Chat Reference service in the fall of 2003, in part to extend services to distance learners, and it will be interesting to see how other students feel about on-site versus technology-based library services.

Focus groups can turn into conversations between librarians and participants unless the facilitator can control the session. The advantage to an outside facilitator is that they are unbiased and generally unknown to the participants. These participants spoke their minds regardless of who was in the room but the sessions did include two USU librarians who were asked questions regarding specific services and problems that sidetracked the session. In the second focus group conducted in Vernal, the USU librarians only participated in the debriefing session in order to avoid this problem. The debriefing sessions were designed to accommodate and encourage conversation and in this, were successful.

Taking focus groups on the road is personally satisfying and professionally effective. Most Utah academic librarians are campus-based and many rural areas only see a public librarian or bookmobile. Academic librarians are hampered by severely reduced travel budgets and this currently limits the number of librarians who can participate in these trips. The Utah Education Network's EDNET system may provide a means to reach multiple sites but the face-to-face interaction and getting out to meet distance learners has made the investment of time and resources worth it.

REFERENCES

Cavill, Patricia M. (2002). The power of focus groups. *PNLA Quarterly, 66*(2), 4-6.

Schafer, Steven A. (1998). Student satisfaction with library services: Results of evaluation using focus groups at Athabasca University. In P. S. Thomas & M. Jones (Comps.) *The Eighth Off-Campus Library Services Conference Proceedings: Providence, RI, April 26-28, 1998* (pp. 245-250). Mount Pleasant MI: Central Michigan University Press.

Shoaf, Eric C. (2003). Using a professional moderator in library focus group research. *College & Research Libraries, 64*(2), 124-133.

State of Utah, Governor's Office of Planning and Budget, Demographic and Economic Analysis. (n.d.). *State and county estimates.* Retrieved November 15, 2003 from http://governor.utah.gov/dea/UPEC/stateandcountypopulationestimates.pdf.

Verny, Roger & Van Fleet, Connie Jean. (2001). Case study 2.2: Conducting focus groups. In Danny P. Wallace, & Connie van Fleet (Eds.), *Library evaluation: A casebook and can-do guide* (pp. 41-51). Englewood, CO: Libraries Unlimited.

APPENDIX A. Focus Group Questions: Distance Education Students

Research Questions:
a. What do distance learners know about information resources available in the library, on the Web, etc.?
b. How do they find information that they need for school research/assignments?
c. What qualities in information sources and services do they value? What do they find useful and why?
d. When and how do they seek help?
e. What barriers do students face?

1. Briefly describe a recent research assignment. How did you begin?
   Prompts/follow-up:
      –How did you hope that this might help?
      –What did you do next?
      –Can you give me an example?
      –What was most useful during the process?

2. Were there times during the research process when you got stuck or did not know what to do next? What did you do?
   Prompts/follow-up:
      –What questions/confusions did you have?
      –How did you get going again?
      –Did you talk to anyone?
      –How did you hope this might help?
      –Can you give me an example?
      –Did you consider using Live Chat or contacting a Librarian?

3. When do you usually conduct research outside of class?
   Prompts/follow-up:
      –What are the most convenient times?
      –Do you work?
      –How many classes are you taking?
      –Where do you have computer access (home, library, ed center)?
      –What problems do you face?
      –Who is your ISP?
      –How far away do you live from class site?

4. How often do you use your local public library?
   Prompts/follow-up:
      –How far away do you live from a public library?
      –How convenient is it to use?
      –What collections do they have (or not) for your classes?
      –Do you have borrowing privileges?

5. Are you aware of library services available to you as an academic student?
   Prompts/follow-up:
      –Has your instructor ever mentioned library services in-class?
      –Have you seen library services advertised in your class syllabus (print/online)?
      –Does your center advertise library services (how)?
      –Have other students told you about library services?

6. What is your preferred method of contacting a librarian?
   Prompts/follow-up:
      –Do you use e-mail?
      –Do you use the phone?
      –Do you have online courses?
      –Have you ever worked face-to-face with a librarian?
      –Have you used the "Live Chat" service?

7. Once you completed your research, what kinds of information sources did you use for your assignment?
   Prompts/follow-up:
   –Why did you choose these sources?
   –Which resources gave you the most useful information? Why?
   –Did you use the library Web page? Did you find it useful? Why or why not?
   –Did you use books?
   –Did you use the Internet or World Wide Web sites?
   –Did you use newspapers or magazines?
   –Did you use people as information sources?
   –Did you use textbooks, e-reserves, syllabi as information sources?

8. What library services would be most helpful to you?
   Prompts/follow-up:
   –Can you explain why?
   –How would you use it?

APPENDIX B. Student Focus Group: Preliminary Survey

Thank you for participating in this focus group. This form asks for some personal and preliminary data that will be expanded on in the focus group where we will ask questions on how you find information and use libraries for class assignments.

Your identity will remain confidential and if you feel uncomfortable answering a question, please leave it blank.

Age:
Status: undergraduate   graduate   concurrent enrollment
Major:
Years completed at USU:

_____

1. How far do you live (in miles) from:

   Campus___   Academic Library___   Local Public Library___

2. Rank the usefulness (1-10) of the following resources for library research by putting 1 as the most useful and 10 being the least useful

Books___	Articles___	Newspapers___	Web Sites___
Textbooks___	Course Notes/Syllabus___	Lectures___	Other Students___
Library Catalogs_____	Other:		

APPENDIX B (continued)

3. What services have you used from an academic library from a distance? Please circle all that apply.

Document Delivery   Research Assistance   Electronic Course   Live Chat
                     (from a librarian)   Reserves

4. What method do you feel <u>most comfortable</u> using to contact a librarian for research assistance? Please circle.

Face-to-Face   Phone   E-mail   Computer:
                                   Chat or Conferencing

Tri-Institutional Library Support:
A Lesson in Forced Collaboration

Paul R. Pival

University of Calgary

Kay Johnson

Athabasca University

SUMMARY. This paper will discuss the trials and tribulations of three separate institutional libraries supporting one new graduate-level academic program. In January 2002, a new distance graduate program in Applied Psychology began with technical, administrative, and academic support provided by three separate institutions. While one institution was initially charged with providing the bulk of library services, in reality, libraries at all three have contributed one service or another. The lead library provides remote database access and document delivery, and initially provided electronic reserves. After the first semester and several glitches, electronic reserves were moved to institutional library #2, which was also hosting the course management system. In the fall of 2002, institutional library #3 began to contribute with an information literacy module that has been incorporated into the orientation for all new students.

KEYWORDS. Collaboration, distance education, library services, technology

[Haworth co-indexing entry note]: "Tri-Institutional Library Support: A Lesson in Forced Collaboration." Pival, Paul R., and Kay Johnson. Co-published simultaneously in *Journal of Library Administration* (The Haworth Information Press, an imprint of The Haworth Press, Inc.) Vol. 41, No. 3/4, 2004, pp. 345-354; and: *The Eleventh Off-Campus Library Services Conference Proceedings* (ed: Patrick B. Mahoney) The Haworth Information Press, an imprint of The Haworth Press, Inc., 2004, pp. 345-354.

http://www.haworthpress.com/web/JLA
Digital Object Identifier: 10.1300/J111v41n03_01

BACKGROUND

The *Campus Alberta Graduate Program in Counselling* was developed by a consortium of three Alberta universities, in partnership with key stakeholder groups in the professional community. The program is jointly sponsored by:

- the Centre for Graduate Education in Applied Psychology at Athabasca University;
- the Division of Applied Psychology at the University of Calgary; and
- the Faculty of Education at the University of Lethbridge.

The *Campus Alberta Graduate Program in Counselling* is a Canadian, collaborative, inter-university, distance education alternative for individuals wishing to prepare for roles as either professional counsellors or counselling psychologists.

The various components of the program are offered through both on-site and distance modes of delivery, drawing on the combined resources and strengths of the participant universities. Students are able to mix and match courses from any of the participant universities.

The program is designed to complement rather than compete with the current on-campus programs in Alberta. The goal is to provide students who face various barriers to completing degrees through traditional programs with the opportunity to further their education. The program will enhance the on-campus programs at the University of Calgary and the University of Lethbridge by providing a high-quality alternative for students in the on-campus programs who face scheduling difficulties.

Finally, the program is designed to foster the continuing professional learning of counsellors and psychologists through access to individual graduate courses. An open registration policy will encourage professionals to continually upgrade their knowledge and skills. Professionals may take additional courses as non-program students or complete a Post-Master's Certificate in one of the areas of specialization.

THE SUPPORTING CAST OF LIBRARIES

The University of Calgary supports approximately 25,000 students, about 1,500 of whom are enrolled in distance programs. The University of Calgary Library has taken a leading role in recognizing that information resources are critical to the success of a student's educational experience. The Library's mandate states that all students, regardless of location, will receive the same resources and services and it strongly advocates equal access to information for all distance learners. The Library has provided both financial and professional support, to develop and deliver services for users outside the physical library, across Canada and outside its borders. The U of C offers full library support to distance students through a service known as Library Connection. Library Connection strives to offer all the services of a University Library to students who are at a distance, including instruction and tutorials, research assistance, and document delivery.

Athabasca University, Canada's Open University, supports over 26,000 students, all of whom are engaged in distance or online learning, and offers approximately 60 programs at master's, bachelor's, diploma and certificate levels. AU is dedicated to removing barriers to university-level studies and to providing quality education across Canada and internationally. The Library supports distance learners through a Web site, e-mail service, a toll free telephone number and delivery of materials through the postal system at the Library's expense. The AU Library Information Gateway provides access to quality information resources including library catalogues, journal databases, online tutorials, selected Internet resources, a digital reference collection (Digital Reference Centre) and an electronic reserves system (Digital Reading Room).

The University of Lethbridge supports approximately 7,200 students, 1,200 of whom are enrolled in distance programs or are taking courses at remote campuses in Calgary and Edmonton. The University of Lethbridge participates with the universities and other post-secondary institutions of Alberta in a variety of co-operative programs and activities. The University Library strives to provide seamless and equitable access to its collections and information literacy programs to all students regardless of their location. Library or research related questions are answered through the Uask@ULeth service available from the Library's home page. The service provides an online form for students to query a librarian as well as a toll free number for personal consultation. Access to the U of L suite of print and online resources, including the full text journal collections is also available to all U of L students.

STATISTICS

The Campus Alberta Applied Psychology program launched in January 2002 with just over 60 students, but quickly settled on 48 as several dropped out. In January 2003, an additional 86 students entered the program, bringing the total number of students served by the three libraries to 134. Approximately 115 students are expected to enroll as the next cohort in January 2004.

Through the Fall 2002 semester, the 48 students enrolled in this program accounted for 1,830 reference and document delivery requests, all to the U of C
Library. To the end of August 2003, there have been 3,782 document delivery
requests sent to the U of C. This seems to put the program on target for an average of 2,000 requests per calendar year, but it would also seem likely this number would rise as more students enter the program. At Athabasca University
from April 2002 to March 2003 approximately 90 requests from CAAP students were received at the Library Information Desk, just over half of which
involved document delivery. The remainder represents requests for assistance
with accessing and/or searching online resources. AU circulation statistics
show 124 items checked out to CAAP students during this period.

Program-specific circulation and database access statistics are not available
from the primary institution, but because student IDs were entered manually
into the patron database at Athabasca, AU is able to determine from the III
Web Access Management System that Campus Alberta Applied Psychology
students initiated 26,359 connects to the AU databases from January 2002 to
August 2003. Independent searching generates some of this database activity,
but it can be assumed that a substantial portion of the total connects were to
persistent links embedded in electronic course reserves. Most interaction between CAAP students and the AU Library occurs through connects to the online databases.

INSTRUCTION

There have been two face-to-face instructional sessions given by the lead library, one during each of the two summer institutes that the program has held.
While the students all receive an online orientation that includes an introduction to library resources and information literacy, the summer institute is the
only time they get to have hands-on instruction with a librarian in the room. In
2002, the Distance Education librarian and psychology Liaison Librarian from
the University of Calgary met with the 48 students for 3 hours, walking them
through the basics of information literacy and database searching. In 2003, the
same librarians met the larger group of new students in two sessions, again
three hours per meeting. Students each had their own PCs for hands-on practice during these sessions.

There was no library session scheduled for the students returning for their
second year, but these students took it upon themselves to request a refresher
meeting for library research outside the normal second year institute hours,
and the psychology Liaison Librarian was able to meet with these students.
General feedback from the summer institutes has been positive.

In the fall of 2002, the Education Librarian at the University of Lethbridge was approached by one of the CAAP faculty members to produce an online guide to Information Literacy that would be included in the orientation session for new CAAP students. This librarian was able to modify a guide to create a comprehensive Web site with program-specific information. This guide was used for the first time in late fall of 2003, when the 2004 students undertook their program orientation.

INITIAL GROWING PAINS AND LEARNING CURVES

This was the first multi-institutional (multi-library) initiative for all three of the libraries, and as expected, there were (and continue to be) bumps along the road. When originally conceived in 1998/1999, each of the three institutions would play a major but separate role in the administration of the CAAP program. Athabasca University would be responsible for development of the learning technologies employed within the program and provision of technological support to students, the U of Calgary would be responsible for registration and library support, and U of Lethbridge would be responsible for central administration of the program (Collins, Hiebert, Magnusson, and Bernes, 2000). This paper, of course, deals with the area of library support.

As the first semester approached, the program made it clear it wanted to offer as much reading material as possible in an online environment. The U of C Library's Copyright Officer has found that it usually requires several months to obtain copyright permission to digitize and post articles and chapters in the electronic reserves module. The program finally presented the Library with a list of 59 readings six weeks before classes were to start. In this short timeframe, copyright holders needed to be found for all 59 readings, permission obtained to digitize, and the Library needed to obtain and scan the articles as well. As the weeks passed and it became apparent that permission would not be forthcoming to post all the articles in time for the first courses to begin, the Library suggested the program consider distributing traditional paper course packs containing those readings that could not be digitized. The campus has a standard license to reproduce readings for course packs at a cost of $.05 per page, so the only issue was who would pay for the packs. The Library suggested that since it was originally going to be covering the copyright costs for the digital copies, it would cover the cost of the course packs for this one semester, since it had been unable to secure permission to digitize in time for the beginning of the course. The program was amenable to this, and the DE Librarian received a crash course in course pack production. Course packs were produced for all 48 students and mailed via priority post at the end of December to ensure students had the readings in time for the beginning of the semester.

RESERVE READINGS

Because this program is delivered entirely online, the administrators wanted to make readings available in this format as well. Canadian copyright law has a "fair dealing" provision that is considerably more restrictive than the "fair use" provision in U.S. copyright law. Fair dealing seems to be lagging in the area of digitization, as the following faculty guidelines from York University (2003) show:

> Generally, according to the Access Copyright license, you *cannot* input copyrighted materials into electronic format except for the sole purpose of producing paper copies. Even then, the electronic copies must be destroyed promptly after the paper copies have been made. The dissemination or distribution of any electronic file in any electronic form in any way is not authorized by the Access Copyright license. Therefore, works which are protected by copyright cannot generally be transformed into a digital or electronic format for electronic distribution. Digital reproduction is not considered to be an acceptable form of reprographic reproduction and thus can easily lead to copyright infringement. (E section, para. 2)

As such, permission to scan articles for posting online, even in a secure environment, must be secured from each copyright holder.

Online readings for the first semester were run through the U of C's homegrown electronic reserves module, Allectra. The campus Copyright Officer obtained permission for all articles posted online. Allectra represents a very secure environment that requires students to be authenticated twice–once to verify campus enrollment, and again to verify enrollment in a specific section of a specific course. This level of security was deemed necessary by the builders of the software to allay the fears of copyright holders that scanned material would be used by students other than those in the course for which permission was granted.

As the CAAP program began, it quickly became apparent that many of the students had not completed the necessary registration paperwork and thus were not listed in the Registrar's database at the U of C. As a result, about one quarter of the students did not have access to their online readings at the start of the course. A generic login and password were distributed to these students, which of course defeated the security of the system. After approximately two weeks, all students had completed their paperwork and all had access to the readings, but by that time Allectra had received a great deal of bad publicity among the students and the program administrators. This would prove to be a fatal blow for Allectra and in subsequent semesters all reserve readings were hosted in the Digital Reading Room developed by Athabasca University.

Athabasca University Library's Digital Reading Room was developed in-house to provide online access to required course readings and supplementary materials. In addition to functioning as an electronic reserves system, the Digital Reading Room (DRR) is also a searchable, multidisciplinary database of learning resources. As of October 2003, there were twenty-one digital reading files for the CAAP program.

The DRR operates on the principle of open access, permitting anyone to view the "digital reading files" for each course, and requiring patron verification only when access to licensed or protected resources is involved. Database articles are linked to by means of persistent URLs and access requires authentication through the Library's proxy server. There are a few resources that require a username and password that are available only to students registered in a course (for example, to control access to a professor's unpublished manuscript or to instructor commentaries). Some of the resources in the DRR are publicly accessible Web sites.

Course developers are able to enhance their digital reading files by including a variety of formats that support a range of learning styles. One instructor, for example, uses audio clips to welcome students to the course. Obtaining copyright permissions for digitization of materials is not the preferred method for adding content to the DRR, although AU Library can accommodate this. In cases where CAAP students have received required course readings or course texts by mail, this is indicated in the digital reading file. Web forms are provided for students to request supplementary materials that are print-based, such as books and photocopied journal articles. When students submit these forms, staff at the AU Library Information Desk receive an e-mail request for the item, process the request and send materials through the postal system.

Generally this system appears to be working well, apart from the need for library staff to occasionally troubleshoot browser configuration or other access problems. Because students are accessing electronic reserves through AU, it was determined that AU Library should perform this function and information to this effect was added to the CAAP Library Web pages. Close coordination between the Library and course developers and instructors is essential to ensure that print-based resources are available from the Library and that relevant Library information is conveyed to students in their courseware.

ID CARDS

Student identification cards are issued by the University of Calgary and bear the logos of all three institutions. The numbers on the cards are used to provide remote access to databases at the U of C. The libraries at Athabasca and Lethbridge manually enter these numbers into their patron databases to allow CAAP students to have remote access to their systems as well. In addition to receiving remote access at all three institutions, CAAP students are also able to check out books at all three institutions, though in reality no students visit more than one library in person; books housed at other libraries (CAAP or other) are obtained through document delivery services by the University of Calgary.

The issue of database access forced an interesting discussion. Database licenses stipulate that databases are only to be made available (especially remotely) to the faculty, staff and students of the purchasing institution. The students enrolled in the CAAP program were certainly U of C students, but they were also considered students of Athabasca University and the University of Lethbridge. After much discussion and counsel, the licenses were interpreted in such a way that they could legally allow access by students in the CAAP program.

In the spring of 2003, the U of C acquired the EBSCO Psychology and Behavioral Sciences collection full text database, which brought the issue of database access for course developers to a head, as the people at Athabasca responsible for working on the Digital Reading Room wanted to have access to this database even though they weren't officially affiliated with the CAAP program. The U of C librarian responsible for database licensing interpreted their license to allow only students and instructors directly involved in the program to have access to U of C databases. This means that if a CAAP faculty member wants to include an online reading that is only available through the EBSCO database, the Electronic Resources Librarian at Athabasca must request the permanent links from the DE librarian at the U of C to then insert into the DRR. While a seemingly cumbersome approach, in reality there have been few articles requested by faculty for inclusion in the DRR that are only available from this one uniquely held U of C database.

CURRENTLY

There are currently 123 students enrolled in the program, which consists of two separate intakes (2002, 2003). In January 2004, an additional 115 students were admitted to the program. Overall library support appears to be successful and thus continues with few modifications. Collection development did not occur as systematically as it should have, but after a formula to share funding between the three supporting institutions was agreed upon, this has continued to improve the holdings to support the curriculum.

One challenge for the librarians supporting the program is that the academic administrators for CAAP rotate every two years. This means ongoing education of what we can and cannot do for the program, and also means there can be swings in the amount of support and understanding the libraries receive from the program (though the funding is locked in).

It is our belief that students need to receive some additional information literacy training. They receive an online orientation before they start the program, and hands on training during their summer institute six months in to the program, but librarians are often contacted to answer questions that were answered in one of those training sessions, so it seems clear that some periodic refreshers or point of need instruction could enhance the student's understanding of the research process and library specifics. It can be challenging for students to learn how to interact with more than one library in terms of how to access different systems, resources, and support. At the same time, the librarians supporting the students in this collaborative program have had to learn how to interact with students who may be more familiar with another institution's library.

THE FUTURE

The CAAP program has expanded through a partnership with the Vancouver (BC) Art Therapy Institute to offer a specialization in Art Therapy. Students complete the first half of their program with the core curriculum, and then specialize in the field of Art Therapy. While this should have little or no impact on library services since these students are already in the CAAP program, in reality the lead library likely needs to improve its collection in this area, and until that is accomplished document delivery may feel an extra burden. The Vancouver Art Therapy Institute does not have a library of its own.

Campus Alberta is proposing to expand the Counselling program by duplicating the current Applied Psychology program with a similar program in Inclusive/Special Education (CAISEI). The University of Alberta, hosting the largest research library in the Province, is a partner in this initiative, so that library may be brought on board in some capacity to support the program. It would be interesting if students in the CAISEI program had access to more resources than the students in the original CAAP program.

CONCLUSIONS

It can be done! It is possible to coordinate various library services from three separate libraries to support a single academic program. It is important to maintain clear lines of communication, and to remember that the goal is to serve the students in the program. Libraries considering similar collaborations need to avoid turf wars. We still have one or two issues that do not feel satisfactorily addressed, but will continue to work together to either come to a satisfactory arrangement, or will develop workaround solutions so that service to students is not negatively affected.

REFERENCES

Athabasca University Library (2003). *Digital reading room.* Retrieved November 7, 2003 from http://library.athabasca.ca/drr/.

Campus Alberta Applied Psychology homepage. Retrieved November 18, 2003 from http://www.abcounsellored.net.

Collins, S., Hiebert, B., Magnusson, K., & Bernes, K. (2000). *Campus Alberta: A collaborative, multi-university counsellor training initiative.* Retrieved August 21, 2003 from http://www.contactpoint.ca/natcon-conat/2001/pdf/pdf-01-03.pdf.

CAAP inclusive/special education initiative concept paper (future). Retrieved August 21, 2003 from http://psych.athabascau.ca/html/CAISEI/Concept_Paper.doc.

Master of Counselling: Art therapy specialization. Retrieved October 23, 2003 from http://www.vati.bc.ca/master.htm.

Pearce, L (2001). Lessons learned: The development of electronic reserves at the University of Calgary. *D-Lib Magazine, 7*(11). Retrieved November 18, 2003 from http://www.dlib.org/dlib/november01/pearce/11pearce.html.

York University (2003). *Copyright and you.* Retrieved November 18, 2003 from http://www.yorku.ca/secretariat/documents/copyright/text7.htm.

Starting Small:
Setting Up Off-Campus Library Services
with Limited Resources

Linda A. Reeves

Northwest Vista College

SUMMARY. How do you provide library services to online students if you have a small staff and a limited budget? First, learn as much as possible about your online students and start small. Librarians at Northwest Vista College, a new community college in San Antonio, addressed the challenge by putting as much help as possible on their library Web site, by targeting groups most in need of these services, and by offering virtual reference service by appointment.

KEYWORDS. Library services, distance learners

Everyone is aware that distance education has experienced phenomenal growth. Features about the increasing popularity of distance education appear nearly every week in newspapers, magazines, and scholarly journals. Probably everyone has seen an increase in the numbers of students enrolling in distance education classes at their own institutions. Indeed, statistics confirm this impression. In the 1997-98 academic year, an estimated 1.3 million students were enrolled in for-credit distance education courses. By the 2000-01 academic year, the number had grown to 2.9 million (Kiernan, 2003). Increas-

[Haworth co-indexing entry note]: "Starting Small: Setting Up Off-Campus Library Services with Limited Resources." Reeves, Linda A. Co-published simultaneously in *Journal of Library Administration* (The Haworth Information Press, an imprint of The Haworth Press, Inc.) Vol. 41, No. 3/4, 2004, pp. 355-364; and: *The Eleventh Off-Campus Library Services Conference Proceedings* (ed: Patrick B. Mahoney) The Haworth Information Press, an imprint of The Haworth Press, Inc., 2004, pp. 355-364.

ingly, distance learners have their choice of more courses and programs, as more and more institutions are offering distance education courses. With the emergence of Web-based technologies, the growth of distance education accelerated, as educators realized that education no longer must be bound by time or place (Explosion, 2002). Enrollment in online courses rose by 20 percent in 2003, and it is now estimated that eleven percent of college students will take at least one course online (Boser, 2003).

How is this growth in distance education affecting academic libraries? It is having a big impact, because academic libraries have an obligation to provide services to faculty and students participating in distance education programs. According to the Association of College and Research Libraries (ACRL), in their *Guidelines for Distance Learning Library Services,* institutions that provide online courses must provide library services that are *equivalent to* the library services offered to on-campus students. According to the *Guidelines*:

> Access to adequate library services and resources is essential for the attainment of superior academic skills in post-secondary education, regardless of where students, faculty, and programs are located. Members of the distance learning community are entitled to library services and resources equivalent to those provided for students and faculty in traditional campus settings. (p. 2)

With distance education students making up an increasingly large portion of their patron base, college libraries are looking for ways to provide services to this population. ACRL'S *2000 Academic Library Trends and Statistics* survey, which focused on distance education, revealed that 90.3 percent of libraries at associate of arts institutions provide library services to distance education students, 83.2 percent of doctoral-granting institutions, 76.1 percent of master's institutions, and 50.6 percent of bachelor's institutions (Thompson, 2002). Library services must be provided to the distance learning population, but how extensive do these services need to be?

The type of library support needed depends on the type of library users. Does the institution provide distance education classes to students who are truly a considerable distance away? In other cities? Other states? Other countries? Or are the "distance learners" actually local students who are taking online classes to have greater flexibility in their schedule? Information reported in the *2000 Academic Library Trends and Statistics* survey indicates that the "distance learners" at a great many colleges are indeed students who live close enough to make at least occasional trips to campus to take advantage of services. For example, 40 to 50 percent of all academic libraries report using *on-campus orientation sessions* to introduce distance learners to library services (Thompson, 2002). Similarly, 57 percent of baccalaureate, master's and doctoral-granting institutions, and 71 percent of associate of arts institutions, use *face-to-face contact* to provide reference service to distance learners (Thompson). As Thompson points out, these statistics suggest that the distance learners at most institutions are engaged in *distributed* learning rather than *distance* learning. That is, students may not be in a traditional classroom, but they are not too far away to be able to come to the campus library. As Barron (2002) points out, the restructuring of the academic environment to provide more Web-based applications has helped to blur the line between "distributed learners" and "distant learners." As Barron observes, "A student who is taking a class from a dorm room or an on-campus studio classroom still has a significant advantage over the student who is 70 (or 500) miles away, because he or she can usually walk across campus to the library if necessary. On the other hand, the restrictions on time, etc., that have led a person to choose an online or televised (distributed) course might also limit his or her access to the library every bit as much as physical distance" (2002, p. 26).

In addition, even students enrolled in traditional, face-to-face courses on campus generally prefer using electronic library resources to using paper materials. In light of these trends, many colleges are opting to provide online library resources and services to all students, in realization that the line between distance education students and local students is no longer clear. The danger of not providing online library resources and services, Barron warns, is that students will turn to the Web, both the free Web and the for-profit vendors of information such as XanEdu and Questia (2002). If a majority of students start using these resources instead of library resources, academic libraries could quickly become obsolete.

Libraries are looking for innovative and cost-effective ways to provide support to this new population of students who are distant from traditional on-campus library resources and services, either in geography or in schedule. Because of the variety of distance learning programs being offered today, the library support solutions that work at one institution may not work at another (Bryant, 2001).

The library support of distance education that we are offering at Northwest Vista College (NVC), a new community college in San Antonio, Texas, continues to evolve as our college grows. The solutions we have found would probably not work for large institutions serving students in other states or countries. However, our solutions might be applicable for other new institutions, for small institutions, for institutions where there are budget issues, and for institutions that want to start providing some of these services without a large outlay of resources.

Northwest Vista College (NVC) is the newest community college in the Alamo Community College District. It began offering classes on its new campus in 1998, and in 2000-01 was listed as the fourth fastest-growing college of its size in the nation. It currently enrolls over 8,000, including approximately 1,000 dual-credit high-school students. The main challenge the college has faced recently is finding classrooms for its growing student enrollment and office space for the faculty needed to teach them. In 2002, the college purchased fourteen portable buildings to provide more space for classrooms and offices, and in 2003 the college began offering classes at an off-site location. The college's growing online learning program has provided another alternative for the many students who want to enroll in classes at the college.

Northwest Vista College launched its online learning program in 1999 with five online courses and a total of 53 students. In the fall semester of 2003, a total of 1,669 students were enrolled in 95 online courses. Eighty-one courses were totally online, and fourteen were "hybrid" courses, combining face-to-face and online learning. The students who enroll in online and hybrid courses at Northwest Vista College tend to fit the definition of "distributed learners" rather than "distance learners." That is, most are local residents, and many also take courses on campus. Many of these online learners have full-time day jobs and family obligations, so they are distant in schedule rather than geography. They opt for online courses for the convenience available through this method of instruction delivery. The task for the Northwest Vista College librarians was to provide access to materials, reference service, and library instruction, with a staff of four full-time librarians and two part-time librarians.

ACCESS TO MATERIALS

In some ways, providing materials for online students was comparatively easy for Northwest Vista College because the library opened when the electronic age was already in full swing. The library started out in the summer of 1998 in rented space in a church downtown and moved into its own space in the fall of 1999. The library at NVC has made an effort to achieve a balance between print and electronic materials. As for periodicals, the trend has been toward purchasing electronic access over print materials. The library subscribes to 75 proprietary databases, all but a couple of which are accessible from off campus. Access to databases is provided 24 hours a day, 7 days a week through an authentication service. Off-campus access is simple; users do not need to configure their browser to a proxy server or memorize several different passwords. On the database page patrons are prompted to enter a single password that gives them off-campus access to virtually all of the databases.

Students also have access to various free online reference sources and to authoritative Web sites in different subject areas that the college librarians have identified and linked from the library Web page.

As for books, students can search the library's online catalog from off campus, and they also have access to thousands of electronic books. Recently the Texas State Library has begun making available electronic books to patrons of academic libraries in Texas. This year the number of full-text, searchable books available online reached 25,000. In addition, college students in Texas can obtain a TexShare card, which gives them borrowing privileges at many public libraries and most academic libraries throughout the state. Because the majority of Northwest Vista's "distance learning" students are local residents, and because TexShare provides access to print and electronic books, the library does not mail materials to students' homes. Therefore, providing access to materials was fairly easy for Northwest Vista College because the library was committed to purchasing electronic access to periodical literature, because TexShare provided a ready-made consortium of libraries with reciprocal borrowing privileges, and because most students were local and could, at some point during open library hours, come on campus to consult or check out a book. Providing reference service and library instruction to distance education students can be more of a problem because these services tend to be labor-intensive.

REFERENCE SERVICE

The majority of reference service at Northwest Vista is delivered face to face. Librarians do answer reference questions sent through e-mail, but their small staff size has not so far enabled them to promote a full-fledged e-mail reference service.

However, Northwest Vista College is experimenting with synchronous online reference service. We were again conservative in that we did not commit ourselves by spending a large amount of money on virtual reference software that might not be used enough to justify its expense. Instead, we used software our district had already purchased, and which could be used by various departments for various purposes. In early 2003, the Alamo Community College District purchased access to Elluminate vClass for 100 concurrent users. Elluminate provides a classroom environment with a whiteboard that can serve as a chalkboard or as a screen on which to show PowerPoint presentations or PDF documents. Elluminate offers not only chat but also the ability to hold voice-over-Internet conversations among participants. The ability to perform co-browsing is especially useful for showing students how to navigate through the dizzying array of online databases and other resources. Moderators can send class members to a Web page or share their desktop to show students a process to follow.

Librarians at Northwest Vista College began piloting the service in May, 2003. A typical session involves chatting with students about their research assignment, showing a PowerPoint presentation about one or more databases appropriate for the topic, turning on application sharing to demonstrate how students can access databases from off campus, and sending students to the library Web page to begin the research process. The librarian moderator uses the chat feature to maintain communication with the student throughout the instruction session. In this way the moderator can immediately address any questions about the instruction being provided.

How are we able to offer live online reference with such a limited staff? We offered virtual reference by appointment only. With assistance from one of our academic computing specialists, we designed an online sign-up form with a drop-down menu from which students select one of the times when a librarian is available for online reference (http://www.accd.edu/nvc/areas/disted/virtualreferencedesk.htm). Thus, we need to staff online reference only those time slots that students have requested. The online form allows us to be efficient in scheduling. The form is also efficient in that it prompts students to provide some basic information, such as their topic and the specifications of their research assignment. This information allows the librarian to prepare for the session, perhaps creating a short PowerPoint presentation or other document, and to load these materials before the session begins.

The academic computing specialist also designed an auto reply form that is generated when the sign-up form is submitted. The auto reply form provides students with logon information and the link to the Elluminate classroom, as well as a link to a tutorial to review before the reference session, if they wish. Having these forms that collect and deliver information saves a lot of time e-mailing back and forth, which we were doing before we developed the forms.

Another way that we were able to offer online reference service with a small staff is to make the service available to just a few classes each semester. Because of our small staff and limited budget, we wanted to pilot virtual reference before making a big investment in software and staff. In order to explore the feasibility of virtual reference without committing ourselves to more than we could handle, we initially offered the service to a few sections of classes taught by instructors who were enthusiastic about participating in the pilot. Having this "buy-in" from instructors is important, because participation in a pilot may involve some class time teaching the student how to access and use the virtual reference software. Furthermore, instructors are able to offer an incentive for students to participate, such as offering extra credit, or assigning use of the service as part of a project.

In order to get information on how the pilot of online reference was going so we could make appropriate changes, we collected feedback from students who had used the service by sending them to a brief online evaluation form after each session. We encouraged students to be honest, and assured them that we would take their suggestions seriously because we are trying to design a service that would be easy for them to use.

According to the feedback we have received, students like our virtual reference service a lot but would like for it to be available on a drop-in basis and for more extended hours instead of by appointment. It would not be difficult for librarians to keep the Elluminate classroom open on their office computer during times when they are not scheduled to work at the reference desk in the library building, and we intend to experiment with this kind of service in the future.

Further study must be done to determine whether the need is great enough to staff online reference service more extensively. Students who are able to come to campus for classes and to visit the physical library probably do not really need online reference. Should the library provide online reference simply because that is how students would like to receive reference assistance? Maybe so. On the other hand, students who are enrolled in online courses probably really need the service, because they are distant either in miles or in time constraints. A complicating factor is that online students are likely to need online reference service at night and on weekends, times when library staffing is ordinarily at a minimum. Therefore, making online reference open to all students and for more hours would probably have a significant impact on staffing. There is talk of forming a consortium with the other colleges in the Alamo Community College District in order to staff online reference more fully, and this idea will be explored more fully. At any rate, it appears that Elluminate vClass holds great promise for providing both reference service and instruction to students who cannot easily come to campus.

LIBRARY INSTRUCTION

The librarians at Northwest Vista knew that they needed to do more than just make resources available to students on the library Web page: they also needed to provide instruction on how to access and use these resources. Every semester, Northwest Vista College librarians use the library teaching lab to teach increasing numbers of library research classes to students whose instructor has requested a session. In September, 2001, librarians taught 13 classes, while in September of 2003, librarians taught 72 classes to 1,200 students in the library teaching lab. However, we wanted to be able to provide library instruction to students in online courses, to dual-credit high school students, to dual-credit home-schooled high school students, to traditional students in classes whose instructors do not schedule library instruction sessions, and to students who do not realize that they need instruction in using the databases until they start working on their research paper—at 10 p.m. the night before it is due.

It was determined that Web-based tutorials would work well at Northwest Vista, since this kind of instruction would be fairly easy to provide and easy for students to access. Because creating Web pages requires less manpower than providing real-time instruction, it was a good option for Northwest Vista's small staff. Furthermore, since so many students have Internet access now, whether at home, at work, or on campus, Web-based library instruction seemed a good way to reach a lot of students at their point of need.

Indeed, research done at other institutions indicates that students prefer Web instruction to other ways of delivering library instruction. At the University of Maryland University College, where student enrollment is almost equally divided between on-campus and online courses, students rated Web-based tutorials and guides as being the most useful publications the college library offers (71.7%). In surveys done at Maryland in 1996 and again in 2001, students reported that they wanted technology-based guides focusing on electronic resources and their use (Kelley & Orr, 2003). To address students' fondness for online research tools and online instruction about such tools, Northwest Vista librarians created tutorials on how to access and use the online catalog, the electronic books, and the most popular subscription databases.

Our first step in developing these instructional Web pages was to study the distance education library Web sites of other colleges to help us decide on the format, design, and content we wanted to use. We selected five Web sites with features we wanted to emulate. We then sketched out a design for our Off-Campus Library Resources opening page and talked about what kinds of information to place on this page—both the existing resources we would provide links to and new resources that we would need to create. Next we identified and gathered graphics that we wanted to use on our Web page.

Our next step was to become more familiar with the Web page design software. We were convinced of the importance of librarians designing and maintaining their own Web site. We were just beginning to learn Web design, and there had been suggestions that the project be given to a non-librarian. One suggestion was to get a graduate student to do our project as a capstone project. Another idea was to use some grant money to hire someone to design our

Web site. However, we resisted such suggestions. We feel that it is important for librarians to learn Web design and be in control of their own Web site. After all, if it is to be a dynamic Web site, librarians will need to know how to make changes and add new materials whenever they need to. Therefore, we applied for and received an instructional innovation grant to purchase the software and acquire the training to make it possible for us to design online tutorials. We purchased Dreamweaver MX and went through various short courses on Dreamweaver.

We re-designed the NVC main library Web page for greater usability and greater consistency with other NVC Web pages (http://www.accd.edu/nvc/lrc/). This included incorporating the standard navigation bar that other college departments use. We also created a new area on the main library Web page for Online Tutorials/Research Guides. Furthermore, we created a page for Off-Campus Services (http://www.accd.edu/nvc/lrc/offcampus.htm), which we linked from the main library Web page. We created online tutorials on the online catalog, accessing the library databases from off campus, critical thinking skills for the Web, and six of the most commonly used online databases. We also provided e-mail and phone contact information for students to reach a real, live librarian. Finally, we contacted appropriate individuals to have the new Off-Campus Services page and links included in the Student Resource Kit for distance education students.

TARGETED MARKETING

Another way in which we are providing off-campus library services in a manageable way is by marketing these services to segments of our population who have the greatest need. At Northwest Vista College these groups include students enrolled in online courses who cannot come on campus, dual-credit high school students, most of whom take courses on their high school campus, and home-schooled, dual-credit high school students. The acquisition of 100 concurrent-use licenses to Elluminate vClass makes it possible to offer online reference service and library instruction to those students enrolled in online courses who cannot come to campus. Information about library resources and services is disseminated to the dual-credit students through a newsletter. Periodically, the librarians at high schools participating in our dual-credit program are invited on campus for conversation and an opportunity to learn about the resources available through the college library. Home-schooled dual-credit students are in particular need of library resources and services because they do not attend class on a high school campus. The college library periodically invites home-schooled dual-credit students and their parents to a reception to learn how to use "their library" at Northwest Vista College.

In conclusion, by providing access through our library Web site to a wide array of useful resources, we have been able to provide assistance 24 hours a day to students enrolled in online classes as well as students enrolled in face-to-face classes. We educated ourselves in Web page design so that we could design and maintain our own library Web page. We redesigned our main library Web page for greater usability and created a separate Off-Campus Services Web page, which consolidated links to online materials and tutorials on their use. For virtual reference, we use multiuse software that our district had already purchased and make the service available by appointment only to students in courses taught by instructors who are committed to working with us on the pilot. Finally, we target our marketing of off-campus library services to those groups who cannot readily come to campus to use the library. In this way we are able to provide some support to students in online courses without making a big dent in the library budget. By starting small and collecting feedback, we hope to be able to expand our off-campus library services as the need for them is demonstrated.

REFERENCES

Association of College & Research Libraries. (2000). *ACRL guidelines for distance learning library services.* Retrieved November 26, 2003 from http://www.ala.org/Content/NavigationMenu/ACRL/Standards_and_Guidelines/Guidelines_for_Distance_Learning_Library_Services1.htm.

Barron, B. B. (2002). Distant and distributed learners are two sides of the same coin. *Computers in Libraries, 22*(1), 24-28.

Boser, U. (2003, October 20). Working on what works best. *U.S. News & World Report 135*(13), 58-61.

Bryant, E. (2001). Bridging the gap. *Library Journal, 126*(16), 58-60.

Explosion of distance education, The. (2002). *ASHE-ERIC higher education report, 29*(4), 1-12.

Kelley, K. B. & Orr, G. J. (2003). Trends in distant student use of electronic resources: A survey. *College & Research Libraries, 64*(3), 176-91.

Kiernan, V. A. (2003). Survey documents growth in distance education in late 1990s. *Chronicle of Higher Education, 49*(48), A28.

Thompson, H. (2002). The library's role in distance education: Survey results from ACRL's 2000 academic library trends and statistics. *College & Research Libraries News, 63*(5), 338-40.

The Impact of Distance Learning Library Services Experience on Practitioners' Career Paths

Beth A. Reiten

Oklahoma State University

Jack Fritts

Benedictine University

SUMMARY. This paper looks at the career experiences of distance learning librarianship practitioners who either attended or presented at one of the first ten Off-Campus Library Services conferences. This is a report on the first phase of the investigation, which utilized a paper survey to identify career patterns and trends. The respondents provided information about distance learning activities along with other library experiences. From a total of 500 initial mailed surveys, the researchers received nearly 200 responses. The second phase of this project, reported on at the 2004 Conference, involves personal contacts with selected respondents.

KEYWORDS. Library services, distance learners, library careers

Central Michigan University in Mt. Pleasant, Michigan, has sponsored ten conferences dedicated to off-campus library services since 1982. From the 66 attendees at the first conference in St. Louis to over 200 at the tenth in

[Haworth co-indexing entry note]: "The Impact of Distance Learning Library Services Experience on Practitioners' Career Paths." Reiten, Beth A., and Jack Fritts. Co-published simultaneously in *Journal of Library Administration* (The Haworth Information Press, an imprint of The Haworth Press, Inc.) Vol. 41, No. 3/4, 2004, pp. 365-374; and: *The Eleventh Off-Campus Library Services Conference Proceedings* (ed: Patrick B. Mahoney) The Haworth Information Press, an imprint of The Haworth Press, Inc., 2004, pp. 365-374.

http://www.haworthpress.com/web/JLA
Digital Object Identifier: 10.1300/J111v41n03_03

Cincinnati, the Off-Campus Library Services Conference has provided a port of entry to more than a thousand librarians facing the task of providing quality service to remote students.

During a discussion session at the Cincinnati conference on the history of the Off-Campus Library Services Conference and on interesting potential research topics, the researchers began to consider the relation of work in distance learning library services to individual career paths. They decided to use the pool of conference attendees and presenters over the twenty-year run of the conference as a sample population to begin studying this question. By looking at the career paths of attendees and presenters at the ten conferences using a mail survey followed by interviews with selected respondents, the researchers hoped to uncover a positive relationship between distance learning librarianship and individual career paths. One area of interest will be the impact, if any, of the ACRL *Guidelines for Distance Learning Library Services* on the career paths of the respondents. The researchers are suggesting that one potential outcome of this research may be some pointers toward models for organizing training for distance learning librarianship.

More academic institutions are entering the distance learning arena each year both as a normal extension of regular programming and as a way to enhance enrollments. Stone, Tudor, Grover, and Orig (2001) provided Steiner's definition of distance learning as:

> an organizational education program that utilizes one or more media tools to deliver instruction to students, who for various reasons, are either unable to utilize the on-campus traditional style of education or have a preference for this high tech instructional format. (p. 3)

This move into increased distance learning opportunities is a logical outgrowth of the growing focus on lifelong learning now seen in many institutions' mission statements and strategic plans. Walsh and Reese (1995) stated:

> Today, the distance learning environment has changed dramatically. Educators increasingly seek new solutions to a myriad of challenges including rising costs, reduced operating budgets, over-utilized resources (from faculty, to the physical plant), and growing competition for a declining student pool. At the same time, advances in both two-way interactive and one-way broadcast video technology have made distance learning more versatile and cost-effective than ever, ideal for a wide range of educational applications. Distance learning has become a core educational strategy in the 1990s, with a reach that extends to a broad cross-section of institutions and curriculum providers around the world. (p. 58)

As institutions continue to move more aggressively into distance learning, the role of the library evolves to keep pace with institutional direction. Librarians increasingly need to shift their focus to provide the necessary service and support. As institutions and students move into new learning modes, librarians also must change with the times. In an article addressed to technology educators Wright (2002) said "Lifelong learning is one of the mantras of career and technical education. Whether one's goal is to learn new skills or update old ones, secure a pay increase or add to one's marketable credentials, education can play an important role" (p. 32). With this mandate, the work of librarians is also shifting to develop a focus on the delivery of service to all institutional patrons regardless of location. The *Guidelines for Distance Learning Library Services* are a tool developed to assist librarians in meeting the specific needs of distant students at a level of service comparable to that afforded on-campus library users. Because the boundary between local and distant learners is blurring, many academic librarians are functioning as distance learning services librarians.

There is not a great deal of literature about library career paths specifically focused on distance learning services. In fact, there is not a great deal of literature tracking careers in librarianship in general, although there is a growing body of literature now appearing that looks at the mid-career librarian and the state of the field from that perspective. In 1999, Gordon and Nesbeitt reported on a survey that looked at librarianship as a career and the growing influence of technology on the field. One of their findings was that librarians show a tendency to remain in the same type of library over a career. They said, "However, the statistics don't reveal that a significant number of librarians–108 of the original 391 (28 per cent)–successfully switched from one library type to another" (p. 37). When asked about recommending librarianship as a career, the majority of the respondents were favorable. The authors also inquired about future expectations of the respondents and found:

> Although librarians' plans for the next five years are as varied as their job titles, 27 percent (106) see themselves moving into an administrative position, such as director or department head. Another 26% (104) are content to stay where they are; many would prefer never to rise into higher-level administration. (p. 39)

Gordon and Nesbeitt also identified an "undercurrent of discontent" (p. 39) regarding the encroaching pervasiveness of technology. This information surfaced through respondents' comments rather than as an outcome of specific survey questions. "Few respondents mentioned technology per se as a draw to the profession. Rather, they emphasized working with people, working with books, and making a difference" (p. 39).

Technology has become a major component of library work, and it does have an impact on the choices people make. As technological applications evolve, the librarian's role has also changed and continues to change. During the late 1980s and into the early 1990s, library technology required more intensive involvement on the instructional side. Librarians needed to teach their patrons how to use the technology itself. Now the trend is shifting to teaching users critical thinking and focusing on information literacy rather than hardware literacy. One aspect of these changes is the blurring of distinctions within librarianship. More librarians are becoming generalists than specialists because there is more overlap between areas. Zemon (2002) said:

> I am startled at how much less "specialized" or "isolated" the library world is these days. The Internet is a leveler in many ways and one of them is in opening quick and easy access to all types of information (both good and bad, organized and chaotic) directly to the user. (p. 671)

In an article describing their individual paths to their current roles as information consultants, Hunt and Falanga (2002) discussed the varied ways in which information professionals develop. They provide some suggestions that could easily apply to the ongoing work of distance learning librarians. They said:

- When the world isn't ready for your vision of what is necessary to complete an information task efficiently, keep trying until the technology catches up.
- Demonstrate your value to management. Make sure your job description accurately describes what you are doing.
- Acknowledge that your personal life is intertwined with your professional life. What may first appear as a constraint, may, in reality, be an opportunity.
- Find a way to do what you feel you need to do in order to grow and take additional leaps. Volunteering and networking are not just ways to get yourself better known, but offer venues to try out new skills in ways that may not be available in your present position. This can take you to places you never imagined going. (p. 18)

In many ways, their list offers good advice for all librarians, not only those involved in distance learning. However, many of these issues apply directly to librarians who have distance learning responsibilities. These suggestions can provide a base for planning for those librarians involved in this area. It is the researchers' hypothesis that such librarians are frequently to be found in the vanguard of the field because of the unique situations in which they operate.

The participants in Central Michigan's Off-Campus Library Services Conferences over the past twenty years provide an identifiable pool of librarians who have been involved in distance learning. The researchers obtained attendee and presenter lists from Central Michigan's Off-Campus Library Services conferences. The lists were entered into spreadsheets and sorted by conference. The final tally identified 1,088 unique names of those who had attended and/or authored papers. The available data included some institutional affiliations and job titles at the time of attendance. Beginning with that information, the researchers began a search program designed to identify current institutional affiliations. The search process utilized Web searches, the ALA Membership directory, the ALA Handbook of Organization and personal contacts. From a total pool of 1,088, the researchers were able to identify current locations for approximately 875. In some cases, the researchers were unable to find current information because participants had retired, left the profession, or were deceased. The researchers did not include conference presenters who were not library practitioners.

A survey instrument (Appendix A) was developed and was mailed in two batches to all attendees for whom address information was available. The instrument asked for professional experiences, job descriptions, and position titles. Open-ended questions sought anecdotal experiences about the impact of distance learning library service on individual career paths. Follow-up interviews were conducted with selected respondents (Appendix B). The personal interviews continue into the spring of 2004 and will be reported during the conference presentation and made available as an addendum to this paper at that time.

During Fall Semester 2003, the authors mailed 500 paper surveys to a randomly selected list of Off Campus Library Services Conference attendees for whom addresses were available. Two hundred returned surveys are included in the following analysis. Other responses continue to trickle in, and will be included in future analysis.

The response rate to the first round of surveys was 40%. Within this sample, the average number of years spent in librarianship was 19.8 years. The average number of years in distance learning librarianship was 6.3 years. Terms that indicate distance learning librarianship (extended campus, off campus, extension, satellite, and distance) appeared in the current titles of 58 individuals, while five respondents started their library careers with position titles indicating involvement in distance learning librarianship.

Ten respondents indicated that they had never worked in distance learning librarianship. Of these, six are in the highest level of library administration (dean/director, assistant dean/assistant director, branch librarian), three are department head level administrators, and one gave no information.

There are 51 respondents who hold positions in the highest level of library administration (dean/director, assistant dean/assistant director, branch librarian), and three retired respondents who held positions at this level at the time of their retirement.

We asked respondents to indicate which part(s) of distance learning librarianship they were/had been involved in, breaking the possibilities into 5 categories: administration, instruction, reference, ILL and other. If "other" was marked, we asked that they gave us some sense of what that entailed. The results were:

Administration	119
Instruction	145
Reference	159
ILL	79
Other	52

Those who indicated "other" listed a number of different activities:

- Publicity and marketing
- Faculty liaison
- Online courseware (Blackboard, WebCT, etc.) involvement
- Digitization of materials and electronic reserves
- Technical support
- Web design
- Remote access administration (EZProxy, IDs, authentication/authorization, etc.)
- Committee work
- Selection, licensing, promotion, administration of electronic resources (databases, e-books, etc.)
- Consulting for larger area projects
- Off-site collection creation and collection development
- Copyright
- Coordinating instructional support agreements
- Cataloging

As we are interested in the career paths of those who have been involved in distance learning librarianship, we used the same categories (administration, instruction, reference, ILL, and other) to look at the respondents' current positions, distance learning-related or not.

For this, we looked at both the Current Position/Title as well as the Current Responsibilities:

	Indicated in Title	Indicated in Description
Administration	112	10
Instruction	12	71
Reference	40	46
ILL	2	17

In addition to these, other responsibilities listed included acquisitions, technical services, and cataloging, to name a few. Some non-library positions include Self-Employed, Grant Program Manager, Homemaker, and Retiree. There were seven respondents who are retired.

One of the researchers' hypotheses was that many of those with experience in distance librarianship would have moved into administrative roles, aided by their experiences with the collaborative nature of work in distance learning. The results of the survey indicated that 51 (about 25%) of the respondents are currently serving in the upper levels of library administration. Forty-one of this group have or have had distance learning experience. Forty respondents (not necessarily from the group of 41) have or have had distance learning administrative responsibility. There are 122 respondents who are currently library administrators at various levels, including coordinators, department chairs, etc. The data seems to support this hypothesis. Even though some respondents may not currently be working specifically as distance learning administrators, a clear majority of the respondents have had library administrative responsibilities in the course of their careers. The follow-up interviews will provide additional information about individual career choices and experiences.

Many respondents also indicated in their general comments that their work with distant learners was exciting, invigorating, and "the most engaging, most fulfilling of any [work] I've done!"

REFERENCES

ACRL. (2003). Guidelines for distance learning library services: A draft revision. *C&RL News, 64*(4), 265-271.

Gordon, R. S. & Nesbeitt, S. (1999). Who we are, where we're going: A report from the front. *Library Journal, 124* (9), 36-39.

Hunt, D. & Falanga, R. (2002, October). Leaping off the edge: Thriving in ever-changing information futures. *Information Outlook, 6*(10), 12-18.

Stone, W. S., Tudor, T. R., Grover, M., & Orig, A. (2001). An empirical investigation of strategic success factors in distance learning programs. *Educational Research Quarterly, 24*(3), 3-9.

Walsh, J. & Reese, B. (1995). Distance learning's growing reach. *T.H.E. Journal, 22*(11), 58-62.

Wright, S. (2002). Never stop learning. *Techniques, 77*(5), 32-33.

Zemon, C. (Bogar). (2002). Midlife career choices: How are they different from other career choices? *Library Trends, 50*(4), 665-672.

APPENDIX A

Survey Instrument

We are conducting a research project for presentation at the Off-Campus Library Services Conference to be held in May 2004. We are tracking the career paths of attendees and presenters from the first ten OCLS Conferences. This survey is part of our data gathering process. Please complete the survey and return it using the included return envelope. Responses will be confidential, although we would like to conduct follow-up interviews with some respondents. If you are willing to be interviewed, please provide your contact information on the back of this survey.

Thank you for your participation in this process.

Part I. Demographics

1. What is your current position/title?
2. Please describe your current responsibilities.
3. How long have you held your current position?
4. How long have you worked in the library field?
5. What was your first (entry) library position/title?
6. How long have you worked in distance learning librarianship?
7. What types of distance learning library work do you/have you been involved in: (check as many as apply)

> Administration _____
> Instruction _____
> Reference _____
> Interlibrary Loan ___
> Other (please describe)

8. What other library positions/titles have you held?
9. For any other library positions listed, please indicate whether they came before or after your distance learning position.
10. Any other comments?

Part II. Contact information for follow-up interviews (optional)

Are you willing to talk with us about your distance learning experiences? If so, please complete the following information:

Name: _____

Title: _____

Institution: _____

Address: _____

Telephone: _____

E-mail address: _____

Thank you very much for your participation in this survey. Please return your completed survey in the enclosed SASE by November 21, 2003.

APPENDIX B

Search Sources Used to Locate Survey Subjects

American Library Association. *ALA handbook of organization.* (2002-2003 ed.). Chicago: American Library Association, 2002.

American Library Directory (55th ed.), 2002-2003. Medford, NJ: Information Today, 2002.

American Library Directory. (56th ed.), 2003-2004. Medford, NJ: Information Today, 2003.

American Library Association. *ALA membership directory.* 2000-2001 ed. Chicago: American Library Association, 2000.

We also utilized Web searches and personal contacts.

APPENDIX C

Personal Interview Questions

How did you initially get involved in distance learning?

Where in your career did this involvement fall?

How long have you been involved in distance learning librarianship?

Do you feel as though that involvement helped you in your career?

How so or not?

Have the ACRL Guidelines helped you in your distance learning work?

What other areas of librarianship have you been involved with?

How do you see distance learning work fitting into the broader range of librarianship?

Would you recommend distance learning librarianship to new librarians?

Why or why not?

Do you have any other comments about distance learning librarianship?

Ahead of the Game:
Using Communications Software
and Push Technology
to Raise Student Awareness
of Library Resources

Tom Riedel

Regis University

SUMMARY. In January 2000, Regis University received a federal grant to form the Learning Anytime, Anywhere Partnership (LAAP) with three other institutions of higher learning and a corporation. As a member of the LAAP Vision Team, I designed a Library Notification Module that works through our Student Information System to identify new students, and then generates an e-mail welcome message to them from the library. The message encourages students to apply for a RegisNET account, essential for remote access to library databases, and provides a hot link to the application form. Messages are tailored to declared programs of study, so students are also directed to Web lists of recommended licensed databases: MBA students, for example, will click on a link to business resources, and nursing students to a guide for health sciences resources.

KEYWORDS. Technology, distance education, Internet

[Haworth co-indexing entry note]: "Ahead of the Game: Using Communications Software and Push Technology to Raise Student Awareness of Library Resources." Riedel, Tom. Co-published simultaneously in *Journal of Library Administration* (The Haworth Information Press, an imprint of The Haworth Press, Inc.) Vol. 41, No. 3/4, 2004, pp. 375-390; and: *The Eleventh Off-Campus Library Services Conference Proceedings* (ed: Patrick B. Mahoney) The Haworth Information Press, an imprint of The Haworth Press, Inc., 2004, pp. 375-390.

http://www.haworthpress.com/web/JLA
Digital Object Identifier: 10.1300/J111v41n03_04

PROLOGUE

Librarians create Web pages that we think are useful, but our patrons may miss them for reasons from poor Web design to low perceived value. Even so, good Web design may not be enough to make sure our distance students know how and when to navigate our library Web pages, and which ones to use when. How do we let a diverse and dispersed population know that we subscribe to resources (with their tuition money) that surpass what they can find through Google? At Regis University, links to the library Web site and to library resource guides for relevant subject areas have been created in on-line courses–but does a student who sees yet another link recognize the value at the other end? We know that if we build it, they may not come, but are the odds improved if we *push* it to them? This project builds on an earlier one (Riedel, 2002) in which I created Web-based resource guides for different subject areas, then worked with instructional design teams to build links to the guides from online courses. These same guides are easily accessible from the library Web page from a "Where to Start" link, but it was my sense that the guides were used primarily as a tool by reference librarians who pushed the pages to students in answer to questions about databases and access or as a tool for library instruction sessions, rather than something students identified as a place to start (even though the "Where to Start" terminology was based on the number of calls we got from students who said they didn't know "where to start"). Add to the other anecdotal evidence that many students who receive library instruction late in their degree programs express irritation that the information they get had not been presented to them at the beginning of their studies. Yet, given the disparities in the way orientations and library instruction are handled across Regis schools and programs, there has been no single, effective way to push information about the library to all new students.

PROFILE

The number and dispersal of Regis students complicate proactive communication from the library. Classes are taught at seven extended campuses, which range from twenty miles to over 700 miles away from the main campus. But the greatest growth area is in online learning, which is available through the School for Professional Studies (SPS) and the School for Health Care Professions (SHCP). Over 13,000 students are enrolled in SPS, and in the previous year, 40% of SPS enrollments were in online courses. Regis students live in over 60 nations, with 32% of the total enrollments outside Colorado. In

SHCP, one online program alone, Registered Nursing to Bachelor of Science in Nursing, is expected to increase by over 120% in 2003-2004. Many Regis online students receive only basic library orientation information, although new online nursing and management students receive a library orientation on CD that includes a tutorial in using basic library systems, databases and services.

OPPORTUNITY

An opportunity presented itself that allowed me to think outside the realm of what I thought was possible in terms of communicating with the invisible constituency of distance learners. In January of 2000, Regis University became a partner in a Learning Anytime Anywhere Partnerships (LAAP) project funded by the federal Fund for the Improvement of Post-secondary Education (FIPSE) and administered by the Western Cooperative for Educational Telecommunications (WCET) of the Western Interstate Commission for Higher Education (WICHE). LAAP projects, which were funded from the late 1990s until 2002, encouraged institutions to "begin using online technologies to reshape the educational enterprise, to foster public-private relationships, and to support innovation where it was prohibitively expensive by shifting the cost structures" (Paulson, 2002, p. 39). What that meant for Regis and its LAAP partners, Kansas State University, Kapi'olani Community College and a software development company, Systems and Computer Technology Corporation (SCT) was to develop homegrown services online. These four entities worked together to address a challenge in online education: developing and providing time and location independent access to a complete array of student support services. The project, funded for a three-year period, was "Beyond the Administrative Core: Creating Web-based Student Services for Online Learners." Each institution focused on developing a plan for specific online student services that would not duplicate the efforts of any partner, then fully implementing components of that plan. SCT was then charged with translating the work of the educational partners into commercial development of online student services that could be used by other institutions.

PROCESS

The Regis LAAP "Vision Team" included institutional representatives that ranged from front-line providers of student services to administrators, representatives from SHCP, SPS, and the libraries. The first year of the project was on reflection and self-study, with the goal of determining the focus the project would take. Also in the first year, Regis students were surveyed to assess their awareness of various student services, their use of them, and their interest in having these services available online. The vision team operated under the basic assumption that we would provide services adaptable for all Regis students and that we would do something that would be carried on after the termination of the project. Members of the team were encouraged to think about what we would like to have online systems accomplish without regard to what we thought it might be possible for the system to do. Push technology, in which the system activates communication at identified stages of the process, was emphasized in planning and development.

When I thought in terms of the need for online library services, I initially considered the problem with remote access, from the perspective of both awareness and mechanics. From anecdotal evidence collected in the office and at the reference desk, by phone and by e-mail, it was clear that students were often not aware of the resources available to them, and even if they were, our Web pages were not making clear to them what they needed to do to gain remote access. At the time the LAAP project was initiated, students registered for a library card, which gave them access to about two-thirds of our databases. To apply for a library card, students needed to know where the online application form was as well as their student ID number to complete the form–often a challenge since distance students do not receive an actual student ID card and may not know they have an ID number. For the LAAP project, I proposed a module that would send students an e-mail message letting them know their ID number and that they needed to apply for a library card for remote access to databases.

VISUAL MODELING

Thinking of what we would like "the system" to do was only the first step in moving our ideas into a working reality. The administrative system in use at Regis is Colleague, a Datatel Student Information System (SIS) that holds all pertinent student information from the application process through matriculation, graduation and into alumnus status. A central piece of the system is communications software and an e-mail server, purchased with LAAP funds, which would provide our primary means of communication for any module we developed. The overall Regis LAAP project was conceived as a single, overarching process that began at the application stage, where push technology would update applicants on their file status, letting them know when the different application materials had been received, what was still missing, and when the file was complete. An applicant moved to student status would then be prompted to apply for a library card. The final module would notify students of the need to set up an advising appointment. However, any module we conceived needed to have code written to make it functional, and since those of us on the team needed to be able to communicate what we envisioned to those in Regis Information Technology Services (ITS) who would be able to implement our vision, we worked with visual modeling and Unified Modeling Language (UML) to work out our scenarios through use case models. Use cases illustrate the system's intended functions, the surroundings, or actors, who interact with the system, and the specific interactions through use case diagrams. While allowing team members to clarify our thoughts about the process and communicate them among ourselves, use cases more importantly provided a vehicle for team members and the system developers "to discuss the system's functionality and behavior" (Quatrani, 2000, p. 21). The following use case diagram (Diagram 1), for example, illustrates the vision team's conception of how the entire project would fit together (Waterman, 2002).

DIAGRAM 1

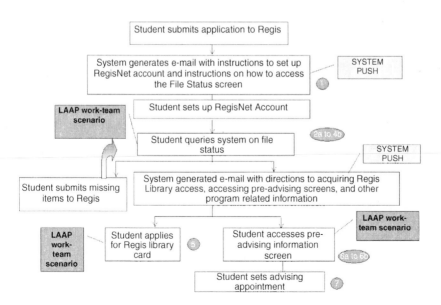

For each use case, each module detailed a sequence with preconditions, goal, actors, other functions involved, and the desired outcome. For example, my first scenario looked like this:

Scenario: Notification of Student ID Number for Library Card Registration

Goal	To contact accepted or registered student who has expressed intent to attend Regis, deliver student ID number, and direct student toward registration for Library Card	
Preconditions	1. Applicant has been accepted to Regis, and moved to student status on Colleague system 2. Student's e-mail address is available	
Step #	**Actor**	**University Systems**
1.		Once preconditions have been met, Colleague contacts student via e-mail: "Welcome to Regis University. Your student number, which is essential to conducting business at Regis, is [00000000]. Now that you have a student ID number, you are eligible to register for a library card [hot link]."
2.	Student clicks on link [http://www.regis.edu/lib/libcard.htm], fills out form and submits	
3.		Form delivered via e-mail to library circulation department
4.	Library staff enters student information in CARL system	
5.		CARL accepts registration, adds student to list of authorized users
6.	Library staff e-mails student, verifying library card number and providing library access information	
Post-Conditions	1. Student knows ID number 2. Student is authorized to use the library online system 3. Student has information about remote access to library online system	

One of the up-front advantages of visual modeling is that I could conceive how I wanted the Colleague system to work without having to *know* exactly how it worked and what was possible within its parameters. By writing down what I expected through a sequence of events, ITS staff could work with me to clarify and move my ideas into a working program. However, this first stab did not get to the point of development since it raised a few questions: could we in fact e-mail student ID numbers? Our Registrar's office determined that FERPA (Family Educational Rights and Privacy Act) regulations would prohibit it. Since tape loads from Colleague update patron records in our ILS, at that time giving new students library card numbers based on their social security numbers, I decided on a second approach. Tape loads were a process between Regis ITS and CARL–with no librarian involved except to nag when it seemed the process wasn't happening as frequently as it should.

One aspect of the new scenario was to move responsibility for tape loads to the library. With the second scenario, we moved to a storyboard format that includes some field-specific information in Colleague.

Library Card Scenario Storyboard

Assumptions

        Student has e-mail address

        Weekly tape load from Colleague to CARL

Trigger

        On the APPN screen field 27 Appl Stat has been changed to MS

        [APPN = application; MS = moved to student]

System generated e-mail:

        Welcome [name]!

        You will soon have full access to Regis University library services and resources. Your Regis library card number will be activated by Saturday, and will consist of A9/your social security number without hyphens, such as A9/123456789. This number will give you access to research databases and full-text articles as well as to important services such as Interlibrary Loan. If you would prefer your library card number to be something other than your social security number, or you would like to expedite the library registration process, please fill out the Web form at http://www.regis.edu/lib/libcard.htm. Please explore our on-campus and extensive online services at our Web site: http://www.regis.edu/lib.

        Thank you,

        Regis University Libraries

        Questions? Contact us:

        303-458-4030 or 800-388-2366, ext. 4030

        circdesk@regis.edu

CONSULTANTS

Consultants were hired for assistance with the Datatel applications (much of what we were proposing to do in Colleague was a departure for the ITS staff who worked with it, as well) and with ADA compliance issues. The Datatel consultant met jointly with the vision team and ITS Business Systems Analysts so that we could walk through our individual modules. By this time, the thrust of the Library Notification Module had changed yet again, since over the long course of development, the library had purchased a proxy server that authenticated remote users by their RegisNET account information, a university-wide standard; a library card for distance learners was no longer needed. I had also decided to incorporate text in the message that would direct students to the recommended subject guides. One valuable suggestion the consultant made, based on my proposed module and his knowledge of Colleague fields and programming, was that the module could be designed so that students could be directed to specific resource guides depending on their declared area of study.

IMPLEMENTATION

My initial understanding of how the project would be implemented led me to believe that once an applicant was moved to student status in the Colleague system, the library notification message would be generated following notification that the applicant was accepted to the university. In fact, one of the aspects of the project for which I had not prepared myself was that I would need to have access to Colleague myself and would have to regularly enter the system to process batches in order to make the Library Notification Module work. Colleague had not been used previously by anyone in the library, although the tape load issue was about to change that. Although I had hoped that I could piggyback on the implementation of the other LAAP modules and not have to have access to Colleague myself, I soon realized the utility of having control over when and how the batches were processed, being able to modify content within the module, and being able to think in terms of other uses for the system.

With the steady guidance of an ITS Colleague specialist, I entered the text of the messages. The learning curve was initially steep–Colleague's interface is akin to a text-based ILS. In creating paragraphs, for instance, the backspace key would delete an entire line of text, so my challenge was to type each line perfectly before moving on to the next. The system is menu-driven, but movement throughout can be expedited by using command language (DPAR, for example, is "define custom paragraphs," which is what I was doing at this point). The ITS specialist then wrote rules in Colleague that would mark a new student in the system to receive an e-mail message from the library when (1) the applicant had been "moved" to student status and (2) the student had an e-mail address. Further rules identifying students by program determine a second paragraph that provides a Web link to a resource guide specific to their declared area of study. For example, MBA students would be directed to a resource guide for Business and Economics, nursing students would be directed to a guide for health care resources. Rules were also written to identify anyone moved to student status who did not have an e-mail address. Those students could then be contacted with the same welcome letter by surface mail (Appendix A).

Each library welcome message consists of three short paragraphs, with the first and last paragraphs common to all messages. The first paragraph welcomes the student by name and encourages him to get a RegisNET account, which is used not only for remote authentication but for e-mail and shared disk space, and provides a link to the university portal where the student fills out a form to set up the account. The third paragraph encourages the student to explore the library Web site and provides contact information for the reference desk and Distance Learning Librarian. The middle paragraph is determined according to rules set up to identify declared programs of study; if any particular rule is passed, the corresponding subject-related paragraph will be added to the e-mail. Individual paragraphs are inserted for different graduate programs: Business, Management, Nonprofit Management, Computer Information Technology, Liberal Studies, Professional Counseling, Teacher Education, Nursing and Health Care Management. All undergraduate students are directed to a single page where they can select subject guides in the above areas as well as communication, history, religious studies, humanities and sociology. Although the same subject guides were available from the library Web page before the Library Notification Module was implemented, I created a parallel set of Web pages that would be linked only to the notification messages in order to have a sense of how often the e-mail messages actually prompted the recipient to follow the link. At the same time, a special departmental e-mail account (distlib@regis.edu) was set up from which the e-mail messages would be generated. Once all the paragraphs had been created and tested, it was time to take it live.

PROCESSING, RETURNS AND QUESTIONS

The first batch of e-mail messages was sent out on August 30, 2002. In order to process a batch, I log into the system and enter "VPC" for "view pending correspondence." I then see a list of e-mail notifications (libemail) and letters (liblet) waiting to be sent. I can choose to process either of these batches, or ignore them for the time being if the numbers or dates don't warrant processing. Each batch is processed, its history updated in the system, then deleted. I process the batches every week or two, paying special attention to the beginning of terms. From the first batch of 155 messages sent out, 21 bounced back. In the first year of the project implementation, 3,782 messages were sent out and 229 (6%) were returned. I take a quick look at returned messages because sometimes the error is a data entry one on the Regis end (for example, nmteddy@earthling.net) and I can correct and resend it. The initial batches of notifications were addressed only to a first name, which hampered this type of troubleshooting, as well as being able to move the problem e-mail cases to a letter notification. Messages are now addressed to full names: "Welcome John Hickenlooper" rather than "Welcome John." The primary reasons that messages have been returned is that the recipients have exceeded their disk quotas in Hotmail and Yahoo accounts, accounts have been discontinued, and mailboxes have not been found. Military accounts have had a high rate of return, and I have also seen messages such as "This message contains suspicious characters in the body" and "NUL characters not allowed." Some have been identified as spam since the user had not listed Regis as a legitimate domain from which to receive mail.

The notification has generated very few questions or comments to the distlib e-mail account. Two students have responded with "thank you" messages. One alerted me to a broken link to the Nonprofit Management resource page. As I had suspected might be the case, some students did not know their student ID numbers at the time of notification. I could tell from other responses that some students were receiving the library notification message before they had been notified of their acceptance to the university. Both issues have been resolved by building in a buffer zone between the days an applicant is moved to student status in the system and when the library notification message is delivered. Another issue was Web design. The first notification message sent students to the Regis INsite portal page and directed them to click on "Apply for a RegisNET account" at the bottom of the page. In the meantime, ITS had redesigned the INsite page so that the link was at the left side of the screen. Others alerted me to mis-entered names in the system ("my name is Burford not Buford"), which kept them from being able to set up a RegisNET account. Still others asked me questions that need to be referred to other university departments.

LOG ANALYSIS AND SURVEY

Soon after the implementation of the Library Notification Module, I began seeing some results of increased student awareness of library resources. At a library orientation session for new graduate students, for example, one asked me if I had sent out "the e-mail message about the library." I now ask each group of new students how many received a message from the library, and nearly half the hands go up. Log analysis of the library Web pages created for the LAAP project showed that in the first year of notification, in which 3,553 e-mail messages had been successfully delivered, the resource lists were hit a total of 664 times, or by an average of about 19% of the recipients. In keeping with the distribution of student enrollments, the largest number of views (251, or almost 38%) was at the undergraduate page. The second most popular page was the one designed for the MBA program, not surprising since the Regis online MBA program makes up the lion's share of graduate enrollments. Perhaps more surprising was the average time viewed per page. The computer science page was viewed 82 times at an average of only 55 seconds, but other pages received more attention, from an average of two minutes for the nonprofit management page, almost five minutes for the MBA page, seven for the management page, and a whopping eight minutes for the undergraduate page. The low percentage of hits on the pages as a whole concerned me, but my expectations were high. Looking at the glass as half full, however, it was good to know that I had influenced nearly 700 hits on the library Web site.

In order to get a better idea of how new students responded to getting the library notification message, I constructed a follow-up e-mail survey (Appendix B). E-mail addresses were saved as part of the batch notification process, and 300 surveys were distributed to students who had been sent the notification message from two weeks to two months prior to sending out the survey. The survey collected only basic demographic information–Regis school of enrollment, and undergraduate or graduate status–but sought to discover whether the recipients remembered getting a library notification message and whether the message prompted them to set up a RegisNET account and visit the library Web site.

Of the 300 surveys sent, 19 bounced back. Of the 281 surveys successfully sent, I received 79 responses, or a 28% response rate. The frequency of response closely mirrored the distribution of Regis enrollment: 79% from SPS, 11% from SHCP and 10% from Regis College, with 68% undergraduate and 32% graduate. Of the 79 respondents, 29, over 36%, said they did not receive the notification message at all. Those who responded negatively to this question were asked to return the survey without further completing it.

Two of my concerns, based on earlier e-mail questions, had been that students did not know their ID numbers in order to set up their RegisNET accounts, and that the library notification was sent out before students were notified that they had been accepted to the university. These concerns were related in that when students are notified of acceptance, they are given their ID numbers. Of the 50 students who received (or remembered receiving) the library notification message, 26% said they received the library message before they had received official notification from the university; but only 14% said they did not know their ID numbers. Although nearly half the respondents did not have a RegisNET account when they received the library notification message, 34% said that they set up the account because of the prompt. Thirty-eight, or 76% of the respondents, had not visited the library Web site before the notification; 48% visited after. Of the number who visited the library Web site after notification, 36% of them were visiting the site for the first time. Twenty-two respondents, or 44%, visited the suggested Web subject resource guide. Extrapolating these numbers to the entire group of notified students, I could assume that 2,249 students remembered getting the notification, that 764 had set up RegisNET accounts, that 1,079 visited the library Web site, and 989 had viewed the resource guides.

The survey also invited comments, some of which indicated that the message arrived too early for some students: "I have not begun my classes and do look forward to the tools." "I have just been enrolled in the SPS program, with classes starting next week. As of now I have yet to use anything from the library, but as the semester continues, I'm sure all of this will come in handy." Another student suggested the library message got lost in the shuffle: "Given the sheer volume of information that new students receive by e-mail and postal mail, it may be beneficial for the library to consider something that really stands out in all the chaos. Maybe a PowerPoint presentation or avi file? For about a 2-week period, I received several e-mails and postal mails every day. It's all still a blur!"

ONWARD

One possible modification to the Library Notification Module is one of timing. Even though the survey numbers are promising, perhaps messages should not be sent out until a month after the student is accepted and is less likely to be receiving other messages from the university, and a secondary reminder message could be sent in a following semester. I have a great deal of latitude in terms of setting up new communications, and have the support of ITS in getting them up and running. Other possibilities include more targeted communication with established students. I could use the Colleague system, for example, to send a message to all MBA students with brief notifications of relevant new developments.

RECREATING THE PROCESS

In order to recreate the process at other institutions, here are some key issues:

- Get the right people involved from the beginning. Working with an intra-institutional team allows librarians to learn a great deal about other departments and functions of the university, and others will become aware of what the libraries and librarians do.

- Determine if applications need to be customized by department or function, and make those accommodations in the design. I did a great deal of investigation into when students became aware of their student ID numbers, for example, and it varied greatly among departments. Similarly, there was some variation among departments of when a student officially becomes a student.
- Clearly define goals and desired outcomes, but be flexible. My vision of what I wanted to accomplish underwent a couple of major changes in response to changes outside the parameters of the project.
- Be aware of policy issues and address them accordingly. Legal considerations (FERPA) had an effect on my project; there may also be university-wide policies regarding communication with students or use of systems to that end.
- Assessment is important. If you are only assuming you have succeeded or failed without getting feedback, you may be wrong.
- Timelines should be shorter than three years. It was difficult to keep motivated and on track when there were great lulls in the action.
- Use a scenario-building process to work through any kind of module. It will help to clarify your ideas and to communicate them to others who don't necessarily speak the same language.

REFERENCES

Learning anytime anywhere partnerships. (2003). Retrieved December 5, 2003, from United States Department of Education Web site: http://www.ed.gov/programs/fipselaap/index.html.

Paulson, K. (2002). FIPSE: Thirty years of learning anytime and anywhere. *Change, 34*(5), 36-41. Retrieved November 30, 2003, from Academic Search Premier database.

Quatrani, T. (2000). *Visual modeling with rational rose 2000 and UML.* New York: Addison-Wesley.

Riedel, T. (2002). Added value, multiple choices: Librarian/faculty collaboration in online course development. In P. Mahoney (Ed.), *The 10th Off-Campus Library Services Proceedings* (pp. 369-375). Mount Pleasant, MI: Central Michigan University.

Waterman, E. (2002). *LAAP at Regis University, 2000, 2001, 2002.* Retrieved November 30, 2003, from http://academic.regis.edu/laap/index.htm.

APPENDIX A

Library Notification Module for MBA

Welcome Firstname Lastname,

One of the benefits of being a Regis student is full access to Regis University library services and resources, no matter where you are located. Before you are able to take advantage of the library databases that provide full-text articles and reference information, however, you must first obtain a **RegisNET** account. If you don't already have an account, you can sign up for one by going to Regis INsite, http://insite.regis.edu. Look for "RegisNET Account" along the left side of the screen. In addition to library access, this account will supply you with a Regis e-mail account.

For a list of useful library databases for the MBA program, follow the link to:

http://www.regis.edu/regis.asp?sctn=lib&p1=list&p2=laapmba

This resource guide suggests sources for full-text articles and other business research.

Please explore our on-campus and extensive online services at our Web site: http://www.regis.edu/lib. We look forward to a productive and rewarding relationship with you as you complete your degree at Regis.

Sincerely,

Regis University Libraries

Questions? Contact us:
Reference desk: library@regis.edu
303-458-4031 or 800-388-2366, ext. 4031
Distance Learning Librarian: distlib@regis.edu
303-458-4261 or 800-388-2366, ext. 4261

APPENDIX B

E-mail Survey of Notified Students

Dear Regis student,

In order for the Regis Libraries to better serve you, we would appreciate if you'd take a few minutes, hit "reply" and answer the following questions. Please add any comments you'd like. We appreciate your input!

1. Are you enrolled in the School for Professional Studies (SPS), School for Health Care Professions (SHCP) or Regis College (RC)? If not enrolled, please answer only this question.

    SPS (62)　　　SHCP (9)　　　RC (8)　　　not enrolled (1)

2. Are you an undergraduate or graduate student?

    Undergrad (54)　　　　graduate (25)

3. Did you receive a "Regis Library Online" e-mail welcome message that included RegisNET account information and Regis library Web links from the Distance Librarian? If your answer is no, please return survey after this question.

    Y (50)　　　N (29)

4. Did you receive the e-mail welcome message from the library *before* you were officially notified that you had been accepted to Regis University?

    Y (13)　　　N (20)　　　don't know (17)

5. Did you already have a RegisNET account (not a WebAdvisor account) when you received the library e-mail message?

    Y (15)　　　N (24)　　　don't know (11)

6. Did you set up a RegisNET account when prompted by the library e-mail message?

    Y (17)　　　N (20)　　　already had account (13)

7. Did you know or have access to your student ID number to set up your RegisNET account?

    Y (38)　　　N (7)　　　didn't set up account (5)

APPENDIX B. (continued)

8. Had you visited the Regis Library Web site before you received the library e-mail message?

   Y (7)   N (38)   don't know (5)

9. Did you visit the library Web site after you received the e-mail message?

   Y (24)   N (24)   don't know (2)

10. Did you visit the Web list of library resources for your program/subject area suggested in the e-mail message?

    Y (22)   N (28)   don't know (0)

Comments?

All in the Family:
Library Services for LIS Online Education

Susan E. Searing

University of Illinois, Urbana-Champaign

SUMMARY. Online distance education is increasingly common in the field of library and information science (LIS). At the University of Illinois, Urbana-Champaign, the departments that work together to meet the information needs of distant LIS students and faculty include: the University Library's central services; the Academic Outreach Library; the Library & Information Science Library; the virtual reference service administered by the Reference Library and the Undergraduate Library; and the instructional technology staff and teaching faculty of the Graduate School of Library and Information Science. The collections and services they provide typify the library support required by distance education programs. However, three factors distinguish LIS from other disciplines: the information-intensive curriculum; the enduring importance of the physical library; and the importance of librarians as role models.

KEYWORDS. Library services, distance education, collaboration

Distance learning has a long history in library and information science (LIS). Over the past century, library educators have used correspondence courses, audio and video broadcasting, and off-campus classrooms to deliver

[Haworth co-indexing entry note]: "All in the Family: Library Services for LIS Online Education." Searing, Susan E. Co-published simultaneously in *Journal of Library Administration* (The Haworth Information Press, an imprint of The Haworth Press, Inc.) Vol. 41, No. 3/4, 2004, pp. 391-405; and: *The Eleventh Off-Campus Library Services Conference Proceedings* (ed: Patrick B. Mahoney) The Haworth Information Press, an imprint of The Haworth Press, Inc., 2004, pp. 391-405.

curricula in both degree programs and post-MLS continuing education. Today, online learning is common. According to the American Library Association, 38 (79%) of the 48 ALA-accredited LIS programs in the United States deliver all or part of their curriculum using some form of distance education technology (ALA, 2001).

These programs reach an impressive number of students. The most recent published statistics from the Association for Library and Information Science Education (ALISE) report an off-campus enrollment total of 2,423.7 FTE in American and Canadian schools in 2001 (ALISE, 2002, p. 132). The figures are inexact, however, because some schools are not included. For example, the Graduate School of Library & Information Science (GSLIS) at the University of Illinois, Urbana-Champaign (UIUC), did not report its off-campus enrollment figures. Furthermore, the ALISE statistics include students in undergraduate as well as graduate courses and encompass all modes of off-campus instruction. Indeed, LIS distance education often blends modes. For example, in GSLIS's distance education option, LEEP, a student begins her studies with an intensive on-campus session, then experiences a mix of synchronous and asynchronous technologies as she pursues her coursework. Some programs require that students be in residence for one or more classes or semesters, while students in other programs never set foot on campus. The University of Washington offers a distinct degree, the dMLIS, while other schools, such as Florida State University, offer online education to both resident and non-resident students in a manner which is highly integrated. In short, one cannot determine definitively how many LIS students are earning their MLS degrees primarily online. But the number is clearly substantial, and it's growing.

This paper examines academic library support for online distance education in LIS, using examples primarily from LEEP and drawing parallels and comparisons to other LIS online distance programs. I briefly describe the library collections and services that are made available to LEEP students and teachers; these are the same core of services that most libraries offer to students at a distance. Integral to the LEEP program, however, are several factors that I believe strongly influence the demand for and provision of library services, and thus help to create and sustain the program's unique "information ecology" (Nardi and O'Day, 1999). I concentrate on three factors in particular–the information-intensive curriculum, the enduring importance of the physical library, and the active modeling of librarianship's professional values–and argue that these factors will impact library support for any LIS distance education program.

LITERATURE REVIEW:
LIBRARIES AND LIS DISTANCE EDUCATION

Librarians have written surprisingly little about the specific challenges and rewards of supporting graduate-level online LIS education. Nor have LIS educators focused much attention on library support for remote learners, as evidenced by the scant mentions of the library in a recent compendium of program descriptions and histories (Barron, 2003). Perhaps this is because, as Mansour A. Alzamil documented, LIS faculty are generally satisfied with the library support for their online courses (Alzamil, 2002). A handful of studies report empirical data on library services for LIS distance education, but none of them zero in on Internet-delivered programs (Kim & Rogers, 1983; Barron, 1987; Hoy and Hale, 1991; Stephens, 1998; Douglas, 2002).

Case studies constitute a substantial portion of the general literature on off-campus library services, yet there are few such studies that focus on LIS programs. Kathleen Burnett and Marilia Painter's description of library support for the Florida State University School of Information Studies Web-based curriculum is a rare but excellent example of this genre, providing a chronology of service development that clearly delineates the various players and the politics involved (Burnett & Painter, 2001). I have written previously about some aspects of library support for LEEP (Searing, 2004).

Also valuable are first-hand accounts by LIS students who have completed their degrees at a distance. Michelle Kazmer interviewed LEEP students and uncovered preferences for library services within the broader context of distant students' learning styles and the rigors of technology-mediated education. She reported that LEEP students want rich online collections, rapid delivery of printed materials, reference service and technical support during evenings and weekends, appropriate training options, and a single point of contact (Kazmer, 2002).

A recent survey, conducted by an LIS student at Southern Connecticut State University, gauged the willingness of library employers to hire graduates of LIS distance education programs. While 82% of the respondents would hire someone with a degree earned online, 18% would not, and nearly a third expressed their preference for a traditional degree. Respondents provided extensive written explanations for their views. Those favoring traditional education most often emphasized the value of face-to-face interactions of students with each other, with instructors, and with librarians. Although none of the survey questions mentioned accessibility of information resources, several respondents asserted the importance of exposure to a sizeable university library collection (Wynkoop, 2003).

Another recent article describes how Don Latham and Stephanie Maatta Smith surveyed the main libraries of the 28 campuses that offered ALA-accredited master's degrees through distance education at the time of their study. Based on responses from 14 libraries (a 50% return rate), they analyzed the services offered and made recommendations in several areas. They also reviewed and evaluated the Web sites of all 28 libraries. Although LIS distance education has expanded since their data was gathered, their study remains the best overview of library services for this constituency.

Latham and Smith's study was guided by four research questions. First, what library services are made available to distant LIS students? Second, how are these services marketed? Third, is special training provided to librarians and staff who work with distance learners? And fourth, are formal evaluation mechanisms in place?

Their mail survey and the Web site evaluation both confirmed that basic services–such as reference, instruction, and access to print and electronic collections–are routinely provided to students in LIS distance education. Libraries engage in various marketing strategies but rely primarily on their Web sites to inform students about available services. Most librarians charged with providing these services have no special training. And finally, needs assessment and evaluation techniques are under-utilized (Latham & Smith, 2003).

CASE STUDY: LIBRARY SUPPORT FOR LEEP

GSLIS shares the number 1 spot in *U.S. News & World Report*'s rankings of LIS programs (U.S. News, 2004). Its LEEP program, which permits students to obtain a master's degree in LIS through Web-based courses, received the prestigious Sloan-C Award for the Most Outstanding Asynchronous Learning Network (ALN) Program in 2001. Most courses are taught as live synchronous sessions, in which instructors and students both utilize text chat. In addition, students hear the voice of the instructor, and guest lecturers participate from the broadcasting studio or by telephone. Slides are displayed during the class sessions, and some teachers incorporate music or pre-recorded audio clips. Most courses also make good use of asynchronous Web pages, e-mail, and Web-based bulletin boards. Class sessions are archived online, so both students and instructors can review the audio and chat logs.

The LEEP instructors are drawn from the resident GSLIS faculty as well as faculty at other schools and professionals located around the country. LEEP students are admitted in "cohorts" each July, when they spend ten intensive days on campus. During that period, which is commonly referred to as "boot camp," they receive training in the technologies and are introduced to library resources. At the same time, they complete an introductory course that requires library-based research. In short, they are immersed in the information world of LIS.

Each semester, students return to campus for one face-to-face class session. These classes are clustered over four or five days, informally known as "LEEP Weekend." Currently, LEEP enrollment has stabilized at around 225 students per year, constituting a full half of the master's-level LIS students at UI.

Access to Collections and Services

LEEP students and faculty expect and deserve the same level of library support that their on-campus peers enjoy. Table 1 lists the many collections, discovery tools, and services that are available to LEEP students. These include:

- An online catalog of print holdings, and increasingly electronic holdings (http://www.library.uiuc.edu/catalog).
- ILLINET Online, a combined catalog for a consortium of fifty-six academic libraries in the state (http://library.ilcso.illinois.edu/ilcso/cgi-bin/welcome).
- A searchable database of thousands of full-text electronic journals and dozens of indexing and abstracting services, many of which also include full-text articles (http://www.library.uiuc.edu/ersearch/).
- Alphabetic menus of subject-specific electronic journals (for example, the LIS list at http://www.library.uiuc.edu/lsx/ejournals.php).
- Numerous online reference tools linked from the UIUC Library Web pages.

In short, the UIUC offers a substantial digital collection, plus useful online tools for mining its print collection. Like most academic libraries, the UIUC Library maintains a proxy server to facilitate off-campus use of licensed resources.

The library's advances in electronic access reflect the inexorable move of academic libraries into the Web environment, to the benefit of all users, not just those at a distance. However, the LEEP program was the impetus for several new online services, including:

- Electronic course reserves (http://www.library.uiuc.edu/lsx/reserves.htm).
- A Virtual New Books Shelf that spotlights new print acquisitions in library and information science (http://www.library.uiuc.edu/lsx/acquis.htm).
- A collection of electronic books in LIS licensed from netLibrary (http://www.netlibrary.com).

TABLE 1

SERVICE	University Library	Academic Outreach Library	LIS Library	Reference Library	Graduate School of LIS
Online catalog	●				
Consortial catalog	●				
E-journals and indexes	●		●	●	
Online reference tools	●		●	●	
Proxy server	●				
E-reserves			●		●
Virtual new books shelf			●		
E-books	●		●	●	
Article delivery		●			
Book delivery		●			
ILL	●				
Toll-free phone reference		●	●		
E-mail reference		●	●	●	
Internet chat reference				●	
On-site tours			●		
On-site training		●	●		●
Live chat training/BI			●		
Online tutorial			●		
Web links, FAQs, etc.	●	●	●	●	●

Of course, despite the wealth of information online, distant students must consult printed materials from the UI library collections. To do so, they place requests for individual items through a Web form. Books are retrieved and sent via a commercial courier to the requester's home or office. Journal articles are retrieved, copied, and sent as either photocopies or password-protected computer files. Distant students are not limited to the UIUC's holdings; they may ask the library staff to obtain books and articles from other libraries on their behalf. Access to print materials is free-of-charge except for the cost of return postage.

Access to librarian-mediated reference and assistance services is arguably as important as access to collections. LEEP students and faculty interact with expert librarians in several ways:

- Toll-free phone numbers to reference and help desks.
- E-mail reference service, provided by both generalist librarians and subject specialists.
- An Internet chat line (also known as "virtual reference" at http://www.library.uiuc.edu/ugl/vr).

UIUC campus libraries also provide various FAQs and search tips through their Web pages. In addition, I regularly scan the general-purpose Web boards maintained by the school for LEEP and on-campus students, looking for queries that I can answer using library resources. Sometimes frantic Web board postings are the first indication that a critical e-resource is "down." The LEEP experience confirms that using multiple media for student-librarian communication promotes the full integration of the library into distance learning.

In such a rich information environment, students can become disoriented and frustrated, especially when trying to navigate among multiple resources from a distance. Therefore, bibliographic instruction is incorporated into the boot camp for incoming LEEP students. I introduce them to the online catalog, core indexes and abstracts, and special features of the library's Web site during two hands-on sessions in a computer lab. They are also taught how to access library resources remotely and how to request delivery of printed materials. In addition, new LEEP students tour the physical library. An optional online tutorial focuses on understanding the concepts of scholarly publishing and peer review and on identifying research articles (http://www.library. uiuc.edu/lsx/tutorial/tutorial.html). Throughout the year, when invited by instructors, I participate in online classes, meet with classes during LEEP Weekend, and prepare class-specific resource guides.

Organizational Structures and Cooperation

As Table 1 indicates, provision of library services for LEEP involves several partners. This is not unusual. Except for a few brand-new online institutions, distance education programs everywhere are layered over existing curricula and campus organizational structures. At a large university like the UIUC, the pre-existing organization is extremely complex, and the library's organization mirrors that complexity. Several units and numerous individuals must work together to meet the information needs of LEEP students and faculty. The five key players are:

- the University Library and its consortial partners, which provide centralized services such as the online catalog and technology support.
- the Academic Outreach Library.
- the Library & Information Science (LIS) Library.
- the virtual reference service administered by the Reference Library and the Undergraduate Library.
- the instructional technology staff and teaching faculty of GSLIS.

Let's take a closer look at what each of these partners contributes. It may seem unnecessary to list basic services such as the online catalog and the proxy server, since these have been installed to benefit *all* our users. Yet without these core infrastructure elements, it would be impossible to deliver quality distance education library services. Continued monitoring and maintenance of electronic services by the University Library's Systems Office is critical. While the LIS Library and the Reference Library bear some costs for acquiring electronic materials, the Systems Office assures that access is rarely interrupted (and quickly restored when interruptions do occur) and is as seamless for the user as technologies and vendors allow. Other central services, including Acquisitions and Cataloging, also provide critical support.

The Academic Outreach Library (http://www.continuinged.uiuc.edu/ao/library) is the unit charged to provide basic library support for distance education at UIUC. Possessing no collections, either physical or digital, of its own, the Academic Outreach Library consists of an office staffed by a librarian and a part-time student assistant, who provide a spectrum of services to off-campus students in all disciplines. The unit is responsible for retrieving and delivering books and articles from the UIUC library collections, and its Web site serves distant students as a gateway to the campus libraries. The Academic Outreach Library is funded and administered through the University's Division of Academic Outreach, which handles student enrollment for off-campus courses and thus certifies that students are eligible for these special no-cost library services. The Academic Outreach Library was earlier known as the Extramural Library, and for a period its funding and staffing were aligned with the University Library's Circulation Department. Today it operates as a separate unit but is still housed in the Main Library building.

The LIS Library (http://www.library.uiuc.edu/lsx) serves the faculty and students of GSLIS, as well as supporting the research and practice of more than a hundred UIUC faculty librarians. It offers a full range of traditional services and houses a collection of books, journals, and non-print media reflecting the range of the LIS curriculum, from information architecture and interface design to cataloging and storytelling. The LIS Library licenses indexes, journals, and other reference materials for online access, and its Web site serves as a gateway to both local and global LIS information. As a "departmental" or branch library, the LIS Library operates semi-autonomously, controlling its own collection budget but depending on centralized cataloging, systems maintenance, and other functions. The discipline-based departmental libraries are fundamental to the library organization at the UI–there are over forty of them–and the LIS Library has long been perceived as the primary provider of services to LIS faculty and students, whether on campus or at a distance. LIS students and faculty are welcome in all campus libraries, but the

LIS Library is their "home library." In addition to myself, the library is staffed by a library specialist, a library clerk, a part-time (.38 FTE) graduate assistant, and several undergraduate student assistants.

A new provider of library service to LEEP students emerged in the spring of 2001, when the Reference Library and the Undergraduate Library began collaborating to provide a real-time text chat reference service over the Web (Kibbee, Ward, and Ma, 2002). The Reference Library and the Undergraduate Library do not have such sharply delineated constituencies as either the Academic Outreach Library or the LIS Library, although organizationally they are positioned like departmental libraries. Their virtual reference service was not developed to support distance education in particular, but rather as a service for the entire UIUC community. Ask-a-Librarian has proven very popular with LEEP students, and the LIS Library actively promotes it.

The final player is GSLIS, which collaborates with the LIS Library on many levels. The school's technology staff facilitated the set-up of software and file transfer processes for the electronic reserves service and continue to provide technical advice and server space. The LEEP home page prominently displays links to library Web pages. Several instructors strengthen connections between students and the library by inviting me to lecture in online class sessions or by scheduling "library time" during LEEP Weekends. When students experience difficulties accessing online information, staff at GSLIS and the library must often cooperate to resolve the problem.

On some campuses, such as the University of Wisconsin-Madison or Florida State University, the LIS library is administratively part of the library school and is co-located with faculty offices and classrooms. At the UIUC, it is part of the University Library and is located within the Main Library complex, about three blocks from the school. This organizational and physical distance makes collaboration more difficult–and all the more valued when it succeeds.

With so many departments involved, coordination and cooperation are the keys to library support for LEEP. The UIUC library service configuration recognizes the strengths and weaknesses of the various cooperating units. The LIS Library staff, for example, is ideally suited, by virtue of their disciplinary expertise, to assist students with in-depth research questions and to introduce them to the literature and search strategies most useful in LIS. However, the LIS Library is not equipped to provide home delivery of materials. The Academic Outreach Library, on the other hand, despite its small staff and the growing demands placed on it, responds quickly to delivery requests. Neither the LIS Library nor the Academic Outreach Library can reply to user queries promptly outside normal office hours, but the virtual reference chat line is available on nights and weekends–a real boon to students in other time zones. The librarians and staff in each unit have forged solid working relationships, make frequent referrals to each other's services, team-teach workshops for new students, and collaborate to solve remote users' technical problems.

LIS DISTANCE EDUCATION: WHAT MAKES IT DIFFERENT?

Most of the dynamics that drive library support for LIS distance education are the same as those in any field. The information needs and learning styles of adult students, and the opportunities and limitations of computer-mediated communication, for example, are dimensions of distance ed librarianship that transcend disciplinary specialties. Nonetheless, I've concluded that three factors are uniquely influential in shaping library services for LIS distance education. They are:

- The nature of the graduate LIS curriculum.
- The physical library.
- The ideals of the library profession.

The Information-Intensive LIS Graduate Curriculum

In professional studies such as LIS, students are expected to attain a high level of disciplinary information literacy, so that they can seek and find the information they will need to stay current throughout their careers. LIS students are frequently required to demonstrate their information skills by producing bibliographies, pathfinders, and Web sites, in addition to traditional term papers. The LIS curriculum is arguably among the most demanding in its emphasis on independent information-seeking, since information retrieval and use lie at the heart of the discipline. This is reflected in statistics compiled by UIUC's Academic Outreach Library. In the spring 2003, LEEP students represented only 21% of the total student population enrolled in distance courses at the UIUC, yet they constituted 63% of the users of the Academic Outreach Library (P. Cardenas, personal communication, December 2, 2003). The LIS subject specialist at the University of Washington Libraries, although unable to provide quantitative measures, confirms that the LIS distance education courses on her campus are "very resource-intensive" (N. Huling, personal communication, December 2, 2003).

The information-intensive curriculum is problematic in light of the relative scarcity of LIS collections (Wagner & Dalrymple, 2003, p. 21). Only forty-nine graduate LIS programs in the U.S. are accredited by the American Library Association; nineteen states have no program within their borders. Paradoxically, while the scarcity of programs contributes to the popularity of distance education options, it complicates the students' task of finding information resources close to home to support their coursework. In other disciplines, such as business, students may turn to nearby colleges or even well stocked public libraries. But institutions that don't offer an LIS degree are unlikely to hold expensive core resources such as *Library & Information Science Abstracts*. Even if nearby libraries subscribe to a few practical journals or purchase how-to guides for their own staff, these in-house professional collections may not be accessible to the general public. The phenomenon of the "victim library" burdened by the demands of unaffiliated users has been noted in the literature (Dugan, 1997), but alas, distant learners in LIS have few libraries to victimize when seeking the specialized literature of the profession. The pressure is squarely on the host institution to satisfy distant LIS students' information needs.

The Enduring Value of the Library as Place

The library is often lauded as the ideal setting for intellectual discovery, contemplation, and inspiration, as embodied in the photographs of Diane Asséo Griliches (1996) or the literary excerpts anthologized by Susan Allen Toth and John Coughlan (1991). What meaning does the physical library hold for the distant learner or teacher? Do distant users need to understand how the physical collections are organized?

As noted earlier, the UIUC library is decentralized, with collections and service points spread over a vast campus. On-campus students and faculty are initially bewildered by the departmental library system, but over time they discover which libraries in addition to their "home" library are necessary to their research. For off-campus students, the physical scatter of collections and expertise is both less and more problematic. On the one hand, they are spared trudging from library to library to retrieve books and articles; they can simply request any materials they need through the Academic Outreach Library. On the other hand, they struggle mightily to comprehend the University Library's organization, perhaps because they don't experience the kinetic learning that cements on-campus students' understanding of what's where.

LEEP students value a systematic introduction to the physical organization of library resources. When asked to evaluate their library orientation sessions, they consistently praise the short tour of the LIS Library and associated service points in the main library building. The tour presents the library in a friendly light and begins the process of building relationships between the LIS Library staff and individual students. It gives students a framework to think about the LIS Library and the wider University Library, which they may unconsciously draw upon as they navigate its Web pages, since large segments of the University Library's Web space mirror the departmental library organization. In an era when many librarians eschew tours in favor of asynchronous online tutorials, the reactions of LEEP students are a reminder that a sense of place still matters.

The Ideals of the Profession of Librarianship

Noting an "obvious connection between the provision of library services and the education of future information providers," Latham and Smith (2003) declare that "it would be especially ironic and vexing if students enrolled in LIS distance education programs were receiving limited and/or inferior services" (p. 122). This does not seem to be the case. In fact, librarians may feel inspired to deliver the highest quality service to this constituency. In the case of the LIS Library at UIUC, the small staff added LEEP support to an already full set of responsibilities. At the same time, LEEP brought new energy and excitement to our work and granted us greater scope to apply the ideals of our profession.

The LIS Library staff members and I believe that students do not learn about LIS solely through reading and in-class experiences, but also through their interactions with information professionals. We share this sentiment with a number of the librarians who participated in Wynkoop's survey. "Library students need role models," one respondent asserted. "It is invaluable to have face-to-face contact with experienced librarians" wrote another (Wynkoop, 2003). On-campus LIS students have many opportunities to form relationships with campus librarians as role models or mentors. The more isolated LEEP students, especially those not concurrently employed in libraries, have fewer opportunities to observe professionals in action and to shape their own service ideals on the basis of the service they receive. Therefore, as the students study the ethics and values of librarianship, we strive to model them by adhering to high standards for service and responsiveness.

It isn't always easy. LEEP has disrupted the familiar rhythm of our academic year. We feel the greatest stress when LEEP students are actually on campus and making intensive use of the library. The ten-day summer boot camp includes a highly condensed course, "Libraries, Information and Society," which features several assignments that require students to seek information beyond the textbook. The mid-semester LEEP Weekends are likewise extremely busy. Every fall, for example, the large "Information Organization and Access" class gathers for a half-day "research fest" in the LIS library. During on-campus sessions, we juggle work schedules to provide extra hours of reference assistance and workshops on evenings and weekends. The LEEP calendar now governs many areas of the LIS Library's operations, from when we send journal volumes for binding to when we take vacations. Even routine interactions take on a distinctive tone. Responding to an e-mail reference question from a LEEP student, I'll embellish the answer with the details of how I found the information. The average library user is only interested in the answer, but students of LIS need to understand the process as well.

Like the students, faculty, and staff of LEEP, the library staff finds energy and inspiration in the community of online learners and teachers to which we now belong. We have a vital role in preparing the new generation of librarians and information workers and in helping to shape new modes of teaching and learning. Within the larger library organization, we are perceived as doing interesting and cutting-edge work, blazing a trail for other departmental libraries.

CONCLUSION

Although LIS distance education programs vary greatly in their delivery modes, they all require adequate library support to produce tomorrow's information professionals. The UIUC provides one model in its library support for LEEP, which involves intensive cooperation and task-sharing both within and outside the library. The experience of providing library services to LEEP suggests that LIS distance education library services, while sharing many attributes with library services to distant learners and teachers in other disciplines, also have three distinguishing features. First, greater demands are made due to the information-intensive nature of the curriculum. Second, students place a high value on understanding the physical nature of the library. And third, the librarians with whom students interact become role models–positive or negative–as the students develop their own ideals of service and professionalism. Librarians serving LIS distance education programs face increased workloads due to these factors, but their role in online learning is the natural outgrowth of the profession's mission and ideals.

REFERENCES

ALA accredited LIS programs that provide distance education opportunities. (2001). Retrieved December 1, 2003, from: http://www.ala.org/Template.cfm?Section= lisdir&Template=/ContentManagement/ContentDispla y.cfm&ContentID=24819.
ALISE library and information science education statistical report 2002. (2002). Reston, VA: Association for Library and Information Science Education.

Alzamil, M. A. (2002). Perceptions of Internet use as academic library services' delivery medium for Web-based courses. *Dissertation Abstracts International, 62,* 3609A. (UMI number AAT 3034039).

Barron, D. D. (1987). Perceived use of off-campus libraries by students in library and information science. In B. M. Lessin (Ed.), *The Off-Campus Library Services Conference Proceedings* (pp. 56-64). Mt. Pleasant, MI: Central Michigan University Press. Retrieved December 1, 2003, from: http://ocls.cmich.edu/3rdOCLSCP.pdf.

Barron, D. D. (Ed.) (2003). *Benchmarks in distance education: The LIS experience.* Westport, CT: Libraries Unlimited.

Burnett, K., & Painter, M. (2001). Learning from experience: Strategies for assuring effective library and information services to Web-based distance learners. In H. A. Thompson (Ed.), *Crossing the Divide: Proceedings of the Tenth National Conference of the Association of College and Research Libraries* (pp. 131-136). Chicago: Association of College and Research Libraries. Retrieved December 1, 2003, from: http://www.ala.org/Content/NavigationMenu/ACRL/Events_and_Conferences/ burnett.pdf.

Douglas, G. (2002). Speaking out: Analysis of experiences and opinions reported by recent graduates of the University of South Carolina's MLIS program. *Journal of Education for Library and Information Science, 43*(1), 16-31.

Dugan, R. E. (1997). Distance education: Provider and victim libraries. *Journal of Academic Librarianship, 23*(4), 315-318.

Griliches, D. A. (1996). *Library: The drama within.* Albuquerque: University of New Mexico Press.

Hoy, C. & Hale, M. L. (1991). A comparison of references cited by on-campus and off-campus graduate library science students. In C. J. Jacob [Comp.], *The Fifth Off-Campus Library Services Conference Proceeding* (pp. 123-127). Mount Pleasant, MI: Central Michigan University. Retrieved December 1, 2003, from: http:// ocls.cmich.edu/5thOCLSCP.pdf.

Kazmer, M. M. (2002). Distance education students speak to the library: Here's how you can help even more. *The Electronic Library, 20*(5), 395-400.

Kibbee, J., Ward, D., & Ma, W. (2002). Virtual service, real data: Results of a pilot study. *Reference Services Review, 30*(1), 25-36.

Kim, M. T. & Rogers, A. R. (1983). Libraries for librarians: Identifying and evaluating resources for off-campus graduate programs in library and information science. In B. M. Lessin (Ed.), *The Off-Campus Library Services Conference Proceedings* (pp. 191-200). Mt. Pleasant, MI: Central Michigan University Press.

Latham, D. & Smith, S. M. (2003). Practicing what we teach: A descriptive analysis of library services for distance learning students in ALA-accredited LIS schools. *Journal of Education for Library and Information Science, 44*(2), 120-133.

Nardi, B. A., & O'Day, V. L. (1999). *Information ecologies: Using technology with heart.* Cambridge, MA: MIT Press.

Searing, S. E. (2004). Reshaping traditional services for non-traditional learning: The LEEP student in the library. In C. Haythornthwaite & M. M. Kazmer (Eds.), *Learning, Culture and Community in Online Education: Research and Practice.* New York: Peter Lang.

Stephens, K. (1998). The library experiences of postgraduate distance learning students or *Alice's Other Story*. In P. Brophy, S. Fisher, & Z. Clarke (Eds.), *Libraries Without Walls 2: The Delivery of Library Services to Distant Users* (pp. 122-142). London: Library Association Publishing.

Toth, S. A., & Coughlan, D. J. (1991). *Reading rooms*. New York: Doubleday.

U.S. News & World Report. (2004). *America's best graduate schools 2004: Library science (ranked in 1999)*. Retrieved December 1, 2003, from: http://www.usnews.com/usnews/edu/grad/rankings/lib/brief/infos_brief.php.

Wagner, M., & Dalrymple, P. (2003). Dominican University (River Forest, IL) and the College of St. Catherine (St. Paul, MN) distance learning experience. In D. D. Barron (Ed.), *Benchmarks in Distance Education: The LIS Experience* (pp. 13-22). Westport, CT: Libraries Unlimited.

Wynkoop, M. (2003). *Hiring preferences in libraries: Perceptions of MLS graduates with online degrees*. Retrieved December 1, 2003, from: http://www.camden.lib.nj.us/survey/default.htm.

Strategic Planning
for Distance Learning Services

Anne Marie Secord
Robin Lockerby
Laura Roach
Joe Simpson

National University

SUMMARY. National University Library began a 12-month journey in 2002-2003 to undergo an intensive self study. It involved the entire central library staff as well as the regional librarians in the Library Information Centers, student and faculty focus groups, staff, and library peers. The outcome of the self study is a strategic plan that identifies mission, vision, goals, and objectives that will strengthen the Library's role as a decisive force of National University's graduates.

KEYWORDS. Library services, distance learners, study

INTRODUCTION

National University is the second-largest private university in California, serving a population of nearly 17,200 full-time equivalent students, principally adult learners. This unique distance learning community is spread out across California at 29 distinct academic learning centers, off-site programs,

[Haworth co-indexing entry note]: "Strategic Planning for Distance Learning Services." Secord. Anne Marie et al. Co-published simultaneously in *Journal of Library Administration* (The Haworth Information Press, an imprint of The Haworth Press, Inc.) Vol. 41, No. 3/4, 2004, pp. 407-411; and: *The Eleventh Off-Campus Library Services Conference Proceedings* (ed: Patrick B. Mahoney) The Haworth Information Press, an imprint of The Haworth Press, Inc., 2004, pp. 407-411.

http://www.haworthpress.com/web/JLA
Digital Object Identifier: 10.1300/J111v41n03_06

as well as a thriving online program. Most classes are offered in the evening on a one course/month format–ideal for working adult learners. The fact that there is no "central" campus is a major challenge in providing timely access to resources and services, both face-to-face and remote.

The Strategic Plan comes at an important point in the Library's development, following the opening in 2000 of a state-of-the-art central library in San Diego and the establishment of satellite facilities–the Library Information Centers (LICs)–at the regional centers. The creation of this new organization offers the opportunity to review and streamline the provision of library and information services on a university-wide basis, in order to take advantage of the new structure and of relevant developments in information technology. The process began with one simple question: How can the library system become a more valuable asset for the National University System as a whole? This, of course, led to more questions which ultimately resulted in the NU Library's Strategic Plan: *Thinking Forward: Innovating, Connecting, and Delivering*.

MISSION AND VISION

National University is dedicated to making lifelong learning opportunities accessible, challenging, and relevant to a diverse population of adult learners. Its aim is to facilitate educational access and academic excellence through exceptional management of University operations and resources, innovative delivery systems and student services, and relevant programs that are learner-centered, success-oriented, and responsive to technology. National University's central purpose is to promote continuous learning by offering a diversity of instructional approaches, by encouraging scholarship, by engaging in collaborative community service, and by empowering its constituents to become responsible citizens in an independent, pluralistic, global community.

As part of the strategic planning process, the Library developed mission and vision statements to serve as a philosophical basis for library planning and to provide a context for the framing of individual goals and objectives. This process began with the central library staff and LIC librarians meeting with an organizational development consultant, George Soete, to examine the relationship of the Library and the University and to identify shared views of what the library should be. The outcomes of this discussion are a revised mission and eight vision statements that further elaborate the mission and serve as guides when later defining the Library's goals and objectives.

- The Library will create an information-literate community through a state-of-the-art instructional program.
- The Library will purchase the electronic and print resources needed by its community of scholars and students, or provide quick access to what it does not own.
- The Library will be proactive and creative in reaching out, in order to anticipate and respond to community needs for resources, programs, and services.
- The Library will be a customer-driven organization, constantly inviting feedback, measuring quality, and making appropriate adjustments.
- The Library will foster learning among its staff, enabling staff to become as skilled and successful as possible.
- The Library will provide for its community the most up-to-date technology possible for the delivery of information resources.
- The Library will join the University in its effort to improve the quality of the National University experience for the entire community.
- The Library will become experienced and successful at fund-raising.

PLANNING PROCESS–A VIEW FROM THE LIC

The National University Library System Strategic Plan is valuable because input was not only solicited but welcomed from a variety of members of the National University community. The regional librarians and center faculty/staff appreciate the opportunity to be part of planning that will directly affect their operations. Other participants in the planning process included external stakeholders, peer group analysis, and review from the Library Management Committee. The LIC librarians were encouraged to participate in several planning meetings with the organizational development consultant and to gather input from their respective campuses through the use of focus groups and/or exit surveys. The result of the LIC participation is that several LIC points of view were included in the Value/Vision and Goal statements.

Participation in the various data processes was varied. Faculty invited to participate as a focus group saw it as a sign of status and came begging to participate. Students, on the other hand, seemed to have their lives scheduled too heavily and it was difficult to solicit their participation or find a convenient time for a focus group to meet. This was true for the central library and the LICs. Online survey, student focus groups, exit surveys, and handing out surveys to library instruction classes all netted low responses, but the results were consistent with other library data from the staff. The whole process was one of active participation for the LIC librarians–front line interfacing with students and staff.

GOALS AND OBJECTIVES

The Strategic Plan sets out a framework within which the Library System can continue to develop as a center of excellence within the National University system. The goals and objectives listed represent the immediate priorities of the Library for the next several years and form the basis for more specific action items and annual assessments. Seven key strategic issues were identified from the numerous sources of input received during the strategic planning process. After extensive discussion and analysis, these were transformed into a set of goals and objectives to guide the annual budget and program planning processes that are tied to the University's six core values: access, relevance, accelerated pace, affordability, and quality. The Library's identified strategic goals and objectives are listed in the appendix of this proposal.

The overall success of this plan will hinge not only on following the actions that are laid out in the goals and objectives, but also in periodically revisiting them to assess their relevance again and again. Time and circumstances can change more rapidly than one expects. Old technologies may lose their usefulness, while new technologies will be developed that need to be embraced quickly. Budget pressures may necessitate mid-course corrections, and finally, as with all such plans, at some point it will reach its intended lifespan. At that time, the cycle should begin again.

CONCLUSION

As a record of where we have been, this plan and the process of developing it have been an enlightening journey for many. The new Central Library stands as a landmark for the library services the NU community can now expect, while the LICs present a cohesive library face to those members of the NU community located outside San Diego. The Library's Web site is and by its nature will always be a work in progress.

As a record of where we plan to go, the process has forced us to think in terms of outward directions. The information business is changing too fast to do otherwise. The change from a strictly bricks-and-mortar institution to a "clicks-and-mortar" one has taken place much faster than we could have anticipated. We must continually assess the information needs of our patrons and work to see that they are satisfied.

For a process that involved all levels of the Library staff and many levels of the University community at large, the result has been worth the effort. The time involved to complete the project has extended beyond original estimates. However, the increased level of communication, from the collective involvement of the staff, was a benefit that could not have been achieved any other way.

The Library will use this plan to shape ourselves and our services over the next several years. At the end of that time, we will be the final arbiters of how well we succeeded.

REFERENCE

National University Library. (2003). *Thinking forward: Innovating, connecting, and delivering: The strategic plan of the National University Library System.* San Diego: National University. From http://libweb3.nu.edu/sp/.

A Systematic Approach to Assessing the Needs of Distance Faculty

Janette Shaffer

Georgetown University Medical Center

Kate Finkelstein

George Washington University Medical Center

Nancy Woelfl
Elizabeth Lyden

University of Nebraska Medical Center

SUMMARY. Beginning in the 1990s, various academic units within our health sciences institution moved aggressively toward providing courses and programs via distance education. Without a centralized campus distance education office, distance library services from our campus evolved sporadically in response to individual needs. In 2001, the library hired its first distance services librarian, whose primary responsibility was to develop a written distance library services plan. In accordance with the ACRL *Guidelines for Distance Learning Library Services*, the library determined that the formulation of an effective plan required a formal needs assessment of the faculty providing distance education. In this paper, we will discuss the process for developing this needs assessment, based on focus groups and a written survey instrument. We will also address some of the challenges we faced with this approach. Preliminary data identified copyright clearance and lack of

[Haworth co-indexing entry note]: "A Systematic Approach to Assessing the Needs of Distance Faculty." Shaffer, Janette et al. Co-published simultaneously in *Journal of Library Administration* (The Haworth Information Press, an imprint of The Haworth Press, Inc.) Vol. 41, No. 3/4, 2004, pp. 413-428; and: *The Eleventh Off-Campus Library Services Conference Proceedings* (ed: Patrick B. Mahoney) The Haworth Information Press, an imprint of The Haworth Press, Inc., 2004, pp. 413-428.

http://www.haworthpress.com/web/JLA
Digital Object Identifier: 10.1300/J111v41n03_07

awareness regarding library services as the major barriers to distance faculty seeking course support from the library.

KEYWORDS. Distance education, library services, assessment, faculty

PURPOSE

Academic units of the University of Nebraska Medical Center have used available technologies to incorporate distance education (DE) methods into their curricula since the 1960s. Beginning in the 1990s, they moved aggressively to begin incorporating computer-based distance courses into course offerings and programs. Without a centralized campus distance education office, distance library services evolved sporadically in response to individual instructors. In 2001, the library hired its first distance services librarian, whose primary responsibility was to develop a written distance library services plan. In accord with the ACRL *Guidelines for Distance Learning Library Services* (2000), the library determined the formulation of an effective plan required a formal needs assessment of the faculty who provide distance education. Through this needs assessment, the McGoogan Library hoped to determine:

- which departments and faculty at UNMC offered courses via distance methods;
- which library services and resources these groups currently used; and
- which library services and resources these groups would like to have.

BACKGROUND

The University of Nebraska Medical Center (UNMC) is one of two health sciences centers in a predominantly rural state. UNMC's mission includes improving the health of Nebraskans and does so by educating many of Nebraska's health professionals. Distance Education at UNMC has grown organically, offering new courses and programs as the needs of a profession, faculty interest, and university or grant resources came together. To provide educational services to students across the state, UNMC has experimented with a number of ways to deliver instruction to a distributed student population. In an effort to gain a unified view of DE across UNMC's colleges and schools, a task force appointed by the Chancellor submitted a document in 2002 describing each college's current and projected distance education activities. The 2002 document revealed that each unit was working independently of the others and that none of the units mentioned support from the Library in their plans. Because students enrolled in these programs need Library support and resource access, McGoogan Library found itself in the position of serving a user population without knowing who they are or what they need. This dilemma became more significant when the Library considered that equivalent library services, will be important when UNMC's distance programs go through accreditation processes.

The Library moved to providing access to more electronic databases, journals, and books and many of those resources allowed off-campus access. Promoting access to those resources raised Library faculty's awareness of access issues experienced by remote users. The Library received frequent calls from scattered students who couldn't connect to its resources through the proxy server. Calls sometimes required hours of research and often led to another access issue requiring further attention. Library instructors also found themselves dealing with increasing questions on remote services during instruction sessions. The Library realized it needed a plan to efficiently apply its resources to the growing population of distant users. The Library looked to the ACRL *Guidelines for Distance Learning Library Services* (2000) to begin establishing a model for service. The guidelines recommend that an effective service plan should be based on a thorough needs assessment of the user population.

After McGoogan Library hired its first Distance Services Librarian, the authors began gathering information about the faculty and students involved in Distance Education at UNMC. However, with no central Distance Education office or similar administrative structure, there was no simple way to determine how many distance courses UNMC offered, nor could the Library identify the faculty and students involved in those courses. Because the Library needed basic data such as who is teaching DE and which classes are offered via distance, Library faculty decided that the most useful information would come from faculty teaching Distance Education. The authors also believed the information they would receive from DE faculty would prove valuable later when trying to understand the needs of distance students.

LITERATURE REVIEW

A number of libraries have conducted surveys to assess distance faculty satisfaction with established library support to their distance classes. A review of the literature indicates that the authors conducting the surveys found the results of their needs assessments useful in determining future directions for their library's distance services programs. One can find much more literature on the topic of needs assessments in general and in libraries in particular. The articles discussed below prove pertinent to this particular study because of their focus on library services to distance faculty.

Lebowitz (1993) performed a survey to better understand whether instructors matched their standard on-campus course outlines, assignments and research requirements to the different needs of their off-campus students. She found that although most faculty were aware of a lack of access to services or materials, they did not adjust their distance course requirements accordingly. She also found that most instructors felt that the library skills of off-campus users compared to those of traditional students, but that off-campus students may not have access to services and materials.

Ruddy (1993) describes a survey of distance faculty with a surprisingly low response rate of 18.5% (p. 230). Such a low response rate does not allow for conclusions drawn on the statistical data. However, Ruddy notes, "that of the 24 faculty members who responded, 18 of them believe that PMA students cannot complete their courses without the use of a library. However, when asked if they require their students to use library resources for the modules they teach, only half of the responses were affirmative" (p. 230).

Along the same lines, Craig and DuFord (1995) surveyed the off-campus faculty in the Central Michigan University Extended Degree Programs and found that "seventy-one percent of undergraduate faculty and 84% of graduate faculty required the use of library services/materials [. . .], but only 42% of undergraduate and 35% of graduate faculty indicated that they offered library instruction to their students" (p. 71).

In another article, Lebowitz (1998) gives an in-depth description of the development of a marketing strategy to counteract the perception some educators have that with the advent of the Internet, librarians are no longer needed to find information. Lebowitz's marketing plan begins with an in-depth analysis of user needs and progresses through developing a mission, objectives and goals, a plan for promotion, and evaluation. She asserts that the plan can help organize a library's activities and provide necessary data to support increases in resources.

Adams and Cassner (2000) look at needs assessment prior to marketing existing distance library services. Respondents indicated that many of the faculty already knew of the Library's services and were satisfied with the level of services currently provided. The authors indicate that they intended their survey, "not only to solicit faculty input but also to increase awareness of library resources and services offered to distance instructors and extended education students" (p. 3).

Finally, Jarebek, McMain and Van Roekel (2002) discuss in detail various methods of conducting needs assessments specifically with a view toward planning distance library services. These authors offer a prescription for progress through the needs assessment process while exploring a variety of methodologies and tools. This paper does not report the results of their specific needs assessment, but serves as a valuable tool to those beginning the assessment process.

METHODOLOGY

Focus Groups

The Library started its needs assessment by conducting focus groups. The primary purpose of the focus groups was to determine the perceptions, attitudes and experiences of UNMC distance faculty toward distance library services. The focus group outcome would serve as the base for a subsequent survey. The authors also asked focus group attendees to help identify further survey participants.

The Library recruited focus group participants from a small pool of faculty whom the authors had identified as already involved in distance education. A total of 13 invitees agreed to participate. The authors divided the participants into two groups–one consisting of UNMC faculty who had considerable experience with distance education, and one of faculty with minimal DE experience.

Faced with the question of how to best facilitate the focus groups, the library provided the funds to hire a professional facilitator with extensive marketing experience. Participants were able to speak freely allowing the facilitator to evaluate the interactions and provided complete transcripts with an executive summary highlighting significant and recurring themes.

Survey

The authors developed the survey instrument directly from the results of the focus groups. With the survey, the authors aimed to capture the distance education experience of faculty, their perceived barriers to using library services and their expectations of distance student's library skills.

The decentralized nature of distance education efforts at UNMC created a challenge to the authors in locating survey participants. In addition to focus group peer recommendations, the authors solicited participants through announcements in the campus daily newsletter. They also gathered attendance lists from DE meetings and conferences held around campus.

The survey process stalled just as the authors began recruiting for the study. Faculty in health care institutions, including librarians, are required to comply with regulations for the protection of human subjects, administered by an Institutional Review Board (IRB). If a publication will result from survey research, the IRB must review the research plan and survey instruments to insure the rights of subjects are not violated. The library had not applied for the appropriate review and as a result, could not publish the findings of the initial focus groups. After completing the necessary paperwork for review of the DE survey, the investigators were informed they could proceed with the survey but only after each member of the research team completed a nationally recognized online course in human subjects protection. Approximately six months elapsed before the library could solicit survey participants.

The Library mailed 60 written surveys via campus mail with a 50% return goal. The survey packet included a letter of introduction containing a return deadline for the survey, and a self-addressed return envelope (Appendix). After approximately two weeks, the authors sent e-mail reminders to all survey recipients. Twenty-nine respondents returned surveys (48%) and the authors regarded them as representative of the target group.

The library compiled the data in MS Excel. The authors consulted a UNMC professional statistician for help in performing inferential analysis.

Results

An eleven-item questionnaire was administered to determine to what extent issues identified by focus group participants could be generalized to the larger population of distance educators at UNMC. Given the promotion of distance education within the entire University of Nebraska system and as a strategic initiative at UNMC, the authors were interested in learning how well distance education had taken root at UNMC. Understanding faculty use of library services and factors that encouraged or discouraged use of library resources were primary objectives.

Ten questionnaire items asked respondents to provide data in the form of yes/no answers and rankings. The eleventh item was an open-ended question that gave respondents a chance to identify library resources or services that would better support their teaching activities. Data related to age, gender, and the respondent's academic unit (i.e., medicine, nursing) were not collected because the subgroups that resulted would have had little value for analytic purposes.

Participants were asked when they had presented their first distance education course (Q1) and the number of unique distance education courses they had developed or taught (Q2). Respondents (n = 29) indicated they had been engaged in distance education an average of six years, seven months and had developed or taught five unique courses. Respondents reported DE teaching experience ranging from 2 to 247 months and it was assumed the longer a faculty member had offered distance education courses, the greater the number of courses he or she had developed. This assumption proved incorrect: there was no association between the total DE teaching time and the number of courses faculty developed (r = .18, p = .38).

Nearly two-thirds of the respondents indicated they had used library resources or services to support their classes (Q3). Subjects were queried about barriers that limited or discouraged use of library resources for class support (Q4). Based on factors identified by focus group participants, they were given ten choices and asked to rank their four most significant obstacles on a scale of 1 to 4, with "1" representing the most significant obstacle. Forcing respondents to limit their choices and rank the barriers served as a weighting mechanism to identify the primary obstacles that discourage DE faculty use of library resources at UNMC. Results are shown in Table 1.

Copyright clearance emerged as the most significant obstacle, with lack of awareness of library services and disqualification from library resources as second and third most significant respectively.

More than seventy percent of the responding faculty (73%) indicated they require distance students to use library resources or services (Q5) and for the most part (92%), they expect distance students to have the same library skills as their campus-based counterparts (Q6). Sixty-eight percent indicated they would be willing to allocate class time to library skills training (Q8).

Table 2 illustrates faculty rankings of various methods of providing distance students with library skills (Q7). Faculty were asked to rank six methods on a scale of 1 to 6 with "1" indicating what they perceived to be the most effective instructional method.

Though many instructional faculty assume distance students have the library skills they need, library faculty face the reality of students of all types who are ill-equipped to take advantage of the available resources. Given the high percentage of faculty requiring use of library resources in their courses and their expectation of distance student competency, these data were correlated with methods of bibliographic instruction. Not surprisingly, faculty who believe students do not need library skills were unwilling to give class time to library instruction (p = .24) as were faculty who assume students will ask a librarian for help (p = .54). Faculty who rated in-class orientation as an important method of student bibliographic training were willing to give class time to it (p = .0027) as were those who try to teach library skills themselves (p = .0035). Some faculty who assume students have library skills were still willing

TABLE 1. Obstacles to Distance Faculty Use of Library Resources

Rank	Score	Obstacles to Use of Library Resources (n = 29)
1	1.46	Obtaining copyright clearance
2	1.5	Unaware of library distance education support services
3	1.66	Class doesn't qualify for library support because it is offered through Division of Continuing Education
4	2.31	Lack of online journals and textbooks for subject
5	2.33	Other
6	2.4	My distance students lack the technology to access the library electronically
7	2.4	Library distance procedures are too complicated for students
8	2.43	Didn't consider using the library for support
9	2.66	Library doesn't subscribe to the materials needed
10	4	Library procedures are too complicated for me

TABLE 2. Methods for Providing Library Skills

Rank	Score	Method
1	2.1	I assume students at this level already have the skills needed
2	2.2	In-class orientation by library faculty
3	2.62	I assume students will ask a librarian for help if needed
4	2.75	I advise students to contact a librarian for help if needed
5	3.78	Students don't need special library skills for my classes
6	5.1	I teach library skills to my students

to give class time (p = .0712) as were those who actively advise students to consult librarians outside class (p = .0712).

To determine how faculty expected students to obtain the required course materials, they were asked to rank five access methods on a scale of 1 to 5, with "1" indicating the most effective/reliable/successful method (Q9). These data are shown in Table 3.

Instructors clearly saw personal copies of printed materials as the most reliable way to deliver course materials to students. Electronic journals, document delivery services, and Internet resources were also seen as useful. As indicated by a fifth place ranking, leaving students to struggle on their own was the least acceptable alternative for faculty.

Because copyright clearance ranked high on the list of instructor barriers to use of library resources, faculty were asked if they had ever chosen a freely available Internet resource over a potentially more appropriate peer reviewed article due the cost or difficulty of obtaining copyright permission (Q10). Fifty-four percent indicated they had done so.

TABLE 3. Delivery of Course Materials

Rank	Score	Method of Delivery (n = 29)
1	1.7	Purchase printed materials (course packs, textbooks)
2	2.2	Electronic journal access or document delivery through library, excluding course reserves
3	2.4	Freely available Internet resources (not through library)
4	2.8	Electronic reserves
5	3.9	Figuring out how to get course materials is part of the student's self-education

When these data were correlated with data regarding barriers to faculty library use (Q4), it was assumed there would be a positive relationship between personal difficulty obtaining copyrighted materials for course use and the choice of freely available Internet resources for students. That is, if a faculty member had difficulty getting access to readings personally, s/he would be unlikely to assign them as course material. Surprisingly, there was no association between these two variables ($p = 1.0$). Faculty who indicated they had experienced copyright difficulties obtaining information did not necessarily refrain from using them as course materials.

DISCUSSION

The lack of association between the time a faculty member had been engaged in distance education and the number of courses developed should be reexamined in light of the outliers previously noted in the data. The lack of association between the two variables suggests that once instructional faculty have translated their traditional lecture materials into a computer-based format, little innovation occurs. The same factors that control the development of lecture-based materials may also apply to distance education materials. Faculty teach within a discipline and subspecialize within the discipline. Once a revolutionary change in format or presentation medium occurs (lecture versus computer), change is incremental. The faculty member, who has mastered both learning curves, becomes comfortable with the content and the technology, forgetting students have a steep learning curve with both the content and the technology. The implication for library support is that librarians find themselves in the position of educating students in the use of these technologies on a one-to-one basis as the students experience problems. A few moments of instruction from the Library to each distance class as a whole could decrease the number of times various librarians have to re-solve the same problems for the same student groups.

Use of library resources to support distance education is the practice with the majority of faculty. Given this fact, one must ask why 34% of UNMC faculty indicate they do not use them. Table 1 indicates the third ranked obstacle to use of library DE resources is disqualification, an obstacle that is closely related to copyright permissions. When signing licenses, the library must have a criterion for identifying authorized users.

The second biggest barrier, lack of awareness of library support for DE, indicates that the Library needs to focus on publicizing those services. The difficulties of marketing to this population are the same difficulties that the authors experienced in trying to identify survey participants. While challenging, the library now knows that identifying DE faculty is not impossible. Continued contact with this group requires focused effort.

Lack of relevant electronic resources emerged as the fourth ranked obstacle to use of library resources. The majority of DE courses at UNMC come from the nursing and allied health disciplines–areas for which there are few electronic resources available. As more electronic materials become available to support those disciplines, McGoogan hopes to lessen the impact of that particular barrier.

Table 2 presents another significant issue: the faculty perception that DE students already have the library skills they need. DE students need two skill sets–research skills (knowledge of search engines and databases) and telecommunication skills that allow them to access the Internet and connect to the appropriate device. Even if instructional faculty correctly assess the research skills, they overestimate student telecommunication skills, especially for their first DE course. This suggests librarians need to target their marketing and interventions to the first DE course. While not statistically significant (p = .0712), the finding that some faculty are willing to give time to library faculty instructors even though they believe students have adequate skills is important.

The survey responses revealed surprising information about DE faculty's attitudes toward copyright. More than 50% of faculty have chosen an Internet resource over a peer-reviewed source from the Library to avoid copyright hassles. These findings present two concerns: first, faculty may not be using the best literature to support their teaching and are not necessarily modeling good scholarly behaviors for their students. Second, faculty appear to assume that because information is freely available on the Internet, copyright does not apply to that material. Although the library provides education on copyright issues, librarians may need to find new ways to communicate information about compliance to UNMC faculty. The Library may also look for ways to assist faculty in the process of obtaining copyright clearance.

CONCLUSIONS

As an unexpected benefit of the process, the authors learned valuable lessons that will save other librarians time and resources as they prepare to conduct future needs assessments.

- Before embarking on any type of research involving people, investigators need to check with the governing agency's Institutional Review Board on human research requirements. Even library research is considered human research and must be reviewed by the IRB. Seeking IRB approval early in the project can save considerable time.
- Hiring a professional focus group facilitator was invaluable to the group process and subsequent evaluation. The benefit of having a professional conduct the facilitation, provide transcripts and an executive summary offset the expense.
- Involve a professional statistician early in the process. The survey instrument for this needs assessment could have been greatly improved with the input of the statistician. The early involvement of the statistician would have facilitated questioning, data correlation and data evaluation.
- Ideally this needs assessment would have offered traditional, paper surveys as well as online versions for participants. The authors recommend allowing plenty of lead-time for electronic survey development, especially if the library requires help from other departments for such a project.

The goal of this needs assessment was to provide the authors with the information necessary to develop a service plan for the Library. However, because of personnel changes at McGoogan Library, the authors did not have time to complete a written plan. The current Library faculty will be able to use the information gathered and analyzed here as the groundwork for developing a plan for DE services.

REFERENCES

Adams, K. E., & Cassner, M. (2000). Marketing library resources and services to distance faculty. In P. S. Thomas (Comp.), *The Ninth Off-Campus Library Services Conference Proceedings: Portland, Oregon* (pp. 1-12). Mount Pleasant, MI: Central Michigan University.

Association of College and Research Libraries (2000). *Guidelines for distance learning library services.* Retrieved October 22, 2003 from http://www.ala.org/Content/

NavigationMenu/ACRL/Standards_and_Guidelines/Guidelines_for_Distance_
Learning_Library_Services.htm.

Craig, M. H., & DuFord, S. (1995). Off-campus faculty perception of the value of library user education. In C. J. Jacob (Comp.), *The Seventh Off-Campus Library Services Conference Proceedings: San Diego, California* (pp. 69-73). Mount Pleasant, MI: Central Michigan University.

Jerabek J. A., McMain L. M., & Van Roekel J. L. (2002).Using needs assessment to determine library services for distance learning programs. *Journal of Interlibrary Loan, Document Delivery & Information Supply, 12*(4), 41-61.

Lebowitz, G. (1993). Faculty perceptions of off-campus student library needs. In Jacob, C. J. (Comp.), *The Sixth Off-Campus Library Conference Proceedings: Kansas City, Missouri* (pp. 143-154). Mount Pleasant, MI: Central Michigan University.

Lebowitz, G. (1998). Promoting off-campus library services: Even a successful program needs a marketing plan. In P. S. Thomas & M. Jones (Comp.), *The Eight Off-Campus Library Services Conference Proceedings: Providence, Rhode Island* (pp. 213-220). Mount Pleasant, MI: Central Michigan University.

Ruddy, M., OSF (1993). Off-campus faculty and students perceptions of the library: Are they the same? In Jacob, C. J. (Comp.), *The Sixth Off-Campus Library Conference Proceedings: Kansas City, Missouri* (pp. 143-154). Mount Pleasant, MI: Central Michigan University.

APPENDIX

Letter of Introduction

March 10, 2003   IRB #: 017-03-EX

Dear Distance Educator,

In response to the growing importance of distance education at UNMC, the McGoogan Library of Medicine seeks to understand the needs of UNMC distance education faculty and administrators regarding library services. McGoogan Library needs your feedback on distance library services so that we can support current and develop future services and collaboration opportunities for improving distance education at UNMC. Even if you have not previously incorporated library services and resources into your classes, we would like to get your feedback on how we might assist you in the future.

Because your needs are important to us, we ask you to share your concerns via the enclosed survey. The entire survey will take about 10 minutes to complete. Please return your completed questionnaire by March 12, 2003 in the envelope provided.

Your participation in this study is voluntary. You may refuse to answer any question, although the study will be most useful if you respond to each item. You will return the survey anonymously and we will not maintain any means of connecting you with the information you provide. We will use the aggregated results of this survey to improve services at McGoogan Library and will share our findings with our colleagues by publishing the aggregated data in a professional library journal.

If you have any questions or concerns about this survey you may contact Janette Shaffer at 559-7097 or via e-mail at jshaffer@unmc.edu.

We appreciate the time you will take to complete this questionnaire. We look forward to future collaborations with you.

Sincerely,

Janette Shaffer, MSLIS   Kate Finkelstein, MLIS
Distance Services Librarian   Head, Education Department

APPENDIX (continued)

Distance Library Services Survey

1. When did you present your first distance education (DE) class?

   __/____ (MM/YYYY)

2. How many unique distance education courses have you taught or planned? Please give the amount (please indicate if this is an estimate).

   _____

3. Have you ever used any of the McGoogan library's services or resources for your DE classes?

   a. yes
   b. no

4. What are some of the barriers that limit your use of the library's services or resources in your DE classes?
   Rank your top 4 barriers, using *1* to indicate your biggest obstacle.

   ___ copyright clearance
   ___ lack of online materials (journals or textbooks not available online)
   ___ library does not subscribe to the materials I need
   ___ my classes are offered through the Office of Continuing Education and therefore don't qualify for library support
   ___ I had not considered using the library for support
   ___ my distance students do not have enough technology (computers, Internet access, or skills) to use the library
   ___ I am not aware of library services to support distance education
   ___ procedures to use the library are too complicated for students
   ___ procedures to use the library are too complicated for me
   ___ Other (please explain): _____

5. Do you require your DE students to use library services or resources?

   a. yes
   b. no

6. Do you expect your DE students to have the same library skills as your on-campus students?

   a. yes
   b. no

7. Where do you expect your DE students to get their library skills? Rank all of the following in order of importance, *1* being most important.

   ___ in-class orientation by library faculty
   ___ I teach library skills to my students
   ___ I assume that students at this level already have the skills they need
   ___ I assume students will ask librarian for help if needed
   ___ I direct students to contact a librarian for help
   ___ students don't need special library skills for my classes

8. Are you willing to give class time for library faculty to teach your students library skills?

   a. yes
   b. no

9. How do you expect your students to obtain their required readings? Rank the following in order of relevance. Use *1* to indicate most relevant.
   ___ print materials purchased by students (textbooks, course packs, etc.)
   ___ electronic reserves
   ___ electronic journal access or document delivery through the library (not reserves)
   ___ figuring out how to get the materials is part of the student's self-education
   ___ freely available Internet resources (not through the library)

10. Have you ever chosen a freely available Internet resource for your class over a potentially more appropriate peer reviewed article because of the cost or difficulty of obtaining copyright permission?

   a. yes
   b. no

APPENDIX (continued)

11. Are there services not presently offered by the McGoogan Library of
Medicine that could facilitate your DE teaching? Please elaborate
(feel free to use the back of this survey for your comments).

Learning to Teach in a New Medium: Adapting Library Instruction to a Videoconferencing Environment

Sheri Sochrin

Springfield College

SUMMARY. The development of a new method of providing instruction involves many different issues. This paper examines a pilot project in which videoconferencing was used to provide library instruction to students at remote campuses. The librarians initiating this new service confronted the issues of training, adaptation of instruction techniques to the new format, and collaboration with faculty and administrative staff. They also dealt with administrative issues such as scheduling classes and facilities and staff scheduling. This paper examines how this cross-departmental project developed and was supported, how the initial training was conducted, and how existing class outlines were adapted. Also discussed are the lessons learned from the initial sessions. Varied administrative and collaborative challenges face the library, faculty, and departmental administrators as this project moves from pilot project status into a regular and required part of the curriculum.

KEYWORDS. Technology, library instruction, distance learners

INTRODUCTION

One challenge faced by librarians in recent years has been finding ways to provide library instruction to students taking classes at remote locations or in

[Haworth co-indexing entry note]: "Learning to Teach in a New Medium: Adapting Library Instruction to a Videoconferencing Environment." Sochrin, Sheri. Co-published simultaneously in *Journal of Library Administration* (The Haworth Information Press, an imprint of The Haworth Press, Inc.) Vol. 41, No. 3/4, 2004, pp. 429-442; and: *The Eleventh Off-Campus Library Services Conference Proceedings* (ed: Patrick B. Mahoney) The Haworth Information Press, an imprint of The Haworth Press, Inc., 2004, pp. 429-442.

http://www.haworthpress.com/web/JLA
Digital Object Identifier: 10.1300/J111v41n03_08

online classrooms. Numerous methods have been used, either singly or in conjunction with each other, including videotaped instruction, in-person instruction (through travel to the remote location), online tutorials, collaborative instruction within online classrooms and other methods. For all these methods, librarians have needed to adapt both their instructional methods and their administrative procedures to adjust to the requirements of the format. One of the methods which has received little discussion is live instruction to remote students using videoconferencing. There have been many articles in the library literature which have discussed videoconference products, technical needs of videoconferencing and/or its use in providing reference services; however, there had been few articles which discussed the instructional *adjustments* that need to be made when using videoconferencing to teach library instruction sessions. This paper offers a look at the development of a library instruction program at a small college, focusing on the practical instructional and organizational issues as opposed to the technological issues.

BACKGROUND

Springfield College is a small private college currently enrolling approximately 5,000 students. The main campus is located in Springfield, Massachusetts. Besides the main campus there are nine remote campuses located in Massachusetts, California, Delaware, Florida, New Hampshire, South Carolina, Vermont, and Wisconsin. All students at these campuses (plus some at the main campus) are part of the School of Human Services (SHS), an adult education program offering both undergraduate and graduate degrees in human services. With the exception of one campus that is experimenting with evening classes, all SHS classes are on the weekends and most classes run all day. Individual courses generally meet four times, one weekend day a month for four consecutive months.

From 1994 to 2003, the School of Human Services expanded from a program with two remote campuses–both within New England and within driving distance of the main campus–to a program with nine remote campuses spread across the country. In 1994, the School enrolled around 700 students, of which approximately 400-450 attended classes at the remote campuses (Enrollment Report, Fall, 1994). According to the Official Enrollment Report, by fall of 2003 this number had grown to nearly 2,000 students (1968), of which almost 1,600 (1,576) were at the remote campuses, several of which are still growing.

At the beginning of this period, Babson Library–the College's library, located at the main campus in Springfield, Massachusetts–was able to provide some in-person instruction on an irregular basis, since the campuses could be reached by car. However, all the travel had to come out of the Library's Professional Development budget, since the Library was not given any funding or other types of support to provide instruction to the students at the remote campuses. As the School of Human Services program began to spread around the country, this was no longer possible. The Library still did not receive funds or support to provide instruction to the remote students, nor could the Library provide the funding out of its existing resources. Travel to the other campuses on the Library's budget was stopped, but the Library continued to advocate for the library instruction needs of the remote students to the School of Human Services and to the College as a whole.

During this period, we (the Library) tried whatever methods we could find to provide some sort of instruction to the remote students: online tutorials, videotaped instruction, instruction via conference phone, occasional in-person classes when the School of Human Services paid for a librarian to travel to a campus (usually because of a licensing or accreditation visit). What we found was that one of the most critical elements of instruction was the live interaction between the instructor and the students, not necessarily for the content but because it built a relationship between the students and the Library, giving them a level of comfort they could draw on later to support them when they considered contacting the Library for further assistance.

Knowing this, and knowing that it was unlikely the College would be able to provide funding for librarians to travel to all campuses on a regular basis, we had been advocating the idea of videoconferencing as a means of providing instruction for years. Although we expected to benefit from it, this would not be a Library project but a project of the School of Human Services in conjunction with the Information and Technology Services (ITS) Department. As a result, we focused our efforts on advocating for it and offering our support if/when it became a reality.

Our efforts were both acknowledged over time and were eventually successful, although many factors came in to play and the Library was only one of them. We were sometimes included when equipment demos were held and it was understood within both the School of Human Services and ITS that, when the College did get videoconferencing, the Library wanted to use it to provide instruction.

Events finally began to move forward in the summer of 2002. The School of Human Services hired a new staff member, the Information Services Coordinator, one of whose primary responsibilities would be overseeing the soon-to-be installed videoconference facilities. The ITS Department soon after hired a new staff member whose primary responsibilities would be handling the technical issues related to running the videoconferencing system.

Perhaps one of the most important changes, also in the summer of 2002, was that the School of Human Services hired a new Dean. The new Dean proved to be a major advocate of providing library services and support to the students and, from the beginning, he developed a strong relationship with the Library. His unflagging support of the Library and his advocacy of the Library to his own staff has helped significantly in smoothing the way, and has contributed to the success enjoyed so far.

INITIATING THE PILOT PROJECT

In January 2003, discussion of using videoconferencing to provide instruction began in earnest between the School of Human Services and the Library. The installation of the videoconference equipment (Tandberg Corporation, Model 6000) was nearing completion and the Dean of the School of Human Services approached the Library about taking the lead in using the system to provide instruction. He was particularly interested in our providing instruction to the undergraduate students and asked our suggestion on the best way to approach this. Based on our experience in instructing the School of Human Services students at the main campus (and occasional other locations over the years), we suggested focusing on a class called Issues in Research. This is the first class that all SHS undergraduates are required to take, although, since they enter the program at different levels, not all of them may take it right away.

The Dean agreed and brought it up with his Campus Directors, obtaining their support to go ahead with the pilot project. Since only a few of the campuses were expected to have finished facilities in time for Spring classes, not all the campuses were to be included; but the Campus Directors of those campuses agreed to alert their regular faculty that the Library would be contacting them to request their participation in the project. The Reference Librarians followed up with the faculty members and explained the pilot project to them in more detail. All agreed to work with us. Most were very interested.

ADAPTING TO A NEW INSTRUCTIONAL MEDIUM

Meanwhile, the Reference Librarians arranged for training on how to use the videoconferencing equipment from the Information Services Coordinator. Each librarian had an individual or small group hands-on session where the Information Services Coordinator explained how the equipment (control panel, cameras, laptop connection, document camera) worked and gave out handouts explaining the different steps. Although the equipment permits us to connect to multiple locations simultaneously, we were asked to start with connecting to single locations only, with the idea that we would learn how to expand to multiple locations later, when everyone was more familiar with videoconferencing. Since we were among the earliest people, trained we gave her feedback to help her train others in the future.

After the initial training, the Reference Librarians arranged individual practice sessions to get comfortable with controlling the equipment. We also began adapting existing class presentations to the new medium. One of the hardest things to adjust to was the need to control and switch between different pieces of equipment while simultaneously giving a presentation. To address this, most of the Librarians began including cues in their outlines. Some added directions directly to our outlines (Figure 1), while others created separate columns, one for the content, one for the equipment commands (Figure 2). In all cases, we tended to put the equipment directions in red so they would stand out and serve as a visual reminder to switch views.

Since videoconferencing significantly limits the instructor's ability to move about the classroom and restricts body language (instructors need to remain in one chair where they can reach the controls and so the camera can focus on them), there was a tendency to try to find and use a wider variety of visual aids. This variety and the switching back and forth between the different types of visuals helps to induce a sense of movement and variety into the presentation

FIGURE 1

Let's talk about public libraries. . . .?
    (ask them about the types of books, etc., they find there)
    Switch discussion to books in academic libs

    Periodicals *(Use slides to discuss mags. vs. journals)*

    (Switch back to camera)

    Databases *(Use slide)*

    (Switch back to camera)

    Internet *(Use slides to discuss Internet and Web eval)*

    (Switch back to camera)

FIGURE 2

STEP 3–INFORMATION SOURCES Let's take a look at a couple of information sources you might consider.	POWERPOINT PRESS SENDS Table PC3 SLIDES 6, 7, 8, 9, 10, 11
STEP 3–SUMMARY For the rest of this session, we'll be looking at some of the databases that Babson Library has available for you. Before we start, do you have any questions?	LEFT CAMERA PRESS SENDS Left Camera–Preset 1

and helped to retain the students' attention. For example, a librarian might use a short PowerPoint slide presentation and, in between slides, go back to the camera for a few face-to-face comments, then switch to the document camera to show a handout, go back to the regular camera then switch to the laptop for an online database demonstration. The Librarian could quickly switch back and forth from any of these as necessary.

INITIAL CLASSES–SUCCESSES AND CHALLENGES

The initial six videoconference classes were held in March 2003. Of the six, two each were held at our Tampa, Milwaukee, and Wilmington campuses. Each of the four Reference Librarians taught at least one of the sessions, with some teaching two. For the most part, the classes were very successful. The student evaluation forms indicated that students found the classes interesting and valuable. The faculty we taught for seemed pleased and, in most cases, enthusiastic. This was reflected in their evaluation forms. In fact, one faculty member sent us the comment "Session very enjoyable. I thought the videoconf. training was quite useful. I want to schedule this for the first class of [Issues in Research] in the summer term." More importantly, during the next semester most of the faculty who participated in the initial pilot classes did request library instruction sessions for their students and encouraged other faculty at their campuses and others to request classes. In our first semester, we taught six undergraduate classes at three campuses; in our second (a summer semester where we traditionally do not get as many classes), we taught six undergraduate and two graduate classes at four campuses.

Not everything went perfectly. Among the positive comments on the evaluation forms, we also received comments (during the pilot classes and after) such as "It was difficult to see the screens. The font on the material seemed small." "Small TV, down low, had to creep around other students to see." "[Should have] bigger screen or up higher." "Got blurry at times." and "It was also a little blurry." Plus the Reference Librarians noted several points of concern. There was lag time between when sound was spoken at one campus and heard at the other, the document camera images were always a bit fuzzy–even when the camera was at its best focus–and the classroom designs at the far end could have significant effects on the class presentations. (While the facilities at the main campus had been designed and built with videoconferencing in mind, the facilities at the remote campuses were all preexisting classroom spaces to which TV monitors, connected to the videoconferencing system, had been added.)

The most obvious difference was whether or not a classroom was set up as a computer lab and contained computer terminals which the students could use for hands-on exercises during the classes, but the shape of the classrooms also mattered. Long, deep classrooms could mean it was hard for the librarian to see students in the back and hard for the students in the back to see the screens. Wide classrooms could mean it was it was necessary to keep swinging the far camera back and forth to see if students had questions, and the seating arrangements in a room could amplify the situation. In some rooms, usually wide ones or ones with the terminals or seating forming a circle around the outside of the room, it was impossible to see all the students at one time. The instructor would have to look at students in one portion of the room then swing the camera all the way to the other side to see the rest of the class. On top of this, although the quality of the image (at the Librarian's end) was sufficient to be able to see everyone fairly clearly, it was not easy or always possible to read facial expressions or body language–especially in a large group of people. As a result, it became very important that we get frequent verbal responses from the class as to how well they were following the presentation. Visual, non-verbal cues, such as expressions or comprehension or puzzlement, for whole classes were simply not clear enough. There were also some technology issues and training/people issues which we ran across, starting in our initial pilot sessions, but becoming particularly apparent during the summer and fall of 2003 as we began to do more sessions.

ADDRESSING THE INITIAL CHALLENGES

For some of the challenges we focused on adapting to them. For example, many of the students complained that they could not see the images well, that they were too small and/or not clear enough. Much of this is because the class-rooms at the far end use 32 inch television screens to project the images. The main videoconferencing room at the Main Campus has two 42 inch plasma screens. (The classroom at the main campus, which was specifically designed for videoconferencing, has 80 inch projection screens.) Until each campus can have a classroom specifically designed for videoconferencing and including large screens, this problem will likely remain. However, there are several things we can do to adjust to the situation including making sure the font sizes on Web pages, handouts, or anything else we display is enlarged, and making sure we continually check in verbally with the students to make sure they are following the presentation. This is less of a problem in classrooms with com-puters, as the students can follow along with any database or Web site demo on their own monitors.

Other problems just require some minor adjustments on the part of the Ref-erence Librarian. For example, if, instead of using the document camera, we open up a Word file of a handout on our laptop, the image that goes through is much clearer. Lengthening our verbal pauses between sections or when we ask for questions or comments to allow for the sound lag time is another relatively simple adjustment to make–although it is not always that easy to do in prac-tice!

Some problems, however, were more serious. During our initial classes, the only serious technology problem was related to the Library's authentication system, not the videoconference system; however, the first class we scheduled after the initial six had to be cancelled because we were unable to connect to the remote campus. We were also unable to connect to the remote campus lo-cations on two other occasions during the first three semesters. Three classes may not seem like a large number but that was approximately 12% of the classes we taught in our first three semesters, a percentage that was disturb-ingly high. There were also several more minor technology problems, includ-ing classes in which the system disconnected during a class and we were able to reconnect or when the sound did not work, although everything else contin-ued working (we used the conference phone in the classroom for sound). In all, 30% of the videoconference classes we taught in the first three semesters ex-perienced videoconference-related technical problems.

These problems were magnified by the fact that one point was overlooked when videoconferencing capability was installed and the supporting staff hired. Despite the fact that just about all School of Human Services classes are taught on weekends or evenings, there is no weekend or evening video-conferencing technology support. When a problem did occur, there was no one to turn to for help. Sometimes the librarian tried asking any of the School of Human Services administrative staff members who might be around if they had any suggestions. In some cases this helped but, since all of us had roughly the same level of training and experience, the help was limited. In some fairly easy cases, we came up with solutions; for example, the time the staff at the far end had not turned on the equipment. Other times we were forced to cancel the class.

In most cases, it turned out the problems were caused by lack of familiarity with the equipment. Essentially, since this is a new service, everyone who uses it, supports it, or even just works at a location that has it is effected by it–or can have an effect on it. Those of us who use it regularly–many of the School of Human Services administrative staff and the Reference Librarians–have been trained to operate the equipment and can figure out how to handle some basic problems (for example, reconnecting to a campus if the connection is lost). Each of the remote campuses is supposed to have someone on their regular staff, trained in the basics of using the equipment, who can serve as a basic support person at their end. Faculty are supposed to be trained in how to operate it before they use it for the first time. Since, at this point, most faculty at the remote campuses are on the receiving end of the conference, mainly they need to know how to turn it on and to wait for the other end to connect.

BE PREPARED FOR ANYTHING

However, being a new service, things do not always work as planned. The most spectacular problem we have had so far occurred during a library instruction session where we were unable to connect at all. Whenever we tried connecting to the remote campus, we received an error message that a "connection was not possible." Since it was a weekend, there was no one available on the main campus who could help diagnose and/or correct the problem. The Librarian called the campus and spoke with both the faculty member and the staff member at the campus who was supposed to have had some training. This was the faculty member's first videoconference class. She had attended a practice session a few days before but was not experienced with the system. The staff member tried her best but was unable to help. It turned out that she had not been fully trained because she was supposed to have been trained along with another person who was on leave at the time and the training had been put off. The class had to be cancelled.

In the end it turned out that someone had moved one of the monitors and a cable had disconnected. A very simple problem, but one that no one at the far end had the training to spot or if they had spotted it, knew how to correct. Problems like this will happen. The equipment at the remote campuses consists of TV monitors and cameras that sit in open classrooms or multipurpose labs. The staff are aware that they are not supposed to move or change any settings on the equipment, but things can happen. The case described above could have been caused by something as simple as a maintenance worker moving a monitor slightly in order to clean around it.

Under the current situation, the practical way to address these issues successfully is through more training and through cultivating awareness on the part of all staff and students of the need not to move or change the equipment. The School of Human Services is doing this. However, there will always be new staff members and students who are inexperienced in using or being around the equipment. This is particularly true of the School of Human Services, which uses a large number of adjunct faculty members.

Another way to address some of these problems is by developing a troubleshooting guide. As individual people gain more experience using the system they will be able to spot and correct minor problems on their own, but, for newer users, a guide with some practical suggestions for diagnosing and correcting problems could be extremely useful. The Reference Librarians suggested to the Information Services Coordinator that she consider creating such a troubleshooting guide. She has agreed and has asked for possible items to include, based on our experience.

A longer term solution–and one that will become more necessary as the use of videoconferencing expands to all the School of Human Services campuses and to multiple points in their curriculum–will be the need for some sort of weekend and/or evening technical support. Since this staffing/support would come from the ITS department, the Library is concentrating on documenting and reporting problems to the School of Human Services and ITS.

MOVING FROM PILOT PROJECT TO ROUTINE–
POSITIVE CHALLENGES

As more campuses received their videoconferencing equipment, we began to try to expand library instruction to other campuses, other faculty, and other classes. The Dean of the School of Human Services was particularly helpful with this. For the second semester, he asked that he be the one to start the ball rolling by sending out a message to his Campus Directors with the procedures for scheduling library sessions. More than that, he added a strong statement of support for library instruction (specifically for its inclusion in the Issues in Research class). When he repeated this message at our request for the third and fourth semester (fall 2003 and spring 2004), he added a message that he expected every campus to have at least one session that semester.

However, success, or expected success, brings its own challenges. In the past, when the Librarians scheduled weekend classes, there were never more than a few of classes who might potentially ask for a session on any particular day, nor was there generally a problem scheduling an appropriate classroom on a weekend. Suddenly, the Library was looking at a situation where potentially up to ten campuses in three different time zones might all have a few classes *each* who could request instruction on the same day. Of course, it was highly unlikely that all of them would choose the same day to request instruction but, because of the School of Human Services schedule, each of these classes meets only four times and almost all class meetings take place on the first two weekends of the month, increasing the likelihood that many instructors could request a session on the same day.

Since the classes are on weekends, the Library also has to contend with weekend staffing patterns. There is always a Reference Librarian working on Saturdays and Sundays but only one and only for eight hours. This Librarian is primarily there to cover the Reference Desk (with student support) but also teaches any weekend classes. When there were only a few weekend classes a semester, this was not a major problem, but with the expected expansion in the number of class requests this became an issue. By fall 2003, eight of the nine remote campuses were expected to have completed videoconference facilities and the Dean of the School of Human Services was pushing the campuses to arrange classes with the Library. There were potentially 15 Issues in Research classes (including those at the main campus) plus requests were expected from at least a few graduate classes and some other undergraduate classes–for a potential total of maybe 25 classes. Almost all of these classes met during the traditional SHS schedule (classes meet one day a month on a day during the first two weekends of the month for four months). Working under the assumption that faculty would not want a session on the last day of class when students should have already completed their research, that meant that most of these classes had only three dates on which they could potentially request a session and, because of the SHS schedule, many of these classes would be looking at the same three dates. The Reference Librarians working on the weekends could not cover all of these and still provide adequate coverage at the Reference Desk.

To address the potential problem, the Reference staff decided to try an instructional rotation schedule for the fall semester. If two classes were scheduled on any one Saturday, the Librarian who normally worked that day would teach the classes and provide coverage/backup coverage at the Reference Desk when not teaching. If a third class was requested, the Reference Librarian who was on rotation would come in to teach the third (and possibly fourth) class. Since we expected more class requests on Saturday than on Sunday, only Saturday was included in the rotation schedule. This made it manageable, as there were only six Saturdays of potential concern and three librarians on the rotation schedule. In no case would one of the librarians on rotation have to come in for more than two extra days in a semester–nor would they have to come in at all unless the third class was scheduled at least a week to ten days before the date in question.

As it turned out, there were only seventeen class requests from SHS of which twelve were for videoconference classes at the remote campuses–quite a few less than expected/hoped for. Even so, there were three occasions when three classes were requested on the same day. One was a Sunday and the Reference Librarian who normally works that day managed to cover them. For one Saturday, the Reference Librarian who normally works made a personal decision to accept a last minute class request when it was too late for the person on rotation to be required to come in. She taught all three classes herself. The last of these days another Reference Librarian did come in to teach. Having a second person in significantly cut the stress level on the regularly scheduled librarian and allowed for a better level of focus on each class as well as better service and staffing at the Reference Desk.

Although there has not yet been much of a test of this weekend rotation system, it seems to be a limited success. It does seem to be much better if the weekend librarians teach no more than two classes a day. Both librarians who did teach three classes on top of their other responsibilities on a weekend reported that it was very hard to do; however, to make the system work it may require being less flexible with the faculty about accepting last minute class requests. It will also mean finding a way to expand the weekend rotation to cover Saturdays as well as Sundays. As of yet, there has not been a great need for a second librarian on the weekends, so it should not be too hard to develop a schedule that doesn't put too much of a burden on any one librarian, but the need may grow. We may need to look into other ways of addressing this issue in the future.

WHAT WE HAVE LEARNED

In every new endeavor, there is something to learn. Among the things we have learned about teaching through videoconferencing are:

- Be prepared for anything–and have a backup plan.
- Practice before you teach. It takes time to learn to teach and run the equipment at the same time.
- Familiarize staff at both ends with how to use the equipment, and each location should have someone who is capable of providing at least basic technical support.
- Take into account the physical shape of the space the students are in. It does matter, as does the layout of the furniture in the room, the size of the screen(s) and the quality of the screen(s).
- Provide terminals to the students whenever possible. Students are better able to follow a demonstration when they can follow along on their own terminals, i.e., hands-on is more effective than a lecture/demonstration.
- Check in with the students verbally and frequently. Don't rely only on facial expressions and body language to make sure a class is following a presentation.
- Adjust speech patterns, especially pauses, to compensate for the time lag.
- Have a way to get in touch with the faculty member if there is a problem.
- Collaborate. What made our efforts a success was the active and willing cooperation of the Dean of the School of Human Services, the Information Services Coordinator, staff members from the ITS department, and both the faculty who participated in the initial classes and those who have joined us since.

FOR THE FUTURE

What comes next? Potentially many things:

- While the Library has no direct control over either the videoconferencing facilities at the main campus or the equipment and space used at the remote campuses, we can advocate to those who do for changes. We can encourage the School of Human Services to look into getting larger screens or finding other ways to make the visuals at the far end larger and/or clearer, we can point out the strengths and weaknesses of the physical set up of different classrooms for classes via videoconference, we can encourage the combination of videoconference facilities and computer labs and we can work with both SHS and ITS to find ways to address or adapt to technology problems.
- Since we are now among the core group of people who are familiar with using the videoconference facilities and the only group who use it to reg-

ularly teach classes (the others use it for meetings and staff training), we can act as a resource to others who want to use it as a teaching medium.

- We can examine and change our own teaching methods to better adapt them to this new format.
- We can look into the possibility of teaching multiple locations simultaneously.
- We can (and will) continue to work with the Dean of the School of Human Services to encourage the addition of a library instruction session in every Issues in Research class and advocate for the same in at least one required graduate level class.
- We can work with the School of Human Services Associate Dean for Curriculum and Instruction and the faculty to integrate information literacy into the curriculum in many ways and at multiple points.
- We can use the videoconferencing equipment as a way to communicate, teach, and learn from the School of Human Services staff. We can use it to attend campus faculty meetings, give workshops, and for individual and committee meetings. We have already used it for this on a limited basis and plan to expand.

We are still at the beginning of this venture but we have learned a lot in a short time and hope to expand on our beginnings and provide reliable, quality information instruction to all our remote students at many points in their curriculum.

REFERENCES

Office of the Registrar. (1994, Sept. 25). *Enrollment report.* Springfield, MA: Springfield College.

Office of the Registrar. (2003, October 17). *Official enrollment report.* Springfield, MA: Springfield College.

Providing Off-Campus Library Services by "Team": An Assessment

Marcia Stockham
Elizabeth Turtle

Kansas State University

SUMMARY. In contrast to many large academic libraries, Kansas State University (K-State) does not have a distance librarian. As a result, the Library Services Project Team (Team) was formed to take a fresh look at current library services for distance learners. Although the Team has been in place for over two years, and has implemented many changes, there was no mechanism for receiving formal feedback from students and faculty about these services. Because it is important to know whether services are being used, two librarians on the Team developed a Web-based survey targeted at distance faculty and students. This paper discusses the assessment project including development of the survey, the university approval process, use of an electronic in-house survey system, administration of the survey, and compilation and analysis of results.

KEYWORDS. Library services, assessment, distance learners, survey

[Haworth co-indexing entry note]: "Providing Off-Campus Library Services by 'Team': An Assessment." Stockham, Marcia, and Elizabeth Turtle. Co-published simultaneously in *Journal of Library Administration* (The Haworth Information Press, an imprint of The Haworth Press, Inc.) Vol. 41, No. 3/4, 2004, pp. 443-457; and: *The Eleventh Off-Campus Library Services Conference Proceedings* (ed: Patrick B. Mahoney) The Haworth Information Press, an imprint of The Haworth Press, Inc., 2004, pp. 443-457.

http://www.haworthpress.com/web/JLA
Digital Object Identifier: 10.1300/J111v41n03_09

INTRODUCTION

The ACRL *Guidelines for Distance Learning Library Services* (ACRL, 2000) state that libraries have the primary responsibility for assessing the value and effectiveness of library resources and services provided for distance learners. It is also recommended that librarians regularly survey distance library users to determine their use of library services and whether their needs are being met. Since it is important, especially in times of budget cuts, to know if current services are ones that students most need, two librarians at Kansas State University (K-State) developed a Web-based survey targeting distance faculty and students.

The objectives of the survey were to learn if students and faculty were aware of the offered library services, if they used the services, how they most often filled their information needs, and what additional services were needed to promote their learning. This paper will present and discuss the assessment of those services. Specifics include the university approval process, use of an electronic in-house survey system, development of the survey, administration of the survey, analysis of results, and recommendations for future changes.

BACKGROUND

K-State is a land-grant university with an enrollment of approximately 23,000 students. The Division of Continuing Education (DCE) offers numerous credit courses to approximately 2,800 distance students. Certificate/endorsement, bachelor's degree completion, and master's degree programs are offered in a variety of disciplines. More than ten years ago, DCE developed a program where they hired a paraprofessional facilitator to offer library services to distance students. The DCE facilitator sent books and photocopies of articles to students and performed limited literature searches. This system worked well for a number of years, but as enrollment grew and more electronic resources became available, it became obvious that the library needed to take a more active role to provide off-campus services. In contrast to many large academic libraries, K-State does not have a defined distance librarian position. Instead, the Library Services Project Team (Team), composed of librarians and representatives from the Division of Continuing Education, was formed to review services provided by both entities. The goal of the Team was to implement changes that would provide equitable library services to the distance population in compliance with the ACRL *Guidelines for Distance Learning Library Services*. Many changes were made including the addition of new Web pages, electronic reserves, remote authentication using EzProxy, promotion of services to students in DCE orientation packets, and a virtual reference service.

After two years of implementing changes suggested by the Team, the authors decided an assessment of services was needed. A Web-based survey was developed and offered to all distance students and faculty enrolled or teaching during the 2003 spring semester.

There are several published studies that document the value of electronic surveys and compare response rates of different methods (Scholar, 2000). Publications also discuss the advantages and disadvantages of Web-based surveys (Wang, 1999), but since neither the library nor DCE could fund the project, the authors pursued this method primarily to avoid mail or telephone costs. In addition, a group at K-State recently developed software for the Web-based K-State Survey System (Kansas State University, 2003) that was freely available to the campus community. Using this system allowed a relatively quick start to the assessment project. The software offered the following features: ease of use; quick creation; multiple question types and distribution formats; live reports; public Web results; raw data files; conditional branching; support for unlimited questions and answers; dedicated secure Web server to host the surveys; training and support; and anonymity for respondents.

PROCEDURE

The campus Committee on Research Using Human Subjects and Institutional Review Board (IRB) approved the proposal for this study. The review included a formal application to the IRB that outlined the purpose and method of the research and proposed survey questions. Investigators were also required to complete online training modules. It was important to complete this review not only to comply with K-State regulations, but also to make it possible to share the results of the research through publication or presentations.

When formulating questions for the survey, a previously published survey for distance students was used as a starting point (Dew, 2001). General information and guidelines about surveys were observed (The Survey Kit, 2002) and questions were developed to elicit specific information. Separate surveys with similar but distinct questions were written for faculty teaching distance courses and distance students. Representatives of the library Public Relations Team, Assistant to the Dean, and the Team, reviewed the questions. After several revisions, the survey was tested by a small number of library faculty and student workers for clarity. The surveys took no more than five minutes to complete (in most cases only two to four minutes) and questions were clear to those testing the survey. The authors wanted to gain a maximum amount of information without asking respondents to spend a lot of time on the survey. The surveys were then sent to 10 individuals from the actual test population, to test both the instrument and the survey system capabilities. The sample confirmed that the system worked as expected. An example section of the student survey form is included as Appendix A. Appendices B and C list the survey questions.

DCE provided electronic files containing e-mail addresses of teaching faculty and students enrolled in one or more distance courses for the semester. The files were imported into the system and parameters were set in the software. These parameters included the survey dates (the surveys were made available for seven days), whether reminders should be sent (one reminder was sent at six days), an e-mail message explaining the purpose of the survey, and contact information for any questions. Since each e-mail address received a unique URL for the survey, all results were anonymous to the authors and the system assured that each participant could respond only once. The system kept track of the e-mail addresses that had not responded within the six days and sent one reminder before the close of the survey.

Results appeared in real time on the Web server and the system automatically calculated percentages for each question. Full text comments by respondents also appeared in the results section. The results could be printed, exported to a spreadsheet, or made available for viewing by others at a separate URL if desired.

RESULTS

Students

In all, 2,801 surveys were sent to student e-mail addresses provided by DCE, and of those, 140 were returned as undeliverable. Of the remaining surveys, 320 were completed and returned for a response rate of 12%. While this response rate was not as high as desired, the information gained from the surveys (especially the comments) was very useful to library staff. See Table 1 for demographic information.

The respondents represented a broad spectrum of disciplines and programs, including business, education, engineering, human nutrition, family studies, psychology, and biology. Seventy-five percent of the respondents indicated they had taken one or more courses requiring research for a paper or project.

Students were asked about their awareness and use of available library services. Less than one-third of the respondents indicated they were aware of any of the listed services. Usage data were even more disappointing with 25% or fewer reporting that they had used any of the services (Table 2).

When asked which one source of information was used the most often, 57% responded with the World Wide Web. Over 65% of those who used the Web

TABLE 1. Student Demographics

Status	Graduate students	59%
	Undergraduates	33%
	Other	8%
Gender	Female	69%
	Male	31%
Age	22 and under	16%
	23-30	29%
	31-44	28%
	45 and over	26%
Type of Program	Degree	54%
	Endorsement	23%
	Other	23%
One or more courses required research		75%

TABLE 2. Student Awareness and Use of Library Services

Service	Indicated awareness of service	Indicated use of service
Distance Learning Web Page	23%	11%
DCE Library Services Facilitator	13%	5%
Off-campus access to KSU electronic resources	33%	25%
Electronic journals	30%	23%
KSU subject librarians and Web-based subject guides	13%	6%
Phone or e-mail help	22%	8%
Mail delivery from DCE	18%	5%
Web-based tutorials	19%	5%

indicated they judged the reliability of the information by the author or sponsoring organization of the Web site, with verification by another source being the second highest response. When asked to rank the three most useful library services, the following were ranked highest: off-campus access to K-State electronic resources (46%), electronic full-text journal articles from K-State Libraries (39%), and the Distance Learning Web Page (24%).

Two survey questions were open-ended asking "What other library services would you suggest that K-State offer to distance students?" and "Any comments you care to make." Sixty-three students answered the first, and 86 answered the second question. These questions elicited a variety of comments from students, but most can be summarized under the following categories: they were not aware of the services; they asked for more publicity through various means; and they expressed frustration with technical or login problems accessing the services. The following list represents examples of student comments:

- I just learned about the services available through the survey.
- Students need to be told about these services–I didn't know that so much was offered.
- I also take on-campus classes and was not aware of many of these available services.
- Send an e-mail to new students informing them of these services.
- I had never been informed about these services. I would have utilized them in my master's program.
- When the classes meet on campus someone from the library should come to give a lecture on using the library and the services available to distance students.
- Instructors should let us know about library services and how to access them.
- I don't want to wait for the mail–I want resources now. Online accessibility is important.
- How do we access these services? We need information on how these resources can be used off campus.
- I have no idea how to use the KSU library for distance learning; I would like the instructors to let us know of library resources and how to access them.

Faculty

Of 196 surveys successfully delivered to faculty, 47 were returned for a response rate of 24%. The survey questions to faculty focused on whether students are required to do research, what resources are suggested, whether faculty are aware of library services available to their students, and whether faculty promote the services. Nearly 80% of the faculty said that they require distance students to do research to prepare papers, reports, or presentations. Over three-quarters (77%) suggest resources for students to use with books (66%), peer-reviewed journals (57%), and the World Wide Web (57%) being the three most frequently recommended. Thirty to seventy percent of the faculty indicated awareness of specific services, but a much lower percentage indicated actual promotion to students (Table 3).

When asked if faculty would be interested in having a librarian participate in a class chat session, message board or live lecture, 32% responded yes with the same percentage responding no. Thirty-six percent responded that they needed more information.

TABLE 3. Faculty Awareness and Promotion of Library Services

Service	Indicated awareness	Indicated they promote service to students
Distance Learning Web Page	45%	26%
DCE Facilitator	36%	19%
Off-campus access to electronic resources	60%	36%
Electronic journals	70%	38%
Library specialists and Web-based subject guides	45%	15%
Phone or e-mail help	43%	15%
Mail delivery from DCE	40%	9%
Web-based tutorials	32%	15%
Library provided guides/instruction	30%	21%
Electronic reserves	38%	13%

The survey included two open-ended questions: "What other library services would you suggest that KSU offer to distance students?" and "Any comments you care to make?" Like the students, some of the faculty expressed surprise that so many services were available for their students. The survey had increased their awareness. Many thanked the authors for requesting their input and for sharing this information. Several suggested that the services be publicized better using various methods: handouts that can be given to students by instructors, librarian-provided guides, awareness sessions of how to use and access the services, periodic information of services available to instructors, and tutorials for new distance faculty. Faculty strongly suggested that the information provided to students be user-friendly.

INTERPRETATION/DISCUSSION

Although the actual student response rate was relatively low, the comments provided by respondents were most interesting and helpful in planning future services. Besides soliciting information about student use of services, the survey itself became a vehicle for publicizing those services. It was evident from many similar responses (". . . I was not even aware that KSU libraries have all of the services mentioned in question 10 . . .") that the survey included new information for some students. Hopefully, the same information was conveyed to those who didn't respond. If nothing else, those students who received the survey had the opportunity to learn that library resources are available to them.

It became obvious that publicizing library services is imperative. During the last two years, the Team recommended information about library services be included in DCE orientation packets. Apparently, students did not absorb this information, possibly due to the timing and format of the packet. DCE recently started sending electronic orientation materials rather than paper at the beginning of each session. The electronic format may have been more difficult for students to read or refer to at a later time. When it is time to use that information (to research a project or paper), students may have forgotten about it or never have seen it. Another source of confusion may be that the library developed Web pages specifically for distance learners focusing on access to electronic resources, while DCE also maintained a Web site geared more to services provided by their facilitator, such as mailing books or articles to students. The library staff assumed that distance learners were finding the pertinent Web pages, when they probably were not.

On the basis of the survey, the authors made the following recommendations to the Team and Library Administration.

- Develop a Marketing/Public Relations plan utilizing designated persons from DCE and the library. This plan should include reorganizing Web pages, producing an FAQ page to address specific questions from the survey responses, informing individual instructors of services, asking instructors to forward information to their students, and including librarians in orientation sessions for new instructors.
- Reallocate resources so that Interlibrary Loan desktop delivery can be instituted for DCE students at the same level as for students on campus.
- Evaluate the role of the DCE facilitator position; noting the way student needs and information delivery methods have changed since the position was created.
- Conduct a second survey at end of fall semester (or after PR implementation) to compare results with first survey.

From these recommendations, the Team felt that publicizing services was the most important strategy. The Team proposed using the faculty as the target audience for the first wave of publicity. This strategy was confirmed by a study that found one of the most effective ways to communicate information about library services to distance students is through class instructors (Kelley and Orr, 2003). The authors developed a series of questions and answers (FAQ) based on survey comments. The document was sent to each individual faculty member with a cover letter explaining the purpose, and was also posted on the distance learner library Web page. Further plans include a second letter from subject librarians encouraging faculty to remind students of K-State library services. Subject librarians are encouraged to increase liaison activities with distance faculty especially in regards to participation in courses through live chat sessions, message boards, or live lecture. In addition, librarians have requested to be included in DCE orientation sessions for new faculty.

The second publicity phase will focus on students. A few weeks into the session, a brief e-mail message will be sent to each distance student listing available library services and contact information. Distance learning Web pages are regularly updated with a priority of making them more student friendly. In addition, the library staff is working with DCE to resolve the problems created by having two sources of Web information for distance learners.

Interlibrary loan desktop delivery for DCE students remains a priority. Library and DCE administrators are working through logistical challenges with staffing and funding to implement the service.

CONCLUSION

The role of the Team has lessened during the last year because many of the original goals have been met with the implementation of new services for distance learners. The team concept was a good way to develop working relationships between DCE and the K-State Library and to increase the library's involvement with distance learners. After two years, it is time for the library to take full responsibility for these services. As there are no plans to hire a distance librarian at K-State, the team concept remains the system in place for coordinating services. The working team now consists of librarians, while the LSP Team functions as a consulting body. The results of these surveys were used as a starting point for discussions and plans between the library and DCE. Due to the varying degrees of involvement, departmental politics, and fees involved, not all recommendations will be implemented immediately. However, steps have been taken to publicize services and improve awareness to both faculty and students. The foundation for providing library service is in place. Now is the time for the library to engage in aggressive publicity of existing user services while moving forward to enhance information resources and services for distance learners.

REFERENCES

Association of College and Research Libraries (2000). *Guidelines for distance learning library services*. Retrieved November 25, 2003, from http://www.ala.org/Content/NavigationMenu/ACRL/Standards_and_Guidelines/Guidelines_for_Distance_Learning_Library_Services.htm.

Dew, S. H. (2001). Knowing your users and what they want: Surveying off-campus students about library services. *Journal of Library Administration, 31*(3/4), 177-93.

Kansas State University. (2003). *K-State survey system*. Retrieved November 26, 2003, from http://survey.ksu.edu.

Kelley, K. B., & Orr, G. J. (2003). Trends in distant student use of electronic resources: A survey. *College & Research Libraries, 64*(3), 176-191.

Schonlau, M., Fricker, Jr., R. D., & Elliott, M. N. (2000). *Conducting research surveys via e-mail and the Web*. Santa Monica, CA: RAND.

The survey kit. (2nd ed.). (2002). (Vols. 1-10). Thousand Oaks, CA: Sage Publications.

Wang, M. C., Dziuban, C. D., & Moskal, P. D. (1999). A Web-based survey system for distributed learning impact evaluation. *The Internet and Higher Education, 2*(4): 211-220.

APPENDIX A. Screen Capture Showing a Sample Excerpt of the Web-Based Student Survey

Question 5

Please indicate your area of study.

(maximum of 50 characters)

Question 6

How many of your KSU distance or off-campus courses have required doing research for papers, reports, or presentations?
- 0
- 1
- 2
- 3 or more

Question 7

For those courses that have required the use of research materials, which sources have you used? Check all that apply
- KSU Libraries
- KSU Division of Continuing Education Library Services Facilitator
- Local Public Library
- Local College or University Library
- Interlibrary Loan through a local library
- World Wide Web
- Other

Question 8

Of these sources which **one** have you used most often?
- KSU Libraries
- KSU Division of Continuing Education Library Services Facilitator
- Local Public Library
- Local College or University Library
- Interlibrary Loan through a local library
- World Wide Web
- Other

APPENDIX B. Student Survey

Library Services for Distance or Off-Campus Students
Survey Description
The results from this survey will be used to determine how Kansas State University Libraries can better serve you, the distance student. All responses will be anonymous. The analysis of these results may be presented at future conferences or in library-related publications, but there will be nothing that ties your identity to specific results.

Opening Instructions
This survey is completely voluntary, but your input is very important to us. It should take you approximately 3-5 minutes to complete and submit the survey. You may skip any questions that you are not comfortable answering. If you have questions concerning the survey, you may contact the following librarians: Marcia Stockham at stockham@lib.ksu.edu or 785-532-7161, Elizabeth Turtle at bturtle@lib.ksu.edu or 785-532-2830. If you have questions concerning the research project, contact Rick Scheidt, Chair, Committee on Research Involving Human Subjects, 1 Fairchild Hall, Kansas State University, Manhattan, KS 66506, (785) 532-3224.

Question 1
Status
  Graduate
  Senior
  Junior
  Sophomore
  Freshman
  Other

Question 2
Gender
  Male
  Female

Question 3
Age
  22 and under
  23-30
  31-44
  45 and over

Question 4
Are you currently enrolled in a KSU distance or off-campus
  Bachelor's degree program
  Master's degree program
  Certificate/Endorsement program
  Other:

Question 5
Please indicate your area of study.

Question 6
How many of your KSU distance or off-campus courses have required doing research for papers, reports, or presentations?
  0
  1
  2
  3 or more

APPENDIX B (continued)

Question 7
For those courses that have required the use of research materials, which sources have you used? Check
all that apply
    KSU Libraries
    KSU Division of Continuing Education Library Services Facilitator
    Local Public Library
    Local College or University Library
    Interlibrary Loan through a local library
    World Wide Web
    Other:

Question 8
Of these sources which one have you used most often?
    KSU Libraries
    KSU Division of Continuing Education Library Services Facilitator
    Local Public Library
    Local College or University Library
    Interlibrary Loan through a local library
    World Wide Web
    Other:

Question 9
If you use the World Wide Web for research, how do you judge the reliability/authority of the information?
Check all that apply
    Author/sponsoring organization
    Web site/domain
    Last update/timeliness
    Non-biased presentation
    Verified with another source
    None of the above
    Other:

Question 10
Are you aware of the following KSU Library Services? Check all that apply.
    Distance Learning Web page at KSU Libraries Web site
    DCE Library Services Facilitator
    Off-campus access to KSU electronic resources (e.g., databases, e-books, e-journals)
    Electronic full-text journal articles from KSU Libraries
    KSU subject specialist librarians and Web-based subject guides
    Telephone or e-mail help from a KSU librarian
    Mail delivery of books or articles from DCE
    Web-based library instruction tutorials through K-State Online

Question 11
Which of the following KSU Library Services have you used? Check all that apply.
    Distance Learning Web page at KSU Libraries Web site
    DCE Library Services Facilitator
    Off-campus access to KSU electronic resources (e.g., databases, e-books, e-journals)
    Electronic full-text journal articles from KSU Libraries
    KSU subject specialist librarians and Web-based subject guides
    Telephone or e-mail help from a KSU librarian
    Mail delivery of books or articles from DCE
    Web-based library instruction tutorials through K-State Online

Question 12
Of the following services, rank the three (1, 2, 3) that you feel are most useful to you as a KSU distance or off-campus student, with "1" being the most useful.
- – 1 2 3 Distance Learning Web Page at KSU Libraries Web site
- – 1 2 3 DCE Library Services Facilitator
- – 1 2 3 Off-campus access to KSU electronic resources (e.g., databases, e-books, e-journals)
- – 1 2 3 Electronic full-text journal articles from KSU Libraries
- – 1 2 3 KSU subject specialist librarians and Web-based subject guides
- – 1 2 3 Telephone or e-mail help from a KSU librarian
- – 1 2 3 Mail delivery of books or articles from DCE
- – 1 2 3 Web-based library instruction tutorials through K-State Online

Question 13
What other library services would you suggest that KSU offer to distance students?

Question 14
How many distance or off-campus courses have you taken (including those you are currently enrolled in)?
1
2-5
6 or more

Question 15
Any comments you care to make

Closing Message
Your input is important to us!

–End of Survey–

APPENDIX C. Faculty Survey

Library Services for Distance or Off-Campus Faculty
Survey Description
The results from this survey will be used to determine how Kansas State University Libraries can better serve you, the distance faculty member. All responses are anonymous. The analysis of these results may be presented at future conferences or in library-related publications, but there will be nothing that ties your identity to specific results.

Opening Instructions
This survey is completely voluntary, but your input is very important to us. It should take you approximately 3-5 minutes to complete and submit the survey. You may skip any questions that you are not comfortable answering. If you have questions concerning the survey, you may contact the following librarians: Marcia Stockham at stockham@lib.ksu.edu or 785-532-7161, Elizabeth Turtle at bturtle@lib.ksu.edu or 785-532-2830. If you have questions concerning the research project, contact Rick Scheidt, Chair, Committee on Research Involving Human Subjects, 1 Fairchild Hall, Kansas State University, Manhattan, KS 66506, (785) 532-3224.

Question 1
Do any of your Kansas State University off-campus or distance courses require student research to prepare papers, reports, or presentations?
Yes
No

APPENDIX C (continued)

Question 2

If so, do you suggest resources for your students to use?

Yes

No

Question 3

If you suggest resources, which of the following do you routinely mention? Check all that apply.

Books

Peer-reviewed journals

Magazines

Newspapers

World Wide Web

Other:

Question 4

Are you aware of the following KSU library services? Check all that apply.

Distance Learning Web Page at KSU Libraries Web site

DCE Library Services Facilitator

Off-campus access to KSU electronic resources (e.g., databases, e-books, e-journals)

Electronic full-text journal articles from KSU Libraries

KSU subject specialist librarians and Web-based subject guides

Telephone or e-mail help from a KSU librarian

Mail delivery of books or articles from DCE

Web-based library instruction tutorials through K-State Online

Librarian-provided guides or instruction to doing research

Electronic Reserves (Reserve material available electronically through K-State Online)

Question 5

Do you promote the use of the following KSU library services to your students? Check all that apply.

Distance Learning Web page at KSU Libraries Web site

DCE Library Services Facilitator

Off-campus access to KSU electronic resources (e.g., databases, e-books, e-journals)

Electronic full-text journal articles from KSU Libraries

KSU subject specialist librarians and Web-based subject guides

Telephone or e-mail help from a KSU librarian

Mail delivery of books or articles from DCE

Web-based library instruction tutorials through K-State Online

Librarian-provided guides or instruction to doing research

Electronic Reserves (Reserve material available electronically through K-State Online)

Question 6

Would you be interested in having a librarian subject specialist participate in one of your class live chat sessions, message boards, or live lecture?

Yes

No

I don't have enough information

Question 7

What other library services would you suggest that KSU offer to distance faculty and students?

Question 8
Degree Program or courses that you teach (optional)

Question 9
Any comments you care to make.

Closing Message
Your input is appreciated.

–End of Survey–

If You Build It, Will They Come?
Creating a Marketing Plan
for Distance Learning Library Services

Terri Pedersen Summey

Emporia State University

SUMMARY. As distance education programs continue to grow, so do the services offered by libraries to the communities created by such programs. However, for these programs to be successful, the people that they are intended to serve need to be aware of the support and services available to them. Without such awareness, the services will go unused. Through a survey, the librarians at Emporia State University learned that making distant students aware of services was essential to the success of distance learning library services. Librarians discovered that creating a marketing plan to guide the marketing process was essential. This tool serves as a road map to visually illustrate the path from the conception of ideas to the realization of the marketing goals and objectives. This paper examines the process of writing a marketing plan and intends to illustrate how it can assist the library in marketing its services to a distant population.

KEYWORDS. Library services, distance learners, planning

Distance learning programs continue to proliferate at academic institutions, resulting in an increasing number of students and faculty at a distance from the traditional campus. These remote learning communities present both chal-

[Haworth co-indexing entry note]: "If You Build It, Will They Come? Creating a Marketing Plan for Distance Learning Library Services." Summey, Terri Pedersen. Co-published simultaneously in *Journal of Library Administration* (The Haworth Information Press, an imprint of The Haworth Press, Inc.) Vol. 41, No. 3/4, 2004, pp. 459-470; and: *The Eleventh Off-Campus Library Services Conference Proceedings* (ed: Patrick B. Mahoney) The Haworth Information Press, an imprint of The Haworth Press, Inc., 2004, pp. 459-470.

lenges and opportunities for the academic library. Consequently, college and university libraries are in a transitional state in attempting to adapt traditional library services to meet the needs of distant learners.

William Allen White Library at Emporia State University conducted a study during the 2000 Spring Semester. The survey used in the study examined the knowledge and use of library services by a distinct distance learning community. Affiliated with the School of Library and Information Management, those surveyed were "library-savvy" individuals. With this in mind, one startling finding from the study was that students were unaware of the services and resources available to them through the campus library. One comment from a respondent was especially straightforward when she wrote, "Better advertisement of the library services than now provided to Distance Students–I had not a clue!" (Fisk, 2000, p. 8). The responses from those surveyed in the "Proposed New Services" section also illustrated this lack of awareness for what the library offers. Respondents chose services already offered as ones that could be added to meet their requests. This need for awareness prompted the library to look at developing a marketing campaign. Resources and services offered by the library to distance learners needed to be promoted to the community that they were designed to help.

Knowing that the library's services and resources are central to the educational mission of the institution, one may question the need to market such a vital component of the learning process. Although the library may be a visible presence on the "brick and mortar" campus, it may not be so obvious to those at a distance from the physical site. In the past, when it came to the provision of information sources and services, the library had a monopoly. This is not necessarily true any longer, because even traditional students physically at the university may look to other sources to meet their information and research needs such as the Internet.

Part of the problem facing libraries is a need for "brand identity." This is a marketing concept that refers to what consumers think of when they think of a product, service, or institution. It includes the look and feel of the library, its slogan, and logo. Another component is making sure that the library's name appears on any electronic resources to advertise who is paying for the access. "Brand Identity" may also refer to what the library does well or the kinds of services that it provides. Unfortunately, libraries are not very good at publicizing what we do and how well we do it. In the book entitled, *Information Ecologies*, the authors Nardi and O'Day (1999) talk about librarians as a "keystone species." In the information ecosystem, they posit that librarians are key to the survival and success of that ecology. Without librarians, the information ecology will cease to function and exist. One finding that Nardi and O'Day discuss is that most people are unaware of what librarians actually do.

This lack of knowledge can then contribute to a lack of knowledge regarding the importance of a library in meeting the information and research needs of individual consumers. A section of the book mentions that because librarians do their job well without a lot of fanfare, it is actually a detriment to their image. People are not aware of the amount of work that transpires in libraries and so they take librarians and the work they do for granted. To be able to sustain old customers and gain new ones, the library needs to take a proactive approach to marketing its resources and services.

In their work, *Marketing Plans That Work*, McDonald and Keegan (1997) write that customers do not always know exactly what they want. With respect to libraries, they know that they want better ways to solve information needs or to make their lives easier. McDonald and Keegan state, "The central idea of marketing is to match the capabilities of a company with the needs and want of customers to achieve a mutually beneficial relationship" (p. 1). Operating a customer oriented library means using business marketing techniques to not only market services, but also to discover the needs of customers and tailor services to meet those needs. There is a core group of services that consumers expect from libraries including the accessibility to books and other materials along with reference and research services.

Various studies though have shown that distance education students do not expect a lot of support services from the parent campus. This makes marketing resources and services provided by the library to these distance students a key to the success of the program. In an article concerning services to remote users, the author Ann Wolpert (1998) writes, "Libraries should approach support to distance education as a new business opportunity, utilizing techniques of market evaluation and analysis" (p. 21). She continues by discussing the need for "brand identity" to create a unique look and feel for the library that becomes recognizable for distant learning students. Marketing is essential for any new venture to do well. Conducting a winning marketing campaign can sometimes be difficult. This is why planning is an integral component of the marketing process.

So what exactly is a marketing plan and who should create it? The marketing plan serves as a road map or guide to the whole marketing process. It answers the following basic questions: Where is the organization at currently? Where does the organization want to ultimately go? and, How will the organization get there? Each plan is unique to the situation and the organization creating it. The smaller the organization, the less formal the plan might be. The written marketing plan is something that emerges out of the planning process and can assist in helping to make things happen. It serves as a starting point for any marketing activity and is a fundamental step in the process. It does not need to be very formal, long or complex. But it is very important to write it down. One just needs to think of all of the unsuccessful unwritten plans that have been developed to realize that writing this in a more permanent form is very important. Putting the marketing plan into writing commits the organization into implementing it and a successful plan is one that is carried out. Although something to keep in mind is that the planning process is almost more important than the final plan itself.

According to David Gumpert (1996), the marketing plan does three things. First, it identifies marketing issues essential for long-term success. Planning involves key players in developing the same goals and assists in having them move in the same direction by getting a commitment to the plan. Finally, success is based on accomplishments and the marketing plan will include ways to measure achievements. The plan also provides stability and serves as a measuring stick with which to measure progress. It forces the organization to think about not only what it does, but what it can do in the future through three to five years of long-term planning. And it provides a focus for the marketing team showing the "big picture" through goals that are set and providing action steps needed to be taken for success. Usually a budget or financial information is included in the plan. This serves as a guide for the allocation of resources. In addition, integrated into the plan is an implementation timetable that includes not only key dates but also indicates responsibility for completion of tasks to direct the distribution of effort. Therefore, the marketing plan is the outline of a design to reach specific goals. It includes action steps, a vision, strategic intent, goals and objectives.

Most marketing plans aim at a higher or administrative audience. Needing to be written clearly, the marketing plan is required to communicate the goals and objectives of the organization. It should take into consideration the decision-making process or hierarchy of the organization. Nevertheless, the plan needs to be able to speak for itself and stand alone, especially outside of the library. This is especially true with a program such as distance education library services that has many ties outside of the library. A marketing plan does not have to be created from scratch. Before embarking on the creation of a plan, one should examine plans that already exist at other institutions and libraries. Another way to get the plan written is to employ a student intern or student employee to draft a plan as part of a marketing class project or assignment. Input during the writing process needs to come from those that will be responsible for its implementation in order for the plan to thrive. Stakeholders in the plan need to be kept informed during its development to insure their cooperation during the execution stage.

A set formula for a marketing plan does not exist and the plan itself will fluctuate depending upon the situation. There are certain elements that should be present in a well thought out plan. At the minimum, a marketing plan should include the following: the mission statement of the institution; a library or community analysis; goals and objectives; an overall marketing strategy; and methods with which to evaluate results. A more complete plan will contain: an executive summary; a table of contents; an introduction; situation or environmental analysis; the SWOT analysis; a description of the target market or market analysis; a brief mission and vision statement; marketing goals and objectives; a marketing strategy; evaluation methods; a timetable and a projected budget.

Each marketing plan should begin with an Executive Summary. This portion of the document will provide an overview of the plan or synopsis. In summarizing the entire plan, the summary will describe the provided service or services. It will include the goals and proposed action steps along with the investment needed for success. The outlay of resources includes not only monetary needs, but also time and personnel requirements. Anticipated results should be included. It may be long or short, but should be succinct. In addition, although this is the first part or introduction to the plan, it may need to be the last portion written.

A Table of Contents that will serve as a guide to the plan itself follows the Executive Summary. This is a necessary part of the plan, even if the marketing plan is short, as it aids in navigating through the plan and locating information. An Introduction follows the Table of Contents. Unlike the Executive Summary that provides an overview of the plan, the Introduction contains the details of the resource or service and its background. The introduction provides the basis for the entire document as it discusses the service, program or part of the library to highlight in the marketing campaign. In order for the plan to succeed it is important to not try to do too much with the plan. Personnel need to decide which service or program that is featured before writing this part of the plan.

An analysis of the situation or environment will come next. Also termed "environmental scanning," this portion of the marketing plan will answer the question, "Where is the institution or library right now?" For this segment, the key question to answer is "What business are we in?" This section of the plan will often include a review of the library situation; market summary, SWOT analysis; a description of the current customers; potential competitors; a picture of services and products already offered; and the marketing strategy being utilized. In the review of the library situation, plan draftees will provide a description of the library, its products and services, the culture and staff within the organization, along with its role or place in the parent institution. The market summary focuses on the demographics or composition of the parent institution along with the community served by the services or resources. It will discuss why the library services and resources targeted with the plan are right for the marketplace or what needs they fulfill. In addition, incorporated into the plan are any future opportunities for the library.

The SWOT analysis that is included in this portion of the plan stands for strengths, weaknesses, opportunities and threats. This strategic planning technique forces the planners to analyze completely the environment in which they operate. The first part of the SWOT analysis examines the library's strengths and weaknesses. To have this section accomplish something, those individuals creating it need to be really honest and forthright. First, the strengths of the library are listed. This part provides something for the institution to build upon. The next part is probably one of the most difficult sections for those intimately involved in the library and its operations to write and that is the weakness section. For this to be useful, plan developers need to critically look at the library, its services and resources. They need to walk in the shoes of the customer and view the library with "outside eyes." In working on this part of the plan, creators need to answer the question, "Can weaknesses be turned into strengths?" Things that need to be eliminated from the library may be included in this section. The opportunity section is a place where a needs assessment could be put. Since expectations are low for services and resources to distant students, much can be included. Services and resources that are, and could be, provided for the remote learning community should be discussed. The final part of this section is threats. This piece of the SWOT analysis will look at external forces that might threaten the library's service offerings and resources. It might include local libraries that are closer to the students' locale and the availability of information on the Internet. The elements included in this section are something that the library needs to be ready to outmaneuver.

In this part of the environmental analysis, the customer base refers to current customers only. Although those that do not use the library are important to examine, the writers will discuss this later in the plan. Here the writers present demographics for current users of the library and services. It may include their opinions of the library, its services and personnel. Library staff can gather these opinions either formally through surveys or informally through conversations. Document creators can use this information later in the market analysis section of the marketing plan.

The competition section of the environmental analysis looks at those elements competing against the library. Creators of the marketing plan need to identify main competitors along with their strengths and weaknesses. This portion of the document examines where non-library users go to have their information and research needs met. The segment of the marketing plan that studies current services and products offered by the library comes next. It goes into depth describing what the library has to offer and the benefits to customers available through using the library and its resources. The final part of the situation analysis looks at the current marketing strategy used by the library. It examines how customers become aware of the library, its services and resources.

The middle part of the document is the main portion of the marketing plan. This section contains a description of the market targeted in the plan; the mission and vision statements; the goals and objectives to reach the goals; and the marketing strategy to implement. The target market is referring to not only those individuals that already utilize the services and resources of the library, but also those that do not. Thus, plan creators describe the current customers along with potential customers. To the people not using the library and its services, the question needs to be posed, "Why not?" Do they have their information needs met elsewhere or are they not aware of what the library can offer to them. The answer to that question will provide valuable information to complete the marketing plan, develop potential services, and guide the purchase of resources. To be successful, the library needs to approach the library, its resources and services from the view of the customer or "walk in their shoes." One marketing concept used here is to look at the USP or "unique selling proposition" of the library. A method to do this is to write a list of what those in the library think their users might want. Asking the customers what they want should follow this up. Library staff can compare the two lists to see how closely they match each other. The library needs to be very honest about the quality of service provided to students, especially those that are at a distance. Is the library meeting the needs of users? If the answer is no, then the question of "Why not?" should be answered. This community analysis of the target market needs to look at geographic factors and lifestyles of the students. In working with distance learning students, this can be very different from the traditional crowd that the library may usually serve.

The mission and vision of the library and the parent organization are included in the next section of the marketing plan. These are important elements as they provide a focus for the rest of the document. Now is a good time to create a mission or vision statement if the library does not have one. If the marketing plan describes a service, library staff may want to create a separate mission or vision for that service. This can be a difficult task to accomplish because it requires the staff involved to think philosophically about the service or program. Staff will analyze the future goals, values, and underlying beliefs of the library. The mission statement needs to be a clear, concise statement concerning what the library is and why. Three questions can help in writing the mission statement. The first, "What type of customer uses the library?" and, "Who should use the library?" helps to define the customer for the mission. The second question, "What does the library do for the user?" looks at the services and programs provided by the library. Last, the library should ask itself, "How does it provide services and resources to users?" The mission statement should be "down to earth" and include levels of service. On the other hand, the vision can "shoot for the moon." It needs to be something that the library strives to attain and needs to be inspirational. Both statements should be short and memorable.

The marketing plan next covers the goals and objectives. What the library would like to achieve becomes the goals. It looks at what the library intends to achieve with the help of the plan. These should be clear, specific and very detailed. They also need to be measurable. Since the goals and objectives are what the library intends to achieve, the next logical section is the marketing strategy or tactics required to achieve the objectives. In looking at marketing in the library, the four strategies to consider are as follows: existing products or services for existing markets; create new products or services for existing markets; extend the existing products or services to new markets or customers; and develop new products for new markets. The decision made on the strategy or tactics to pursue influences the marketing plan. The marketing strategy is composed of action steps to promote the product or service. This is how the library intends to get to the end result. Marketing should be a continual and dynamic process. The Marketing Strategy section allows the library to focus on the goals and set priorities. The four Ps of marketing are included in the part of the document: product, price, promotion, and place. These principles and answers to them will guide the marketing campaign.

The next part of the marketing plan describes implementation details. Here the writers lay out the timetable for results. The library staff creates short milestones and deadlines to meet. This will keep the plan and the campaign moving forward. Document creators should build delays into the timetable, as they are inevitable. The resources needed to carry out the marketing strategies and plan are described. Resources include equipment, supplies, and a proposed budget, along with the people and the time needed to complete the campaign. Personnel need to assign responsibility to the tasks laid out on the marketing plan or the action steps. This will assist in accountability for completing responsibilities in a timely manner.

The most crucial part of the document is the assessment or evaluation techniques that conclude the plan. These look at the effectiveness of the marketing planning process. It should be formative and take place through the entire process, not only at the end. Those responsible for the campaign and plan will complete a summative evaluation at the conclusion of the campaign. The evaluation step is very important as it not only looks at the effectiveness of the campaign, but also the document and process. As assessment is done throughout the process, the plan may be changed and modified periodically. The marketing plan should be a fluid document that is flexible and can be adapted to different circumstances that might arise.

As mentioned earlier, the marketing plan will vary with the situation. It needs to identify key issues, serve as a way to mobilize resources and use them efficiently, and include methods to measure accomplishments or results. It is a policy document, a strategic planning document, a management tool and implementation document. The plan will also serve as an assessment tool with built-in evaluation processes and measures. Although there is not a set formula to follow, there are certain elements that should be included and particular questions that need answers. The other thing to remember is that the marketing plan is never really completed and needs to be continually updated and revised. This goes along with the fact that the planning process is just as important as the final plan. The process forces the library to consider its current situation and the future directions that it would like to go. Throughout the process, staff at all levels needs to be consulted and involved in creating the final product.

In the past, libraries have not taken a very proactive stance with regards to marketing themselves and their services. In our current technological age, when inventions such as the World Wide Web compete with the library as providers of information, the library needs to take a more active role in making people aware of what they have to offer to customers. This is especially true of the distance learning communities that are increasing in numbers at most colleges and universities. The remote population is especially hard to reach because they are not physically present in the library. To contact this population, the library should develop "brand identity" or a look and feel that is accessible online. In order to conduct a successful marketing campaign, the marketing plan is an essential piece. It allows library personnel to look at the "big picture" and assists in the visualization of what the library would like to accomplish. Creating a plan can help stimulate thinking and make better use of limited resources. It assists with organizing the campaign and the assignment of tasks, responsibilities and deadlines. Finally, it serves as a road map leading the library from the inception of the plan to the accomplishment of the goals and objectives (Cohen, 2001).

REFERENCES

Cohen, W. (2001). *The marketing plan.* (3rd ed.). New Jersey: John Wiley and Sons.

Fisk, J. (2000). *A community analysis and library services needs assessment of the students of the School of Library and Information Management of Emporia State University: An executive summary.* Unpublished research project, Emporia State University.

Gumpert, D. E. (1996). *How to really create a successful marketing plan.* (3rd ed.). Massachusetts: Goldhirsh Group, Inc.

McDonald, M. H. B., & Keegan, W. J. (1997). *Marketing plans that work.* Boston: Butterworth-Heinemann.

Nardi, B., & O'Day, V. (1999). *Information ecologies: Using technology with heart.* Boston, MA: MIT Press.

Wolpert, A. (1998). Services to remote users: marketing the library's role. *Library Trends, 47(1),* 21-41.

APPENDIX

Creating a Marketing Plan for Distance Library Services

Activity Sheet

A Marketing Plan for: _____(Name of Library)

Introduction: (What is the service or product to be featured in the marketing campaign? Why was the plan written? What are the overall goals of the plan or what is to be accomplished?)

Situational or Environmental Analysis: (Where is the library or institution right now? What is offered? What business is the library in and who are they serving?)

- Describe the library situation. (Library services, personnel, culture and environment)

- Describe the current market. (Describe the parent institution of community culture surrounding the library. Also the demand for services and resources that are offered.)

- SWOT Analysis:
  - Strengths: (What the library does well?)

- Weaknesses: (What areas need improvement?)

- Opportunities: (What services and resources could be provided by the library?)

- Threats: (Who are the chief competitors or external forces shaping the library?)

- Current Customers: (Who is currently using the services and resources–demographic characteristics?)

- Services and Products Offered: (Describe current services and resources.)

- Current Marketing Strategy: (Describe the current marketing tactics employed, if any.)

Market Analysis: (Describe the market to be reached. Existing services to existing customers; new services to existing customers; existing services to new customers; and new services to new customers.)

Mission and Vision:

- Mission Statement: (Down to earth. What the library is, to whom, and why. Include beliefs and assumptions.)

- Vision Statement: (Shoot for the moon. What the library would like to be.)

Goals and Objectives: (What is to be achieved?)

APPENDIX (continued)

Marketing Strategies: (Specific action steps to achieve the goals and objectives.)

Implementation Details: (Budget, timetable, responsibilities, and resources needed.)

Assessment or Evaluation: (How will success be measured?)

Executive Summary: (For administrators, write a summary of the document. This goes at the beginning, but is written last.)

Date Completed:
Authors:

Yeah, I Found It!
Performing Web Site Usability Testing to Ensure That Off-Campus Students Can Find the Information They Need

Beth Thomsett-Scott

University of North Texas

SUMMARY. A well-designed and user-friendly Web site is essential with the large and rapid increase in the number of off-campus users. Web site usability studies can help ensure that libraries provide effective and efficient access to their Web site for both on- and off-campus users. Formal usability studies, focus groups, and cognitive walkthroughs are usability techniques that can be incorporated into a Web site study. These three techniques will be discussed with real life experiences added in to provide the reader with suggestions of how to and how not to use the techniques.

KEYWORDS. Technology, distance learners, study, evaluation

INTRODUCTION

The number of off-campus users of library sites is rapidly increasing as computers become more prevalent among students and online courses grow in number and popularity. Library Web sites are not always designed to allow their patrons to use the site efficiently and effectively without assistance or

[Haworth co-indexing entry note]: "Yeah, I Found It! Performing Web Site Usability Testing to Ensure That Off-Campus Students Can Find the Information They Need." Thomsett-Scott, Beth. Co-published simultaneously in *Journal of Library Administration* (The Haworth Information Press, an imprint of The Haworth Press, Inc.) Vol. 41, No. 3/4, 2004, pp. 471-483; and: *The Eleventh Off-Campus Library Services Conference Proceedings* (ed: Patrick B. Mahoney) The Haworth Information Press, an imprint of The Haworth Press, Inc., 2004, pp. 471-483.

frustration. Dickstein and Mills (2000) state that a Web site must be designed for the users of the site, not for the librarians or the creators. Libraries are beginning to adopt the concepts of "usability" that have been used by software companies for a number of years. The interest in providing Web sites that are seen as "useable" and "helpful" by our patrons comes not only from a desire to provide the best possible service but also from other factors. One of these factors is that the increase in distance learning and off-campus users necessitates additional concern about the efficiency and effectiveness of a library's Web site (Cockrell and Jayne, 2002). As well, libraries are spending more and more of their budgets on Web-based resources and it is essential that users be able to access and use these resources efficiently and effectively.

A useable Web site is defined by Rubin (1994) as being useful (doing what the user wants it to do), effective (the ease of use while achieving the user's goals), learnable (the ability to grow from a novice to a skilled user), and satisfying (how well the user enjoyed their time on the site). McMullen (2001, p. 7) states that a useable Web site is essential as it is the interface between the "information professional and the individual who is seeking information." Usability studies gather information on how users actually use the site (Campbell, Walbridge, Chisman, and Diller, 1999). Battleson, Booth, and Weintrop (2001) state that usability studies replace "opinion" with user-centered data. Usability studies put the end users first and assist in understanding the needs of the users (Norlin and Winters, 2002). Collins and Aguinaga (2001) describe their amazement at how differently the study participants used the site than the staff or the designers of the site expected it to be used. Incorporation of usability testing into Web site development increases the value of the site and enhances user satisfaction (Norlin & Winters, 2002).

The purpose of this paper is to discuss several Web site usability techniques using real life experiences to provide the fundamentals of the techniques and to help prepare the reader to use them in a Web site usability study. The author's experience is with academic libraries; however, Web site usability testing can be used on any Web site. Some knowledge of Web site usability is assumed. For readers who are unfamiliar with the topic, Campbell (2001a) and Norlin and Winters (2002) are both good sources for background information.

BACKGROUND TO THE REAL-LIFE STUDIES

Two Web site usability studies were conducted at the University of North Texas (UNT) Libraries. The first study was performed on the Ask A Librarian sub site and the second on the home page. Thirty students were hired for each study. The participants were divided into three categories: undergraduates, graduates, and those experienced with online learning.

Both studies used the techniques of formal usability studies and focus groups. The formal usability study technique was incorporated as it involves users directly in the process and was performed first as the results formed the basis of the discussion in the focus groups. Jeffries and Desurvire (1992) suggest that the best evaluations come from multiple methods. Focus groups were included as they provide group discussion and often promote the synergy of ideas. Significant additional information was gleaned from the groups in both studies. Often participants are more relaxed in a group situation than in one-on-one situations (Canning, 1995), and this may be the reason for the additional usefulness of the focus groups.

FORMAL USABILITY STUDIES

The Basics

Formal usability studies, also referred to as task-based testing, are the ultimate way to involve library users in the design of the site. They allow researchers to observe how the site is used, find any errors in the design, and determine which elements or terminology participants find confusing. Since formal usability studies provide both qualitative and quantitative data, they give greater scope and breadth to the study (Norlin & Winters, 2002). Formal usability studies find the more serious difficulties that users have with the site (Jeffries & Desurvire, 1992).

Formal usability studies involve the observation of users performing specific tasks on a Web site. Observation can be direct where a moderator, and sometimes an observer as well, watches the participants while in the same room; or indirect using a two-way mirror, video recorder and/or screen capture equipment. It is usually only the bigger companies or institutions that have two-way mirrors and the more advanced set-ups. Most research is still done using direct observation with the addition of screen capture software. Screen capture software, often called tracking software, collects information on the users' paths while they complete the tasks. Basic screen capture software will record the time taken between each mouse click and track the URLs of the pages viewed. More advanced systems, and more costly, will record screen images and some even produce a video of the transaction.

There are usually eight to twelve questions with very specific answers and paths, as the goal of usability studies is to determine how the individual pages and overall site can be improved to allow users to find the information they need in less time and with fewer steps. The tasks are based on the actual purposes of the site, such as finding the catalog, locating the hours page, finding a liaison librarian, etc. The difficulty in writing the tasks is avoiding using the terminology that is actually on the page. Tasks are the most critical part of the design (Campbell, 2001b), and need to be solvable without "leading" the participant through the use of keywords from the "correct" link. The wording and the order of the tasks are the keys to a successful study (Battleson et al., 2001). Chisman, Diller and Walbridge (1999) suggested that tasks should not be built on one another as this will prevent unsuccessful students from answering the next question as well.

Each test session usually lasts between one and a half hours and two hours. The data collected can vary among researchers; however, most record the success rate, the time taken to complete each task, the number of clicks, and the pathway. The pathway is useful in determining the common mistakes that participants make. Some researchers will record body language observations as well to help them determine at what point the participants become frustrated with the question.

There is some debate about timing the sessions, both whether it should be done and how long to do it for. Some researchers do not time at all and allow the participants to continue searching for the answer as long as they want to. Other researchers stop the participants at one minute as they believe that if the participant is not successful after one minute, they will not be able to find the correct answer at all. However, the standard still appears to be a three minute maximum.

Task-based testing can be as minimalistic or as extensive as needed. Rubin (1994) states that four to five participants will find eighty percent of the errors and fifteen will find all the errors at the page level. Participants must be homogeneous for the above to be true. If differences among populations are being considered, more participants will be needed to ensure a minimum of four to five homogenous participants in each population. Skelton (1992) notes that any changes based on a single test can actually worsen the site. Therefore, after applying the results of the usability study to a redesign, iterative testing, which involves the testing the changes in a less formal atmosphere before revealing them to the public, should be performed to ensure that the study results were interpreted correctly (Campbell et al., 1999). This process is also called "cookie testing."

Comments and Thoughts

Dickstein and Mills (2000) used eight to twelve participants across several populations and noted that the first four to five participants found the major errors, but added that additional participants always revealed something valuable and unique. Each of the ten participants in each population in the UNT studies provided some useful information, although the more "serious" errors were discovered after the fourth to sixth participant in each population.

There were eight questions in the first study and ten in the second. Ten questions are recommended as the maximum number to use. After the tenth question, participants were showing signs of fatigue and becoming more easily frustrated.

Beta testing the tasks prior to the study is highly recommended. If different populations are being examined, the beta testing needs to be performed across all the populations. Hudson (2000) discussed the importance of beta testing across populations as well. An entire beta test should be conducted to determine any potential pitfalls so they can be resolved prior to the main study. Data collection and analysis should also be beta tested to ensure that the necessary data will be gathered properly and entered in a manner to facilitate successful analysis.

Both a moderator and observer were used when possible. The moderator's role was to introduce the test, ask the participants to read the questions aloud, and prompt them if they left the site. The observer would time the test and record the pathway taken for each question. Approximately a third of the second series of tests only had a moderator present due to unavailability of volunteers to serve as recorders; thus, the moderator was required to also act as the observer.

The time allotted for each participant to complete all the tasks was one and a half hours, although both series of tests ended before that time. However, the extra time allowed a relaxed debriefing period and casual conversation, if the participants desired this, which added to the overall positive feeling that a number of the participants commented on.

Three minutes was the maximum time allowed for each task and this worked well. Only two participants became frustrated enough that the question had to end prior to the three minutes. In both cases it was the same question that caused the problem. It has been discussed in the literature that if the participants cannot find the correct path after one minute, they would not be successful at completing the task (Gullikson, Blades, Bragdon, McKibbon, Sparling, & Toms, 1999); however, the results do not support this. In fact, there were a number of times when the question was successfully answered just before the three minute mark, although three minutes did seem to be the longest participants wanted to, or were able to, look for the answer. Battleson et al. (2001) allowed three minutes as the outside marker for closing the question, but used three incorrect choices as the time to intervene.

Participants were asked to read the questions aloud, as suggested by Battleson et al. (2001), to encourage the participants to continue to think aloud while completing the question. However, most participants did not vocalize unless they were reading the question. Walbridge (2000) notes that the think-aloud technique reveals the thought processes of the participants, which can indicate why they make particular choices. It is recommended that usability participants be encouraged to think aloud as the information obtained should be well worth the effort.

A video capture software was used which provided high quality videos, and allowed the researchers to go back and check any pathway or timing questions they had. McGillis and Toms (2001) used tracking software exclusively. The video capture software was particularly important in the UNT studies due to the high number of sessions where only a moderator was present.

Participants were allowed to choose either Netscape or Internet Explorer to complete the tasks. McGillis and Toms (2001) suggest that participants be allowed to use the browser of their choice to avoid any variation in usability caused by an unfamiliar browser. Many students were content with Netscape, the default on the terminals, but others appreciated the ability to use the browser they were most comfortable with.

Tasks were printed out and available for the participants to look at while doing the study. Participants appreciated having the questions in front of them, although it had to be made clear several times that participants were not expected to write the path on the sheets! A number of students would pick the question up and look at it or glance down at it. Chisman et al. (1999) notes that non-English speakers had difficulty understanding some of the test questions, thus supporting our decision to provide the questions in written form as it is frequently easier to understand information presented in written form than in verbal form.

At the end of the session, participants were offered a chocolate bar or box of candy to provide "immediate gratification." Participants appreciated the chocolate bars as some were "down" after the session and the candy perked them back up. This is highly recommended as the immediate gratification effect seemed to overcome any negative feeling from the study. It is important to have participants feel good about the process, especially if you want them to return for another part of the study or to be available for the next study.

A posttest questionnaire, which asked the participants for their likes and dislikes of the site as well as what made it easy and difficult to use, was administered after the formal usability test. The posttest questionnaire elicited a lot of useful information. Most students did not fill in all the blanks and this was permitted as forcing them to fill in all the blanks would make it more like a "test." It was more important that the participants left with a good feeling about the library. Often the comments reflected what had been observed, so overall there wasn't as much data missing as the empty blanks would suggest. McGillis and Toms (2001) note that posttest surveys provide the participants' perceptions of using the site and the features. Questionnaires are useful to balance the feedback from the study (Campbell, 2001a). Participants were also asked to fill in a demographic questionnaire.

The use of a posttest questionnaire allowed students some time to relax and led into the debriefing sessions. Debriefing sessions for the moderator and observers were also included as time permitted. Chisman et al. (1999) state that debriefing participants and test administrators after each study is essential for a quality result. Walbridge (2000) notes that debriefing offers an opportunity to provide information literacy training to the participants. Debriefing also allows the moderator and observers to examine the results. Rubin (1994) notes that the debriefing portion is the key to fixing the problems indicated by the study results. The informal comments provided by the participants during the debriefing were often enlightening (Battleson et al., 2001), possibly because the "test" had concluded.

Data Recording, Analysis, and Presentation of Results

A results sheet was used for each participant and included the names of the moderator and observer, the time taken to complete the task, whether the task was successfully completed, what pathway was taken to complete the task, and what problems were encountered. The observers were encouraged to note the behavior of the participants and to include any comments that were expressed as part of the "think-aloud" process on the sheet. Recording the pathway, as well as the number of mouse clicks or pages viewed, provides information on common mistakes which helps to determine what items need to be changed to make the pages more useable. Participants were required to return to the home page before beginning the next question in order to provide a standard starting point for each question.

Using Excel, the success rate, time taken, and number of clicks were recorded for each question across all participants. The average, mode, and median were calculated. Pathway information was recorded in a Word table using the name of the link the participant chose. Posttest questionnaire responses were also recorded in a Word table. The participant number was attached to all data.

The Excel data provided quantitative information on how difficult the Web site was to use and which tasks were more difficult. The pathways were examined to see where the students took a "wrong turn." This information was correlated to determine which links or terminology needed revising. The posttest questionnaire provided additional insight into the usability of the Web site.

Results were presented with suggestions for improvement based on common errors and page problems found during the study.

FOCUS GROUPS

The Basics

The focus group technique has been used for many years in marketing, psychology, and sociology research. Focus groups are an inquiry method that looks at users' opinions or perceptions. Libraries use focus groups primarily for user satisfaction studies, although they are beginning to use them to determine marketing strategies and to incorporate them into Web site redesign projects. Canning (1995) described focus groups as a cost-effective and quick means to elicit relevant information about services and resources. Focus groups can also be part of Web site usability studies.

When incorporated into usability studies, focus groups are used in several different ways. Groups can be used to look at a site initially, usually copies rather than live sites, and discuss issues about the site. This preliminary information is used to create prototypes for the revised site. Other researchers use focus groups after formal usability studies. Some researchers will perform the formal usability studies in a group setting and then immediately have a focus group (Palmquist, 2001), while others work with the usability participants individually and then bring them together for a focus group.

When used in usability studies, focus groups are conducted similarly to other disciplines. There are usually eight to twelve participants, a moderator and perhaps an observer, it may be audio and/or video taped, have eight to ten questions, and last for approximately two hours. Focus groups are another relatively cheap way of gathering input from users as they can be small, with one or two groups, or large, with several to many groups.

Thoughts and Comments

The UNT focus groups ranged from four to six participants. The small size of the groups worked well, especially as participants were allowed to digress from the questions. The researchers believed that this promoted a more positive feeling for the experience and also, for the same reason, would answer very quick, specific reference questions. An example of this process was several participants asked why UNT did not have an online form for interlibrary loans. The moderator replied that there was a form, quickly discussed where the form was located, and used the question as an example of why the studies were being performed! Responding to some questions at the point of need increased participant satisfaction and showed that the Libraries were interested in students needs and not just in gathering data.

Participants were asked for their first comment in a round robin manner to create a comfort level among the group members. After the first set of comments, participants were allowed to offer comments in free form. Generally, after each person had given an answer, there was more interaction among the attendees. Students were respectful of others' opinions as had been requested at the beginning of the group.

When using focus groups after formal usability studies, an Internet accessible computer should be available or screen shots of the main pages should be provided. Frequently, participants wanted to review the pages to remember specific comments they had during the task completion. Screen shots were included in the second series of focus groups and the participants provided many more useful and specific comments.

Another very important lesson learned from the UNT studies was to ensure that the focus groups were held in a welcoming environment. The first set of focus groups were held in a lecture-like room with dark brick walls and it was a frequently used room so the researchers were unable to "decorate" it with homey touches. Participants who had been outgoing and verbal in the usability studies were quieter during the focus groups, which is the inverse to the expected situation. The second series of focus groups were held in the same room as the usability studies which, although significantly smaller, worked very well. Even participants who were subdued during the usability studies were comfortable during the focus groups. Collins and Aguinaga (2001) note that they took great care to make the test room homey and comfortable.

Participants were provided with comment sheets that had each question written on them, with one question per page. The sheets were introduced by the moderator as a place to write down comments participants didn't have time to make during the discussion or comments they didn't want to vocalize. Pens were provided to avoid any concerns that their comments could be traced back to them as anonymity had been assured. The comment sheets were generally not utilized, although there were several occasions where students used them when they did not agree with the general consensus of the group and wanted to ensure that their comments were recorded. Since the groups were small and there was plenty of time allowed, it is possible that students didn't have many more comments to add. Comment sheets will be provided in subsequent studies as the few comments received were very valuable.

Data Collection, Analysis, and Presentation of Results

Data collected from focus groups can be difficult to analyze as it is primarily qualitative information rather than quantitative. One method to deal with this is to put the comments in a Word table. Then, assign a subject heading or category to each comment. Using this method makes it easy to gather comments with the same subject or category together using the sort command in Word. Another way is to enter all comments, scan them for trends, decide on major categories or subjects, and cut and paste comments into the appropriate category. The number of positive and negative comments in each category can then be counted to gather some quantitative information on each category. Comments are broken into very small pieces using this technique. Participant numbers or identification should be assigned to each comment to track the owner of the comments especially if trends across different populations are being looked for.

Examples of categories include design issues, such as colors and navigation; comments on specific pages; terminology; and desired links–links users would like to see on the home page or other pages. Categories will vary depending on the questions asked and the discussion threads. A study by Thomsett-Scott (2004), utilized both focus groups and formal usability studies to explore the best and the worst of the UNT Libraries' home page and three other academic library home pages. During the focus groups, the participants pulled out links and terminology that were missing for the UNT page and discussed design elements, such as a direct catalog search box on the home page, which would improve the usability of the UNT home page.

COGNITIVE WALKTHROUGHS

The Basics

The cognitive walkthrough is an inspection technique where "usability experts" or designers work through the Web site using scenarios that approximate the users' experiences. The scenarios are often very complex and require the walkthrough team to completely get into the users' point of view. For example, a common scenario is "I am a first year student and need to find three magazine articles on anemia. I have never used the library before and don't know what anemia means." In a face-to-face situation, the librarian would initiate a reference interview and guide the student through the steps necessary to find information on their topic. Unfortunately, this student is not in the library but on the Internet approaching an unfamiliar and possibly complex Web site.

Although the word "expert" is included in the previous paragraph, a well-prepared and user-passionate team of library staff can do almost as well. The essential characteristic of an effective cognitive walkthrough team is being able to look at a question and find the correct route to locate the answer from a user's perspective (Campbell, 2001a). There are usually two to three members on the team.

There are often eight to ten tasks, frequently based on the most common or essential tasks that the Web site is able to answer (Campbell, 2001a). These tasks often necessitate finding the catalog, databases, interlibrary loan forms, contact information, online reference services, subject guides, tutorials, and more. The age and library experience of the user are identified as well as any special circumstances, such as a disability.

The team will go through the steps involved to complete each task. As they move through the Web pages necessary to answer the task, a list of the pages and the errors or usability issues discovered will be kept. Issues can be direct errors, such as wrong or outdated information, or indirect, such as terminology issues (library speak, multiple terms for one item), and design issues (links not changing color, poor background colors, etc.). Essentially, the team needs to look for anything that inhibits the user's ability to locate the information they need. Required changes can then be prioritized. Some of these will be easy to fix, while others will require additional effort, such as needing the agreement of colleagues when deciding whether the catalog should be titled "online catalog," "library catalog," "catalog of books and more," etc. Other "big deal" modifications include changing titles of pages which may affect navigation elements, color standardization among different departments of the library, re-arranging the information or links on pages, and similar issues.

Thoughts and Comments

Cognitive walkthroughs were not selected for the UNT studies as direct user participation was desired. However, they are highly recommended, especially before the formal usability study technique. The benefit of performing a cognitive walkthrough is that the usability team will catch many of the more obvious errors that detract from the usability of the site. While observing participants during the formal usability studies, the UNT researchers discovered two incidences of this type of error: the response time to e-mail questions was listed as twenty-four, forty-eight and twenty-four to forty-eight hours on various pages and several of the links on the home page of the sub site did not change color after being clicked while the remaining ones did. These two errors occasionally distracted participants during the task-based tests. It is worthy of note that the site was examined six months prior to the study. This suggests that reviewing the site without considering the user will find some issues, such as outdated information, grammar and spellings mistakes, but will not catch all of the usability mistakes.

Cognitive walkthroughs are a relatively cheap method of cleaning up a Web site. Since walkthroughs don't involve actual users, they can be done at anytime and as frequently as desired. A simple way to get volunteers is to solicit several librarian friends, order in pizza, develop some scenarios and go for it! As mentioned above, the primary qualification for the "walkers" is the ability to put themselves in the user's shoes. However, there is no substitute for involving the users as even the best cognitive walkthrough team will still miss things that usability studies with real users will find (Campbell, 2001a).

CONCLUSION

With the rapid and still-growing increase in the number of users accessing library resources from off-campus, it is more important than ever that libraries have Web sites that are "useable" without library staff mediation. Web site usability testing will help to achieve this. Task-based testing, focus groups, and cognitive walkthroughs are relatively easy and effective Web site usability testing methods that can be modified to fit most library budgets. Learning from the results of previous studies can increase the usefulness of the next study. Libraries serving off-campus users will find user satisfaction with their Web site increase through the use of Web site usability testing.

REFERENCES

Battleson, B., Booth, A., & Weintrop, J. (2001). Usability testing of an academic library web site: A case study. *Journal of Academic Librarianship, 27*(3), 188-198.

Campbell, N. (2001a). Usability methods. In N. Campbell (Ed.), *Usability assessment of library-related web sites*, (pp. 1-10). Library and Information Technology Association, Chicago.

Campbell, N. (2001b). Conducting a usability study. In N. Campbell (Ed.), *Usability assessment of library-related web sites*, (pp. 11-15). Library and Information Technology Association, Chicago.

Campbell, N., Walbridge, S., Chisman, J., & Diller, K.R. (1999). Discovering the user: A practical glance at usability testing. *Electronic Library, 17*(5), 307-311.

Canning, C.S. (1995). Using focus groups to evaluate library services in a problem-based learning curriculum. *Medical Reference Quarterly, 14*(3), 75-81.

Chisman, J., Diller, K., & Walbridge, S. (1999). Usability testing: A case study. *College & Research Libraries, 60*(6), 552-69.

Cockrell, B., & Jayne, E. (2002). How do I find an article? Insights from a web usability study. *The Journal of Academic Librarianship, 28*(3), 122-132.

Collins, K. & Aguinaga, J. (2001). Learning as we go: Arizona State University West Library's usability experience. In N. Campbell (Ed.), *Usability assessment of library-related web sites,* (pp. 16-29). Library and Information Technology Association, Chicago.

Dickstein, R. & Mills, V. (2000). Usability testing at the University of Arizona Library: How to let users in on the design. *Information Technology and Libraries, 19*(3), 144-151.

Gullikson, S., Blades, R., Bragdon, M., McKibbon, S., Sparling, M., & Toms, E. G. (1999). The impact of information architecture on academic web site usability. *Electronic Library, 17*(5), 293-304.

Hudson, L. (2000). Radical usability (or, why you need to stop redesigning your website). *Library Computing, 19*(1/2), 86-92.

Jeffries, R. & Desurvire, H. (1992). Usability testing versus heuristic evaluation: Was there a contest? *SIGCHI Bulletin, 24*(4), 39-41.

McGillis, L. & Toms, E. G. (2001). Usability of the academic library web site: Implications for design. *College and Research Libraries, 62*(4), 355-368.

McMullen, S. (2001). Usability testing in a library web site redesign project. *Reference Services Review, 29*(1), 7-22.

Norlin, E. and Winters, C. (2002). *Usability testing for library web sites.* American Library Association, Chicago.

Palmquist, R.A. (2001). An overview of usability for the study of users' web-based information retrieval behavior. *Journal of Education for Library and Information Science, 42*(2), 123-136.

Rubin, J. (1994). *The handbook of usability testing: How to plan, design and conduct effective tests.* New York: Wiley.

Skelton, T. (1992). Testing the usability of usability testing. *Technical Communications, September,* 343- 358.

Thomsett-Scott, B. (2004). *Pick and choose: Incorporating other library web sites into a web site usability study to see what works best for your users.* Unpublished manuscript.

Walbridge, S. (2000). Usability testing and libraries: The WSU experience. *ALKI, 16*(3), 23-24.

Pests, Welcomed Guests, or Tolerated Outsiders? Attitudes of Academic Librarians Toward Distance Students from Unaffiliated Institutions

Johanna Tuñón

Nova Southeastern University

Rita Barsun

Walden University

Laura Lucio Ramirez

Nova Southeastern University

SUMMARY. Librarians are seeing increasing numbers of distance students from other institutions using proximal library facilities for their research. Academic librarians were surveyed to learn more about their attitudes toward these unaffiliated distance students. The 107 responses to the survey found that, overall, academic librarians reflected a service attitude. Few expressed overtly hostile attitudes, but there were concerns about the strains unaffiliated distance students put on their libraries' resources and services.

KEYWORDS. Distance learners, librarian attitudes, study

[Haworth co-indexing entry note]: "Pests, Welcomed Guests, or Tolerated Outsiders? Attitudes of Academic Librarians Toward Distance Students from Unaffiliated Institutions." Tuñón, Johanna, Rita Barsun, and Laura Lucio Ramirez. Co-published simultaneously in *Journal of Library Administration* (The Haworth Information Press, an imprint of The Haworth Press, Inc.) Vol. 41, No. 3/4, 2004, pp. 485-505; and: *The Eleventh Off-Campus Library Services Conference Proceedings* (ed: Patrick B. Mahoney) The Haworth Information Press, an imprint of The Haworth Press, Inc., 2004, pp. 485-505.

http://www.haworthpress.com/web/JLA
Digital Object Identifier: 10.1300/J111v41n03_12

Libraries are seeing increasing numbers of distance students from other, unaffiliated institutions using their library research facilities. This trend is facilitated because state university libraries are usually open to state residents and many private academic institutions either offer free access or are willing to permit access for a fee. Anecdotal evidence has indicated that, in spite of the service philosophy of libraries, the librarians often resent this influx of distance education students from other institutions as "pesky outsiders" who come as "stealth" users to make use of the library resources of other libraries. To examine this issue, a survey was constructed to examine academic librarians' attitudes toward unaffiliated distance students from other institutions that came to use their libraries.

BACKGROUND

Unaffiliated users who expect to avail themselves of the services and resources of academic libraries are in competition with, and may hinder service to, the parent institution's faculty and the students whose tuition contributes significantly to the library's budget. Students' use of *proximal* libraries (nearby geographically) rather than their *home* libraries (those supported by the colleges or universities where they are enrolled) is not a new phenomenon. More than 30 years ago E. J. Josey wrote of "considerable evidence" that undergraduate students from colleges with "woefully inadequate" libraries were turning to other academic libraries (1969, p. 66). In fact, the pressure from students in other institutions on academic libraries in the Chicago area was so acute that a conference was called to discuss the problem and seek a solution (67). Librarians in the Washington, DC, region were confronted with a similar situation in the 1980s because of the presence of many faculty and students who were "lured by internships, fieldwork, and employment opportunities" to the area and far from their own institutions (Kelley, 1985, p. 147). A survey in the late eighties of academic libraries in Virginia revealed that students from other colleges or universities were the most "frequent types" of unaffiliated users (McCulley and Ream, 1988, p. 10).

Because of the phenomenal growth in courses and programs offered at a distance, libraries are seeing increasing numbers of distance learners from other institutions (Allen & Seaman, 2003; National Council on Education Statistics [NCES], 1999; NCES, 2002; NCES, 2003). Although there is an increase in this class of users, the situation is also not a new one. Students enrolled in distance education programs or courses have been included among those making demands on college and university libraries since the sixties. William Archie wrote of "unheard-of-pressures" on academic librarians because of the exploding student population as well as "unheard-of-demands" from all segments of the "non-academic public," including adults studying television courses (1964, pp. 43-44). Five years later there was a noticeable growing demand for college libraries to support individuals in nearby communities taking extension courses from universities that had made no provision for library services (Josey, 1969, p. 70). David Kaser commented on the lack of library support offered by the "open universities, universities without walls, and external degree experiments springing up rapidly" in the seventies (1974, p. 281). As in the past, many distance learners look to local academic libraries as a supplement to, or in place of, service from their home libraries, the libraries of the institutions to which they pay tuition (Dugan & Hernon, 1997; Goodson, 1996; Sutherland, 2000; Unwin, Stephens, & Bolton, 1998). What is the effect on academic librarians faced with expectations for service by outsiders, especially students from other educational institutions?

Service to all and free access to information lie at the very heart of the library profession. For example, Carla Stoffle, in her valedictory message as president of ACRL, reminded readers that a commitment to the free flow of information compels academic librarians to extend services to the communities in which their parent institutions are located (1983, p. 227). More recently, Larry Oberg called "generous service to an unaffiliated public" a moral obligation (1998, para 4). However, as Nancy Courtney noted in a recounting of libraries' responses to the needs of unaffiliated users over a period of 50 years, librarians are often caught between their instinct to provide services to all and "the realities of budgets, space, and the needs of their own clientele" (2001, p. 473). George Bailey lamented that the dream of most librarians to throw open the doors of their libraries to everyone is often shattered by hard facts, perhaps chief of which is the struggle to provide adequate service to their own students and faculty (1961, p. 669). John Waggoner cautioned against any action that would impede service to a library's own academic community (1964, p. 56). One author compared the library trying to serve unaffiliated users to a man trying to support two families on wages barely enough for one (Josey, 1969, p. 66). David Kaser called equality of access to information "almost an article of faith" but also recognized that librarians have a responsibility to manage resources for the best interests of their own institutions (1974, p. 280). W. B. Mitchell was concerned that a library's charge from the state is not being fulfilled when serving others interferes with service to the institution's students or faculty (1982, p. 13). Prince and Nelson were concerned that implementing the right of free access would interfere with service to their primary clientele (1985, p. 26). Masters and Flatness noted that, although helping users "to the fullest extent we can" is a "basic tenet of our profession," doing so might deprive a library's primary users of the service they need (1985, p. 66).

Fred Heath wrote of his philosophical transformation in reconciling "the conflict between a personal commitment to cooperative effort [serving outside users] and responsibilities to a private university community that has purchased enhanced library services at a premium" (1992, p. 16). His story brings into sharp focus Lloyd Jansen's comment on the conflict between idealistic voices that consider offering service to all as an ethical obligation and practical voices that view an academic library's priority as "providing the finest resources and services to its primary users" (1993, p. 10). Charles Wiggins described free access to information as a "basic philosophical commitment" among librarians (1999, para 6) yet acknowledged that one might shortchange primary customers in order to serve secondary users (para 28).

Few academic librarians entered the profession anticipating the need to categorize clients (Ford & Likness, 1989, p. 24). Although the notion of a primary clientele directly contradicts the profession's service ethic (Martin, 1990, p. 24), librarians are "in the last resort the servants of particular [academic] communities" (Flesch, 1997, p. 187). Even the ACRL *Guidelines for the Preparation of Policies on Library Access* recognized the need for "necessary distinctions between primary and other users" (1992, Preamble section). Why must such a distinction be made? Respondents to Nancy Courtney's recent survey of 527 academic libraries included these reasons: security, seating space, impact on library materials, and impact on staff (2003, p. 4). Like her, others have cited security risks or the need to devote resources to security as concerns (Johnson, 1984, p. 405; Johnson, 1998, p. 9; Stoffle, 1983, p. 229; Verhoeven et al., 1996, p. 392) in addition to the competition for seating space (Verhoeven et al., 1996, p. 392; B. Johnson, 1984, p. 405).

Impact on materials involves at least two areas, lost books and the competition for them. For example, in 1978 unaffiliated borrowers at Montana State University accounted for only about 5.5% of total circulation, but the loss rate for them was more than one third of the annual replacement budget (Mitchell, 1982, p. 11). Citing that report, Lloyd Jansen commented that apparently those not directly affiliated with the institution felt no compunction to return the materials (1993, p. 10). As Patricia Kelley noted, the lending library takes all the risks (1985, p. 151). Of 68 library directors surveyed in 1992, 41 restricted or blocked circulation to unaffiliated users because of the number or value of lost items (Mitchell, 1992, p. 38). Another impact on materials is that books needed by students for classes or for papers may have been checked out by outsiders (Bobp & Richey, 1994, p. 7; Jansen, 1993, p. 10; Josey, 1969, p. 73).

Nicewarner and Simon warned that, because unaffiliated users' services and information needs often differ from those of the academic community, librarians might be hard-pressed to meet their needs (1996, p. 435). The effect on staff is mainly in terms of time. Inexperienced outsiders are seldom familiar with the library's space or resources and often require a disproportionate amount of one-to-one assistance (Hammond, 1989, p. 134; Jansen, 1993, p. 9; Masters & Flatness, 1985, p. 67; Verhoeven et al., 1996, p. 396). Time spent with outside users can hamper service to the parent institution's students and faculty, who may have to wait in line or be put on hold while their librarians try to serve others. Such situations may lead to stress, as librarians are torn between their philosophical commitment to serve all comers and the practical constraints of limited resources coupled with budget cutbacks.

The extra time spent with unaffiliated users is a hidden cost, especially to the administrators who allocate funds on the basis of FTE (full-time equivalent) students. Ideally, informing funding agencies of the number and percentage of unaffiliated users would result in additional financial support (Piternick & McInees, 1979, p. 303; Judd 1984, p. 128). Chances are, however, that the funding agencies would not understand the disproportionate time and effort needed to serve such users (Parnell, 2002; Verhoeven et al., 1996, p. 396). David Kaser, almost 30 years ago, estimated that serving an average student user costs $500 a year and a heavy user $2,000 a year (approximately $2,200 and $8,650 respectively in today's figures if one assumes an average 5% annual cost-of-living increase). He then explained that unaffiliated users who make a special effort to visit an academic library are probably heavy users in need of extra assistance because of their unfamiliarity with the system (1974, p. 284). However, seldom are libraries compensated–or compensated adequately–for serving non-affiliated users (Holley, 1972, p. 185).

Limitations on access or service are not only abhorrent to librarians committed to the ideal of free access, but also such limitations can cause further stress because of the attitude of the outside users. The response of a gentleman who retired to New York City in the nineties in anticipation of using the rich library resources there is not atypical. He wrote, " . . . citizen access to the library has dangerously corroded in recent years because the private university library, necessary adjunct to the public library, has withdrawn from public service" (Cohn, 1993, p. 182). In his opinion, there are many ways in which private institutions are supported in part by public monies and should therefore be open to the general public (p. 183). That is apparently a view shared by others, especially with regard to publicly supported (i.e., by taxes) academic libraries. Because they are unaware of the relatively small contribution of tax dollars to a library's overall budget (Jansen 1993, p. 10), unaffiliated users expect to be granted the same level of access and service as the students paying tuition to the parent institution (Russell, 1979, p. 39). They do not realize that the portion of a student's tuition used to support the library is far greater than the amount from their state taxes (Johnson, 1998, p. 10). Librarians are often the ones who bear the brunt of the ire of users denied access or limited in any way.

Advances in technology make the provision of information faster and more convenient, but they can also threaten free availability and open access to materials (Potter, 1987, p. 293). More and more computer center staff or database vendors are insisting on authentication for logging on to a library's databases or even to its computers (Courtney, 2003, p. 5). Librarians who wish to let outsiders take advantage of rich electronic resources can do nothing about the restrictions. Furthermore, they are put into a position of having to act as advocates for policies they do not necessarily support personally or professionally.

If a librarian in the early sixties could describe library budgets as "frequently below the minimal needs for satisfactory service" (Bailey, 1961, p. 669), how much greater is the discrepancy now in light of recent budget cuts, especially the decreases in support for higher education at the state level? Publicly supported colleges and universities are struggling to keep their share of shrinking state budgets, a losing battle in view of the fact that "higher education is the single largest chunk of discretionary spending in the state budget," the amount left over after all other spending decisions have been made (Selingo, 2003, Eroding Foundation section). Even an incomplete list of cuts to higher education funding reads like a sad litany: a decrease of about $19.5 million to the University of Massachusetts (Tynan, 2001, p. 2); universities in at least nine states warned to expect midyear budget cuts (Yudoff, 2002); a $14.8 million decrease in funding to the University of Illinois-Urbana/Champaign, $30 million to the University of Iowa, with five other states–Florida, Massachusetts, Missouri, and Nebraska–experiencing similar cuts (Zeman, 2002); the University of Virginia's expected 30% cut for the 2002-2004 fiscal year and the possibility of Dartmouth College's closing the Sanborn Library in response to a drop in endowments (Albanese, 2002, p. 16); hiring freezes, cancelled serials, and contract delays in the University of California and California State University systems (Albanese, 2003, 18); a 15% slash in funding for New York state libraries (Rogers, 2003, p. 22); and the moving of the allocation for TexShare and Texas libraries to support for K-12 schools (Oder, 2003, p. 24). When the university's budget suffers, the library's budget suffers with shortened hours, hiring freezes, book and serial orders cancelled or put on hold. At the same time, librarians are trying to provide the best service to their primary clientele possible as well as trying to respond as fairly as feasible to demands of students from other institutions.

DEMOGRAPHICS ABOUT THE RESPONDERS' LIBRARIES AND UNAFFILIATED WALK-IN USERS

In an attempt to better understand librarians' attitudes toward unaffiliated distance students who use proximal facilities, academic librarians on a variety of electronic discussion groups including Offcamp (Off Campus Library Services), ILI-L (Information Literacy Instruction Listserv), DIG_REF (Discussion of digital reference services), and PACS-L (Public Access Computer Systems Forum) were invited to participate in a survey in the spring of 2003. An e-mail was distributed on these electronic discussion groups with a description of the purpose of the survey and a Web address where the survey was posted.

The survey was used to gather quantitative evidence to answer several related questions:

- Do unaffiliated distance students use library services from other academic institutions?
- What kinds of library services can unaffiliated distance students access from the home libraries of other institutions?
- Do the academic librarians feel that their resources are adequate to serve students from unaffiliated institutions?
- What attitudes do academic librarians have about providing these services to students from unaffiliated institutions?
- What attitudes do academic librarians have about the home institutions offering these distance programs?
- Is there any difference in attitudes toward unaffiliated users between librarians from public and private institutions?
- Do the responding librarians have distance programs at their own institutions, and if so, how do they view their own efforts to provide library services for their own distance students?

(See the Appendix for a complete list of questions and responses.)

A total of 107 surveys were returned via e-mail with almost 62% or 66 of the responses from librarians at state institutions in either community college or state academic libraries, 34% or 36 responses from librarians at private institutions, and 4% (5 responses) from other types of libraries (Question 1). Of the types of libraries represented, 32% were from libraries with research-level or large collections with more than 500,000 volumes. Another 31% of the libraries had medium-sized collections of 200,000 to 500,000 volumes, and 37% came from libraries with collections with less than 200,000 volumes (Question 2).

Perhaps not surprisingly given the increasing popularity of distance education in the last decade, 88% of librarians at state academic libraries reported that unaffiliated distance students from other institutions were using their libraries' services (Question 3). When asked in question 4 if the librarians knew which institutions' students used their facilities, the librarians mentioned the

University of Phoenix (13), Emporia State University (4), and Nova South-eastern University (4) most frequently. (See Question 4 for the complete list.) Surprisingly, 86% of the librarians working at private institutions reported that they too had unaffiliated distance students using their services.

RESPONDERS' PERCEPTIONS OF THE SUPPORT PROVIDED BY OTHER INSTITUTIONS FOR THEIR HOME STUDENTS IN DISTANCE PROGRAMS

Questions 5, 6, and 7 in the survey were designed to see what attitudes the responding librarians had about the library services being provided by the distance students' home institutions. Question 5 asked librarians how adequate they thought the library services provided by the home institutions were to support the needs of the home institution's distance students. Opinions were about evenly divided between librarians who thought that the home libraries were providing adequate services, librarians who thought they were not, and librarians who were not sure. One comment, however, was rather pointed about the services of one of the for-profit universities: "[x university's] 'state of the art library' which they advertise on TV is useless. All their local students end up at our library. We are in effect giving free library service to [x university]. This ups their profit margin I am sure." Overall, however, it is worth noting that librarians at state university and community college libraries had more positive attitudes about the library services provided by the home institutions than did librarians at private academic institutions. About one-third of the librarians said that they had contacted the librarians at the students' home institutions, and librarians at public institutions were more likely to do so than librarians at private institutions (Question 6). On the other hand, the third of the librarians with negative attitudes indicated that they based these attitudes most often on the comments and requests made by unaffiliated students (Question 7).

RESPONDERS' PERCEPTION OF THE ADEQUACY OF THEIR LIBRARY COLLECTIONS TO SUPPORT RESEARCH NEEDS OF UNAFFILIATED WALK-IN USERS

Question 8 was designed to see if librarians considered their libraries adequate to support the research needs of the distance students who are walk-in users of their facilities. The frustration of some librarians was reflected in one librarian's comment, "[The collection is] not adequate for our own students, much less anyone else." Nevertheless, over 50% of the librarians responding thought that their libraries were adequate to meet the research needs of the unaffiliated walk-in users from other institutions. Librarians at state academic libraries were most satisfied with the adequacy of their home collections, followed by libraries at private academic institutions. Not surprisingly, librarians at community colleges were least likely to consider their resources adequate to meet the research needs from unaffiliated distance students.

Comments about Question 8 reflected some other frustrations as well. One librarian noted, "We are a small campus and can only serve our own student's subject areas. Students from other units often get 'stroppy' when they find the resources they want aren't here." Another librarian challenged why libraries should even feel responsible for trying to support the research needs of students from other institutions with the comment, "But is that my institution's responsibility?"

Question 9 raised the most issues. Overall, the general attitudes toward distance students from other institutions were either positive or neutral or ambivalent. Fewer than 10% of the respondents reported negative feelings while mixed feelings were reported about as frequently as positive attitudes in the various types of libraries. Not surprisingly, more public academic librarians reported positive attitudes toward walk-in users than librarians working in private academic institutions. Librarians generally had a genuine service attitude as was reflected in this comment by a private academic librarian: "Of course, our own students and faculty are the priority, but we are happy to help anyone."

A number of themes emerged in the comments that responders made to Question 9. Some librarians expressed irritation about serving unaffiliated distance students. One librarian complained about students using his/her library because it was more convenient than driving to the students' library. The librarian noted that these students were "a drain on time and resources." Other negative comments included:

- Although we are the largest library in the area, we ourselves are not so large that we can easily accommodate other students. We feel that they take time, computer space, and materials from our own students.
- I do think some of the distance education institutions are relying all too much on the kindness of their colleagues. No wonder they can charge less tuition. I believe in reciprocal agreements with the emphasis on reciprocal.
- Students/faculty from non-partner institutions that don't contract with us for library services are frowned upon.

Other comments expressed some frustrations with the students from other institutions:

- We try to be very helpful, but sometimes when the students are expecting the world, I point out that we're providing a very nice service to them for nothing.
- [Distance students] are frequently very demanding and some have been quite rude about the "lack of resources" to meet their study needs. They also frequently complain about not having access to networked material.
- We do not ask if they are a distant ed. student or a regular student. [The attitude toward walk-in distance students by librarians is] generally positive, but for those students at the nearby private institution that are in here in droves–it takes time to teach them how to use our system, and also teach them about the research process in general.
- We welcome community people in our library, but if they want a similar degree from a similar institution, why use our resources to get a degree elsewhere? We pay for the resources, but someone else gets the student's tuition.

A number of librarians drew a distinction between their feelings toward the students from other institutions and their feelings toward the policies of the institutions that students attend:

- I am very positive about the students themselves, less enthusiastic about the home institution.
- Positive toward the student but negative toward the institution–seen as a "for profit parasite."
- As usual some students are clueless, some are not, but in some cases the schools are failing the students and we are left to pick up the pieces.
- If they've just been told to go out and find a library, we resent it; if they're looking for something special that only we have, that's fine.

The time spent helping unaffiliated distance students was reported to be an issue by 30% of the respondents. One-third (34%) thought that it was OK to provide students from other institutions with a lower level of service than their own students. A total of 62% of librarians who responded reported that they wanted to help distance students learn to use their home libraries. However, only 44% of these librarians assumed that the unaffiliated students did not know about their home institutions' library services because of a lack of bibliographic instruction on the part of the home libraries. Comments included: "Distance students tend to take up a lot of time particularly on weekends when the Info desk is only manned by one person." and "I don't mind helping, but I also try to encourage them to use the resources that they are paying for and to become aware of them."

LIBRARY SERVICES THAT DISTANCE STUDENTS FROM UNAFFILIATED INSTITUTIONS CAN ACCESS AT LOCAL LIBRARIES IN THEIR AREAS

Question 10 was designed to learn more about which services walk-in users could access free or for a fee at various types of institutions. Librarians reported an impressive array of services available at no charge to walk-in distance students from other institutions. These included in-house use of print materials (97%), in-house access to proprietary databases, (87%), in-house access to the Internet and non-proprietary databases such as ERIC (86%), references services in person (93%), and virtual reference by phone, chat, or e-mail (63%). Some state academic and community college libraries (8%) even offered free interlibrary loan to walk-in users.

Assumptions that libraries funded by state institutions would have more liberal rules toward non-students did not always hold true. Only one librarian out of the 107 responses reported that his or her library provided no library services of any kind to any outside users, and that individual happened to be from a state institution. Free services available for walk-in distance students at state institutions included in-house use of print materials (100%), in-library access to proprietary databases (88%), in-house access to the Internet and non-proprietary databases such as ERIC (90%), reference services in person (94%) and by phone, chat, or e-mail (75%). A surprising number of private academic libraries reported providing at least some free services to unaffiliated students, and all but one private academic library permitted walk-in users from unaffiliated institutions to have at least in-house access to print materials.

Overall, the attitudes reported by all types of institutions were relatively positive toward unaffiliated walk-in distance students, as reflected by the answers to Question 11. Librarians who responded were asked to report about any attitudes observed at their libraries and not just about their own feelings. Positive attitudes reported included 50% of responders feeling that unaffiliated distance students were taxpayers who should be able to use resources and 72% thought that unaffiliated distance students were usually appreciative of the library services provided by the host library. Positive comments included:

- Our library sees relatively few DE students from other univ[ersities], so we are able to handle them on a case-by-case basis. Our overall philosophy is to try to acquaint them with the services and resources from their own univ[ersities] and to try to help them with their initial comfort level so that they will be comfortable doing so.

- My attitude is that we are a public university, and should give reference assistance to these students and allow them to use our resources to the best of our ability.
- I try to be as helpful as I can. I think most librarians here feel the same.

Other responses were more ambivalent. One librarian commented, "I am very positive about the students themselves . . . Some of my coworkers share my attitude; others see these students as moochers." However, another librarian noted, "For my 2 cents, it is not the students fault, but there are institutions who are certainly willing to take their money and then expect other institutions to support them." More clearly negative attitudes included comments about unaffiliated students from other institutions who demanded services that they were not paying for (29%), unaffiliated students being "clueless" (37%), "moochers" (7%), and/or "outsiders" (13%). Comments included:

- The other institutions see distance ed programs as a "cash cow"–they bring in all these students, yet don't do anything about providing access to library resources. Our students pay for the resources, and these other institutions seem to think it's OK to send their students to us without paying for their share of the services.
- It can get very frustrating to deal with students who demand services that they haven't paid for via tuition.

DISTANCE PROGRAMS OFFERED BY THE HOME INSTITUTIONS OF THE SURVEY RESONDERS

Questions 12, 13, and 14 were included in the survey to see if the respondents worked at institutions that offered distance education programs of their own and if their attitudes differed toward their own distance students. A total of 85% of the responders worked at academic institutions that offered distance education programs of their own (Question 12). As one librarian noted, "[It is] the same old story everywhere–The old folks are wary of technology and its role in education AND the young whippersnappers actively push the envelope. Ahhhh–the winds of change will blow you away sometimes." Interestingly enough, 58% reported positive attitudes toward their own distance students and their research needs versus 36% toward distance students from other institutions. Negative attitudes also dropped from 8% toward unaffiliated distance students from other institutions to 2% toward distance students from the home academic institutions (Question 13). In Question 14, 53% of the librarians felt that their libraries should be responsible for providing library services to their own distance students rather than having a different academic department handling the students.

CONCLUSIONS

Many of the same themes and concerns expressed by the academic librarians responding in this survey to questions about unaffiliated *distance* students were consistent with past attitudes expressed by other librarians about unaffiliated *local* students' use of their libraries. Distance education seems to have accelerated the numbers of unaffiliated library users using libraries other than those at their home institutions. Librarians responding to this survey reflected a strong commitment to free access to information and a service philosophy that is characteristic of the library profession as a whole. Libraries at both private and public institutions provided a wide array of services to unaffiliated students of all types. Not surprisingly, however, state academic libraries and community college libraries did provide more services to walk-in users from the public than did private institutions. Several librarians commented on the fact that they tried to avoid categorizing students by type of user (home or unaffiliated) or the level of service these users should be entitled to receive. Comments indicated that librarians, particularly at smaller institutions, also worried about the appropriateness of their collections to meet the research needs of unaffiliated users. Librarians expressed concerns in their comments about the drain on staff and financial resources that unaffiliated patrons created. Having said that, most librarians reported that their libraries did provide unaffiliated students with walk-in access to the host library's proprietary databases. Although some librarians did report resenting institutions that send their students out to "mooch" library services from other institutions, the majority of librarians reported a positive attitude toward serving individual users both on their own part and that of their colleagues.

Attitudes of entitlement to services at unaffiliated libraries by some walk-in library users were reported as one irritant for some of the responding librarians. In spite of considering many unaffiliated users as "clueless" on how to use the host libraries, most librarians did not fault the home libraries for these unaffiliated users not having basic library skills to locate information effectively. Perhaps one reason was that most of the responding librarians worked at institutions with distance programs of their own, and they better understood the challenges of providing library training and services to distance students. Librarians responding to the survey certainly saw serving their home institutions' distance students as part of their libraries' responsibilities. It would be interesting to see if the attitudes of public librarians towards distance students differ greatly from those of academic librarians.

REFERENCES

Albanese, A. (2002). Academic library budgets squeezed by lowered revenue. *Library Journal, 127*(2), 16.

Albanese, A. (2003). California universities face massive budget cuts. *Library Journal, 128*(1), 18.

Allen, I. E., & Seaman, J. (2003). *Sizing the opportunity: The quality and extent of online education in the United States, 2002 and 2003.* The Sloan Consortium. Retrieved November 19, 2003, from http://www.aln.org/resources/sizing_opportunity. pdf.

Archie, W. C. (1964). The college library and the community. *North Carolina Libraries, 22*(2) 42-47.

Association of College and Research Libraries. (1992). *Guidelines for the preparation of policies on library access.* Retrieved November 15, 2003, from http://www. ala.org/Content/NavigationMenu/ACRL/Standards_and_Guidelines/Guidelines_ for_the_ Preparation_of_Policies_on_Library_Access.htm. First published in *College & Research Libraries News, 53*(11), 709-711.

Bailey, G. M. (1961). Demands on college and university libraries in metropolitan centers. *Illinois Libraries, 43*, 667-675.

Bobp, M. E., & Richey, D. (1994). Serving secondary users: Can it continue? *College & Undergraduate Libraries, 1*(2), 1-14.

Cohn, W. (1993). Private stacks, public funding. *American Libraries, 24*(2), 182-183.

Courtney, N. (2001). Barbarians at the gates: A half-century of unaffiliated users in academic libraries. *The Journal of Academic Librarianship, 27*, 473-480.

Courtney, N. (2003). Unaffiliated users' access to academic libraries: A survey. *The Journal of Academic Librarianship, 29*(1), 3-7.

Dugan, R. E., & Hernon, P. (1997). Distance education: Provider and victim libraries. *The Journal of Academic Librarianship, 23*, 315-318.

Flesch, J. (1997, September). Which library is mine? The university library and the independent scholar. *Australian Academic & Research Libraries, 28*, 181-187.

Ford, B. J., & Likness, C. S. (1989). Varied clientele, services objectives and limited resources: The academic library in transition. *Urban Academic Librarian, 6/7*, 20-24.

Goodson, C. (1996, Summer). A continuing challenge for librarians. *MC Journal: The Journal of Academic Media Librarianship 4*(1). Accessed November 24, 2001, from http://wings.buffalo.edu/publications/mcjrnl/.

Hammond, C. B. (1989). Aliens in the house: Those other students who use your library. *Research Strategies, 7*(3), 134-137.

Heath, F. (1992). Conflict of mission: The midsize private university in an urban environment. In G. B. McCabe (Ed.), *Academic libraries in urban and metropolitan areas: A management handbook* (pp. 15-23). New York: Greenwood Press.

Holley, E. G. (1972). Organization and administration of urban university libraries. *College and Research Libraries, 33*(2), 175-189.

Jansen, L. M. (1993). Welcome or not, here they come: Unaffiliated users of academic libraries. *Reference Services Review, 21*(1), 7-14.

Johnson, B. I. (1984). A case study in closing the university library to the public. *College and Research Libraries News, 45,* 404-407.

Johnson, P. (1998). Serving unaffiliated users in publicly funded academic libraries. *Technicalities, 18*(1), 8-11.

Josey, E. J. (1969). Community use of academic libraries. *Library Trends, 18*(1), 66-74.

Judd, B. (1984). Community use of public academic libraries in New York State: A CUNY/CUNY survey. *The Bookmark, 42*(11), 126-134.

Kaser, D. (1974). Library access and the mobility of users. *College and Research Libraries, 35*(4), 280- 284.

Kelley, P. M. (1985). Library privileges for off-campus faculty and students: The view from an impacted library. *The Off-Campus Library Services Conference Proceedings* (pp. 147-156). Mount Pleasant, MI: Central Michigan University.

Klotsche, M. J. (1969). The role of the academic library in urban development. *College and Research Libraries, 30*(2), 126-129.

Martin, R. R. (1990). The paradox of public service: Where do we draw the line? *College and Research Libraries, 51*(1), 20-26.

Masters, D., & Flatness, G. (1985). Yours, mine and ours: Reference service and the non-affiliated user. *The Reference Librarian, 12,* 65-71.

McCulley, L., & Ream, D. (1988). Public use of academic libraries in Virginia. *Virginia Librarian, 34,* 9-12.

Mitchell, E. S. (1992). General circulation policies for private citizens: The practices of publicly supported academic libraries. In G. B. McCabe (Ed.), *Academic libraries in urban and metropolitan areas: A management handbook* (pp. 33-44). New York: Greenwood Press.

Mitchell, W. B. (1982). Formulating a policy for academic library service to unaffiliated borrowers: Some problems and considerations. *PNLA Quarterly, 46*(3), 10-17.

National Center for Education Statistics. (1999). *Distance education at postsecondary education institutions: 1997-1998.* Retrieved November 19, 2003, from http://nces.ed.gov/surveys/peqis/publications/2000013/.

National Center for Education Statistics. (2003). *Distance education at postsecondary education institutions: 1997-1998.* Retrieved November 19, 2003, from http://nces.ed.gov/pubsearch/pubsinfo.asp?pubid=2003017.

National Center for Education Statistics. (2002). *A profile of participation in distance education: 1999-2000.* Retrieved November 19, 2003, from http://nces.ed.gov/pubsearch/pubsinfo.asp?pubid=2003154.

Nicewarner, M., & Simon, M. (1996). Achieving community borrower compliance with an urban university library's circulation policies: One university's solution. *The Journal of Academic Librarianship, 22,* 435-439.

Oberg, L. R. (1998). Non-primary clientele: An emerging concern for college librarians. *Moveable Type: The Newsletter of the Mark O. Hatfield Library, 5*(2). Retrieved November 12, 2003, from http://library.willamette.edu/publications/movtyp/spring98/oberg.htm.

Oder, N. (2003). Texas governor aims to redirect TIF. *Library Journal, 128*(5), 24.

Parnell, S. (2002). Redefining the cost and complexity of library services for open and distance learning. *International Review of Research in Open and Distance Learning, 3*(2). Retrieved November 12, 2003, from http://www.irrodl.org/content/v3.2/parnell.html.

Piternick, A. B., & McInnes, D. N. (1975). Sharing resources: Outside use of academic libraries in British Columbia. *Canadian Library Journal, 32,* 299-308.

Potter, W. G. (1987). Libraries, computing centers, and freedom of access: Libraries and computing centers: Issues of mutual concern. *The Journal of Academic Librarianship, 13,* 293-394.

Prince, W. W., & Nelson, W. N. (1985). Public access to academic libraries. *Tennessee Librarian, 37*(1), 25-28.

Rogers, M. (2003). New York governor's budget spurs furor. *Library Journal, 128*(5), 22-23.

Russell, R. E. (1979). Services for whom: A search for identity. *Tennessee Librarian, 31*(4), 36-40.

Selingo, J. (2003). The disappearing state in public higher education: When the recession ends, appropriations may not rebound. *The Chronicle of Higher Education, 49*(25), A22. Retrieved November 18, 2003, from http://chronicle.com/free/v49/i25/25a02201.htm.

Stoffle, C. (1983). ACRL President's report: 1982-1983. *College & Research Libraries News, 44,* 227-232.

Sutherland, J. (2000). *Library use among adult distance learners: Its implications for local public and academic libraries.* Unpublished capstone project, University College, University of Denver.

Tynan, T. (2001). Massachusetts' colleges stunned by doubled state budget cuts. *Community College Week, 4*(9), 2.

Unwin, L., Stephens, K., & Bolton, N. (1998). *The role of the library in distance learning: A study of postgraduate students, course providers and librarians in the UK.* New Providence, NJ: Bowker-Saur.

Verhoeven, S., Cooksey, E. B., & Hand, C. A. (1996). The disproportionate use of reference desk service by external users at an urban university library. *RQ, 35,* 392-397.

Waggoner, J. P. (1964). The role of the private university library. *North Carolina Libraries, 22*(2), 55-57.

Wiggins, Charles P. (1999). *Services to unaffiliated patrons in public college and university libraries.* Accessed November 20, 2003, from http://web.archive.org/web/20020305183906/ http://home.att.net/~cpwiggins/librarianship/portfolio/unaff_pat.html.

Yudof, M. G. (2002). Point of view: Is the public research university dead? *Chronicle of Higher Education, 48*(18), B24.

Zeman, Elizabeth. (2002, January 16). Budget cuts hit public universities. *Daily Illini.* Retrieved November 18, 2003, from http://www.uwire.com/content/topnews011602001.html.

APPENDIX

Question 1: I work at a:

Community college library (CC)	15
State academic library (SA)	51
Private academic library (PR)	36
Other (OTH)	5
TOTAL =	107

Question 2: Size of library collection:

	Total = 107	SA = 51	PR = 36	CC = 15	OTH = 5
More than 1,000,000 volumes	18	17	1	-	-
Between 500,000 and 1,000,000 volumes	16	11	4	-	1
Between 200,000 and 500,000 volumes	33	17	14	1	1
Less than 200,000 volumes	40	6	17	14	3

Question 3: Are you aware of any distance students from other institutions using or asking to use services at your library?

	Total = 107	SA = 51	PR = 36	CC = 15	OTH = 5
Yes	92	45	31	11	5
No	-	-	-	-	-
Not sure	15	6	5	4	-

Question 4: Identify institutions that your walk-in distance students are most commonly affiliated with. (Total noted in parentheses if more than one occurrence.)

Argosy
Augsburg
Baker University
Barry University (2)
Barton College
BC Campus
Bluefield College
Bowie State University
Brock University
California State University, Dominguez Hills
California State University, Los Angeles
California University of Pennsylvania
Carson-Newman College
Charles Stuart
Colorado State
Colorado Tech
Community colleges, unnamed (8)
Concordia College
Devry
Duke

Eastern Kentucky University
Eckerd College (2)
Empire State College (2)
Emporia State University (4)
Florida State University (2)
Fort Lewis College
Gainesville College
George Fox University
George Washington University
Hawaii Pacific University
Hawkeye Community College
Iowa Central Community College
James Madison University
Johns Hopkins University
Jones International University
Kaplan Higher Education
Lincoln Memorial University
Linfield College
Louisiana State University
Loyola University (2)

APPENDIX (continued)

Marshall University
McDaniel College
McNeese State University
Medical College of Georgia, School of Nursing
Mineral Area College
Montana State University-Northern
Morningside College
National American University
National Louis University
National University
NC AHECs
Northern Arizona University
Northern Michigan University
Norwich University
Notre Dame College
Nova Southeastern University (4)
OLA
Old Dominion University
Pitt Community College
Pittsburgh State University (2)
Pratt
QUT
Reinhardt College
Roberts Wesleyan College
San Jose State (2)
SFU
Southern Connecticut
Southern Cross
Southern University
St. Leo College
Texas A&M Commerce
Three Rivers Community College
Towson State University
Troy State (2)
Tulane University
UNBC
University of Arizona
University of Central Florida
University of Colorado at Boulder

University of Hawaii
University of Hawaii at Manoa
University of Houston
University of Iowa (3)
University of Kansas
University of Laverne
University of Louisville
University of Maine
University of Maryland University College
University of Nebraska
University of New Orleans
University of North Carolina-Chapel Hill
University of North Texas (3)
University of Northern Colorado
University of Northern Iowa (3)
University of Phoenix (13)
University of Redlands
University of South Dakota (2)
University of South Florida (2)
University of Southern Queensland
University of Utah
University of Virginia
University of Wisconsin
University of Wisconsin-LaCrosse
Upper Iowa University (2)
Valencia Community College
Virginia Tech
Viterbo University
Walden University
Washburn University (2)
Wayland Baptist U
Webber College
Weber State University
Webster University
West Virginia University
Western Baptist College
Western Kentucky University
Wilson Technical College

Other answers:

It's only happened a few times; I can't recall any particular institution
Mainly from other brick and mortar academic institutions in the state
Many are students at other universities, but not distance ed students
Many others
Minnesota schools
Occasional walk-ins taking distance courses from out-of-state institutions
One guy I know of getting his Ph.D. from a California University, not sure which one
Other colleges in our state
Other Michigan academic institutions
Other online places
Other out-of-state institutions (but within 40 miles) that have less resources
Other similar institutions elsewhere in country
Other state institutions with less resources
Other state system universities
Other state universities within South Dakota
Other University of Texas System schools
Other Wisconsin state system schools
Others unknown
Our "sister institution" that has less resources
Private institutions nearby that have limited resources
Several different seminaries

Several others
State distance program
State universities
The list is endless . . .
Too many to mention
Universities in East Carolina
Varies widely
Various inquiries about borrowing books
We don't ask walk-ins for affiliation
We're in an urban area, so we get a few from various places from time to time

Question 5: To the best of your knowledge, do these institutions' libraries provide their distance education students adequate library services?

	Total = 107	SA = 51	PR = 36	CC = 15	OTH = 5
Yes	34	19	6	6	3
No	30	14	11	4	1
Not sure	38	17	17	3	1
Not answered	5	1	2	2	-

Question 6: Have you ever communicated with the librarian(s) at that institution about library services offered to their distance students?

	Total = 107	SA = 51	PR = 36	CC = 15	OTH = 5
Yes	37	22	7	7	1
No	65	28	28	6	3
Not answered	5	1	1	2	1

Question 7: If you answered that the institution is not providing adequate library services for its distance students, which of the following best explains why you reached these conclusions:

	Total = 107	SA = 51	PR = 36	CC = 15	OTH = 5
Student comments or requests	34	16	13	3	2
Info you had about the institution in question	6	4	1	1	-
Other	4	2	-	1	1
Not answered	63	29	22	10	2

Question 8: Do you consider your library's collection adequate to meet the research needs of the walk-in students from the institution(s) you identified in Question 4?

	Total = 107	SA = 51	PR = 36	CC = 15	OTH = 5
Yes	57	36	14	3	5
Not for the topics that students research	11	4	7	-	-
Not for the level of research students need	15	6	3	6	-
Other	17	5	8	4	-
Not answered	6	-	4	2	-

APPENDIX (continued)

Question 9: Which of the following choices best describes the general attitude of you and other librarians toward distance students from other institutions using your library?

	Total = 107	SA = 51	PR = 36	CC = 15	OTH = 5
Positive	39	24	7	6	2
Negative	9	3	6	-	-
Neutral	17	8	7	2	-
Mixed	40	15	16	6	3
Not answered	2	1	-	1	-

Question 10: Please check any services available in your library to walk-in distance students from other institutions:

	Total = 107	SA = 51	PR = 36	CC = 15	OTH = 5
In-house use of print materials	104	51	35	13	5
Circulation privileges	53	32	7	11	3
Fee-based "Friends of the Library" card to check out books	39	20	16	3	-
In-library access to proprietary databases	93	45	30	13	5
In-house access to Internet & non-proprietary databases (e.g., ERIC)	92	46	27	14	5
Free interlibrary loan	9	6	-	3	-
Fee-based interlibrary loan	10	3	2	3	2
Fee-based entry for non-students	2	1	1	-	-
Fee-based access to databases	1	-	1	-	-
Face-to-face reference	100	48	34	13	5
Virtual reference (phone, chat, and/or e-mail)	69	38	18	9	4
No services are available to individuals from other institutions	1	1	-	-	-
Services restricted to outside users with consortial agreements	4	2	1	1	-

Question 11: Check every choice that reflects negative and/or positive attitudes that you have observed among the librarians at your institution toward walk-in distance education students from other institutions:

	Total = 107	SA = 51	PR = 36	CC = 15	OTH = 5
Distance students are taxpayers who should use resources.	54	36	7	9	3
Distance students from other institutions are usually appreciative.	77	40	20	14	3
Librarians should help students learn about own libraries.	66	31	21	9	4

	Total = 107	SA = 51	PR = 36	CC = 15	OTH = 5
Librarians from home don't do BI for their students.	47	25	16	6	-
Distance students demand services without paying.	31	12	14	2	3
It is OK not to provide same level of help.	36	9	19	6	2
The time spent with others is a drain on librarians.	32	14	16	2	-
Distance students from other institutions seem "clueless."	40	20	15	5	-
Distance students from other institutions are "moochers."	8	2	5	-	1
Distance students from other institutions are treated as "outsiders."	14	5	9	-	-

Question 12: Does your own academic institution offer distance or distributed programs?

	Total = 107	SA = 51	PR = 36	CC = 15	OTH = 5
Yes	91	46	26	15	4
No	16	5	10	-	1

Question 13: What would you say is the sentiment among librarians in your library regarding your own distance students' library and research needs?

	Total = 107	SA = 51	PR = 36	CC = 15	OTH = 5
Positive	62	33	16	10	3
Negative	2	-	2	-	-
Neutral	15	4	7	3	1
Mixed	17	11	4	2	-
Not answered	11	3	7	-	1

Question 14: Should distance students at your institution be handled by a department specifically designed and funded to serve distance students rather than by your library?

	Total = 107	SA = 51	PR = 36	CC = 15	OTH = 5
Yes	10	5	3	2	-
No	57	25	21	8	3
Don't know	6	2	2	-	1
Mixed opinion	25	17	4	4	-
Varies from one branch campus to another	1	1	-	-	-
Not answered	8	1	5	1	1

80 Miles from the Nearest Library, with a Research Paper Due Monday: Extending Library Services to Distance Learners

Allyson Washburn
Jessica Draper

Brigham Young University

SUMMARY. This presentation reports the results of a project to extend the services and resources of Brigham Young University's Harold B. Lee Library to distance education students located in many areas of the world. Focusing on students enrolled in university-level English courses, the project team created a one-stop, integrated Web portal of library services and resources in Independent Study courses. This Library portal includes links to subscription databases, interlibrary loan, and personal reference services such as Ask a Librarian Live. The project team promoted faculty members' use of library research in the assignments for their Independent Study English courses. Finally, to ascertain the success of the project and make recommendations for further implementation and improvement, the project team tracked the students' use of library resources for their English courses and evaluated their experience with the portal. The ALA SIRSI's Leader in Library Technology Grant provided funding for the project.

KEYWORDS. Library services, distance learners, evaluation, library resources

[Haworth co-indexing entry note]: "80 Miles from the Nearest Library, with a Research Paper Due Monday: Extending Library Services to Distance Learners." Washburn, Allyson, and Jessica Draper. Co-published simultaneously in *Journal of Library Administration* (The Haworth Information Press, an imprint of The Haworth Press, Inc.) Vol. 41, No. 3/4, 2004, pp. 507-529; and: *The Eleventh Off-Campus Library Services Conference Proceedings* (ed: Patrick B. Mahoney) The Haworth Information Press, an imprint of The Haworth Press, Inc., 2004, pp. 507-529.

http://www.haworthpress.com/web/JLA
Digital Object Identifier: 10.1300/J111v41n03_13

INTRODUCTION

The Harold B. Lee Library is located on the campus of Brigham Young University (BYU), in Provo, Utah. The library holds memberships in the Utah Academic Library Consortium, Great Western Library Alliance, Online Computer Library Center, Research Libraries Group, and other library organizations. Through these memberships, BYU students and employees may also use the facilities of other Utah college and university libraries and major research libraries in the United States. Libraries operated by the Church of Jesus Christ of Latter-day Saints are also available to BYU students and employees, including the library of the Church Historical Department located in Salt Lake City.

The Lee Library facilities are open to students on and off campus, faculty, alumni, and other community patrons. Currently, the Library serves an extensive on-campus and off-campus population, including:

1,502	full-time instructional faculty
28,401	full-time undergraduate and graduate students
4,370	part-time undergraduate and graduate students
20,019	off-campus annual enrollments through Independent Study
1,863	off-campus enrollments in University-level English courses (2000-2001)

The Lee Library's collection numbers over three million volumes, including books, periodicals, government documents, microfilm, and other media and non-print items. The library is a depository for United States and Canadian government documents and regularly receives publications of state and local governments. The Utah Valley Regional Family History Center (UVRFHC) supports family history research through an extensive collection of microfilm and microfiche. The Special Collections and Manuscripts department houses non-circulating books and manuscripts related to Mormonism, western Americana, incunabula, Victorian and Edwardian literature, historical manuscripts and photographs, motion pictures, and items dealing with many other disciplines. The Library provides excellent teaching and research support for faculty and other university personnel.

Brigham Young University has a strong commitment to providing Web-based learning via courseware to off-campus students. The Independent Study program offers over 530 paper and 340 Web-based courses for distance learners. The Library supports BYU's extensive Independent Study program, including approximately 1,800 students enrolled in university-level English courses, and over 20,000 students taking a wide variety of university-level courses. Independent Study currently offers thirty English courses, from basic

College Reading and Writing, to Creative and Technical Writing, English and American Literature, Shakespeare, Poetry and Novels.

BACKGROUND OF THE PROJECT

Suzanne (name changed to protect privacy), a student pursuing a degree through distance education, had been successfully completing assignments for English 251, Fundamentals of Literary Interpretation and Criticism, when she suddenly hit a roadblock. The assignment required her to find two critical reviews of a short story she had read–but she lives 80 miles from the nearest library. After searching the Internet to no avail, she called the librarian who serves remote users. The librarian checked the extensive online resources at the library and quickly located several critical reviews, which she then sent to the student. Problem solved–for the moment.

Many Independent Study students find themselves in Suzanne's situation–especially those students enrolled in BYU's Independent Study program. These students live all over the world as they pursue academic degrees through both paper and Web-based courses. Thus, their access to the research resources they need for their academic experience varies widely. For many of these students, finding high-quality, academic research materials are virtually an impossibility.

Until the library worked with Independent Study to devise an authentication system for the students many instructors at BYU regretfully omitted challenging research assignments when designing their Independent Study courses. Faculty members often feel they cannot include assignments that their students may not have the resources to complete. While this is a valid consideration, it does rob the students of the opportunity that on-campus students have to hone their academic and research skills.

The lack of access to academic resources is the specific problem this project addressed. " . . . much of the distance education literature as well as the discipline-related literature dealing with distance delivery contains minimal reference to the use of the library or library resources by students studying off-campus" (Lebowitz 1997, p. 303). "A review of articles on the topic . . . shows that only a few mention issues related to library access or resource integration" (Beagle 2002, p. 367).

To begin to address this problem, the Library hired a Distributed Learning Coordinator in January of 2002 to specifically support distance education students. One of the major responsibilities of the position is to work with Independent Study employees and faculty to discover ways to incorporate library resources into their courses working together with the Library's Electronic Licensing and Resources Coordinator–who had previously negotiated access for remote users with many of the library's vendors of online databases. Additionally, the Library began working with Independent Study employees early in 2002 to design and implement technological solutions to provide off-campus access to these subscription databases for all students enrolled in Independent Study courses. As a result of these efforts, the students now have access to 53 of the library's online databases, some of which provide full-text content. Thus, the Library is able to extend educational opportunities to the Independent Study students that are equivalent to those available to full-time, on-campus students. This means that faculty members, especially those in the English Department, who expressed frustration over the limitations imposed by the students' lack of access to library resources, can now incorporate those resources into the assignments in their courses.

Simply offering access through the Library Web page, however, is not the same as fulfilling and supporting the students' research needs. The project took the next vital steps by:

- Integrating library services, particularly the live Ask a Librarian feature that provides both live chat and e-mail reference assistance, into a one-stop Web interface
- Incorporating the Library page into English courses, making it easily accessible 24/7 through the course itself
- Conducting formal evaluations with students enrolled in Independent Study English courses (the target population for the project) to elicit feedback on the project's successes, failures, and overall utility
- Publicizing the available library services to both instructors and students in the Independent Study program
- Working with faculty members (initially in the English Department, then campus-wide) to include library and research assignments in the Independent Study courses they develop and refine

This project supports several of the Harold B. Lee Library's stated 5-year objectives, and the 2002-03 Public Service Division's Goals, including (1) reinventing reference services by studying and adapting to the changing teaching and learning environment at BYU and responding to evolving student needs for library support, (2) managing resources wisely by collecting and analyzing data on library operations and services and fostering positive change, (3) licensing common access to commercial digital resources that support undergraduate education, (4) creating digital collections and services that support distributed learning environments, and (5) promoting library services to faculty and students through a variety of channels at every opportunity. In addition, extending vital library services and resources to Independent Study students, then evaluating the program for further refinement, supports BYU's important overall goal to extend the blessings of learning to students all over the world.

PREVIOUS NEEDS ASSESSMENT

In June, 2002, the Department of Continuing Education surveyed students taking courses through Independent Study to assess their experiences with the program, including their responses to three library-specific questions. [See Appendix A for detailed information about the survey.] The survey was sent to all formally admitted Independent Study Bachelors of General Studies students, 700 via e-mail and 489 by telephone, with 179 e-mail responses and 100 telephone responses received. The library-specific questions were:

14. What is your first choice when searching for additional information resources to complete coursework (select ONLY one)?

    Most students (52%) use an Internet search engine to locate resources. A much smaller group (17%) turned to their local libraries. Only 1% used the remote services available at that time through the Lee Library.

15. Which of the following Harold B. Lee Library services are you aware of or have you used in your BGS program?

    The vast majority of students were not aware of library services such as electronic reserve materials, asking for help from a librarian via e-mail or live chat, use of full-text databases (journals, newspapers, encyclopedias, etc.), or instruction in the use of library resources. Being unaware of these services, the students did not use them.

16. The following services are currently available or being considered at the Harold B. Lee Library. How would you rate the helpfulness of each service when completing your coursework? (1 = Not Very Helpful, 7 = Very Helpful)

    Students indicated that several services would be very helpful to them, including remote access to full-text databases, indexes or abstracts; e-mail, toll-free telephone number, and/or real time access to librarians; and guides to doing research in a subject area.

With this information in hand, the target group selected for this project was students enrolled in university-level English courses through BYU's Independent Study program. With over 1,800 individual enrollments, this group had a large enough population to yield valuable, generalizable results. In addition, the English faculty members are actively involved in creating courses and assignments that demand a high degree of rigor to complete, and depend on access to high-quality academic resources.

OBTAINING THE GRANT

In the fall of 2002, the Library became aware of an ALA grant that could support this project. The ALA SIRSI's Leader in Library Technology Grant is an:

> annual award consisting of $10,000 and a 24k gold-framed citation of achievement which is given to encourage and enable continued advancements in quality library services for a project that makes creative or groundbreaking use of technology to deliver exceptional services to its community. Eligible libraries are public, academic, school, and special (i.e., medical, law, government, corporate, or museum). Donated by the SIRSI Corporation. (American Library Association, 2003, SIRSI section)

Although the library had not worked extensively with grants in the past, the Associate University Librarian for Public Services was supportive of the project and of a grant as a way of financing the first phase. A meeting was scheduled with the Distributed Learning Coordinator, the Process Improvement Specialist, the Library Information Systems Department Chair and the Director of the Center for Instructional Design. All parties were extremely supportive of the project and of applying for the grant. Various members contributed information for the grant application and it was submitted in December of 2002. The Distributed Learning Coordinator was notified in February of 2003 that the grant had been awarded.

PROJECT PLANNING PHASE

The objectives for this project were:

1. Create and implement an online portal page for library resources
2. Integrate the library resources page with the portal created for Independent Study students through University's learning-management system (Blackboard)

3. Publicize the availability, location, and access methods for the Library's online portal to all Independent Study students
4. Publicize the availability, location, and access methods for the Library's online portal to faculty members
5. Evaluate students' use of, reaction to, and experience with the Library Services Portal
6. Evaluate English faculty members' use of library resources in the assignments in their courses
7. Use evaluation data to improve, update, expand, and modify the program as needed

The first step in the project planning phase was to have the Library's Project Management Team vet the project and assign it a priority. Previously, the library administrators and others had received training in the University's Project Planning and Management approach. The library administration adopted a scoring model for all projects involving technology (computer) resources and personnel. This project was presented at a project management meeting and it received a high score, placing it at the top of the list of priorities.

Subsequently, the project director, the Distributed Learning Coordinator, decided to use the project planning and management process to plan and administer the project. The project team was identified and invited to be part of the project. The team consisted of:

- Project sponsor, the Assistant University Librarian for Public Services
- Project manager, the Distributed Learning Coordinator
- Department Chair of Library Information Systems
- Assistant Director of Independent Study
- Assistant Director of the Center for Instructional Design
- Instructional Design Architect
- Senior Production Designer
- Instructional Design Architect/English
- Library's Process Improvement Specialist
- Subject Librarian for English
- Programmer from Library Information Systems

The early team meetings consisted of orientation to the project, its goals and timeline, and gaining buy-in from the major stakeholders. Once the commitment was obtained from all campus units involved, the team began the process of defining the various parts of the project, constructing a task breakdown, assigning tasks to the appropriate personnel and constructing a timeline for completion of tasks.

PROJECT BUILDING PHASE

Originally, the project was designed to deliver the library services via the University's Blackboard portal. However, the University was in the midst of implementing Blackboard 6.0 and needed to complete major infrastructure upgrades and address issues of server stability. Since Independent Study courses already use online pages to deliver course-related features, the team decided that Blackboard would not be the delivery vehicle for the first phase. With this decision, the team turned to its in-house Web production expertise. The Library Information Systems Department Chair and a programmer determined a way to build and deliver the portal in a browser-friendly format that fit within the online Independent Study courses and included a simple URL that could appear in the paper versions of the courses as well. Therefore, the plan for this part of the project was revised to specify that the Center for Instructional Design (CID) programmers would implement the new library services portal for the courses.

After the delivery mechanism was decided upon, the Distributed Learning Coordinator and two Instructional Design Architects from CID decided on the general content categories for the portal. Once the list of categories was determined, a CID Senior Production Designer took the information and designed a portal interface that corresponded quite closely with the look and feel of the library home page. Independent Study students previously used the library home page to find research resources, and the team wanted the students to associate the new portal with the services they were familiar with. The Library Information Systems programmer then implemented interactivity on the portal page, making the links active and implementing the page in HTML.

The static links on the page were built first. Since the project dealt only with English courses, some of the links led to content that would apply to any English course. One section of the portal includes several short explanations of how to find articles, books, news sources and e-books. A Writer's Toolbox contains links to Web versions of bibliographies, dictionaries, maps, quotations, thesauri and acronyms, and style manuals. Other links let students search the online catalog and provide access to information about the Library's delivery service for books and articles. Last, but certainly not least, the page provides a link to the Ask a Librarian e-mail and chat reference service, as well as the subject librarian's name, phone, and e-mail contact information. The page also provides an e-mail feedback form so that students can communicate with the Distributed Learning Coordinator if they have problems with any of the portal services while completing their course.

After the programmer constructed the static links, he built a database to supply the dynamic, course-specific content which included research guides and online databases. Since Independent Study offers such a wide range of English courses, the team decided early in the project, that the content would be specific to each course rather than general content for any English course–all to make the portal useful and relevant to the students. Once the programmer had constructed the portal, the Distributed Learning Coordinator and the Instructional Design Architect from CID tested it to ensure that the links worked and that the interface for adding online research guides and databases functioned properly [see Appendix B].

Adding course-specific resources required the assistance of several subject librarians. Each librarian reviewed the course manual for the course(s) he or she was assigned and determined the most appropriate online research guides and online databases for the particular course. With the online form and database already in place, the process of adding the appropriate resources to the portal page was efficient and took a minimum amount of the subject librarians' time [see Appendix B].

As noted previously, the original plan was to implement the page in the University's Blackboard portal, however, it was determined earlier in the project that the Blackboard portal would not be ready by the time the library services portal needed to be active in the Independent Study Courses. Therefore, the programming teams implemented the portal for each of the English courses.

PROJECT PUBLICITY

The next phase in the project was to develop a public relations and marketing plan to make faculty and students aware of the library portal. This phase of the plan included (1) publicizing the Library Services Portal (the portal) to all students enrolled in Independent Study English courses, and (2) publicizing the availability, location, and access methods for the portal to faculty members. The Distributed Learning Coordinator met with the Independent Study marketing team to discuss ways to market and advertise the portal. The marketing team identified and implemented marketing efforts to coincide with the initial rollout of the portal, with the goal of promoting the portal and making current students aware of this new and useful resource. A serendipitous development in the marketing meeting was that a member of the marketing team was a recent graduate of the University in English and was very familiar with the library and its resources. She was extremely eager to make students aware of the resources in the portal and their value in completing their courses.

The team decided to use the following marketing efforts to publicize the service:

1. The Center for Instructional Design consultant assigned to work with the English faculty and the Distributed Learning Coordinator met with instructors developing or upgrading Independent Study courses to make them aware of the portal and suggest ways they could incorporate assignments/activities into their courses to utilize this resource.

2. The library liaison from CID-trained instructional designers on the portal so that they could encourage the faculty members to include rigorous assignments in their courses as they were working with the instructional designer to design the course.

3. Marketing personnel from Continuing Education:

   - Created a digital and paper insertion for Web and paper courses to make new students aware of the portal, and mailed an announcement of this resource to the 1,800 students already enrolled in English courses.
   - Placed an announcement on Independent Study's home page that the portal is now available for all university-level English courses.
   - The Distributed Learning Coordinator, CID, and Independent Study personnel developed a virtual tour of the portal and placed it on the Independent Study Web site. It was constructed to give students an idea of how the portal works and what the features and benefits are to those that use it.
   - Wrote and distributed a press release about the portal.
   - Wrote an article about portal in Independent Study's eNewsletter to counselors.
   - Prepared and sent a mailer to Bachelor of General Studies students enrolled in English courses.
   - Created and inserted an icon for portal in the Independent Study online catalog, CD catalog, and paper catalog.

EVALUATION PHASE

The final task in the Project Building Phase was to design both summative and formative evaluations for this project with the goal of using the evaluation data to improve the portal. The team will collect data for a summative evaluation at the conclusion of the pilot phase, using survey results from students who have completed their courses. This data will help us determine the value of the portal, focusing the outcome for the students. The team will also collect formative evaluation data during the pilot phase, which will assist us in determining the utility of the portal as students complete their course assignments.

The formative evaluation of this project began with inserting an e-mail feedback link on the portal. This link lets students send their comments to the Distributed Learning Coordinator as they work through the course, and provides immediate feedback on both the implementation of the portal and the library services.

In addition to the feedback link, Independent Study uses a course-completion survey to gather information about students' experiences with the course. When students complete a course and take their final exam, they also receive this survey. The Library project team and the Independent Study team included another survey for the students in University-level English courses, asking specifically about the students' experience with the portal [see Appendix C]. The Distributed Learning Coordinator constructed the survey and the Library's Process Improvement Officer, who conducts surveys, and collects, compiles and analyzes all statistics for the library, vetted the form, questions, and language. It was then sent to the Center for Instructional Design and published in .PDF format. As the CID evaluation-team employees published the survey, they evaluated it for clarity, conciseness, and consistency. This provided feedback from a student point of view, so that the team knew the survey was asking the right questions to obtain the data needed to evaluate the portal. The survey was designed to be as short as possible without sacrificing the quality and quantity of information that was collected. Independent Study agreed to send out the survey with the student's final exam or make it part of their final exam in order to have a sufficient returns for evaluation. In return for completing the survey, names of five students will be drawn from the list of those who choose to participate, and they will receive a tuition reimbursement for their course.

In addition to the self-reported survey data, the Library, Independent Study, and the CIDs Quality & Assurance Evaluation personnel will expand the summative evaluation of the project using authentication data to track the students' use of the portal and the resources contained within the portal. Shortly after developing the portal page, the Library programmer also built a tracking mechanism to collect the number of "hits" the portal had within each course. The tracking mechanism could not determine which of the resources the student used after entering the library portal, so the team decided to collect that information in the survey given to the students at the completion of their course. The team hopes to gather sufficient data to effectively evaluate the portal and its use in Independent Study courses. The Distributed Learning Services Coordinator and members of the project team will report on results of these surveys and tracking program after April 1, 2004, when the evaluation team completes the first survey of the data.

With the portal in place, we expect to see several outcomes:

- Independent Study students will have easy online access to necessary academic research materials, expert assistance, and other library resources, which will overcome obstacles to completing their coursework
- Instructors for English and other Independent Study courses will be free to create challenging, academic assignments that depend on access to high-quality research materials
- Independent Study students will use the resources available through the Lee Library to complete and enhance their coursework

CONCLUSION

Throughout the entire process of the project, there has been phenomenal cooperation between the personnel of the Library, the Center for Instructional Design and Independent Study. Each person who worked on the project completed assigned tasks in a timely manner–and often ahead of schedule. Additionally, the Center for Instructional Design and Independent Study personnel contributed many hours of in-kind service. This was due, we believe, to the commitment of each campus unit to the success of the project which, we feel, will greatly enhance the quality of the courses.

The team is already looking forward to phase two of this project. We hope to (1) improve the variety of databases accessible to Independent Study students, (2) improve the authentication mechanism the students use to gain access to the portal, (3) provide improved library-use instruction, and (4) implement this portal in other Independent Study courses in a phased approach. As the library continues to expand the range of library resources and services available to Independent Study students, we hope to make their experience more productive–and as close as possible to what they would experience on-campus.

REFERENCES

American Library Association. (2003). *Grants & fellowships.* Retrieved February 9, 2004 from http://www.ala.org/Template.cfm?Section=grantfellowship.
Beagle, D. (2002). Web-based learning environments: Do libraries matter? *College and Research Libraries, 61*(4), 367-79.
Lebowitz, G. (1997). Library services to distant students: An equity issue. *The Journal of Academic Librarianship, 23*(July), 303-8.

APPENDIX A

BGS Survey
Administered June 7 to June 23, 2002

The following survey was sent to all formally admitted BYU Independent Study Bachelors of General Studies students (700 via e-mail and 489 by telephone) with 179 e-mail responses and 100 telephone responses.

1. Do you have access to the Internet at home or at the place where you study the majority of the time?

Yes   265
No   11

2. If "Yes," what is your Internet connection speed?

High speed connection (i.e., DSL, cable modem, etc.)	88	32.84%
56K	105	39.18%
Slower than 56K	24	8.96%
Don't know	51	19.03%

3. How often do you use the Internet?

Daily	204	75.28%
Once a week	56	20.66%
Once a month	8	2.95%
Less than once a month	3	1.11%

4. Which do you prefer?

Taking courses over the Internet	82	30.65%
Taking courses by paper manuals and materials	186	69.35%

Why?

5. Which of the following enrollment options would you prefer?

A semester-long course that starts and ends on specific dates and includes scheduled activities that allow you to work and interact with other students in the course	54	19.71%
A course that you can begin anytime and finish on your own schedule, but limits opportunities to work and interact with other students	220	80.29%

6. What types of interactions would you like to have with other *students* in independent study courses? (select all that apply)

The ability to communicate with other students by posting and reading questions and comments on an *unscheduled* online discussion board	156	55.91%
The ability to chat with other students during *scheduled* times using an online chat forum	68	24.37%
The ability to participate with other students in *scheduled* online activities and lectures	83	29.75%
The ability to work with other students on projects and assignments	46	16.49%
None, I prefer to work independently	103	36.92%

APPENDIX A (continued)

7. Please rank the following in order of importance. (1 being the most important)

The ability to work independently *with* the benefit of determining your own schedule
76% of the respondents ranked this option 1st and 16% ranked it 2nd

The ability to interact with other students *without* having to work on a set schedule
73% of the respondents ranked this option 2nd and 15% ranked it 1st

The ability to work with other students *with* the benefit of a structured course schedule
80% of the respondents ranked this option 3rd

8. Would you be willing to pay an additional fee or increased tuition for the ability to work with other students in independent study courses?

Yes   52
No   222

9. If "yes," how much would you be willing to pay for this option?

$10-$25 per course, if it were more than this I would not want the option	46	77.97%
$25-$50 per course, if it were more than this I would not want the option	12	20.34%
$50-$75 per course, if it were more than this I would not want the option	1	1.69%
$75-$100 per course, if it were more than this I would not want the option	0	0.00%
Over $100 per course, I really need the student interaction	0	0.00%

10. What types of interactions would you like to have with instructors or teaching assistants in independent study courses? (select all that apply)

The ability to contact the instructor or teaching assistant by e-mail or telephone	248	88.88%
The ability to post questions and comments using an unscheduled online discussion board	185	66.31%
The ability to participate in *scheduled* online activities and lectures with an instructor or teaching assistant present or leading	111	39.78%
None, I prefer to work independently	17	6.09%

11. Please rank the following in order of importance. (1 being the most important)

The ability to work independently *with* the benefit of determining your own schedule
51% of the respondents ranked this 1st, 38% ranked this 2nd

The ability to interact with the instructor or teaching assistant *without* having to follow a course schedule *41% of the respondents ranked this 1st, 53% ranked this 2nd*

The ability to interact with an instructor or teaching assistant *with* the benefit of a structured course schedule *83% of the respondents ranked this 3rd*

12. Would you be willing to pay an additional fee or increased tuition for the ability to interact with instructors and teaching assistants in independent study courses?

Yes   138
No   137

13. If "Yes," how much would you be willing to pay for this option?

$10-$25 per course, if it were more than this, I would not want the option	95	67.86%
$25-$50 per course, if it were more than this I would not want the option	41	29.29%
$50-$75 per course, if it were more than this I would not want the option	3	2.14%
$75-$100 per course, if it were more than this I would not want the option	1	0.71%
Over $100 per course, I really need the faculty interaction	0	0.00%

The following questions relate to references used for your independent study courses. *(These questions were added, at the request of the library, three days into the survey. For this reason, the first 55 respondents did not respond to these questions.)*

14. What is your *first* choice when searching for additional information resources to complete coursework? (select ONLY one)

An Internet search engine (e.g., Yahoo!, Google, Ask Jeeves, etc.)	117	52.23%
A local bookstore	7	3.12%
Your local library	37	16.52%
The Harold B. Lee Library via remote access	3	1.34%
Course does not require the use of additional resources	49	21.88%
Other	11	4.91%

15. Which of the following Harold B. Lee Library services are you aware of or have you used in your BGS program?

	Not aware	Aware but have not used	Have used
Check-out materials	154 **(69%)**	49 **(22%)**	19 **(9%)**
Electronic reserve materials	182 **(83%)**	25 **(11%)**	13 **(6%)**
Order copies of articles	183 **(83%)**	31 **(14%)**	7 **(3%)**
Asking for help from a librarian via e-mail or live chat	172 **(79%)**	37 **(17%)**	8 **(4%)**
Use of full-text databases (journals, newspapers, encyclopedias, etc.)	161 **(73%)**	38 **(17%)**	22 **(10%)**
Instruction in the use of library resources	167 **(77%)**	35 **(16%)**	16 **(7%)**

APPENDIX A (continued)

16. The following services are currently available or being considered at the Harold B. Lee Library. How would you rate the helpfulness of each service when completing your coursework? (1 = Not Very Helpful, 7 = Very Helpful)

	1	2	3	4	5	6	7	% ≥ 5*
E-mail, toll-free telephone, and/or real time access to librarians	13	17	11	32	40	30	65	65%
Remote access to full-text databases, indexes or abstracts	13	12	10	18	27	41	87	75%
Delivery of books, photocopied articles, or other materials to your home or work	14	6	14	19	37	42	77	75%
Guides to doing research in a subject area	13	9	12	25	42	44	60	71%
Instruction on how to use the library for research	17	13	12	29	34	36	67	66%
Written or Web-based information describing library services, resources and policies	13	10	13	29	36	30	77	69%
Technical assistance for using e-mail, connecting to online library catalogs, databases, etc.	13	15	20	24	28	35	73	64%

*This column lists the percent of respondents that rated each category as a five or higher. We can assume that these respondents feel that a service is or would be helpful to them.

17. Do you have any additional comments or suggestions?
    These open-ended responses are found below

Appendix (of BGS survey)

Complete Responses to Question 17*

Additional Comments and Suggestions

47% of respondents answered this question

*Comments edited to include only those that applied specifically to the library (and for spelling). Contact the authors if you would like the full comments section.

42 I don't think these last questions are applicable to me because I go to my local library anytime I need more information.

90 I am truly enjoying my courses. They give me a lot of information. I am new to the program and am not taking, at this time, terribly challenging course that I need reference materials. However, in the future I am sure they will be greatly appreciated.

97 I had no idea that I could use the BYU library system to do research. I wish it was general information shared with every course. I would like to know how to use it without getting caught up in too many technicalities. Make it simple. I would also like to have answers to my questions in a course done quicker. Sometimes these questions slow down or almost stop my progression in the course. I don't think it has to be that slow. If

I were on campus I would just go to the office or resource center, but in independent study it is just as important to get answers quickly.

111 I think I have only seen one reference to library services since I've been in the program (an e-mail). I haven't needed the library (yet) with the courses I've taken, but I am sure I will need to use it in the future. I would sure appreciate more information on library services for research, etc.

PS Some of your questions are duplicates.

125 I assume that the last two questions refer to services provided by the HB Lee Library and not my local library.

129 I feel that the additional help needed from an instructor should not be a fee, but should be part of the course cost. Also, I am not aware of any of the services available to me. I have never been told of them.

138 So far I haven't had to do any outside research for any of my Independent Study Courses. But after looking at the section of the survey about the library, I realize that I'd better learn what library services exist, and how to use them.

140 Although I struggled with the self-paced and independent aspects of Independent Study courses with my first few classes, I really learned to value learning at my own pace, learning to be disciplined, and forcing myself to learn by myself not relying on the lectures of the teacher to glean what I should or the opinions of other students to base my own opinions. I've really found this way of learning very valuable.

142 Instructor interaction has been the greatest tool I have had in my independent study courses. However, it has only been in my English courses that the instructors have made themselves available. Additionally, I have not had to pay extra for this service, I would be most unhappy if I had to start paying to receive this help.

146 I send in written papers for assignments and I've never received any kind of comments on them. I just receive a grade. I'm not even sure anyone even reads my papers.

147 Some of my responses to these questions are very dependant on the type of course I am taking. There are courses where I value the ability to work on my own above all else. However, I am currently taking a math course and I would love to have access to online lectures and/or help sessions.

148 My biggest problem has been that I must wait for assignments to be graded before I take the final. This policy is evidently to protect me from burning bridges (can't redo assignments after the final), but it slows the course completion sometimes by several weeks. Changing the policy to all assignments SUBMITTED would help. If I am capable of earning a degree from BYU while in Colorado, I believe that I am capable of planning the time table for my courses. (If an instructor doesn't get around to grading written assignments for a week or two, with the mailing lag time and library processing time, it can add three weeks or a month to a course's time.) What if IS students signed a waiver? "I will not get mad when I don't do well on an assignment graded after the final, because I can't retake it."

160 I have no problem finding the information I need to complete my work. But I do find that finding a place to take my final exams is very frustrating. If the Internet could be used in this sense I feel I would like that option, but other than that I am having no problems doing my courses with the literature and information that is already available to me.

168 I have not needed more information than what has been provided by my teachers, except for the Children's literature class I just finished and the library was the most practical place to get my books I needed to read. That answer really only fit that class and may not be indicative of the rest of the courses I may take.

173 I prefer to use the University of Utah Library when I need to do research–it's closer to my home. Training for using libraries online where people live may be helpful, too.

180 I tried to access online journal articles, but had so much trouble getting my remote access password to work that I ended up making the 1 1/2 hour drive in to use the library twice. The online chat was helpful and I was referred to a technical support person who could not help me, thus the problem was never resolved. I was not aware that I could order copies of journal articles or I would have done that.

193 I know that there is some type of access available from the Harold B. Lee Library for BGS students, but I really don't know much about it. Those services would be beneficial to me as I live in a very small community and have to rely on interlibrary loan for most of my research books.

197 There are limited library resources where I live. Extensive access to the BYU Library would be wonderful. Technical information and assistance will be a must for it to work properly. I would also like access to

APPENDIX A (continued)

more information for my classes. I have found especially with the 100 level courses that the textbook is the only source of information. Why have 3 hours of lectures every week, even a lab in some cases, if everything can be learned from reading the text? I feel like we're missing out on some interesting and vital information taking classes through IS. My thought is that a scheduled class on the Internet would make it possible to compensate for that.

198 Please let me know how to access the library via the Internet. I would be very interested in this.

207 I currently work at a local public library and use its resources for most of my library needs.

220 I think we would be able to interact with instructors without paying more. I am interested in learning more about library services.

228 Thanks for asking. It sounds like you have some exciting ideas that could be really helpful. I am now mostly finishing general ed requirements, but I can see that I may need more access to research materials as I get into my higher level classes, and these things will help me more then.

229 This may seem rather obvious, but I believe more is better. The more opportunities to learn the coursework, the better off the student will be, whether that means interacting with other students, with faculty, or by making use of library resources. I also believe some students may be more comfortable with one resource than another; therefore the more resources that are made available the better "coverage" you will have in helping students learn the coursework.

235 My Internet Web course did not require a textbook or other materials other than a CD-ROM that I was disappointed was not sent with confirmation of course registration. I completed the course without the use of this CD-ROM. In the future, if the course work does require such an item, it would be most helpful to include it with the letter of course confirmation. Thank you.

APPENDIX B. Library Services Portal and Administrative Interfaces

Library Services Portal

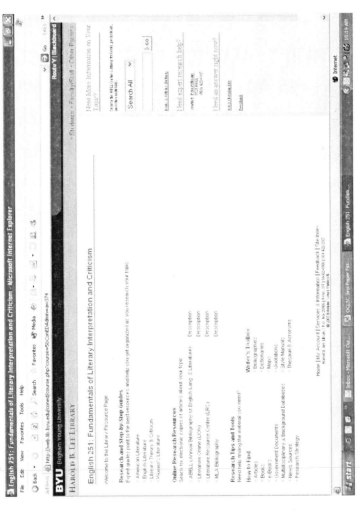

APPENDIX B (continued)

Librarians' Administrative Interface Class List

My Class List - Microsoft Internet Explorer

File   Edit   View   Favorites   Tools   Help

Back • ⌂ • ⌧ ⌧ | Search Favorites Media | ...

Address: https://www.lib.byu.edu/coned/classlist.php

Welcome

User Administrator   Usage Stats   Logout

Course Name and Preview	Add	Delete	Add	Delete	Add	Delete
Computer Science 251 Data Structures	Research Guides		Step-by-Step Guides		Online Resources	
English 115 College Reading and Writing	Research Guides		Step-by-Step Guides		Online Resources	
English 218Q Section 10 Creative Writing	Research Guides		Step-by-Step Guides		Online Resources	
English 220 Writing Personal History	Research Guides		Step-by-Step Guides		Online Resources	
English 230 Introduction to Literature Fiction, Drama, Poetry	Research Guides		Step-by-Step Guides		Online Resources	
English 251 Fundamentals of Literary Interpretation and Criticism	Research Guides		Step-by-Step Guides		Online Resources	
English 291 British Literary History 1	Research Guides		Step-by-Step Guides		Online Resources	
English 292 British Literary History 2	Research Guides		Step-by-Step Guides		Online Resources	
English 293 American Literary History	Research Guides		Step-by-Step Guides		Online Resources	
English 312 Persuasive Writing	Research Guides		Step-by-Step Guides		Online Resources	
English 315 Writing in the Social Sciences	Research Guides		Step-by-Step Guides		Online Resources	
English 316 Technical Writing	Research Guides		Step-by-Step Guides		Online Resources	
English 319R Section 5 Writing of Poetry	Research Guides		Step-by-Step Guides		Online Resources	
English 320R Section 5 Writing for Children and Adolescents	Research Guides		Step-by-Step Guides		Online Resources	
English 333 The English Novel	Research Guides		Step-by-Step Guides		Online Resources	
English 336 The American Novel	Research Guides		Step-by-Step Guides		Online Resources	
English 350 The Bible as Literature	Research Guides		Step-by-Step Guides		Online Resources	
English 359 The Short Story	Research Guides		Step-by-Step Guides		Online Resources	
English 361 American Literature to the Mid-Nineteenth Century	Research Guides		Step-by-Step Guides		Online Resources	
English 362 Late Nineteenth and Early Twentieth Century American Literature	Research Guides		Step-by-Step Guides		Online Resources	

Internet

Start   Inbox - Microsoft Out...   OCLC SiteFinder Fin...   My Class List - Micro...   10:00 AM

Librarians' Interface for Adding Resources

Research Guides - Microsoft Internet Explorer

File   Edit   View   Favorites   Tools   Help

Back   Search   Favorites   Media   Go   Links

Address   https://www.lib.byu.edu/coned/research.php?action=showList&course=5

Add / Delete Research Guides for English 251: Fundamentals of Literary Interpretation and Criticism

Check Add Research Guides;
Uncheck to Delete Research Guides

- [ ] Adolescent Literature
- [ ] African Studies
- [ ] Agriculture
- [ ] American Art Research
- [ ] American History
- [x] American Literature
- [ ] American Sign Language
- [ ] Anthropology
- [ ] Apocrypha
- [ ] Archaeology
- [ ] Architecture Research
- [ ] Art Education Research
- [ ] Art History Research
- [ ] Art Web Sites
- [ ] Asian Religions
- [ ] Asian Studies
- [ ] Behavioral Science
- [ ] Bibles & Literature
- [ ] Biology
- [ ] Book of Mormon
- [ ] Brazilian and Portuguese Literature
- [ ] Business - Business Biographical Information
- [ ] Business - Business Management
- [ ] Business - Business Newspapers
- [ ] Business - Business Statistics

- [ ] Government Documents
- [ ] Government Publications, U.S.
- [ ] Graphic Design & Illustration Research
- [ ] Graphic Design Web Sites
- [ ] Hispanic American Studies
- [ ] History, Worldwide
- [ ] Home Economics
- [ ] Humanities Research
- [ ] Iconography Research
- [ ] Italian History & Politics
- [ ] Italian Language & Literature
- [ ] Italian Studies
- [ ] Juvenile Literature
- [ ] Latin American Studies
- [ ] LDS Guides
- [ ] Library Film Journals
- [ ] Linguistics & TESOL
- [x] Literary Theory & Criticism
- [ ] Local History
- [ ] Maps, Atlases & Gazetteers
- [ ] Mathematics
- [ ] Middle East Studies
- [ ] Music
- [ ] New Testament
- [ ] Nutrition, Dietetics, and Food Science

Done   Internet

start   Inbox - Microsoft Out...   SKESE Strix Paper File...   Research Guides - Mi...   10:21 AM

APPENDIX C

Library Survey

Library Services Portal Survey Questions

The Lee Library is conducting a pilot of library resources and services in your Independent Study English course. Your feedback is critical! Please help us by completing and returning this survey. It will take approximately 10 minutes to complete.

Once you have completed the survey, you will have the option of entering into a prize drawing where five winners will receive tuition reimbursement for this course! You can enter by providing your name and e-mail address at the end of the survey. This information will be separated from the survey itself and your responses will be kept confidential. We hope you take the time to respond and enter the drawing, because your responses are important to us in our efforts to evaluate and improve the services the Lee Library provides.

1. Were you aware of the resources and services available from the Harold B. Lee Library as you completed your coursework? ☐Yes ☐No
   If yes, please answer the following questions about your experience using the Library Services Portal.

2. How did you become aware of the Library Services Portal (the services)?

3. Which of the services did you use in your Independent Study English course? (Scale: Never = 0; Seldom = about once a month; Occasionally = about every other week; Often = weekly; Very often = nearly everyday)

	Never	Seldom	Occasionally	Often	Very Often
Research Guides	○	○	○	○	○
Step-by-Step Guides	○	○	○	○	○
Online Research Resources	○	○	○	○	○
Research Tips and Tools	○	○	○	○	○
Writers Toolbox	○	○	○	○	○
Lee Library's Online Catalog	○	○	○	○	○
Books and Articles Delivery Service	○	○	○	○	○
Subject Librarian Assistance	○	○	○	○	○
Ask a Librarian LIVE Assistance	○	○	○	○	○
Feedback Form	○	○	○	○	○

4. How would you rate the overall usefulness of the services in completing course assignments? Mark the appropriate circle.

Not useful   Extremely useful
○---------○---------○---------○---------○---------○---------○

5. As you did your coursework, how helpful were the following services?

	Not helpful	Seldom helpful	Occasionally helpful	Very helpful	Extremely helpful
Research Guides	○	○	○	○	○
Step-by-Step Guides	○	○	○	○	○
Online Research Resources	○	○	○	○	○

	Not helpful	Seldom helpful	Occasionally helpful	Very helpful	Extremely helpful
Research Tips and Tools	○	○	○	○	○
Lee Library's Online Catalog	○	○	○	○	○
Books and Articles Delivery Service	○	○	○	○	○
Subject Librarian Assistance	○	○	○	○	○
Ask a Librarian LIVE Assistance	○	○	○	○	○
Feedback Form	○	○	○	○	○

6. How would you rate the availability of the services? Mark the appropriate circle.

Never available   Always available
○---------○---------○---------○---------○---------○---------○

7. How would you rate the ease of use of the services? Mark the appropriate circle.

Not useful   Extremely useful
○---------○---------○---------○---------○---------○---------○

8. Where did you access the services? Check all that apply.
   ☐ At home
   ☐ At work
   ☐ At BYU, other than in the Lee Library
   ☐ At the Lee Library
   ☐ Other, please explain _____

9. What type of computer did you use?

   ☐ PC   ☐ Mac   ☐ Other

10. What is the speed of your Internet connection?

   ☐ 14.4   ☐ 28.8   ☐ 33.6   ☐56K   ☐DSL   ☐ Cable   ☐ Don't know

11. Do you have any additional comments or suggestions for the people providing the Library Services Portal?

_____

Thank you for participating!

Please enter your name and e-mail address below if you wish to have your name included in the drawing for tuition reimbursement.

Name: _____

E-mail: _____

Selecting Electronic Document Delivery Options to Provide Quality Service

Cherié L. Weible

University of Illinois at Urbana-Champaign

SUMMARY. Providing electronic document delivery (EDD) services to off-campus students can be a challenge. Methods of delivery that work well for one group of users might not work at all for another group. Knowing and using the different EDD service options to accomplish the goal of providing quality service to students results in a win-win situation. Student expectations of timely delivery of material are met and the department develops a reputation of dependable quality service. Library users have raised expectations from the 24/7 services available through the World Wide Web. Providing EDD of information to the researcher's desktop helps the library meet these needs and expectations. However, the options for desktop delivery can also be overwhelming, so knowing how and why different software and delivery methods work enables the practitioner to control the outcome of the transaction. This control over the service also ensures that quality service expectations are met by the library since the practitioner has the ability to use a variety of delivery options to the user's desktop.

KEYWORDS. Library services, technology, distance learners

INTRODUCTION

A variety of software like Ariel, Prospero, Odyssey, and Adobe Acrobat are widely used to deliver materials electronically through e-mail and HTTP. The

[Haworth co-indexing entry note]: "Selecting Electronic Document Delivery Options to Provide Quality Service." Weible, Cherié L. Co-published simultaneously in *Journal of Library Administration* (The Haworth Information Press, an imprint of The Haworth Press, Inc.) Vol. 41, No. 3/4, 2004, pp. 531-540; and: *The Eleventh Off-Campus Library Services Conference Proceedings* (ed: Patrick B. Mahoney) The Haworth Information Press, an imprint of The Haworth Press, Inc., 2004, pp. 531-540.

proliferation of electronic means for delivering information to the desktop has empowered librarians by giving them choices about the best options available to deliver documents to students. E-mail and HTTP, or combinations of the two technologies, also offer a variety of means for delivery. While the library may implement one primary method of delivery, other methods are often employed to ensure quality service. Successfully meeting the document delivery needs of today's users requires knowledge of the many delivery options available through various technologies.

The goal of this paper is to clarify EDD options and illustrate the relative ease with which the various methods of delivery for off-campus users can be quickly implemented in small or large library settings. This paper will also discuss which methods of EDD have worked in different environments. These methods can be implemented by the interlibrary loan, document delivery, or access services department or they can be employed directly by the off-campus service department. A final purpose of the paper is to empower the reader with additional knowledge, a better understanding, and more confidence selecting and adjusting an electronic desktop delivery service.

SOFTWARE CHOICES

The focus on streamlining the workflow of production based library operations like Interlibrary Loan has created an environment where numerous software packages are available for a variety of uses (Fuller, 2002, p. 20). In the past few years most of these software programs have developed a desktop delivery feature either as a stand alone product or as a piece of a larger product. Prospero, Ariel, Odyssey, and Adobe Acrobat are software programs that can be obtained and used independently of an ILL management system. Several of these programs were created to work in conjunction with, or independently of, one another, creating a variety of options for libraries implementing EDD services. The programs listed above enable the lending library's staff to scan materials and deliver them to another library or to a user's desktop, or alternatively, for a library to scan materials from their collections to be delivered to students located on or off-campus.

For example, Ariel was originally created so libraries could scan materials and deliver them via the Internet to other libraries with Ariel software in a .TIFF format. Since .TIFF viewers were not widely available or used by the academic population, the library's only choice for delivery was to print the documents out and provide the user with the research materials they requested. At the time, this was still a huge improvement over faxing materials for three reasons. First, the images and overall quality of the documents delivered through Ariel were much better. Second, the Internet transmissions were free whereas the faxed materials required the cost of a telephone line and connection time. Third, the turnaround time for delivery was dramatically improved (Stabler, 2002, p. 64; Sellen, 1999, p. 71). Delivery between libraries was also improved when the software was engineered to increase the options available for transmission. Ariel allows for delivery from the lending library to the borrowing library through e-mail if the borrowing library is not equipped with the software. A simple configuration in the borrowing library's e-mail allows them to receive documents from libraries that prefer to scan and send using Ariel software (Lindsay, 2000, p. 82).

Prospero was created to work with the Ariel software so that incoming documents could be transformed from .TIFF files into .PDF files (Schnell, 1999, p. 95). The software has two options for delivery to the user which will be discussed in the "Methods of Delivery" section of this paper. Essentially, Prospero allowed for a way to eliminate the paper printing and mailing steps of each item for each individual and further reduced the overall delivery time of the documents from the library to the user (Weible & Robben, 2002, p. 80). Elimination of the printed document not only saves time, but also money spent on reams of paper (Weible & Robben, p. 82). Prospero also allows for delivery to only the user who had requested the material, which meant that libraries were still adhering to the fair use guidelines as listed in the copyright laws. Additionally, a copyright notice is inserted as the first page of each document delivered to the desktop and a purge program eliminates the digital images of the document after a reasonable time so the images are not saved or distributed to another user (Rodman, 2002, p. 69).

The next generation of the software versions for these products contains a scan, send, and EDD feature all contained in the same package. This means that Ariel, Prospero, Odyssey, and Adobe Acrobat can all function separately, without working in conjunction with other software, which has reduced the cost, training, and maintenance factors for libraries in addition to streamlining the workflow of the EDD process. Other software programs such as ILLiad, ILL Manager, VDX, and Clio also allow the library to work with incoming and outgoing documents by depending on the EDD features of Prospero, Ariel, Odyssey, or Adobe Acrobat. The borrowing library can electronically accept the incoming materials and then deliver them to the users' desktops. Libraries can now easily implement an EDD service due to the wide range of software available with a variety of options for workflow and delivery. From this availability and ease of creating an effective EDD service enables libraries to include their off-campus users in the delivery service.

Depending on the departmental and staff organization at the library, off-campus users can be served through traditional ILL services, separate units dedicated to this unique population and their needs, or from a combination of the two (Casey & Grudzien, 2002, pp. 112-113). If traditional ILL services are involved in serving the off-campus population the staff will likely be aware of potential difficulties in delivery methods of EDD documents. However, if the off-campus population is served entirely by a separate unit, staff will need to become familiar with EDD delivery options and learn the advantages and dis-advantages of each.

Along with the proliferation of EDD options, numerous articles have been written about the selection, implementation, and pilot project experiences of other institutions that are now successfully using some form of EDD. Regard-less of whether or not the ILL department (or equivalent) is involved in the EDD process, the appropriate articles should be identified and the experiences of other institutions should be taken into account when evaluating EDD op-tions.

METHODS OF DELIVERY

There are two methods used to deliver documents to the users' desktops. Both methods require the user to have an e-mail account and both methods have their advantages and their disadvantages. The first way to deliver docu-ments electronically is to simply send the item as a .PDF attachment to a user's e-mail account. The advantage to using this method is that users can instantly access the document from their e-mail message by clicking on the attachment and opening the file with Adobe Acrobat Reader. Another advantage of deliv-ering the document in .PDF is the fact that this format can be read using differ-ent computer operating systems and the software is free and easy to use (Kriz, 2000, p. 27).

Although this method would seem straightforward and simple to use, some-times it is just not possible to successfully deliver materials in this manner. The disadvantage in sending the document as a .PDF attachment is that once materials are scanned the file sizes can become quite large, especially if it is not a simple text document. Images and graphs can create large file sizes and if color scanning is required the files can become enormous. Difficulty arises in successfully delivering the material as a .PDF attachment to the user's e-mail account when the attached file size is larger than the e-mail account can han-dle. Additionally, if the user has requested more than one document, as is often the case to satisfy his or her research needs, the problem then increases since multiple items are now undeliverable if the e-mail account reaches quota.

The second way to deliver documents electronically is to post the document to a Web server and then send the user an e-mail that includes the URL for the

Web site where the documents can be accessed, instructions for accessing and using the file, and usernames and PINs as needed to open the documents that are for their use. The login process is simple and secure, but firewalls and the Web server need to be maintained by knowledgeable staff. The advantage to using this method is that the size of the e-mail received by the patron is usually quite small in size and it can contain as much or as little information about the process as needed, and as determined by the library in a standardized e-mail. One library noted that posting the file to the Web server "leaves the file more within our domain of control" (Sayed, Murray, & Wheeler, 2001, p. 67). This is beneficial for troubleshooting purposes since the library staff can easily re-access the article and print it out for paper delivery to the user when it cannot be obtained electronically.

The disadvantage of using this method is that instead of one click to open the file, multiple steps are now involved for the user to successfully complete the transaction. First, the library's Web server must be up and running so the user can open a Web browser and then correctly type in the URL to load the Web page. Next, the user must correctly type in a username and a PIN that has been assigned to them and submit the information to the Web server to see the documents that are available to them. At this point, the user can then click on a link that will open the document in Adobe Acrobat reader so it can be read, printed, saved, or deleted. Documents posted to a Web server are purged after a selected amount of time to comply with copyright restrictions. If the user has not accessed their document by the time these materials have reached the purge date, the documents are no longer available to the user and the process of ordering the material may need to be repeated. (See Table 1.)

Since both methods of delivery have their advantages and their disadvantages, libraries serving off-campus users must be able to use both methods to achieve the highest possible level of service. Users, regardless of location, may experience difficulty using one or both methods. This is why the library should have the option of using a different method of delivery if one method fails. For example, if an off-campus user cannot access materials posted to the

TABLE 1. Advantages and Disadvantages of EDD Delivery Methods

	E-mail attachment in .PDF	Post document to Web server
Advantages	Instant access upon opening	Large files can be delivered
	No firewall involved	Secure login process
	No Web server involved	More control for the library
Disadvantages	Large files are undeliverable	Multiple step process for user
	Many requests fill up e-mail quota	Accidental deletion of file

Web server, the library can attempt to send the documents as an e-mail attachment. If the user has a campus e-mail address, they should have enough space in their account to receive at least one document at a time into the account. Once the document is successfully received the user can clear the file from their account and then receive the next document after corresponding with the staff of the off-campus service department.

TESTING AND EXPERIMENTATION

It is important to experiment with new installations before implementing them for production. Testing consists of sending documents to yourself, your colleagues, and a limited group of users who are willing to report back to you about their experience. A short period of testing helps identify any errors in the software setup, gives another opportunity to proofread Web pages and e-mail notices, and to fix these errors before they impact large groups of users.

Experimenting with the software and various methods of delivery will also help increase confidence when users call with troubleshooting questions that have resulted from technical glitches.

Tips for Testing and Experimentation Stage of Implementation

- *Do* experiment with more than one method of delivery
- *Do* seek input from users who are willing to serve as testers
- *Do* be ready to spend time proofreading e-mail notifications and Web-based instructions
- *Don't* assume that testing will solve all problems ahead of time
- *Don't* make the delivery workflow too complicated
- *Don't* hesitate to implement as soon as possible

Although testing and experimentation is a valid step of the implementation process, caution should be taken to prevent technical difficulties from derailing the entire project. Users are generally willing to work with new systems especially when they can understand how it will benefit them.

TROUBLESHOOTING

Unfortunately, after all the setup, testing, and experimentation there will be times when a user has difficulty and frustration using the desktop delivery system. At this point, some limited additional experimentation may be necessary.

Unless a user is pressed for time, most people will participate in the trouble-shooting process and are grateful to have assistance to obtain their materials through EDD.

One of the most common mistakes is the accuracy of the e-mail account address. A simple typo in the e-mail address when entered into the EDD software will completely prevent the material from reaching the user. Also, users may try to access a different e-mail account than the one to which the document has been delivered. Many users have multiple e-mail accounts which are both campus approved and free or fee based services available from online sources. Free e-mail accounts often have a very limited space available for incoming messages and experience has shown that e-mail attachments of .PDF files are often too large to be delivered successfully. Another problem is that newer versions of Web browsers allow users to set their own profiles and preferences and now have more sophisticated protection to prevent the user from submitting personal information over the Web. This can cause problems when the user attempts to login to their account to retrieve their documents that have been posted to the Web. Recent upgrades to newer versions of Web browsers can create new problems for methods of electronic document delivery that were previously working under the older versions of the Web browsers.

In addition to Web browser versions creating problems for access to documents, home computer firewall programs have settings that prevent access to documents posted to the Web. Other settings to check include cookies, java script, and Adobe Acrobat Reader. Cookies and java script should be turned on for the user to access materials posted to the Web. And, for any user, Adobe Acrobat Reader should always be upgraded to the most recent version to remove any problems that are caused by older versions of the software.

Troubleshooting can be time consuming, but it is a necessary part of providing quality service. Keep track of any advanced troubleshooting efforts, any problems that seem specific to your campus, and the questions that are frequently asked by users so the information can be added to the tips, tricks, and FAQs of an online troubleshooting guide created to assist users (Weible, p. 80). Online troubleshooting guides for EDD services have become popular and are easily found by performing a few searches on the Internet (see the "Additional Resources" section at the end of this paper). Most institutions will allow their guide to be copied and tailored by another institution so the creation of this type of Web document is relatively quick and easy. Creating options for users to solve problems on their own is a helpful part of the troubleshooting process (Weible & Robben, p. 83). In spite of possible derailments from various versions and options in software programs and e-mail account settings, electronic document delivery can be quite successful and a beneficial service for the majority of users.

CONCLUSION

Implementing an EDD service for the off-campus population is just one aspect of providing a complete program for this unique group of users and libraries have strategically included this main campus service as a part of their distance education programs (Bibb, 2003, p. 5). Although providing a quality EDD service means an investment and commitment of time, the fact remains that the options available to implement this kind of service are numerous and flexible. Library staff can easily implement and maintain just the basic of EDD services and reduce delivery time and increase patron satisfaction. Every library's situation is different and the software and methods chosen by each will vary with the factors involved in making the EDD service selection process. However, the variety of options available to libraries has created an environment where no library has a valid reason not to implement some form of an EDD service for at least some, if not all, of their off-campus users.

Despite the fact that most documents can be delivered directly to the off-campus users' desktops, there will occasionally be times when this service fails to live up to the expectations of the end user or the librarian. If the EDD service fails individual users on occasion it is important to remember that the information can still be delivered via private courier or the U.S. postal service. Although these methods of delivery are not as instant in the 24/7 world in which the library researchers live and work, the material will still reach the end user in a timely and (hopefully) acceptable manner. Testing, experimentation, and troubleshooting are all parts of the implementation and maintenance process. Support from fellow librarians at other institutions, discussion lists, and help desks all make the troubleshooting and maintenance issues easier to cope with as they arise. Providing quality service should be the goal of every unit that supports off-campus students and choosing an EDD service has never been easier. Make it your goal today to re-evaluate your current methods of document delivery and implement an EDD service for off-campus users as soon as possible.

REFERENCES

Bibb, D. D. (2003). Distance center students deserve main campus resources. *Collection Building, 22*(1), 5-9.

Casey, A. M. and Grudzien, P. A. (2002). Increasing document delivery to off-campus students through an interdepartmental partnership. In P. Mahoney (Ed.), *The Tenth Off-Campus Library Services Proceedings*, Cincinnati, Ohio, April 17-19, 2002, (pp. 111-117). Mount Pleasant, MI: Central Michigan University Press.

Fuller, D. H., Jr. (2002). Distance learning and interlibrary loan: A look at services and technology. *Journal of Interlibrary Loan, Document Delivery & Information Supply, 12*(4), 15-25.

Kriz, H. M. (2000). Electronic interlibrary loan delivery with Ariel and ILLiad. *Journal of Interlibrary Loan, Document Delivery & Information Supply, 10*(4), 25-34.

Lindsay, G. (2000). Ariel via e-mail: New possibilities for the non-Ariel equipped library. *Journal of Interlibrary Loan, Document Delivery & Information Supply, 11*(1), 81-85.

Rodman, R. L. (2002). 3D: The paperless document delivery project at the Prior Health Sciences Library. *Journal of Interlibrary Loan, Document Delivery & Information Supply, 12*(4), 63-77.

Sayed, E. N., Murray, S. D. & Wheeler, K. P. (2001). The magic of Prospero. *Journal of Interlibrary Loan, Document Delivery & Information Supply, 12*(1), 55-72.

Sellen, M. (1999). Turnaround time and journal article delivery: A study of four delivery systems. *Journal of Interlibrary Loan, Document Delivery & Information Supply, 9*(4), 65-72.

Schnell, E. H. (1999). The Prospero electronic document delivery project. *Journal of Interlibrary Loan, Document Delivery, and Information Supply, 10*(2), 89-100.

Stabler, K. (2002). Benchmarking interlibrary loan and document delivery services: Lessons learned at New Mexico State University. *Journal of Interlibrary Loan, Document Delivery & Information Supply, 12*(3), 57-73.

Weible, C. L. (2002). Providing electronic document delivery services: Juggling user needs, delivery options, and quality service. In C. J. Ury & V. Wainscott (Eds.), *Brick and Click Libraries: Changes and Challenges* (pp. 77-82). Maryville, MO: Northwest Missouri State University.

Weible, C. L. and Robben, C. (2002). Calming the tempest: The benefits of using Prospero for electronic document delivery in a large academic library. *Journal of Interlibrary Loan, Document Delivery & Information Supply, 12*(4), 79-86.

ADDITIONAL RESOURCES

Prospero
Prospero home page: http://bones.med.ohio-state.edu/prospero/
Discussion group: http://lists.med.ohio-state.edu/mailman/listinfo/hslprospero

Ariel
Home page: http://www4.infotrieve.com/ariel/
Discussion group: http://www4.infotrieve.com/ariel/arie-l.html

Odyssey
http://216.54.31.120/Documentation.html
http://www.oclc.org/illiad/about/features/delivery/
Discussion group: http://www.oclc.org/illiad/about/features/delivery/

Patron Delivery Using Ariel 3.01 by The University of Chicago
http://www.lib.uchicago.edu/e/using/ill/ariel_config.html

Adobe Acrobat Products
Home page: http://www.adobe.com/products/acrobat/readstep2.html

NLM's DocView, DocMorph, and MyMorph
Home page: http://docmorph.nlm.nih.gov/docview/

ILL Management Software Incorporating the EDD Function:
Clio http://cliosoftware.com/
ILLiad http://www.oclc.org/illiad/
RLG's ILL Manager http://www.rlg.org/illman/index.html
Fretwell-Downing's VDX http://www.fdusa.com/products/vdx.html

Electronic Document Delivery Troubleshooting Guides:
University of Illinois at Urbana-Champaign
     http://gateway.library.uiuc.edu/irrc/eddhelp.htm
University of Michigan http://docdel.lib.umich.edu/ddTroubleShootingGuide.html
University of Massachusetts at Boston
     http://www.lib.umb.edu/prospero/troubleshooting.html

Contributor Index

Adams, Kate E.
  and Mary Cassner: *A Survey
  of Distance Librarian-
  Administrators in ARL
  Libraries: An Overview of
  Library Resources and
  Services*, 85-96
Adams, Tina M.
  and R. Sean Evans: *Educating
  the Educators: Outreach to
  the College of Education
  Distance Faculty and Native
  American Students*, 3-18

Baird, Constance M.
  and Linda L. Lillard, Pat
  Wilson: *Progressive
  Partnering: Expanding
  Student and Faculty Access
  to Information Services*,
  227-242
Barsun, Rita
  and Johanna Tuñón, Laura
  Lucio Ramirez: *Pests,
  Welcomed Guests, or
  Tolerated Outsiders?
  Attitudes of Academic
  Librarians Toward Distance
  Students from Unaffiliated
  Institutions*, 485-505
Bedi, Shailoo
  and Rosie Croft: *eBooks for a
  Distributed Learning
  University: The Royal Roads
  University Case*, 113-137

Behr, Michele D.
  *On Ramp to Research:
  Creation of a Multimedia
  Library Instruction
  Presentation for Off-Campus
  Students*, 19-30
Bickford, David
  *Using Direct Linking
  Capabilities in Aggregated
  Databases for E-Reserves*,
  31-45
Black, Nancy E.
  *Blessing or Curse? Distance
  Delivery to Students with
  Invisible Disabilities*, 47-64
Buchanan, Elizabeth A.
  *Institutional Challenges in
  Web-Based Programs:
  Student Challenges and
  Institutional Responses*, 65-74
Buehler, Marianne A.
  *Where Is the Library in
  Course Management
  Software?* 75-84

Casey, Anne Marie
  and Lana Ivanitskaya, Ryan
  Laus: *Research Readiness
  Self-Assessment: Assessing
  Students' Research Skills and
  Attitudes*, 167-183
Cassner, Mary
  and Kate E. Adams: *A Survey
  of Distance Librarian-
  Administrators in ARL
  Libraries: An Overview of
  Library Resources and
  Services*, 85-96

http://www.haworthpress.com/web/JLA
Digital Object Identifier: 10.1300/J111v41n03_15

Chakraborty, Mou
    and Shelley Victor: *Do's and
    Don'ts of Simultaneous
    Instruction to On-Campus
    and Distance Students via
    Videoconferencing*, 97-112
Croft, Rosie
    and Shailoo Bedi: *eBooks for
    a Distributed Learning
    University: The Royal Roads
    University Case*, 113-137

Dew, Stephen H.
    and Evadne McLean:
    *Assessing the Library Needs
    and Preferences of
    Off-Campus Students:
    Surveying Distance Education
    Students, from the Midwest to
    the West Indies*, 265-302
Draper, Jessica
    and Allyson Washburn: *80
    Miles from the Nearest
    Library, with a Research
    Paper Due Monday:
    Extending Library Services to
    Distance Learners*, 507-529

Evans, R. Sean
    and Tina M. Adams:
    *Educating the Educators:
    Outreach to the College of
    Education Distance Faculty
    and Native American
    Students*, 3-18

Finkelstein, Kate
    and Janette Shaffer, Nancy
    Woelfl, Elizabeth Lyden: *A
    Systematic Approach to
    Assessing the Needs of
    Distance Faculty*, 413-428

Fritts, Jack
    and Beth A. Reiten: *The
    Impact of Distance Learning
    Library Services Experience
    on Practitioners' Career
    Paths*, 365-374

Guillot, Ladonna
    and Beth Stahr: *A Tale of
    Two Campuses: Providing
    Virtual Reference to Distance
    Nursing Students*, 139-152

Hufford, Jon R.
    *User Instruction for Distance
    Students: Texas Tech
    University System's Main
    Campus Library Reaches Out
    to Students at Satellite
    Campuses*, 153-165

Ivanitskaya, Lana
    and Ryan Laus, Anne Marie
    Casey: *Research Readiness
    Self-Assessment: Assessing
    Students' Research Skills and
    Attitudes*, 167-183

Jerabek, Judy Ann
    and Lynn M. McMain:
    *Assessing Minds Want to
    Know: Developing Questions
    for Assessment of Library
    Services Supporting
    Off-Campus Learning
    Programs*, 303-314
Jones, Marie F.
    *Creating a Library CD for
    Off-Campus Students*, 185-202

Johnson, Kay
    and Elaine Magusin:
    *Collaborating on Electronic
    Course Reserves to Support
    Student Success*, 255-264
Johnson, Kay
    and Paul R. Pival:
    *Tri-Institutional Library
    Support: A Lesson in Forced
    Collaboration*, 345-354

Kayler, Grant
    and Paul R. Pival: *Working
    Together: Effective
    Collaboration in a
    Consortium Environment*,
    203-215
Kern, M. Kathleen
    *Chat It Up! Extending
    Reference Services to Assist
    Off-Campus Students*, 217-226

Laus, Ryan
    and Lana Ivanitskaya, Anne
    Marie Casey: *Research
    Readiness Self-Assessment:
    Assessing Students' Research
    Skills and Attitudes*, 167-183
Lillard, Linda L.
    and Pat Wilson, Constance
    M. Baird: *Progressive
    Partnering: Expanding
    Student and Faculty Access
    to Information Services*,
    227-242
Lockerby, Robin
    and Anne Marie Secord,
    Laura Roach, Joe Simpson:
    *Strategic Planning for
    Distance Learning Services*,
    407-411

Lockerby, Robin
    and Divina Lynch, James
    Sherman, Elizabeth Nelson:
    *Collaboration and Information
    Literacy: Challenges of
    Meeting Standards When
    Working with Remote
    Faculty*, 243-253
Lyden, Elizabeth
    and Janette Shaffer, Kate
    Finkelstein, Nancy Woelfl: *A
    Systematic Approach to
    Assessing the Needs of
    Distance Faculty*, 413-428
Lynch, Divina
    and Robin Lockerby, James
    Sherman, Elizabeth Nelson:
    *Collaboration and
    Information Literacy:
    Challenges of Meeting
    Standards When Working
    with Remote Faculty*, 243-253

Magusin, Elaine
    and Kay Johnson:
    *Collaborating on Electronic
    Course Reserves to Support
    Student Success*, 255-264
McLean, Evadne
    and Stephen H. Dew:
    *Assessing the Library Needs
    and Preferences of
    Off-Campus Students:
    Surveying Distance
    Education Students, from the
    Midwest to the West Indies*,
    265-302
McMain, Lynn M.
    and Judy Ann Jerabek:
    *Assessing Minds Want to
    Know: Developing Questions
    for Assessment of Library
    Services Supporting
    Off-Campus Learning
    Programs*, 303-314

Mikesell, Brian L.
*Anything, Anytime, Anywhere:
Proxy Servers, Shibboleth,
and the Dream of the Digital
Library,* 315-326
Morrison, Rob
and Allyson Washburn:
*Taking Assessment on the
Road: Utah Academic
Librarians Focus on
Distance Learners,* 327-344

Nelson, Elizabeth
and Robin Lockerby, Divina
Lynch, James Sherman:
*Collaboration and
Information Literacy:
Challenges of Meeting
Standards When Working
with Remote Faculty,*
243-253

Pival, Paul R.
and Grant Kayler: *Working
Together: Effective
Collaboration in a
Consortium Environment,*
203-215
Pival, Paul R.
and Kay Johnson:
*Tri-Institutional Library
Support: A Lesson in Forced
Collaboration,* 345-354

Ramirez, Laura Lucio and Johanna
Tuñón, Rita Barsun: *Pests,
Welcomed Guests, or
Tolerated Outsiders?
Attitudes of Academic
Librarians Toward Distance
Students from Unaffiliated
Institutions,* 485-505

Reeves, Linda A.
*Starting Small: Setting Up
Off-Campus Library Services
with Limited Resources,*
355-364
Reiten, Beth A.
and Jack Fritts: *The Impact of
Distance Learning Library
Services Experience on
Practitioners' Career Paths,*
365-374
Riedel, Tom
*Ahead of the Game: Using
Communications Software
and Push Technology to
Raise Student Awareness of
Library Resources,* 375-390
Roach, Laura
and Anne Marie Secord,
Robin Lockerby, Joe Simpson:
*Strategic Planning for
Distance Learning Library
Services,* 407-411

Searing, Susan E.
*All in the Family: Library
Services for LIS Online
Education,* 391-405
Secord, Anne Marie
and Robin Lockerby, Laura
Roach, Joe Simpson: *Strategic
Planning for Distance
Learning Services,* 407-411
Shaffer, Janette
and Kate Finkelstein, Nancy
Woelfl, Elizabeth Lyden: *A
Systematic Approach to
Assessing the Needs of
Distance Faculty,* 413-428
Sherman, James
and Robin Lockerby, Divina
Lynch, Elizabeth Nelson:
*Collaboration and
Information Literacy:
Challenges of Meeting
Standards When Working
with Remote Faculty,* 243-253

Simpson, Joe
and Anne Marie Secord,
Robin Lockerby, Laura
Roach: *Strategic Planning
for Distance Learning
Services*, 407-411

Sochrin, Sheri
*Learning to Teach in a New
Medium: Adapting Library
Instruction to a
Videoconferencing
Environment*, 429-442

Stahr, Beth
and Ladonna Guillot: *A Tale
of Two Campuses: Providing
Virtual Reference to Distance
Nursing Students*, 139-152

Stockham, Marcia
and Elizabeth Turtle:
*Providing Off-Campus
Library Services by "Team":
An Assessment*, 443-457

Summey, Terri Pedersen
*If You Build It, Will They
Come? Creating a Marketing
Plan for Distance Learning
Library Services*, 459-470

Thomsett-Scott, Beth
*Yeah, I Found It! Performing
Web Site Usability Testing to
Ensure That Off-Campus
Students Can Find the
Information They Need*,
471-483

Tuñón, Johanna
and Rita Barsun, Laura Lucio
Ramirez: *Pests, Welcomed
Guests, or Tolerated
Outsiders? Attitudes of
Academic Librarians Toward
Distance Students from
Unaffiliated Institutions*,
485-505

Turtle, Elizabeth
and Marcia Stockham:
*Providing Off-Campus
Library Services by "Team":
An Assessment*, 443-457

Victor, Shelley
and Mou Chakraborty: *Do's
and Don'ts of Simultaneous
Instruction to On-Campus
and Distance Students via
Videoconferencing*, 97-112

Washburn, Allyson
and Rob Morrison: *Taking
Assessment on the Road:
Utah Academic Librarians
Focus on Distance Learners*,
327-344

Washburn, Allyson
and Jessica Draper: *80 Miles
from the Nearest Library,
with a Research Paper Due
Monday: Extending Library
Services to Distance
Learners*, 507-529

Weible, Cherié L.
*Selecting Electronic
Document Delivery Options
to Provide Quality Service*,
531-540

Wilson, Pat
and Linda L. Lillard,
Constance M. Baird:
*Progressive Partnering:
Expanding Student and
Faculty Access to
Information Services*,
227-242

Woelfl, Nancy
and Janette Shaffer, Kate
Finkelstein, Elizabeth Lyden:
*A Systematic Approach to
Assessing the Needs of
Distance Faculty*, 413-428

Index

Numbers followed by n indicate notes.

Academic success, relationship with
    control, 59
Accord bridge, 103
ACRL. *See* Association of College and
    Research Libraries
Adaptive computer technology, 56-58
Administrators, distance learning
    librarians as, 370,371
    survey of, 85-96
        methodology of, 87-88
        results, 88-95
Adobe Acrobat, 270,532,540
Adobe Acrobat Reader, 534,535,537
AIX, 179
Alamo Community College District,
    358,359,361
ALISE (Association for Library and
    Information Science
    Education), 392
American Library Association (ALA),
    392
    information literacy definition of,
        177
    Master of Library and Information
        Science program
        accreditation by, 392,400-401
    SIRSI's Leader in Library
        Technology Grant, 512
Americans with Disabilities Act of
    1990, 58
    Title II, Section 202, 52
Apache HTTP server, 179,180
Apsangikar, Kedar, 179
Arial software, use in document
    delivery, 9

Ariel software
    .TIFF format of, 532-533
    use in document delivery, 531,
        532-533,539
Arizona. *See also* Northern Arizona
    University
    economic conditions in, 6-7
    educational attainment levels in, 5-6
    student enrollment statistics in, 5
Arizona State Library, 9
ARL. *See* Association of Research
    Libraries
Assistive Technology for Individuals
    with Disabilities Act, Section
    508, 52
Association for Library and Information
    Science Education (ALISE),
    392
Association of College and Research
    Libraries (ACRL)
    *Emergency Technologies in
        Instruction Committee*, 24
    Focus on the Future Task Force, 86
    *Guidelines for Distance Learning
        Library Services*, 48,85-87,
        106,150,227-228,274,356,
        366,367,444
    *Guidelines for the Preparation of
        Policies on Library Access*,
        488
    *Information Literacy Competency
        Standards for Higher
        Education*, 171,244,245
    president of, 487
    *2000 Academic Library Trends and
        Statistics*, 356-357

© 2004 by The Haworth Press, Inc. All rights reserved.

Association of Research Libraries (ARL)
    definition of, 86
    SPEC Kit, 87
    survey of distance learning
        librarian-administrators,
        85-96
Athabasca University, distance learning
        library services of, 347
    for Campus Alberta Graduate Program
        in Counselling, 347,348,349,
        351,352
    Digital Reading Room, 255-264,
        347,351
        benefits to students, 260-262
        as collaborative project, 258-260
        copyright law and, 260-261
        definition of, 257
        Digital Reading Files, 257,258
        eduSource Canada learning
            objectives repository project
            and, 260
        faculty's concerns about, 259-260
        Help Centre and, 262-263
        information literacy and, 262
        as multidisciplinary knowledge
            database, 258
        open access principle of, 257-258
        Required Readings, 257
        Supplementary Materials, 257,
            258,259,261
    Digital Reference Centre, 347
    Library Information Gateway, 347
Athens (Access Management
        Services), 323-324,325
Attention-deficit/hyperactivity
        disorder, 49
Attention-getting strategies, in library
        instruction tutorials, 187-188
Authentication, for electronic resources
        access
    for e-reserves access, 81-82
    with FirstClass course management
        software, 81-82
    implication for unaffiliated library
        users, 490

with IP (Internet Protocol), 316
    advantages of, 317
    process of, 316-317,318
need for, 317-318
with proxy servers, 315-326
via direct linking, 38-39,40,41-42,44

Bias, in questionnaire design, 311-312
Bibliographic instruction. *See also*
        Library instruction
    transition to information literacy,
        99-111
Blackboard (course management
        system), 140,228,232
    versions 2.0-5.0, 83
    Virtual Classroom of, 241
"Bobby," 57
Bookmarked electronic documents, 32
Books
    electronic. *See* eBooks
    Utah distance learners' use of, 337
Bowling Green State University,
        FALCON library instruction
        tutorial use at, 24
Brand identity, of libraries, 460,461,
        467
Brigham Young University, Harold B.
        Lee Library, 507-529
    collection, 508
    consortia memberships, 508
    distance learning library services
        project, 507-529
        American Library Association
            grant for, 512
    distance learning library services
        project of, 507-529
        background to, 509-511
        correlation with library's goals,
            510-511
        correlation with library's
            objectives, 510
        evaluation phase of, 516-517
        evaluative survey of, 517,
            528-529

marketing of, 515-516
needs assessment for, 511-512,
519-524
planning phase of, 512-515
portal and administrative
interfaces of, 517-518,
525-527
Brown, John Seely, 169
Budgets
for distance learning library services,
86-87,89-92,93,95
at small institutions, 355-364
for universities, decreases in, 490

California State University, decreased
funding for, 490
Campus Alberta Graduate Program in
Counselling
definition of, 346
description of, 346
enrollment in, 347-348,352
sponsorship for, 346
tri-institutional library services
support for, 345 -354
Athabasca University
participant, 347,348
future developments in, 353
library instruction, 348-349
reserve readings, 350-351
student identification cards, 352
University of Alberta participant,
353
University of Calgary participant,
346-347,348,349-352
University of Lethbridge
participant, 347,348,349-352
Canada, adaptive computer technology
use in, 57-58
Canadian Charter of Rights and
Freedoms, Section 15(1), 51
Canadian Human Rights Act, 51-52
Canadian Library Association,
*Guidelines for Library Support
of Distance and Distributed
Learning in Canada*, 48,204,
206

Canadians, learning disabilities
prevalence among, 49
CANCORE, 260
Careers, of distance learning librarians,
365-374
Caribbean Development Bank, 273
Catalogs
online, budget support for, 89
online public access catalog
(OPAC), 310-311
Utah distance learners' use of, 337
CAUL (Coalition of Atlantic
University Libraries), 210
CD-ROM-based library instruction
tutorials, 185-202,377
adult learning theory and, 187
components of, 187-192
assessment of student
performance, 191
attention-getting strategies,
187-188
elicitation of student
performance, 191
feedback, 191
guided learning, 189-191
humor, 190-191
length of presentation, 190,202
multimedia, 190
objective-setting, 188-189
organization of presentation, 190
presentation of material, 189-191
recall of prior learning, 189
content of, 192-193
InfoTrac tutorial, 193
music video/library tour, 193
off-campus library services
directory, 193
Texas Information Literacy
Tutorial (TILT), 192
Two-Minute Web site Tour,
192-193,194,196-201,202
Voyager Library Catalog, 193
in multimedia library instruction,
26,27-28,190
rationale for, 186

technology for, 193-201
    Dreamweaver (HTML editor),
        193,194,202
    PowerPoint, 192,193,196-201,
        202
Central Michigan University,
        Off-Campus Library Services
        conferences held at, 365-366
    survey of participants, 369-374
Central Michigan University
        Off-Campus Library
        Services, 170-181
    document delivery services, 170
    Research Readiness Self-Assessment
        (RRSA) survey by, 171-181
    attitudes assessment component
        of, 172,173,175,180-181
    content of, 172-174
    design of, 172-174
    health professions component of,
        174
    multidisciplinary version of, 174
    technical overview of, 178-180
    uses for, 180-181
    validation of, 174-177
Certification programs, distance
        learning-based, 88
CGI programming language, 178,180
Chadwick-Healy, 42
Chronicle of Higher Education, The, 86
Church of Jesus Christ of Latter-day
        Saints, 508
Clio software, 533
Coalition of Atlantic University
        Libraries (CAUL), 210
Cobrowsing software, 142-143,
        146,147
Collaboration, in distance learning
        library services. *See also*
        Consortia
    in e-reserves system development
        and use, 258-260,263
    faculty-librarian
        in course management software
            use, 77-79,82-84,94

in information literacy, 245,246,
        247-248
    in library instruction, 76
    in reference services for distance
        learners, 360-361
    in information literacy
        faculty-librarian, 245,246,
            247-248
        outreach component of, 249-251
        for Master of Library and Information
            Science students, 397-400
    in online library instruction,
        227-242
    tri-institutional, 345-354
Colleague Data (student information
        system), 378,381-382
College of Eastern Utah, 328
    distance learning focus group study
        at, 329-335
    distance learning library services of,
        328
Communication
    among distance learning students,
        66,70-71
    between institutions and students,
        67,68-70
Community colleges, library services
        for unaffiliated students, 495,
        497
Concorde 4500, 103
Consortia, distance learning library
        services of
    of Council of Prairie and Pacific
        University Libraries
        (COPPUL), 203-215
    projected trends in, 95
Content analysis, 306
Control, relationship with academic
        success, 59
Copyrighted material, Internet access
        to, 169
Copyright law
    digitalized material and
        in America, 350
        in Canada, 349,350-351
    e-reserves systems and, 260-261

Cost. *See also* Budgets
   of distance learning library services,
      149-150
Coughlan, John, 401
Council of Prairie and Pacific University
      Libraries (COPPUL), 116
   Distance Education Forum, 203-215
      annual meeting of, 206-208
      document delivery/interlibrary
         loan services, 212-213
      examination of commercial
         library alternatives project,
         207-208
      goals, 205
      information literacy Web site,
         209-210
      mandate for, 204-205
      objectives, 205-206
      reciprocal borrowing project,
         208-209
      resources, 213
      user survey, 212
      Virtual Western Canadian
         University Library
         (VWCUL), 210-211
   member libraries, 204
Course management software
   Blackboard, 140,228,232
      versions 2.0-5.0, 83
   budget support for, 92
   faculty-librarian collaboration
         regarding, 77-79,82-84,94
   FirstClass, 76,79-80,81-82
      e-reserves component of, 81-82
      history function component of,
         80
      library pathfinder component of,
         82
   Prometheus, 76,77-78,80
      Course Content Module of, 79
      e-reserves component of, 78
   use at Rochester Institute of
         Technology, 77-84
   faculty-librarian collaboration
         in, 77-79,82-84

myCourse class in, 77-78
      pathfinders for, 76-77
      Prometheus, 78,79
Course notes, as distance learners'
         information source, 337
CSS, 259
Cultural awareness and sensitivity, in
         distance learning library
         services, 12-13
Culturally-sensitive materials, use in
         distance learning library
         services, 13-14

Dartmouth College, Sanborn Library,
         490
Databases
   budget support for, 90
   unaffiliated distance learning
         students' access to, 495,497
   Utah distance learning students'
         lack of knowledge about,
         338,339
Database servers, 178-179
Digital object identifiers (DOIs), 42-43
DIG_REF (discussion group), 490-491
Direct linking, with aggregated
         databases, 31-34
   copyright clearance for, 32-33
   with digital object identifiers
         (DOIs), 42-43
   with EBSCO platforms, 34,35
      EBSCOhost, 36-38,41,44,45
      Page Composer, 34
   with Gale platforms, 34,35,38-39
   with Infomarks, 38-39,45
   with JSTOR, 44
   with Lexis-Nexis Academic, 44
   OpenURL standards-based,
         34,41-42,43
   with Ovid platforms, 35,39-40
   with ProQuest platforms, 35-36
      Durable Links, 45
      "My Research Summary," 41

OpenURL standards-based,
41-42,43
SiteBuilder, 33-34,40-41,42,43
recommendations regarding, 42-44
software tools for, 33-44, 45
via cross-platform linking, 43-44
WilsonWeb, 44
Distance education. *See* Distance learning
Distance learning
comparison with distributed
learning, 357
definition of, 366
prevalence of, 88
relationship with lifelong learning,
366
Distance learning librarians
as administrators, 370,371
survey of, 85-96
careers of, 365-374
as online library science course
co-instructors, 227-242
connectivity issues and,
231-232,235-236
students' reactions to, 235-240
Distance learning programs
enrollment in, 355-356
increase in, 154
planning strategies for, 66-68
Distance learning students
assistance for, 69-70
awareness of distance learning-related
library services, 375-390
definition of, 219
demographic profile of, 48
lack of social interaction among, 98
online mentors for, 71,73n
from unaffiliated institutions. *See*
Unaffiliated distance learning
students
virtual lounges for, 70-72,73n
Distributed learning, comparison with
distance learning, 357
Document delivery services, for
distance learners
access and delivery options for, 92
budget support for, 90

non-electronic alternatives to, 538
at Northern Arizona University
Cline Library, 9
at Nova Southeastern University, 106
projected trends in, 95
user surveys of
Council of Prairie and Pacific
University Libraries
(COPPUL), 212
University of Iowa, 268,271,
289,290
Utah distance learners' use of, 337
via e-mail, disadvantages of, 535,537
in virtual reference services, 221-222
at Western Michigan University
Libraries, 20
Docutek, ERes, 255-256
Docutek VRLplus software, 20-21
DOIs (digital object identifiers), 42-43
Dreamweaver (HTML editor), 193,
194,202
Dreamweaver MX, 363
Drucker, Peter, 250
Dual-credit students, library services
for, 362,363-364
Durable Links, 45

East Tennessee State University,
CD-based library instruction
tutorials, 185-202
adult learning theory and, 187
components of, 187-192
assessment of student
performance, 191
attention-getting strategies,
187-188
elicitation of student
performance, 191
enhancement of learning
retention and transfer, 192
feedback, 191
guided learning, 189-191
humor, 190-191
length of presentation, 190,202

multimedia use, 190
objective-setting, 188-189
organization of presentation, 190
presentation of material,
    189-191
recall of prior learning, 189
content of, 192-193
    InfoTrac tutorial, 193
    music video/library tour, 193
    off-campus library services
        directory, 193
    Texas Information Literacy
        Tutorial (TILT), 192
    Two-Minute Web site Tour,
        192-193,194,196-201,202
    Voyager Library Catalog, 193
rationale for, 186
technology for, 193-201
    Dreamweaver (HTML editor),
        193,194,202
    PowerPoint, 192,193,196-201,
        202
eBooks, 113-137
availability to Texas libraries, 359
budgetary support for, 90
Council of Prairie and Pacific
    University Libraries
    evaluation of, 207-208
in LEEP program, 395,396
Royal Roads University collections,
    113-137
    ebrary, 117-118,122
    Electronic Library Network
        (ELN), 116
    faculty and student user surveys
        of, 119-132
    ITKnowledge, 117
    most frequently accessed titles,
        117
    netLibrary, 116,117,118,120,129
    usage rates, 116,117-118
University of Rochester, Rush
    Rhees Library collection, 129
University of Texas collection, 118

EBSCO
    direct linking tools of
        EBSCOhost, 36-38,41,44,45
        Page Composer, 34
    Psychology and Behavioral
        Sciences database collection,
        352
EDNET system, 341
Education Tutorial, 25
EduServ, 323
eduSource Canada, learning objectives
    repository project, 260
Electronic books. *See* eBooks
Electronic course reserves. *See*
    Reserves, electronic
Electronic resources. *See also* eBooks;
    Journals, electronic
    distance learning students' access
        to, 223-224
    IP (Internet Protocol) access to
        advantages of, 317
        process of, 316-317,318
    versus print resources, 357
    proxy server access to, 315-326
        alternatives to, 322-326
        comparison with IP (Internet
            Protocol), 316-317
        definition of, 318-319
        manually-configured, 320,321
        problems with, 319-321
        URL-rewriters for, 320,321-322
        students' preference for, 357
    University of Iowa focus group
        survey of, 268
Elluminate vClass, 359-360,361,363
E-mail reference services, 217-218,359
    budget support for, 91
    University of Iowa user survey of,
        268,271,289,291
    Utah distance learners' use of, 338
*Emergency Technologies in Instruction
    Committee*, 24
Employment satisfaction, of learning
    disabled individuals, 58-59

Employment statistics, from Arizona,
      6,7
Emporia State University, 460,491-492
Environmental (scanning) analysis,
      463-465,468
ERes, 255-256
e-reserve systems. *See* Reserves,
      electronic
ERIC, 25,495, 495
      ED documents, 106
Excel, 248,249,251,270,477
Explorer, 321
EZproxy software, 28,320,321-322,325

Face-to-face library instruction/
      reference services, 357,359
      HyperCard tutorial in, 22
      limitations to, 21-22
      for nontraditional students, 21-22
      versus remote-access services,
            228,337,338,339-340
      Utah distance learners' preference
            for, 337,338,339-340
      versus videoconferencing, 101-102
      Web browser use in, 22
Faculty, in distance learning
      involvement in online library
            instruction, 228,229,234
      library outreach to, 15-17
      software used by, 225
      training in distance learning
            pedagogy, 67
Faculty-librarian collaboration
      in course management software use,
            77-79,82,84,90
      in library instruction, 105,108
      in reference services for distance
            learners, 360-361
FALCON library instruction tutorial, 24
Family Educational Rights and Privacy
            Act, 380,387
Financial services, for distance learning
            students, 69

FIPSE (Fund for the Improvement of
            Post-Secondary Education),
            377
FirstClass, 76,79-80,81-82
      e-reserves component of, 81-82
      history function component of, 80
      library pathfinder component of, 82
FirstSearch, 25,28
Florida State University, School of
            Information Science, 392,393
      Library of, 399
Focus groups
      for evaluation of distance learners'
            information-seeking
            behavior, 327-344
      at College of Eastern Utah,
            329-335
      debriefing sessions in, 339-341
      future use of, 340
      informed consent for, 336
      institutional review board
            permission for, 335
      methodology, 330-331,335-336
      summary of responses, 331-333
      at Utah State University Moab
            Education Center, 329-335
      at Utah University, Uintah Basin
            Branch Campus, 335-338
      with learning disabled students, 61
      online, 68
      use in Web site usability studies,
            473,478-480
Formal (task-based) testing, 473-478
      basics of, 473-474
      beta testing of tasks prior to, 475
      debriefing sessions in, 477
      "gratification effect" in, 476-477
      posttest questionnaire in, 476-477
      screen capture (tracking) software
            use in, 473,476
Fund for the Improvement of
            Post-Secondary Education
            (FIPSE), 377

Gale Group
  direct linking tools, 34,35
  Infomarks, 38-39,45
  InfoTrac periodicals database, 38
General Disability Internet Resources
  Web site, 58
Glossary of Education Terms and
  Acronyms, 252
Goodson, Carol, 140
Graduate programs, distance
  learning-based
  library services for, 356
  prevalence of, 88
Graduate students, multimedia library
  instruction tool for, 22-30
  CD-ROM files use in, 26,27-28
  content modules of, 26-28
  development and implementation
    of, 24-28,29
  EZProxy software use with, 28
  goals of, 23-24,25
  Macromedia Flash MX software
    use with, 26
  Teaching and Learning with
    Technology (TILT) Grant
    for, 23,24
"Gratification effect," 476-477
Greater Western Library Alliance, 508
Griliches, Diane Asséo, 401
Guided learning, in library instruction,
  189-191
Guidelines for Distance Learning
  Library Services (Association
  of College and Research
  Libraries), 48,85-87,106,
  150,227-228,274,356,366,
  367,444
Guidelines for Library Support of
  Distance and Distributed
  Learning in Canada
  (Canadian Library
  Association), 48,204-206
Guidelines for the Preparation of
  Policies on Library Access
  (Association of College and
  Research Libraries), 488

Harvard University Extension School,
  168,169
Home-schooled students, library
  services for, 362,363-364
Hoover, Mike, 43
Hopis, as Northern Arizona University
  students, 4
House Rules (television program), 304
HTML, 259
Humor, use in library instruction, 190-191
HyperCard, 22

Identification (ID) cards, for distance
  learning students, 68
  for database remote access, 352
  for user survey participation,
    269-270,272
ILI-L (Information Literacy Instruction
  Listserv), 490-491
ILLiad software, 25,28,533
ILLINET Online, 395
Illiteracy, learning disabilities
  associated with, 49-50
ILL Manager, 533,540
Income levels, in Arizona, 6,7
Indexes, online, budget support for, 90
Infomarks, 38-39,45
Information Ecologies (Nardia and
  O'Day), 460-461
Information Excavation, 25
Information literacy
  bibliographic (library) instruction
    transition to, 99-111
  definition of, 177
  faculty-librarian collaboration for,
    245,246,247-248
  research skills and, 169
Information Literacy Competency
  Standards for Higher
  Education (Association of
  College and Research
  Libraries), 171,244,245
Information Literacy Instruction
  Listserv (ILI-L), 490-491

Information-seeking behavior, of
distance learners, focus group
studies of, 327-344
awareness of library services, 333
at College of Eastern Utah, 329-335
first study, 329-335
methodology, 330-331,335-336
obstacles to library services use,
333,339
preferred sources of information,
337
summary of responses, 331-333
at Utah State University, Uintah
Basin Branch Campus,
335-338
at Utah State University Moab
Education Center, 329-335
InfoTrac periodicals database, 38
InfoTrac tutorial, 193
Innovative Interfaces Inc., 257
Institute of Electrical and Electronics
Engineers (IEEE), Learning
Object Metadata (LOM)
standards of, 260
Interlibrary loan services, for distance
learners
budget support for, 90-91
consortial
budget support for, 90-91
of Council of Prairie and Pacific
University Libraries
(COPPUL), 212
of Northern Arizona University
Cline Library, 8
of Nova Southeastern University,
106
reserve readings as percentage of,
32
for unaffiliated distance learning
students, 495
in virtual reference services,
221-222
of Western Michigan University
Libraries, 20

Internet
impact on library usage, 167-168
unaffiliated distance learning
students' access to, 495
Internet Education Project, 24
Internet Explorer, 321
Internet Netscape, 321
IP (Internet Protocol) authentication,
316
advantages of, 317
process of, 316-317,318
iPowers, 103
Iron Chef (television program), 304
ITKnowledge ebooks, 117
ITS, 322

JavaScript, 259
Job satisfaction, of learning disabled
individuals, 58-59
Jones e-global library, 207
Journal articles, Utah distance learners'
use of, 337
Journals, electronic, budget support
for, 90
Journals@Ovid, Jumpstarts, 39-40
JSTOR, 44

Kansas State University, 377
Library Services Project Team
survey, 443-457
background to, 444-445
Distance Learning Web Page,
445,447
faculty's responses, 448-449
awareness of library services,
448,449
promotion of library services,
448,449
recommendations for
improvement of, 449
response rates, 448
survey form, 455-457

institutional review board
  approach for, 445
interpretation of results, 449-451
procedure of, 445-446
recommendations based on,
  450-451
students' demographics, 447
students' responses, 446-448
  awareness of library services,
    446,447
  library usage rates, 446,447
  preferred library services,
    447
  recommendations for library
    services
    improvements,
    447-448
  response rates, 446
  survey form, 453-455
  World Wide Web use
    statistics, 446-447
Kapi'olani Community College, as
  Learning Anytime Anywhere
  Partnership (LAAP) partner,
  377
Knock First (television program), 304

Laus, Ryan, 179
Law, John, 42
Leader in Library Technology Grant,
  512
Learning Anytime Anywhere
  Partnership (LAAP), 375-390
  administration of, 377
  funding for, 377
  Library Notification Module of,
    378-390
    Colleague Data (student
      information system),
      378,381-382
    consultants for, 381-382
    e-mail message processing in,
      383-384

e-mail user survey of, 385-386,
  389-390
Family Educational Rights and
  Privacy Act and, 380,387
implementation of, 382-383
push technology use in, 378-379
Unified Modeling Language
  (UML) use in, 379
visual modeling in, 379-381
Vision Team of, 377-378
Learning disabilities
  definition of, 49,50-51
  as "hidden" disabilities, 49
Learning Disabilities Association of
  Canada (LDAC), 49,50,58
  Facts Sheets of, 54,58
Learning disabled students
  academic environment for, 53-56,
    60
  academic success of, characteristics
    required for, 53,54-56,59,60
  distance learning environment for,
    52-53
  distance learning library services
    for, 47-64
    adaptive computer technology,
      56-58
    barriers to, 52-53,60
    improved access to, 61,62
    legislation affecting, 51-52,
      53-54,58
    focus groups with, 61
    reframing process utilization by, 55
    scaffolded instruction for, 55
    transition into careers, 58-59
Learning objectives repository project,
  260
Learning Object Metadata (LOM)
  standards, 260
Learning styles, of Native-American
  students, 12-13
Lectures, as distance learners'
  information source, 337

LEEP program, 392,393
    Academic Outreach Library and,
        398,399-400,401
    access to library collections and
        services in, 395-397
    case study of, 394-403
    cooperative approach in, 397-400
    enrollment in, 395
    instructors for, 394
    library instruction component of,
        394-395,397
    as Most Outstanding Asynchronous
        Learning Network, 394
    organizational structure of, 397-400
    program structure of, 394-395
    reference services for, 396-397,399
    students' preferences in, 393
Lenger, John, 168
LexisNexis, 224
LexisNexis Academic, 44
Librarians. *See also* Distance learning
    librarians
    attitudes toward technology,
        367-368
    attitudes toward unaffiliated
        distance learning students,
        485-505
        equality of access ethic and,
            487-488,489,493
        negative attitudes, 493-495,
            496-497
        positive attitudes, 493,495-496
Librarianship
    generalized *versus* specialized, 368
    ideals of, 402-403
    impact of technology on, 367-368
    public's lack of knowledge about,
        460-461
Libraries. *See also* names of specific
    libraries
    brand identity of, 460,461,467
    as physical places, 401-402
    "victim," 401
Library and Information Science
    Abstracts, 401

Library careers, of distance learning
    librarians, 365-374
Library instruction, for distance
    learners
    Association of College and Research
        Libraries guidelines for, 48,
        85-87,106,150,227-228,
        356,366,367,444
    budget support for, 91-92
    CD-ROM-based tutorial in,
        185-202,377
    adult learning theory and, 187
    attention-getting strategies in,
        187-188
    components of, 187-192
    content of, 192-193
    Dreamweaver (HTML editor)
        use in, 193,194,202
    elicitation of student
        performance, 191
    guided learning in, 189-191
    humor use in, 190-191
    InfoTrac tutorial, 193
    length of presentation, 190,202
    multimedia, 190
    music video/library tour, 193
    objective-setting in, 188-189
    off-campus library services
        directory in, 193
    organization of presentation, 190
    PowerPoint use in, 192,193,194,
        196-201,202
    presentation of material, 189-191
    rationale for, 186
    recall of prior learning in, 189
    technology for, 193-201
    Texas Information Literacy
        Tutorial (TILT), 192
    Two-Minute Web site Tour,
        192-193,194,196-201,202
    Voyager Library Catalog, 193
    face-to-face
        HyperCard tutorial in, 22
        limitations to, 21-22
        for nontraditional students, 21-22
        Web browser use in, 22

FALCON tutorial in, 24
multimedia, 22-30
  CD-ROM files use in, 26,27-28
  content modules of, 26-28
  development and implementation
    of, 24-28,29
  EZProxy software use with, 28
  goals of, 23-24,25
  Macromedia Flash MX software
    use with, 26
  Teaching and Learning with
    Technology (TILT) Grant
    for, 23,24
for Native-American students,
  11-14
at small colleges/libraries, 361-363
Southern Association of Colleges
  and Schools guidelines for,
  105
videoconferencing-based, 97-112,
  429-442
  background to, 430-432
  benefits of, 100-101
  college administration's support
    for, 432,438-439,441,442
  document delivery and
    interlibrary loan services in,
    106
  expansion of use of, 438-440
  extended library instruction
    classes in, 105-106,108
  face-to-face instruction *versus*,
    101-102
  faculty-librarian collaboration
    in, 105,108
  faculty's response to, 434-435
  faculty's training in, 437
  future developments in, 441-442
  guidelines for, 105-106
  initial class in, 434-435
  instructional techniques in,
    432-434,435,436
  librarians' training in, 432-434,
    435,436,437
  limitations to, 101

pilot project in, 432-438
recommendations for, 440-441
recommendations regarding,
  110-111
scheduling of, 439-440
technical problems in, 435,
  436-438
trouble-shooting guide for, 438
weekend/evening technical
  support for, 438
Web-based tutorials in
  Education Tutorial, 25
  FALCON, 24
  Information Excavation, 25
  at small colleges/libraries,
    362-363
  of Western Michigan University,
    19-30
Library services, for distance learners.
  See also Reference services,
  for distance learners
  cost of, 149-150
  impact on distance learning
    librarians' careers, 365-374
  with limited staff and budget,
    355-364
  marketing of, 148-149,333,363-364
  on-campus orientation to, 356-357
  prevalence of, 356
  projected trends in, 94-95
  strategic planning for, 407-411
Library usage, impact of the Internet
  on, 167-168
Linux, 178,179
Local libraries, use by distance learning
  students, 222-223
Lounges, virtual, 70-72,73n
Loyola University of New Orleans, 142

Macromedia Flash MX software, 26
*Management: Tasks, Responsibilities,
  Practices* (Drucker), 250
Manuals, for distance learning
  students, 70

MARC, 260
Marketing, of distance learning library
    services
  at Brigham Young University,
      515-516
  targeted marketing, 363-364
  at Utah State University, 333
  of virtual reference services, 148-149
Marketing plan, for distance learning
      library services, 459-470
  activity sheet for, 468-470
  definition of, 461
  documentation of, 461-462
  elements of, 462-467
    evaluation methods, 463,466,
        467,470
    executive summary, 462-463,
        470
    introduction, 463
    library or community analysis,
        462-463
    market analysis, 463-464,465
    marketing goals and objectives,
        463,465,466,469
    marketing strategy, 463,
        464-465,466,470
    mission statement and vision,
        462-463,465-466,469
    situation or environmental
        (scanning) analysis, 463-465,
        468
    SWOT analysis, 463,464,
        468-469
    table of contents, 463
    timetable and projected budget,
        463,466,470
    "unique selling proposition"
        (USP) concept, 465
  functions of, 462
  need for, 460-461
Marketing Plans That Work
      (McDonald and Keegan), 461
Master of Library and Information
      Science, distance learning
      programs in, 65-74,391-405

employability of graduates, 393
enrollment in, 392
Florida State University program,
      393,394
online mentors in, 71
planning strategies for, 66-68
students' problems with, 68-69
students' virtual lounge in, 70-72
University of Illinois,
      Urbana-Champaign LEEP
      program, 392-403
  Academic Outreach Library and,
      398,399-400,401
  access to library collections and
      services in, 395-397
  case study of, 394-403
  cooperative approach in, 397-400
  enrollment in, 395
  factors affecting, 400-403
  graduate LIS curriculum and,
      400-401
  ideals of librarianship and,
      402-403
  instructors for, 394
  library instruction component of,
      394-395,397
  as Most Outstanding
      Asynchronous Learning
      Network, 394
  organizational structure of,
      397-400
  physical library and, 400,
      401-402
  program structure of, 394-395
  reference services for, 396-397,
      399
  students' preferences in, 393
University of Washington program,
      392,400
Master of Library and Information
      Science programs, American
      Library Association-accredited,
      392,400-401
Mentors, online, 71,73n

Microsoft
    Excel, 248,249,251,270,477
    PowerPoint, 102,105,192,193,
        196-201,202,246,248,249,
        251,359,360,434
    SQL Server, 178
    Word, 27
Montage MCU, 103
Mormons, 508
Most Outstanding Asynchronous
        Learning Network award, 394
Multimedia-based library instruction,
        22-30
    CD-ROM files use in, 26,27-28,190
    content modules of, 26-28
    development and implementation
        of, 24-28,29
    EZProxy software use with, 28
    goals of, 23-24,25
    Macromedia Flash MX software
        use with, 26
    Teaching and Learning with
        Technology (TILT) Grant
        for, 23,24
MySQL, 178-179,180,259

National Institute for Literacy,
        49-50,58
National University, description of,
        407-408
National University Library System,
        distance learning library
        services of Information
        Literacy Plan for, 243-253
    compliance with ACRL
        Information Literacy
        Standards, 244,245
    faculty-librarian collaboration
        in, 245,246,247-248,249-251
    at Fresno Academic Center,
        247-249
    implementation of, 244-245
    outreach component of, 249-251

    at Sacramento Information
        Center, 249
    at San Jose Academic Center, 247
    self-assessment component of,
        251-252
    technological resources for, 246
    time limitations to, 245
    Library Information Centers (LICs)
        and, 244,408,409-410
    Strategic Plan for, 407-411
    goals and objectives of, 408,
        410-411
    mission and vision statements,
        408-409
    planning process for, 409-410
Native-American students, distance
        learning library services for,
        3-18
    cultural awareness and sensitivity
        in, 12-13
    culturally-sensitive materials in,
        13-14
    demographic factors in, 4-7,12,17n
    faculty and student outreach
        component of, 15-17
    Internet-based chat rooms for, 11
    Internet-based courses for, 14-15
    library instruction, 11-14
    obstacles to, 11-12
    students' learning styles and, 12-13
    via IITV, 11,14,16
    WebQuest module use in, 14-15,18n
Navajo Reservation and Trust Lands
    distance learning library services
        for, 10-17
    culturally-sensitive materials in,
        13-14
    faculty and student outreach
        component of, 15-17
    Internet-based courses, 14-15
    WebQuest module use in,
        14-15,18n
    economic and employment
        conditions in, 6-7
    educational attainment levels in, 5-6

educational enrollment levels in, 5
    student enrollment statistics, 5
Navajos. *See also* Navajo Reservation
    and Trust Lands
    as Northern Arizona University
        students, 4
Nelson, Elizabeth, 249
netLibrary, 207
Netscape, 321
Networking, 368
Newspapers, Utah distance learners'
    use of, 337
New York State libraries, decreased
    funding for, 490
Northern Arizona University, Cline
    Library, distance learning
    library services
    Ask-A-Librarian (AAL) service,
        10-11,18n
    current services provided, 9-11
    demographic background to, 5-7
    as Distributed Library Service, 8-9
    Document Delivery Services, 9
    for education programs, 7-18
    Field Services Office, 8-9
    history of, 8-9
    interlibrary loan services, 8
    Library Technology Services unit,
        10
    for Native-American students, 10-11
        cultural awareness and sensitivity
            in, 12-13
        culturally-sensitive materials in,
            13-14
        demographic factors in, 4-7,12,
            17n
        faculty and student outreach
            component of, 15-17
        Internet-based chat rooms, 11
        Internet-based courses for, 14-15
        library instruction, 11-14
        obstacles to, 11-12
        students' learning styles and,
            12-13
        via IITV, 11,14,16

WebQuest module use in,
        14-15,18n
    telephone reference services, 9,11
    via IITV, 4,8
    via the Internet, 4,8
Northwest Vista College, distance
    learning library services,
    357-364
    access to materials, 358-359
    library instruction, 361-363
    reference services, 359-361
    targeted marketing of, 363-364
Nova Southeastern University,
    35,491-492
    Alvin Sherman Library, Research
        and Information Technology
        Center, Distance and
        Instructional Library Services
        Department, 106,107
    Education Tutorial, 25
    Electronic Library Web page of,
        108
    library instruction programs, 104-110
    Major Applied Research Projects
        (MARPs), 106
    videoconferencing-based library
        instruction use at, 104-111
Nursing students, virtual reference
        services for, 139-152,139-152
    institutional context of, 140-141
    instructional model for, 141-144
    pilot program in, 143,144-147
        evaluation of, 145,147-150
        follow-up of, 145,146-147
        implementation of, 145,146
        planning of, 145-146
    Tutor.com (cobrowsing) software
        use in, 142-143,146,147

Objective-setting, in library
        instruction, 188-189
OCLC. *See* Online Computer Library
        Center
Odyssey software, 531,532,539

OECS (Organization of Eastern
Caribbean States), 273
Offcamp (Off Campus Library
Services), 490-491
Off-Campus Library Services
Conferences, 266,268,365-366
Onelog, 322-323
Online Computer Library Center
(OCLC), 228,508
E-Learning Task Force, 150
Online public access catalog (OPAC),
310-311
OPAC (online public access catalog),
310-311
Operating systems, 178
Oracle, 178
Organization of Eastern Caribbean
States (OECS), 273
Outreach, in distance learning library
services, 15-17,249-251
Ovid, Journals@Ovid, Jumpstarts,
39-40

PACS-L (Public Access Computer
Systems Forum), 490-491
Page Composer, 34
PDF. *See* Portable Document Format
(PDF)
PERL/CGI programming language,
178,179,180
Peters, Thomas, 204
Phoenix Public Library, 35
PHP scripting language, 259
PictureTel, 102-103
Plagiarism, 78,168-169
Planning, for distance learning library
services, 66-68
marketing planning, 459-470
activity sheet for, 468-470
definition of, 461
documentation of, 461-462
elements of, 462-467
functions of, 462
need for, 460-461
strategic planning, 407-411

goals and objectives of, 408,
410-411
mission and vision statements,
408-409
planning process for, 409-410
Polycom Ipower system, 103
Portable Document Format (PDF),
92,359
of electronic reserves, 32
Poverty levels, in Arizona, 6,7
PowerPoint, 102,105,192,193,202,
246,248,249,251,359,360,434
use in interactive tutorial design,
196-201,202
PowerPoint XP, 194
Print materials
unaffiliated distance learners'
access to, 495
Utah distance learners' use of, 337
Prometheus, 76,77-78,80
Course Content Module of, 79
e-reserves component of, 78
ProQuest, direct linking tools of, 35-36
Durable Links, 45
"My Research Summary," 41
OpenURL standards-based, 41-42,
43
SiteBuilder, 33-34,40-41,42,43
Prospero software, 531,532,539
Proxy servers, 315-326
alternatives to, 322-326
Athens, 323-324,325
Onelog, 322-323
problems with, 325-326
Shibboleth, 324-325
virtual private networks (VPNs),
323,324
comparison with IP (Internet
Protocol) authentication,
316-317
definition of, 318-319
manually-configured, 320,321
problems with, 319-321
bandwidth consumption, 320
security, 319-320
URL-rewriters for, 320,321-322

Public Access Computer Systems
Forum (PACS-L), 490-491
Public libraries
Phoenix Public Library, 35
Utah distance learners' use of, 334,
338,339
Push technology, 378-379

Qualitative research, questionnaire
design for, 306-307,312
Quantitative research, questionnaire
design for, 306-307,312
Questia, 207,357
Questionnaire design, for assessment
of distance learning library
services, 303-314
bias avoidance in, 311-312
closed-ended questions, 309-310,
312
context of questions in, 307
double negative avoidance in, 311,
312-313
guidelines for, 304-305
jargon avoidance in, 310-311,312
language and wording of, 305,
310-313
method effect and, 308
open-ended questions, 308-309,312
order of questions in, 308
for qualitative research, 306-307,
312
for quantitative research, 306-307,
312
relationship with
research methodology, 308,312
survey's purpose and goals, 305,
312
research objective definition in,
307-308
self-administered questionnaires,
for user surveys
close-ended questions in, 275
design of, 267-268
open-ended questions in, 267

pre-testing of, 268
question format of, 267
use by University of Iowa, 268,
283-294
use by University of the West
Indies, Mona Campus,
275-276,295-302
survey structure and, 310

RDS Business Reference Suite, 35
Reference materials, Internet-based.
See also Electronic resources
budget support for, 90
Reference services, for distance
learners
chat
budget support for, 91
for nursing students, 142,143,
149
Utah distance learners' use of,
337,338
e-mail, 217-218,359
budget support for, 91
University of Iowa user survey
of, 268,271,289,291
Utah distance learners' use of,
338
face-to-face, 357,359
versus remote-access services,
228,337,338,339-340
Utah distance learners'
preference for, 337,338,
339-340
versus videoconferencing,
101-102
faculty-librarian collaboration in,
360-361
for LEEP program, 396-397,399
limited staffing for, 360
for nursing students, 139-152
institutional context of, 140-141
instructional model for, 141-144
pilot program in, 143,145,
144-147

Tutor.com (cobrowsing)
software use in, 142-143,
146,147
synchronous online, 359-360
telephone, 217-218
budget support for, 91
of Northern Arizona University
Cline Library, 9,11
unaffiliated distance learners'
access to, 495
University of Iowa user survey
of, 268,271,288,290
Utah distance learners' attitudes
toward, 338
for unaffiliated distance learners,
495
virtual, 217-226,228
by appointment, 360
definition of, 219
document delivery services,
221-222
librarians' knowledge of academic
programs in, 224-225
offered by small colleges/
libraries, 359-361,364
print collection access with,
221-222
service policy for, 219-221
trouble shooting in, 223-224
for unaffiliated distance learning
students, 495
of Western Michigan University
Libraries, 20-21
Reframing process, utilization by
learning-disabled students, 55
Regis University, Learning Anytime
Anywhere Partnership
(LAAP), 375-390
administration of, 377
funding for, 377
Library Notification Module of,
378-390
Colleague Data (student
information system),
378,381-382

consultants for, 381-382
e-mail message processing in,
383-384
e-mail user survey of, 385-386,
389-390
Family Educational Rights and
Privacy Act and, 380,387
implementation of, 382-383
push technology use in, 378-379
Unified Modeling Language
(UML) use in, 379
visual modeling in, 379-381
Vision Team of, 377-378
Research Libraries Group, 508
Research process, Utah distance
learners' lack of knowledge
about, 338
Research Readiness Self-Assessment
(RRSA) survey, 171-181
attitudes assessment component of,
172,173,175,180-181
content of, 172-174
design of, 172-174
health professions component of,
174
multidisciplinary version of, 174
technical overview of, 178-180
uses for, 180-181
validation of, 174-177
Research skills. *See also* Research
Readiness Self-Assessment
(RRSA) survey
effect of the Internet on, 167-169
Reserve readings, *versus* electronic
reserves (e-reserves), 32
Reserves, electronic
at Athabasca University, 255-264
budget support for, 90
developed internally, 32
FirstClass course management
software-based access to, 81-82
outsourced, 32
Portable Document Format
(PDF)-based, 32

at Rochester Institute of
    Technology, 78,81
for tri-institutional graduate
    program, 350-351
Utah distance learners' use of, 337
via direct linking with aggregated
    databases, 31-34
    copyright clearance for, 32-33
    with digital object identifiers
        (DOIs), 42-43
    with EBSCO platforms, 34,35,
        36-38,44
    with Gale platforms, 34,35,
        38-39
    JSTOR, 44
    Lexis-Nexis Academic, 44
    OpenURL standards-based, 34,
        41-42,43
    with Ovid platforms, 35,39-40
    with ProQuest platforms, 33-34,
        35,40-42,43,44
    recommendations regarding,
        42-44
    software tools for, 33-44,45
    via cross-platform linking, 43-44
    WilsonWeb, 44
Reserves, electronic course. *See*
        Electronic course reserves
Rochester Institute of Technology,
        course management software
        use at, 77-84
    Blackboard, versions 2.0-5.0, 83
    faculty-librarian collaboration in,
        77-79,82-84
    FirstClass, 76,79-80,81-82
        e-reserves component of, 81-82
        history function component of,
            80
        library pathfinder component of,
            82
    myCourse class in, 77-78
    pathfinders for, 76-77
    Prometheus, 76,77-78,80
        Course Content Module of, 79
        e-reserves component of, 78

Royal Roads Military College, 113
Royal Roads University, 113-116
Royal Roads University Act, 113-114
Royal Roads University Library,
        eBook collections, 113-137
    cost of, 118
    ebrary, 117-118,122
    Electronic Library Network (ELN),
        116
    faculty and student user surveys of,
        119-132
        access methods to eBooks,
            125-126,129-130
        data analysis of, 126-131
        eBook database accounts, 124-125
        ebrary evaluation, 120,122,124,
            127,129,131
        faculty survey form, 135-137
        netLibrary evaluation, 120,122,
            124,129,131
        preference for print collections,
            122-123,128
        reasons for using eBooks, 125,
            126,129
        response rate, 120
        satisfaction rates, by academic
            discipline, 126,127,128,131
        satisfaction rates, faculty *versus*
            students, 123-124,128
        student survey form, 133-135
        usage rates, 120-121,127
        usage rates by academic
            discipline, 121,127,128
    ITKnowledge, 117
    most frequently accessed titles, 117
    netLibrary, 116,117,118,120
        MARC records for, 116,118,129
    usage rates, 116,117-118
Ruzmetov, Sherzod, 179

SACS. *See* Southern Association of
        Colleges and Schools
Sage, 44
San Diego State University, 32

Scaffolded instruction, 55
Scheduling, of virtual reference
    services, 148
Screen capture (tracking) software,
    473,476
Search engines, limitations to, 169
SearchPath, 22-23
Self-administered questionnaires, for
    user surveys
    close-ended questions in, 275
    design of, 267-268
    open-ended questions in, 267
    pre-testing of, 268
    question format of, 267
    use by University of Iowa, 268,
        283-294
    use by University of the West
        Indies, Mona Campus,
        275-276,295-302
Self-efficacy, relationship with job
    satisfaction, 58-59
Self-regulation, relationship with job
    satisfaction, 58
Servers, 178-179
Sherman, James, 247-249
Shibboleth, 324-325
SiteBuilder, 33-34,40-41,42,43
Situation or environmental (scanning)
    analysis, 463-465,468
Sloan-C Award, 394
SNOW (Special Needs Opportunity
    Windows) Project, 54,58
Soete, George, 408
Solaris, 178,179
Southeastern Louisiana Collaborative
    Digital Reference Service,
    142
Southeastern Louisiana University,
    Simis Memorial Library,
    virtual reference services for
    nursing students, 139-152
    institutional context of, 140-141
    instructional model for, 141-144
    pilot program in, 143,144-147

evaluation of, 145,147-150
follow-up of, 145,146-147
implementation of, 145,146
planning of, 145-146
Tutor.com (cobrowsing) software
    in, 142-143,146,147
Southern Association of Colleges and
    Schools (SACS)
accreditation review by, 156-157
distance learning library instruction
    guidelines of, 105
Special Needs Opportunity Windows
    (SNOW) Project, 54,58
Springfield College, Babson Library,
    videoconferencing-based
    library instruction use,
    429-442
background to, 430-432
college administration's support
    for, 432,438-439,441,442
expansion of use of, 438-440
faculty's response to, 434-435
faculty's training in, 437
future developments in, 441-442
initial class in, 434-435
instructional techniques in,
    432-434,435,436
librarians' training in, 432-434,
    435,436,437
pilot project in, 432-438
recommendations for, 440-441
scheduling of, 439-440
technical problems in, 435,436-438
trouble-shooting guide for, 438
weekend/evening technical support
    for, 438
SQL Server, 178
Staffing, for distance learning-related
    library services, 92-93
for online reference services, 360
Stoffle, Carla, 487
Strategic planning, for distance
    learning library services,
    407-411

goals and objectives of, 408,
410-411
mission and vision statements,
408-409
planning process for, 409-410
Survey(s). *See also* User surveys
of distance learning librarian
administrators, 85-96
of distance learning librarians,
369-374
of librarians' attitudes toward
unaffiliated students, 485-505
background to, 486-390
equality of access ethic and,
487-488,489,493
methodology, 491
negative attitudes, 493-495,
496-497
positive attitudes, 493,495-496
respondents' demographics,
490-492
SWOT analysis, 463,464,468-469
Syllabus, as distance learners'
information source, 337
Systems and Computer Technology
Corporation, 377

Task-based (formal) testing, 473-478
basics of, 473-474
beta testing of tasks prior to, 475
debriefing sessions in, 477
"gratification effect" in, 476-477
posttest questionnaire in, 476-477
screen capture (tracking) software
use in, 473,476
Teaching and Learning with Technology
(TILT) Grants, 23,24
Team approach, in online library
instruction, 227-242
Technology
impact on librarianship, 367-368
librarians' attitudes toward, 367-368
Telecommunication Act, 52
Telephone reference services, 217-218
budget support for, 91

of Northern Arizona University Cline
Library, 9,11
unaffiliated distance learners'
access to, 495
University of Iowa user survey of,
268,271,288,290
Utah distance learners' attitudes
toward, 338
Tenth Off-Campus Library Services
Conference, 266
Term paper banks and services, 168
Texas Information Literacy Tutorial
(TILT), 192
Texas libraries, decreased funding for,
490
Texas State Library, 359
Texas Technical University, Hill
County Library, distance
learning library services,
153-165
background to, 154-155
document delivery services, 155-156
Hill Country Higher Education
Steering Committee and, 154
interlibrary loan services, 156
library instruction, 155-156
reference services, 155-156
Southern Association of Colleges and
Schools accreditation-related
review of, 156-157,159
Web-based library instruction
course, 157-160
course requirements, 162
enrollment in, 160
goal of, 157
promotion of, 159,160
reading assignments, 163-165
syllabus, 161-165
WebCT use in, 158
Web page, 156-157
TexShare, 156,359,490
Textbooks, Utah distance learners' use
of, 337
10th Off-Campus Library Services
Conference, 268
TILT (Teaching and Learning with
Technology) Grants, 23,24

TILT (Texas Information Literacy
Tutorial), 192
Toth, Susan Allen, 401
Tutor.com (cobrowsing) software,
142-143,146,147
Two-Minute Web site Tour,
192-193,194,196-201,202
*2000 Academic Library Trends and
Statistics* (Association of
College and Research
Libraries), 356-357

U.S. *News and World Report*, 394
Unaffiliated distance learning students
adequacy of library collections for,
492-495,497
book loss rate among, 488
economic costs of, 489,490
impact on library staff, 488-489
increase in, 486-487
library seating space for, 488
library services offered to, 495-496
types of, 495
security concerns about, 488
survey of librarians' attitudes
toward, 485-505
background to, 486-390
equality of access ethic and,
487-488,489,493
methodology, 491
negative attitudes,
493-495,496-497
respondents' demographics,
490-492
at University of Iowa, 285
in Utah, 334,338,339
Undergraduate programs, distance
learning-based
library services for, 356
prevalence of, 88
Unemployment statistics, from
Arizona, 6,7
Unified Modeling Language (UML),
379

"Unique selling proposition" (USP),
465
Universities. *See also* names of
specific universities
distance learning curriculum
prevalence in, 88
University College of the West Indies,
272
University endowments, decline in, 86
University graduates, employment
satisfaction of, 58-59
University of Calgary, as Campus
Alberta Graduate Program in
Counselling participant,
346-347,348,349-352
University of California, decreased
funding for, 490
University of Florida, decreased
funding for, 490
University of Illinois,
Urbana-Champaign,
decreased funding for, 490
University of Illinois,
Urbana-Champaign,
Graduate School of Library
and Information Science,
distance learning coursework
enrollment in, 392
LEEP program, 392,393
Academic Outreach Library and,
398,399-400,401
access to library collections and
services in, 395-397
case study of, 394-403
cooperative approach in,
397-400
enrollment in, 395
instructors for, 394
library instruction component of,
394-395,397
as Most Outstanding
Asynchronous Learning
Network, 394
organizational structure of,
397-400

program structure of, 394-395
reference services for, 396-397,
    399
students' preferences in, 393
University of Iowa, 266
decreased funding for, 490
user surveys of distance learning
    library services
    1998-1999, 268-269,270
    2003, 269-272,283-294
    cover letter for survey, 294
    Distance Education Library
        Services Web site evaluation,
        286,287
    document delivery services
        evaluation, 268,271,289,290
    e-mail reference services
        evaluation, 271,289,291
    identification of most useful
        library services, 289-292
    library handouts evaluation,
        287-288
    library instruction sessions
        evaluation, 271,288
    library services evaluations, 271,
        285,286
    methodology of, 269-270,272
    other libraries' services
        evaluation, 285
    other UI Web sites evaluation,
        286,287
    response rates, 283
    responses to, 271,285-293
    student profiles, 279-283
    students' academic program
        enrollments, 284
    students' CD use, 293
    students' e-mail access, 293
    students' FAX machine access,
        293
    students' Internet access,
        271-272,293
    telephone reference services
        evaluation, 271,288,290
University of Lethbridge, as Campus
    Alberta Graduate Program in
    Counselling participant,
    347,348,349-352
University of Maryland University
    College, 362
University of Massachusetts, decreased
    funding for, 490
University of Michigan, 106
University of Missouri, decreased
    funding for, 490
University of Nebraska, decreased
    funding for, 490
University of New Orleans, 142
University of North Texas Libraries,
    Web site usability studies at,
    472-473,474-475,478-480,
    481-482
University of Phoenix, 35,491-492
University of Texas
    eBook collection, 118
    Information Excavation library
        instruction tutorial use at, 25
    Teaching and Learning with
        Technology (TILT) Grant
        for, 23
University of the South Pacific, 273
University of the West Indies
    distance education at, 273
    history of, 272-273
University of the West Indies, Mona
    Campus, 266
    distance services and library
        support at, 273-274
    user survey of distance learning
        library services, 274-280
        background to, 274
        cover letter for, 302
        evaluation of other libraries'
            services, 299
        evaluation of UWI library
            services, 298-299
        findings and recommendations
            based on, 276-279,295-302

new services recommendations, 300-301

objectives and methodology for, 274-275

profile of distance learning students, 295-297

self-administered questionnaire for, 274-275

students' Internet access, 299-300

students' program enrollments, 297

University of Utah, Spencer S. Eccles Health Sciences Library, 328

University of Virginia, decreased funding for, 490

University of Washington, 392,400

University of Wisconsin-Madison, Library and Information Science School Library, 399

University of Wisconsin-Milwaukee, School of Information Studies, 73n

UNIX-like operating systems, 178

Usability studies, of Web sites, 471-483

with cognitive walkthroughs, 480-482

with focus groups, 473,478-480

with formal (task-based testing), 473-478

basics of, 473-474

beta testing of tasks prior to, 475

debriefing sessions in, 477

"gratification effect" in, 476-477

posttest questionnaire in, 476-477

screen capture (tracking) software use in, 473,476

goal of, 473-474

at University of North Texas Libraries, 472-473,474-475, 480,481-482

User surveys, of distance learning library services, 265-302

by Council of Prairie and Pacific University Libraries (COPPUL), 212

of eBook collections, 119-132

access methods to eBooks, 125-126,129-130

data analysis of, 126-131

eBook database accounts, 124-125

ebrary evaluation, 120,122,124,127,129,131

faculty survey form, 135-137

netLibrary evaluation, 120,122,124,129,131

preference for print collections, 122-123,128

reasons for using eBooks, 125,126,129

response rate, 120

satisfaction rates, by academic discipline, 126,127,128,131

satisfaction rates, faculty *versus* students, 123-124,128

student survey form, 133-135

usage rates, 120-121,127

usage rates by academic discipline, 121,127,128

at Kansas State University, 443-457

literature review of, 266-268

self-administered questionnaires for close-ended questions in, 275

design of, 267-268

pre-testing of, 268

question format, 267

use by University of Iowa, 268,283-294

use by University of the West Indies, Mona Campus, 275-276,295-302

University of Iowa surveys 1998-1999, 268-269,270

2003, 269-272,283-294

cover letter for survey, 294

Distance Education Library
 Services Web site evaluation,
 286,287
document delivery services
 evaluation, 271,289,290
e-mail reference services
 evaluation, 271,289,291
identification of most useful
 library services, 289-292
libraries' services evaluation,
 285
library handouts evaluation,
 287-288
library instruction sessions
 evaluation, 271,288
library services evaluations, 271,
 285,286
methodology of, 269-270,272
other UI Web sites evaluation,
 286,287
response rates, 283
responses to, 271,285-293
student profiles, 279-283
students' academic program
 enrollments, 284
students' CD use, 293
students' e-mail access, 293
students' FAX machine access,
 293
students' Internet access,
 271-272,293
telephone reference services
 evaluation, 271,288,290
University of the West Indies,
 Mona Campus survey,
 272-279,295-302
background to, 274
comparison with University of
 Iowa survey, 279-280
cover letter for, 302
evaluation of other libraries'
 services, 299
evaluation of UWI library
 services, 298-299

findings and recommendations
 based on, 276-279,295-302
new services recommendations,
 300-301
objectives and methodology for,
 274-275
profile of distance learning
 students, 295-297
self-administered questionnaire
 for, 274-275
students' Internet access,
 299-300
students' program enrollments,
 297
Utah, population distribution in,
 327-328
Utah Academic Library Consortium,
 508
purpose of, 328
Utah Academic Library Consortium
 Distance Education
 Committee, focus groups
 studies by, 328-341
at College of Eastern Utah, 329-335
debriefing sessions in, 339-341
first, 329-335
future use of focus groups, 340
informed consent for, 336
institutional review board
 permission for, 335
methodology, 330-331,335-336
rationale for, 329
summary of responses, 331-333
at Utah State University Moab
 Education Center, 329-335
at Utah University, Uintah Basin
 Branch campus, 335-338
Utah Education Network, 328
EDNET system, 341
Utah State University
distance learning focus group
 studies at, 329-335
at Moab Education Center,
 329-335,340

at Uintah Basin Branch Campus,
335-341
distance learning programs of, 328
Utah Valley Regional Family History
Center, 508

Vancouver Art Institute, 353
VDX software, 533
Vendors, direct linking tools offered
by
from EBSCO
EBSCOhost, 36-38,41,44,45
Page Composer, 34
Infomarks, 38-39,45
from ProQuest, 35-36
Durable Links, 45
"My Research Summary," 41
OpenURL standards-based,
41-42,43
SiteBuilder, 33-34,40-41,42,43
Vennues 2000, 103
"Victim libraries," 401
Videoconferencing
definition of, 99-100
in library instruction, 97-112,
429-442
background to, 430-432
benefits of, 100-101
budget support for, 438
college administration's support
for, 432,438-439,441,442
comparison with on-campus
students, 102,109
document delivery and
interlibrary loan services in,
106
expansion of use of, 438-440
extended library instruction
classes in, 105-106,108
face-to-face instruction *versus*,
101-102
faculty-librarian collaboration
in, 105,108
faculty's response to, 434-435

faculty's training in, 437
future developments in, 441-442
guidelines for, 105-106
initial class in, 434-435
instructional techniques in,
432-434,435,436
librarians' training in, 432-434,
435,436,437
limitations to, 101
pilot project in, 432-438
problems associated with, 106-108
recommendations for, 110-111,
440-441
scheduling of, 439-440
technical problems in,
435,436-438
trouble-shooting guide for, 438
weekend/evening technical
support for, 438
students' acceptance of, 100
in virtual reference services, 219
budget support for, 91
Videotaped library instruction, budget
support for, 92
Virtual private networks (VPNs),
323,324
Virtual Western Canadian University
Library (VWCUL), 210-211
Visual impairments, learning
disabilities-associated, 50-51
Volunteering, 368
Voyager Library Catalog, 193

Wayne State University, 106
WCET (Western Cooperative for
Educational
Telecommunications), 377
Web Accessibility Initiative (WAI), 57
Web-based tutorials, in library
instruction
Education Tutorial, 25
FALCON, 24
Information Excavation, 25
of Western Michigan University,
19-30

WebCT, 158,269-270,272
Web pages
    design of, 362-363
    for distance learners, 89
    Utah distance learners' attitudes
        toward, 338
WebQuest, 14-15,18n
Web sites
    design of, 472
    unstable nature of, 31-32
    usable, definition of, 472
    Utah distance learners' use of, 337
Web site usability studies. *See*
        Usability studies, of Web
        sites
Wellesley College, 168
Western Cooperative for Educational
        Telecommunications
        (WCET), 377
Western Illinois University, University
        libraries, 204
Western Interstate Commission for
        Higher Education (WICHE),
        377
Western Michigan University
        Libraries, distance learning
        library services of, 19-30
    document delivery services, 20
    face-to-face library instruction
        HyperCard tutorial use in, 22
        limitations to, 21-22

    for non-traditional students,
        21-22
    Web browser use in, 22
    interlibrary loan services, 20
    reference services, 20-21
    student demographics and, 20
    Web-based multimedia library
        instruction tool use in, 22-30
    CD-ROM files use in, 26,27-28
    content modules of, 26-28
    development and
        implementation of, 24-28,29
    EZProxy software use with, 28
    goals of, 23-24,25
    Macromedia Flash MX software
        use with, 26
    Teaching and Learning with
        Technology (TILT) Grant
        for, 23,24
WICHE (Western Interstate Commission
        for Higher Education), 377
WilsonWeb, 44
Windows 2000, 178
Windows XP, 178,179
Wu, Xinin, 179

XanEdu, 207,357

Young offenders, learning disabilities
        prevalence among, 49

The Future of Information Services, edited by Virginia Steel, MA, and C. Brigid Welch, MLS (Vol. 20, No. 3/4, 1995). *"The leadership discussions will be useful for library managers as will the discussions of how library structures and services might work in the next century."* *(Australian Special Libraries)*

The Dynamic Library Organizations in a Changing Environment, edited by Joan Giesecke, MLS, DPA (Vol. 20, No. 2, 1995). *"Provides a significant look at potential changes in the library world and presents its readers with possible ways to address the negative results of such changes. . . . Covers the key issues facing today's libraries . . . Two thumbs up!"* *(Marketing Library Resources)*

Access, Ownership, and Resource Sharing, edited by Sul H. Lee (Vol. 20, No. 1, 1995). *The contributing authors present a useful and informative look at the current status of information provision and some of the challenges the subject presents.*

Libraries as User-Centered Organizations: Imperatives for Organizational Change, edited by Meredith A. Butler (Vol. 19, No. 3/4, 1994). *"Presents a very timely and well-organized discussion of major trends and influences causing organizational changes."* *(Science Books & Films)*

Declining Acquisitions Budgets: Allocation, Collection Development and Impact Communication, edited by Sul H. Lee (Vol. 19, No. 2, 1994). *"Expert and provocative. . . . Presents many ways of looking at library budget deterioration and responses to it . . . There is much food for thought here."* *(Library Resources & Technical Services)*

The Role and Future of Special Collections in Research Libraries: British and American Perspectives, edited by Sul H. Lee (Vol. 19, No. 1, 1993). *"A provocative but informative read for library users, academic administrators, and private sponsors."* *(International Journal of Information and Library Research)*

Catalysts for Change: Managing Libraries in the 1990s, edited by Gisela M. von Dran, DPA, MLS, and Jennifer Cargill, MSLS, MSEd (Vol. 18, No. 3/4, 1994). *"A useful collection of articles which focuses on the need for librarians to employ enlightened management practices in order to adapt to and thrive in the rapidly changing information environment."* *(Australian Library Review)*

Integrating Total Quality Management in a Library Setting, edited by Susan Jurow, MLS, and Susan B. Barnard, MLS (Vol. 18, No. 1/2, 1993). *"Especially valuable are the librarian experiences that directly relate to real concerns about TQM. Recommended for all professional reading collections."* *(Library Journal)*

Leadership in Academic Libraries: Proceedings of the W. Porter Kellam Conference, The University of Georgia, May 7, 1991, edited by William Gray Potter (Vol. 17, No. 4, 1993). *"Will be of interest to those concerned with the history of American academic libraries."* *(Australian Library Review)*

Collection Assessment and Acquisitions Budgets, edited by Sul H. Lee (Vol. 17, No. 2, 1993). *Contains timely information about the assessment of academic library collections and the relationship of collection assessment to acquisition budgets.*

Developing Library Staff for the 21st Century, edited by Maureen Sullivan (Vol. 17, No. 1, 1992). *"I found myself enthralled with this highly readable publication. It is one of those rare compilations that manages to successfully integrate current general management operational thinking in the context of academic library management."* *(Bimonthly Review of Law Books)*

Vendor Evaluation and Acquisition Budgets, edited by Sul H. Lee (Vol. 16, No. 3, 1992). *"The title doesn't do justice to the true scope of this excellent collection of papers delivered at the sixth annual conference on library acquisitions sponsored by the University of Oklahoma Libraries."* *(Kent K. Hendrickson, BS, MALS, Dean of Libraries, University of Nebraska-Lincoln)* *Find insightful discussions on the impact of rising costs on library budgets and management in this groundbreaking book.*

The Management of Library and Information Studies Education, edited by Herman L. Totten, PhD, MLS (Vol. 16, No. 1/2, 1992). *"Offers something of interest to everyone connected with LIS education–the undergraduate contemplating a master's degree, the doctoral student struggling with courses and career choices, the new faculty member aghast at conflicting responsibilities, the experienced but stressed LIS professor, and directors of LIS Schools."* *(Education Libraries)*

Library Management in the Information Technology Environment: Issues, Policies, and Practice for Administrators, edited by Brice G. Hobrock, PhD, MLS (Vol. 15, No. 3/4, 1992). *"A road map to identify some of the alternative routes to the electronic library."* *(Stephen Rollins, Associate Dean for Library Services, General Library, University of New Mexico)*

Managing Technical Services in the 90's, edited by Drew Racine (Vol. 15, No. 1/2, 1991). *"Presents an eclectic overview of the challenges currently facing all library technical services efforts. . . . Recommended to library administrators and interested practitioners."* *(Library Journal)*

Budgets for Acquisitions: Strategies for Serials, Monographs, and Electronic Formats, edited by Sul H. Lee (Vol. 14, No. 3, 1991). *"Much more than a series of handy tips for the careful shopper. This [book] is a most useful one–well-informed, thought-provoking, and authoritative."* *(Australian Library Review)*

Creative Planning for Library Administration: Leadership for the Future, edited by Kent Hendrickson, MALS (Vol. 14, No. 2, 1991). *"Provides some essential information on the planning process, and the mix of opinions and methodologies, as well as examples relevant to every library manager, resulting in a very readable foray into a topic too long avoided by many of us."* *(Canadian Library Journal)*

Strategic Planning in Higher Education: Implementing New Roles for the Academic Library, edited by James F. Williams, II, MLS (Vol. 13, No. 3/4, 1991). *"A welcome addition to the sparse literature on strategic planning in university libraries. Academic librarians considering strategic planning for their libraries will learn a great deal from this work."* *(Canadian Library Journal)*

Personnel Administration in an Automated Environment, edited by Philip E. Leinbach, MLS (Vol. 13, No. 1/2, 1990). *"An interesting and worthwhile volume, recommended to university library administrators and to others interested in thought-provoking discussion of the personnel implications of automation."* *(Canadian Library Journal)*

Library Development: A Future Imperative, edited by Dwight F. Burlingame, PhD (Vol. 12, No. 4, 1990). *"This volume provides an excellent overview of fundraising with special application to libraries. . . . A useful book that is highly recommended for all libraries."* *(Library Journal)*

Library Material Costs and Access to Information, edited by Sul H. Lee (Vol. 12, No. 3, 1991). *"A cohesive treatment of the issue. Although the book's contributors possess a research library perspective, the data and the ideas presented are of interest and benefit to the entire profession, especially academic librarians."* *(Library Resources and Technical Services)*

Training Issues and Strategies in Libraries, edited by Paul M. Gherman, MALS, and Frances O. Painter, MLS, MBA (Vol. 12, No. 2, 1990). *"There are . . . useful chapters, all by different authors, each with a preliminary summary of the content–a device that saves much time in deciding whether to read the whole chapter or merely skim through it. Many of the chapters are essentially practical without too much emphasis on theory. This book is a good investment."* *(Library Association Record)*

Library Education and Employer Expectations, edited by E. Dale Cluff, PhD, MLS (Vol. 11, No. 3/4, 1990). *"Useful to library-school students and faculty interested in employment problems and employer perspectives. Librarians concerned with recruitment practices will also be interested."* *(Information Technology and Libraries)*

Managing Public Libraries in the 21st Century, edited by Pat Woodrum, MLS (Vol. 11, No. 1/2, 1989). *"A broad-based collection of topics that explores the management problems and possibilities public libraries will be facing in the 21st century."* *(Robert Swisher, PhD, Director, School of Library and Information Studies, University of Oklahoma)*

Human Resources Management in Libraries, edited by Gisela M. Webb, MLS, MPA (Vol. 10, No. 4, 1989). *"Thought provoking and enjoyable reading. . . . Provides valuable insights for the effective information manager." (Special Libraries)*

Creativity, Innovation, and Entrepreneurship in Libraries, edited by Donald E. Riggs, EdD, MLS (Vol. 10, No. 2/3, 1989). *"The volume is well worth reading as a whole. . . . There is very little repetition, and it should stimulate thought." (Australian Library Review)*

The Impact of Rising Costs of Serials and Monographs on Library Services and Programs, edited by Sul H. Lee (Vol. 10, No. 1, 1989). *". . . Sul Lee hit a winner here." (Serials Review)*

Computing, Electronic Publishing, and Information Technology: Their Impact on Academic Libraries, edited by Robin N. Downes (Vol. 9, No. 4, 1989). *"For a relatively short and easily digestible discussion of these issues, this book can be recommended, not only to those in academic libraries, but also to those in similar types of library or information unit, and to academics and educators in the field." (Journal of Documentation)*

Library Management and Technical Services: The Changing Role of Technical Services in Library Organizations, edited by Jennifer Cargill, MSLS, MSEd (Vol. 9, No. 1, 1988). *"As a practical and instructive guide to issues such as automation, personnel matters, education, management techniques and liaison with other services, senior library managers with a sincere interest in evaluating the role of their technical services should find this a timely publication." (Library Association Record)*

Management Issues in the Networking Environment, edited by Edward R. Johnson, PhD (Vol. 8, No. 3/4, 1989). *"Particularly useful for librarians/information specialists contemplating establishing a local network." (Australian Library Review)*

Acquisitions, Budgets, and Material Costs: Issues and Approaches, edited by Sul H. Lee (Supp. #2, 1988). *"The advice of these library practitioners is sensible and their insights illuminating for librarians in academic libraries." (American Reference Books Annual)*

Pricing and Costs of Monographs and Serials: National and International Issues, edited by Sul H. Lee (Supp. #1, 1987). *"Eminently readable. There is a good balance of chapters on serials and monographs and the perspective of suppliers, publishers, and library practitioners are presented. A book well worth reading." (Australasian College Libraries)*

Legal Issues for Library and Information Managers, edited by William Z. Nasri, JD, PhD (Vol. 7, No. 4, 1987). *"Useful to any librarian looking for protection or wondering where responsibilities end and liabilities begin. Recommended." (Academic Library Book Review)*

Archives and Library Administration: Divergent Traditions and Common Concerns, edited by Lawrence J. McCrank, PhD, MLS (Vol. 7, No. 2/3, 1986). *"A forward-looking view of archives and libraries. . . . Recommend[ed] to students, teachers, and practitioners alike of archival and library science. It is readable, thought-provoking, and provides a summary of the major areas of divergence and convergence." (Association of Canadian Map Libraries and Archives)*

Excellence in Library Management, edited by Charlotte Georgi, MLS, and Robert Bellanti, MLS, MBA (Vol. 6, No. 3, 1985). *"Most beneficial for library administrators . . . for anyone interested in either library/information science or management." (Special Libraries)*

Marketing and the Library, edited by Gary T. Ford (Vol. 4, No. 4, 1984). *Discover the latest methods for more effective information dissemination and learn to develop successful programs for specific target areas.*

Finance Planning for Libraries, edited by Murray S. Martin (Vol. 3, No. 3/4, 1983). *Stresses the need for libraries to weed out expenditures which do not contribute to their basic role–the collection and organization of information–when planning where and when to spend money.*

Planning for Library Services: A Guide to Utilizing Planning Methods for Library Management, edited by Charles R. McClure, PhD (Vol. 2, No. 3/4, 1982). *"Should be read by anyone who is involved in planning processes of libraries–certainly by every administrator of a library or system." (American Reference Books Annual)*

BOOK ORDER FORM!

Order a copy of this book with this form or online at:
http://www.haworthpress.com/store/product.asp?cku=5563

The Eleventh Off-Campus
Library Services Conference Proceedings

_____ in softbound at $49.95 ISBN-13: 978-0-7890-2785-6.   ISBN-10: 0-7890-2785-2.
_____ in hardbound at $69.95 ISBN-13: 978-0-7890-2784-9.   ISBN-10: 0-7890-2784-4.

COST OF BOOKS _____

POSTAGE & HANDLING _____
US: $4.00 for first book & $1.50
for each additional book
Outside US: $5.00 for first book
& $2.00 for each additional book.

SUBTOTAL _____
In Canada: add 7% GST. _____

STATE TAX _____
CA, IL, IN, MN, NJ, NY, OH & SD residents
please add appropriate local sales tax.

FINAL TOTAL _____
If paying in Canadian funds, convert
using the current exchange rate,
UNESCO coupons welcome.

❏ **BILL ME LATER:**
Bill-me option is good on US/Canada/
Mexico orders only; not good to jobbers,
wholesalers, or subscription agencies.

❏ **Signature** _____

❏ **Payment Enclosed: $** _____

❏ **PLEASE CHARGE TO MY CREDIT CARD:**
❏ Visa ❏ MasterCard ❏ AmEx ❏ Discover
❏ Diner's Club ❏ Eurocard ❏ JCB

Account # _____

Exp Date _____

Signature _____
(Prices in US dollars and subject to change without notice.)

PLEASE PRINT ALL INFORMATION OR ATTACH YOUR BUSINESS CARD

Name

Address

City   State/Province   Zip/Postal Code

Country

Tel   Fax

E-Mail

May we use your e-mail address for confirmations and other types of information? ❏ Yes ❏ No We appreciate receiving
your e-mail address. Haworth would like to e-mail special discount offers to you, as a preferred customer.
We will never share, rent, or exchange your e-mail address. We regard such actions as an invasion of your privacy.

Order from your **local bookstore** or directly from
The Haworth Press, Inc. 10 Alice Street, Binghamton, New York 13904-1580 • USA
Call our toll-free number (1-800-429-6784) / Outside US/Canada: (607) 722-5857
Fax: 1-800-895-0582 / Outside US/Canada: (607) 771-0012
E-mail your order to us: orders@haworthpress.com

For orders outside US and Canada, you may wish to order through your local
sales representative, distributor, or bookseller.
For information, see http://haworthpress.com/distributors

(Discounts are available for individual orders in US and Canada only, not booksellers/distributors.)

Please photocopy this form for your personal use.
www.HaworthPress.com   BOF05